To Ashley

SELECT LEGAL TOPICS

Civil, Criminal, Federal, Evidentiary, Procedural, and Labor

My Colleague

Andrew J. Schatkin

Andy Schatkin

University Press of America,® Inc.
Lanham · Boulder · New York · Toronto · Plymouth, UK

Library of Congress Control Number: 2009926590
ISBN: 978-0-7618-4644-4 (paperback : alk. paper)
eISBN: 978-0-7618-4645-1

♾™ The paper used in this publication meets the minimum
requirements of American National Standard for Information
Sciences—Permanence of Paper for Printed Library Materials,
ANSI Z39.48-1992

To my mother and father who throughout their lives, and to this day, have inspired me and directed me in my literary efforts.

Table of Contents

Preface

Since 1978, I have had the opportunity and privilege to practice law in the State of New York, in both the State and Federal Trial and Appellate Courts. As a result of this experience, I have had the chance to gain knowledge in many areas of law. These areas include Federal Procedure; Evidence; Civil Procedure; Family Law; Labor and Employment Law; and Criminal Law. Many and most of the articles offered to the reader and reprinted here are the result of my intensive work practicing in these fields. Each of these articles covers and presents specific issues of law. They are primarily New York in character, but they also touch on Federal practice, to some extent on a policy level. The articles present my thoughts and reflections on law as I have encountered it and reflected on it. It is hoped that the practicing lawyer, the law professor, and even the general reader may be led, by reading these articles, to a deeper understanding and knowledge of both the law and the legal system in the United States. These articles, although sometimes specialized in character, can be seen as more general reflections on these fields in which I have developed my thinking and knowledge

If the reader does not have the chance to read them all, some of them may lead the reader to the case law and statutory sources of my many years of reflection in these fields.

Finally, I wish to acknowledge the great help and assistance of the legal intern in my office, Umair Hussain, who rendered me invaluable assistance in assembling and assisting me in the preparation of this book.

Introduction to Criminal Law Reprinted Articles

These articles, almost exclusively on New York Criminal Law, cover such areas as speedy trial; specific statutory issues; issues of suppression, whether confessions, issues of identifications, show ups, or line ups or issues of suppression of tangible matter; issues connected with Driving While Intoxicated; search issues; and many more. These issues are specific and discrete in their presentation and in the references that support and buttress these essays on Criminal Law. Some articles are recent, and some are not, but all represent my developing thinking in this constitutionally impacting field.

Chapter 1
Criminal Law Reprinted Articles

1. The Right to a Speedy Trial: C.P.L Sec. 30.20: An Overview

C.P.L. Sec 30.20 entitled Speedy Trial, in general, simply states, in terse and economical language, that, after a criminal trial is commenced the defendant is entitled to a speedy trial (sub. 1) and that, insofar as practicable (sub. 2), the trial of a criminal action is to be given preference over that of a civil action, and that of an incarcerated defendant awaiting trial over that of the paroled defendant.

The statute is very general and is to be distinguished from the "ready for trial" rules of C.P.L. Sec. 30.30 and the constitutional speedy trial guarantee of the Sixth Amendment of the U.S. Constitution held binding to the states through the due process clause of the 14th Amendment. See *Klopfer v. North Carolina,* 386 U.S. 213; 87 S. Ct. 988, 18 L. Ed.2d 332 (1962). As stated, the statute is simply stated and, apparently, eminently clear. The problem this article proposes to consider is how this general trial guarantee of the Criminal Procedure Law has been interpreted by the courts of this state.

The leading case for this consideration is *People v. Taranovich,* 37 N.Y.2d 442, 373 N.Y.S.2d 79 (1975). The issue in *Taranovich* was whether the twelve month delay between the appellant's arraignment and his subsequent indictment was violative of his constitutional and statutory right to a speedy trial. The County Court granted the defendant's motion to dismiss the indictment on speedy trial grounds. The Appellate Division reversed and reinstated the indictment. The facts in *Taranovich* are as follows: a police officer of the Nassau County Police Department stopped a vehicle being operated in an erratic manner on the highway. When the defendant refused to open the car window and exhibit his operator's license and car registration, the officer proceeded to return to his police car for assistance and, while he was doing so, the defendant placed his car in reverse and ran over the officer with his vehicle. The officer was hospitalized for his injuries, the defendant apprehended and charged with Attempted Murder; Possession of a Dangerous Drug in the Sixth Degree; Resisting Arrest; Leaving the Scene of an Accident; Operating a Motor Vehicle While Impaired; and Operating a Vehicle Without a License. The defendant was arraigned, admitted to bail and remained free on bail. On February 10, 1972, the Grand Jury indicted the defendant for Assault in the First Degree and Leaving the Scene of an Accident but the defendant was not tried until January 19, 1973, due to the fact, on the People's admission, that the papers in the defendant's case were inadvertently misplaced due to a clerical error.

Initially the court noted that there is no specific time frame after which a defendant automatically becomes entitled to release for denial of a speedy trial but that the issues raised by the defense required the court to examine the defendant's speedy trial violation claim in light of the particular factors in the specific case.

The court held the following factors should be considered and balanced by the court to reach a correct determination in a C.P.L. See. 30.20 deprivation claim:

1. the extent of the delay
2. the reason for the delay
3. the nature of the underlying charge
4. whether or not there has been an extended period of pretrial incarceration.
5. whether or not there is any indication that the defense has been impaired by reason of the delay.

As regards the first factor, *the extent of the delay*, the court noted that the greater the delay the more probable the accused has been harmed by the delay. The court went on to state, however, there is no per se period beyond which a criminal prosecution may not be pursued.

With respect to the second factor, *the reason for the delay*, the court stated that in this case, the delay was in the appellant's favor since the failure to indict was due to a clerical error in the District Attorney's office but not, the court noted, a deliberate attempt by the prosecution to hamper the defendant in the preparation of his case. The court noted, however, that this in itself was insufficient to merit the drastic remedy of dismissal of the indictment.

The third factor, *the nature of the underlying charge*, i.e., Assault in the First Degree, although the defendant was arrested for Attempted Murder, was in the People's favor since they would be expected to proceed on such a serious charge with much more deliberateness and thoroughness of preparation.

The fourth factor, *the length of the pretrial incarceration*, would be, the court stated, a factor here persuasive of dismissal of the indictment, since the defendant, except for eight days, was released on bail for the entire period of time. The court stated this factor was of the greatest import, since the speedy trial guarantee affords a safeguard against prolonged pretrial incarceration and bears on possible prejudice since the incarcerated defendant is at a disadvantage in assisting in the preparation of his case.

The court held the fifth factor, *impairment of the defense*, the most critical in this case. The court stated the defendant need not show he was prejudiced by the delay but that a questionable period of delay may be unreasonable depending on whether the likelihood of an acquittal has been affected thereby such as where the delay resulted in the defendant being unable to call certain witnesses or whether the duration of the delay dimmed the memory of a witness or witnesses.

In this case, the court held, only two witnesses were present: the appellant and the police officer who was run over. The police officer would be expected to remember what had transpired. Balancing these factors—the one year delay between the occurrence of the crime and the indictment on the Serious Class C Felony—the court held that even where the delay is due to prosecutorial misconduct, dismissal is not mandated where there is no lengthy period of pretrial incarceration and no apparent impairment of the defense caused by the delay.

The court added the caveat, however, that it was not departing from the traditional view that where the delay is great enough there need be no proof of prejudice to the defendant required.

Taranovich states the balance test of the factors to be taken together that may result in dismissal of an indictment pursuant to C.P.L. Sec. 30.20 but adds, or rather indicates, that where the delay is extended, regardless of prejudice, dismissal may result.

The Factors Applied

In 1975 the Court of Appeals applied the *Taranovich* balancing test in *People v. Johnson,* 38 N.Y.2d 271, 379 N.Y.S.2d 735 (1975). In *Johnson*, the defendant was incarcerated for eighteen months awaiting trial on an indictment charging him with Murder 2 and Possession of a Weapon as a Misdemeanor. He was indicted on January 27, 1972, and finally on July 2, 1973, pled guilty to Manslaughter in the Second Degree. Only thirty days of the eighteen months were chargeable to the defendant and the trial was delayed due to cases of older vintage being ahead of it on the calendar in the prosecutor's office and the prosecutor being engaged in trial on other cases. The defendant alleged prejudice because, in the period of the delay, an important witness had left the area. The court initially noted that the eighteen month delay was questionable, that the defendant had been incarcerated during this period of time and that there was an indication the defense had been prejudiced by the delay through the loss of a key witness.

In response to the argument of the People, that the seriousness of the crime and the cause of the delay being due to backlog in the prosecutor's office outweighed the other three factors and so the indictment should not be dismissed under C.P.L. Sec. 30.20, the court noted that while it was true the more serious character of the crime required greater preparation, the need for preparation in this case was not the cause for the delay, but rather the delay was due to the shortage of trial assistants in the prosecutor's office and the concomitant priority system of trying cases in order of their age and depending on whether the defendant was incarcerated.

The court noted, moreover, that no consideration was given to the fact that the defendant was not charged with the delay, that the evidence of guilt was not overwhelming, that the defense raised a genuine issue for trial and that the defendant's case depended upon proof of susceptibility to loss by the passage of time.

The court concluded that if the priority system of the prosecutor's office were the only factor favoring dismissal, there would be a close question whether the delay here had not violated C.P.L. Sec. 30.20. The court stated that this factor could not outweigh the fact that the defendant had been incarcerated eighteen months awaiting trial and the delay had prejudiced his case.

The cases following *Taranovich* and *Johnson* have consistently and uniformly applied the *Taranovich* test. Most recently in 1992 the Appellate Division, Second Department, held in *People v. Tulloch*, 179 A.D.2d 794, 579 N.Y.S.2d 442 (2d Dept. 1992), that, although eleven years had elapsed from the time of the indictment until the defendant's arraignment, the reason for the delay was the defendant's deliberate avoidance of apprehension; that the police exercised due diligence in attempting to discover the defendant's location and secure his presence for trial; that the defendant was charged with the serious crime of murder; that the defendant was not incarcerated for any extended length of time before his trial; and that the defendant failed to demonstrate his suffering any prejudice by reason of the delay.

Similarly, the Third Department held in *People v. Acevedo*, 176 A.D.2d 1007, 575 N.Y.S.2d 174 (3rd Dept. 1991), that although the post indictment delay was approximately two years, for approximately three months during the summer of 1989 defense counsel was not available due to his engagement in Federal Court trial and for one week the defendant was on trial on an unrelated indictment. The court noted these periods of time were not chargeable to the People as well as the one hundred and sixty eight days of post indictment motion practice. The court noted that the remaining time was due to calendar congestion. The court further noted that the defendant suffered no period of pretrial incarceration. The court rejected the defendant's claims of prejudice because of the death of a codefendant who would have allegedly offered favorable testimony on behalf of the defendant and the arrest and conviction of two defense witnesses during the period of delay.

The cases following *Taranovich* and *Johnson* are reflected in all the trial courts and appellate departments of this state. See *People v. Flores*, 151 Misc.2d 185, 573 N.Y.S.2d 233 A (New York City Criminal Court, 1991); *People v. Shafer*, 175 A.D.2d 564, 473 N.Y.S.2d 231 (4th Dept. 1991); *People v. Pearson*, 170 A.D.2d 889, 567 N.Y.S.2d 183 (3rd Dept. 1991); *People v. Watts*, 86 A.D.2d 964, 448 N.Y.S.2d 299 (4th Dept. 1982), affd. 57 N.Y.2d 299, 456 N.Y.S.2d 677, 442 N.E.2d 1188 (1982); *People v. Delvas*, 167 A.D.2d 977, 562 N.Y.S.2d 315 (4th Dept. 1990); *People v. Rosado*, 166 A.D.2d 544, 560

N.Y.S.2d 825 (2d Dept. 1990); *People v. Gwynn,* 161 A.D.2d 1174, 555 N.Y.S.2d 520 (4th Dept. 1990); *People v. Drew,* 160 A.D.2d 1100, 554 N.Y.S.2d 742 (3rd Dept. 1990); *People v. Moore,* 159 A.D.2d 521, 552 N.Y.S.2d 389 (2d Dept. 1990); *People v. Thorpe,* 586 N.Y.S.2d 519 (2d Dept. 1992); *People v. Crandall,* 5896 N.Y.S.2d 158 (3rd Dept. 1992); *People v. Dury,* 580 N.Y.S.2d 871 (2d Dept. 1992); *People v. Felder,* 583 N.Y.S.2d 697 (4th Dept. 1992).

The Extent of the Delay

Although, for the most part, *Taranovich* and its critical factors, so delineated in the case, have governed and continue to govern all applications pursuant to C.P.L. Sec. 30.20, there is a line of cases, following the discrete language in *Taranovich,* that an unanswerable unexcused delay will result in dismissal, regardless of a showing of prejudice to the defense. These cases, although following the *Taranovich* exception, constitute an effectual caveat to the general applicability of *Taranovich.*

Thus, for example, in *People v. Minicone,* 28 N.Y.2d 279, 321 N.Y.S.2d 570 (1971), the Court of Appeals held that a delay of almost four years between the indictment of the defendants in September of 1965 and their trial in June of 1969 at which they were convicted of Assault in the Second Degree, effectively deprived them of their constitutional and statutory right to a prompt trial. The court noted that although the People showed some excuse for the delay attributable to pretrial procedures, there remained a long unexplained period of delay.

In *People v. Staley,* 41 N.Y.2d 789, 396 N.Y.S.2d 339, 364 N.E.2d 111 (1977), the defendant was arrested and charged with Criminal Possession of Stolen Property and Reckless Endangerment. He was arraigned the next day and spent four days in jail before bail was posted. On September 31, 1972, the complaint was dismissed at the request of the district attorney so that charges could be directly presented to the Grand Jury and the bail was discharged. Two and one half years later, in March of 1975, the case, apparently forgotten during that period, the defendant was indicted. The defendant was found guilty, after trial, of Unauthorized Use of a Vehicle and was sentenced to one year in prison. At trial, his motion to dismiss the indictment for failure to prosecute was denied. The defendant sought reversal of his conviction and dismissal of the indictment for violation of his so-called constitutional right to a speedy trial pursuant to C.P.L. Sec. 30.20.

The Court of Appeals reversed, holding that the thirty-one month delay, without excuse or justification being offered, mandated dismissal of the indictment. The Court reiterated the rule that where the delay is long enough, the charges must be dismissed without the need for proof that the defendant's ability to present a defense has been shown to have been hampered.

Most recently, the Third Department in *People v. Charles,* 580 N.Y.S.2d 99 (3rd Dept. 1992), held that where there is a delay of forty-three months between the defendant's arrest and trial and the People make no showing or justification for the extended delay, an unjustified delay of this extent obviates any need on the part of the defendant to show prejudice, and dismissal pursuant to C.P.L. Sec. 30:20 is mandated.

The extent of the delays in *Charles* was the one year gap between decision on defendant's omnibus motion and commencement of the suppression hearing; the fifteen months between the conclusion of the suppression hearing and the Court's determination of the motion to suppress; and the one year between that determination and trial. For none of these periods, the court held, did the People offer a sufficient explanation of the delays.

One Final Point

In *Taranovich*, the Court of Appeals, citing *People v. Ganci*, 27 N.Y.2d 418, 318 N.Y.S.2d 484, 267 N.E.2d 263 (1971), and *People ex. rel. Franklin v. Warden*, 31 N.Y.2d 448, 341 N.Y.S.2d 604, 244 N.E.2d 199 (1973), noted that a delay in prosecution, caused by calendar congestion or inadequate facilities or personnel weighs less heavily against the state, because it furnishes a more neutral reason than one wholly subject to the prosecutor's control such as a shortage of trial assistants as was the case in *People v. Taranovich, supra*.

In sum, *Johnson* established a caveat that calendar congestion may be a factor taken into account for the delay and so the delay thereby resulting may be weighed less heavily against the People than delay caused by the action or inaction of the People.

This rule set forth in *Johnson* has since been followed by the appellate courts of the state. Thus, the Fourth department in *People v. Watts*, 86 A.D.2d 964 (4th Dept. 1982), noted that although a sixteen-month delay generally attributable to the State is not excessive, a great portion of the delay was due to court scheduling, an excuse which would weigh less heavily against the State. See also *People v. Collins*, 98 A.D.2d 947, 472 N.Y.S.2d 796 (4th Dept. 1983); *People v. Walker*, 141 A.D.2d 991, 530 N.Y.S.2d 644 (3rd Dept. 1988); *People v. Charles, supra* at 102.

Conclusion

The *Taranovich* factors, in particular the necessity for a showing of prejudice and the importance of a sustained period of pretrial incarceration during the delay, must govern all motions pursuant to C.P.L. Sec. 30.20. If the delay is sufficiently excessive, the time passage alone, in the absence of any showing of prejudice, is enough to cause dismissal of the indictment.

Finally, as a caveat, delay caused by calendar congestion or court scheduling will weigh less heavily against the State than a delay caused by the direct action or inaction of the prosecutor.

2. Suppressing the Beeper in the Drug Sale

The carrying of a beeper has become something of a fixture not only in the business and professional world but has become, as it were, a fashion. In a word, beepers may frequently be found on many sorts and kinds of persons ranging from teenagers wishing to keep up with the times to Doctors and Lawyers desiring to keep tabs on the patients and clients, cases and responsibilities.

By the same token, if a person is arrested for Criminal Sale of a Controlled Substance he may be found, upon subsequent search, to be in possession of a beeper. The People will voucher this item and seek to introduce it into evidence in their direct case as probative of the defendant's intent to engage in the trade and business of the sale of narcotics.

The criminal practitioner thus is confronted with the situation of a beeper sought to be admitted into evidence by the People which may, if admitted, be highly prejudicial to his client's case. The question is what, in fact, can be done by defense counsel to prevent this eventuality.

There are few cases on this particular issue and all rule for admissibility of the beeper into evidence. The leading cases are *People v. Calada*, 154 A.D.2d 700, 546 N.Y.S.2d 681 (2d Dept. 1989), and *People v. Ortiz*, 152 A.D.2d 755, 544 N.Y.S.2d 204 (2d Dept. 1989).

Calada was an appeal from a judgment of the Supreme Court of Queens County for Criminal Possession of a Controlled Substance in the Third Degree and Criminal Sale of a Controlled Substance in the Third Degree. The facts were that the defendant was convicted, after a jury trial, of having sold two glassine envelopes of heroin to an undercover officer during a buy and bust operation in Corona, Queens. He was arrested immediately after the sale and a search of his person produced a glassine envelope containing heroin, a beeper and $281.00 in cash of which $20.00 was prerecorded buy money. Defendant contended on appeal that the introduction of the beeper and cash into evidence constituted reversible error. The court held that the crime, P.L. 220.16, Criminal Possession of a Controlled Substance with Intent to Sell, required the People to prove beyond a reasonable doubt that the defendant possessed the heroin with the specific intent to sell it. The court concluded that the introduction of the beeper was proper since the jury could properly infer that the defendant was using it in his business of narcotics dealing to keep in touch with his customers. Thus the court stated that the evidence that the defendant possessed a beeper was probative of his intent to sell narcotics.

Ortiz was an appeal from the order of the Supreme Court of Queens County granting the defendant's motion to dismiss the indictment charging him with selling a controlled substance. Specifically, the appeal was from an order of the

Supreme Court granting the defendant's motion to dismiss in the furtherance of justice the counts of the indictment charging the defendant with Criminal Sale of a Controlled Substance in the Second Degree; Criminal Sale of a Controlled Substance in the Third Degree and Criminal Possession of a Controlled Substance in the Third Degree. The court noted, indicta, that the defendant had been an alcohol and narcotics abuser since age 14 and stated that ". . . the foregoing in conjunction with the defendant's use of an electronic beeper belies defense counsel's assertion that the defendant was a "dabbler" and an "amateur" in narcotics. . . ." *People v. Ortiz, supra* at 205.

See also *People v. Melendez,* 160 A.D.2d 739, 553 N.Y.S.2d 808 (2d Dept. 1990); *People v. Debiasi,* 160 A.D.2d 952, 554 N.Y.S.2d 673 (2d Dept. 1990).

It would appear that the few cases on this subject do not support the exclusion of the beeper in evidence as prejudicial. Yet there is a way out of this dilemma. First, if the paper has been vouchered, it may be made the subject of a Mapp hearing. If it is successful at the hearing, the beeper, by this method, may be excluded from use in evidence by the People.

If the Mapp Hearing is lost, the beeper should be sought to be excluded from use in evidence by the People as inherently prejudicial as tending to show the defendant is in the business of selling narcotics. *Calada* may be distinguished as dealing with Possession with Intent to Sell, P.L. Sec. 220.16, where the beeper was held probative of the defendant's specific intent to sell narcotics, an element of the People's case. *Ortiz,* it should be argued, involved a Clayton motion. Moreover, in *Ortiz* the beeper was in point of fact used directly in the undercover sale and so was more directly an element of proof.

Finally, and this is most important, an argument by an analogy should be made to the cases that hold that cash found on the defendant and then sought to be admitted into evidence by the People where the charge is a single sale, is inherently prejudicial. See *People v. Jones,* 62 A.D.2d 356, 404 N.Y.S. 2nd 865 (1st Dept. 1978); *People v. Whitfield,* 144 A.D.2d 915, 534 N.Y.S.2d (4th Dept. 1988).

It is the position of this writer that although the case law does not directly support exclusion of the beeper for use in evidence by the People in their case-in-chief in a Sale Case, the obvious prejudice and the reasoning of the cases following *Jones* argue most strongly for exclusion. Indeed, this writer recently successfully excluded a beeper for use in evidence by the People in a Drug Sale case in Queens County, along with cash, on this very ground although the case was ultimately lost.

It should be noted that even if the notion in limine is lost, a proper record of objection to the use of the beeper in evidence should be made by defense counsel for preservation of the issue for appeal. Ultimately, this issue will most surely be resolved by the Appellate Division of this State.

3. Due Diligence Under C.P.L. Sec. 30.30(4)(c.): A Recent Development

Introduction

Sec. 30.30 of the Criminal Procedure Law defines the specific criteria and conditions whereby the defendant, provided certain periods of chargeable times are met, may obtain dismissal of an indictment, misdemeanor, or violation, or in the alternative, if incarcerated be released. The idea behind the statute, simply stated, is that a defendant, whether incarcerated or not, is entitled to a speedy trial within the ambit of the statutory limitations and conditions, and that if the People are not in a state of readiness within the proper period of time set forth in the statute, or to put it with greater clarity, are, due to prior periods of unreadiness, counting in the excludable period of time chargeable to defendant, not ready for trial within the statutory temporal frame of reference, the accusatory instrument is subject to dismissal with prejudice. It is beyond the scope of this article to analyze and consider at length this most complex and technical statute or the companion constitutional speedy trial statute, C.P.L. Sec. 30.20. What will be considered in this article is the question of what, if any, "due diligence" must be shown by the People to locate the absent or unavailable defendant under C.P.L. Sec. 30.30(4)(c), so that the period of this delay may be charged to the People. This is most important, and of seminal significance, since if the period of this delay is, in fact, charged to the People, where the defendant's absence or unavailability is due to the purported lack of "due diligence" on the part of the People to locate and produce the defendant for trial and that delay is at or beyond the statutory period in which the People must be in a state of readiness for trial, the result will be that the accusatory instrument will be dismissed. The defendant, under this scenario, will effectively obtain the benefit of his possible deliberate absence and evasion of and from the jurisdiction of the court.

Prior to 1984, Sec. 30.30(4)(c) stated that the excludable or time to be charged to the defendant was

> the period of delay resulting from the absence or unavailability of the defendant. A defendant must be considered absent whenever his location is unknown and he is attempting to avoid apprehension or prosecution, or his location cannot be determined by due diligence. A defendant must be considered unavailable whenever his location is known but his presence for trial cannot be obtained by due diligence.

It would appear, under this statutory section, that the time of the defendant's absence or unavailability, if the People have failed to exercise "due diligence" to locate and produce him for trial, may be charged to the People, with resulting possible dismissal of the accusatory instrument. The exception, under the statute, to the requirement of the People exercising "due diligence" is where the absent defendant's location is unknown and it can be shown he is attempting to avoid apprehension or prosecution.

What constitutes a proper degree of "due diligence," prior to 1984, to locate the absent or unavailable defendant has been variously defined by the courts of this state. *People v. Manley*, 63 A.D.2d 988, 406 N.Y.S.2d 109 (2d Dept. 1978), is a good example of how an appellate court chose to define "due diligence" prior to 1984. *Manley* was an appeal by the people from an order of the Supreme Court of Kings County, which granted the defendant's motion to dismiss the indictment pursuant to C.P.L. Sec. 30.30. The Appellate Division reversed, stating that the actions of the police and District Attorney's Office in attempting to locate the defendant, including interviews with neighbors at his last known address and with the letter carrier, were sufficient to meet the statutory standard of "due diligence" under C.P.L. Sec 30.30(4)(c). The court noted further that there was evidence that the defendant was attempting to avoid prosecution by the use of a false name and different address, covering the same period. Under these facts, given the People's efforts to locate the defendant and his effort not to be located, the Appellate Division reversed the trial court and denied the defendant's motion to dismiss the indictment on statutory speedy trial grounds. See also *People v. Wittman*, 73 A.D.2d 1053, 425 N.Y.S.2d 416 (4th Dept. 1980). In *Wittman* the defendant appealed from a conviction of Driving While Intoxicated on the ground, among others, that he was denied a speedy trial. The facts in *Wittman* were that the defendant was arrested on June 5, 1976, and appeared with his attorney in court on June 16, 1976. He was arraigned on that date, posted $500.00 bail, and the case was adjourned to July 27, 1976. The defendant and his attorney heard nothing about the case until October of 1977, some 16 months later. Thereafter the defendant was indicted on December 4, 1977, and, some twenty-two months after his arrest, moved for dismissal of the indictment pursuant to C.P.L. Sec. 30.30. A hearing was held on the issue in May of 1978 and the defendant's application to dismiss was denied. Again on February 1, 1979, the defendant moved to dismiss the indictment and without a hearing the court denied the motion. At trial, the defendant was convicted of the charges.

The Court noted that on July 26, 1976, the defendant's case was adjourned to August 9, 1976, and that, inasmuch as the defendant did not appear on that day a bench warrant was issued for his arrest. The court added, however, that neither the defendant or his attorney were notified of the adjourn date of August 9, 1976. At the Speedy Trial Hearing in May of 1978, the officer testified that on August 24, 1976, he went to the defendant's last known address and did not find him there. The court stated that no other attempt was made to serve the defendant, nor was inquiry made of the post office or Social Security office concerning the defendant's whereabouts, nor was his attorney of record contacted concerning his possible whereabouts.

The court also noted that the defendant testified at the Speedy Trial Hearing that he moved on August 1, 1976, notified the post office and Social Security Office of his change of address, received mail at both addresses, and was in regular contact with his attorney during this period. Moreover, the court pointed out that the defendant's attorney retained his same address throughout this period.

The court held, on all these facts, that since the defendant, after his arrest, was available to the People and that they could have contacted his attorney concerning his whereabouts, that the trial court erred in denying his C.P.L. Sec. 30.30 motion in May of 1978. Thus, the Appellate Division, Fourth Department, reversed and dismissed the indictment.

See also on this *People v. Cullen,* 99 Misc.2d 646, 416 N.Y.S.2d 1011 (S. Ct. Kings County, 1979); *People v. Schiavo,* 118 Misc.2d 776, 461 N.Y.S.2d 689 (Westchester County Court, 1983).

The Law Since 1984

In 1984 the legislature amended C.P.L. Sec. 30.30(4)(c) to more specifically exclude the period of time from the delay on which a bench warrant is issued for the defendant who fails to appear in court on that day, to the day he subsequently appears in court pursuant to the bench warrant, whether voluntarily or otherwise. The defendant may have either escaped from custody, been released on bail, or have been released on his own recognizance when the warrant was issued. This amendment, apparently, was designed to overrule two Court of Appeals Decisions, *People v. Sturgis,* 38 N.Y.2d 625, 381 N.Y.S.2d 860, 345 N.E.2d 331 (1976), and *People v. Colon,* 59 N.Y.2d 921, 466 N.Y.S.2d 319, 453 N.E.2d 548 (1983), which held, respectively, that where the absence or unavailability of the defendant did not actually prevent the filing of the indictment or the conversion of the misdemeanor complaint to an information, the delay caused by the failure to file the indictment or convert the misdemeanor complaint to an information did not "result" from the defendant's absence and so did not constitute excludable time. See also on this *People v. Bratton,* 103 A.D.2d 368, 480 N.Y.S.2d 324 (2d Dept. 1984), affd. 65 N.Y.2d 675, 491 N.Y.S.2d 623, 481 N.E.2d 255 (1985); *People v. Leone,* 105 A.D.2d 757, 481 N.Y.S.2d 186 (2d Dept. 1984), affd. 65 N.Y.2d 674, 491 N.Y.S.2d 481, 481 N.E.2d 255 (1985).

It is interesting to note, however, that despite this amendment to the statute in 1984, its purpose being to exclude the time where the defendant absconds from the jurisdiction of the court when a bench warrant is issued to the time he is returned to court, whether voluntarily or otherwise, the language of "due diligence" was still retained in the statute.

Since 1984 the appellate courts of this state have, despite the statutory emendation in 1984 to C.P.L. Sec. 30.30(4)(c), deliberately and specifically excluded the time the defendant warrants from the jurisdiction of the court to the time of his return, for speedy trial purposes, and have continued to apply to the absconding defendant the benefit of the "due diligence" statutory standard of C.P.L. Sec. 30.30(4)(c), thus entitling the warranting defendant to this statutory speedy trial protection. The cases are legion. *People v. Lugo,* 140 A.D.2d 715,

528 N.Y.S.2d 895 (2d Dept, 1988), app. den. 72 1043, 34 N.Y.S.2d 946, 531 N.E.2d 666 (1988), illustrates this principle. In *Lugo* the defendant appealed from a judgment of the County Court of Westchester County convicting him of Robbery in the Third Degree upon a jury verdict and imposing sentence. The court considered the defendant's contention that his statutory right to a speedy trial under C.P.L. Sec. 30.30 had been violated by the prosecutor's failure to exercise due diligence in locating him after a warrant had been issued for his arrest. The court noted that the record established that investigators had visited the defendant's last known address on three occasions, interviewing neighbors, locating the defendant's apartment and had found no one home, and interviewing the defendant's mother and sister who informed them that the defendant knew he was wanted and was living on the street. They then left a card and asked them to have the defendant call them. When they returned to headquarters they had "wanted posters" prepared and circulated. The court concluded, under the facts, that "due diligence" was exercised.

It is clear under the holding in *Lugo* that the "due diligence" statutory standard of C.P.L. Sec. 30.30(4)(c) subsequent to the 1984 statutory amendment to C.P.L. Sec. 30.30(4)(c) continued to be applied.

Similarly, in *People v. Liss* 131 A.D.2d 595, 516 N.Y.S.2d 302 (2d Dept. 1987), app. den. 70 N.Y.2d 714, 519 N.Y.S.2d 1049, 513 N.E.2d 1317 (1987), where the defendant appealed from a conviction of Robbery in the First Degree in the County Court of Nassau County, the Appellate Division held that the defendant's statutory right to a speedy trial was not violated where, although the defendant was a fugitive from justice from March 12, 1981, to February of 1982, the time was not chargeable to the People, since the court properly found the police had exercised due diligence in attempting to locate the defendant.

See also *People v. Cruz.* 155 A.D.2d 683, 548 N.Y.S.2d 61 (2d Dept. 1989); *People v. Jackson*, 150 A.D.2d 609, 541 N.Y.S.2d 478 (2d Dept. 1989); *People v. Shannon*, 128 A.D.2d 395, 512 N.Y.S.2d 680 (1st Dept. 1987), app. den. 64 N.Y.S.2d 1009, 517 N.Y.S.2d 1043, 511 N.E.2d 102 (1987); *People v. Taylor,* 139 A.D.2d 543, 526 N.Y.S.2d 624 (2d Dept. 1988); *People v. Machowe*, 131 A.D.2d 785, 517 N.Y.S.2d 73 (2d Dept. 1987), app.den. 70 N.Y.2d 705, 519 N.Y.S.2d 1040, 513 N.E.2d 717 (1987); *People v. Hutchenson*, 136 A.D.2d 737, 524 N.Y.S.2d 76 (2d Dept. 1988); *People v. Garrett*, 575 N.Y.S.2d 93 (2d Dept. 1991).

It is clear that subsequent to the statutory amendment of 1984 the standard of requisite "due diligence" continued to be applied to the absent or unavailable defendant, albeit the subject of a bench warrant, unless it was established that his location was unknown and he was attempting to avoid apprehension or prosecution.

A Fairly Recent Case

In January of 1992 the Appellate Division, Second Department, decided a most seminal decision on the meaning of and, in fact, the actual need for a showing of "due diligence" on the part of the People where the defendant has been the subject of a bench warrant and has either voluntarily or involuntarily returned on the outstanding warrant. That case is *People v. Bolden*, A.D.2d 578 N.Y.S.2d 914 (2d Dept. 1992).

Bolden was an appeal from a conviction in the Supreme Court of Kings County of Attempted Robbery in the First Degree and Criminal Possession of a Weapon in the Fourth Degree. The facts were that two days after the defendant's arrest for allegedly robbing at knife-point one Aron Turner of two dollars, the defendant was arraigned on a felony complaint in the Criminal Court. On September 22, 1987, three days after his arraignment, he was released on his own recognizance and the matter was adjourned to November 14, 1987. On November 14, 1987, an indictment was issued charging the defendant with Robbery in the First Degree and the matter was adjourned to November 24, 1987, for the defendant's arraignment on the indictment. The defendant failed to appear on that date and on December 7, 1987, a bench warrant was issued. The defendant was returned on the warrant 143 days later on April 28, 1988. After a jury trial the defendant was convicted of Attempted Robbery in the First Degree and Criminal Possession of a Weapon in the Fourth Degree.

Prior to trial the defendant moved to dismiss pursuant to C.P.L. Sec. 30.30(4)(c), arguing that the People were obligated to and had not exercised "due diligence" in the entire 143 day period between the issuance of the Warrant and the defendant's return. The defendant further argued that, together with a further delay of 55 days, a total of 198 days was chargeable to the People, exceeding the statutory maximum of six months. The People argued, in opposition to the defendant's 30.30 motion, that the People were under no obligation to ascertain the defendant's whereabouts after the issuance of the bench warrant on December 7, 1988, and that those 143 days were properly excludable time.

In an order dated July 5, 1988, the Supreme Court denied the defendant's speedy trial motion concluding that, under C.P.L. See. 30.30(4)(c), the People in fact were not required to exercise "due diligence." The Appellate Division, Second Department Affirmed.

The court reasoned that in 1984, Sec. 30.30(4)(c) was amended so as to legislatively override two Court of Appeals holdings, *People v. Colon, supra*, and *People v. Sturgis, supra*. In *Sturgis* and *Colon* the court noted that the Court of Appeals ruled that the absence of the defendant had not prevented the People from filing accusatory instruments and so any delays attributed to failure to so file did not "result" from the defendant's absence and so are not excludable pursuant to C.P.L. Sec. 30.30(4)(c).

The court went on to state that the 30.30(4)(c) statutory section excluded the period of time when the defendant had been the subject of a bench warrant to the time of his return, as chargeable to the People. The Court further held that it was now extending its holding in *People v. Garrett, supra*, where the court had concluded that, where a bench warrant had been issued, the People were not required to exercise "due diligence" where it had been established that the defendant was absent, i.e., that his location was unknown and that he was attempting to avoid apprehension, to the rule that the People need only establish that a bench warrant had been issued in order to exclude the ensuing period of delay attributed to the defendant's failure to appear in court. The court then went on to state that the review of the legislative history underlying C.P.L. Sec. 30.30(4)(c) showed that the intent of the 1984 amendment was to exclude the period of delay extending from the issuance of the bench warrant to the defendant's return on the warrant, and so to overcome the holdings of the Court of Appeals in *Sturgis* and *Colon*.

The court therefore rejected the defendant's argument that the amended 1984 statute still imposed the requirement of "due diligence" which existed prior to 1984, since the court reasoned that was contrary to the legislature's clear intent.

Finally, the court noted that the imposition of the "due diligence" obligation was inconsistent with the logic of the 1984 amendment, which was not to afford the absconder the subject of a bench warrant speedy trial protection.

The *Bolden* decision represents a clear and distinct break with the prior case law as set forth and analyzed in this article concerning the requirement to prove "due diligence" under C.P.L. Sec 30.30(4)(c). There is no doubt, in this writer's view that the requirement of "due diligence" continued until *Bolden* to be required despite the statutory amendment of 1984, to the warranting absent or unavailable defendant whose location cannot be determined by "due diligence." [See *People v. Rodriquez*, 580 N.Y.S.2d 24 (1st Dept. 1992); See *People v. Garrett*, 574 N.Y.S.2d 188 (1st Dept. 1991)].

Thus, it is the view of this writer that, despite the *Bolden*'s court's reading of the legislative history leading to the enactment of the statutory amendment of 1984, largely in respect to the *Sturgis* and *Colon* decisions, the *Bolden* court has done nothing more nor less than, in fact, read out the language of "due diligence," specifically left in the statute by the legislature, with no real basis for doing so. If the legislature had intended to eliminate that language it would have done so. Prior to *Bolden* neither the legislature nor any appellate court of this state had actually and effectively read out that statutory language. In this sense, *Bolden*, in the opinion of this writer, is incorrect in its reading and construction of this statutory section. Of course, it remains to be seen what the Court of Appeals will hold on this subject since leave to appeal *Bolden* has been granted.

It is interesting to note that most recently the Appellate Division, First Department, in *People v. Wilds,* 574 N.Y.S.2d 188 (1st Dept. 1991), upheld the "due diligence" requirement under C.P.L. Sec 30.30(4)(c). *Wilds* was an appeal from an order of the Supreme Court, Bronx County, dismissing the indictment charging the defendant with criminal possession of a weapon in the Third Degree on the ground that his right to a speedy trial had been denied pursuant to C.P.L. Sec 30.30(4)(c).

The facts were that a bench warrant was issued on July 26, 1988, when the defendant, after arraignment, failed to appear. The People conceded, as of August 17, 1988, that a criminal history search revealed, or should have revealed, to the District Attorney's office that the defendant was known by an alias and had been known at an address other than the one provided by him in connection with his arrest. At the Speedy Trial Hearing the investigating officer testified that between August 17, 1988, and November 11, 1988, he ran computer checks based only upon pedigree information provided by the defendant, but which did not include the alias and other address provided by the defendant in connection with his arrest.

The court initially held that the People had failed to sustain their burden of demonstrating that the defendant was either absent or unavailable under the statutory language of C.P.L. Sec 30.30(4)(c) as amended in 1984. The court, however, rejected the people's arguments that the 1984 amendment to C.P.L. Sec 30.30(4)(c) relieved the prosecution of demonstrating "due diligence." The Court reasoned that the only circumstance where "due diligence" need not be established is where the defendant is deemed absent because his location is unknown and he is attempting to avoid apprehension or prosecution. The Court further stated that the People conceded that the defendant's location was known as early as August 17, 1988, and that the People also bear the burden of establishing that although the defendant's location is known, his presence for trial cannot be obtained by due diligence. The Court noted that since the minimal attempts to secure the defendant's presence for trial between August 17 and November 11, 1988, did not include an attempt to locate the defendant at a known address, this did not constitute the exercise of due diligence.

It is the legislature, in response to the will of the People, that enact the law. *Bolden*, most obviously, chose to read out statutory language that the legislature deemed fit and proper to retain in the amended statute. Perhaps the *Bolden* court, more for reasons of policy and popular opinion than adherence to the rule of law, objected to rewarding absconding defendant for his possible malfeasance by dismissal of the indictment. It is not for the court, however, to misconstrue and misapprehend clear statutory language for any policy. The will of the People in their policy is expressed in the statutory enactment. It is not the court, bowing to a perception of the wind of the popular will, to sua sponte amend the statute when the legislature has failed so to do. There can be no doubt that the *Bolden* issue will ultimately and finally be resolved by the Court of Appeals given the split in the Appellate Departments on this most significant issue.

Addendum

The outcome of the law of *Bolden* was and finally has been resolved by the Court of Appeals in a decision rendered on February 25, 1993. The Court of Appeals ruled in *People v. Bolden*, on appeal from the Appellate Division, Second Department, in a 4-2 decision, that the 30.30 statute required the People to make reasonable efforts to enforce the warrants issued by the lower court judges. The Court went on to state, in reversing the Appellate Division, Second Department, that the 1984 amendment did not affect due diligence requirement in the statute. The Hon. Vito Titone concluded that the quid pro quo in the amendment was that the People had to obtain a bench warrant as a condition of availing themselves of the relaxed burden of proof to claim an exclusion from the readiness rule and that the legislature did not intend the bench warrants to be treated as empty paper symbols. It is clear that the Court of Appeals has blown the last trumpet on the proper interpretation and import of C.P.L. Sec. 30.30(4)(c) and that the inevitable and logical conclusion was reached, with no bias to the People or the defense bar, that the language of the statute enunciating the requirement of due diligence where a bench warrant has been issued had a purpose and was there for a purpose and cannot, in sum and effect, be read out of the statute for a policy purpose.

Copyright 1993 by the Queens County Bar Association and the Queens Bar Bulletin. Reprinted with permission.

4. C.P.L. Section 30.30: A Sequel

In a previous article, this writer considered past and recent case law interpreting and construing the statutory language and requirement of "due diligence" on the part of the People to locate the absent or unavailable defendant and apprehend him for trial under C.P.L. 30.30(4)(c).

In this article the same language of "due diligence," this time under the companion section of C.P.L. Sec. 30.30(4)(e), will be examined in terms of the prior, and also the more recent, case law construing the section.

C.P.L. Sec. 30.30(4)(e) essentially states that the period of delay resulting from the defendant's detention in another jurisdiction will constitute excludable time and will not, thus, be charged to the People, provided the District Attorney is aware of such detention and has been diligent and has made reasonable efforts to obtain the presence of the defendant for trial.

The question is, assuming the defendant is incarcerated in another state, another county within New York State, or in a federal facility, what constitutes diligent and reasonable efforts to obtain the presence of the defendant for trial on the part of the People? The issue is a significant one, since if, in fact, it can be shown that the People have not made the requisite, adequate and reasonable efforts to obtain the presence of the defendant for trial, a potentially serious indictment may be dismissed under the section.

The case law is somewhat unclear as to what constitutes the required effort by the People under this section to produce the defendant. Compliance with C.P.L. Sec. 560.10 (securing attendance of defendants confined within the state) is necessary if the defendant is held within a neighboring county within the state. Here an order to produce must be filed. If the defendant is confined in a penal institution of another state there must be compliance with C.P.L. Sec. 580.20, *Interstate Agreement on Detainers.* Compliance is had here by the filing of a detainer or warrant. If the defendant is confined in a federal facility, the requirements of C.P.L. Sec. 580.30 must be followed. This section, entitled *Securing attendance of defendants confined in federal prisons,* requires the filing of a writ of habeas corpus *ad prosequendum,* filed with the Attorney General of the United States, to produce the defendant for trial in the State of New York.

The question is what degree of compliance is necessary? Is the filing of a mere warrant or detainer in and of itself enough, if the defendant is lodged in another state's institution, to constitute both compliance with the Interstate Agreement on Detainers and fulfill the statutory requirement of C.P.L Sec. 30.30(4)(e)?

In an earlier case, *People vs. Brandfon,* 4 A.D.2d 679 (2d Dept. 1957), the Second Department held this was sufficient. Thus, in *Brandfon,* the Second Department reversed the granting of the Speedy Trial motion at the trial court level, holding that the delay in bringing the action to trial was due to the fact that the defendant was imprisoned in a foreign state prison under an indeterminate sentence and that, in fact, a warrant of arrest and detainer was indeed filed in such prison. On these facts the Second Department reversed the granting of the speedy trial motion by trial term.

Brandfon, although prior to the enactment of C.P.L. Sec. 30.30(4)(e), is clear that the filing of the detainer alone in the companion state facility constituted sufficient efforts for Speedy Trial purposes and that the time was completely excludable.

More recently, in *People vs. Mainor,* 77 Misc. 2nd 946, 355 N.Y.S.2d, 263 (S. Ct. New York County, 1974), where the defendant was confined in a Youth Correctional Center in New Jersey, the New York County Supreme Court held that where a detainer was filed pursuant to the provisions of the Interstate Agreement on Detainers (C.P.L. Sec. 580.20) and an extradition proceeding initiated along with the warrant, and the request to produce the defendant was dishonored by the New Jersey State authorities because the defendant was a youth, this constituted the requisite due diligence under C.P.L. Sec. 30.30(4)(e).

Mainor seems to indicate that the mere lodging of a warrant would not be enough, but there must be substantial compliance with C.P.L. Sec. 580.20, the Interstate Agreement on Detainers.

More recently in *People vs. Wojciechowski,* 143 A.D.2d 164 (2d Dept. 1988), the Second Department dismissed an indictment on Speedy Trial grounds and stated that compliance with Sec. 30.30(4)(e) is had when the proper statutory procedures are followed with respect to securing the presence of the defendant for trial whether C.P.L. Sec. 560.10 (*Securing Attendance of Defendants Confined in other State Institutions*); C.P.L. Sec. 570.02 (*Securing Attendance of Defendants Confined Outside of the State*); C.P.L. Sec. 580.20 (*Agreement on Detainers*); or C.P.L. Sec. 580.30 (*Securing Attendance of Federal Prisoners*).

Thus in *People vs. Brown,* 136 A.D.2d 715 (2d Dept. 1988), the Second Department declared that the filing of three writs to produce the defendant for trial in New York State on the federal authorities satisfied the Due Diligence requirement of C.P.L. Sec. 30.30(4)(e). See also *People vs. Jameson* 89 A.D.2d

697 (3rd Dept. 1982); *People vs. Jensen* 109 Misc.2d 813, 441 N.Y.S.2d 333 (Suffolk County District Court, 1981); *People vs. Mucciolo,* 104 A.D.2d 905 (2d Dept. 1984); *People vs. Smith,* 138 A.D.2d 972, 526 N.Y.S.2d 303 (4th Dept. 1988); *People vs. Lowman,* 102 A.D.2d 896 (2d Dept. 1984); *People vs. Left-wich,* 1266 A.D.2d 748, 511 N.Y.S.2d 138 (2d Dept. 1987*); People vs. Chan,* 81 A.D.2d 765, 439 N.Y.S.2d 112 (1st Dept. 1981); *People vs. Lloyd,* 141 A.D.2d 669, 529 N.Y.S.2d 801 (2d Dept. 1988).

The Issue

It would appear, based on this review of past and recent case law on the subject, that at least facial compliance with C.P.L. Sec. 560.10; C.P.L. Sec. 580.20; C.P.L. Sec. 570.02; and C.P.L. Sec. 580.30, mechanisms, respectively, for securing attendance of prisoners in neighboring counties within the state, prisoners in other states, and prisoners in federal facilities fulfills, depending on the discrete facts, the requirement of C.P.L. Sec. 30.30(4)(e) of diligent and reasonable efforts on the part of the People to obtain the presence of the defendant for trial.

There is, however, a line of cases that seems to indicate that the mere filing of a detainer, order to produce, or, if the defendant is confined in Federal custody, a writ of habeas corpus *ad prosequendum,* constitutes insufficient compliance with the mandate of C.P.L. Sec. 30.30(4)(e) of "due diligence."

People vs. Melendez, 92 A.D. 904 (2d Dept. 1983), is relevant. In *Melendez,* the defendant allegedly robbed and attempted to murder three persons in Queens County on March 31, 1980. The following day he was arrested and incarcerated in Rensselaer County on an unrelated weapons charge and on April 4, 1980, a felony complaint was sworn to in Queens County and an arrest warrant was issued and warrant was lodged as a detainer in Rensselaer County on April 7, 1980. Finally, on February 20, the defendant was removed from Rensselaer County on the basis of the detainer and was produced the next day in Queens County. The court noted that, although the people were aware of the defendant's whereabouts from April 7, 1980, to date, the warrant was lodged as a detainer, no evidence was offered that any effort was made to obtain the presence of the defendant for prosecution in Queens County, other than the fact that an arrest warrant had been lodged as a detainer in Rensselaer County, some ten and one-half months prior to the defendant's production in Queens County. The Second Department held that the mere filing of a detainer did not satisfy the statutory speedy trial requirement of C.P.L. Sec. 30.30(4)(e) and so affirmed the holding of Trial Term dismissing the indictment.

Again, the Second Department held in *People v. Orse,* 118 A.D.2d 816, 500 N.Y.S.2d 173 (2d Dept. 1986), that the mere filing of a detainer did not satisfy the due diligence requirement and that the People should have availed themselves of the procedure under C.P.L. Sec. 560.10. See also *People vs. Billups,* 105 A.D.2d 795, 481 N.Y.S.2d 430 (2d Dept. 1984); *People vs. McLaurin,* 38

N.Y.2d 123 378 N.Y.S.2d 692 (1975); *People vs. Partman,* 70 A.D.2d 814, 417 N.Y.S.2d 477 (2d Dept. 1979).

The thrust of these cases is obvious—namely, that the lodging of a warrant, detainer, or the filing of an order to produce is simply insufficient compliance with the statutory mandate of C.P.L. Sec. 30.30(4)(e).

If then the lodging of a mere detainer is not enough to fulfill the requirement of "due diligence" under C.P.L Sec. 30.30(4)(e), what in fact is required?

The answer, as previously indicated, is there must be full compliance with the relevant statutory procedures of C.P.L. Sec. 560.10, C.P.L Sec. 580.20, C.P.L. Sec. 580.30 or C.P.L. Sec. 570.02 .

People vs. Mucciolo, 104 A.D.2d 905, 480 N.Y.S.2d 516 (2d Dept. 1984), illustrates the rule well. *Mucciolo* was an appeal by the People from an order of the Supreme Court which granted the defendant's motion to dismiss the indictment. In reversing the trial court, the Appellate Division held that the period from February 25, 1981, to April 16, 1981, was properly excludable, since the People did not merely lodge a detainer with the federal authorities where the defendant was incarcerated, but fully complied with C.P.L Sec. 580.20, the Interstate Agreement on Detainers. See also *People vs. Leftwich, supra*; *People vs. Jensen, supra*; *People vs. Smith, supra*; and *People vs. Wojciechowski, supra.*

In short, it is clear that for compliance with the "due diligence" requirement to be had, there must be full and not facial compliance with the statutory mechanisms under the C.P.L. (C.PL. Secs. 560.10; 580.20; 580.30; 570.02). Moreover, it is also clear that such facial compliance as the mere filing of a warrant or detainer, without full use of the relevant statutory mechanisms, will not pass muster under C.P.L. Sec. 30.30(4)(e).

5. A Note on Burglary in the Second Degree

P.L. Sec. 140.25, the crime defined as Burglary in the Second Degree, is one of the most frequent denizens of the criminal courts of this state as well as one of the most, in a sense, heinous of crimes since, as set forth in the statutory language, it involves the knowing entry or remaining in a building which is a dwelling, i.e., a personal residence, whether a rented room, leased apartment or private house, with the intent to commit a crime therein.

The definitional language in the statute is eminently clear. There is a point of neat distinction, however, where, under certain facts, it may be not at all clear that a Burglary has been committed under P.L. Sec. 140.25 and that the statute has been violated, even though for all intents and purposes an individual's residence has been burglarized.

Let us posit this factual scenario: Two roommates share a one-bedroom apartment and both have keys. May one burglarize the other's leased portion of the premises? Or, what of when a common law spouse effectively burglarizes the other's portion of the leased premises?

The case law is clear that certain facts must be present for a burglary to be committed where the premises are shared, if not by a formal leasehold agreement with separately rented portions of the premises with each party having a key, then with a more informal arrangement where rent is shared, paid in common, and a common area is occupied and shared. The leading case is *People v. DelaCruz,* 162 A.D.2d 312, 556 N.Y.S.2d 892 (1st Dept. 1990). In *DelaCruz* the defendant was convicted in the Supreme Court of New York County of Burglary in the Second Degree and two counts of Assault in the Third Degree and was sentenced to indeterminate terms of imprisonment of 3-4 years for the Burglary and 1 year for the Assault charge, all terms to run concurrently. The First Department Affirmed. The court noted that the defendant had a common law relationship where the defendant would sleep over on a regular basis at the complainant's apartment where the complainant lived with her son and daughter. After a few months the defendant became physically abusive and in March of 1987 the defendant knocked at the complainant's door; when there was no response, he entered the apartment and began to assault the complainant. The defendant was arrested shortly after the police arrived. The Appellate Division held that the proof elicited at trial was sufficient to affirm the Burglary in the Second Degree conviction, noting that the defendant paid no rent; that his name was not on the lease; that he did not have a key and that his knocking down the apartment door was inconsistent with any notion that he had a license to enter.

DelaCruz is clear that occasionally sharing a common premises is insufficient to justify a burglary where the person has no license or basis to be or remain on the premises, whether by way of a name on the lease, the payment of rent, or having a key.

More recently in *People v. Clarke,* 585 N.Y.S.2d 738 (1st Dept. 1992), the Burglary occurred between persons occupying separate apartments on separate floors in a family-owned dwelling. The Appellate Division First Department sustained the Burglary Conviction noting that the building, though family-owned, was divided into distinct living units; that the complainant's apartment was one such unit and that the complainant and not the defendant had the key for it. The court concluded, on these facts, that the defendant had no license or privilege to enter the complainant's apartment.

People v. Smith, 144 A.D.2d 600, 534 N.Y.S.2d 1021 (2d Dept. 1988), follows *DelaCruz* and *Clarke* stressing the necessity for a license or privilege to enter even where a mere rented room is involved. In *Smith* the defendant was convicted of Burglary in the Second Degree and Criminal Mischief in the Fourth Degree and appealed. The facts in *Smith* were that the defendant was charged with Burglary after he entered the bedroom of a co-tenant and removed some belongings. The defendant claimed, in support of his argument for reversal, that the bedroom of the co-tenant was not a building within the meaning of P.O. Sec.

140.25 and that since he was privileged to be in the main area of the house he could not have committed a Burglary. The court rejected the defendant's contention stating that the co-tenant's room was independent of the rest of the house, should be considered as a separate dwelling within the building and that the fact that the defendant was licensed or privileged to be in the common areas did not give him a license to enter the bedroom of another tenant. See also *People v. Bull,* 136 A.D.2d 929, 524 N.Y.S.2d 909 (4th Dept. 1988).

In conclusion, the subject of this brief article raises and has perhaps resolved the issue of whether a true charge of burglary may be sustained where roommates, friends or common-law spouses inhabit nearby or shared premises. It is clear that a Burglary charge can not be proven where there is a true and clear license or privilege to enter the area where the alleged burglary occurred. That is to say, where rent is paid, premises are shared, names are on a common lease and both parties have keys to the apartment, there can be no bona fide burglary. Where none of these facts are present, either one or all, then a mere familiar living arrangement between persons or an occasional visitor of the opposite sex may well, not withstanding, give rise to a charge and conviction of Burglary in the Second Degree.

6. Brady: Part One

It is the law, under *Brady v. Maryland,* 373 U.S. 33, 88 S. Ct. 1053 (1963), as codified under Sec. 240.20(1)(h) of the Criminal Procedure Law, that the prosecution is mandated, with or without demand by the defense, to disclose evidence in its possession favorable to the defendant or which is material to guilt or punishment. *Brady* material has been held, also, to include material which may tend to impeach the People's witnesses.

It is the purpose of this article to explore and analyze what, in fact, may be included under the rubric of *Brady* material. *People v. Cotto,* 28 A.D.2d 1116, 285 N.Y.S.2d 247 (First Dept. 1967), and the later Court of Appeals decision *People v. Novoa,* 70 N.Y.2d 490, 522 N.Y.S.2d 504 (1987), present two significant categories of what may constitute *Brady* material.

Cotto was an appeal to the Appellate Division, First Department, from a conviction of Murder in the First Degree. The First Department reversed and ordered a new trial. The facts in *Cotto* were that during the trial, the District Attorney accepted the codefendant's plea of guilty to Manslaughter in the Second Degree and it developed that prior to the plea the codefendant stated to the police and the District Attorney that the defendant was not present at the scene of the stabbing. The District Attorney at trial failed to respond to the request of defense counsel, who had some information that the codefendant had said the defendant was not involved, that the prosecution reveal the codefendant's statement to the defense. The Appellate Court held, under *Brady*, that the defendant was entitled to this information to determine whether to call the codefendant as a witness.

In *Novoa*, the defendant was charged with Murder in the Second Degree and alleged a justification defense. The wife of the victim testified that one Pablo Rodriguez told her the day after the shooting that the defendant had attacked her husband with a metal pipe and then shot him. This same Pablo Rodriguez, the defendant's witness, had previously testified for the defense that the defendant had acted in self-defense in shooting the victim, who had attacked him with a machete. Afterward it was revealed that the wife, Anita Ortiz, was facing indictment for selling drugs to an undercover police officer. Mrs. Ortiz, in response to a question of the prosecutor, stated that no one had promised her anything with respect to her pending case. The defendant was ultimately convicted of Second Degree Murder and sentenced to a term of imprisonment of twenty-five years to life.

A year later, in the course of a second murder trial in which the defendant was acquitted, the defendant testified that Mrs. Ortiz, again a witness for the People, had, after the first trial, pled guilty and received a non-incarceratory sentence of lifetime probation for the drug charges pending against her at the time of the first trial. The defense argued prosecutorial misconduct in permitting Mrs. Ortiz to testify in the first murder trial that no promise had been made when he knew, or should have known, that Mrs. Ortiz had been promised probation in exchange for her cooperation.

At the C.P.L. Sec. 440.10 hearing, the District Attorney in charge of the prosecution of Mrs. Ortiz under the indictment for drug sale revealed that Anita Ortiz, upon conviction for the drug charges pending against her at the time, faced a sentence of three years to life, that she agreed to cooperate by providing information on other drug transactions and a homicide case, and that the District Attorney promised to evaluate her cooperation and inform the Special Narcotics prosecutor who would decide whether to recommend a sentence of lifetime probation. Mrs. Ortiz, in fact, pled guilty and received lifetime probation.

The trial assistant at the hearing testified she was unaware of any cooperation agreement and was not informed of it at any time. The trial court denied the defendant's C.P.L. Sec. 440 motion, finding no promise had been made to Mrs. Ortiz with respect to her pending case.

Citing *People v. Owikla*, 46 N.Y.2d 434, 414 N.Y.S.2d 102 (1979), the Court of Appeals held that the existence of an agreement between the prosecution and the witness made to induce testimony of the witness is evidence which must be disclosed under the *Brady* requirement.

The court also noted that, as a further ramification of the *Brady* rule, the prosecutor had an obligation to correct the misstatement of the witness concerning her original response to this query, as cited here. The court found that the failure of the prosecution to reveal the existence of the agreement and correct the witness's misstatement at trial constituted a *Brady* violation, entitling the defendant to reversal and a new trial.

What constitutes *Brady* material runs the gamut and must be subject to particular individual analysis. For further examples of *Brady* material, see:*People v. Boone*, 49 A.D.2d 559, 370 N.Y.S.2d 613 (First Dept. 1975), (reports that crime or occurrence took place at another location); *People v. Velez,* 118 A.D.2d 116, 504 N.Y.S.2d 404 (First Dept. 1986), (failure to provide defendant with information that main prosecution witness may have had overriding animosity against defendant because witness blamed defendant for prior offense committed against his wife); *People v. Anderkavich,* 117 Misc.2d 218, 457 N.Y.S.2d 718 (Co. Ct., Nassau County 1982), (People required under *Brady* to supply exculpatory material of names and addresses of witnesses who could identify the defendant at lineup); *People v. Ambrose*, 52 A.D.2d 850, 382 N.Y.S.2d 506 (2d Dept. 1976), (prior inconsistent statements); *People v. Lowe,* 96 Misc.2d 33, 408 N.Y.2d 873 (Criminal Court, Bronx County 1978) (mental illness of witness).

This brief review of the case law of this state of what may, in a criminal case, constitute *Brady* material under C.P.L. Sec. 240.20(1)(h) leaves the sense that the defense must be continually alert and cognizant of what may impact as *Brady* material at a criminal trial and that what may even constitute *Brady* material must be determined on an ad hoc, case by case basis.

7. Conspiracy: The Necessity of an Overt Act

Article 105 of the New York State Penal Law defines the various elements and degrees of the crime of conspiracy. Conspiracy in many ways is a mental or intellectual crime, since the crime is primarily founded in an agreement to commit a crime or a plan to do so. The Conspiracy Statute enables the state to prosecute a plan to commit a crime, and thereby, in a sense, functions in a preventive mode, or rather, seeks to prevent and attack nascent or imminent planned criminal conduct. Conspiracy in the sixth degree, Section 105 of the Penal Law, states that a person is guilty of Conspiracy in the sixth degree when, with intent that conduct constituting a crime be performed, he agrees with one or more persons to engage in or cause the performance of such conduct. Conspiracy in the sixth degree is a class B misdemeanor.[1] Other statutes defining the various degrees of Conspiracy are Conspiracy in the fifth degree, PL 105.05;[2] Conspiracy in the fourth degree, PL 105.10;[3] Conspiracy in the third degree, PL 105.13;[4] Conspiracy in the second degree, PL 105.15;[5] and Conspiracy in the first degree, PL 105.17.[6] Conspiracy in the fifth degree is a class A misdemeanor; Conspiracy in the fourth degree is a class E felony; Conspiracy in the third degree is a class D felony; Conspiracy in the second degree is a class B felony;[7] and conspiracy in the first degree is a class A-I felony.

In addition to the planning or thinking element of Conspiracy, it is also the law that it must be shown in pleading and proving the crime an overt act. This legal requirement is codified in Section 105.20 of the Penal Law entitled Conspiracy; pleading and proof; necessity of overt act.

The leading and seminal case setting forth the elements of conspiracy is *People v. Berkowitz.*[8] In that case, the Court of Appeals stated that the core of conspiracy is the illicit agreement. *Berkowitz* held that the defendant must have entered into the requisite agreement with at least one other person and that once the illicit agreement is shown, the requirement of an overt act of any conspirator may be attributed to other conspirators to establish the offense of conspiracy. It is beyond the parameters of this article to exhaustively analyze the elements, thrust, and total understanding of the crime of conspiracy, on which many law review articles, books, and book chapters have been written. This essay proposes to examine, under New York law, what may be said to constitute the "overt act" required to complete the crime.

In general, overt act has been defined variously as functioning to manifest the fact that conspiracy is at work. The conspiracy statute does not specify any particular conduct to satisfy the requirement that there be an overt act in furtherance of the conspiracy. It is the law that the overt act must be an independent act that tends to carry out the conspiracy, but need not necessarily be the object of the crime. See *People v. Arroyo.*[9] In *People v. Canale,*[10] the Appellate Division Third Department stated that the overt act, once again, in furtherance of the conspiracy, need not be the object of the crime and can even include acts of concealment occurring before, during, or in some cases after the conspiratorial objective. In *Robinson v. Snyder,*[11] the Appellate Division First Department further refined and defined the reach of the requirement of the "overt act" in stating that the overt act is merely an element of the crime that has as its basis the agreement and that the overt act of any conspirator may be attributed to other conspirators to establish the offense of conspiracy.

People v. Ortiz[12] gives a more exact definition of the overt act of a conspiracy, stating that that act signals the intent to move the project forward from talk to action; provides corroboration of the existence of the agreement; and indicates that the agreement has reached a point where it poses a sufficient threat to society to impose sanctions. Thus far, we have seen that the overt act requirement need not be the object of the crime; functions to show that a conspiracy is at work; can be an act of concealment; and provides evidence of the agreement and of the intent to move the project forward from the mere planning and thinking stage to the point where a threat to society is apparent. Finally we have seen that an overt act of any co-conspirator becomes the legal act of the rest.

We will now consider, more specifically, what may be said to constitute or not constitute the "overt act." It has been held that passive acts or omissions cannot constitute an overt act. Thus, in *People v. Abedi*[13] it was held that alleged omissions of failing to inform an attorney over a period of five years of the means by which bank holding company stock was purchased; the failure by two defendants to inform their law partners over the same period of the means by which stock was purchased; and, when informing the auditor of the loans, failing to mention their non-recourse nature were not "overt acts" as required for a conspiracy in the prosecution arising from the investigation into the relationship between the corporation and bank holding company.

Similarly, in *People ex rel. Conte v. Flood*[14] it was held that although the "overt act" must be specific, affirmative, independent and identified as done to further the conspiracy, the allegation that the conspirators threatened victims during the period of conspiracy with physical harm did not allege an overt act.[15] On the other hand, conversations among conspirators may constitute an overt act in furtherance of the agreement and conversations which attempt to elicit others may also constitute such an act.[16] In the same way, telephone conversations have been held to be "overt acts." Thus, in *People v. Sorentino*[17] the Appellate Division First Department held that there was sufficient evidence of overt acts connecting the defendant to a conspiracy charge to sustain his conviction for Conspiracy in the first degree, where the timing of the defendant's telephone call to an intermediary and of the intermediary's phone call to the union official informant, coupled with the intermediary's payment of $1,000 to the informant as a bribe by a private contractor who was using non-union employees, constituted overt acts in furtherance of the conspiracy.[18]

Another play on a telephone conversation constituting an "overt act" in furtherance of a conspiracy is where tape recordings are involved. In *People v. Surpris*[19] the Appellate Division Second Department held that a conviction for conspiracy to sell narcotics was sufficiently supported by evidence of tape-recorded conversations between the defendant, the confidential informant, and the undercover police officer, which indicated that the defendant had entered into an agreement to sell a controlled substance and actively pursued consummation of the deal.[20]

It is has also been held that the fact of a common scheme or plan can constitute an "overt act" in furtherance of a conspiracy. Thus, in *People v. Ozarowski*[21] the trial court held that the fact of rapid, continuous, and related sequence of events on the night of the assault and the planned character of the group action, among other things, supported the trial judge's conclusion that there was a common plan or scheme hatched among the defendants and that overt acts in furtherance of the conspiracy took place. The law has also established that a meeting or series of meetings can constitute an overt act or acts in furtherance of a conspiracy. Thus, in *People v. Sher,*[22] the trial court held that, where it was alleged that one defendant in Albany County communicated with a second defendant in Kings County for the purpose of compelling a third person to pay a gambling debt; and that later the first defendant met with such person in Greene County for the purpose of arranging payment; and that thereafter a third defendant collected money from the person and, upon default, assaulted him, the meeting in Greene County was an overt act in furtherance of the conspiracy to collect the gambling debt and all defendants were within the jurisdiction of the Greene County Court.[23]

Another example of an overt act that fulfills that requirement for a conspiracy, it has been held, is a solicitation. Thus, in *People v. Bongarzone*[24] the Court of Appeals held there was sufficient circumstantial evidence upon which to infer performance of an overt act of conspiracy by defendant charged with crimes stemming from alleged conspiracy to arrange for the murder of the eyewitness to the automobile accident; the evidence included admissible statements made by defendant to others that he had spoken, and would again speak, to his mother and sister to further the conspiratorial objective by providing payment and photograph of victim; statement to undercover officer posing as hitman that defendant would make telephone call to his mother immediately; specific instructions to the undercover officer about following up on the telephone call to the defendant's mother; and provision of his mother's phone number to undercover officer with description of instructions he intended to give her.[25]

It should further be noted that it is also the law that money payments can constitute an overt act or acts in furtherance of a conspiracy. Thus, the Appellate Division Fourth Department held in *People v. Ortiz*[26] that the payment of $50 to an undercover officer, who would not perform previously arranged conspiracy to use physical force to collect a debt until payment was made, was an "overt act" of the conspiracy and not an act to cement the conspiracy or secure the participation of the officer in the conspiracy. Similarly, in *People v. Teeter*[27] the Appellate Division Fourth Department again held, as it did in *People v. Ortiz*,[28] that even if the undercover officer to whom money was allegedly paid for the purpose of having certain persons killed was not a co-conspirator, the payment of money would constitute an "overt act" required for first-degree conspiracy conviction.[29]

It has also been held that drug sales and evidence as to drug sales can constitute an overt act in furtherance of a conspiracy. For example, in *People v. Weaver*[30] the Appellate Division Third Department held that a co-conspirator's delivery of cocaine and his use of County airport to import cocaine were overt acts in furtherance of the conspiracy involving the defendant, even though the cocaine handled by the co-conspirator did not come from the defendant; the co-conspirator went to Florida to get cocaine from the defendant; and he turned to another supplier when he was unable to do so. On this area of drug sales, *Borzuko v. City of New York Police Dept. Property Clerk*[31] is instructive. In that case, the trial court held that evidence of a trip from New York to Florida with $50,000 with which the accused intended to purchase drugs was sufficient showing of an overt act to support a finding of conspiracy.[32]

A final point should be noted. Overt acts in furtherance of a conspiracy which took place later than during the date specified in the indictment can be admitted into evidence and even when the overt act was in furtherance of the conspiracy completed despite the eminence of the actual commission of the murder.[33]

Conclusion

This brief review of what the law has held may be said to constitute an overt act in furtherance of a conspiracy reveals a number of rules. Threats cannot constitute an "overt act" in furtherance of a conspiracy, nor can passive actions or omissions. Conversations can and that includes telephone conversations and tape recordings. Meetings and evidence of a rapid sequence of events indicating a common scheme of plan have been held to be overt acts in furtherance of a conspiracy. Solicitation, payments, and drug sales all have been held to be overt acts in furtherance of a conspiracy. It is the law as well that an overt act in furtherance of a conspiracy need not necessarily be the object of the crime and can include acts of concealment. It is also the law that once a defendant is shown to be a member of a conspiracy all overt acts performed by any of the co-conspirators become the legal act of every other. Finally, an act close to the consummation of the crime or even afterward, at least as to the date of the indictment, are admissible as an overt act. It is hoped that this cursory review of the law of "overt act" in furtherance of a conspiracy will prove useful to the practitioner faced with this sort of case or issue.[34]

This article is reprinted from Atticus, *the Newsletter of the New York State Association of Criminal Defense Lawyers, 2007, with permission.*

8. Brady, Part Two

In a previous article, this writer examined, in part, what may constitute *Brady* material required to be disclosed to the defense by the prosecution pursuant to C.P.L. Sec. 240.20(l)(h). Unlike the rule for the disclosure of *Rosario* material as codified under C.P.L. Sec. 240.45, which states that *Rosario* material must be made available to the defendant after the jury has been sworn and before the prosecutor's opening statement in the case of a jury trial, or, in the event of a bench trial, after the commencement of trial and before the submission of evidence, the rule as to the time at or before trial when *Brady* material must be revealed to the defense differs from the *Rosario* rule as the following cases will show.

In *People v. Cortijo*, 70 N.Y.2d 868, 523 N.Y.S.2d (1987), the Court of Appeals stated the rule. In *Cortijo* the defendant was convicted of Attempted Murder in the Second Degree and Criminal Possession of a Weapon in the Third Degree. Prior to trial, the defendant demanded the People disclose all *Brady* material. In the course of the People's case, the defense found that the People knew of two eyewitnesses to the incident not called as witnesses at trial and whose identity had not been revealed to the defendant. Pursuant to a court order, the People produced one eyewitness along with a statement that he had given to the police. The defense decided, after interviewing the eyewitness, not to call him as witness or to use his statement for cross-examination. The defense argued that the statement given by the eyewitness was exculpatory and that the People's failure to disclose it prior to trial was a *Brady* violation requiring reversal. The Court of Appeals held that there was no *Brady* violation, stating that the defendant's right to a fair trial is not violated as long as he is given a meaningful opportunity to use the allegedly exculpatory material to cross-examine the People's witnesses or as evidence during his case.

In *People v. White*, 178 A.D.2d 669, 578 N.Y.S.2d 227 (2d Dept. 1991), Second Department reached a similar conclusion. *White* was an appeal from a judgment of the Supreme Court of Kings County, convicting the defendant of Robbery in the First Degree; Robbery in the Second Degree; Assault in the Second Degree; Grand Larceny in the Fourth Degree and Criminal Possession of a Weapon in the Fourth Degree. The defense argued a *Brady* violation in the failure of the People to turn over, until after the beginning of trial, a laboratory report which confirmed the presence of human blood on the defendant's pants but was inconclusive as whether the blood found was that of the complainant. The Second Department held that there was no *Brady* violation, stating that the rule of *Brady* does not require that disclosure be made at any particular point in the trial, but that it must be made in time for the defendant to use it effectively. The court concluded that the report was produced for the defense during the cross-examination of the complainant and so the defense was given a full opportunity to utilize it. See also *People v. Fernandez*, 135 A.D.2d 867, 522 N.Y.S.2d 264 (3rd Dept. 1987).

In sum, unlike the *Rosario* rule, *Brady* material need not be disclosed and made available to the defense prior to the commencement of trial or after voir dire and before the prosecutor's opening statement in the case of the jury trial, but need only be made available in time for the defense to utilize it effectively and to be given a "meaningful opportunity" to make use of it.

Although the *Brady* rule differs from the rule of *Rosario* in respect to the period of time allowed for disclosure, it is the view of this writer that the better procedure for the timely disclosure of *Brady* material would be to compel the People to produce it at least prior to the opening of the trial testimony. The rule of *Brady* that exculpatory material must be disclosed and be made available to the defense is a role of fundamental fairness and due process. To permit the prosecutor in the midst of the heat of trial to produce what fairness and due process mandate the production of to the defense early on, thus allowing the defense little or no time to consider its relevance and importance, and to permit this kind of surprise and obvious prejudice in the midst of trial is to hamper the total disclosure of truth, or at the very least, hamper its unearthing, which is, after all, the purpose of trial by jury.

Although the appellate courts of this state hold otherwise as to the proper time for the disclosure of *Brady* material, to assure total fairness the rule should be similar to the *Rosario* rule, since the need for the earliest possible disclosure of exculpatory or impeaching evidence is all the more pressing than *Rosario*, where oftentimes the material may largely consist of mere witness inconsistencies. Perhaps the time will come when the appellate courts of this state will see that there is no true "meaningful opportunity" to utilize exculpatory or impeaching evidence unless it is produced before the trial testimony has commenced. Nothing less is fair and nothing less will lead to meaningful and ultimate justice.

9. The Accidental Showup

The showup in criminal practice, wherein the defendant, with a police presence, is displayed to the complainant for the purpose of an effectual identification, is the most common form of pretrial identification procedures, along with the lineup and photo identification. The showup procedure often occurs within minutes, hours or days of the criminal transaction and may occur at the scene, or nearby, pursuant to canvas of the area of the crime. It can even occur at the police station house although this is most suspect and subject to the severest scrutiny by the courts.

In general, it is the law that the police arranged or induced showup is condemned as inherently suggestive, as opposed to the fairer lineup procedures, and is generally disfavored. *People v. Lane,* 102 A.D.2d 829, 476 N.Y.S.2d 365 (2d Dept. 1989); *People v. Ford*, 100 A.D.2d 941 (2d Dept. 1984).

The showup procedure may be defined as a police arranged or induced identification procedure where the complainant, in the deliberate presence of a police officer or officers, identifies the defendant as the perpetrator.

This article, however, proposes to deal not with the law concerning the most common police arranged showup, on the subject of which the cases are legion, but with the law concerning the chance or accidental showup identification of the defendant. *People v. Gonzalez* 46 N.Y.2d 1011, 416 N.Y.S.2d 239, 389 N.E.2d 834 (1979), states the rule on this well.

In *Gonzalez*, the defendant was convicted in the Supreme Court of Bronx County of First Degree Robbery and the Supreme Court, Appellate Division Affirmed. The Appellate Court simply stated that the showup was accidental, the identification spontaneous and there was an absence of unnecessarily suggestive, untoward police conduct to taint the identification.

It would appear, pursuant to the rule stated in *Gonzalez*, that a similar standard of suggestive and unfair police conduct will be applied both to the accidental and deliberately police arranged showup, and the fact that the showup is accidental is of no matter.

In *People v. McLamb*, 140 A.D.2d 717, 528 N.Y.S.2d 897 (2d Dept. 1988); app. den. 72 N.Y.2d 959, 534 N.Y.S.2d 673, 534 N.E.2d 305 (1988), the Second Department further stated and defined the *Gonzalez* rule. In *McLamb,* the defendant was convicted of Robbery in the First Degree; Robbery in the Second Degree; and Assault in the Second Degree and appealed. The Second Department affirmed the trial court's denial of defendant's motion to suppress eyewitness testimony stating the identification was by chance and spontaneous. The facts were, in *McLamb*, that the witness was making a statement to a detective in the precinct when she identified the defendant who was brought in by a police officer, who was unaware the witness was in the squad room. The court held the showup accidental and stated the more exact rule that the accidental showup at the police station is not impermissibly suggestive when the identification is unavoidable and not the result of any malfeasance or misdirection on the part of the police.

Under the rule stated in *McLamb*, an accidental showup, albeit at the police station house, is not unduly suggestive unless the direct product of deliberate police misconduct and planning, in fact police urged. Again in *People v. Musial*, 120 A.D.2d 682, 501 N.Y.S.2d 913 (2d Dept 1986); app. den. 68 N.Y.2d 815, 507 N.Y.S.2d 1033, 449 N.E.2d 882 (1986), the Second Department held the showup identification of the defendant at the station house accidental. Here the police officer who arrested the defendant handcuffed him to the railing where the other suspect had been placed. The arresting officer, after being treated for an injury incurred in the course of the arrest of the codefendant, returned to the station house with the eyewitness who noticed the defendant handcuffed to the railing and identified him. It was the testimony of the witness that no one directed her to identify the defendant. The court noted that here there was no reason to believe that the eyewitness knew the police had in fact apprehended the defendant. The court thus held the showup accidental and sustained the trial court's determination not to suppress.

It is clear that unless the so-called accidental or chance showup can be shown to be deliberately police induced and arranged and the product of unfair police procedure, it will not be suppressed.

See also *People v. Cummings,* 109 A.D.2d 748, 485 N.Y.S.2d 847 (2d Dept. 1985) (Held: Accidental encounter between witness and defendant was to appear not unduly suggestive); *People v. Martin,* 38 A.D.2d 536, 327 N.Y.S.2d 53 (1st Dept. 1971); affd. 32 N.Y.2d 771, 344 N.Y.S.2d 957, 298 N.E.2d 119 (1973) (Held: Accidental identification by complainant of defendant while being interrogated accidental, not police urged, and so not bar to in court identification); *People v. Tatum,* 129 Misc.2d 196, 492 N.Y.S.2d 999 (S. Ct. Queens County 1985) (Held: Where the defendant waived his appearance at Wade Hearing, chance viewing of defendant by witness in courtroom accidental and not the result of police or prosecutorial action).

Conclusion

The cases on accidental or inadvertent showups, on analysis, state a rule that unless the so-called inadvertence can be shown to be the direct result of deliberate police or prosecutorial malfeasance or unfairness, it will not be held to be unduly suggestive and so not suppressed. The obvious difficulty facing the defense lawyer under this scenario is proving police unfairness when all the circumstances show chance, not deliberation, was involved. Hence, it is the task of defense counsel to obtain any chance at suppression, to paint the totality of the circumstances to show effectively in fact that the showup could not have been the product of accident or chance, that happenstance is not in the likelihood of the chain of events. This is most difficult and one can only conclude from the case law that accidental showups will generally not be suppressed.

10. Psychiatric Examination of the Complainant in Criminal Law: Some Case Law

The mental and psychiatric status, condition, impairment or history of the complainant in a criminal case, whether the charge be rape, sexual abuse, murder, manslaughter or robbery, is rightly of more than passing interest to the criminal defense counsel. If, in fact, it is known to defense counsel that the complainant has a past and/or continuing history of psychiatric treatment, in order to properly discredit the complainant's allegations of wrongdoing and malfeasance against the defendant and counter them, it is highly desirable that not only the psychiatric records of the complainant's treatment, but the records of hospitalization and of outpatient medical treatment, be obtained; and also a thorough psychiatric examination of the complainant be obtained by court order, either by a court appointed psychiatrist or a psychiatrist of the defendant's own choosing. In this way, it may be shown, should the complainant have a history of treatment for psychosis due to schizophrenia or a manic depressive illness, through the cross-examination of the complainant and the trial testimony of the examining psychiatrist, that the complainant's allegations are insubstantial and the product of delusion, paranoia, or manic depressive illness. In addition, if the complainant has a past history of psychiatric treatment, it may be shown in this way that the complainant's recollection and perception were impaired due to his past and continuing mental disability.

Some Pertinent Cases

The cases are few in number that have reached the issue of, whether upon application of the defendant, the court may order a psychiatric examination of the complainant. Most are trial court decisions. *People v. Griffin,* 138 Misc. 2nd 279 (S. Ct. Kings County 1988), is an interesting decision. In *Griffin,* the defendants were indicted for committing, *inter alia,* the crime of aggravated sexual abuse. Defendant Mann moved for an order directing that the complaining witnesses be made available for psychiatric evaluation by a doctor chosen by the defense. Codefendants joined in the motion.

The basis for the relief sought was that an examination by the office of Dr. Schiffman of the complainant's psychiatric records, provided by the prosecution for 1982 and 1983, revealed that the complainant, in the past, had suffered from a mental illness, still suffered from it and that it had possibly gotten worse over the past several years. The doctor also stated, in a letter, that to determine to a degree of medical certainly whether the complainant still suffered from a mental illness, it would be necessary for him to interview the complainant. The motion was made in anticipation of a request to preclude the complainant's testimony, to receive his testimony unsworn pursuant to C.P.L. Sec. 60.20 and impeach his testimony on the basis of his psychiatric history.

The court first reviewed the older authorities in this general area, including Wigmore on Evidence, the language and purpose of the New York Rape Shield Law, C.P.L. Sec. 60.42 and the law that a medical person with personal knowledge of the complainant's condition may testify for the limited purpose of helping the jury evaluate his credibility, citing *People v. Parks*, 41 N.Y.2d 36.

The court went on to state that no appellate decision in New York had ruled on the issue of whether a trial court had the power to order a psychiatric examination of the complainant, although the court noted that the federal courts had held that the decision on whether to order a psychiatric examination of the complainant was within the sound discretion of the trial court. The court went on to note that in *Ballard v. Superior Court*, 64 Cal 2nd 159, 49 CA. Rprt. 3002, the court held that the trial judge has the discretion to order a psychiatric examination of the complaining witness in a sex violation case when the defendant presents a compelling reason for the same. The California court suggested that a compelling reason would generally arise only whether little or no corroboration supported the charge and the defense raised the issue of the effect of the complaining witness's mental or emotional condition upon her veracity.

The court stated that it was in agreement with the *Ballard* holding stating that although no specific statutory authority existed in New York for a complaining witness to undergo a psychiatric examination and no case law could be found to support such a procedure, nevertheless the court had the power and discretion to devise a remedy. The court held, thus, that it was within the discretion of the trial judge to order the complainant to submit to a psychiatric examination, but such examination could only be ordered in light of the particular facts of a given case and only where a compelling reason is present. The court held that, although the complainant's credibility is always in issue, the complainant is not on trial and a balance must be struck between the necessity to protect the rights of the mentally disabled and the right of the defendant to a fair trial.

Although the court did hold, in *Griffin,* that the trial court could, given the showing of a compelling reason under the facts of particular case scenario, order a psychiatric examination of the complainant, in this case it declined to do so since there was no showing of a compelling reason. The court stated the defense speculated on medical records more than four years old that the complainant still suffered from a mental illness and that his condition had deteriorated over the past four years. The court further stated that there was no allegation in the defense affirmation, or the Doctor's letter, that the complainant's illness, should it exist, would affect the witness' competency or capacity to testify or that the results of an examination were needed to aid the jury is assessing the credibility of the witness.

In sum, the *Griffin* court held that the speculation and conclusory allegation of the defense did not present a sufficiently compelling reason based on fact and not on speculation and conclusion, for the trial court to order a psychiatric examination of the complainant .

People v. Lowe, 96 Misc.2d 33 (Criminal Court, Bronx County 1978), precedes *Griffin,* but agrees on reasoning and result. In *Lowe*, the defendant was charged with burglary, petit larceny and criminal mischief, arising from alleged incidents in the complainant's apartment on two separate occasions. The felony charges were reduced and the matter remanded for trial. The Defendant moved for discovery of the complainant's medical records and for a psychiatric examination of the complainant. At the preliminary hearing, the complainant, a fifty-four year old disabled veteran, testified that he had suffered a brain injury during the Second World War. He also testified that he could not remember certain things, such as the dates of the alleged incidents or how long he had lived in his present apartment. His testimony was in part confused and contradictory. He changed his testimony several times as to how many people were involved, who they were, and how they had entered his apartment At another point, he testified that he could not see very well and later stated that he had been wearing his glasses on the day in question.

Subsequent to the hearing, defense counsel's investigation revealed that the complainant had been hospitalized at a psychiatric hospital in New Jersey and that psychiatric evaluations were performed on him at the Veterans Administration Hospital. The defendant sought production of these records.

The court reasoned that due process considerations pursuant to *Brady v. Maryland,* 373 U.S. 83, required the disclosure to the accused of evidence favorable to him which is material to guilt or punishment and would affect the credibility of a particular witness. The court went on to state that the long standing mental illness of a complaining witness who is the sole eyewitness to the crime, and where such condition may affect the accuracy, perception and comprehension of his testimony, must be disclosed to the defendant, including the case records of the complainant's psychiatric history.

What is most important, however, is the dicta of the court that upon a proper factual showing, a showing not made in this case, a psychiatric examination of the complainant may be ordered. The court noted that in two New Jersey cases, *State v. Falcetano*, 107 N.J. Super 375, and *State v. Franklin*, 49 N.J. 286, the trial courts had ordered a psychiatric evaluation and examination of the complaining witness. In *Falcetano*, that court held that where a homicide victim's son, who had been indicted with the defendant but turned State's evidence, had exhibited signs of traumatic shock and exhibited violent behavior, a psychiatric examination should be ordered. The *Franklin* court ordered a psychiatric examination of the main prosecution witness in a murder trial where the witness had once been committed to a hospital for the insane.

In short, the *Lowe* court, like *Griffin,* held that in the particular case, it is within the discretion of the trial court based on the totality of the facts and circumstances to order a psychiatric examination of the complainant in a criminal case. However, it declined to do so in the case before it, citing two New Jersey cases for the proposition that such examination is appropriate where violent behavior of the witness is evidenced or the witness has had a prior psychiatric hospitalization. See also *People v. Freshley,* 87 A.D.2d 104 (1st Dept. 1982); *People v. Passenger,* 175 A.D.2d 944 (3rd Dept. 1991); *People v. Souvenir,* 83 Misc.2d 1038 (Criminal Court, New York County 1975). For a most recent case analyzing this issue, see *People v. Lucy Costanza,* N.Y.L.J. 5/5/93, p. 27 col. 1 (Westchester County Court).

Conclusion

There has been no appellate decision in this state specifically giving its imprimatur to a trial court ordering a psychiatric examination of the complainant in a criminal case. In *Passenger,* the Third Dept. holds that it may be in the discretion of the trial court to do so and that the criterion for ordering or not ordering the examination is compelling proof of mental or emotional instability. *Griffin* found that the trial court has the power to do so under Sec. 2 b(3) of the Judiciary law, an enabling statute that states that a court of record has the power to devise and make new process and forms of proceedings necessary to carry into effect the power and jurisdiction possessed by it. Like *Passenger, Griffin* holds that a compelling reason must be present to order a psychiatric examination of the complainant. *Lowe* holds the same, but does however hold that a showing of compulsion be present as long as the facts of the case warrant it. It is clear, although *Costanza* most recently holds otherwise, that it is within the discretion of the trial court to order a psychiatric examination of the complainant in a criminal case on a proper factual showing. Whether the criteria be a compelling reason, as in *Griffin* and *Passenger,* or the totality of the circumstances, as *Lowe* holds, there is authority, both trial and appellate, for the trial court to order such an examination. If such power exists, it may be of clear and inestimable benefit to the defense and, if properly used at trial, may serve to discredit the perception, recollection and overall credibility of the complainant.

11. A Question of Value

It is the law of the State of New York, as codified in C.P.L. Art. 60 *Rules of Evidence,* and C.P.L. Art 190.30(1) *Grand Jury, Rules of Evidence,* that, in the Grand Jury, as at trial in general, only direct, non-hearsay evidence may be admitted into evidence for the Grand Jury's consideration. Sec *People vs. Percy,* 74, Misc.2d 552, 345 N.Y.S.2d 276 (Suffolk County Court, 1973), affd. 45 A.D.2d 284, 358 N.Y.S.2d 434 (2d Dept. 1974); affd. 38 N.Y.2d 806, 382 N.Y.S.2d 39 (1975); *People vs. Sutton,* 49 Misc.2d 672, 564 N.Y.S.2d 646 (S. Ct. Bronx County 1990); *People vs. Jackson,* 148 Misc.2d 886, 561 N.Y.S.2d 398 (S. Ct. Kings County 1990).

Thus, with some exceptions to be considered at a later point in this article, an indictment is only authorized when, on the basis of direct non-hearsay evidence, the evidence before the Grand Jury is legally sufficient to establish that such person committed such offense and competent and admissible evidence before the Grand Jury provided reasonable cause to believe that such people committed such offense. C.P.L. Sec. 190.65, 1, 2 *Grand Jury, When Indictment Authorized.*

There are, however, as codified in C.P.L. Sec. 190.30 subs. 2, 3, two exceptions to the rule that only direct non-hearsay evidence is appropriate and available to obtain a legally sufficient and valid indictment. C.P.L. Sec. 190.30(2) dispenses with the necessity of the direct Grand Jury testimony of chemists, coroners, medical examiners, ballistics experts, handwriting experts, fingerprint experts or an expert or technician in some comparable scientific or professional field.

The section provides that a certified report of such expert may be received in the Grand Jury proceeding as evidence of the facts stated herein.

The idea behind the section is that the certified reports of such experts in their particular scientific field are as valid as direct testimony on the subject and such testimony would only repeat the scientific finding, as articulated in the sworn certified report.

The second exception to the requirement of non-hearsay direct evidence in the Grand Jury is C.P.L. Sec. 190.30(3). That section provides in pertinent part that a written or oral statement, under oath, is legally sufficient evidence to be considered by the Grand Jury, even though it is technically hearsay, where the written certified report is evidence of

1. that person's ownership of the premises and of the defendant's lack of license or privilege to enter or remain thereupon;
2. that person's ownership or possessory right in property and the monetary amount of any damage and the defendant's lack of right to damage or tamper with the property;
3. that person's ownership of property, its value and the defendant's lack of superior or equal right to possession thereof;

4. that person's ownership of a vehicle and the absence of his consent to the defendant's taking, operating, exercising control over or using it. (C.P.L. Sec. 190.30(3)(A-D)

This section clearly envisions and provides for and dispenses with the need for a necessity for the personal appearance in the Grand Jury of the owner of stolen or damaged property, including a vehicle, and premises the subject of a Criminal Trespass or Burglary. In short, these relevant sections provide that in case of Larceny, Burglary, Criminal Mischief, Criminal Trespass and Vehicular Theft, that the owner of the stolen, damaged or trespassed upon property need not personally appear before the Grand Jury to prove ownership, value or damage to property.

This section, in Sec. 190.13(e), (f), also dispenses with the personal appearance with respect to that person's qualifications as a dealer or other expert in appraising or evaluating a particular type of property, his expert opinion as to the value of a certain item or items of property of that type and the basis for his opinion; (C.P.L. Sec. 190.30[e]) and that person's identity as an ostensible maker or drafter of a written instrument and of its falsity within the meaning of section 170.00 of the penal law. (C.P.L. Sec. 190.30, 3[f]).

It would appear that the essential purpose of C.P.L. Sec. 190.30(A-F) was to allow the owners of stolen property, damaged property, trespassed upon premises, or forged instruments from having to make personal appearances before the Grand Jury to testify as to ownership of damages or value of the property. The apparent idea behind this statute was, in a word, to allow indictment by affidavit, relieving the property owner from having to personally appear before the Grand Jury.

A Recent Case

Although the wording of the statute, and its apparent purpose, is eminently clear, a recent case in the Supreme Court of the County of Queens, affirmed by the Appellate Division, Second Department, has interpreted and in a sense amended what in fact this affidavit must contain and cast into doubt the intent of the statutory language that the affidavit alone of the owner of the premises or the stolen or damaged property is sufficient to allow an indictment pursuant to C.P.L. Sec 190.30(3) and C.P.L. Sec. 190.65. That case is *People vs. Ricardo Lopez.*

The facts in *Lopez* were that on August 8, 1990, in the County of Queens, the police saw a 1985 Pontiac with a towel wrapped around its steering column and with a broken rear vent window. The vehicle was stopped. The vehicle was driven by the co-defendant, Mr. Nuñez. Mr. Lopez was the front seat passenger. The police then arrested both occupants of the vehicle after a VIN check and when the driver, upon request of the police, failed to produce ownership papers, the steering column was found to be broken and the car's trunk and luggage rack broken.

Pursuant to the law, the affidavit of the owner was admitted into evidence before the Grand Jury attesting, in pertinent part, that the damage to the vehicle was in excess of $250.00 and that its value was over $2500.00.

The defendants, based on this affidavit, were indicted for Grand Larceny in the Fourth Degree; Criminal Possession of Stolen Property in the Fourth Degree; Criminal Mischief in the Third Degree; and Unauthorized Use of a Motor Vehicle in the Third Degree. Upon a motion to inspect, dismiss and/or reduce the indictment, the Hon. Pearle Appleman of the Queens County Supreme Court dismissed the Counts in the Indictment of Grand Larceny in the Fourth Degree, Criminal Possession of Stolen Property in the Fourth Degree and Criminal Mischief in the Third Degree, to Petit Larceny, Criminal Possession of Stolen Property in the Fifth Degree and Criminal Mischief in the Fourth Degree, in a decision and order dated January 9, 1991.

Judge Appelman reasoned that the owner's unsupported opinion as to the value of the property or damage was insufficient to establish valuation, citing *People vs. Bernard,* 123 A.D.2d 324 (2d Dept. 1986).

The People appealed this order of Judge Appelman and in a decision and order dated May 31, 1991, the Appellate Division, Second Department held, citing *Bernard,* that the evidence before the Grand Jury was legally insufficient to establish the value of the property that was allegedly stolen and damaged, holding thereby that the Supreme Court did not err in reducing the Felony Courts in Misdemeanors.

In the Appellate Division decision, what is more significant, the Appellate Division rejected the People's contention that C.P.L. Sec. 190.30(3) required the conclusion that the contents of the affidavit, provided under this section to the Grand Jury, which may be received in evidence by that body, constitute legally sufficient evidence per se.

It would seem that J. Appelman of the Queens County Supreme Court and likewise the Appellate Division, Second Department, were concerned that a mere affidavit of ownership, value or damage to property, without more, is insufficient to indict. Neither Judge Appelman nor the Appellate Division suggested that C.P.L. Sec. 190.30(3), which provides for this paper procedure in certain categories of property offenses, was in any way improper or that the owner of such stolen or damaged property should be required to personally testify before the Grand Jury. What the lower court, per Judge Appleman, held, as did the Appellate Division, was that something more was required than the conclusory allegations of the owner as to value and damage, as occurred in this case. There is no indication in the lower Court decision or the Appellate Court holding as to what more is or would be required. Perhaps an itemized repair bill or estimate would be required to establish damage before the Grand Jury. Perhaps an affidavit from an expert as to the value of the stolen vehicle would be required, or an affidavit as to the present fair market value of the car in its present condition.

In that opinion, the court defined the issue to be whether an affidavit, submitted to the Grand Jury pursuant to C.P.L. Sec. 190. 30(3), where the owner states in conclusory terms the worth of allegedly stolen property and the dollar amount of physical damage to it, without indicating the basis for that valuation, can sustain an indictment where value is an element of the offense charged.

After reviewing the facts and procedural history of the case, the court held that C.P.L. Sec. 190.30(3), although it allows an owner of property to furnish a written or oral statement, made under oath, to establish the monetary value of or damage to that person's property, thereby eliminating the need to have the complainant appear personally before the Grand Jury, did not change the requirement in New York Law that more is required, under New York Law, to sustain an indictment under these circumstances than a lay witness' unsupported statement of value without indicating a basis for that valuation.

The Court held that the complainant need not be actually present, but that the affidavit must contain a basis of knowledge for the witness' statement so that the Grand Jury can reasonably infer and not speculate that property or damage to the property has the requisite value to satisfy the statutory threshold requirement.

The Court of Appeals, in affirming the Second Department, has done no more than ensure that a person will not be held in these cases on the speculation or conclusion, but on a showing of the basis of the alleged truth. It is only fair and right that a defendant, held most possibly in pretrial detention on the basis of an indictment obtained by affidavit, not be held on mere opinion or conclusion, but on an established basis of fact. It remains to be seen what, as the courts apply the Court of Appeals' opinion in *Lopez,* may be required and deemed sufficient. It may be a repair bill; it may be an assessment from an expert under C.P.L. Sec. 190.30(e). It may be an affidavit as to the cost of purchase of the automobile and its present fair market value. The Court of Appeals has assured, whatever the specifics that may follow in its wake, that no man or woman will ultimately be prosecuted under C.P.L. Sec. 190.30(c) by conclusion, speculation or opinion.

This much is clear—more than, as occurred in *Lopez,* the conclusory allegations of the owner by way of sworn affidavit is needed to indict. What more is needed and necessary is not articulated by the lower court or the Second Department. There is an indication in the citation of *Bernard,* however, as to what more may possibly be required.

Bernard was an appeal from a judgment of the Supreme Court of Kings County, convicting the defendant of Burglary in the Second Degree, Grand Larceny in the Third Degree and imposing sentence.

The Appellate Division modified on the law, reducing the conviction of Grand Larceny in the Third Degree to Petit Larceny and vacating the sentence imposed thereon. The court held that, in fact, the People proved beyond a reasonable doubt that the defendant burglarized the apartment and stole $100.00 in coins and a stereo. The court went on to state, however, that the only evidence as to the value of the stereo was the victim's testimony that it was worth $700.00.

The witness never testified, although the court noted that photographs of the stereo were admitted into evidence, as to the basis of his opinion, when the stereo was purchased, the price paid or its condition.

The court concluded, that this evidence was insufficient to establish the stolen property as having an aggregate value over $1,250.00, necessary for the conviction of Grand Larceny in the Third Degree.

It is clear from both courts' citation of *Bernard* that what more is necessary may be evidence as to the purchase price of the stolen property, its present condition or the cost or estimate of repair, if there is a charge of criminal mischief.

Lopez is a most important and significant decision since it points toward a rule that something more is required and needed under C.P.L. Sec. 190.30(3) to sustain indictment on affidavit alone than the mere conclusory statement of the owner as to value of property or the degree of damage.

This is simple fairness. It is only right that if indictment is to obtained by affidavit, it should contain more than a summary conclusion. Where indictment is obtained by affidavit, the Appellate Division held, and a defendant may be held in pretrial incarceration as a result of that affidavit, more than a mere conclusion is required, albeit sworn.

Epilogue

If there can be any doubt as to the validity and effect of *Lopez,* that question was laid to rest by the Court of Appeals in its affirmance of the order and decision of the Second Department in *People vs. Ricardo Lopez,* N.Y.L.J., p. 26, col. 3 (1992) (Court of Appeals).

12. Express Consent and the Two Hour Rule

The Driving While Intoxicated Charge, V.T.L. Sec. 1192(2),(3) is one of the most frequent denizens of the criminal courts of this State. For one who is subject to this charge, whether founded under V.T.L. Sec. 1192(2), where the crime is based on the results of a breath or blood test, or V.T.L. Sec. 1192(3), where it is based on the common law observations of the officer or civilian witness who happened to observe the defendant in his allegedly intoxicated condition, it is often the defendant's first brush with the criminal justice system and the possible penalty of one year's incarceration and the concomitant stigma of a criminal conviction will undoubtedly have a deleterious effect on the defendant's future career and personal life.

For the most part, the People will often base the strength of their case on the chemical or blood test or alcohol test given to the defendant within two hours of his arrest or within two hours after a screening test. V.T.L. Sec. 1194(2).

The statute also states in pertinent part that

> any person who operates a motor vehicle in this state shall be deemed to have given consent to a chemical test of one or more of the following: breath, blood, urine, or saliva, for the purpose of determining the alcoholic and/or drug content of the blood provided that such test is administered by or at the direction of a police officer with respect to a chemical test of breath, urine or saliva, or with respect to a chemical test of blood. . . . V.T.L. Sec. 1194(2).

The statute is clear then in two main aspects. First the chemical test, if the People wish to introduce it into evidence at trial and possibly succeed in obtaining a conviction for this offense, must be administered within two hours of arrest or administration or a screening test. Second, absent a refusal to take the test, the consent is deemed to have been given under the statute and, apparently, no express consent is needed.

The Problem

The subject of this article is, first, the effect on admission of the test results at trial of administering the test after the needed two hour period of time has elapsed and, second, whether an express consent to take the test beyond the two hour framework has any effect on admission of the test results at trial.

These issues are most significant in DWI litigation since determining the evidentiary effect of the two hour rule on admissibility of the test results at trial and determining whether an express consent may essentially obviate the apparently mandatory character of the two hour rule, can make or break the case for the defense. In sum, the question and relationship of the two hour rule in V.T.L. Sec. 1194(2) to an express consent to take the test beyond that time, is a most significant point for the attorney or client in the throes of Driving While Intoxicated litigation.

It has long been the law of this state that it is the People's burden to show that the test has been administered within two hours and their further burden to establish this fact lest preclusion or suppression of the test results in evidence be ordered. The leading case is *People v. Brol*, 81 A.S.2d 739, 438 N.Y.S.2d 424 (4th Dept. 1981). In *Brol* the defendant was convicted of Manslaughter in the Second Degree; Assault in the Third Degree; Driving Under the Influence of Alcohol and Failure to Keep Right. The charges arose from an automobile accident. At trial, evidence was admitted that the defendant had refused to take a blood/alcohol test after the accident. The defendant, noting there was testimony as to two different times of arrest, two hours apart, contended that under the two hour rule, his test refusal was inadmissible into evidence. The Fourth Department remitted the case for a hearing to determine the time of the defendant's arrest and also to determine that compliance was had with the two hour rule of

V.T.L. Sec. 1194(2). The court held, however, most specifically and in no uncertain terms, that the test or evidence of a refusal must occur within the two hour time limit and that absent this the test results and/or evidence of a refusal are incompetent evidence and not admissible.

Brol would seem to be most specific in holding that the test results and/or evidence of a refusal are either not admissible or are subject to suppression if not obtained within the two hour framework of V.T.L. Sec. 1194(2).

Five years later in 1986, the Second Department in *People v. Mills*, 124 A.D.2d 600, 507 N.Y.S.2d 743 (2d Dept. 1986), considered the issue whether an express consent can render admissible, or no, test results not obtained within the requisite two hours.

In *Mills* the defendant appealed from a judgment of the County Court of Orange County, convicting him of Criminally Negligent Homicide upon his plea of guilty and imposing sentence. On appeal, the defendant contended that the court erred in denying his motion to suppress the results of the blood alcohol test administered to him beyond the required two hours following his arrest, although he expressly consented to the test. The Second Department affirmed.

The court held that V.T.L. Sec. 1192(4) provides a method whereby a blood sample may be obtained from a driver who is suspected of Driving While Intoxicated without obtaining his express consent to do so, provided that the test is administered within two hours after the driver's arrest. The court went on to state that the requirement that the blood sample be obtained within two hours after his arrest is relevant to blood samples obtained in cases where no express consent has been given. Thus, the court noted that it has been recognized that this two hour requirement does not extend to blood samples obtained by court order pursuant to V.T.L. Sec. 1194-a, where there has been a refusal to submit to a test and that a blood sample may be obtained pursuant to a validly issued search warrant without resort to V.T.L. Sec 1194. The Court held that V.T.L. Sec. 1194 and its construing case law are designed to govern situations in which a blood sample is obtained by implied consent or court order and has no bearing upon cases where there has been an express consent.

The holding of the appellate court in *Mill* is clear: namely, that the presence of an express consent effectively nullifies the two hour rule with respect to the admissibility of chemical test results under V.T.L. Sec. 1194(2). See also *People v. Morse*, 127 Misc.2d 468, 486 N.Y.S.2d 621 (Essex County Court 1985), (Held: Two hours period for administration of blood alcohol test, under deemed consent statute, not applicable to court ordered test); *contra People v. D'Angelo*, 124 Misc.2d 1050, 478 N.Y.S.2d 539 (S. Ct. Queens County, 1984). Since *Mills* is the only appellate court to address this issue, it is at least the law in the Second Department that express consent to chemical test, otherwise valid under V.T.L. Sec. 1192(2), precludes the evidentiary effect of the two hour rule.

Some Recent Case Law

Of late, however, a number of trial courts have considered this same issue and reached differing results on whether an express consent can effectively obviate the effect of the two hour rule. *People v. Dillin,* 150 Misc.2d 311, 567 N.Y.S.2d 991 (New York City Criminal Court, 1991), is an interesting decision. In *Dillin* the defendant was charged in an information with Operating a Motor Vehicle While Under the Influence of Alcohol, a violation of V.T.L. Secs. 1192(2) (3). The defendant had previously moved to dismiss the V.T.L. Sec. 1192(2) charge on the ground that V.T.L Sec. 1194 requires that a chemical breathalyzer test to determine the blood alcohol level must be administered within two hours for its result to be admissible and that, in this case, the test was administered more than two hours after the defendant's arrest. The People argued that the defendant's express consent obviated the applicability of the two hour requirement, citing *People v. Kates,* 53 N.Y.2d 541, 444 N.Y.S.2d 446 (1981), and *Schermber v. California,* 384 U.S. 757, 86 S. Ct. 1826, 16 L.Ed.2d 908 (1960).

The court rejected the defendant's claim of coercion—that the refusal warnings given by the police effectively coerced or induced his consent.

Most importantly, the court held that the fact that the test was administered more than two hours after the defendant's arrest was irrelevant to the voluntariness of the defendant's consent. The court reasoned that the two hour period was applicable only to the "deemed consent" portion of the statute and not to the instant case where the consent was express and consensual. The court, while recognizing that the warnings concerning the consequences of a refusal do not render an express consent involuntary, also added that the consent here was knowingly, freely and voluntarily given but that if the motorist claims that he did not understand the warnings, or force or the threat of force is used, then the consent may be involuntary. The court held, in sum, that since the defendant had not alleged any coercive police action than the giving of the warnings and did not claim that he did not comprehend their import the consent here was not involuntary.

Dillin holds that where the test is administered after two hours from arrest, and there is an express consent then, absent police coercion, the two hour rule has no applicability.

People v. Sesman, 137 Misc.2d 676, 521 N.Y.S.2d 626 (Criminal Court, Bronx County, 1987), an earlier case, reaches a different result. In *Sesman* the defendant was charged with Driving While Intoxicated, under V.T.L. Sec. 1192(2), (3). The facts were that on February 13, 1987, based on observations of an officer that the defendant had a cracked windshield and his further erratic driving, he was stopped, given an alcohol sensor test, advised of his Miranda warnings, and, with his consent, given a breathalyzer test, on which he registered a 0.21. The pivotal issue before the court was the defendant's motion to suppress the Breathalyzer test.

The court held, based on a review of all the relevant evidence, that the People had not proven beyond a reasonable doubt that the test had been administered within two hours of the defendant's arrest. The court went on to state that the defendant's consent did not constitute a waiver of the two hour rule, holding that the defendant could not retrospectively be held to have waived the two hour requirement or his right to contest any aspect pertaining to the admissibility of the test, by acquiescing to the procedure. The court held that to hold the two hour requirement did not apply would be to nullify the purpose and intent of V.T.L. Sec. 1994.

Sesman is a significant decision since it holds the two hour requirements applicable where there is an alleged express consent. *Sesman* would appear to part way with *Mills* but attempts to distinguish *Mills* stating that, unlike *Mills* where there was an express consent, in this case the defendant merely declined to revoke his deemed consent, declining to have his driving privileges revoked.

Three recent trial court decisions have freshly considered the issue which is the subject of this article: *People v. Kennie Edwards,* N.Y.L.J., p. 26, col. 6, 5/12/92 (Criminal Court, New York County); *People v. Donald Resinger,* N.Y.L.J., 5/12/92, p. 27, col. I (Criminal Court, New York County); *People v. Glenn Flora,* N.Y.L.J., p. 22, col. 6, 6/23/92 (Criminal Court, New York County).

In *Edwards* the defendant was charged with violating V.T.L. Sec. 1192(1), (2) and (3) and moved to suppress the results of a breathalyzer test on the ground that the test was not conducted within two hours of the defendant's arrest as required by V.T.L. Sec. 1194. The People, although conceding the test was not given within two hours after arrest, argued the two hour rule did not bar untimely use of the breathalyzer test where the defendant expressly consented to the test.

The court, after a review of some recent trial court decisions including *Dillin* and *Sesman* as well as appellate court decisions, held the People are required to prove compliance with the two hour rule to sustain a conviction under Sec. 1192(2) of the V.T.L., reasoning that the plain language of the statutes incorporates the requirements of V.T.L Sec. 1994, including the two hour rule. The court reasoned that the two hour requirement is an element of the case to be proved beyond a reasonable doubt by the People and so cannot be waived by the defendant. The court distinguished *Mills* since in *Mills* the defendant was charged with Criminally Negligent Homicide and *Dillin* where the court stated it improperly limited the applicability of the two hour rule only to a deemed consent and not to express consent. Thus, the court held that the People could not rely on an untimely chemical test to make out a violation of V.T.L. Sec. 1192(2).

Resinger differs from *Edwards*. In *Resinger* the defendant was charged with a violation of V.T.L. Sec. 1192(2) pursuant to a test administered under V.T.L. 1194. He registered a blood alcohol level of 0.19 and moved to suppress the test results on the ground that the test was administered more than two hours after his arrest. The People argued the test results were admissible because of the defendant's express consent. The court after a review of the relevant case law, including *Brol, Mills* and *Dillin*, agreed with the reasoning of *People v. Bezer*, N.Y.L.J., 11/18/91, p. 25, col. 3 (Criminal Court, Bronx County), which held, concurring with *Dillin* and *Mills,* that the two hour rule has no applicability where there is an express consent, but noted that *Bezer* held that the burden is on the People to show that the consent was knowingly, freely, and voluntarily given. Thus, the *Resinger* court concluded that the results of the Intoximeter test should be admissible provided that the People could establish beyond a reasonable doubt that the defendant's consent was given freely and voluntarily given.

Most recently in *People v. Glenn Flora, supra*, Judge Walsh rejected the applicability of the two hour rule where there has been an express consent. In *Flora* the defendant was charged with a violation of V.T.L. Secs. 1192(3) and (4), Driving While Intoxicated, and Driving While Impaired by Drugs, and moved to preclude the results of the urinalysis which showed the presence of P.C.P., on the ground that it was not taken within two hours of his arrest. The People argued, once again, that although the test was not given within two hours of his arrest, it was admissible since the defendant expressly consented to take the test. The court, after reviewing the pertinent case and legislative history, following *Mills* and *People v. Byington*, N.Y.L.J, 12/8/89, p. 21, col. 1 (App. Term, First Dept.), held that an express consent obtained after two hours from the time of arrest is no bar to the admission of chemical test results into evidence.

The court held, however, that immediately prior to trial there should be a hearing to determine if the defendant's consent was knowingly, freely and voluntarily given, by a standard of clear and convincing evidence.

See also *People v. Ali*, 573 N.Y.S.2d 575 (New York County Criminal Court 1991), (Held: Results of breathalyzer test obtained by express consent but not within two hours of admissible); *People v. Keane*, 76, A.D.2d 963, 428 N.Y.S.2d 972 (3rd Dept. 1980).

Conclusion

This brief review of past and present cases on the interaction and the interconnection of the two hour rule to an express consent and specifically to where the express consent was rendered beyond the requisite two hour period of V.T.L. 1194 reveals a jumbled scenario with two lines of cases, appellate and trial, appearing in the picture. *Mills,* the leading appellate decision on the issue, says the two hour rule has no application where there is an express consent under the aegis of the deemed consent statute. *Dillin* is in accord with *Mills* with the caveat that the consent must be freely and voluntarily given without police coercive action. *Sesman* differs, holding that express consent or no, the test must be administered within two hours. *Edwards* agrees with *Sesman. Resinger* holds the two hour inapplicable to an express consent, with the burden on the People to show the consent was knowingly, freely, and voluntarily given, beyond a reasonable doubt. *Glenn Flora*, like *Mills* and *Dillin* agrees that the two hour rule has no applicability where there exists an express consent but like *Resinger* mandates a burden on the People, by the standard of clear and convincing evidence, to prove in a hearing prior to trial that the consent was knowingly, freely and voluntarily given.

It is the view of this writer that, although *Mills* would appear to be the law on this subject, at least in the Second Department, *Sesman* and *Edwards* are closer to the mark. The two hour rule is codified in the V.T.L. It is the statute law of this state and essentially ensures that the test result, if obtained, will be accurate. To read this legislation out of the statutory scheme, based on an express rather than a deemed consent, is to read out not only the applicable state law, but to parlay over what and what is not consent. There can be no true consent of any type when the arrested is uninformed either by action or words, of the two hour rule of law pertinent to and bearing on the legality of the test results. It is for the legislature to read out the language of the will of the People's legislators and not the courts. The two hour rule should not be read out of the statute and the case based on a technical hairsplitting distinction between implicit and actual consent. It is the legislative mandate for this class of cases, and it is hoped that one day it will be applied uniformly to all DW litigation where the chemical test is obtained in violation of statute by express consent. For there can be no true consent where a state of ignorance of a legal right governs the outcome of the case.

13. Notice and the Confirmatory Identification

It has long been established law in the State of New York that, in general, the defense in a criminal case is not entitled to a so-called Wade Hearing where the identification is confirmatory in character. The confirmatory indicia of the identification can be either in the context of a so-called buy and bust operation, where the undercover officer, subsequent to the sale transaction, does a later drive-by identification to the arresting backup team that the right man has been nabbed, or where the parties are sufficiently related or known to each other to preclude the question of any suggestiveness. See *People v. Morales*, 37 N.Y.S.2d 262, 372 N.Y.S.2d 25 (1975); *People v. Wharton,* 74 N.Y.2d 921, 550 N.Y.S.2d 260, 549 N.E.2d 462 (1984); *People v. Gissendanner.* 48 N.Y.2d 543, 423 N.Y.S.2d 8, 399 N.E.2d 424 (1979); *People v. Tas,* 51 N.Y.2d 915, 434 N.Y.S.2d 978, 415 N.E.2d 967 (1980). With some exceptional circumstances delineated in the case law, in general where the identification is confirmatory, the defense is not entitled to a Wade Hearing. Hence, it would appear that where the People deem the identification to be confirmatory no 710.30(b) notice is required. It follows that, no notice being required, the People will not be precluded from moving the unnoticed confirmatory identification facts into evidence at trial.

The fact of the matter is, however, that often, at least in the Queens County Criminal Court, 710.30(b) notice is in fact given in most if not all confirmatory identifications. The question therefore arises, and it is the subject of this article, whether, indeed, notice is required where there has been a confirmatory identification since if it is, then the defense, on notice of the possible identification, will naturally move for a Wade Hearing, and if notice is not mandated, then the People, depending on the facts of the confirmatory identification, will either be allowed to introduce the identification into evidence at trial without a pre-trial Wade Hearing or be precluded from doing so.

On the issue of whether the People must give notice under C.P.L. Sec. 710.30(b) of what they may deem a confirmatory identification, the case law varies.

The leading appellate case on this issue is *People v. Newball*, 76 N.Y.2d 587, 561 N.Y.S.2d 898 (1990). In *Newball*, the defendant, convicted primarily upon the testimony of two undercover officers, contended that the identification testimony of one of the officers should have been precluded since the People did not serve notice pursuant to C.P.L. Sec. 710.30(b) with regard to that testimony, even though the officer had previously identified the defendant within the meaning of the statute. The facts in *Newball* were that Undercover John Smith bought cocaine and Undercover Doe observed the sale from approximately fifty to seventy-five feet away. Officer Smith, upon completion of the sale, radioed a description of the seller to the backup unit but by the time the backup unit arrived to make the arrest, the subject had left and could not be found afterwards.

Thereafter on November 18, 1986, Officer Smith, in the course of his duties, spotted the former subject from the October 21, 1986 sale, radioed his backup unit, giving the subject's description and location and, on arrival at the scene, Officer Doe identified the defendant as the subject of the October 21, 1986 sale.

Prior to trial the defendant was not served with C.P.L. Sec. 710.30(b) notice pertaining to Officer Doe's previous identification and at trial Officer Doe identified the defendant as the person he had seen doing the October 21, 1986 sale and as the person he identified twenty-eight days later. On the basis of the testimony of Officers Smith and Doe, the defendant was convicted of Criminal Sale of a Controlled Substance in the Third Degree.

On Appeal the Appellate Division rejected the defendant's arguments that C.P.L. Sec. 710.30(b) had been violated, citing *People v. Gissendanner, supra*, and *People v. Wharton, supra*. The Court of Appeals reversed.

The People argued, on appeal to the Court of Appeals, that Officer Doe's identification did not constitute a previous identification within the meaning of the statute since it was not a police arranged identification procedure, but was the product of a chance meeting on the street. The Court of Appeals held, however, that, like a showup, the identification here occurred at the deliberate direction of the state. The Court of Appeals also rejected the People's reliance on

Gissendanner, stating that the October 21, 1986, identification did not make the defendant and the officer known to each other within the meaning of *Gissendanner.*

The Court also rejected the People's contention that the November 18, 1986 identification of the defendant was confirmatory within the meaning of *Wharton.* The Court held the November 18, 1986 viewing was not a part of integral police procedure. The Court also noted that the lapse of four weeks called into question the reliability found to exist in *Wharton.* In sum, the Court concluded that this case presented the type of special circumstances which called for a C.P.L. Sec. 710.60(4) Hearing and therefore required notice under C.P.L. Sec. 710.30(b). The Court concluded that, given the lack of required notice, it was error to admit Officer's Doe's identification testimony into evidence.

The holding of *Newball* is not entirely clear. It would appear that if certain discrete special circumstances are present, such as the lapse of time between arrest and subsequent identification, C.P.L. Sec. 710.30(b) notice, though not ordinarily required, is mandated. *Newball* holds that, but for the time lag between identification and arrest, the identification would be confirmatory and with the time lapse it is not confirmatory and, in the absence of C.P.L. Sec. 710.30(b) notice, preclusion would result.

The Supreme Court of New York County in *People v. Naranjo,* 140 Misc.2d 43, 529 N.Y.S.2d 953 (Supreme Court, New York County, 1988), reached a different result. In *Naranjo* the defendant was charged with Criminal Sale and Possession of a Controlled Substance in the Third Degree and moved to preclude the identification testimony of the undercover based on the prosecutor's failure to serve identification notice within fifteen days of the defendant's arraignment. The People opposed the defendant's request on the ground that the identification was confirmatory under *Morales.* The Court held that the prosecutor's characterization of the identification procedure as confirmatory did not relieve the People of their statutory obligation to provide notice pursuant to statute since the determination that an identification or viewing is confirmatory is a question of fact and law to be decided by the Court pursuant to a motion to suppress made by the defendant, and does not reside in the unfettered discretion of the prosecutor.

The *Naranjo* court distinguished *Morales* noting that in that case the court determined the identification was confirmatory, nevertheless the trial court determination on the issue was made pursuant to a Hearing held at the defendant's request.

The court further stated that in some cases a hearing has been held where there has been an undue delay between the sale and arrest, although the identification would ordinarily be considered confirmatory, citing *People v. Rubio,* 118 A.D.2d 879, 500 N.Y.S.2d 366 (2d Dept. 1980), (27 days), and *People v. Wright,* 47 A.D.2d 894, 367 N.Y.S.2d 261 (1st Dept. 1975), (7 weeks). The court thus concluded that, having failed to serve the required fifteen days notice or establish good cause for the failure to do so, the court precluded the sought for admission of the identification evidence by the People.

Naranjo differs in reasoning and result from *Newball*. Whereas in *Newball* notice is apparently required only when the special circumstances of a delay or lapse of time occurs between identification and arrest, *Naranjo* holds that notice is always required since the decision as to the confirmatory character of the identification is a question for the court and not to be left to the total judgment and discretion of the People. *Naranjo* effectively holds that absent notice of any purported identification procedure, preclusion must inevitably follow. *People v. Rolison*, 141 Misc.2d 318, 533 N.Y.S.2d 661 (S. Ct. New York County 1988), presents a different perspective from both *Newball* and *Naranjo*.

In *Rolison*, the defendant moved to preclude the in-court identification on ground that the prosecutor failed to provide notice within the intendment of C.P.L. Sec. 710.30(b). The People argued notice was not required because the identification was confirmatory in nature and so not subject to provisions of C.P.L. Sec. 710.30(b).

The facts in *Rolison* were that on March 14, 1988, Police Officer McKeon observed the defendant inside a 1985 Toyota automobile and sought to stop the defendant. Thereupon an auto chase ensued with the eventual apprehension of the defendant by other police officers. Shortly thereafter in the vicinity of the Toyota, Officer McKeon arrived at the scene and identified the defendant as the person he had seen seated in the car. The defendant was arrested and charged with Criminal Possession of Stolen Property in the Third Degree.

Following the reasoning of *Morales* the court initially held the subsequent identification by Officer McKeon was confirmatory in nature and not the subject of a pretrial motion to suppress. The court then considered the question of whether, under these facts, notice was required under C.P.L. Sec. 710.30(b). Initially the court rejected the argument of the defendant that notice was required on the ground that the determination whether an alleged confirmatory identification is one is reserved for the court and not the prosecutor. The court thus rejected the *Naranjo* viewpoint.

The court concluded that notice was not required under the statute, reasoning, somewhat inexplicably, that confirmatory identifications are not within the intendment of the statute.

Rolison, in the opinion of this writer, puts the cart before the horse, assuming an identification is confirmatory because it has been denominated as such by the prosecutor. Indeed *Rolison* specifically distinguishes *People v. Brown*, 140 A.D.2d 266, 528 N.Y.S.2d 563 (1st Dept. 1988), which held that any statement is the subject of the notice and Hearing process and refused to analogize Wade Notice and Hearing to that decision.

Finally, there is *People v. Doyle*, 134 Misc.2d 338, 510 N.Y.S.2d 987 (S. Ct. Kings County 1987). In *Doyle* the defendant moved to suppress identification of him as the perpetrator of the crime on the ground that it was impermissibly suggestive. The People, in opposition to the motion, alleged the identification in question involved two confirmatory views by an undercover officer not subject to the strictures of the Wade rule.

The court initially noted that C.P.L. Sec. 710.60(3)(b) relieves the defense, in these motions, of alleging a factual basis for the legal ground stated and that at first blush it would appear that the defense was entitled to a Hearing. The court then noted that the People argued that under *Morales* and *Gissendanner*, the identification here was a confirmatory identification and not under the intendment of the statute.

The court went on to note that there may be factual settings which would warrant a hearing in these cases, citing *Rubio, supra*. The court then noted that the People had served notice in this case yet notice was not required, under the decisional law, where the previous identification involved a confirmatory identification.

The court stated that the People, having served notice, the defense was entitled to a hearing, absent withdrawal of the notice by the People, and possible ultimate preclusion of the evidence.

In conclusion, the court summarily denied the defense motion on condition that the People do explicitly what they had done implicitly—withdraw the notice. Should the People fail to withdraw the notice a Wade Hearing would be mandated.

Doyle is a significant decision holding as it does that if the People give Wade notice then the defense is entitled to a hearing should a Wade application be made. *Doyle* further states that if the People regard the identification as confirmatory then notice should be withdrawn. In effect, what *Doyle* holds is that if the People give Wade notice, they are presumed to do so sincerely and honestly, believing that the identification is confirmatory and not within the intendment of the statute.

This short summary of whether notice is required when the claimed identification is confirmatory reveals a multiplicity of views. *Newball* requires notice if the facts are that the confirmatory rubric is inapplicable such as when there has been a lapse of time between observation and arrest. Significantly, *Newball* is the only appellate court to directly rule on this subject. *Naranjo* holds that notice is required regardless the People's ex parte opinion that the viewing was confirmatory since it is for the court to decide this issue and question of law and fact. *Rolison* directly rejects the *Naranjo* ruling, holding that the People may have their cake and eat it too. *Doyle* says if the People give notice they must abide by it or in all honesty withdraw it if the identification is in fact confirmatory. *Doyle* in effect follows and parallels *Naranjo*, leaving the ultimate decision on whether to give notice to the prosecutor, but emphasizing if given the giving must be bona fide.

It is the view of this writer that *Naranjo* presents the better perspective on this subject. Whether a viewing and identification is confirmatory should be left to the ruling and decision making power of the court and not to the unfettered power, judgment and total discretion of the prosecutor. Whether an identification is confirmatory is really a question of fact, and should not be the result of an ex parte determination of an attorney who bases his decision on interviews with the identifying individual or examination of the Grand Jury Minutes if there is an indictment. The purpose of our adversarial system is to reach a conclusion somewhat approaching to the truth, and truth cannot be reached by crediting one man or woman's opinion. It is true that *Newball* required notice where certain special circumstances are present. Often however the particular circumstances may not become palpable until after a hearing. Whether suggestiveness is present in any identification is properly the subject of a full adversarial hearing rather than the silent hidden decision of the prosecutor.[1]

14. Juror Note Taking

This article proposes to consider when, how, and under what circumstances, if any, a juror or jurors in a criminal trial will be permitted to take and use notes of any aspect of the trial proceedings, whether testimony or charge, in their deliberations under New York Law.

The first New York appellate case to consider the broad issue of whether a juror or jurors will be permitted to make and use any notes of a portion of the trial proceeding in their deliberations, albeit in a civil and not a criminal context, was *Bolm vs. Triumph Corporation,* 58 A.D.2d 1014 (4th Dept. 1977). *Bolm* was an appeal by the plaintiff from a judgment in favor of the defendants entered after a jury trial. The original complaint alleged causes of action sounding in negligence, breach of express and implied warranty and strict liability in tort, wherein the plaintiff received serious physical injuries when the motorcycle he was driving, manufactured and distributed by the defendants, collided with an automobile approaching him in the main highway.

The plaintiff alleged, as one of the purported trial court errors, that the charge was so unclear that reversal was required in the interests of justice. The court noted that the juror requested the court to explain the various theories of negligence, implied and express warranty and strict liability in tort, that the trial complied with this request and that thereafter the jury returned two hours later with a verdict of no cause of action. The court went on to state that the several elements of the various causes of action were presented by the court in such a confused manner that the jury could not have understood the difference between the cause of action grounded in negligence and the other causes of action such as to render an intelligent decision on the matters before them. Most important, as the eventual basis for the court mandating a reversal and a new trial, was that the trial court, in an effort to fix the various elements of proof in the jurors' minds, instructed one juror to take notes on the key parts of the charge, for the benefit of the other members of the jury, leaving the selected juror to determine what were the key parts of the charge and what were not. The Appellate Division,

Fourth Department, held that the responsibility for explaining the law rests on the court and not on a lay juror and that the court should not have directed the note taking. This error, the court held, and the confusion in the charge mandated reversal and a new trial.

The broad holding of the Fourth Department would appear clear: that the trial court sua sponte, so to speak, should not delegate its law directions and explaining function to the jury by directing note taking of the charge by one of the members of the jury.

In 1982, the Second Department had occasion to consider this same issue, in that instance a criminal trial. The case was *People v. DiLuca*, 85 A.D.2d 439, 448 N.Y.S.2d 730 (2d Dept. 1982). *DiLuca* was an appeal from a conviction in the Supreme Court of Suffolk County of Attempted Grand Larceny in the First Degree and Criminal Usury in the Second Degree. In the first trial a Mistrial was declared. At the second trial after both sides had rested and prior to the commencement of summations, the trial judge, over the objection of both defense counsel, announced it was his desire to allow the jurors to take notes during the summations and charge and thereafter between six and eight jurors were observed taking notes during the summation, the court's charge, and during a readback of taped conversations received in evidence. The court gave no advice with respect to the taking of notes nor were the jurors instructed regarding their proper use. Neither defense counsel, other than their general objection to the notes, requested that cautionary instructions be given to the jury. After two days of deliberations defendant Petrizzo was found guilty of Attempted Grand Larceny in the First Degree and Criminal Usury in the Second Degree. Defendant DiLuca was found guilty of Criminal Usury in the Second Degree.

The court initially noted that both the federal courts and some states have allowed note taking and that, absent an abuse of discretion, these courts have ruled that it is within the trial court's discretion to allow the jury or a juror to take notes. The court went on to state that the basis of the decision of the Fourth Department in *Bolm* was the improper delegation of the law-explaining function of the trial court to the jury by allowing the taking of notes during the charge and allowing these notes to be used and examined during the jury's deliberations.

The court further noted that the New York Pattern Jury Instructions provided for a cautionary instruction by the court with respect to juror note taking and that while the former Code of Criminal Procedure allowed for notes to be taken and used by deliberating jurors, the present Criminal Procedure Law omitted this portion of the older predecessor statute. The court opined that note taking in the appropriate case can be helpful as a memory aid for the jurors, as an attention focusing device during the trial proceedings, while the court noted the dangers in note taking by jurors, in that the juror may place greater significance in their notes than in their own independent recollection, that the notes may be inaccurate or misleading, that the juror with the best notes will influence or mislead the other jurors and that the actual taking of the notes will distract the jurors from the proceeding.

The court concluded, after this lengthy review of arguments pro and con on the issue, that the matter is properly left to the discretion of the trial court and that absent an abuse of discretion the trial court's decision on this issue should not be disturbed.

The court added, however, that in any case, prior to allowing the note taking and at the time of the court's charge, the trial court should issue certain cautionary instructions. These are (1) that the note taking should not distract the jurors from the actual proceeding; (2) that the notes are only an aid to the juror's memory and should not take precedence over their independent recollection; (3) that those jurors who do not take notes should rely on their independent recollection of the evidence and not be influenced by the fact that another juror has taken notes; (4) that the notes are for the note takers' personal use in refreshing his recollection of the evidence; (5) that the jury should be told that should any discrepancy exist between their recollection of the evidence and their notes, they should request that the record of the proceeding be read back and that it is the transcript that must prevail over their notes; (6) that in a special case a further cautionary instruction might be needed such as where, for example, one juror is a highly skilled note-taker. In this situation it might be appropriate to instruct the other jurors that they need not pay special attention to that one juror's notes.

The Second Department in *DiLuca* held these cautionary instructions "critical" and that although in the *DiLuca* case no cautionary instructions were given and the defendants made no request therefore and technically the issue had not been preserved for appellate review as a question of law, nevertheless, the court held that the defendant's guilt had not been established by overwhelming evidence, and since counsel for the defense did object at the outset to permitting the juror to take notes, the court did not apply the harmless error rule since the court stated the giving of cautionary instructions to be essential for proper jury deliberations. In sum, the court held that a reversal and a new trial, in the interests of justice, was required here.

DiLuca did not, unlike *Bolm*, base its decision on the fear that to permit the jury to take notes on the charge and use these notes in their deliberations constituted an improper delegation of the court's law explaining and delivering task. The *DiLuca* court, rather, based its opinion on the view that the complete failure to give cautionary instructions at the outset permitting the note taking and in the charge constituted form of per se reversible error.

The First Department, more recently, in two cases, *People vs. Anderson*, 151 A.D.2d 335, 542 N.Y.S.2d 592 (1st Dept. 1989), and *People vs. Morales*, 159 A.D.2d 86 (1st Dept. 1990), had occasion to consider the legal effect of juror note taking.

Anderson was an appeal from a conviction for Forgery in the Second Degree. At the close of trial the judge instructed the jury on the charges of Forgery in the Second Degree and Criminal Possession of Stolen Property in the Fourth Degree. After the commencement of the deliberations the jury sent a note requesting a rereading of the five elements of Forgery in the Second Degree. The trial judge complied with this request. The judge then, sua sponte, suggested the jury take notes on the charge and offered to provide paper for that purpose. One juror replied that he had already done so and the judge then repeated the five elements of the Forgery Charge. When the jury left the room to resume its deliberations, defense counsel objected to the jurors being allowed to take notes.

The Appellate Division, First Department, reversed on the ground that this procedure was improper and reversed and remanded for a new trial. Citing *People vs. Owens*, 69 N.Y.2d 585, 516 N.Y.S.2d 619, 509 N.E.2d 314 (1987), where the Court of Appeals held that where defense counsel objects, it is improper for the trial court, after reciting its instructions orally, to distribute only certain portions of its charge in writing for the jury's use in its deliberations, the court held the risk of unreliability was even greater here where the portions of the written charge taken into the jury room are the product of a juror's note taking, citing *Bolm* and *DiLuca*. The court held the issue was preserved for appellate review, since defense counsel objected to the jurors being permitted to take notes during the court's charge of the elements of Forgery in the Second Degree and the defense did not consent as required to written portions of the charge being made available to the jury, citing C.P.L. Sec. 310.30 which allows a statute to be distributed to the jury with the consent of defense counsel. *Anderson* follows *Bolm* with its concern that the law prerogative of court, with the allowance of note taking on the charge, would pass to the jury or juror, who may be inaccurate in his or her note taking, emphasize only certain portions of the charge, deliberately mislead and assume with these notes a position of importance in the deliberative process. Significantly, *Anderson* makes no mention of the cautionary instructions emphasized in *DiLuca*, although it cites the case and language from it. *Anderson*, however, in part, analogizes its decision on the requirement of C.P.L. Sec. 310.30 already mentioned, which forbids, without the consent of counsel, for the text of a statute to be distributed to the jury. It would appear that the error in *Anderson* is based on *Bolm*, C.P.L. Sec. 310.30 and *Owens* rather than on the failure to give the *DiLuca* cautionary instructions.

Morales is highly similar both in its facts, reasoning and result to *Anderson*. *Morales* was an appeal from a judgment of conviction, convicting the defendant of Criminal Sale of a Controlled Substance in the Third Degree, and Criminal Possession of a Controlled Substance in the Third Degree. In *Morales*, the trial court, after receiving a request for a written copy of the charge, refused, but said it would allow the jury to take notes.

Citing *Owens*, *Bolm*, *DiLuca* and *Anderson,* the First Department held the procedure improper. The court noted that here, while the court did give a cautionary instruction to the effect that if there was any discrepancy between one juror's recollection and the other's notes they were to come back and have the instruction reread, most of the cautionary instructions required in *DiLuca* were omitted. Specifically, the Appellate Division, First Department, noted that the trial court merely suggested that if any discrepancy existed between one juror's notes and the other's personal recollection they were to have the instructions read back, and did not require this, as *DiLuca* held appropriate. The First Department in *Morales* held that this did not rise to the level of the required cautionary instruction as set forth in *DiLuca*. The Appellate Division further held that the court prejudiced the defendant by saying that it would have given the whole written charge with the consent of the attorneys to the jury but no one would consent, implying that but for the defense counsel's consent the jury could have had the whole written charge. *Morales* reached the same conclusion on much the same reasoning as *Anderson*, putting greater emphasis, however, on its decision on the lack of cautionary instructions as required by *DiLuca*.

Finally, there is *People vs. Tucker*, 77 N.Y.2d 862 (1991). *Tucker* was an appeal by permission from orders of the Appellate Division, First Department, affirming judgments of the Supreme Court, New York County, convicting the defendants of Two Counts of Robbery in the First Degree and Two Counts of Robbery in the Second Degree. The facts in *Tucker* were that during its deliberations the jury asked for reinstruction in the elements of First and Second Degree Robbery. While the judge was explaining these elements, a juror was taking notes and noting this the judge instructed the jurors that if disagreement arose between a juror's recollection and the notes, the jurors must request a readback of the instruction. After this cautionary instruction defense counsel asked the court to direct the juror to rip the notes and the court denied the application. Defense counsel argued it was error to permit the juror's notes to be taken into the jury room, likening the procedure to taking a copy of a statute into the jury room, which a jury may only be given with the parties' consent (C.P.L. See. 310.30) or to taking partial written charge into the jury room, citing *Owens*.

The Court of Appeals held the procedure here proper and affirmed. The court held that there was no danger the jury would infer the matter contained in the notes was of due importance; that the judge's cautionary instruction removed any possibility of undue reliance on the notes as opposed to their independent recollection; that the notes would not be subject to misuse such as when a copy of a statute is given to the jury.

In *Tucker*, it would appear, that the Court of Appeals breaks from the concerns evident in *Anderson, Morales, DiLuca* and *Bolm*. The Court of Appeals in *Tucker* does not require the full panoply of cautionary instruction prior to note taking and during the charge, as mandated by the Second Department in *DiLuca*. In *Tucker* only one instruction was given. Glossed over is the argument from *Owens* that the court is giving law in written form without the consent of the parties. Not mentioned is the concern of *Bolm* that the court in allowing the jury to take notes on the charge and use these notes in their deliberations is in abdication of the law giving and interpreting task of the trial court. Yet the facts in *Tucker* are in essence similar to *Anderson, Morales, DiLuca* and *Bolm*. All concern the juror being permitted to take notes during the court's charge and making use of these notes in their deliberations. If *Tucker* is the last blow of the trumpet on this issue, it differs greatly from the prior Appellate Division holdings on this subject and seems to evidence little or none of the lower court's serious reservations and concerns on the subject.

In short, *Tucker* seems to hold that if one required cautionary instruction is given that the notes are not to take precedence over the juror's memory, then note taking is permitted. The overriding concerns of the First, Second and Fourth Department are rejected. The highest court of this state has ruled on this issue on a discrete set of facts. The opinion could be read as a kind of carte blanche with the requirement of one limited instruction. It is the view of this writer, however, that as more and more cases are litigated on the subject that the law will not remain static but will remain live and quick in future case law. *Tucker* may have opened the door, yet the flood will flow through the dike requiring future explanation and resolution.

15. Recent Batson Developments

In 1986 the United States Supreme Court decided the seminal case of *Batson vs. Kentucky*, 476 U.S. 79, 106 S. Ct. 1712, 90 L. Ed.2d 69 (1986). In *Batson,* the facts were that the prosecutor used peremptory challenges to strike four black jurors from the jury so that the defendant, also a black man, was tried by an all white jury. The United States Supreme Court held that the Equal Protection Clause of the Fourteenth Amendment forbade the use of peremptory challenges solely for racial reasons. The Supreme Court found that a prima facie case of racial discrimination had been established and the court reversed the judgment of conviction and remanded for the prosecutor to provide racially neutral reasons for his peremptory strikes, or, in the absence of such reasons, for a new trial. In its opinion the court set forth a threefold test to establish a prima facie case of purposeful discrimination in petit jury selection. The defendant must show 1) that he or she is a member of a cognizable racial group, 2) that the prosecutor's use of peremptory challenges resulted in the exclusion of members of the defendant's racial group from the jury, and 3) that the facts and other relevant circumstances are sufficient to raise an inference that the prosecutor used the peremptory challenges for discriminatory purposes. If the People cannot establish race neutral reasons for their exercise of peremptory challenges the remedy of the defense is either an application for Mistrial or the seating of the heretofore excluded jurors. On Appeal a "Batson" violation if found can result in reversal and a "Batson" hearing or even a new trial.

The New York State Appellate Courts, in general, have applied the "Batson" rule, in the past to where there has been firstly and initially a pattern of racially exclusionary peremptory challenges. See *People vs. Scott*, 70 N.Y.2d 420 (1987); *People vs. Kern*, 75 N.Y.2d 638 (1990); *People vs. Hernandez*, 75 N.Y.2d 350 (1990). Of late, however, at least in two cases decided by the New

York Court of Appeals there has been an apparent shift or modification in the requirement that a cognizable pattern of discriminatory peremptory challenges need be established by the defense to claim a prima facie *Batson* violation. The relevant cases are *People vs. Jenkins*, 75 N.Y.2d 550 (1990); and *People vs. Bolling*, N.Y.L.J., 4/8/92, p. 25, col. 1 (Court of Appeals).

Jenkins was an appeal from an order of the Appellate Division, First Department, reversing the defendant's conviction, after a jury trial, because the prosecutor purposefully excluded blacks from the petit in violation of the Equal Protection Clause of the Fourteenth Amendment, citing *Batson*.

The facts were that the defendant and codefendant Jackson, both black, were indicted for crimes arising out of an armed robbery of a supermarket in the Bronx and a subsequent exchange of gunfire with pursuing police officers. The Indictment charged the defendants with Two Counts of Attempted Murder of a police officer, Robbery in the First and Second Degree and Criminal Possession of a Weapon.

During the Voir Dire at the ensuing trial, the prosecutor exercised ten peremptory challenges, seven of which were exercised against seven of the ten blacks on the panel. Only three were used against the thirty-seven white and Hispanic members of the panel. Defense counsel used two peremptory challenges against blacks with law enforcement associations and prior jury experience and the petit jury was eventually composed of one black and eleven white jurors. The defense, based on *Batson*, moved for a mistrial. The application was denied by the trial court. The Appellate Division, however, reversed and remanded for a new trial because of the violation of the Equal Protection Clause of the Fourteenth Amendment and in violation of *Batson vs. Kentucky*.

The Court of Appeals also concluded a *Batson* violation based on a pattern of racially discriminatory strikes against prospective black jurors based solely on the assumption that black jurors cannot be impartial as regards a black defendant.

Most important for this article is the language of the Court of Appeals in *Jenkins* that, in response to the argument of the People that the jury impaneled was in fact representative of the proportion of the black community in the Bronx at that time, that

> for the purposes of equal protection, the constitutional violation is the exclusion
> of any blacks solely because of their race. If any blacks are so excluded, it is of
> no moment that the jury nevertheless contains a token number of blacks. *People vs. Jenkins, supra* at 559.

It would appear from the above language in the *Jenkins* decision that the exclusion of any black or blacks can give rise to a claim by the defense of a *Batson* violation and that the former law that a pattern of discriminatory strikes need be established to claim such a violation is no longer good law.

The more recent case of *People vs. Bolling* and *Steele, supra*, follows suit. In these two cases counsel for the defendants alleged *Batson* violations by the prosecutions use of peremptory racially based strikes. The *Batson* violation was sustained in *Bolling* while in *Steele* it was denied. The Court of Appeals, citing *Jenkins*, held, albeit *in dicta*, that the exclusion of any blacks solely because of their race is constitutionally forbidden and that "the wrong may occur after only one strike and the prosecution cannot defer the objection and later overcome it with evidence that the jury as finally selected, contained a proportionate number of African-Americans." *People vs. Bolling, supra*, at 25.

Based on this review of the language in *Jenkins* and *Bolling* it is the opinion of this writer that the Court of Appeals has moved to the view that a *Batson* violation, prima facie, can be established by the defense solely on strikes by the People of one minority juror, and that a pattern of racially motivated strikes need not be shown by the defense, the apparent former law on this subject. *Jenkins* and *Bolling* both hold and may a be quoted for the proposition that one racially discriminatory peremptory strike against one black, Hispanic or Asian may give rise to a *Batson* violation with the burden shifting to the People to show a racially neutral reason for the peremptory strike on pain of a Mistrial, or what is more likely, the juror being seated.

It is clear on the strength of these two Court of Appeals cases that defense counsel, given one apparent racial peremptory strike by the People, can establish a prima facie *Batson* violation which can result in a Mistrial, the juror being seated, and if the *Batson* issue is lost at the trial level, a reversal on appeal and even the granting of a new trial based on the Violation.

16. Border Searches: An Overview

It has long been the law of the State and Federal Courts that a warrant is not required for customs officials to search a person entering this country, whether at an actual physical border crossing or disembarking from a ship or plane. The search may range from the minimally intrusive examination of the person's belongs to the more extensive pat down, strip search, or body cavity search. For each type of search, there are differing sets of rules of law governing the level of intrusiveness allowed under the State and Federal cases.

It is therefore the purpose of this article to examine the rules governing these various types of searches, varying in personal intrusiveness and invasion of the individual's privacy, in order to afford a guide to the criminal practitioner whereby he may know how and when he may be successful in a Mapp Motion to suppress the contraband recovered from the person as a result of the search at the border.

Searching Belongings

The least intrusive form of search, and most common, is a search of the entering person's belongings at the border crossing. Under both the State and Federal cases no level of suspicion, however minimal, is required to justify this type of search. Thus, in *People v. Luna*, 73 N.Y. 2nd 173, 535 N.E.2d 1305, 538 N.Y.S.2d 765 (1989), the Court of Appeals specifically stated that the brief detention of incomers and examination of their belongings is constitutionally permissible at border crossing without any suspicion at all of criminal activity. *People v. Luna, supra*, at 767. See also *People v. Materon*, 107 A.D.2d 408, 487 N.Y.S.2d 334 (2nd Dept. 1985); *U.S. v. Montoya De Hernandez*, 473 U.S. 531, 538, 195 S. Ct. 3304, 3309, 87 L.Ed. 2nd 381, 389 (1985); *U.S. v. Ogberaha*, 771 F.2d 655, 657 (2d Cir. 1985), *U.S. v. Asbury*, 586 2d 973 (2d Cir. 1978).

"Pat Down" Searches

The second, more intrusive search which may occur at the border is the pat down or Terry type search. The Federal Courts and the New York State Court of Appeals appear to differ on the level of suspicion, if any is required, to justify this somewhat more intrusive type search. Reference is made again to *People v. Luna* for the New York perspective. In *Luna*, the defendant, a 48-year-old Ecuadorian, traveling alone, having presented his passport and luggage at the inspection station, appeared physically agitated and nervous.

The defendant's appearance and behavior, and the fact that he was traveling alone from a "high profile country," led the custom official to suspect he was a drug courier. A subsequent pat down search revealed a bulge around the defendant's two ankles which consisted of two packages of cocaine. The defendant contended on appeal that the same reasonable suspicion of stop and frisk law in domestic situations should apply. The People argued the pat down was incidental to a routine border search for which no justification was required. The Court held, after an extensive review of the Federal and State case law, that a pat down at the border must be justified by some level of suspicion but the suspicion need not be as objectively clear as that required for the usual stop and frisk. The Court went on to state, however, that the suspicion must be real and based on legitimate factors other than race, gender, whim, or caprice. Applying this standard, the Court held the pat down was proper, given the defendant's behavior, and his arrival alone with one suitcase from a source country. See also *People v. Materon*, 107 A.D.2d 408, 487 N.Y.S.2d 334 (2d Dept. 1985) (Articulated suspicion required to justify pat down on arrival at international airports).

The Federal Courts, however, appear to differ on the suspicion, if any, required for a pat down search at the border. *U.S. v. Charleus*, 871 F.2d 265 (2d Cir. 1989), is apropos. In *Charleus*, the appellant arrived with a male companion at JFK International Airport from Haiti. The male companion, Louis, appeared hesitant, startled and nervous, was searched, and taped packages were found around his back and waist containing cocaine. Louis was placed under arrest.

Thereafter, the appellant was approached by the same customs officer where a pat down of his back revealed a taped bulge containing cocaine. The Trial Court denied the defendant's motion to suppress, and subsequent to conviction after a jury trial, the defendant contended on appeal that the pat down search was not a routine border search and so required some level of suspicion.

The Court held the search to be a routine border search not requiring reasonable suspicion, despite the fact that the defendant was patted down and, upon noting of the bulge, was asked to remove his shirt. See also *U.S. v. Nieves*, 609 F.2d 642, 646 (2nd Cir. 1974) (Removal of shoes incident to routine border search); *U.S. v. Ramos*, 645 F.2d 318, 322 (5th Cir. 1981); *U.S. v. Braks*, 842 F.2d 509 (1st Cir. 1988).

Strip Search and Body Cavity Search

The next types of border searches to be considered are the strip search and the body cavity search. These searches are the most intrusive and there is some slight differentiation of the level of suspicion required under New York State and Federal Law, at least for body cavity searches. *People v. Materon, supra,* states the New York perspective. In *Materon,* the defendant disembarked at JFK Airport from a flight from Colombia. The defendant was observed to be nervous, had trouble closing her suitcase, was unable to flex her knees and moved awkwardly. The defendant was approached by a customs agent who, after examining her passport and declaration form, noted the ticket had an open return, had been purchased with cash, and that the defendant had made two previous trips to Colombia within a short period of time. The defendant was then subjected to a pat down search, which revealed a bulge in her crotch area containing four condoms filled with a white powder that later tested positive for cocaine.

The defendant was then subjected to two strip searches which revealed two more condoms that fell from her vagina. The defendant then admitted she had two more condoms in her anal cavity, was given a laxative and excreted cocaine-filled condoms. The defendant moved to suppress and after a hearing, the motion was denied. Midway through trial, she pled guilty to Criminal Possession of a Controlled Substance in the Second Degree and was sentenced to five years to life.

The Appellate Division held, as noted previously, that the initial pat down search was justified by some or a mere suspicion of criminal activity, based on the aforementioned articulable factors. The Court went on to state, however, that the strip searches, in the context of a border search, required a real or reasonable suspicion of illegal concealment such as to cause a customs officer to have a substantial as opposed to a mere suspicion that the person is concealing contraband. The Court also held that a body cavity search may not be performed absent a "clear indication" of smuggling; although the Court went on to state that probable cause is not the standard for a body cavity search. The Court stated that there must be a definite reason to believe that contraband will be found in the particular area of the body being searched.

The Court held, in conclusion, given the totality of the factors and circumstances, including the fact that the defendant was traveling alone from a source city, was unusually nervous, frequently changed lines at the inspection area, and had difficulty moving and bending her knees, had been in Colombia for two weeks, had an open return ticket, had purchased the ticket with cash, and had made two prior trips to Colombia in a relatively short period of time, gave justification for the pat down search, and that the discovery of the cocaine-filled condoms justified the subsequent strip and body cavity searches.

The Federal Courts, however, have a significantly different standard to justify body cavity searches under the Fourth Amendment. *U.S. v. Ogberaha*, 771 F.2d 655 (2nd Cir. 1985), represents an articulation of the federal standard on this issue. The facts in *Ogberaha* were that in May of 1984, two female Nigerian nationals, traveling separately on the same flight arrived at JFK Airport from Lagos, Nigeria. Each, after examination of her documents, was subjected to a body cavity search that revealed heroin-filled condoms in the vagina. Defendants moved to suppress and the motions were denied. The defendants, after a non-jury trial, were convicted and sentenced, respectively, to five years incarceration and to treatment and supervision pursuant to the Federal Youth Corrections Act.

The Court agreed with the New York standard in *Materon* that there must be a reasonable suspicion, based on articulable factors, to justify a strip search at the border. The defendant argued, citing *U.S. v. Mastberg*, 503 F.2d 465, 471 (9th cir. 1974), and apparently following the *Materon* standard, that the most intrusive search should require not merely a reasonable suspicion, but a clear indication that the person is concealing contraband within his body, a level of suspicion falling somewhere between "reasonable suspicion" and "probable cause." The Court, however, rejected this standard for a body cavity search at the border, citing *U.S. v. Asbury*, 586 F.2d 973 (2d Cir. 1978).

Twelve Factors in Determining Suspicion of Smuggling

The Court noted that the *Asbury* Court suggested twelve factors pertinent to determining the reasonableness of a border official's suspicions concerning possible smuggling activity. These were: 1) excessive nervousness, 2) unusual conduct, 3) an informant's tip, 4) computerized information showing pertinent criminal propensities, 5) loose-fitting or bulky clothing, 6) an itinerary suggestive of wrongdoing, 7) discovery of incriminating matter during routine searches, 8) lack of employment or a claim of self-employment, 9) needle marks or other indications of drug addiction, 10) information derived from the search or conduct of a traveling companion, 11) inadequate luggage, and 12) evasive or contradictory answers.

The Court then noted that, applying the relevant *Asbury* factors, both defendants traveled from a drug source country; planned a short stay in this country;

carried a small amount of luggage inconsistent with international travel; appeared nervous and disoriented; and had purchased their tickets in cash prior to departure.

The Court went on to state that the presence of *at least four* of the *Asbury* factors, including excessive nervousness, unusual conduct, loose fitting or bulky clothing, a suggestive itinerary, and inadequate luggage, raised a reasonable suspicion of internal concealment that justified the body searches.

Thus, the standard stated in *Ogberaha* for both strip and body cavity searches is a reasonable suspicion. The clear indication standard of *Materon* is rejected, for body cavity searches. See also *U.S. v Handy,* 788 F.2d 1419 (9th Cir. 1986) (Strip search at border is justified by a real subjective suspicion supported by objective articulable facts that would reasonably lead an experienced customs officer to suspect that a particular person, seeking to cross the border, was concealing contraband); *U.S. v. Charleus, supra,* at 296; *U.S. v. Pino,* 729 F.2d 1357 (11th Cir. 1984); *U.S. v. Montoya De Hernandez, supra.*

This brief summary review of some pertinent New York State and Federal border search cases reveals first that a search of a person's luggage and personal effects, under both New York State and Federal case law, requires no justification or level of suspicion. New York and Federal case law differs, however, on the level of suspicion required for a pat down. The New York Law is that some level of suspicion is required. The Federal Courts differ, holding that a pat down search constitutes no more than a routine border search and requires no level of suspicion.

Again, the New York Courts and Federal Courts differ on the standard required to justify a body cavity search at the border, the Federal Courts making use of a reasonable suspicion standard, for the most part; the New York Courts, at least as reflected in the *Materon* decision emanating from the Appellate Division Second Department, using a clear indication standard. This clear indication standard, although good law in the Second Department, is specifically rejected by the Second Circuit in *Ogberaha.* The standard of a reasonable suspicion to justify a strip search would appear to be the same for the State and Federal Courts of this state.

Hopefully this brief overview of border search law in New York State and the Federal Courts will afford a guide to the practitioner when confronted with a border search issue.

17. AIDS Dismissal and the Clayton Motion

The problem of individuals HIV-infected or with full blown AIDS has become a city as well as a national crisis. Just recently in the May 18, 1991, issue of the *Daily News*, there was a headline, "AIDS From the Grave." The substance of the story was that 50 transplant patients six years ago received organs or tissues from an AIDS-infected donor and that three had since died of AIDS.

The criminal defense lawyer has ample reason to be familiar with this crisis since many defendants are found to be HIV positive either at the initial arraignment or at a later date in the course of the litigation. Many defendants are persons involved in undercover or observation drug sales; sometimes they are charged with more violent crimes. Whatever the charge, the criminal defense lawyer is always faced with a formidable task.

Using the Clayton Motion

If the client, however, has AIDS or is even merely HIV infected, although the case may not be winnable on the merits and the only apparent viable alternative may be for the client to plead guilty to a lesser offense and so receive less jail time than if the defendant were to be convicted after trial, an additional avenue of defense exists, and that is to make a Clayton motion or a Motion to Dismiss the Indictment or information in the Furtherance of Justice pursuant to C.P.L. Sec. 210.40 if the charge is an indictment, or pursuant to C.P.L. Sec. 170.40 if the charge is a simplified traffic information, prosecutor's information, information, or a misdemeanor complaint.

This motion may be made at any time in the course of the litigation, even at conviction after trial. The statutes list a number of factors to be considered by the Court in the determination whether to grant the motion. These include the seriousness and circumstances of the offense; extent of harm caused by the offense; the evidence of guilt whether admissible or inadmissible at trial; the history, character, and condition of the defendant; any exceptionally serious misconduct of law enforcement personnel in the investigation, arrest, and prosecution of the defendant; the purpose and effect of imposing upon the defendant a sentence authorized for the offense; the impact of a dismissal on the safety or welfare of the community; the impact of a dismissal upon the confidence of the public in the criminal justice system; the attitude of the complainant or victim with respect to the motion; and any other relevant fact indicating that a judgment of conviction would serve no useful purpose.

Defense counsel would be wise then, if the client is at all HIV infected, to make this motion. Counsel has nothing to lose and everything to gain. It is imperative that the medical records attesting the defendant's condition be obtained and attached to the motion papers. It would be appropriate also to obtain a letter from an independent physician concerning the existence and severity of the defendant's condition. The factors listed in C.P.L. Secs. 210.40 and 170.40 must be covered and fleshed out at length in the motion papers. Of course, the decision whether or not to grant the motion is totally within the discretion of the Court and the decision to deny it is at worst no more than an abuse of discretion, and so is not a viable appellate issue.

Nevertheless, even if the motion is not granted, a better plea may well be obtained. Thus, for example, this writer filed, in the Queens County Supreme Court, Clayton motions for felons in two cases, a Robbery II Case (PL. 160.10), and an Undercover Drug Sale (PL. 220.39). In the Robbery, a Misdemeanor plea with time served was offered by the People and taken by the defendant and in the latter case, the minimum under the law was offered by the People—2-4 years incarceration—and taken by the defendant although in both cases the motion itself was denied.

It should be noted that until very recently for a dismissal to be obtained pursuant to a Clayton Motion for a person affected with AIDS, there had to be a showing that the defendant was actually terminal. Thus in *People v. Carmago*, 135 Misc.2d 987 (S. Ct. Bronx Co.) 986, the Court held that where the defendant with AIDS had five to six months to live, the indictment charging third degree sale and possession of cocaine, Class B Felonies, was dismissed. See also *People v. Roman*, N.Y.L.J. 10/5/90 p. 25, col. 4; *People v. Quinn*, N.Y.L.J., 10/20/88, p. 29, col. 5; *People v. Williams,* N.Y.L.J., 9/18/87, p. 12, col. 4; *People v. Vasquez*, N.Y.L.J., 6/20/88, p. 30, col. 2.

Recent Developments in the Courts

The climate of the Courts in this respect may be changing. Two recent cases demonstrate how favorable the Court may be to a defendant who is HIV infected and not necessarily terminal and also how harsh. *People v. Suarez*, N.Y.L.J. 2/1/91, p. 22, col. 4 (S. Ct. New York County), evinces how favorable a Trial Court may be to a Clayton motion made on behalf of an HIV-infected defendant. In *Suarez*, the defendant was charged with criminal sale of a controlled substance in the fourth and fifth degrees, P.L. Sec. 220.34 and 220.30, and criminally possessing a hypodermic instrument. The facts were that acting in concert with the codefendant, the defendant delivered one codeine pill and one glutehimide pill to an undercover officer in exchange for prerecorded buy money later recovered from the person of the defendant. The People offered the defendant a plea to an open "D." The Court noted that this plea, if taken, could result in no incarceration, although the prosecutor recommended incarceration, given the lack of medical care available to this homeless defendant. The Court granted the Clayton motion, citing a number of cases where dismissal on a Clayton application was granted where the defendant was terminal, but noted the defendant did not suffer from full blown AIDS and was not in any sense terminally ill. The Court, however, went on to state that the Court should not act like an ostrich; where the defendant was homeless, the Court stated, and in economically deprived condition, he was effectually terminal.

The Court reviewed at length the severe symptoms the defendant was suffering from including weight loss, diarrhea and multiple abscesses. The Court noted that this was the defendant's first drug arrest, that the amount of controlled substance was small, that the buyer was an undercover officer, and that therefore the harm defendant caused to the community was minuscule. The Court stated that a non-jail sentence would serve neither the defendant nor the community, that making the defendant a predicate felon would serve no purpose due to the defendant's limited life span, that the People's argument that the defendant's medical condition would be better treated in jail was to make the criminal justice system a dumping ground for all the homeless and economically deprived. Hence, after reviewing all these facts and all the applicable factors in C.P.L. Sec. 210.40, the Court granted defense counsel's Clayton Motion.

Suarez is most helpful to defense counsel since it takes the case law one step further away from the older body of case law that the defendant must be actually proved terminally ill to merit an HIV Dismissal, to the point that HIV infection alone is sufficient to warrant dismissal, given the appropriate fact pattern and the relevance of the factors set forth in C.P.L. Sec. 210.40.

A Differing View

People v. Luis Soto Gray, N.Y.L.J., 3/15/91, p. 27, col. 1 (S. Ct. Kings County), reaches a different result. In *Gray,* the defendant was charged with Robbery I and I, Assault II, Grand Larceny IV, Criminal Possession of a Weapon II and III, Criminal Possession of Stolen Property III and IV and Unauthorized Use of a Vehicle.

Defense moved to dismiss pursuant to C.P.L Sec. 210.40 on the ground that the defendant had been diagnosed as having AIDS with a life expectancy of one to one and one half years. Under the First Indictment, the defendant was charged with unauthorized use of a vehicle and Criminal Possession of Stolen Property III and IV in that the defendant was observed in an unoccupied parked car. A chase ensued ending with the defendant crashing into a parked vehicle. He was later apprehended while attempting to flee. The vehicle was subsequently found to have been stolen.

While out on bail for this offense, defendant was again arrested for Robbery I, Assault II, Criminal Possession of a Weapon I and IV, in that the defendant and an unapprehended other approached the complainant and took money and other personal property at gunpoint and when the defendant demanded more money and none was forthcoming, he shot the complainant in the thigh and fled.

The Trial Court proceeded to review the applicability of the ten factors listed in C.P.L. Sec. 210.40 noting first the cases against the defendant were most strong based on the Court's review of the Grand Jury minutes. The Court went on to state that the defendant had a long prior criminal history and had in fact recently recovered from pneumonia, the first symptom of this illness. The Court then proceeded to review the growing body of case law on this issue and concluded that this case was distinguishable from the line of cases where dismissal was granted when the defendant was terminally ill with AIDS and not merely HIV infected.

Finally, the Court reviewed the purpose and effect of sentence, found the statutory sentencing fully applicable, concluded that the impact of dismissal upon the confidence of the public in the Criminal Justice System and on the safety and welfare of the community would be deleterious since it would be a signal for any HIV-infected person to commit further anti-social acts and that the remaining three factors in the statute did not indicate that dismissal was appropriate.

Thus, the Court in *Gray* denied the Clayton motion of the defense. The Court stated, however, that its decision was based on the particular facts and that these cases should be decided on an ad hoc cause by case basis.

Gray is obviously not favorable to defense counsel. In the opinion of this writer, however, it presents a unique factual scenario, given the defendant's multiple indictments, the degree of the crimes charged, their violent character, defendant's conduct and his long prior criminal history. In short, *Gray* is distinguishable from *Suarez*, a non-violent undercover drug sale, where the harm was slight. What distinguishes *Gray,* in the view of this writer, is the fact that defendant was charged with violent crimes and not a non-violent drug sale.

In sum, although the growing body of case law on this subject still seems to hold that the defendant must be terminally ill with AIDS to warrant dismissal by way of Clayton motion, there is a trend, however, slight, to treat the HIV-infected defendant in similar fashion, particularly where the crimes charged is a drug sale to an undercover officer or even an observation sale.

18. Dismissal of an Indictment under 190.50 of the C.P.L. (Part Two)

In a previously published article in the May, 1991, issue of the *Brooklyn Barrister,* entitled "Dismissal of an Indictment under Sec. 190.50 of the Criminal Procedure Law," this writer, analyzing the case law construing Sec. 190.50 of the Criminal Procedure Law, concluded that there were four common contexts, scenarios, or situations whereby the defendant is so effectively deprived of his right to testify before the Grand Jury such that dismissal under Criminal Procedure Law Sec. 190.50(5)(c) may result, if motion is made by defense counsel within five days of arraignment on indictment. They were (1) untimely or unreasonable notice to defense counsel of the prospective Grand Jury Presentation; (2) failure of the Department of Corrections to produce the defendant in time before actual presentment of the case by the People to the Grand Jury; (3) unavailability of defense counsel to be present on the date or dates of presentment; and (4) excessive or unfair or prejudicial cross-examination of the defendant by the prosecutor.

In this article, the subject of dismissal, pursuant to C.P.L. Sec. 190.05(5)(c), will again be revisited and a fifth ground, rarely used but nevertheless available, will be explored and analyzed whereby defense counsel may obtain a dismissal under this section due to a deprivation of the defendant's right to testify before the Grand Jury.

The Law

The Fifth ground, as suggested by this writer, such that dismissal of an indictment pursuant to C.P.L. 190.50(5)(c) may be obtained, is where the felony complaint, under which the defendant is arraigned and given notice of the charges or charges on which he is to base his decision whether or not to testify, varies materially from the charges under which he is eventually indicted. Under this argument, if the charges for which the defendant is indicted are either a higher level or more serious charge, or a lower level or less serious charge, and so vary from the charges under which the defendant is arraigned on the felony complaint, then the defendant, at the time he was arraigned on the felony complaint, was not given actual or effectual notice of the charge for which he was eventually indicted; had he known the nature of the charges for which he was actually indicted, his decision whether or not to testify might well have been a different one. The essential basis for a motion to dismiss under this scenario is that the defendant did not have true and bona fide notice of the nature of the Grand Jury Presentation which resulted in this indictment.

The case supporting this further ground for dismissal pursuant to Sec. 190.50(5)(c) of the C.P.L. is *People v. Suarez*, 103 Misc.2d 910, 427 N.Y.S.2d 187 (S. Ct., New York County, 1980). The facts in *Suarez* were that on January 13, 1980, the defendant was arrested for Attempted Murder in the Second Degree; Criminal Possession of a Weapon in the Second Degree; and Criminal Possession of a Weapon in the Third Degree. On January 14, 1980, the defendant was arraigned on the felony complaint and was served with Grand Jury Notice. The felony complaint charged two counts of Criminal Possession of a Weapon in the Third Degree only. On January 15, 1980, indictment was voted charging him with Criminal Possession of a Dangerous Weapon in the Second Degree, an Armed felony; Reckless Endangerment in the Second Degree; Menacing; and Criminal Possession of a Weapon in the Third Degree.

The defendant moved to dismiss pursuant to C.P.L. Sec. 190.50(5)(c), arguing that because the felony complaint charged a more serious crime, an Armed Felony, than that for which he was eventually indicted, the notice given by the People was ineffectual. In addition, he argued that the indictment was defective and subject to dismissal under C.P.L. Sec. 190.50(5)(c) since the defendant was not actually apprised of the charges for which he was eventually indicted and based his decision, whether or not to testify, on the lesser charge before him at the time of his decision.

The court concluded that the District Attorney, by denying the defendant the relevant information, whether or not to testify before the Grand Jury, rendered ineffectual the notice served by the People, consequently prejudicing the defendant's right to appear as a witness on his own behalf before the Grand Jury and by implication his constitutional right to effective assistance of counsel.

The court initially reasoned that the Criminal Procedure Law, Section 190.50(5)(a), states that the defendant is entitled to actual notice that the prosecution is submitting charges to the Grand Jury and distinguished the instant case from the decision in *People v. Root*, 87 Misc.2d 482 (S. Ct. Bronx County, 1976). In *Root*, the court held that because the defendant, an attorney, was aware, via independent sources, of the nature and scope of the charge being investigated by the Grand Jury, the prosecutor's refusal to inform him of the nature and scope of the charges was not so prejudicial as to deny the defendant his statutory right to appear as a witness. The court noted that, in *Root*, the defendant did not fall within the statutory class of persons whom the prosecutor had an affirmative duty to notify as the defendant in the instant case and that the *Root* court decision turned on the defendant's having actual effective notice, not present in this case.

In sum the *Suarez* court concluded that the defendant had no notice of the gravity of the charges from the Grand Jury Notice or Felony Complaint, noting that the defendant was not a lawyer who could incidentally gather information from courthouse gossip; in fact his attorney had little time to investigate the case, before the voting of the indictment.

The court noted also that the Criminal Procedure Law mandates that where an offense constituting an Armed Felony is includable in an accusatory instrument, the description "armed felony" must be included in the applicable count.

Thus the court in *Suarez* concluded that the notice given by the People was ineffective, as failing to give effective notice of the Armed Felony charge to be presented against him since the prosecution knew that this charge was to be presented to the Grand Jury and failed to state good cause for not giving notice. The court further stated that where the prosecutor does not know of the armed felony charges from the outset and such evidence emerges in the course of the Grand Jury Proceeding, an opposite outcome would not have been a problem.

Suarez remains good law, if only in the First Department. Its reasoning is cogent—simply that the defendant and his attorney are entitled to honest and actual notice of the charges he is to face, should he decide and choose to testify. *Suarez* concludes that where the People know that a higher and more serious charge under the Penal Law, subjecting the defendant to possible greater incarceratory exposure, is in fact to be presented to the Grand Jury, the notice to the defendant of a less serious charge in the felony complaint is inadequate notice, so requiring dismissal of the indictment pursuant to Sec. 190.50 of the Criminal Procedure Law.

The *Suarez* decision, despite its logic and cogency, however, has not been consistently followed by the courts of this state.

For example, in *People v. Scott,* 141 Misc.2d 623 (S. Ct. Queens County 1988), the defendant was arraigned in court on a felony complaint on July 2, 1988, charging her with Vehicular Assault in the Second Degree; Reckless Endangerment in the Second Degree; Criminal Possession of Stolen Property in the Third Degree; and Unauthorized use of a Vehicle in the Third Degree.

At the arraignment the People served the defense with Sec. 190.50 notice that they intended to present the matter to the Grand Jury, and the defense served cross 190.50 notice of her intention to testify before the Grand Jury. On July 7, 1988, the matter was presented to the Grand Jury and the defendant did not appear to testify. Subsequently, she was indicted for Attempted Murder in the Second Degree; Assault in the First Degree; Leaving the Scene of an Accident Without Reporting; Reckless Endangerment in the First Degree; Unauthorized Use of a Vehicle in the Third Degree; Criminal Possession of Stolen Property in the Third Degree; and Endangering the Welfare of a Child. The defendant, relying on *Suarez,* moved to dismiss, arguing that the notice she received was ineffective since it did not apprise her of the more serious charges for which she was subsequently indicted. The court reasoned that the defendant knew in advance the nature and essential seriousness of the charges to be presented to the Grand Jury, although not the specific charges for which she was subsequently indicted, but stated that the notice need not be so specific, as *Suarez* would appear to require. In short, the court held that the defendant was aware of the basic gravity of the charges pending against her prior to indictment, and so could know, and have anticipated, that more serious charges might have been contemplated by the Grand Jury and so declined to dismiss the indictment pursuant to C.P.L. Sec. 190.50(5)(c).

See also *People v. Fletcher,* 140 Misc.2d 389 (S. Ct. Queens County 1988) (Felony Complaint charged Assault II and the defendant was indicted for Assault IV. The court did not dismiss, under *Suarez* pursuant to C.P.L. Sec. 190.50(5)(c)).

However, in *People v. Diaz,* 144 Misc.2d 766 (S. Ct. Bronx County 1989), the trial court dismissed where the defendant testified before the Grand Jury concerning one incident involving Assault charges but did know, was not questioned, and did not speak about a prior incident, which had also been presented to the Grand Jury and which resulted in additional Counts in the indictment; at the time he testified he had no knowledge that this separate incident would be addressed. The court held that by presenting evidence of a totally distinct and separate criminal transaction, while not effectively informing the defendant of its intention to do so, the District Attorney failed to comply with the requirement of C.P.L. Sec. 190.50; the entire indictment was dismissed as the result of a presentment unduly prejudicial to the defendant and lacking in essential fairness.

In the view of this writer, *Suarez* as affirmed by the First Department continues to be good and compelling law. It is simply unfair to the defendant to expect him to base his decision to testify on a notice that is, in effect, no notice at all.

The decision in *Fletcher* is understandable since it is logical that notice of the lesser included offense of Assault II is sufficient even where the defendant is ultimately indicated for Assault I. The decision in *Scott*, in the view of this writer, is aberrational. To be given notice, as in *Scott*, where the Felony complaint charge Assault in the Second Degree and Reckless Endangerment, and then be indicted for Attempted Murder, is no notice at all.

Suarez is valid and good. Indeed, as an example of its continued vitality, most recently, pursuant to *Suarez,* Judge Rosenzweig of the Queens County Supreme Court dismissed an indictment with leave to represent pursuant to C.P.L. Sec. 190.50 where the felony complaint charged Robbery I and that defendant was indicted for Assault I. The court, in a terse memorandum opinion, reasoned that notice was ineffective under the felony complaint when the resulting indictment was for Assault I.

In short, *Suarez* presents defense counsel with an additional arrow in the quiver of grounds available for dismissal of an indictment under C.P.L. 190.50(5)(c) for deprivation of the defendant's right to testify before the Grand Jury.

Copyright 1993 by the Kings County Criminal Bar Association. Reprinted with permission.

19. Sandoval and Severance

In 1974, the Court of Appeals decided the landmark case of *People v. Sandoval,* 34 N.Y.2d 371, 357 N.Y.S.2d 849 (1974). In that case, in order that the defendant not be totally impeached in his case through his prior convictions, should he choose to testify, or actually be deterred from taking the stand by the threatened use by the People of his prior convictions, the court approved the procedural device whereby the defense, in a pretrial motion, can have the determination by the court as to which convictions the People may use to impeach him should he choose to testify. The balancing test devised was the probative value of the impeachment evidence as weighed against the risk of unfair prejudice to the defendant. The Court of Appeals and the lower appellate courts of this State have held that the *Sandoval* rule only applies to the criminal defendant as witness and not to the defendant's witnesses, the prosecution's witnesses or to a civil case.

Since 1974, the *Sandoval* rule has been broadly and uniformly applied by the Courts of this State to all criminal defendants who may choose or not choose to testify on their own behalf at trial.

In 1986, however, the Court of Appeals, in a most significant decision, refused to apply the *Sandoval* rule where the codefendant, jointly tried with the defendant, seeks to bring out the defendant's prior convictions and/or prior bad acts. In that case, *People v. McGee,* 68 N.Y.2d 328, 501 N.E.2d 576, 508

N.Y.S.2d 927 (1986), the court held the *Sandoval* rule had no bearing or applicability to the above particular circumstances. The Court of Appeals also held in that decision that the remedy by the defendant to avoid such prejudicial cross-examination by a co-defendant was a timely motion for severance under Sec. 200.40 of the Criminal Procedure Law.

McGee bears careful consideration. In *McGee* the defendant and co-defendant Amer were jointly tried on charges stemming from a robbery in Buffalo. The defendant was convicted of Robbery in the First Degree and Criminal Possession of a Weapon in the Second Degree. The Appellate Division affirmed without issuing an opinion.

On Appeal to the Court of Appeals the defendant argued for reversal on the ground that because the trial court had improperly refused to give him a *Sandoval* ruling as to the questions the co-defendant might ask him on cross-examination concerning previous convictions and bad acts, that refusal made it impossible for him to testify and he was thereby deprived of a fair trial.

The Court of Appeals rejected this argument and affirmed. The Court initially noted that *Sandoval* applied only to the defendant and not to the ordinary witness. The court went on to state that a problem arose, however, where two defendants are tried jointly and one desires to testify but in doing so may incriminate the other. Thus, the defendant, as witness in this context the court noted, testifies in a dual role, both on his own behalf and as witness for the prosecution since what he said may tend to incriminate the co-defendant.

The Court then noted that the defendant, in *McGee*, had sought a *Sandoval* ruling to protect him in his dual roles as a defendant and witness since if the *Sandoval* ruling did not apply both to cross-examination by the prosecution and co-defendant the ruling was of no use since co-defendant's prosecutor had been precluded and the damage would be done.

The Court, however, rejected this reasoning, stating the People, in their cross-examination, would seek to attack the defendant's credibility while counsel for co-defendant in cross-examination would be merely exercising his client's right to confrontation. The court, weighing the procedural right of a defendant to a Sandoval ruling as against the right of a co-defendant to confront and cross-examine the witness possibly testifying against him, held the former must yield to the more fundamental constitutional right of the co-defendant to confront and cross-examine his accusers. The Court, thus, held that in a joint trial a *Sandoval* ruling made as to the defendant did not apply to limit the scope of cross-examination of that defendant by the co-defendant.

The Court, held, however, that there was a remedy and way out of this dilemma. The court stated that where, in a joint trial there are conflicting defenses, the remedy is a timely motion for severance under C.P.L. Sec. 200.40.

The Court concluded, in this particular case, that since the defendant's attorney neither joined in the co-defendant's motion for a severance or applied for it on his own, the issue of a possible abuse of discretion by the trial court had not been preserved.

The holding of *McGee* is clear, namely that where there is a joint trial with possible conflicting theories of defense the *Sandoval* ruling applies only to the prosecution and not to co-defendant's cross-examination of the defendant. If the accused, under *McGee*, wishes to avoid either a joint trial where there are conflicting theories of defense and the eventuality that his client will be cross-examined by the co-defendant with respect to his prior convictions and bad acts, should they exist, the remedy would be a timely motion for severance pursuant to C.P.L. Sec. 200.40.

McGee has since been consistently followed by all the lower appellate courts of this State. See *People v. Sanders*, 162 A.D.2d 327, 556 N.Y.S.2d 903 (1st Dept. 1990); *People v. Rogers*, 156 A.D.2d 598, 549 N.Y.S.2d 107 (2d Dept. 1989); *People v. Woods*, 146 A.D.2d 662, 536 N.Y.S.2d 554 (2d Dept. 1989); *People v. Williams*, 142 A.D.2d 310, 536 N.Y.S.2d 814 (2d Dept. 1988).

One final point should be noted. If the defendant wishes a severance under *McGee*, he must allege antagonistic defenses. The fact that the co-defendant is not bound by the *Sandoval* ruling with respect to the defendant under *McGee*, is not enough, if alleged to obtain a severance. *People v. Sanders, supra*, is apropos. In *Sanders* the defendant was convicted of Robbery in the Second Degree, and Attempted Robbery in the Second Degree. The facts were that the defendant moved for a severance on the eve of trial, after a *Sandoval* ruling, on the ground that if he were to take the stand the co-defendant, who was not bound by the *Sandoval* ruling, could cross-examine him as to all his prior convictions and that this would inhibit him from testifying on his own behalf.

The Court held that since the defendant had failed to state that his defense was antagonistic to the co-defendant, the denial of his motion for a severance was not an abuse of discretion by the court.

It is clear under *McGee* that if the defendant, for reasons of strategy, and to avoid possible cross-examination by the co-defendant on his prior convictions, wishes a severance, he must assert, to obtain a severance and thus avoid the possible damage of cross-examination by the co-defendant as to these prior convictions and/or possible bad acts, that his client would be prejudiced and how so, by the antagonistic defense of his co-defendant.

McGee is a foundation decision in that it refuses to extend *Sandoval* beyond its original intent and limit to prosecution's cross-examination of the defendant. Yet it has a wider implication. This is that if the defendant wishes to avoid a deleterious joint trial and possible prejudicial cross-examination by the co-defendant on his prior convictions, should he take the stand, or choose not to do so because the co-defendant will not be bound by the original *Sandoval*, this potential disaster may succinctly be averted by our relevant and timely motion for severance under the criteria set forth in *McGee* and *Sanders*. If the proper allegations per *McGee* and *Sanders* are made, a potentially prejudicial joint trial may be successfully avoided.

20. Production of the Complainant in a Wade Hearing: Some Recent Law

It had heretofore been the law, that, in a Wade Hearing, where the People have the initial burden of going forward to show the reasonableness of the police conduct and the defense the burden, by a preponderance of the evidence, to show a tainted identification procedure, be it a showup, lineup or photo identification, the complainant could not be compelled to testify, unless, in fact, the procedure had been shown to be unduly suggestive, so requiring proof of an independent source. *People v. Martin*, 35 A.D. 786, 315 N.Y.S.2d 201 (1st Dept. 1970), aff. 32 N.Y.2d 771, 344 N.Y.S.2d 957 (1973), is a good example. In *Martin*, Welch, the victim of the robbery, was present outside the building in which the defendant was encountered by the police and saw him as he left police custody. At the hearing, defense counsel asked that he be produced by the District Attorney. The hearing Court denied this request. The Appellate Court held that the victim's version of the circumstances at the time he saw the defendant would have been relevant concerning the issue of possible suggestion and that he should have been called, even by the Court, at the pre-trial hearing. The Appellate Court held it immaterial that the witness testified at trial and was subject to cross-examination. Thus, the Appellate Division re-opened the pre-trial hearing.

Hence, the result was, under the prior case law, that, in general, the complainant's production at the Wade Hearing, could rarely be compelled by defense counsel, unless there had been a previous showing of taint or suggestion established and so the necessity shown for an independent source of the identification.

In 1990, however, the Court of Appeals determined in the case of *People v. Chipp*, 75 N.Y.2d 327, 553 N.Y.S.2d 72 (1990), cert. den. U.S., 111 S. Ct. 99 (1990), that there were other criteria and circumstances whereby the complainant could be compelled by the defense to testify at a Wade hearing. This case bears careful analysis.

In *Chipp*, defendant was convicted, after a jury trial, of First Degree Sexual Abuse; First Degree Attempted Sodomy; Endangering the Welfare of a Child; and Fourth Degree Criminal Possession of a Weapon. The Appellate Division affirmed without opinion. On appeal, the essential issue presented by the defense was that the hearing Court's refusal to call the complaining witness to testify at a combined Huntley and Wade hearing, denied him the constitutional and statutory right to present relevant evidence on the issue of the suggestiveness of the pre-trial lineup identification procedures and on whether the lineup identification should have been suppressed as the fruit of an unlawful arrest.

The facts were that on April 7, 1986, Shanice F. was allegedly sexually abused by the defendant while on her way to school. One of the tenants of the building, Shermain Thompson, heard her screams and when the girl described her attacker, Ms. Thompson realized she was describing the defendant, whom she knew to be a friend of her brother, Sherman Thompson.

Detective Francisci interviewed the complainant at the hospital where she was taken and she described her attacker as a light skinned, black male, with short black hair, wearing a black baseball cap with white writing on the front and black framed glasses. The Detective also interviewed Shermain and Sherman Thompson and they also recognized and described the alleged assailant. Two days later, in response to a 911 call directing them to the 131st Street building, police officers found a number of civilians holding the defendant and were told he was the man who had "raped" a 10-year-old girl two days before. The defendant was arrested, and after giving an exculpatory statement having been given his Miranda warnings, he was identified by the complainant.

At the combined Wade-Huntley hearing, defense counsel requested that the People be required to produce Shanice to sustain their burden of going forward to establish the propriety of the pre-trial identification.

The People argued that a bifurcated hearing should be held to determine, initially, the possible suggestiveness of the lineup procedure, and, if so, to then proceed to determine whether the complainant witness' identification was grounded on an independent basis. The Court agreed with the People's contention and ordered a bifurcated hearing. Counsel for the defense, when the photograph and lineup form were received in evidence, argued that because the fill-ins had significantly darker complexions than the defendant, who had been described as light skinned, the lineup was prima facie suggestive, thus mandating the People to call Shanice to sustain their burden. This application was denied and the hearing proceeded.

At the hearing, defense counsel renewed his application to call the complainant. The Court denied the application finding no undue suggestiveness had been shown and concluding there had been no showing of a need to call the complaining witness to establish an independent basis for an in-court identification.

Thereafter, in a written decision, the Court denied suppression of the defendant's statement and the lineup identification, concluding that no undue suggestiveness had been demonstrated and so there was no need to produce the complaining witness at the Hearing. The Appellate Division affirmed.

The defendant argued to the Court of Appeals that he had a basic right to call the complainant at the pre-trial Wade Hearing, since she viewed the lineup and that this therefore was the only way to challenge the People's case. The defense further argued that the complainant should have been called as a matter of fairness, since he had the burden of showing the ultimately suggestive character of the lineup and that this right derived from the Compulsory Process Clause of the Constitution and C.P.L. 60.15.

The Court of Appeals rejected these arguments. The Court reasoned that the right of compulsory process is essentially a trial right and that the right alleged here involved only a Wade Hearing. Thus, the Court held that the right to compulsory process, critical at trial, does not absolutely attach to a pre-trial Wade Hearing and may be outweighed by countervailing policy concerns. Thus, the Court held that policy considerations militate against a rule making the complaining witness subject to compulsory process at the behest of the defendant at a Wade Hearing absent some indicia of suggestiveness. The Court went on to state, however, citing *People v. Ocasio,* 134 A.D.2d 293, 294, 530 N.Y.S.2d 620 (2d Dept. 1987), that the complainant's testimony might well become necessary if the hearing evidence raises issues as to the constitutionality of the lineup.

The key word here is necessary. The Court of Appeals seems to be creating a rule that although no absolute right exists on the part of the defense to have the complaining witness called at a Wade Hearing, absent a showing of suggestiveness at the Hearing and the concomitant need to establish an independent source, nevertheless facts may come to light at the Hearing, where the constitutionality or fairness of the identification procedure are cast in question by the defense. Under these circumstances, the complainant may be called. It is unclear, under *Chipp,* however, what precisely these circumstances in fact are, when the complainant may be called by the defense at a pre-trial Wade Hearing absent suggestive taint being shown.

Most of the cases following *Chipp* have simply adhered to the older general rule of thumb that the defense has no absolute right to call the complaining witness at a Wade Hearing absent a showing of suggestiveness. Thus, in *People v. Priester,* 162 A.D.2d 633, 556 N.Y.S.2d 951 (2d Dept. 1990), the Second Department held that since the defendant had failed to identify any indicia of suggestiveness in the photographic and lineup identification procedures employed, the hearing Court properly declined to compel the production of the complainant, citing *Chipp.* See, also, *People v. Griffin,* 161 A.D.2d 799, 556 N.Y.S.2d 131, 133 (2d Dept. 1990); *People v. Bernard,* 162 A.D.2d 362, 557 N.Y.S.2d 319, 320 (1st Dept. 1990); *People v. Peterkin,* 75 N.Y.2d 985 (1990). (Held: No abuse of discretion denying the defense request to call the complainant at the Wade Hearing absent some indicia of suggestiveness of the identification procedure employed, citing *Chipp*); *People v. Habersham,* 162 A.D.2d 370, 557 N.Y.S.2d 36, 37 (1st Dept. 1990); *People v. Cromwell,* 163, A.D.2d 410, 559 N.Y.S.2d 18 (2d Dept. 1990).

Other cases following *Chipp* have simply stated, in general terms, that absent a showing of a suggestive identification at the Wade Hearing, the complainant may be called, under *Chipp,* with a showing of special circumstances. Thus, in *People v. Peterkin, supra,* the Court added that in addition to the act that the defendant had made no showing of suggestiveness at the Wade Hearing, there was no contention by the defense that the complainant's testimony would have differed from that offered by the People's witnesses, citing *Chipp.* See, also, *People v. Habersham, supra.* In *People v. Allen,* 103 A.D.2d 396, 558 N.Y.S.2d 121 (2d Dept. 1990), interpreting *Chipp,* the Court held that the defendant, under *Chipp,* has no unqualified right to call the complainant at the Wade Hearing. The inquiry, if this is to occur, must focus on whether the hearing evidence raises substantial issues as to the constitutionality of the identification procedure, whether the People's evidence is incomplete with respect to the identification procedure or the defendant otherwise establishes a need for the testimony.

Two cases, however, flesh out the holding of *Chipp* in regard to under what particular circumstances the complainant may be called where, at the Wade Hearing there are no indicia of suggestiveness. They are *People v. Ocasio*, 134 A.D.2d 293, 520 N.Y.S.2d 620 (2d Dept. 1987), and *People v. Sokolyansky*, 147 A.D.2d 722, 538 N.Y.S.2d 69 (2d Dept. 1989). Indeed *Ocasio* was cited in *Chipp*. Both *Ocasio* and *Sokolyansky* bear careful review.

In *Ocasio*, the defendant was convicted in the Supreme Court, Kings County, of Manslaughter. On appeal the defendant contended the photographic identification procedure employed was unduly suggestive and that the Court erred in refusing to allow him to call the identifying witnesses to testify.

The facts were that at the Pre-trial Wade Hearing, the People called Detective O'Flaherty and that he testified that four witnesses came to the precinct to view a photographic array. Each witness was then taken into a separate room to view the photographic array and after each witness identified the third photograph as that of the perpetrator, they were instructed not to discuss their identification of the defendant with the remaining witnesses. The detective stated, however, that he could not state whether the witnesses followed these instructions, leaving open the possibility that a witness who had already viewed the array suggested or influenced a subsequent witness' identification of the defendant. Following direct and cross-examination by the defense, defense counsel requested the People produce the identifying witnesses or that he be permitted to subpoena them on the defendant's behalf. The Court denied these requests.

The Second Department initially held that the photo array and identification procedure were not unduly suggestive. The Court held, however, that the trial Court erred in refusing to allow the defendant to call the identifying eyewitnesses. The Court stated that the defendant had a right to explore the circumstances under which the identification of the photo was made by the various witnesses and was not required to accept the Detective's incomplete testimony at face value. The basis for the holding in *Ocasio*, cited by *Chipp*, would seem to be that where the testimony of the officer at the Wade Hearing reveals some break or question in the identification procedure, then the defense has a right to have the identifying witness or witnesses produced for examination.

Sokolyansky is also instructive. In *Sokolyansky* the defendant appealed from a conviction of Robbery in the Third Degree. The facts were that at the suppression hearing, the detective testified that the two identifying witnesses selected the defendant's photograph from a three photograph array. Subsequently, the witnesses came to police headquarters to view a lineup at which the defendant was to be a participant. While fillers were gathered for the lineup, the two witnesses were left in the presence of the detectives for twenty minutes and then each was taken individually to the viewing room and then identified the defendant as the perpetrator. At the close of the People's case the defense sought to call one of these witnesses to the stand arguing that the witness' identifications were possibly influenced by the suggestive police conduct and that the examination of the detective could not be solely relied on with respect to this issue. The Trial Court denied defense counsel's request and on appeal, the defense contended that the Supreme Court erred in denying his request to call one of the identifying witnesses to the stand at the Wade Hearing. The Appellate Division agreed with the defense, citing *Ocasio* and stating the defense was not required to accept the Detective's incomplete testimony at face value when it, in fact, moved in good faith and timely fashion to call these witnesses. Thus, the Appellate Division remitted the matter to the Supreme Court for a de novo suppression hearing.

Again, the holding in *Sokolyansky* is that where there is some sort of break or defect in the identification procedure, the identifying witness may be called by the defense to flesh out the appropriateness of the identification procedure where it is apparently incomplete and possibly suggestive and based heretofore on police testimony alone.

In sum, *Chipp* is a most important decision since although it upholds the prior law that a showing of the suggestiveness of the identification must be generally shown before the complaining witness must be called at a Wade Hearing, it also describes and suggests the particular circumstances and conditions which the complaining witnesses must be called upon a showing of need or necessity.

21. Undercover Closure

The undercover sale is one of the most common species of drug felonies. The courts of the Metropolitan New York area are literally inundated with this type of crime. Inevitably, in order to present their direct case, the people must produce the undercover police officer and therefore subject him to cross-examination by defense counsel. At this juncture of the trial the prosecutor will often apply to have the Court closed to the public, arguing that the undercover's life may be endangered, or his work as an undercover threatened, if he is subject to a public direct and cross-examination.

It is essential that defense counsel, at this point, object and insist that the courtroom remain open to the public. The right to a public trial is a fundamental right. The subjection of the prosecutor, judge, jury and witness to public scrutiny must inevitably and obviously ensure and preserve a fair trial for the defendant.

Thus, the question arises, and it is one of importance and significance, what in fact is the law when the application by the People, under these circumstances, is made, and how defense counsel may successfully avoid courtroom closure and, in point of fact, assure the fairness and integrity of the trial.

The leading case establishing the proper criteria for closure when an undercover officer is produced to testify is *People v. Jones*, 47 N.Y.2d 409, 418 N.Y.S.2d 359, 391 N.E.2d 1335 (1979); cert. den. 444 U.S. 946. In *Jones*, the defendant was convicted of charges arising out of the sale to two undercover police officers. The first undercover officer, Officer Howard, took the stand, and in the midst of his testimony, the trial judge was asked by the prosecutor to close the courtroom to the public because an undercover was testifying. The District Attorney stated that he wished the courtroom closed, but the undercover at that point indicated that he was not fearful of testifying and the issue was dropped. The next day, as Brown was about to be called as a witness by the People, the District Attorney again applied for closure on the ground that the witness feared for his life. The application was granted, over the objection of the defense counsel, that no information supporting that claim had been presented to the Court either by way of testimony or Colloquy.

When the courtroom was closed, the undercover testified that he was no longer engaged in undercover activity and that his present work as a uniformed officer was far from his former theater of operation. The Appellate Division, on appeal, affirmed, holding that the decision of the trial judge to close the courtroom had not seriously deprived the defendant of a fair public trial. The Court of Appeals after an extensive analysis of the fundamental character of the right to a full public trial as essential to a fair trial, concluded that either an inquiry by the trial judge concerning the present possible threat to the undercover's safety or his ongoing investigations should have been conducted or, if necessary, an evidentiary hearing held on the issue. The Court held this error was not harmless, was inherently prejudicial, and that the Court should not have relied for its decision to close the courtroom on its own vague notion of the general danger incumbent on undercover activity. Indeed, the Court noted that the trial judge continued to close the courtroom even when the undercover testified that he was no longer engaged in undercover work and had not done so for the past six months and that, apparently, the threat to his life and safety was *de minimis*.

The holding in *Jones* is clear. In the event that the undercover officer is produced to testify and the People apply for closure of the courtroom, defense counsel must apply either for an extended Colloquy concerning the issue with the prosecutor and Court, requesting immediate justification under *Jones* of the application to close or, what is more preferable, insist on an evidentiary hearing where the undercover is subject to cross-examination concerning his present work, its location and whether and how his life and work may be threatened should he testify in an open courtroom.

The trial and appellate courts of this State have consistently followed *Jones* with some modification. Thus, in *People v. Cordero*, 76 N.Y.2d 757, 541 N.Y.S.2d 917 (1989), the Court of Appeals again reiterated the rule in *Jones*, holding it reversible error to close the courtroom when the undercover testifies, without further inquiry by the Court.

Similarly, in *People v. Gutierrez*, 133 A.D.2d 647, 519 N.Y.S.2d 756 (2d Dept. 1987), the Second Department held it error to close the courtroom based on the mere assertion of the District Attorney that the undercover feared for his safety should he testify in an open courtroom. The Court insisted that a further factual showing was necessary. Cf., however, *People v. Santos*, 154 A.D.2d 284 (1st Dept. 1989), where the First Department held the closure of the courtroom proper, where the undercover detailed in a closed hearing that he was still working actively as an undercover in the Bronx and that his safety would be threatened in the event of his testifying in an open courtroom. The Court held that when the fact of the undercover's work in the community is elicited from the witness himself, that is a justifiable reason to close the courtroom to the public during the undercover's testimony. See also *People v. Wharton*, 143 A.D.2d 958, 533 N.Y.S.2d 557 (2d Dept. 1988) (Evidentiary hearing detailing present undercover activities held sufficient basis to close the courtroom).

The courts of this State, however, seem to be moving to a rule of law that mere inquiry by the trial judge of the undercover concerning his present work activities, under *Jones*, for possible closure is insufficient to preserve the integrity of a fair and open trial and that, in fact, a full evidentiary hearing should be held. Thus, the Second Department held, in *People v. Romain*, 137 A.D.2d 848, 525 N.Y.S.2d 313 (2d Dept. 1988), that when no hearing on the issue of closure was conducted, this constituted reversible error, particularly where the defense counsel was not provided with an opportunity to examine the undercover or even be heard prior to the decision to close the courtroom. See also *People v. Davis*, 72 A.D.2d 798, 421 N.Y.S.2d 629 (2d Dept. 1979) (Proper closure where evidentiary hearing held detailing that testimony by the undercover in open Court might endanger her life since there were unresolved cases in which she had participated and she was presently working as a security officer); *People v. Cuevas*, 50 N.Y.2d 1022, 431 N.Y.S.2d 686, 409 N.E.2d 1360 (1980) (Improper closure where the Court, in response to the People's application for closure, did not make an adequate inquiry of the witness). See also on this *People v. Boucher*, 112 A.D.2d 310, 491 N.Y.S.2d 757 (2d Dept. 1985); *People v. Thompon*, 151 A.D.2d 626, 542 N.Y.S.2d 700 (2d 1989); *People v. Tinsley*, 145 A.D.2d 448, 534 N.Y.S.2d 415 (2d Dept. 1988).

Although it is clear under *Jones* that the Court may proceed by Colloquy or evidentiary hearing, the cases following *Jones* seem to indicate that some sort of full hearing should be held in which at least the judge examines the witness under oath as to his present activities and the actual threat to his life, safety or present work, should he be compelled to testify in an open courtroom. Preferably this hearing should include the opportunity to cross-examine the witness by defense counsel.

What then is the proper course to follow should Court closure be applied for by the District Attorney when an undercover is produced to testify?

Defense counsel should, citing *Jones* and the cases following it, insist that an actual evidentiary hearing be held in which he is given the right to cross-examine the undercover. If this is not granted, counsel should insist that the judge examine the undercover and inquiry be made under the *Jones* criteria. Counsel should insist, in either event, that the trial judge make findings of fact on the record justifying closure If closure is granted, counsel should reiterate his objection, in chambers, to closure on the record.

Finally, it should be noted, that if counsel fails in timely and vigorous fashion to object to closure, the error will surely not be preserved for appellate review.

The right to a public trial is a fundamental right. It assures and ensures that the actions of the Court and the prosecutor will be visible and that their errors and abuses, should they occur, will not be hidden from public view. Any abrogation of the right to an open trial is anathema and antithetical to our republican and democratic system of government which abhors secret proceedings and Star Chamber inquiries. The rule of *Jones*, if raised in timely fashion by defense counsel, is a lynch pin of this fundamental right and will assure that the openness of our system of law will be preserved.

Copyright 1993 by the Queens County Bar Association and the Queens Bar Bulletin. Reprinted with permission.

22. The Confirmatory Identification: Wade Hearing or No

It is the law that where there is a hint of suggestive police arranged identification of the defendant by showup or lineup, the defendant, under *U.S. vs. Wade,* 388 U.S. 218 (1967), is entitled to a so-called Wade Hearing. In fact, the showup, the most common form of police arranged identification, is the most suggestive procedure available. *Stovall vs. Denno,* 388 U.S. 293 (1967); *People vs. Adams,* 53 N.Y.2d 241 (1981). An apparent exception, under New York Law, to the rule of law wherein a Wade Hearing is usually granted, is the confirmatory identification. Simply put, a confirmatory identification is nothing more than an indication by a police office to other law enforcement officials or an official that the right man has been nabbed. The context is, in general, where an undercover officer has made a narcotics sale to the defendant, radios the description of the alleged perpetrator to the backup team, and, in a subsequent driveby or other form of identification, indicates to the backup team that the defendant, who allegedly made the sale to him, is the right man, thereby effectuating the eventual arrest of the defendant. The Courts of the State of New York, have, for the most part, held that this confirmatory identification is not subject to the granting of a Wade Hearing since what is involved is nothing more than good police procedural work in the course of effecting the arrest of the defendant.

The leading case articulating this rule is *People vs. Morales,* 37 N.Y.2d 262, 372 N.Y.S.2d 5 (1975). The facts of *Morales* were that in September of 1970 an undercover officer purchased 15 glassine envelopes from the defendant. The officer then informed the backup team, by prearranged signal, that he had completed the drug purchase. The undercover officer then rendezvoused with the backup team where he vouchered the purchase in police property envelopes and wrote a detailed description of the defendant Morales on the envelope. The detective then cruised the neighborhood until he saw Morales again and then radioed the backup team, directing them to arrest Morales, the man he had described and whom he had seen earlier. Six hours after the arrest the undercover officer went to the precinct where Morales was being held and viewed and identified the prisoner through a two-way mirror, through which he could see and identify the defendant without being seen.

At trial the undercover officer, over objection of the defendant, testified to his stationhouse observation of the defendant.

The defendant was convicted of criminally selling a dangerous drug. The Appellate Division, however, reversed, holding in part, that the defendant's due process rights had been violated by the admission into evidence of the police officer's testimony of that stationhouse identification of the defendant.

The Court of Appeals held that the stationhouse viewing was confirmatory only and that the trial court was correct. The Court of Appeals distinguished a police officer's identification from that of the ordinary citizen, stating it was consonant with good police work. The court noted, particularly, that the identifying officer had been trained for such a role and could be expected to be careful. The courts of this state, trial and appellate, have interpreted *Morales*, for the most part, to mandate denial of a Wade Hearing under the circumstances of a confirmatory identification. See *People vs. Leftwich,* 82 M.2d 993, 372 N.Y.S.2d 888 (S. Ct. New York County 1975); *People vs. Laurain,* 84 M.2d 970, 378 N.Y.S.2d 599 (S. Ct. New York County 1976); *People vs. Stanton,* 108 A.D.2d 688, 485 N.Y.S.2d 998 (1st Dept. 1985); *People vs. Smith,* 103 M.2d 513, 426 N.Y.S.2d 420 (Westchester County Court 1980); *People vs. Marrero,* 110 A.D.2d 785, 487 N.Y.S.2d 853 (2d Dept. 1985).

A number of trial and appellate courts, however, have, depending on the circumstances, taken exception to the *Morales* rule of law. *People vs. Rubio,* 118 A.D.2d 879, 500 N.Y.S.2d 366 (2d Dept. 1986), is apropos. *Rubio* was an appeal from a judgment of conviction of Criminal Sale of a Controlled Substance in the Third and Seventh Degrees. The matter was remitted, by the Second Department, for a Wade Hearing. The case, in essence, arose out of an undercover sale in which the defendant acted as intermediary between the seller and the undercover officer. No arrest was made at the time of the transaction and when the police returned several hours later the suspects could not be located.

Twenty-seven days later the informant spotted the defendant in the area of the location of the sale, the police were notified and the defendant was arrested and brought to the stationhouse where he was identified by the undercover officer through a two-way mirror. The defendant's pretrial motion to suppress the undercover's stationhouse identification was denied by the trial court and, at trial, the officer testified regarding his observation and identification of the defendant at the precinct. The Second Department held that the question whether the stationhouse identification should be regarded as merely confirmatory of the previous identification, or improper, should have been determined by Wade Hearing. The Appellate Court noted that *Morales* should not be viewed or read as having dispensed with a Wade Hearing invariably under all these circumstances and that the particular facts in hand may suggest that a reasonable possibility exists that the officer's identification of the defendant might be the product of the stationhouse viewing rather than the observations made during the commission of the crime.

Similarly, in *People vs. Williams*, 79 A.D.2d 929 (1st Dept. 1981), the First Department also held that the Wade application by the defense should have been granted where the identification by the undercover was confirmatory in character. The court noted, in *Williams*, that the identification was made only after the sergeant told the undercover officer that the purchase money had been found on the defendant and after the cap and glasses found in the transporting car were placed on the defendant. Before that the undercover had been unable to successfully identify the defendant. For cases following *Rubio* and *Williams* see *People vs. Lugo*. 62 A.D.2d 1024, 403 N.Y.S.2d 550 (2d Dept. 1978); *People vs. Doyle,* 132 M.2d 338, 510 N.Y.S.2d 987 (S. Ct. Kings County 1987); *People vs. Baron,* 154 A.D.2d 710, 553 N.Y.S.2d 195 (2d Dept. 1990); *People vs. Wright*, 47 A.D.2d 894 (1st Dept. 1975) (Seven week delay between the undercover's initial observation at the scene and confirmatory identification. Held: improper to deny Wade Hearing); *People vs. Larando,* N.Y.L.J. 5/9/91, p.24. Col. 5.

It is clear that although the general rule of law in this state is that a Wade Hearing will be denied where there is apparently a confirmatory identification only, it is also clear that, depending on the discrete facts alleged, particularly if there is a gap of time between the initial observations of the undercover officer and the confirmatory identification, that a Wade Hearing may be granted. It would also appear that where a confirmatory identification occurs at the stationhouse, that this is an additional factor that must be taken into consideration by the trial court in the determination of whether to grant a Wade hearing. Hence, it is essential that defense counsel, if he would gain a Wade Hearing in the context of a confirmatory identification, must, contrary to the specific requirement of law and practice under the C.P.L., allege specific facts.

A final point is to be noted. Even where the identification is completely confirmatory in nature, notice must be given under C.P.L. Sec. 710.31(b). If this notice is not given, the case law of this state holds that the People will be precluded from introducing the confirmatory identification into evidence. See on this *People vs. Naranjo,* 140 M.2d 43, 529 N.Y.S.2d 953 (S. Ct. New York County 1988); *People vs. Newball*, 76 N.Y.2d 587, 561 N.Y.S.2d 898 (1990).

23. The Confirmatory Identification

In an article published in the April 1992 *Queens Bar Bulletin,* entitled "The Confirmatory Identification: Wade Hearing or No," this writer examined the question of when and under what specific circumstances the defense may be entitled to a Wade Hearing when the identification is labeled confirmatory by the People, meaning that in an undercover buy and bust operation, there has been a subsequent identification after the sale by the undercover officer. This writer concluded that, without some lapse of time occurring between the time of the sale and the subsequent identification by the undercover officer, a Wade Hearing will not be granted by the trial court.[1]

In this article, a second prong of the confirmatory identification exception to the normal Wade Hearing procedure will be examined and recent case law considered on the subject. The confirmatory identification exception, under the law, can be said to include not only where a police officer makes an identification within minutes, hours or days after the occurrence, such as occurs in an undercover sale, but also where the People seek to introduce identification evidence where the parties allegedly know each other or have some sort of relationship, familial or amicable. Here, the courts of this state have held, in general, that the defense, under this factual scenario, is not entitled to a Wade Hearing.

The seminal and still leading case on the subject is *People v. Tas,* 51 N.Y.2d 915, 434 N.Y.S.2d 978, 415 N.E.2d 967 (1980). *Tas* was an appeal, by the defendants, from two counts of Sodomy in the First Degree. The Court of Appeals held that the trial court was correct in denying the defendant's motion to preclude evidence relating to the victim's identification on the ground that the People had failed to give notice. The Court of Appeals, citing the Appellate Division decision that the defendant and victim were inmates in the same tier of cells for one month prior to the attack and so the victim and perpetrator were known to each other, held there was no identification within the meaning of C.P.L. Sect. 710.30(b). See also *People v. Gissendanner,* 48 N.Y.2d 543, 423, N.Y.S.2d 893, 399 N.E.2d 925 (1979). The courts of this state, following *Tas* and *Gissendanner,* both trial and appellate, have labeled such identification where the victim and defendant are known to each other as confirmatory and not the subject of C.P.L. Sec. 710.30(b) notice, the Hearing process, or ultimate suppression. See *People v. Butler,* 150 A.D.2d 789, 542 N.Y.S.2d 220 (2d Dept. 1989); *People v. Walker,* 150 A.D.2d 515, 541 N.Y.S.2d 111 (2d Dept. 1989); *People v. Epps,* 155 A.D.2d 933, 547 N.Y.S.2d 755 (4th Dept. 1989); *People v. Stewart,* 144 A.D.2d 601, 534 N.Y.S.2d 439 (2d Dept. 1988); *People v. Ambroise,* 142 A.D.2d 647, 531 N.Y.S.2d 13 (2d Dept. 1988); *People v. Baity,* 577 N.Y.S.2d 262 (1st Dept. 1991).

Some Recent Law

Of late, however, the legal sands would appear to be shifting on the issue of whether, based on the bald assertion of the People, the parties were known to each other and so identification is not an issue as labeled confirmatory. The Appellate Courts of this state seem to be reaching toward a modified rule that where there is some issue of fact raised by defense on the actual extent of the parties alleged relationship and/or acquaintance, the defense may be entitled to a Wade Hearing on the issue.

People v. Mosley, 136 A.D.2d 500, 523, N.Y.S.2d 820 (1st Dept. 1988), is a precursor. *Mosley* was an appeal from a judgment of the Supreme Court of New York County convicting the defendant of Robbery in the First Degree and sentencing him to a term of 10-20 years incarceration. On appeal the issue was the trial court's denial of the defense motion to suppress identification evidence. In *Mosley* the defendant was arrested and charged with Robbery in the First and Second Degree. After the arraignment on the indictment the defendant moved to suppress, alleging a suggestive show-up and denying ever having seen the complainant. The prosecutor, who opposed the motion, alleged the identification procedure used in the case was a confirmatory show-up and that the complainant knew the defendant from the building. Thereafter, the trial court denied the defense counsel application for a Wade Hearing on the ground that the identification procedure used was not an issue, based solely on the People's assertion that the parties knew each other.

At trial, identification was an issue before the jury. The complainant testified that his familiarity with the defendant arose from his allegedly having, through a peephole, seen him passing in the hallway and once allegedly having passed him on the stairs.

The court reasoned that the allegations made in support of the defendant's motion would, if contradicted, have been sufficient to warrant suppression and that the People's response did no more than raise an issue of fact which could be resolved only upon a hearing. In short, the court held that where the motion papers submitted by the defense raise an issue of fact, a Wade Hearing is appropriate and necessary. Thus, the Appellate Division, First Department, remanded to the Supreme Court for a hearing on the defendant's motion to suppress the identification evidence.

Mosley is a groundbreaking decision in that the Appellate Division, in essence, held that where, despite the People's denomination of the identification as confirmatory due to the parties' prior familiarity with each other, the defense in its motion papers raises an issue of fact as to the extent of the defendant's and complainant's acquaintanceship with each other or whether they actually knew each other, a Wade Hearing is mandated. See also *People v. Marte,* 149 A.D.2d 335, 539 N.Y.S.2d 912 (1st Dept. 1989), where citing *Mosley* the First Department held, this time in the context of the defense application for a Mapp Hearing, that where the defense counsel's affirmation in support of his motion for

Mapp relief was sufficient to place in issue the lawfulness of the defendant's arrest and the reply affirmation of the Assistant District Attorney did not resolve the issue, a hearing should be granted.

It would appear that the First Department has been moving to a rule that where an issue of fact is raised in the defendant's motion papers, be it an application for Wade or Mapp relief, a hearing is appropriate if, in fact, the factual assertions of the People are contradicted by the defense.

If there can be any doubt but that the courts of this state are moving to the *Mosley* perspective, then the recent case of *People v. Rodriguez*, N.Y.L.J. p. 22, Col. 1, 5/12/92 (Court of Appeals) lays all doubts and fears to at least limited rest.

The facts in *Rodriguez* were that on August 22, 1986, David Benito noticed a group of people from below his apartment window. He noticed two men arguing, saw one shove the other, whereupon the latter drew a gun, shot the other man to death and fled. Two hours later, Benito reported his observations to the police, was shown two or three photographs, but did not identify any one as the assailant. Three days later, Benito identified, from a single photograph shown him by a detective, the gunman. The defendant, on being arrested in an unrelated incident, was charged with the August 22nd murder. After the filing of the indictment, the defendant moved for a Wade Hearing to explore the suggestiveness of the photo identification. The People relied on the Grand Jury testimony of Benito wherein he testified that he had seen the defendant four dozen times as a customer in the grocery store. The People, in opposing the motion for Wade relief, stated that Benito was very familiar with the defendant and therefore suggestiveness was not an issue. The trial court summarily denied the defendant's motion. At the conclusion of the pretrial Mapp Hearing the defendant renewed his application for a Wade Hearing, stating that his client was not familiar with Benito and that Benito was a long time police informant. Again the court denied the motion. The defendant moved at trial for a Wade Hearing, again denying any familiarity with Benito and adding that defense investigations revealed that a criminal case pending against Benito had been A.C.D. on the day of the defendant's arrest. The motion was again summarily denied.

At trial, Benito made an in-court identification of the defendant but, in contrast to his Grand Jury Testimony, he testified that he had seen the defendant a few times prior to the crime as one of the guys in the neighborhood. He also stated he was neither a friend or acquaintance of the defendant. The defendant, on the testimony of the photo showup and in-court identification, was convicted of Second Degree Murder and Weapons Possession.

On appeal to the Appellate Division, the defendant argued that the trial court, in summarily denying a Wade Hearing, was in error. The Appellate Division affirmed. The Court of Appeals, however, reversed and remitted for a Wade Hearing.

In its decision, the Court of Appeals first reviewed the mechanism for and the importance of testing the reliability of identification testimony before trial through the schemata of C.P.L. Sec. 710.20, 710.30 and 710.60.

The court then noted that a narrow exception existed with respect to the notice requirement for suggestive pretrial identification. This exception was where the defendant and complainant and/or witness are sufficiently acquainted with or known to each other, the so called confirmatory identification exception. The court went on to state that, as indicated in *People v. Collins,* 60 N.Y.2d 214 (1933), whether the exception applies depends on the extent of the prior relationship. The court noted that the exception may be confidently applied where the protagonists are family members, friends, acquaintances, spouses, or have lived together for a time. On the other hand, the court stated the exception does not apply where the alleged familiarity emanates from a brief encounter. In the case before it, the court held that there was an issue as to the extent of Benito's familiarity with the defendant and whether, although Benito might have seen the defendant four dozen times, such witness, nevertheless, could be influenced by suggestiveness to make a misidentification. The Court of Appeals held that without more information the trial court had no basis for ruling that the witness was impervious to suggestion and that the trial court should have granted the defendant's request for a hearing to explore Benito's alleged prior familiarity with the defendant. The Court of Appeals suggested that at this, as it were Pre-Hearing, the court should consider such factors as the number of times Benito viewed the defendant prior to the crime, the duration and nature of the encounters, the setting and period of time over which these encounters occurred, the time that elapsed between the crime and the previous viewings and the question whether the two had any conversations.

The court also stated that the confirmatory identification to C.P.L. Sec. 710.30 requires the exception to be usually applied to situations where suggestiveness is not a concern. Hence, the court held the People must show the protagonists are known to each other or know each other so well as to be impervious to police suggestion.

The court also rejected the People's argument that the defendant was not entitled to a hearing because, as a matter of pleading, the defendant did not create a factual issue as to Benito's familiarity with him. In fact, the court noted that the defendant denied knowing Benito and these facts, despite the uncontroverted allegation of the People that Benito had seen the defendant four dozen times in the grocery store, entitled the defense at least to a pre-hearing as to the issue of Benito's prior familiarity with the defendant.

In sum, the court held that where the People did not allege a mutually defined relationship, whether familial, spousal or an extended friendship, and defendant denied any prior familiarity with Benito, the court should have applied the confirmatory identification pursuant to *Tas* and *Gissendanner*. If after that hearing it is found that the People have not sustained their burden of establishing the requisite degree of familiarity, a full Wade Hearing should be ordered.

Rodriguez is an important decision since the Court of Appeals in essence holds that the defense, although not entitled to a Wade Hearing where the People allege an extended relationship of prior familiarity arising from family, marriage, common law marriage or simple friendship, is entitled to a so called Pre-hearing to establish the requisite knowingness and prior familiarity where the extent of the relationship is cast into issue by the defense.

Thus it would seem that in the absence of an established spousal, familial or amicable relationship, where there is question of fact as to the extent of the familiarity, the defense is entitled to a pre-Wade Hearing on this issue for the People to successfully invoke the confirmatory/identification exception.

Rodriguez does not go so far as *Mosley* or *Marte* which state that any question of fact raised by the defense in his Wade or Mapp papers entitled him to a hearing. It does say, however, that outside of certain relationships, where familiarity is made an issue, there must be a Pre-Hearing to resolve this question of fact.

Conclusion

Mosley and *Marte* hold that an issue of fact, if raised, entitles the defense to a pretrial Wade or Mapp Hearing. *Rodriguez* is more limiting. In the view of this writer, *Mosley* is closer to the true mark. To allow, based on the ex parte Grand Jury Proceeding, or an ex parte interview with the complaining witness, that a prior relationship exists and so allow the confirmatory identification to apply even where that relationship is denied by the defense, and so to deny a Wade Hearing, is illogical and contrary to the letter and spirit of the law. Relationships are fleeting. Spouses separate and are divorced. Fleeting common law relationships are increasingly prevalent in our fast moving society. Brothers may neither know nor see each other. These relationships, excluded by *Rodriguez* from being the subject of a Wade Hearing, constitute questions of fact to be resolved by our adversarial system and not by the secret decision of the prosecutor to claim a label. All question of fact, as suggested by *Mosley,* in Wade motion papers should be resolved by a hearing on the issue. *Mosley* is the kindling spirit. *Rodriguez* hesitates to join the fire. It is hoped that, in time, the Appellate Courts of this state will see that to allow the People to invoke the confirmatory identification exception based on a supposed relationship is to deny the resolution of facts that may only be revealed by a hearing. The purpose of our adversarial system is the unearthing of truth and truth will never, however imperfectly, be brought to light by ex parte decisions that may well serve to hide the truth and the facts.

24. Violation of Probation in Criminal Law: One Small Point

The criminal practitioner in the State of New York who, depending, of course, on the strength of the People's case, can obtain from the People an offer of a non-incarceratory sentence of probation for his client, whether Five years probation when the client is charged with a Felony; Three years when the client is charged with a Class A Misdemeanor; or One year when he is charged with a Class B Misdemeanor; will often, so to speak, seize the moment and urge his client to avail himself of this possibility of a non-jail disposition when the alternative may be, if there occurs a conviction after trial, a lengthy period of incarceration, particularly if the charge is a Class B or Class C Felony.

The sentence of probation is, to be sure, no free ride for the defendant. He remains under the jurisdiction and supervision of the State and if he is re-arrested, or fails to report to his probation officer, or in some other fashion violates his sentence of probation, he may be subject to a re-sentence to the maximum of the underlying charge. Thus, for example as often happens where, in a defendant's first B Felony Drug Sale or Drug Possession offense, he chooses to plead guilty to Attempted Sale of a Narcotic Drug, or to Attempted Possession of a Narcotic Drug, a Class C Felony, and receives a sentence of Five Years Probation, and is subsequently violated based on a re-arrest or failure to report to probation, he can receive a maximum sentence of five to fifteen years incarceration based on the violation alone and can receive consecutive time if there is a conviction after trial based on the new arrest which formed the basis of the Violation of Probation.

The Problem

The problem this article seeks to explore is when a re-arrest is the subject of the Violation of Probation, can the defendant be violated on the re-arrest alone, without actual evidence of a conviction, and if so, can, as a logical corollary of the latter, the Violation of Probation hearing precede the actual trial on which the arrest is based. This is a most important point since the standard of proof on which an adjudication of violation of probation is based is by a preponderance of the evidence, and the result may be, under the above scenario, that the client, if the Violation of Probation Hearing precedes the trial, may be faced with a lengthier period of incarceration, based on a lower standard of proof than a conviction, should there be one, after trial, since the re-arrest which forms the basis of the Violation of Probation may be a lesser grade Felony than the conviction which formed the basis of the sentence of probation.

Thus, in effect, the threat of a Violation of Probation Hearing preceding trial, based on a new arrest, if allowed under the law can, since it is a hearing based on a lower standard proof than that required for a conviction after trial, which is beyond a reasonable doubt, and could result in a lengthier period of incarceration than would occur if first the defendant were found guilty on the new arrest after trial, function as a threat by the court to force the defendant to plead guilty first to the Violation of Probation thereby not going to trial on the new charge and also pleading guilty.

The question this article proposes to consider is whether this unfortunate scenario may be avoided by defense counsel and whether the court may be forced to try the new charge forming the basis of the Violation of Probation first, and be forced to obtain a conviction before it can proceed to the Violation of Probation Hearing, rather than proceeding first on the Violation of Probation, thereby effectively threatening the client with an adjudication based on a lower standard of proof than the beyond a reasonable doubt standard, obtained without the benefit of a jury and possibly involving the imminent possibility of a greater period of incarceration than if the new charge, forming the basis of the Violation of Probation, had been tried first.

It is the view of this writer that, based on the weight of authority in this state, a Violation of Probation should not ideally be obtained based on the specification of a new arrest alone, that a conviction based on that arrest is necessary for a probationer to be violated and that, therefore, the trial should precede the Violation of Probation Hearing under these circumstances.

The relevant and leading case is *People vs. Diaz*, 101 A.D.2d 841, 475 N.Y.S.2d 504 (2d Dept. 1984).

Diaz was an appeal from an amended judgment of the Supreme Court of Kings County, rendered in April of 1982, which, after a hearing, adjudicated the defendant to be in violation of probation and sentenced him to a term of imprisonment. The facts in *Diaz* were that the defendant was convicted of Robbery in the Third Degree in July of 1975, upon his plea of guilty, and was sentenced to five years probation on condition he remain at a particular therapeutic facility. The defendant absconded from the facility and committed a series of offenses. In November of 1978 the defendant failed to report to his probation officer, failed to appear in Kings County Criminal Court in connection with an arrest for Burglary and Criminal Possession of Stolen Property for which a bench warrant was issued, and in December of 1978 was arrested in White Plains for Petit Larceny. A violation warrant was issued in March of 1979 and in April of 1979 the defendant failed to appear in New York County Criminal Court and a bench warrant was issued.

In May of 1979 Criminal Term in New York County so ordered a recommendation that the defendant be declared delinquent and issued a bench warrant. The defendant's whereabouts remained unknown until December of 1981, when he was arrested in New York County for Petit Larceny and Possession of Stolen Property.

In April of 1982, a final revocation hearing was held and the defendant was adjudicated in Violation of Probation, on 1979, 1981 New York County convictions and his failure to report to his probation officer. The defendant was adjudicated in violation of his probation and sentenced to 1-3 years incarceration to run concurrent with the two eight month sentences he was serving.

The court rejected the defendant's arguments that reversal was warranted because his term of probation, which was to have expired in July of 1980, was never tolled because no declaration of delinquency was filed and so the court was without jurisdiction to proceed; and that even if a declaration had been issued, the failure to bring him before Criminal Term for a final delinquency determination within the original probationary period warranted reversal.

The court also held that the delay in locating the defendant for a final adjudication of delinquency was not due to any lack of due diligence on the part of the People, but due to the defendant's own actions.

What is important here, however, is the holding of the *Diaz* court that evidence that a probationer has been arrested for a new offense is not sufficient reasonable cause to support issuance of a warrant or a declaration of delinquency. The court went on to note, however, that in this case the evidence that the probationer had absconded from the facility he was to be associated with as a condition of his probation, his failure to report and his new arrest in another county provided reasonable cause to believe that the probationer had violated a condition of his sentence and based upon such conduct revocation of probation and resentencing to a term of imprisonment was proper.

The language of *Diaz* is clear—that a violation warrant, declaration of delinquency and, by inference, ultimately an adjudication of probation violation cannot be obtained based on evidence of a new arrest alone. If other bases are present, such as failure to report, then the arrest warrant declaration of delinquency and adjudication may possibly be had. An arrest alone, however, is insufficient. By implication there must be a conviction based on the new arrest before a probation warrant, declaration of delinquency, or adjudication of violation of probation is possible.

See also *People vs. Amaro*, 358 N.Y.S.2d 900 (S. Ct., New York County 1974), where the trial court held, referring to the Model Penal Code of the American Law Institute and the 1973 National Advisory Commission on Criminal Justice Standards and Goals, that the showing of a new arrest did not, in the absence of exigent circumstances, authorize issuance of a warrant for probationer's arrest or a judicial declaration of delinquency and did not support any judicial action upon the probationer except service of a notice to appear. *Amaro*, however, like *Diaz*, failed to rule specifically on the issue whether an actual adjudication of violation of probation can be obtained based on an arrest alone, although that is the clear implication and inference to be drawn from both cases.

But, note however, *People vs. Crandall*, 51 A.D.2d 841 (3rd Dept. 1976), where the Third Department held, noting it was aware of the recommendations of the Model Penal Code of the American Law Institute and the National Advisory Commission on Criminal Justice Standards and Goals, that revocation of probation for commission of a new offense should be deferred until the criminal violation is formally tried and that the charge should not be used as a basis for revocation, that all the precautionary steps had been taken here including issuance of a formal charge by the Probation Department, issuance of an arrest warrant, a notice to appear to the Defendant, the assignment of counsel to the defendant and the holding of a full adversary hearing.

It would appear that the Third Department rejects the *Amaro* and *Diaz* view of this issue as well as the recommendations of the Model Penal code and the National Advisory Commission of Criminal Justice Standards and Goals that the court, at least, should not issue a probation warrant and file a declaration of delinquency and, by implication, adjudicate one in violation of probation based on a mere arrest, and that trial or disposition of the new arrest forming the violation of probation should proceed first, enabling the trial court to base its violation of probation on a conviction after trial or, should there be an acquittal, allowing the probation department, in its discretion, to withdraw the specification of the new arrest and restore the defendant to probation. It is interesting to note, however, that the Fourth Department in *People vs. Brink*, 124 A.D.2d 966, 508 N.Y.S.2d 799 (4th Dept. 1986), held that the Monroe County Court erred in finding a violation of probation based on proof of two arrests.

Conclusion

It is clear that, although the Fourth Department and Third Department have specifically ruled on the issue the subject of this article, whether a mere arrest, without an actual conviction, can result in a violation of probation, the Fourth Department saying it cannot, the Third saying it can provided certain precautionary steps are taken, the Second Department in *Diaz* did not actually reach this issue, although the inference can be drawn in *Diaz* that an arrest cannot found an adjudication of violation of probation, since *Diaz* held that an arrest is not sufficient reasonable cause to support issuance of a probation warrant or the filing of a declaration of delinquency. *Amaro*, a trial court decision, says the same.

There can be no doubt, given the split in the Third and Fourth Department and the failure of the Second Department to reach this issue, that law will ultimately be made in the future on this subject, the particular issue will remain open and will ultimately be resolved by the Court of Appeals, given the conflicts in the Departments.

25. Defendant's Presence at Trial: Recent Developments

The right of the criminally accused to be present at all stages of the criminal proceeding is a subject that has lately tested the interest of the Appellate Courts of this State. It can be generally stated that the defendant has a constitutional right to be present at all critical stages of the criminal litigation.

Thus, the defendant has the right to appear and testify before the Grand Jury. That right, however, can be waived and, under certain discrete circumstances, due to the action or lack of action of the prosecutor, can result in dismissal of the indictment. C.P.L. Sec. 190.50(5); C.P.L. Sec. 210.20.

Under certain classes of accusatory instruments, such as the Simplified Information or a summons or desk appearance ticket, the defendant's appearance may be waived by counsel. C.P.L. Sec. 170.10(a), (b).

It is also the law that a defendant may choose not to appear at a pre-trial hearing. By the same token, under C.P.L. Sec. 260.20 the defendant may, by his disruptive conduct, cause his removal from the trial or he may, under C.P.L. 340.50, by filing a written and subscribed statement, waive his right to be personally present. It is beyond the scope of this article, however, to examine in complete depth and complexity when, how, and under what circumstances the defendant's presence at any and every stage of the criminal litigation may be required or, as a matter of law, be waived.

The Problem

Specifically, this article will consider the distinct problem as to the circumstances, under the present state of the case law, that defendant's presence, as a matter of due process and statute, is required at certain stages of the criminal proceeding such as voir dire challenge conferences, charge conferences, or side bar or in chambers proceedings. The appellate courts of this State have, of late, been most active in ruling on this issue of due process.

People v. Velasco, 77 N.Y.2d 469, 568 N.Y.S.2d 721 (1991), is a most significant case. In *Velasco*, the defendant was convicted of Manslaughter in the First Degree, a charge arising from an argument in which the victim was stabbed with a Ninja knife. The Appellate Division, First Department, affirmed the judgment of conviction. The defendant, in his brief address to the Court of Appeals, argued that the judgment of conviction should be reversed because of his absence and exclusion from a pre-charge conference, side bar voir dire, and a conference in the robing room to discuss peremptory challenges and challenges for cause. The defendant claimed that, as a result of his exclusion from these particular stages of the proceeding, his constitutional and statutory right to be present at all material stages of the criminal proceeding was denied. Citing *People v. Mullen*, 44 N.Y.2d 1, 403 N.Y.S.2d 470, 374, N.E.2d 369 and *Snyder v. Mass.*, 241 U.S. 97, 108, 54 S. Ct. 330, 333, 78 L.Ed. 674, and C.P.L. 260.20, the court noted that the pre-charge conference was conducted in the court's robing room where the attorneys for both parties, but not the defendant, were present. The court went on to state that the parties discussed a stipulation concerning the contents of a medical record, the scheduling of the rest of the trial, the court's instructions to the jury and certain motions of the defendant. Thus, the court concluded that the conference involved only questions of law and procedure and so the defendant's presence was not required.

The court also rejected the defendant's contention that he had a right to be present at the side bar voir dire where, following the court voir dire any juror wishing to respond to the court's questions was directed to approach the bench where further discussion was held by the court and attorneys, but outside the presence of the defendant and the jury panel. Following these side bar conferences some prospective jurors were excused by the court and some returned to the jury box. The court held, in response to the defendant's contention that he had a right to be present during these conferences, that the process of actual disqualification of a juror was a matter for the court and that the defendant had no statutory or constitutional right to be present during these discussions. The court noted that the defendant was present during the initial questioning of the jurors and represented by counsel during the discussions at the bench.

Finally, the court also rejected the defendant's contention that his right to be present during the impaneling of the jury was impaired by his absence from the conference in the robing room, during which counsel advised the court of the challenges for cause and the peremptory challenges. The court held that the defendant's statutory and constitutional rights were not violated by this procedure since the defendant was present during the initial voir dire and the exercise of the challenges in open court leading to the removal of the jurors.

Velasco is a landmark decision. The Court of Appeals, most probably acting more for reasons of judicial economy and smooth procedure than the right of due process, held, effectively, that the defendant had no constitutional or statutory right to be present at the pre-charge conference, side bar court voir dire whereby some jurors are removed or in chambers voir dire discussions where both counsel advise the court of their peremptory challenges or challenges for cause.

People v. Lowe, 117 A.D.2d, 755 (2d Dept. 1986), seems to be a precursor of *Velasco* by the Second Department and, in a sense, both follows and extends it. *Lowe* was an appeal from a judgment of conviction of the Supreme Court of Queens County convicting the defendant of First and Second Degree Robbery. The defendant argued on appeal that he was denied due process of law because he was not present at all in camera and side bar proceedings in which his attorney appeared on his behalf. Citing *People v. Mullen, supra*, the Second Department rejected this argument. See also *People v. Rodriguez*, 76 N.Y.2d 918, 563 N.Y.S.2d 55 (1990) (Defendant's right to be present during jury instructions, including read back, did not require defendant's presence at Colloquy outside presence of jury concerning sufficiency of read back.) But cf. *People v. Turaine*, 78 N.Y.2d 871 (1991) (Error to exclude the defendant from a hearing during trial outside the presence of the jury to determine if witness would be permitted to testify whether the defendant threatened the witness to prevent him from testifying. The proceeding where testimony is received is a material part of the trial and the defendant should be present to advise counsel of errors and inconsistencies in his testimony and be able to confront this adverse witness.)

It is clear that one conclusion may be drawn from this review of some recent decision articulating the extent to which the defendant as a matter of statute and due process may be mandated to be present at all stages of the criminal trial. That conclusion is that at this point in time, the appellate courts of this state have held that his presence is not required at the pre-charge conference, side bar voir dire, and challenge conference, under *Velasco,* and the defendant, under *Lowe,* is not required to be present at any and all in camera proceedings. (The Appellate Courts of the State of New York have apparently concluded that inasmuch as the defendant is fully and adequately represented by counsel at these various stages of the criminal litigation and that since he is present in the courtroom whereby the results, for example, of the voir dire and challenge conferences are implemented and since they do not involve the taking of evidence or confrontation or cross-examination of a witness, as in *Turaine,* his presence is not required as a matter of law.)

It is also clear, however, to this writer, that the extent to which the defendant's presence is required at every stage of the criminal proceeding will remain a question to be litigated by the trial and appellate courts of this State and, indeed, nation. In a word, the question of the defendant's required presence will, in this writer's view, stay open and controversial and law, in point of fact, will surely be made in the near future on the issue.

Copyright 1992, Andrew J. Schatkin.

26. Recent "Payton" Decisions

Payton v. New York, 445 U.S. 573, 100 S. Ct. 1371, 63 L. Ed.2d 639 (1980), is one of the seminal Supreme Court decisions in the field of the Fourth Amendment provision against unreasonable searches and seizures. The Supreme Court of the United States, in *Payton,* concluded, considering two companion cases decided to the contrary by the New York State Court of Appeals, that the Fourth Amendment of the United State Constitution forbade the arrest or seizure of a person in his home absent a warrant. The Supreme Court, however, declined to articulate what, if any, exigent circumstances might provide the exception to this most significant rule of law.

The criminal practitioner in the State is frequently confronted with the warrantless arrest of a person in his home and a subsequent search of the home premises or person of the defendant whereby property, whether narcotics, a knife, a gun or other evidence is seized and sought to be admitted into evidence at trial.

The argument is made by the State that the warrantless arrest, seizure and search were justified without an actual and legal arrest warrant because of certain exigent circumstances. What these so-called exigent circumstances may be are covered by the whole spectrum and panorama of police and ultimately human conduct.

It is the purpose of this article, therefore, to consider a number of recent decisions of the courts of this State to determine what, in fact, has lately been determined by the courts of New York to constitute exigent circumstances.

In this article, this writer will consider not only the cases specifically articulating what may constitute exigent circumstances but will also examine two subcategories of the rule: (1) The Emergency Doctrine, and (2) Primary or Third Party Consent.

First, some recent cases examining the doctrine of exigent circumstances proper as an exception to the *Payton* rule otherwise barring warrantless home entries and searches.

People v. Klinger, N.Y.L.J., 3/20/89, p. 24, Col. 4 (S. Ct. Bronx County), is instructive on the doctrine. In *Klinger*, the defendant was charged with Criminal Possession of a Controlled Substance in the First Degree, (P.L. 220. 21[1]); Criminal Possession of a Controlled Substance in the Third Degree, (P.L. 220.16 [1]); and Criminal Possession of a Weapon in the Fourth Degree (P.L. 265.01 [1]).

The defendant moved to suppress physical evidence seized and certain statements made to law enforcement officers. The facts were that one Nate Callaghan reported to the 46th Precinct that a man displayed a gun during an argument with Callaghan's mother in their apartment in the Bronx. Pursuant to a radio run, two uniformed officers met Callaghan in front of the multiple dwelling in question, who informed them that his mother's boyfriend had hit her and displayed a revolver and that the defendant was armed in the apartment. The police went to the apartment, entered it and encountered an unarmed defendant without a shirt. The defendant, in answer to the officers' inquiry, said there was a revolver in the bedroom inside a closed dresser drawer. An unloaded gun was recovered. Cocaine was also found in a plastic bag on the bed. The defendant said this cocaine was his as well as the cocaine found by the police in the bedroom closet. Money was also found by the police in a pouch on the bed and the defendant admitted it was drug money. The defendant was subsequently arrested and the prosecutor sought, in a suppression hearing, to gain admittance of these items into evidence at trial.

The court held that the facts adduced established the exigent circumstances necessary to permit this warrantless entry into the defendant's home. The court noted that the following factors should be considered to determine whether exigent circumstances exist to permit a warrantless entry into a person's home:

1. the gravity of the offense charged;
2. whether there is reason to believe the suspect is armed;
3. whether there is reasonable trustworthy information to believe the suspect committed the crime;

4. whether there is a strong reason to believe the suspect is in the premises to be entered; and

5. the likelihood the suspect will escape if not quickly apprehended.

The court, analyzing these factors as applied to the facts of the case before it, noted the information received should be deemed reliable by the police. Mr. Callaghan, an eyewitness, had observed the defendant display a revolver; he told the officers the armed defendant was inside the apartment. The unlocked door revealed a bruised, partially clothed suspect. The gun had yet to be recovered. The police, therefore, had sufficient probable cause to apprehend and arrest the defendant without the gun.

This court, it is to be noted, also held the emergency doctrine, as set forth in *People v. Mitchell*, 39 N.Y.2d 173 (1976), cert den. 426 U.S. 953, applicable to the facts of this case, a rule of law to be considered in detail at a later point in this article.

The court, however, held that although sufficient exigent circumstances were present to justify the warrantless entry into the apartment and a subsequent security check of the premises for persons who might pose a threat to the officers' safety or destroy possible evidence, nevertheless, the full blown warrantless search of the bedroom was overly intrusive and the court, thus, suppressed the gun, drugs, and money seized. See also *People v. Debra Brathwaite,* N.Y.L.J., 10/17/89, p. 27, Col. 4, (S. Ct. Kings County); *People v. Dennis Powell,* N.Y.L.J. 3/13/89, p. 23, Col. 4, (S. Ct., N.Y. County); *People v. Jose Lopez,* N.Y.L.J., 2/28/89, p. 24, Col. 2, (S. Ct. Bronx County); *People v. Marcos Lopez,* N.Y.L.J. 3/14/89, p. 25, Col. 2, (S. Ct. Bronx County); *People v. Angel Guevara,* N.Y.L.J. 1/31/91, p. 28, Col. 1, (S. Ct. Bronx County).

The second category of "exigent circumstances," whereby a warrantless entry and search in a private premises is justified, is under the emergency doctrine as stated by the Court of Appeals of this State in *People v. Mitchell*, 39 N.Y.2d 173 (1976), cert. den sub. nom *Mitchell v. New York,* 426 U.S. 953. Although the emergency doctrine is often considered separate and apart from the rule of exigent circumstances as an exception to the Payton rule, this writer rather considers it a subcategory of that rule of law.

The emergency doctrine, as stated in *Mitchell*, consists of three basic elements:

1. The police must have reasonable grounds to believe that there is an emergency at hand.

2. The search must not be primarily motivated by an intent to arrest and seize evidence.

3. There must be some reasonable basis, approximating probable cause, to associate the emergency with the area or place to be searched.

People v. Pedro Calderon, N.Y.L.J. 12/1/89, p. 28. Col. 4 (Crim. Ct. Bronx County), is illustrative of an application of the emergency doctrine. In *Calderon*, the defendant was charged with Criminal Possession of a Weapon in the Fourth Degree, Assault in the Third Degree, Reckless Endangerment in the Second Degree and Criminal Mischief in the Fourth Degree. The defendant moved to suppress physical evidence seized. The facts of the case were that two officers responded, while on routine patrol, to a radio transmission of shots fired. Upon arrival at the location, the complainant brought them to a car with damage to its window caused by a beebee gun. Another person emerged during this interview and stated that earlier in the afternoon, she had been hit in the neck by a beebee. The officers were informed by the children of this complainant and another person that the damage and injuries had been caused by a young man living in a building across the street on the second floor.

One officer then proceeded to the second floor of this building, knocked and spoke to the defendant's thirteen year old sister who, in answer to the officer's question, stated her brother was not at home. Ms. Calderon then admitted the officer into the apartment and directed him to the defendant's room where the officer saw and seized a packet of pellets in open view. A more extensive search revealed a beebee gun and a .22 caliber pistol hidden under the defendant's mattress. The defendant later came to the stationhouse, pursuant to the request of this same officer, and was arrested. He denied ownership of the gun both in a statement over the phone and at the stationhouse. The defendant sought to suppress the gun and pellets.

The People argued against suppression on the ground of the emergency doctrine. The court held the emergency doctrine inapplicable since first, there was no basis to believe there was an emergency at hand and an immediate need of assistance for protection of life and property. The Court noted that the warrantless entry was not contemporaneous with the emergency but was two hours after the reported shots were fired. Moreover, the officer, the court stated, believed the emergency had passed, since he stated that he did not believe the defendant was in the apartment when he conducted the search. Second, the court noted, the officer's warrantless entry into the bedroom was not to allay a volatile situation but to seize the beebee gun. Hence, the court held the emergency doctrine inapplicable since there was no need for immediate assistance and the officer's action was primarily motivated by an intention to seize evidence. Hence, the court, partially on this ground, granted the motion to suppress. On the emergency doctrine, see also *People v. Jose Vasquez*, N.Y.L.J., 7/3/89, p. 25, Col. 2 (S. Ct. Bronx County); *People v. Wayne Jackson*, N.Y.L.J., p. 24, Col. 2, 6/6/89 (S. Ct. Bronx Co.); *People v. Klinger, supra*; *People v. Angel Guevara, supra.*

The third category and ground under which a warrantless arrest and search of a home premises may be allowed, as exception to *Payton*, is under the doctrine of primary or third party consent. Although this category and doctrine, like the emergency doctrine, does not, according to the courts of this state, come under the rubric of exigent circumstances, nevertheless, since it is an exception, as the emergency doctrine is, to the *Payton* prohibition against warrantless home arrests and searches, it is useful to consider it under the denomination of exigent circumstances.

The court in *People v. Pedro Calderon, supra*, considered the applicability of the consent doctrine as well as the emergency doctrine in granting the defendant's motion to suppress. The facts of this case, which have previously been summarized, do not bear repetition. Suffice to say that pursuant to a complaint of a beebee gun shooting damaging a car and injuring a person, the police knocked at the door of the defendant's apartment and were admitted into the defendant's bedroom by the defendant's 13-year-old sister where the beebee gun, pellets and a gun were recovered.

The People urged that a third party consent to this search was given by the defendant's 13-year-old sister. The court held not true third party consent was given. The court noted that to sustain a third party consent to a search, a three pronged test must be satisfied:

1. The permission of the third party must be knowing and voluntary.
2. The person must have or appear to have authority to allow the search.
3. The police officer's reliance on the third party's authority to consent to a search must be reasonable.

The court went on to state that to determine the voluntariness of the consent the factors to be considered include the personal background of the consenter, including age and prior experience with law enforcement authorities as well as whether the police advised the consenter of the right to refuse consent.

With regard to the second prong of the third party consent requirements, the court stated that the general rule is that an individual who shares with another common authority over a premises has no right to prevent a search made with the consent of a co-occupant of equal authority. Where a child is involved, the court stated that the authority of the child to give an effectual third party consent rests on the age of the child and the scope of the consent given. With respect to the third prong of this test, the officer's reliance on the third party's authority to consent to the search, the court applied a totality of the circumstances test.

Analyzing this test and the foregoing factors, the court held the consent given by the sister invalid given her age and failure of the officers to advise her of her right to refuse consent. The court held that what occurred here was not a knowing and voluntary consent but an acquiescence to police authority.

The Court held further that even if the consent were deemed voluntary, this thirteen-year-old girl did not have authority to allow the search of the defendant's room, and the officer's reliance on the apparent authority of the sister was unreasonable because of his failure to inquire into the basis of the sister's authority.

In short, the trial court held invalid the alleged and argued for third party consent and granted the defendant's motion to suppress. On the consent doctrine, see also *People v. Klinger, supra*; *People v. Guevara, supra*.

In sum, it is hoped that this review of a recent spate of trial court decisions illustrating and articulating what may constitute the exigent circumstances justifying a warrantless arrest or search of a home premises and the consideration of what this writer considers two subcategories under the rubric of exigent circumstances, the emergency doctrine and primary or third party consent, will serve as a guide to the criminal practitioner in this State when confronted with a *Payton* issue.

27. *Standing Under Wesley*

In 1989 the Court of Appeals decided the seminal case on the issue of establishing standing in a criminal prosecution where the defendant is charged with constructively possessing or acting in concert to possess contraband. That case, *People v. Wesley*, 73 N.Y.S.2d 353, 540 N.Y.S.2d 757, bears careful review. In *Wesley,* the defendant was arrested following a search of the house occupied by his girlfriend and her infant son pursuant to a search warrant. In the master bedroom closet upstairs, were found two suitcases containing seventy-five pounds of marihuana. In addition marihuana, a handgun and $1,800.00 in cash were found in a dresser containing men's clothing and masculine toilet articles. A wallet and items of identification in Mr. Wesley's name were found in a dresser that contained women's clothing. Wesley's driver's license, birth certificate, unopened mail addressed to him and an address book with his parole officer's name were found elsewhere in the bedroom. Also several scales, nickel bag drug packaging and $18,000.00 in cash were found in three metal boxes in another bedroom closet. One of the boxes contained the defendant's photograph.

A search of a second bedroom disclosed men's and women's clothing in a closet, a box containing the defendant's correspondence, photographs and other personal items.

Photographs of the defendant were found in the living room, and a pistol and an ammunition clip were found in the kitchen cupboard. At the time of the search, the defendant's girlfriend said all the items upstairs belonged to the defendant. The defendant's girlfriend and the defendant were charged with possession of the guns, and marihuana and, before trial, both defendants sought to suppress the fruits of the search. The motion to suppress was denied for lack of standing since the defendant, in his motion papers, failed to allege any privacy interest in the premises and testified to that effect before the Grand Jury. Following trial, the defendant was convicted of possession of marihuana and the guns. The Appellate Division reversed the defendant's conviction citing *People v. Millan,* 69 N.Y.2d 514, 516 N.Y.S.2d 168 (1987), and *People v. Mosley,* 68 N.Y.2d 881, 508 N.Y.S.2d 931 (1986); rearg den. 69 N.Y.2d 707, 512 N.Y.S.2d 1031, cert. den. 482 U.S. 914, 707 S. Ct. 3185, for the proposition that the defendant had standing because the People may not charge the defendant on the theory of constructive possession of the drugs because he was present on the premises at the time the search warrant was executed and simultaneously deprive him of standing to challenge the legality of the search.

The Court of Appeals reversed the Appellate Division's decision, holding the defendant had failed to establish standing. The Court initially noted that an exception to the general rule of standing whereby the defendant had to have a possessory interest in the seized property or premises had been the rule of automatic standing, so conferred where the criminal defendant was charged with a constructive possessory offense. *Jones v. U.S.,* 362 US. 257, 80 S. Ct. 725 (1960).

The Court went on to reason, however, that subsequent Supreme Court decisions had done away with the automatic standing rule for possessory offenses, holding that a defendant must show a legitimate expectation of privacy in the searched premises, and that trial standard was adopted by the Court of Appeals of New York as a matter of State constitutional law in *People v. Ponder,* 54 N.Y.2d 160, 445 N.Y.S.2d 57 (1981). Thus, the Court of Appeals held, in sum, that where a defendant is charged with constructively possessing contraband or acting in concert to do so, he must assert some sort of privacy interest in the premises searched in order to obtain the requisite standing to suppress the fruit of a purported illegal search, be it a gun, money, drug paraphernalia or narcotics.

The Court, however, created an exception to the rule of standing it articulated. That exception was that standing is automatically conferred where the possession of the contraband was the result of a statutory presumption of possession under P.L. Sec. 265.15 and P.L. Sec. 220.25.

The standing rule of *Wesley,* along with the exception it carved out, has since been consistently followed by all the lower appellate and trial courts of this state (*People v. Pearson,* 150 A.D.2d 732, 541 N.Y.S.2d 601 (2d Dept. 1989) (No standing conferred where the defendant was observed exiting a grocery store containing the drugs, immediately after the officer announced his presence. The court noted that the store contained little or no merchandise on the shelves); *People v. Pierce,* 150 A.D.2d 948, 541 N.Y.S.2d 866 (3rd Dept. 1989) (No standing conferred when defendant failed to establish any proprietary interest or relationship to the apartment); *People v. Brewer,* 151 A.D.2d 985, 541 N.Y.S.2d 1003 (4th Dept. 1989); *People v. Daniel,* 152 A.D.2d 742, 544 N.Y.S.2d 941 (2d Dept. 1989) (Where the drugs were found, did not possess a key and kept no property there, he failed to establish a reasonable expectation of privacy in the premises and was without standing.); *People v. Stewart,* 153 A.D.2d 597, 544 N.Y.S.2d 386 (2d Dept. 1989) (Where drug charges were based upon the open room presumption under P.L. See. 220.25, the trial court erred in holding the defendant lacked standing); *People v. Williams,* 144 Misc.2d 688, 545 N.Y.S.2d 457 (S. Ct. Kings County, 1989).

In light of the holding in *Wesley,* the question arises, and it is an interesting one, as to how defense counsel may, as it were, overcome *Wesley* and obtain a suppression hearing where the defendant is charged with constructively possessing contraband or acting in concert to do so, and lacks the benefits of the statutory presumptions under P.L. Secs. 265.15 or 220.25.

The answer is to rely on the People's evidence and assert it in the affirmation in support of the motion to suppress, to the effect that the defendant has a legitimate expectation of privacy in the premises searched.

For example, in a case where the defendant wishes to assert a privacy interest where contraband is discovered and the defendant is on the premises and charged with constructively possessing contraband or acting in concert and the facts as revealed by the People in their felony complaint, indictment, disclosure form, police report, or based on conversations with the prosecutor, are that the defendant was there, had a key, or had items of personal identification there, or frequently used the premises to stay or was engaged in a common law relationship with the codefendant there, these facts should be asserted in the affirmation in support of the motion to suppress. The affirmation, however, should not contain wording that is based on information gleaned from the defendant, since this could be considered an admission of dominion and control and so could effectively destroy the defense's case, should the defendant choose to testify and be therefore subject to cross-examination. It should be based upon information and belief and no more.

If this tactic fails, then the testimony of the codefendant at his suppression hearing, should there be one, that the defendant had access to the premises, or the testimony at trial of the defendant's connection with the premises, could suffice for the granting of a suppression hearing, at either of these junctures.

One final point should be noted. It is inadvisable for the defendant to testify before the Grand Jury and allege any connection with the premises or contraband since this could be used as a ground for denial of the motion to suppress. Of course this decision, i.e., whether or not testify, must be made on a case-by-case basis. Thus, if the defendant has a strong defense and has witnesses, it may be advisable for the defendant to testify before the Grand Jury in the hope of a favorable result at that juncture.

This article previously appeared in an edition of The Nassau Lawyer, a publication of the Nassau County Bar Association, and is being reprinted here with the permission of The Nassau County Bar Association.

28. Advocacy Over Etiquette: Preserving the Prosecutor's Misconduct in Summation as Reversible Error

Summation can be the critical point for the defendant in a criminal case. The defense, of course, sums up first; the prosecutor, last. Summation is the final opportunity for the defendant to present his arguments and version of the events in the case. Often, however, if the defense summation is not objected to by the prosecution, there is a tendency on the part of the defense counsel to remain silent during the prosecutor's summation out of what is, so to speak, a sense of politeness, rectitude and fairness. Although perhaps proper etiquette, this is an incorrect stance for defense counsel. For the prosecutor's summation may be replete with reversible error.

Hence, it is essential that defense counsel pay careful attention to the prosecutor's summation and duly object so that if the defendant is convicted, the prosecutor's improper comments are preserved as grounds for reversal and a new trial. There are various forms of prosecutorial misconduct in summation. The prosecutor may attempt to inflame the passions of the jury, vouch for the credibility of his own witnesses, denigrate the defendant or his defense, comment on the defendant's failure to testify, shift the burden of proof, or usurp the court's prerogative on the law. This article will highlight some recent cases wherein the judgment of conviction was reversed and a new trial granted on the basis of the prosecutor's improper conduct in summation.

First, a case illustrating inflammatory comments by the prosecutor, *People v. Henry Thompson,* A.D.2d, 555 N.Y.S.2d 266 (1st Dept. 1990), is apropos. *Thompson* was an appeal from a judgment convicting the defendant, after a jury trial, of Assault in the Second Degree and sentencing him to an indeterminate term of imprisonment from one and one-half to four and one-half years. The complainant, an acquaintance of the defendant, confronted him in the street about five dollars she had given him to procure marijuana. The complainant accused him of having neither returned with the marijuana nor refunded the money. The defendant denied the accusation. The disagreement escalated and the complainant threw the defendant's bicycle, which he had been riding, onto the street. The prosecutor's theory was that the defendant then deliberately unleashed his pit bull to attack the complainant. The defendant denied any intentional action. The Appellate Division, First Department, reversed on the ground that the prosecutor's highly inflammatory comments during summation had unduly prejudiced the defendant and denied him a fair trial.

Specifically, the *Thompson* court held that, in describing the pit bull's attack, the prosecution had impermissibly doubled the duration of time estimated by the witnesses and resorted to grotesque rhetoric and gruesome analogies. *Id.* at 267-268. The court also ruled that the prosecutor's closing statement mischaracterized the defense by accusing defense counsel of claiming that the defendant was justified in sicking the pit bull on a woman. *Id.* at 268. In conclusion, the *Thompson* court determined "[t]he 'appeals to passion and sentiment' and the other 'myriad of improper comments' which comprised the prosecutor's summation . . . served to deprive defendant of a fair trial." *Id.* (citations omitted).

Similarly, the Appellate Division, Second Department, in *People v. Gomez,* 156 A.D.2d 462, 463-464 (2d Dept. 1989) (citations omitted), reversed murder conviction where "the prosecutor improperly attempted to inflame the passions of the jurors" throughout his summation. And, in *People v. Hubert Chin,* 138 A.D.2d 389, 389-391 (2d Dept. 1988), the Second Department ordered a new trial in a rape case because "during summation, the prosecutor sought to inflame the jury by arguing that the defendant and one of his character witnesses may have made a habit of molesting little girls" and "tried to convey to the jury, by insinuation, suggestion and speculation, that the defendant may have committed or may have been planning to commit offenses similar to the one for which he was being tried."

Nor may the prosecutor vouch for the credibility of his witnesses in summation. This too, if duly objected to by defense counsel, is a ground for reversal and a new trial. Here, *People v. Durham,* 154 A.D.2d 615 (2d Dept. 1989), is illustrative. *Durham* was an appeal from a judgment convicting the defendant of Operating a Motor Vehicle while Intoxicated As a Felony and imposing sentence. The Second Department reversed, in part, due to the prosecutor's repeated vouching for his witnesses. *Id.* at 616.

The court also condemned the prosecutor's improper characterization and attacks on the defendant and his testimony in referring to the defendant as a "loud drunk" and his testimony as a "creation, a fabrication." *Id.*

Likewise, reversible error was found in *People v. Hall,* 138 A.D.2d 404 (2d Dept. 1988). The *Hall* prosecutor had acted improperly in arguing to the jury that defense counsel had not discussed his client's testimony in summation because the testimony was "a crock" and "a lie" and in repeatedly accusing the defendant of lying on the witness stand. *Id.* at 404-405. Thus, it is clear that inflammatory attacks by the prosecutor on the defendant's credibility or his case will not be tolerated. The Second Department also noted that the prosecutor had impermissibly advanced his personal opinion on the merits of the case during summation. *Id.* at 405.

Finally, there is *People v. Antonio Roman,* 150 A.D.2d 252 (1st Dept. 1989). *Roman* demonstrates a number of bases whereby a prosecutor's summation, if properly objected to by defense counsel, may result in reversal. *Roman* was an appeal from a murder-robbery on which the defendant was sentenced to concurrent indeterminate terms of imprisonment of 25 years to life and 12 1/2 to 25 years. In sum, the First Department held that although the evidence at trial was sufficient to establish the defendant's guilt beyond a reasonable doubt, "the improper statements by the District Attorney during summation had the cumulative effect of depriving defendant of a fair trial." *Id.* at 253. The *Roman* Court noted that the prosecutor had improperly vouched for his own witnesses, flagrantly appealed to the jurors' emotions, usurped both their fact-finding role and the court's function as legal adviser, wrongly assailed the defendant's witnesses as liars, erroneously contended that the defendant's presence at his family home in Rhode Island was actually evidence of flight and improperly instructed the jury they should convict if they doubted the defendant's alibi witnesses. *Id.* at 253-257.

Hopefully, this overview of some recent appellate decisions concerning prosecutorial misconduct during summation will remind defense counsel to be aware of the myriad of possibilities for reversible error and to preserve the same for review by opting for advocacy over etiquette in duly objecting during summation.

This article previously appeared in an edition of The Nassau Lawyer, a publication of the Nassau County Bar Association, and is being reprinted here with the permission of The Nassau County Bar Association.

29. Possession as "Dominion and Control"

The Class A misdemeanors of Criminal Possession of Stolen Property in the Fifth Degree, Penal Law Section 165.40, and Unauthorized Use of a Vehicle in the Third Degree, Penal Law Section 165.05, are two of the most common petty possessory crimes with which the criminal practitioner is confronted. Section 165.05(1) states that "[a] person is guilty of unauthorized use of a vehicle in the third degree when, knowing that he does not have the consent of the owner, he takes, operates, exercises control over, rides in or otherwise uses a vehicle." The statute goes on to add that "[a] person who engages in any such conduct without the consent of the owner is presumed to know that he does not have such consent." Clearly, this statute is directed against a temporary taking of a vehicle without the consent of the owner ("joy riding").

Penal Law Section 165.40 provides that "[a] person is guilty of criminal possession of stolen property in the fifth degree when he knowingly possesses stolen property, with intent to benefit himself or a person other than the owner thereof or to impede the recovery by an owner thereof." Although Section 165.40 is addressed to the knowing possession of all forms of stolen property, commission of this crime often manifests itself in some form of alleged unlawful possession of cars or vehicles, albeit temporary, under Section 165.05.

Both Criminal Possession of Stolen Property in the Fifth Degree (165.40) and Unauthorized Use of a Vehicle in the Third Degree (165.05[1]) are "possessory" offenses. Therefore, Penal Law Section 10.00(8) mandates that some form of dominion or control, constructive or actual, exercised over the vehicle by the defendant, be proven by the People beyond a reasonable doubt. Absent such proof, the People's case must fail.

In 1989, the Appellate Division, Second Department, decided two seminal cases on the degree of dominion and control necessary for conviction under Penal Law Sections 165.40 and 165.05. The first was *People v. Gregory* 147 A.D.2d 497 (2d Dept. 1989). The *Gregory* court addressed the dominion and control required to prove Criminal Possession of Stolen Property where the property involved is a vehicle.

Gregory was an appeal from a judgment of conviction of Criminal Possession of Stolen Property in the First Degree, Unauthorized Use of a Vehicle in the Third Degree, and Possession of Burglar's Tools. The evidence was that Chatten, the driver of the vehicle, knew that the car was stolen and had invited the defendant to visit his girlfriend's sister, whereupon the defendant as passenger, accompanied Chatten in the automobile. After a plate check revealed that the car was stolen, it was stopped, both occupants were arrested, and a screwdriver was found jammed in the ignition.

The Second Department reversed the convictions for Criminal Possession of Stolen Property in the First Degree and Possession of Burglar's Tools. The appellate court held that the proof at trial was insufficient to establish that the defendant, as a passenger, exercised in concert with the driver "dominion and control" over the vehicle. The Court added, "Nor can the defendant's mere presence in the automobile be equated with his possession thereof." *People v. Gregory, supra*, 147 A.D.2d at 498 (citations omitted). The evidence of the defendant's possession of the screwdriver was similarly insufficient.

The holding in *Gregory* is most significant. It effectively rules out conviction for Criminal Possession of Stolen Property (and possibly for Possession of Burglar's Tools, depending on the particular circumstances), where the defendant is merely a passenger in the stolen vehicle. Thus, where a Misdemeanor Information charging Criminal Possession of Stolen Property alleges that the defendant was only a passenger, a motion to dismiss the information, on the ground of facial insufficiency, should be made under Sections 100.15, 100.40 and 170.35 of the Criminal Procedure Law (C.P.L.).

If dismissal is denied, then a pre-trial motion in limine, preferably on written papers, should be made, citing *Gregory*. If this is not granted then, at the conclusion of the People's case, counsel should seek a trial order of dismissal, under C.P.L. Sections 290.10 and 360.40, on the grounds that the evidence was legally insufficient. If unsuccessful, this application should be renewed at the conclusion of all the evidence. If, despite these efforts, the defendant is convicted of Criminal Possession of Stolen Property in the Fifth Degree, and was, in fact, only a passenger in the stolen vehicle, a compelling basis for appellate reversal exists under the current state of the law, as articulated in *Gregory*.

The second case this article will consider concerns the degree of possessory dominion and control needed to prove Unauthorized Use of a Vehicle in the Third Degree (Penal Law 165.05[1]). The pivotal case is *In re Ruben P.*, 151 A.D.2d 485 (2d Dept. 1989). *Ruben P.* was an appeal from an order of disposition of the Family Court of Queens County, adjudicating the appellant a juvenile delinquent based upon his having committed an act which, if committed by an adult, would have constituted the crime of Unauthorized Use of a Vehicle in the Third Degree. The Second Department reversed on the ground of deficient proof of dominion and control by the appellant.

At the fact-finding hearing, the People's witness, a police officer, testified that he received a radio run of two males stripping a car. Upon arrival on the scene, the police officer stated that he saw the appellant inside the vehicle but did not see what he was doing. On cross-examination, the officer testified that he saw the appellant exiting the vehicle's passenger side. The officer recounted that the vehicle had no front fenders, bumper, hood or front seat, that the front console was damaged, the ignition was popped and the motor was running.

The appellant testified that while walking along the street, he passed the damaged vehicle and looked inside. He stated that the floor of the car had a lot of glass on it, and that the car had no front, no seats, no radio, a broken dashboard, a popped ignition, and no steering wheel. The appellant recalled how he had reached into the automobile to pick up some change, turned around, and then observed the police at the corner, who ordered him to "freeze."

The Second Department held that the appellant's momentary presence did not constitute the dominion and control contemplated by Penal Law 165.05. The appellate court noted, "The People offered no evidence to show, either directly or by inference, that the appellant exercised control over this stripped vehicle." *In re Ruben P. supra,* 151 A.D.2d at 487, citing *People v. Butler,* 119 Misc.2d 1071, 1073 (Sup. Ct. N.Y. Cty. 1983). The Second Department concluded that some degree of control over the confines of the car or its mechanism must be shown by the People.

The ruling in *Ruben P.* is not so broad as *Gregory,* since it does not per se, declare that passenger status is insufficient dominion and control to prove Unauthorized Use. The case is, however, helpful to defense counsel in holding that mere momentary presence in a vehicle is not enough. It is clear that the Second Department envisions more. See, *In re Archangel O.,* 551 N.Y.S. 2nd 785 (2d Dept. 1990), reiterating that mere momentary presence in a vandalized auto does not amount to dominion and control requisite to Unauthorized Use.

In sum, the Appellate Division, Second Department, as evidenced in *Gregory* and *Ruben P.* is limiting the former outer perimeters of sufficient dominion and control under Penal Law 165.40 and 165.05(1). With these cases in hand, and depending on the facts presented, counsel has an added chance to successfully defend against charges of both Criminal Possession of Stolen Property in the Fifth Degree and Unauthorized Use of a Vehicle in the Third Degree.

This article previously appeared in an edition of The Nassau Lawyer, a publication of the Nassau County Bar Association, and is being reprinted here with the permission of The Nassau County Bar Association.

30. Dismissal of a Misdemeanor Complaint: Victory Before Trial

The criminal lawyer is often faced with the difficult choice of negotiating a plea of guilt and thereby subjecting his client at least to a possible criminal conviction and at most to possible incarceration. The facts may be against him no matter how much the investigation of the case uncovers. Trial, on the other hand, is a calculated risk. The lawyer may be faced with the prospect of not placing his client on the stand and facing the testimony of a complainant and/or a police officer whose credibility the court or jury may be inclined to credit wholly.

Thus, it behooves the criminal lawyer to make every effort to remove his client from the Scylla of a plea and the Charybdis of a conviction after trial.

Is there, therefore, a way out of this dilemma? One way, and it is the way this article will examine, is dismissal of the misdemeanor information based on factual insufficiency. The codification of this rule of law of the State of New York is found in the Criminal Secs. 100.15(1) and (3) and 100.40(1). C.P.L. 100.15(1) states, in brief, that an information or misdemeanor complaint must contain an accusatory part and a factual part and that the factual part must contain a statement of the complainant stating facts of an evidentiary character supporting the charges. That statute goes on to state in C.P.L. 100.15(3) that the factual allegations may be based on personal knowledge of the complainant or upon information and belief.

C.P.L. Sec. 100.40(1), an analog and addition to C.P.L. 100.15(1) and (3), states that an information is sufficient on its face when it substantially conforms to the requirements of C.P.L. 100.15; the allegations of the factual part, together with any accompanying supporting depositions which provide reasonable cause to believe the defendant committed the offense charged, and non-hearsay allegations of the factual part of the information and/or supporting depositions establish every element of the offense charged and defendant's commission thereof.

In sum, for a misdemeanor information to pass muster and not be subject to dismissal, the factual section of the accusatory instrument must allege facts of an evidentiary character, in the form of non-hearsay allegations establishing, factually, every element of the offense charged and providing reasonable cause to believe the defendant committed the offense (C.P.L. Secs. 100.15[1] and [3]; C.P.L. Sec. 100.40[1]).

The accusatory instrument, improper factually under these statutes, is jurisdictionally defective and is subject to dismissal at any stage of the criminal proceeding, including appeal.

The seminal case articulating and explaining this rule of law is *People v. Alejandro,* 70 N.Y. 2nd 133, (1987). In *Alejandro* the defendant was charged with resisting arrest (P.L. 205.30), was tried before a jury, and convicted on the basis of a misdemeanor information which set forth no factual allegations stating that the police were effecting an authorized arrest, an essential element of the charge. The Appellate Term reversed on the law and dismissed the information as jurisdictionally defective since it failed to contain non-hearsay allegations establishing that the defendant had attempted to resist an authorized arrest. The Court of Appeals affirmed. The Court first noted that the misdemeanor information for resisting arrest was insufficient on its face under C.P.L. 100.40 since it is an essential element of the statute for resisting arrest that the arrest be authorized whether by warrant or probable cause and the essential factual allegations to support this were lacking in the information. Second, the Court held the defect jurisdictional under C.P.L. Secs. 100.15 and 100.40. The court reasoned that, unlike prosecution by felony complaint, which is often followed by a preliminary hearing or Grand Jury Proceeding, a misdemeanor information, which requires the showing of a prima facie case, is the sole instrument upon which a defendant may ultimately be prosecuted for a misdemeanor or petty offense. The People need not, prior to trial, present actual evidence demonstrating a prima facie case unlike an indictment following a felony complaint. While a felony complaint need show only reasonable cause to believe the defendant committed the felony in question, a misdemeanor complaint must show both reasonable cause and a prima facie case.

People v. Alejandro makes clear that a misdemeanor information must allege facts of an evidentiary character establishing every element of the offense in question and that, absent the latter, the accusatory instrument is subject to dismissal.

People v. Dumas, 68 N.Y.2d 729 (1986), a decision of the Court of Appeals, preceding *Alejandro* by one year, is a case in which the Court of Appeals essentially reiterates the reasoning of *Alejandro* under a different factual scenario. In *Dumas* the defendant was charged with criminal sale and possession of marijuana in the Fourth degree. The factual part of the complaint simply stated that the defendant sold two plastic bags of marijuana to an undercover officer for a sum of U.S. currency. Citing C.P.L. 100.15(3) the Court of Appeals noted that the complaint contained a conclusory statement that the defendant sold marijuana unsupported by evidentiary facts, showing the basis for the conclusion the substance actually was marijuana. The Court went on to state that there were no allegations that the officer was an expert in identifying marijuana or that the defendant represented the substance as being marijuana. Thus, the Court of Appeals held that the misdemeanor complaint was factually defective under C.P.L. 100.15(3) and reinstated the criminal court orders of dismissal which the Appellate Term had reversed. See also *People v. Fasanaro,* 134 Misc. 2nd 141, (New York City Criminal Court, 1986).

Hence, every misdemeanor information must be examined by counsel for factual sufficiency under the relevant statutes. If the charge, for example, is harassment, and there is no allegation that the striking or shoving was done with the intent to harass, annoy, or harm another person, it is factually defective. See *People v. Hall,* 48 N.Y.2d 927 (1979); *People v. Miles,* 64 N.Y.2d 731 (1984).

See also *People v., Maksymenko,* 109 Misc.2d 171, 442 N.Y.S.2d 699 (Supreme Court, App. Term 1981) (Harassment, P.L. 240.25, and Resisting Arrest, P.L. 205.30); *People v. Shapiro* 61 N.Y.2d 880 (1984) (P.L. 120.20); *People v. Keestanuk,* 135 Misc.2d 456, 511 N.Y.S.2d 203 (District Court, Nassau County, 1987) (Unauthorized Use of a Motor Vehicle in the 3rd Degree, P.L. 165.05); *People v. Wilson,* 122 Misc.2d 55 (City Court, Rochester 1983) (Trespass, P.L. 140.05); *People v. Harvin,* 126 Misc.2d 775, 483 N.Y.S.2d 913 (New York City Criminal Court, 1984) (Possession of a Weapon, P.L. 265.01); *People v. Farley,* 129 Misc.2d 925 (Suffolk County District Court, 1985) (Operating Motor Vehicle While License is Suspended, V.T.L. 511(2)).

In conclusion, the law is well settled under C.P.L. Secs. 100.15 and 100.40 that any misdemeanor complaint must contain evidentiary allegations in full support of the Penal Law charges. The Court of Appeals in *Alejandro* and *Dumas* has blown the last trumpet on this issue and the lower courts have followed suit. At the outset, the practitioner must examine every misdemeanor complaint for factual sufficiency.

This article previously appeared in an edition of The Nassau Lawyer, *a publication of the Nassau County Bar Association, and is being reprinted here with the permission of The Nassau County Bar Association.*

31. Suppressing Cash in a Drug Sale Case

The drug sale is one of the most frequent species of case with which the criminal practitioner is confronted. Under Penal Law Section 220.39, Criminal Sale of a Controlled Substance in the Third Degree, a Class B Felony, the scenario may be either an undercover sale, where an undercover officer solicits a purchase of drugs from the defendant in return for prerecorded buy money and, thereafter, radios a description of the defendant to the backup team who then some minutes later proceed to arrest the defendant; or the sale may be what is known as an observation sale where the arresting officer observes, from some distance, the sale of a controlled substance between two persons and based on his observations proceeds to arrest the defendant who made the sale.

In the undercover sale, prerecorded buy money, if used, may or may not be recovered. Obviously, in the observation sale, it not recovered, since it has not been used.

When cash, however small or large an amount, is recovered from the person of the defendant, the People seek to use this cash at trial as a means of showing that the defendant is in the business of selling drugs. May this cash be excluded from evidence by motion of defense counsel?

The first and still the leading case to examine this issue is *People v. Jones,* 62 A.D.2d 356, 404 N.Y.S.2d 865 (1st Dept. 1978). In *Jones* defendant appealed from a judgment convicting him of criminal sale of a controlled substance in the third degree. The trial court denied the defendant's motion to suppress $831.00 in cash found on the defendant's person, following a search conducted at the police precinct after his arrest. No "buy money" or drugs were found on the defendant's person. The trial judge reasoned that possession of so large a sum of cash confirmed the identification of the defendant. The issue on the appeal was the admission of police testimony that this $831.00 in cash had been found on the defendant's person.

The First Department held the testimony inadmissible. The court stated the testimony as to the cash found on the defendant's person following his arrest was irrelevant since it did not aid in the identification of the defendant and was prejudicial since the testimony placed before the jury proof of possible crimes with no apparent relationship to the crime charged, a single sale of drugs. The court noted the prejudice was obvious since it tended to show the defendant was in the business of selling narcotics, when in fact he was charged with a single sale. On this ground, therefore, the judgment of conviction was reversed and the matter remanded for a new trial.

It is clear, then, that under *Jones* where cash, in whatever amount, is recovered from the defendant's person subsequent to a P.L. Sec. 220.39 arrest, it should be excluded from evidence as irrelevant and prejudicial.

The rule articulated in *Jones* by the First Department in 1978 has since been consistently followed by the Appellate Courts of this state. Thus, in *People v. Whitfield*, 144 A.D.2d 915, 534 N.Y.S.2d 25 (4th Dept. 1988), the defendant was convicted of criminal sale of a controlled substance in the third degree, arising from a single sale of narcotics. The issue on appeal was whether the admission of evidence that the defendant had a "wad" of money on his person at the time of the alleged drug sale, coupled with comments by the prosecutor about this money both in his opening statement and summation, deprived the defendant of a fair trial. Following the *Jones* holding, the Fourth Department held that the testimony as to the money and the comments of the prosecutor were highly prejudicial to the defendant since although the defendant was charged with a single sale, the evidence of the possession of the money was probative of the sale of drugs as a business and, in essence, put before the jury evidence of uncharged crimes. The Fourth Department reversed, on this basis, and granted the defendant a new trial.

In 1987 the Second Department had occasion to consider this issue in *People v. Morales*, 133 A.D.2d 90, 518 N.Y.S.2d 437 (2d Dept. 1987). In *Morales* the defendant was convicted of criminal possession of a controlled substance in the second degree. At trial the People were permitted to elicit from a police officer, over objection of defense counsel, that the defendant, when questioned by the officer, had in his possession a wad of five, ten and twenty dollar bills. The Second Department held that the testimony of the officer as to the cash was of no relevance and highly prejudicial since it suggested the defendant was engaged in the sale of narcotics as a business.

See also *People v. Symbato*, 72 A.D.2d 780, 421 N.Y.S.2d 404 (2d Dept. 1979) (where the defendant was charged with Burglary in the Third Degree and Grand Larceny in the Third Degree and it was adduced at trial that the defendant was unemployed and in possession of more than $700.00 in cash and, in addition, the People, during summation, asked the jury where an unemployed person could get $700.00 in cash. The Second Department held the fact of the defendant's possession of the money irrelevant to the People's case, admission of it prejudicial under *Jones* and the prosecutor's comments with respect to it, improper in summation.); *People v. Reyes*, 72 A.D.2d 512, 421 N.Y.S.2d 5 (1st Department, 1979) (Evidence that defendant had a large sum of money when arrested irrelevant and prejudicial).

The rule first articulated in *Jones* and since followed by the courts of this state is clear. Where a single narcotics sale is alleged, evidence of cash recovered from the person of the defendant cannot be testified to or referred to by the prosecutor, upon pain of reversal and a new trial.

What then is the proper course for defense counsel? First, upon being given notice of recovery of cash by the People, a motion to suppress the cash should be made. By this method, if a hearing is granted pursuant to the motion, at least valuable discovery will be obtained and at most suppression will be obtained. If, after the hearing, suppression is not granted, a motion in limine should be made, immediately prior to trial, arguing exclusion of any reference to the cash at trial by the People or their witnesses. Preferably the motion should be made on papers. If the motion in limine is not granted, then, if a reference is made to the cash recovered from the person of the defendant at trial, a paper record should be made at trial by defense counsel, including objection to any reference to the cash and the legal basis for the objection.

If, after all these efforts, the cash is not suppressed or reference to it excluded, as the cases cited here indicate, a most strong basis lies for appeal and eventual reversal and new trial.

This article previously appeared in an edition of The Nassau Lawyer, a publication of the Nassau County Bar Association, and is being reprinted here with the permission of The Nassau County Bar Association.

32. The Requirements of a Physical Injury in Assault Cases

One of the most frequent and common cases the criminal practitioner is confronted with particularly on the misdemeanor level (P.L. Sec. 120.00, Assault in the Third Degree) is the assault charge. The context may be a husband-wife domestic verbal dispute, which has unfortunately escalated into physical combat; a fight between friends; a dispute between strangers; or even, in the context of resisting arrest, an alleged attack on a police officer (P.L. 120.05[3], Assault in the Second Degree). Whatever the context, the police are summoned by the injured wife, friend or stranger and the client is confronted by either a petty charge of Assault in the Third Degree, P.L. Sec. 120.00, bringing in its wake possible incarceration of up to one year or, if the attack is on a police officer, bringing with it a charge of Assault in the Second Degree, P.L. Sec. 120.05, a Class D Felony, with far more serious consequences, particularly for the client who is a "predicate" felony offender, that is, one previously convicted of a felony.

Hence, the criminal practitioner, whose counsel is sought by a client so charged, whether by misdemeanor information or indictment, has a grave responsibility. It is true that in the charge of assault, the client is entitled to a jury trial. Trial, however, is always a risk, and if a way may be found to exonerate one's client and avoid trial, this path to victory must be explored by defense counsel and thus the following analysis is commended to your attention.

Assault in the Third Degree, P.L. Sec. 120.00, and Assault in the Second Degree, P.L. Sec. 120.05(3), if the assault is on a police officer, both require that for the assault to pass legal muster, there must be a showing of a physical injury by the People. Sec. 10.00(9) of the Penal Law , entitled "Definitions," states that "a physical injury means impairment of physical condition or substantial pain."

The courts of this state, taking these sections together, have been most careful to define what constitutes a physical injury requiring an objective level of what constitutes a physical injury, meaning to exclude such things as petty slaps, shoves, kicks and even punches. If a certifiable physical injury is not shown as required by law, it is the position of this writer that the information or indictment should be dismissed under the law. If the accusatory instrument is not dismissed, the issue is assuredly preserved for appeal. In any event, if the case does go to trial, the issue of an objective physical injury is an issue for the fact finder and, if the jury is rightly charged on this rule of law, the case may still be won for the defense.

The leading case is *Matter of Philip A.,* 49 N.Y.2d 198, 424 N.Y.S.2d 418, 400 N.E.2d 358 (1980). In *Philip A.* a juvenile appealed from an order of the Appellate Division, First Department, which affirmed an order of the Bronx County Family Court that the appellant committed an act which, if committed by an adult, would constitute the crime of assault in the third degree and so adjudicated the appellant a juvenile delinquent. It was shown at trial that the appellant twice hit the respondent in the face causing him to cry, causing pain and causing red marks. The trial court found the respondent suffered substantial pain. The Appellate Division, First Department, affirmed. The Court of Appeals held that, generally, the substantial pain necessary to establish Assault in the Third Degree is a question for the trier of fact but, nevertheless, there is an objective level below which the question is one of law and the charge should be dismissed. The court concluded that the unspecified pain of the respondent, his crying and the red marks failed to establish substantial pain beyond a reasonable doubt, and reversed.

Similarly, in *People v. McDowell,* 28 N.Y.2d 373, 321 N.Y.S.2d 894 (1971), which involved an assault on a police officer under P.L. Sec. 120.05, the Court of Appeals, in this earlier case, held that the incidental reference to a black eye, without any development of its seriousness, appearance, swelling or suggestion of pain, was insufficient to sustain the conviction of Assault in the Second Degree on a police officer. The Court held there was insufficient showing of a true physical impairment.

See also *People v. Jiminez,* 55 N.Y.2d 895, 449 N.Y.S.2d 22, 433 N.E.2d 1270 (1982) (One centimeter cut about lip proved neither substantial pain or a physical impairment); *Application of Derrick M.* 63 A.D.2d 932, 406 N.Y.S.2d 88 (1st Dept. 1978) (Appellant struck respondent with chain; Respondent's rib cage became black and blue but there was no bleeding or medical attention given. Held: no statutory physical injury.) *Matter of Edward B.,* 109 A.D.2d 1103, 487 N.Y.S.2d 205 (4th Dept. 1985); *People v. Chandler,* 120 A.D.2d 542, 502 N.Y.S.2d 47 (2nd Dept. 1986) (Blow to head, without more, insufficient to establish substantial pain); *People v. Ciccari,* 90 A.D.2d 853, 456 N.Y.S.2d 103 (2nd Dept. 1982) (Complainant's subjective testimony that defendant hit her and she screamed in pain insufficient to establish impairment of physical condition or substantial pain required for 1st Degree Burglary conviction); *People v. Brown,* 145 A.D.2d 301, 535 N.Y.S.2d 366 (1st Dept. 1988) (Complainant struggled with the defendant, bumped her head. Her body was sore for some time and her neck was swollen. Complainant did not visit a doctor or go to a hospital. Held: No physical injury under Sec. 10.00(9) of the Penal Law); *People v. Melcherts*, 147 A.D. 594, 537 N.Y.S.2d 889 (2nd Dept. 1989) (Complainant's testimony of pain, after defendant punched her in the stomach, insufficient to establish physical injury for Assault in Third Degree); *People v. Tabachnik*, 131 A.D.2d 611, 516 N.Y.S. 312 (2nd Dept. 1987) (Complainant kicked in thigh by defendant and complained of soreness. Thigh was black and blue. Held: No physical injury to sustain charge of P.L. 120.00, Assault in Third Degree); *People v. Contreras*, 198 A.D.2d 627, 485 N.Y.S.2d 261 (1st Dept. 1985); *People v. Reed*, 83 A.D.2d 566, 441 N.Y.S.2d (2nd Dept. 1981) (blows to side of head and nose resulting in bruises, headache and minor pain. Held: no physical injury); *People v. Jackson*, 139 A.D.2d 766, 527 N.Y.S.2d 514 (2d Dept. 1988); *People v. Oquendo*, 134 A.D.2d 203, 521 N.Y.S.2d 5 (1st Dept. 1987); app. den. 70 N.Y.2d 959, 525 N.Y.S.2d 842 (1988); *Matter of Antonio J.*, 129 A.D.2d 988, 514 N.Y.S.2d 156 (4th Dept. 1987) (Victim testified he had black and blue face and sore and bruised ribs. Held: no physical injury).

It is clear, from this brief summary of some relevant case law, that the courts of this state, including the Court of Appeals, the Appellate Divisions, and the lower trial courts, require an objective level of injury to sustain an assault charge. Hence, counsel, when confronted with a client charged with assault or kindred crimes also requiring a physical injury as defined in Sec. 10.00(9) of the Penal Law, should first examine the misdemeanor or felony complaint. If, for example, punching with a black and blue mark resulting is alleged, it is most likely, under the case law, that the pleading will be dismissed. If the complainant was hospitalized, the hospital record should be immediately obtained to determine the extent of the injuries, if any. Perhaps, the complainant was only taken to the emergency room and not admitted to the hospital. In any event, even if the complainant was treated at the hospital, there still may be no true physical injury, whether physical impairment or substantial pain, as required by statute.

Where there is a statutory physical injury as a question of law, counsel, if not successful in dismissing the misdemeanor information or indictment may yet win on this issue at trial or on appeal. Thus the careful, thoughtful and well-informed defense counsel may succeed on this ground where victory did not seem possible at the outset.

This article previously appeared in an edition of The Nassau Lawyer, a publication of the Nassau County Bar Association, and is being reprinted here with the permission of The Nassau County Bar Association.

33. Unconstitutional DWI Checkpoints: A Basis for Suppressing the Chemical Test

Both federal and state court decisions prohibit the random unbridled stopping of motorists on public highways. The officer must have a reasonable basis for pulling over a vehicle, such as a traffic infraction. A vehicular stop cannot be based on whim.

The DWI checkpoint is an exception to the general rule. Simply stated the DWI checkpoint is a standardized uniform procedure for the police to stop intoxicated drivers. The important point is that a standard or uniform procedure must be followed, and certain standard criteria followed, for the checkpoint to be effective and withstand constitutional challenge. For example, every other or third vehicle must be stopped. Signs are essential. The roadblock must be obvious. The checkpoint should be well lighted.

It is not, however, the purpose of this article to consider the effectiveness of DWI checkpoints or the criteria for them to pass constitutional muster. Rather, it is to suggest that if a DWI checkpoint does not follow that necessary standard procedure and have the required uniformity, and so lack intrusiveness, the chemical test, if given after a motorist is stopped and is suspected to be intoxicated, can be suppressed, after a hearing is applied for to the court and given.

The leading case on this subject is the Court of Appeals Decision, *People v. Scott*, 62 N.Y.2d 518, 483 N.Y.S.2d 649, 473 N.E.2d (1984). In *Scott*, the defendant was stopped by a roadblock established pursuant to the order of the sheriff of Genesee County. The defendant was directed to the side of the road and asked to produce his license, registration and insurance card. The defendant fumbled with his wallet and the officer noticed the defendant's eyes were watery and bloodshot and that there was a strong odor of alcohol on his breath. The defendant, on inquiry, admitted he had just left a bar and was asked to step out of the car. He was then unstable on his feet and could not successfully perform field sobriety tests, such as the heel to toe and finger to nose tests. Based on the defendant's failure to successfully perform these tests, and also based on the results of an alco-sensor breathing screening test which the defendant consented to take, the deputy concluded the defendant was intoxicated and placed him under arrest.

Constitutionality Upheld

The court upheld the constitutionality and validity of the checkpoint. The court initially noted that the checkpoint was established pursuant to specific guidelines. The roadblocks were established once each month between midnight and 3:00 a.m. at predetermined locations. Four sites had been selected on the date of this matter, September 25, 1982. The roadblock was maintained at each location for 20 to 30 minutes before moving on to the next site. At the third location, where the defendant was stopped, warning signs were set up on the shoulders facing traffic in both directions, 300 feet in advance of the checkpoint. Two police vehicles exhibited flashing lights and their headlights illuminated the signs. Flares were placed in the center of the road. The checkpoint was manned by law enforcement officers and all vehicles approaching from either direction were stopped.

The court then noted that in determining the appropriateness of the DWI checkpoint stop, such as occurred in this case, the legitimate governmental interests concerned in this case, DWI enforcement, or the apprehension of possible drunk drivers and the deterrence of drunk driving, must be balanced against the intrusiveness of the DWI checkpoint procedure. The court further stated that the importance of the governmental interest is proved by the carnage caused by drunk drivers, and that the intrusiveness of the DWI checkpoint was limited and bounded by the fact that the checkpoint was operated in accordance with a uniform procedure ". . . which afforded little discretion to operating personnel, and that adequate precautions as to safety, lighting and fair warning of the existence of the checkpoint were in operation." *People v. Scott, supra* at page 652.

The Court further stated that the fact that the plan called for not stopping every car did not affect its validity since the pattern of selection was not discriminatory. Nor was the plan invalid because of its deterrent purpose or because the checkpoints were shifted after short periods of time.

The Court held that deterrence is a legitimate governmental purpose and that deterrence by fear of apprehension is a proper means of keeping drunk drivers off the highways. The court also stated that constitutionality was not affected by the shifting and temporary feature of the checkpoints in this case, since, first, whether the roadblock was there for hours or for 15 minutes did not change the subjective effect of the checkpoint on the approaching driver's observation of it, which would be measured in minutes if not seconds, and second, the checkpoint had visible signs of authority, such as signs, lighting and police vehicles. The court concluded that the shifting DWI checkpoint could not be analogized to a roving stop, holding that [the DWI checkpoint procedure] "is a sufficiently productive mechanism to justify the minimal intrusion involved." *People v. Scott supra* at 654.

The holding in *Scott* upheld the particular DWI checkpoint procedure of the County of Genesee. *Scott*, however, held that roadblocks are neither constitutional nor unconstitutional per se, and may be unconstitutional. The constitutionality and legal validity of the checkpoint must be evaluated by balancing the intrusion of a warrantless search and seizure without particularized suspicion or reasonable cause against the legitimate governmental interest in the apprehension of drunk drivers and the deterrence of drunk driving. Whether a checkpoint is so intrusive as to rise to the level of unconstitutionality is measured by the existence of a set plan and written rules, the specificity of these rules, the persons who promulgate the rules, the discretion of the operating officers and the presence of signs, light, and police vehicles. If a roadblock is not operated in accordance with set procedure, is without signs, without adequate lighting and without lighted police vehicles, it is the view of this writer that, under *Scott*, a motion may be made to suppress the chemical test, if given, and the result may be suppressed on these grounds under *Scott.* To be sure the test was not suppressed in *Scott* but, again, if the necessary criteria and elements are not present it may well be. In short, if a DWI checkpoint is operated in a nonuniform and discriminatory manner, and there is no real basis to justify the stop, the test result may be suppressed. See also *Little v. State,* 479 A.2d 902, 300 MD. 485 (Court of Appeals of Maryland, 1984).

The DWI charge strikes often at the client without a prior criminal record. The client is faced with the possibility of a misdemeanor conviction and having his license suspended for a period of time. Future life possibilities may be severely affected by this conviction. Counsel, therefore, must explore every avenue of defense. It is the firm view of this writer that, under *Scott,* a motion to suppress can be made. If the client was stopped under a DWI checkpoint and, upon investigation, the checkpoint lacked the necessary *Scott* criteria, the motion should be granted.

Hence, counsel must carefully question his client as to whether, in the first instance, there was a checkpoint stop and, if so, whether there was proper lighting, signs, marked police cars and a uniform procedure used. The DWI procedure and plan of the police department, if they exist , should be obtained.

Even if a hearing is denied or the hearing itself lost, the issue will have been preserved for appeal.

This article previously appeared in an edition of The Nassau Lawyer, a publication of the Nassau County Bar Association, and is being reprinted here with the permission of The Nassau County Bar Association.

34. Dismissal of Interfamily Disputes

Sections 812.2 of the Family Act and 530.11 of the Criminal Procedure Law of the State of New York together give the Family and Criminal Courts concurrent jurisdiction over any proceeding

> concerning acts which would constitute disorderly conduct, harassment, menacing, reckless endangerment, an assault in the second degree, or assault in the third degree or an attempted assault between spouses or between parent and child or between members of the same family or household except that if the respondent would not be criminally responsible by reason of age pursuant to Section 30.00 of the penal law, then the family court shall have exclusive jurisdiction over such proceeding.

Section 812.2 of the F.C.A.. and Section 530.11 of the C.P.L further mandate that law enforcement officials inform any petitioner or complainant bringing a proceeding against members of the same family or household, before the proceeding is commenced, of the procedures available for the institution of family offense proceedings.

Thus Sections 812.2 of the F.C.A. and C.P.L. 530.11(d) state:

2. Information to petitioner or complainant. The chief administrator of the courts shall designate the appropriate probation officers, warrant officers, sheriffs, police officers or any other law enforcement officials, to inform any petitioner or complainant bringing a proceeding under this article, *before such a proceeding is commenced,* [emphasis added] of the procedures available for the institution of family offense proceedings, including, but not limited to the following:

(a) That there is concurrent jurisdiction with respect to family offenses in both family court and criminal courts;

(b) That a family court proceeding is a civil proceeding and is for the purpose of attempting to stop the violence, end the family disruption and obtain protection. Referrals for counseling, or counseling services are available through probation for this purpose;

(c) That a proceeding in the criminal courts is for the purpose of prosecution of the offender and can result in a criminal conviction of the offender;

(d) That a proceeding or action subject to the provisions of this section is initiated at the time of filing of an accusatory instrument or family court petition, not at the time of arrest, or request for arrest if any;

(e) That subject to the provisions of section eight hundred thirteen of this article, the filing of such an accusatory instrument or family court petition constitutes a final choice of forum after seventy-two hours have elapsed from such filing and bars any subsequent proceeding in an alternative court based on the same offense. However, in the event that a finding by the court on the merits of such a complaint or petition occurs before seventy-two hours have elapsed, such a finding shall be deemed to constitute a final choice of forum and shall bar any subsequent proceeding in an alternative court based on the same offense;

(f) That an arrest may precede the commencement of a family court or criminal court proceeding, but an arrest is not a requirement for commencing either proceeding.

Further, Section 812.5 of the Family Court Act states that

5. Notice. Every police officer, peace officer or district attorney investigating a family offense under this article shall advise the victim of the availability of a shelter or other services in the community, and shall immediately give the victim written notice of the legal rights and remedies available to a victim of a family offense under the relevant provisions of the criminal procedure law, family court act and the domestic relations law. The division of criminal justice services shall prepare the form and content of such written notice and distribute copies thereof to the appropriate law enforcement officials pursuant to subdivision nine of section eight hundred forty-one of the executive law. No cause of action for damages shall arise in favor of any person by reason of any failure to comply with the provisions of this subdivision except upon a showing of gross negligence or willful misconduct.

In order to understand the legislative intent of these statutes it is necessary to look at the legislative history of FCA Section 812. Prior to September 1, 1977, The Family Court Act required an action involving assault by members of the same household originating in the Criminal Court to be transferred to the Family Court for determination as to whether or not its procedures were appropriate. In 1977 the legislature abolished that provision of Article 8 and instead granted a right of election by a victim in certain enumerated "family offenses" between members of the same household. The purpose of the right of election was to ensure that the aggrieved party proceed in either Family Court if reconciliation was desired or Criminal Court if sanctions and/or punishment was desired. In enacting the scheme the legislature was cognizant of the fact that a complainant in a "family offense," not the Court, would decide the future course of the family. See FCA Sec. 812; Judiciary Law Sec. 216; *People v. Garcia*, 98 Misc.2d 907, 415 N.Y.S.2d 175 (Criminal Court, New York County 1979); *People v. Harris*, 113 Misc.2d 46, 448 N.Y.S.2d 961 (Suffolk County Court 1982); Practice Commentary, Douglas J. Besharov, McKinney's Consolidated Law, PCA Sec. 812, pp. 132-143.

In *People v. Garcia, supra,* at 177 the Court stated,

> Where the legislature contemplated a "poor person's court" for the unsophisticated litigant, it must be held to have imposed a positive duty upon that court itself to ensure that litigants in fact understand precisely what legal process they have activated.

The question arises, and it is the subject of this article, that if the petitioner or complainant is not advised of his or her right of election under Sec. 812 of the FCA and Sec. 530.11 of the C.P.L. nor of the ramifications or benefits available to him or her depending on the choice of forum whether there is a remedy. Let us assume that a defendant is arrested pursuant to a complaint by his wife during a family dispute. The defendant is arraigned in criminal court and none of the persons enumerated in Sec. 812 of the FCA advises the complainant of her right of election under Section 812. Assume she wishes to proceed in the Family Court. Is there a remedy or is she compelled to proceed in the Criminal Court? In the view of this writer the proper remedy is dismissal of the Criminal Court complaint.

People v. Garcia is relevant. In *Garcia* the defendant-husband was charged with attempted third-degree assault and criminal possession of a weapon in the fourth degree based on his throwing a bottle at his wife thereby placing her in fear of imminent physical injury. In questioning the complainant, the court found that the complainant-wife was not interested in prosecuting her husband criminally but in help for his alcoholism. The wife testified she was never advised of her right of election and had she been so told she would have elected to proceed in the Family Court.

The court held that the admonitions under Section 812 of the FCA constitute a condition precedent which must be met before a binding election of remedies is imposed. *People v. Garcia, supra*, at 177.

The court stated that, lacking these admonitions, the complainant would pursue her remedy in the Family Court and dismissed without prejudice such proceeding since the statutory machinery for transfer is now non-existent.

People v. Harris, supra, follows *Garcia* at least in its reasoning if not in its result. In *Harris* the defendant pled guilty to the charge of attempted criminal possession of a weapon in the third degree. The defendant moved for an order dismissing the indictment and transferring the subject matter of the indictment to the Family Court on the ground that his wife had never been advised that she had a right to choose the forum in which to proceed—the Family Court or the Criminal Court. The defendant stated his wife had not been so advised of her choice of forum and if she had been so advised she would have selected Family Court. The wife stated the defendant worked at two jobs to support his children. The People conceded the arresting officer did not advise the complainant of her rights in this respect. The People argued that the motion should be denied because the defendant's plea of guilt had waived any procedural defect.

After a review of the statutory scheme under FCA 812 and citing *Garcia* the court held that

> where the complainant was not advised of the statutory right of election and now expresses a desire to do so, then the only way to effectuate the purpose of the statute is to permit an exercise of that right. In a proper case that may be accomplished by a dismissal of the charge and either a transfer of the subject matter to the Family Court or the institution of an original proceeding in that court. This remedy is not available where, as here, the defendant has pled guilty to the charge. (See *People v. Mack, supra*.). *People v. Harris, supra* at 964.

Both *Harris* and *Garcia* hold that the proper remedy, absent a plea of guilty, for failure to advise a petitioner-complainant of her choice of forum under Section 812 of the FCA is dismissal of the charge and transfer to the proper forum.

It is true that the Court of Appeals in *People v. Mack*, 53 N.Y.2d 803, 422 N.E.2d 572, 439 N.Y.S.2d 912 (1981), seems to contradict this view. In *Mack* the defendant appealed from his plea of guilt of assault in the second degree on the grounds that his wife, as complainant, was never advised of the procedures available for the institution of family offense proceedings in the Family Court in compliance with Section 812 of the FCA. The court held that by his plea of guilt the defendant waived his right in this regard, and that the directives of FCA 812.2

> consist of a threshold, statutory directive with respect to procedures to be followed for access to the family court or to the criminal courts, unrelated to the judicial competence of those courts. Nothing in the statute or in the legislative history of its enactment suggests that it was intended or even visualized that the consequence of failure to give the advice contemplated would oust either Family Court or the criminal courts, or conceivably both courts (which are ex-

pressly given concurrent jurisdiction), or authority to entertain prosecutions concerning family offenses. *People v. Mack, supra* at 913.

It is true that the language of *Mack* seems to limit defendant's right to use the failure to inform the petitioner-complainant of his or her rights under FCA 812. *Mack*, however involved a plea of guilt, as the Court of Appeals emphasized in its decision. Once that is made, the choice of forum is fixed and cannot be altered since the plea of guilt waived any rights in this regard.

It is thus the conclusion of this writer, based on an examination of the limited case law on this subject, that the defendant has a remedy of dismissal of the petition-complaint if the petiole-complainant was not advised of the directives mandated under FCA 812 as long as a plea of guilt has not been entered which would constitute a waiver of those rights.

Copyright 1989 by the Queens County Bar Association and the Queens Bar Bulletin. Reprinted with permission.

35. *Residue of Cocaine*

The question whether possession of a mere "residue" of Cocaine, without discernable and definite weight or volume, is sufficient to sustain a statutory charge is one which, of late, has teased the lower Trial Courts and apparently has been resolved by the highest Appellate Court of this State. This Article proposes to trace the evolution of this issue in the recent case law and point toward the final resolution of the question.

The earliest case to examine this issue is *People v. Irwin Ifill*, 137 Misc.2d 14, 519 N.Y. Supp.2d 584 (Criminal Court, New York County 1987). In *Ifill*, the defendant was arrested and charged with the Criminal Possession of a Controlled Substance in the Seventh Degree (P.L. Sec. 220.03) and Unlawful Possession of Marijuana (P.L. Sec. 221.05). The accusatory instrument stated that the defendant knowingly and unlawfully possessed one clear plastic bag of Marijuana, six vials of Cocaine and one glass pipe containing residue of Cocaine. The laboratory report disclosed that no Marijuana was present, but that Cocaine residue was present in the six glass vials and the glass pipe. The defendant moved to dismiss the information pursuant to C.P.L. Section 170.30(1)(a) and Section 170.35(l)(a), for factual insufficiency on the ground that possession of Cocaine residue was insufficient to sustain the charge of Criminal Possession of a Controlled Substance in the Seventh Degree.

Under Sections 100.40 and 100.15 of the C.P.L. one of the requirements of sufficiency is that every element of the offense charged and the defendant's commission of that offense must be established by non-hearsay allegations of the factual part of the information.

The Court then defined the issue to be whether a residue of a quantity of controlled substance which the legislature said was criminal to possess constituted the corpus of the crime of knowingly and unlawfully possessing a controlled substance and so is an element of the crime.

Citing the Webster definition of residue as that which remains after a portion is taken, separated, removed, or designated, and the New York City Police Crime Laboratory Report as that which is not measurable, the Court defined Cocaine residue as

> that which remains in the vial, pipe, or other packaging after the Cocaine has been removed or used and exists in such small quantity that it cannot be measured. *People v. Ifill*, 519 N.Y. Supp.2d at 586.

The Court concluded that the residue of Cocaine was no longer the drug in usable form, that the defendant could not use the substance to ". . . engage in the types of conduct the drug possession statute was meant to prohibit—i.e., the defendant could not use this substance to induce an artificial state, transfer it for another person's use or sell it. . . ." *People v. Ifill, supra,* at 586.

The Court concluded, in light of the fact that the drug could not be used for the criminal purposes contemplated by the statute, that the possession of a mere residue of Cocaine did not violate P.L. Section 220.03.

Ifill is a groundbreaking decision since it bases its decision that a residue cannot constitute the element of possession necessary in P.L. Section 220.03 on the ground that it is unusable and cannot be used for the prohibited conduct contemplated by the statute.

People v. Shelton, 136 Misc.2d 644, 519 N.Y.S.2d 102 (Criminal Court, Bronx County 1987) closely follows *Ifill* in time and also follows it in its reasoning on this issue. In *Shelton*, the defendant was arrested and charged with, among other charges, Criminal Possession of a Controlled Substance in the Seventh Degree. (P.L. Section 220.03). The defendant moved, pursuant to C.P.L. Sections 170.30 and 170.35, to dismiss the complaint for facial insufficiency on the ground that possession of a residue of Cocaine was not sufficient to sustain a charge of Criminal Possession of a Controlled Substance in the Seventh Degree. The defendant also filed a Supplemental Motion to dismiss under C.P.L. Section 170.45 for the reason that the People had not opposed the original motion. The Court noted that the original misdemeanor complaint charged the defendant with knowingly and unlawfully possessing a Controlled Substance in the Seventh Degree, to wit, 26 vials containing residue of alleged Cocaine on the defendant's person. The laboratory report indicated 26 vials containing residue of Cocaine and two smoking devices also containing a residue of Cocaine.

The Court reserved decision on the People's Application to have the complaint deemed on information based on the laboratory report, pending decision on the defendant's motion to dismiss. The Court received no answering papers on the main or supplemental motion to dismiss of the defendant, on behalf of the People.

The Court noted that, in this case, the defendant alleged as a ground constituting a legal basis for dismissal that possession of Cocaine residue was insufficient as a matter of law to establish a violation of P.L. 220.03 which required a knowing and unlawful possession of a controlled substance to come within its ambit.

The Court cited *People v. Ifill, supra,* which had recently examined the issue whether Cocaine residue was sufficient to sustain a charge of criminal possession of a controlled substance. The *Ifill* Court, the *Shelton* Court noted, held that Cocaine residue was no longer Cocaine in usable form since it could neither be possessed nor sold and that residue was by definition what was left after Cocaine was removed. For these reasons, the *Shelton* Court noted, the *Ifill* Court dismissed the case before it.

The *Shelton* Court, for all the above reasons, granted the defendant's motion to dismiss. The *Shelton* Court, it is true, based its decision to dismiss, in part on the fact that the People had failed to dispute the defendant's application to dismiss the complaint. The *Shelton* Court, however, closely followed the reasoning of *Ifill*, holding that a residue of Cocaine could neither be used nor sold and, in any event, was not measurable in any defined quantity.

The last of this trio of lower Court decisions on the issue of whether a residue of Cocaine can constitute possession under the statute is *People v. Riley Mason*, 136 Misc.2d 968, 519 N.Y. Supp.2d 609 (Criminal Court, Bronx County 1987). In *Mason*, the defendant was again charged with Criminal Possession of a Controlled Substance in the Seventh Degree; again, the defendant moved to dismiss the complaint for facial insufficiency on the ground that possession of Cocaine residue is insufficient to sustain a charge of Criminal Possession of a Controlled Substance in the Seventh Degree. The *Mason* Court granted the motion to dismiss the possession charge holding that the possession of Cocaine residue is insufficient to establish a violation of the statute prohibiting possession of Cocaine.

The *Mason* Court stated that the misdemeanor complaint stated that the defendant knowingly and unlawfully possessed a controlled substance—one vial containing Cocaine and six vials with residue of Cocaine. The subsequent laboratory report indicated one vial, no controlled substance, six vials of Cocaine containing residue, and one glass pipe containing residue with no controlled substance. The Court defined the issue to be whether the possession of Cocaine residue constituted a violation of P.L. 220.03 which requires a person to knowingly and unlawfully possess a controlled substance. The *Mason* Court cited *Ifill* to the effect that residue was no longer Cocaine in usable form in that it could neither be used nor sold and was what remained after the Cocaine had been removed.

Examining the dictionary definitions of residue, the Court held that

> one does not know whether "Cocaine residue" is even the same in chemical composition as Cocaine. The term can refer to what is left after all the smokeable or 'freebase' Cocaine is smoked, or it may consist of impurities with which Cocaine, or some other substance was mixed. *People v. Mason*, 519 N.Y. Supp.2d at 611.

The *Mason* Court also noted that Cocaine residue was not susceptible of measurement and concluded that "where the substance cannot be measured, the individual in question cannot be said to be in knowing possession of the substance." *People v. Mason, supra,* at 611.

The *Mason* Court based its decision on three factors: Cocaine residue
1. was not Cocaine in usable form,
2. was not susceptible in measurement, and
3. may not be Cocaine at all.

This trio of Criminal Court decisions is indicative of a trend to find Cocaine residue insufficient to support a charge of knowing drug possession under the relevant statutes, primarily for the reason that it is not Cocaine in usable form, cannot be measured and has no defined weight or volume and may not be Cocaine at all, but different in chemical composition.

A recent Appellate Term decision followed these cases. In *People v. Irving Mizell,* 139 Misc.2d 286, 530 N.Y.S.2d 503 (1988), the Appellate Term for the 2nd and 11th Judicial Districts had before it an information charging the defendant with Criminal Possession of a Controlled Substance in the Seventh Degree, in that the defendant possessed two vials of Cocaine. The Trial Court had dismissed the information on the basis of a laboratory report indicating that the vials contained only a residue of Cocaine. The Court concluded that ". . . it is our opinion that proof of only a non-quantifiable amount of a controlled substance is insufficient, without more, to support a conviction for a criminal possession of a substance *People v. Mizell,* Ibid.[1]

The last trumpet on this issue which apparently resolves once and for all the matter is from the Court of Appeals of this State in *People v. Mizell,* 72 N.Y.2d 651 (1988), an appeal from the latter Appellate Term decision. In *Mizell* the defendant was arrested for criminal mischief in the fourth degree, for allegedly using a metal pipe to damage the door lock of a Staten Island apartment. In the course of the arrest two vials were recovered from the defendant's possession and the police department laboratory report noted cocaine residue on both sides of the vials. The Criminal Court, on motion of the defendant, dismissed the accusatory instrument concluding that cocaine residue was not a controlled substance and the Appellate Term affirmed, as noted.

The Court of Appeals defined the issue to be whether a charge of Criminal Possession of a Controlled Substance in the Seventh Degree, P.L. Sec. 220.03 is sustainable when the quantity involved is unusable residue.

The Court concluded that cocaine residue, though unusable, is a controlled substance that can give rise to criminal liability under P.L. Sec. 220.03. The Court reasoned that P.L. Sec. 220.03 is unambiguous since it does not specify any minimum amount. The Court noted that the legislature, in the possession crimes, six degrees in all ranging from a Class A misdemeanor to a Class A-I felony, when it wanted to do so, did indicate a minimal amount of a particular substance.

In short the Court concluded that because of the language and structure of the New York Statute, and its relevant history, cocaine in any amount can sustain a criminal charge under P.L. Sec. 220.03.

Mizell apparently is the last word on this short but winding subject. It is the law that a residue of Cocaine can sustain a charge under P.L. Sec. 220.03, regardless of the amount, though mere unusable residue.

36. The Presentence Report in New York Law

Section 390.20 of the Criminal Procedure Law states that the Court must order, where a person is convicted of a felony, a presentence investigation and may not pronounce sentence until it has received a written report of such investigation. (C.P.L Section 390.20[1]).

The section further states that where a person is convicted of a misdemeanor a presentence report is not required but the Court may not pronounce a sentence of probation, a sentence of imprisonment for a term in excess of ninety days or consecutive sentences of imprisonment for terms aggregating more than ninety days, unless it has ordered a presentence investigation of the defendant and has received a presentence investigation of the defendant and has received a written report of such investigation. (C.P.L. 390.20[2A, B, C]). Finally, the section states that the Court may, in its discretion, order a presentence investigation and report whether such investigation and report is required.

This part of the Criminal Procedure Law mandates a presentence investigation and report in three instances: felony matters, three categories of misdemeanor convictions, and instances where the trial court, in its discretion, deems the report necessary. The requirement, thus, that a presentence report be ordered and received by the trial court before sentence is imposed, where there is a Felony Conviction, a misdemeanor conviction with a sentence of probation or a sentence in excess of ninety days, or where the Court sua sponte has ordered the report, is mandatory in character and cannot be ignored by the Court. *People v. Selikoff,* 30 N.Y.2d 227, 360 N.Y. Supp.2d 623 (1974), stay den. 419 U.S. 1086, 95 Supreme Court 677, 42 Lawyers Edition 679 (1974), cert. den. 419 U.S. 1122, 95 S.C. 806, 42 L.E.2d 822 (1975).

The defendant is not required to request the report, and in the case of a sentence of more than ninety days, the report is required unless knowingly waived. *People v. McCarthy,* 177 Misc.2d 442, 459 N.Y. Supp.2d 959 (1st Dept. 1983), is illustrative of this point. In *McCarthy* the defendant pled guilty to petit larceny and waived a presentence report at the time of the plea of guilt. The case was adjourned for sentencing and the defendant, in the interim, was allowed to participate in a community service program with the understanding that a sentence of imprisonment might be imposed should her conduct, in this interim period, warrant it. The defendant failed to appear on the date of sentencing and was then, later, brought before the Court on a warrant. The sentencing Court, noting the defendant's prior waiver of the presentence report, after hearing comments from both the prosecution and defense counsel concerning sentence, sentenced the defendant to term of seven months imprisonment. The Appellate Division, First Department, held that the defendant's waiver of a presentence report at the time when no sentence was imposed, was not controlling when a jail sentence in excess of ninety days was, thereafter, actually pronounced.

The Appellate Division concluded that the sentencing Court should have ordered a presentence report, since the sentencing Judge at the time of sentencing must exercise his wisdom and discretion in light of current information obtained from the presentence report and on the basis of facts known to him at the time of sentencing, rather than depending on any facts known at the time of plea.

The requirements and conditions set forth in C.P.L. 390.20, whereby a presentence investigation must be ordered and a report received by the sentencing court before sentence is pronounced in certain classes of crimes, is clear in its form, mandatory in character, and has been strictly construed by the Courts of this State.

Thus, it has been uniformly held by the Appellate Courts of this State that it is legal error to pronounce sentence without first receiving a presentence report where there is felony conviction or a misdemeanor conviction with a sentence in excess of ninety days. *People v. Grice,* 64 A.D.2d 718, 407 N.Y. Supp.2d 533 (2nd Dept. 1978); *People v. Scalasny,* 67 App. Div.2d 801, 472 N.Y. Supp.2d 505 (3rd Dept. 1979); *People v. Bentley,* 78 Misc.2d 578, 359 N.Y. Supp.2d 391 (Supreme Court App. Term, 1974); *People v. Aiss,* 29 N.Y.2d 403, 328 N.Y. Supp.2d 438 (1972); *People v. Klein,* 78 A.D.2d 743, 432 N.Y. Supp.2d 735 (3rd Dept. 1980); *People v. Brook,* 48 A.D.2d 790, 369 N.Y. Supp.2d 154 (1st Dept. 1975); *People v. Almstead,* 42 A.D.2d 743, 346 N.Y. Supp.2d 295 (2nd Dept. 1973); *People v. Phillips,* 42 A.D.2d 719, 346 N.Y. Supp.2d 103 (2nd Dept. 1973).

The proper remedy for failure to secure the presentence report as required by this statute is vacatur of the sentence and remand to the trial court for resentencing. *People v. Aiss, supra*; *People v. Scalasny, supra*; *People v. Grice, supra*; *People v. Ex Rel. Hall on Behalf of Haralambou v. LeFevre,* 92 A.D.2d 956, 460 N.Y. Supp.2d 640 (3rd Dept. 1983). The requirement of the presentence report under C.P.L. 390.20 has been applied where probation is revoked following a conviction by plea or otherwise. Hence, it is the law that following a conviction of probation, a new presentence report must be rendered and considered by the trial court prior to sentencing on the previous conviction that gave rise to the sentence of probation. *People v. Halaby,* 77 A.D.2d 717, 430 N.Y. Supp.2d 717 (3rd Dept. 1980); *People v. Rossi,* 96 A.D.2d 646, 466 N.Y. Supp.2d 511 (3rd Dept. 1983); *People v. Stanton,* 96 A.D.2d 652, 466 N.Y. Supp.2d 517 (3rd Dept. 1983).

The report is even necessary, under the law of this State, where there has been a substantial passage of time between the original date set for sentencing and the date sentence was imposed. The Court's failure to obtain an updated presentence report before imposing sentence, under this particular circumstance, requires vacatur of the sentence and a remittal for resentencing. *People v. Sierra,* 99 A.D.2d 472, 470 N.Y. Supp.2d 51 (2nd Dept. 1984); *People v. Criz,* 89 A.D.2d 569, 451 N.Y. Supp.2d 1001 (2nd Dept. 1982).

The Issue

The importance of the presentence report, its mandatory character, and the strict construction given the Courts of this State to the requirements of C.P.L. 390.20, give rise, in the view of this writer, to a particular question, seemingly innocuous, but nevertheless of significance. This question, the specific subject of this article, is that whether, at the date of sentencing, there must be mention, or note by the sentencing judge, on the record, that he has received and considered the report before passing sentence. This is no minor matter since without some mention of this fact by the trial judge, neither defense nor prosecution has true assurance that the report has been considered by the Court other than the vague and hazy assumption that the statute has been followed.

The presentence report and the requirements of C.P.L. 390.20 are of too great import and significance to be relegated to the fantasy land of regularity of action and the metaphysics of a priori assumptions. The defendant must be assured that the report has been prepared and received on the trial record, by the trial judge on the date of sentencing. This is particularly important when we consider that the defendant is not required to request or order the report, but this is a responsibility within the purview of the sentencing court. *People v. McCarthy,* 117 Misc.2d 442, 459 N.Y. Supp.2d 959 (lst Dept. 1983).

The case law of this State supports the idea that the sentencing court must note, on the record, that the report has been prepared and received and considered by it in determining sentence. In *People v. Kenneally,* 50 A.D.2d 949, 376 N.Y. Supp.2d 21 (3rd Dept. 1975), the defendant was convicted before the County Court of Greene County of Grand Larceny in the third degree. The Court held that

> the record does not show the trial court did not have the presentence investigation report on defendant before sentencing. The record does show the trial court proceeded to order a presentence report. On sentencing the defendant, the trial court referred to the record showing defendant was sentenced by the Judge's father in 1949. This record was undoubtedly the presentencing report. *People v. Kenneally, supra,* at 21.

Similarly in *People v. Kellar,* 56 A.D.2d 682, 391 N.Y. Supp.2d 730 (3rd Dept. 1977), the defendant appealed from a conviction of robbery in the first degree. The Third Department held that the affidavit of Rensselaer County Judge Cholakis, who presided at the trial, that he reviewed and considered a presentence report prepared by the Rensselaer County Department of Probation, satisfied the requirements of Section 390.20 of the Criminal Procedure Law. *People v. Kellar, supra*, at 731.

The legal implications of both *Kenneally* and *Kellar* are clear: There must be an indication in the record, by the trial court, that the report was before the Court at the time of sentencing. As was true in *Kenneally*, the reference can be to the report on the record or, as was the case in *Kellar*, an affidavit by the sentencing Judge that he reviewed and considered the presentence report, will be sufficient to satisfy the statutory requirements.

To interpret the holdings of *Kenneally* and *Kellar* otherwise is to effectively ignore the conclusion of these cases since, if there were no requirements that under C.P.L. 390.20 that the sentencing Court specifically note on the record that it has received and considered the presentence report before sentencing, the issues considered in *Kenneally* and *Kellar*, and their conclusion with respect to these issues, would be nothing more than an exercise in verbal surplusage, since the reports no doubt existed in some form and could be found in the Court file.

Conclusion: The presentence report is a significant link in the chain and machinery of the Criminal Justice System. The requirements surrounding it are set forth in C.P.L. 390.20.

The case law interpreting this section, it is the thrust of this article, have fleshed out a requirement, not entirely obvious, that the sentencing Court must note on the record that it has received and considered the presentence report prior to sentencing. Total compliance with C.P.L. 390.20 requires nothing more and nothing less. It is a small price to pay where there may be loss of liberty and is a sure assurance that the report has not only been prepared, at some point, but has been before the Court and truly considered in the determination of sentence.

37. Bolstering, Part One: Notes Toward Definition

In a criminal trial, improper bolstering occurs where another witness, not an eyewitness of the incident, testifies that he witnessed the primary witness make a pretrial identification of the defendant. Improper bolstering may be direct, when the second witness repeats the facts of the pretrial identification, or indirect, when the circumstances are repeated. C.P.L. Sec. 60.25 entitled Rules of evidence; identification by means of previous recognition in absence of present identification and C.P.L. Sec. 60.30, entitled Rules of evidence; identification by means of previous recognition in addition to present identification, together constitute statutorily codified exceptions to the rule against improper bolstering.

Improper Bolstering, in a criminal trial, is barred as inadmissible hearsay and as a prior consistent statement. See *Crawford v. Nilan,* 289 N.Y. 444 (1943); *People v. Davis,* 44 N.Y.2d 269 (1978); *People v. Ramos,* 70 N.Y.2d 639 (1987); *People v. Trowbridge,* 305 N.Y. 471 (1953); *People v. Henry,* 150 Misc.2d 706 (S. Ct. Monroe County 1991).

There is also a case law exception to the bar against improper bolstering, apart from the statutory exceptions, where the evidence is sought to be admitted to counter a charge of recent fabrication. *People v. McLean,* 69 N.Y.2d 426 (1987); *People v. McMillian,* 139 A.D.2d 674 (2d Dept. 1988).

The issue this article proposes to briefly consider is how defense counsel can effectively determine in the course of a criminal trial when an instance of improper bolstering occurs and how and when to properly object and so preserve the trial record for appellate review. The case law must be consulted. *People v. Green,* 104 A.D.2d 451 (2d Dept. 1984), is a good example of where improper bolstering at trial resulted in prejudicial error and reversal of the judgment of conviction. In *Green,* the defendant was convicted, after a jury trial, of Grand Larceny in the Third Degree. The facts in the case were that the complainant was walking in the street and had her pocketbook taken by one of four youths. The police were called and the complainant gave a description of the youth who had stolen her pocketbook. The description was then broadcast by the police as a radio bulletin. A specific description was given, a canvas of the area made by the complainant, and two officers and the complainant pointed out the defendant as the person who stole her bag. The defendant was arrested and the complainant's pocketbook recovered. The problem at trial was that following the complainant's testimony as to the identification of the defendant from the police car, the arresting officers were permitted, over objection, to testify as to the particulars of the complainant's description of the defendant and her identification of the defendant at the scene. The court held this, under *People v. Trowbridge,* 305 N.Y. 471. *People v. Randall,* 91 A.D.2d 838 (4th Dept. 1982), is another example of where an appellate court of this state, in the case the Fourth Department, reversed on the ground of improper bolstering. In *Randall,* the facts were that an emergency room doctor's repetition of what the complainant said in his presence were held to be improper bolstering.

The instances of what the case law defines as improper bolstering are legion. See, for example, *People v. Roff,* 67 A.D.2d 806 (4th Dept. 1979). Improper bolstering, in this case, was held where a detective in his trial testimony repeated what the complainant said to him when she looked at the defendant's photograph and identified him as the perpetrator. See also *People v. Luciano,* 64 A.D.2d 614 (2nd Dept. 1978). Here it was held that improper bolstering occurred when the undercover officer testified as to what he repeated to members of the backup team after the sales were made and after the defendant's arrest, after having testified at the trial about the two sales of narcotics made by the defendant to him.

In short, improper bolstering, or *Trowbridge* error, is an ever-present possibility in any criminal trial, and defense counsel must be ever vigilant to preserve the record for appellate review, first by an initial impression in limine on the subject, timely objection when perceived bolstering occurs at trial and, in addition a motion for a mistrial. It is only in this way, ever aware of the manifold factual scenarios wherein bolstering may occur, that defense counsel by timely motion and objection may obtain a possible reversal on appeal and salvage an otherwise hopeless case.

Copyright 1993, Andrew J. Schatkin.

38. Bolstering, Part Two: A Recent Case

Improper bolstering, whether direct or inferential, is barred as inadmissible hearsay and as a prior consistent statement. In a previous article, this writer considered what the case law considered instances of improper bolstering.

In this article, a case recently decided by the Court of Appeals will be analyzed and considered. That case, *People v. Huertas*, 75 N.Y.S.2d 487 (1990), constitutes a significant decision on the issue of what may be considered bolstering since in *Huertas* the Court of Appeals apparently permitted what would otherwise seem to be bolstered complainant description testimony.

The facts in *Huertas* are these: The complainant encountered the defendant on March 27, 1986, while walking home from her sister-in-law's house in Brooklyn. The defendant approached the complainant, drew a gun and pushed it into her side. The complainant described the lighting as bright. Eventually, the defendant forced the complainant to an overhang in the schoolyard playground and raped her. Subsequently, after the complainant dressed and ran from the playground, she encountered three police officers to whom she reported that she had been raped. She was then taken to the hospital, where she provided a description of the assailant. The defendant was arrested twelve days after the rape when the complainant observed the defendant and reported that fact to a nearby police officer, who then arrested the defendant.

Prior to trial, defense counsel requested that neither the complainant or officer testify that she had identified the defendant to the police and that the officers be prohibited from testifying that they had arrested the defendant as a result of a conversation with the complainant. Defense counsel also argued that the complainant should not be allowed to testify that she had given any description to the police, since such testimony would constitute improper bolstering.

The prosecutor agreed that there would be no police testimony concerning what the complainant had said to police witnesses, but argued, and the trial court agreed, that the complainant would testify that when she saw the defendant twelve days after the rape, she went to the police and told them.

The defendant, on appeal, did not raise this issue, but did contest the trial court's holding that allowed the complainant's testimony about the description she gave to the police after the rape as bearing on the accuracy and reliability of the identification of the defendant.

The Court of Appeals initially noted that the description given by the complainant to the police was inadmissible hearsay unless it fell within one of the hearsay prohibitions. The Court of Appeals held that this evidence, in this case, was admissible, through hearsay, as bearing only on the accuracy and reliability of the identification of the defendant and was not offered for its truth. The Court of Appeals specifically stated that this evidence assisted the jury in evaluating the witness's opportunity to observe at the time of the crime and reliability of her memory at the time of the identification.

Huertas, in the view of this writer, is an aberrational and incorrect decision, contrary to the long line of cases barring bolstering. To allow this testimony, as the Court of Appeals did, on the ground that the jury would only be allowed to consider it as bearing on the witness's ability to observe at the time and the reliability of the memory is to allow for nothing more nor less than its truth, since the jury would be led to match that description, albeit offered for limited purpose with a limiting instruction by the court, with the defendant's appearance in court, and it would lead them to the inevitable and unfair conclusion that he was the perpetrator, based on the conclusion that the complainant's memory and ability to observe was good. In this case *Huertas* evades, by a virtual word play, the effect on the jury of this type of bolstered testimony.

It is noteworthy that the cases following *Huertas* have given it very limited application. Thus, in *People v. Rice*, 75 N.Y.2d 929 (1990), the Court of Appeals barred the admission, as an exception to the hearsay rules, of the testimony of the police concerning a description a rape victim gave of her assailant. Similarly in *People v. Williams*, 167 A.D.2d 295 (1st Department 1990), the First Department admitted the fact that the description had been given by the robbery victim to the police to the fact of the description and not for its substance and truth. See also *People v. Guerra*, 168 A.D.2d 394 (1st Department 1990).

In sum, the rule against bolstering is of long-standing force in the state, the subject and object of case law statute. *Huertas* drives a wedge in this role and constitutes an exception to the rule against bolstering. The statutory and case law exceptions to allowable bolstering have long stood the test of time. The holding in *Huertas* goes beyond the allowable exceptions and it is to be hoped the Court of Appeals will see that the permitted exceptions to bolstering and the rule itself have their genesis in providing against unreliable and prejudicial testimony and that the appellate courts of this state will be most cautious in giving it any wide application.

39. A Note on Chargeable Time

The question of chargeable or excludable time, in the context of a motion for the violation of the defendant's speedy trial right, is an important one since the time that is charged to the People will, obviously, determine the outcome of any speedy trial motion pursuant to C.P.L. Sec. 30.30. In this article, the status of the current case law will be examined and analyzed on the issue of whether the time from the defendant's arraignment on the felony complaint, or, more exactly, the time from when bail is set, to the time of his actual arraignment on the indictment, is chargeable to the People or is excludable, under C.P.L. Sec. 30.30.

This is a question of great import since the time frame encompassing these events can be as much as three weeks to a month, at least in the County of Queens, almost one sixth of the People's total allowable speedy trial time to answer ready for trial on the indictment. Until recently, the case law was divided on this point, the weight of authority allowing this time to be charged to the People. *People v. Range,* 80 A.D.2d 812, 437 N.Y.S. 312 (2d Dept. 1981), is an example of an appellate court holding that the time frame from initial arraignment on the felony complaint when bail is set or not, to arraignment on the indictment is chargeable to the people. The facts in *Range* were that on October 8, 1977, it was alleged that the defendant and two others forcibly stole various items of personal property from the complainant. The defendant was apprehended later that day and a three-count indictment was filed five days later, charging the defendant with the crimes of Burglary in the First Degree and Robbery in the First and Second Degrees. The defendant's two accomplices were later arrested and indicted. The last indictment was filed on December 14, 1977. Thereafter, six months elapsed and the defendant was not brought to trial. The defendant then moved to dismiss the indictment pursuant to C.P.L. Sec. 30.30 and the trial court granted the motion. Although the Appellate Division reversed, the First Department specifically stated that the first time period of twenty-seven days from the date of the defendant's arrest to the date of his arraignment on the indictment was correctly charged to the People.

Similarly, in *People v. McCaffery,* 78 A.D.2d 1003, 433 N.Y.S.2d 909 (4th Dept. 1980), the Fourth Department held, on appeal from a judgment of conviction for Criminal Possession of a Controlled Substance in the Third Degree, on review of the denial of the defendant's speedy trial motion by the trial court, that the first period of 162 days from November 9, 1978—the date of the preliminary hearing—to April 20, 1979—the date when the defendant was arraigned on the indictment—was chargeable to the People since the date of presentment to the Grand Jury was wholly under the control of the People and there was nothing the defendant could do to prevent the delay in presentment of his case to the Grand Jury. See also *People v. Green,* 134 A.D.2d 612 (2d Dept. 1987), where the Appellate Division, Second Department, held that the delay between the filing of the indictment and the defendant's arraignment thereon was properly charged to the People; also *People v. Toro,* 151 A.D.2d 142 (1st Dept. 1989);

People v. Williams, 132 Misc.2d 549, 504 N.Y.S.2d 364 (S. Ct. New York County 1986); *People v. Smith,* 97 A.D.2d 485, 468 N.Y.S.2d (2d Dept. 1983).

There is another line of cases, however, that establishes less than the apparently set and opaque rule of constraint, so to speak, that automatically charges to the People from the time of the setting of bail on the felony complaint to the time of arraignment on the indictment. These cases hold that there is no set rule and automatic measure, but the People are to be allowed a reasonable time for this purpose. *People v. Traficante,* 147 A.D.2d 843, 538 N.Y.S.2d 331 (3rd Dept. 1989), illustrates this point. In *Traficante,* the defendant, upon a jury trial, was found guilty of Escape in the First Degree. He appealed from the County Court's determination that his speedy trial rights under C.P.L. Sec. 30.30 had not been violated in that the number of days of delay allowable to the People was less than the statutory requirement. The Appellate Division reversed, holding that the delay resulting from the defendant's being incarcerated in a different county required an order to produce and transport and was to be charged to the People since there was no indication in the record that the People had exercised due diligence in producing him.

What is most important in this decision was the Third Department enunciation of a rule that the People, upon an appropriate showing, will be allowed a "reasonable time" in which to arrange for the defendant's arraignment on the indictment. *People v. Traficante, supra* at 333. See also *People v. Lopez,* 149 A.D.2d 735, 540 N.Y.S.2d 518, 519 (2d Dept. 1989), and *People v. Baker,* 131 A.D.2d 491, 516 N.Y.S.2d 106, 107 (2d Dept. 1987), where the Second Department also set forth a similar reasonable time period rule. It would appear that there is a perspective in the Second and Third Departments allowing the People a "reasonable time" to arraignment on the indictment as opposed to the First and Fourth Departments' perspective, at times, that the time is totally chargeable to the People.

The Last Word

The Court of Appeals has blown, however, the last trumpet on this issue, in a terse memorandum opinion in *People v. Correa,* 77 N.Y.2d 930 (1991). In that opinion, the Court of Appeals stated in no uncertain and in mandatory language that delays between indictment and arraignment on the indictment, like other court congestion, do not prevent the People from being ready for trial and so are not excludable under C.P.L. Sec. 30.30. The Court rejected the People's contention that they were legally blocked from asserting their readiness for trial prior to arraignment on the indictment because the defendant might not yet be represented by counsel since C.P.L. Sec. 30.30(4)(f) explicitly exempts this period during which the defendant is without counsel, and also found unpersuasive the People's alternate contention that it would be impractical to require them to prepare for trial prior to arraignment because the defendant could plead guilty at the arraignment. The court stated, with respect to this second argument, that the fact that the defendant might plead guilty, at arraignment or any other time, does not excuse the People from being ready for trial within the necessary period. More recently, in *People v. Palacios,* 79 N.Y.2d 897 (1992), the Court of Appeals on review of submissions pursuant to Section 550.5 of the rules of the Court of Appeals (22 N.Y.C.R.R. 400.4) again reiterated the continued vitality and validity of the *Correa* rule of readiness.

In sum, despite the "reasonable time" rule articulated by some few appellate decisions in this state, the weight of authority and indeed the rule mandated and set forth by the Court of Appeals is that the time from the arrest and setting of bail to arraignment on the indictment is within the discretion and control of the People. There is no excuse for their failure, and the time is to be charged to the State.

40. The Undefined Bulge and Probable Cause

In criminal practice in the State of New York, one of the most frequently encountered factual patterns in the Search and Seizure scenario is the so-called "bulge" case where a police officer justifies a search and recovery of a gun from the defendant's person on the basis that he observed a bulge on the defendant's person, suspected a weapon, and feared for his personal safety. The officer then proceeded to search and subsequently recover a weapon from the defendant's person, thereby justifying the search and seizure.

At first blush, there would appear to be no legal objection to the legality and constitutionality of this search and seizure. The case law, however, holds otherwise. In fact, under the law of this state, a mere bulge, without the distinct outline of a weapon, is insufficient in itself to justify this type of search and seizure.

People v. Prochilo/v. Goings/v. Bernard, 41 N.Y.2d 759 (1977), states the rule well. The *Prochilo* court upheld the denial of suppression. In *Prochilo,* an officer on patrol in Brooklyn observed the defendant watching other officers interviewing passing pedestrians. From a short distance, the officer saw the defendant making continuous hand motions to his side. Noticing an object on the defendant's right hip, the officer left his car, approached the defendant who was still making hand motions; and the officer observed, through the defendant's tight-fitting clothing, the complete outline of a gun at his side. The officer then reached out and removed a revolver from the defendant's waist band. The Court upheld the constitutionality of the search, stating that the officer could reasonably fear for his personal safety where the basis of his suspicion was justified by the presence of an outline of a gun.

The same was true in the companion case of *Goings,* where the officer observed a bulge in the defendant's right hand jacket pocket, which had the configuration of a hand gun. See also *People v. Trulio*, 135 A.D.2d 758 (2d Dept. 1987).

On the other hand, the courts of this state have not upheld a search resulting in the recovery of a gun from the defendant's person where the officer merely observed an undefined bulge. Thus, the Second Department held in *People v. Harris*, 149 A.D.2d 730 (2d Dept. 1989), that suppression was warranted where the testimony at the suppression hearing was that the officer observed nothing more than a bulge at the defendant's right waist band. See also *People v. Bernard*, 41 N.Y.2d 759 (1977).

In conclusion, this brief analysis of some pertinent cases on the subject of waist band bulges reveals that the observation of a mere bulge, without something more, does not and cannot, absent the distinct outline and configuration of a gun, justify a search and recovery of a weapon from the person of the defendant.

This is correct. We all, as citizens of this Republic, may carry a heavy wallet or small package on our persons. To permit a stop and search on the basis of the bulge of an unknown item, without the distinct configuration of a weapon, whatever the community and whatever the race of the defendant, is to intrude on the freedom to be free of an unwarranted intrusion by the state on the privacy of the individual. In short, something more is rightfully needed to justify a search under these circumstances than an undefined bulge or wad.

41. Three Pretrial Hearings

The Criminal Law, in recent years, has given rise to numerous and various hearings. Thus, there is the *Dunaway* Hearing, *Dunaway v. New York,* 442 U.S. 200, 99 S. Ct. 2248 (1979), to determine whether the People's evidence should be suppressed due to lack of probable cause for the defendant's arrest; the *Wade* Hearing, *U.S. v. Wade,* 388 U.S. 218, 87 S. Ct. 1926 (1967), a hearing to determine whether an in-court identification should be suppressed due to the suggestive taint of an out-of-court identification procedure; a *Huntley* Hearing, *People v. Huntley,* 15 N.Y.2d 72, 255 N.Y.S.2d 838 (1965), to determine the voluntariness of a confession or inculpatory statement or whether it was obtained in violation of the defendant's Fifth and Sixth Amendment rights.

The various kinds and types of hearings have proliferated. Most recently, in *People v. Rodriguez,* 79 N.Y.2d 445, 583 N.Y.S.2d 814 (1992), the Court of Appeals mandated, as it were, a pre-Wade hearing, to determine whether an identification was confirmatory or not based on an inquiry into the degree of familiarity existent between the defendant and the witness.

This article proposes to consider, define and analyze three little known Pretrial Hearings in New York State Criminal Law. The first case and hearing to be considered is the *Gomberg* Hearing, so named after *People v. Gomberg*, 38 N.Y.2d 307, 379 N.Y.S.2d 769 (1975).

In *Gomberg* the defendants were convicted before the Supreme Court of New York County of Arson in the Second Degree and they appealed. The Appellate Division affirmed. The principle issue on appeal arose out of the joint representation of all three defendants by the same attorney; in short, the question of the effectiveness or possible ineffectiveness of counsel. The Court of Appeals held that the trial court must be satisfied, where the representation is joint, that the defendant's decision to proceed with his attorney is an informed one and stated that the court may even inquire as to whether counsel himself has perceived the conflict and apprised the client of the risks involved. The Court of Appeals concluded that where two or more defendants are represented by the same attorney, the court must conduct an inquiry on the record whether each defendant was, or is, aware of the potential risks involved and has knowingly consented to the fact of joint representation. Hence, the *Gomberg* Hearing involved an inquiry by the court directed both to the defendants and their counsel as to the propriety and potential risk of joint representation by the same attorney.

The second hearing to be analyzed in this article is the *Issacson* Hearing, so named after *People v. Issacson*, 44 N.Y.2d 511, 406 N.Y.S.2d 714 (1978). In *Issacson*, the defendant was convicted of Criminal Sale of Controlled Substance in the First Degree. The Appellate Division affirmed. *Issacson* involved substantial police brutalization, trickery and deceit directed to the defendant resulting in the defendant being involved in the sale of drugs. The Court held that under these circumstances that there must be an inquiry by the court as to whether, under the principle of due process and fundamental fairness, the defendant's rights have been violated by such egregious misconduct by the prosecutor or state such as to mandate dismissal of the indictment. In fact, the *Issacson* hearing is an inquiry by the court on the issue of possible prosecutorial, police or state misconduct.

The third and final little known pretrial hearing to be considered in this article is the *Alfinito* Hearing, named after *People v. Alfinito*, 16 N.Y.2d 181, 264 N.Y.S.2d 243 (1965). *Alfinito* involved a prosecution for alleged violation of a statute proscribing policy gambling. The Criminal Court granted the defendant's pretrial motion to suppress. The People appealed to the Appellate Team and the Appellate Team reversed. Both the defendant and the People directly appealed to the Court of Appeals. The issue on appeal was whether the defendant may question the truth of the allegations in support of the search warrant. The Court held that under the law there may be an inquiry as to whether the affiant's statements were perjurious, that the burden of proof is upon the person attacking the warrant, and that any doubt arising from the testimony of the suppression hearing as to whether the affiant's statements were perjurious should be resolved in favor of the warrant.

In conclusion, this article, in brief and sum, has considered three little known but important pretrial hearings in addition to the most common, the

Dunaway, Wade, Huntley, and *Rodriguez* Hearings. These hearings may arise in the course of the litigation of a criminal case and defense counsel should be aware and cognizant of the existence of these hearings as they may arise in the course of a New York State criminal practice.

42. Sandoval and the Grand Jury: A Recent Case

In 1974, the Court of Appeals decided the landmark case of *People v. Sandoval,* 34 N.Y.2d 371, 357 N.Y.S.2d 849 (1974). In that case, in order that the defendant not be totally impeached, should he choose to testify, through his prior convictions, or actually be deterred from taking the stand through the use by the People of his prior convictions, the court approved the procedural device whereby the defense, in a pretrial motion, could have the determination by the court as to which convictions the People could use to impeach him should he choose to testify. The balancing test devised was the probative value of the impeachment evidence as weighed against the risk of possible unfair prejudice to the defendant. The Court of Appeals and the lower appellate court of this state have held that the *Sandoval* rule only applies to the criminal defendant as witness, and not to the defendant's witnesses, the prosecution's witnesses or to a civil case. Since 1974, the *Sandoval* rule has been broadly and uniformly applied by the Courts to all defendants who may choose to testify on their own behalf at trial.

In general, the rule of *Sandoval* had not been applied to the Grand Jury proceeding. The traditional procedural remedy devised by the appellate courts of this state has been the motion pursuant to C.P.L. Sec. 190.50 of the Criminal Procedure Law. See *People v. Miller,* 144 A.D.2d 44, 537 N.Y.S.2d 318 (3rd Dept. 1989); *People v. Lerman,* 116 A.D.2d 665, 497 N.Y.S.2d 733 (2nd Dept. 1986); *People v. Davis,* 119 Misc.2d 1013, 465 N.Y.S.2d 404 (S.Ct. Queens County 1983).

In a recent trial court decision, however, the court suggested extending the rule of the *Sandoval* compromise to Grand Jury proceedings. That case is *People v. (Jeff) Thomas,* N.Y.L.J. p.25, col. 6, 1/19/94. In *Thomas,* the defendant, in an omnibus motion, sought dismissal of the indictment on two grounds. The first alleged lack of evidence. The court ruled that it had inspected the minutes of the Grand Jury and stated it had found sufficient evidence to sustain both counts of the indictment and so denied that part of the motion to dismiss for lack of evidence.

The second part of the defendant's motion alleged that the District Attorney failed to notify defense counsel, after inquiry, of his intention to use specific convictions to impeach the credibility of the defendant before the Grand Jury. In sum, the court stated that the defendant sought to apply the *Sandoval* principles at the Grand Jury level.

The defendant in this action was indicted and charged along with the codefendant with Criminal Sale of a Controlled Substance in the Third Degree and Assault in the Second Degree. The defendant, prior to the Grand Jury's deliberations, exercised his statutory right to appear as a witness on his own behalf. His attorney, prior to the defendant's appearance before the Grand Jury, requested that the prosecutor inform her as to what convictions the People intended to utilize in their cross examination but the prosecutor refused to divulge this information. The defendant then testified before the Grand Jury and testified, essentially, that he was in the area of the drug transaction on the day in question, that he borrowed two dollars from the codefendant to buy cigarettes in a local store, and while in the store, was grabbed by someone and arrested on a drug charge. The defendant maintained that he was not involved in an illegal act and volunteered the information that he had been previously in jail, that he had been convicted of other crimes and was currently involved in a parole violation.

On cross-examination, the District Attorney inquired extensively with respect to the defendant's criminal record and the defendant was forced to admit that he had been previously convicted of Reckless Endangerment. The People also brought out that the defendant had been previously convicted of Criminal Possession of a Controlled Substance as well as Attempted Unauthorized Use of A Motor Vehicle.

In response to a question of a Grand Juror that when the defendant was arrested for criminal sale of a controlled substance, did he possess drugs at the time, the defendant stated he was "in possession" and also "on drugs."

Based on the District Attorney's quasi-judicial duties to protect the rights of the accused and to see that justice would be done, the defense counsel requested that a *Sandoval* compromise be had before the defendant testified at the Grand Jury, in order to limit the use of his prior convictions. The prosecutor refused to agree prior to the Grand Jury presentation to limit his cross examination of the defendant.

The defense further alleged that the cross-examination by the prosecutor and the question posed on behalf of a Grand Juror as to "sale" rather than "possession" was highly prejudicial, as criminal sale was the charge being presented to the Grand Jury.

The defendant also asserted that the District Attorney had failed to grant him the initial *Sandoval* relief of knowing which crimes could be used against him, thus forcing him to testify against himself, and the lack of such information resulted in unfair and inappropriate cross-examination, nullifying his right to testify effectively on his own behalf. The People contended that the defendant was given the opportunity to complete his entire statement before cross-examination and that the prosecutor's questioning was proper and impartial.

Initially, the court stated that in deciding whether to apply the *Sandoval* principles at the Grand Jury level, the following issues must be considered:

1. Can the District Attorney be required to advise defense counsel in advance of his intention to use convictions to impeach the credibility of the defendant when the defendant chooses to testify before the Grand Jury?
2. Does the court have the right to make evidentiary rulings which affect the presentation of evidence to the Grand Jury?
3. Would a *Sandoval* ruling applicable only to Grand Jury presentment result in a greater number of defendants exercising their rights to testify before the Grand Jury?

The court answered all these questions in the affirmative. The court held that advising the defendant as to his impeachment by his prior convictions, prior to a Grand Jury appearance, is a valid exercise of the District Attorney's duty under *Sandoval* and that such an act insures the integrity of the Grand Jury. The court further stated, citing *People v. DiFabio,* 79 N.Y.2d 836, that it was within the trial court's power to participate in the Grand Jury proceedings, that that power was not curtailed by statute, and that it should follow that the trial court has the right to make an evidentiary ruling as to the use of the defendant's prior convictions, not only prior to trial, but prior to his appearance before the Grand Jury. The court also cited *People v. Hargrove,* 80 Misc.2d 317 (S.Ct. Westchester County), where that court held that the prosecutor had violated the rationale and spirit of *Sandoval* by knowingly prejudicing the defendant with the use of his prior drug convictions before the Grand Jury and so dismissed the indictment, based on the *Sandoval* violation. The court went on to distinguish the holdings in *People v. Adams,* 80 Misc.2d 528, and *U.S. v. Dionisio,* 410 U.S. 1, stating that a *Sandoval* ruling prior to a Grand Jury appearance by the defendant would ensure that competent evidence would be presented and that prejudice to the defendant would be eliminated.

Thus, the court held that the emphasis on the defendant's past drug convictions and erroneous reference to a sale conviction resulted in prejudice to the defendant's credibility in this case and deprived him of a meaningful opportunity to testify, thus nullifying his rights pursuant to C.P.L. Sec. 190.50.

The court concluded that in order to preserve the integrity of the Grand Jury and permit the defendant a meaningful opportunity to testify, the application of the *Sandoval* principles was required at the Grand Jury level and to hold otherwise would defeat the spirit and intent of *Sandoval.*

The *Thomas* decision, therefore, is a landmark one, representing a significant development of the law. The District Attorney's right, at the Grand Jury proceeding, to cross-examine the defendant is often unfettered and the defendant is left with no other remedial recourse than a motion pursuant to C.P.L. Sec. 190.50, a motion that may take weeks to decide and implement. It is only fair that the rule of *Sandoval* be extended to the Grand Jury proceeding. The Grand Jury is a critical stage of a criminal proceeding, as critical as the trial itself. If the People are left with unlimited discretion to cross-examine and impeach the defendant through the use of prior convictions, the defendant will often hesitate to testify and should he do so, will face total discrediting and impeachment by the prosecutor, leading the Grand Jury to inevitably conclude that "where there is smoke, there is fire." The defendant's only remedy under the circumstances is the motion under C.P.L. Sec. 190.50, with the defendant left languishing in jail for weeks or months, awaiting a decision that may not even be favorable.

It is no argument that judicial economy dictates that the *Sandoval* rule be applied only at the trial itself and should not be equally applied to the Grand Jury stage. The rights of the accused to a total, fair and speedy proceeding at all levels of litigation must override any consideration of time and trouble. Neither more, nor less, is necessary to assure a totally fair trial, where the defendant's rights and case may be speedily determined in all fairness. The considerations of fairness and substantial justice must always be the paramount consideration. The *Thomas* court has seen this, and it is to be hoped that the appellate courts will take cognizance of this decision and give its idea force throughout the state

43. A Question of Weight

The Penal Law of this state under P.L. Section 220.00 categorizes and defines the various types of Possessory Controlled Substance Offenses. All these Possessory Offenses, in their respective statutes, stipulate knowingness or knowledge of possession of the Controlled Substance as an element of the offense.[1] Many of these possessory statutes also stipulate *weight* as an element of the offense. For example, P.L. Sec. 220.06(5) defines the possessory offense to be the knowing possession of five hundred milligrams or more of cocaine and P.L. Sec. 220.09 states the offense to be the knowing possession of one or more preparations, compounds, mixtures, or substance of an aggregate weight of one-eighth of an ounce or more containing a narcotic drug. The list and subcategories are numerous: suffice it to say that at least one subcategory of every drug possessory offense of this state defines *weight* to be an element of the offense.

Until recently, however, the courts of this state have not held actual or inferred knowledge of the weight of the controlled substance to be an element of the possessory crime and so part of the People's burden, despite the clear statutory requirement of knowing possession.

A recent case, however, decided by the Court of Appeals, has modified the law in this respect and so requires careful consideration and analysis. That case is *People v. Robert Ryan*, N.Y.L.J., 12/20/93m, p. 25, col. 1. The facts in *Ryan* are these: the defendant was charged with Attempted Second Degree Possession, P.L. Sec. 220.18(5), for arranging to obtain a shipment of hallucinogenic mushrooms. A police chemist testified at trial that the total weight of the mushrooms was about two pounds and that a 140 gram sample of the package contained 796 milligrams of psilocybin, a hallucinogen. The chemist, however, did not know the process by which psilocybin appears in mushrooms or how much psilocybin would typically appear in two pounds of mushrooms.

At the close of the People's case, the defendant moved to dismiss for insufficient proof that he knew the level of psilocybin in the mushrooms and also requested a charge-down to second degree attempted criminal possession, which had no weight element. Both applications were denied and the defendant was convicted as charged and sentenced to ten years to life as a Second Felony. Offender. The Appellate Division affirmed, holding that the defendant must know the nature of the substance possessed but declined to read the statute as requiring that the defendant have actual knowledge of the weight, holding that the term "knowing" should be interpreted to refer only to the element of possession and not weight.

The Court of Appeals reversed, noting that the offense of P.L Sec. 220.18 provides that a person is guilty of Criminal Possession of a Controlled Substance in the Second Degree when he knowingly and unlawfully possesses six hundred twenty-five milligrams of a hallucinogen. The Court defined the issue to be whether, in addition to knowledge of the possession and nature of the Controlled Substance, the defendant must also know the weight of the matter possessed. The Court reasoned that the knowledge of weight, under a sample reading of the statute itself, the rules of statutory construction, and an overall analysis of the drug possession laws, mandates the conclusion that weight is an element of this crime. It was significant, the court noted, that if actual knowledge of the weight was not to be an element of this possessory drug offense, then the crime would become a strict liability statute. Referring to the legislative history of the statute itself, its language, and the rules of statutory construction, the court further noted that the various grades and degrees of possessory drug offenses are keyed to the weight of the controlled substance and that the degree of punishment and incarceration increases with the weight of substance possessed. The Court also noted that the case law also suggested that knowledge of the weight should be an element of the crime. The Court rejected the People's contention that it would be prohibitively difficult to secure convictions in these cases if they were required to prove definite weight and knowledge of the weight.

The Court of Appeals suggested ways by which knowledge of the weight could be circumstantially proved. These included evidence of negotiation concerning weight, potency, or price. For controlled substances measured on an "aggregate weight" the court stated that knowledge of the weight could be inferred from the defendant's handling of the material.

As to substances measured by pure weight such as psilocybin, the court noted that the showing might be difficult where minuscule doses are involved and they are customarily combined with other substances to facilitate handling and use. The court suggested that the actual knowledge of the weight under these circumstances could be satisfied with evidence that the pure weight of the controlled substance possessed by the defendant is typical for the particular form in which the drug appears. This correlation, the court reasoned, between the pure weight typically found and the pure weight actually possessed, substantially reduces the possibility that a person would be unjustly convicted for a more serious crime.

The Court then considered under the foregoing principles and analysis whether there was sufficient evidence to convict the defendant of Attempted Second Degree Possession, an A I Felony. The Court held that although there was sufficient evidence here from which a jury could conclude beyond a reasonable doubt that the defendant attempted and intended to possess a two pound box of hallucinogenic mushrooms, it was also undisputed that the mushrooms in the particular box the defendant attempted to possess contained more than 650 milligrams of psilocybin and that the issue the Court must decide was whether sufficient evidence was presented at trial from which it could be inferred that the defendant had the requisite knowledge of the weight. The Court held that the sole evidence that the defendant attempted to possess two pounds of mushrooms could not satisfy the People's burden of proof since only a small portion of the mushrooms was pure psilocybin and there was no evidence linking psilocybin weight to mushroom weight and no evidence showing what weight of psilocybin would typically appear in two pounds of mushrooms.

Ryan is a clear, credible, and convincing interpretation of the statute law. The Court of Appeals correctly analyzed and concluded that weight is an element of every single drug possessory offense of this state and that knowledge of both the nature of the controlled substance and its weight is keyed to all these statutory offenses, knowledge both of the nature of the controlled substance, its possession, and its weight. As weight increases, the Court of Appeals significantly noted, the incarceratory exposure of the defendant increases. Knowledge of the weight of the controlled substance possessed, however inferred or circumstantially proved, is merely to provide for the implementation of the will of the legislature, which stated knowledge to be an aspect of both possession and weight under the rules of statutory construction and a clear reading of all these statutes. The Court's decision is cautious and conservative, refusing to read out an element of these statutes that the legislature willed. It is no small price for fairness that where the legislature, reflecting the will of the People, provides both knowledge and weight to be elements of the offenses and a part of the mens rea of the statute, that the People should be held to proving their complete case as the statute and codification of the law has defined it. The law properly does not punish negligence, but leaves this, instead, to the civil courts. Where the law does, however, define the element of the offense, it is proper that the People be held to the responsibility of proving their case beyond a reasonable doubt as defined by statute and not as defined by some notion of policy that evades the will of the People as defined in their enactment. In this way, the Court of Appeals rightly concluded that neither more nor less than total adherence to the statutory elements is necessary should the People choose to prosecute and attempt to convict for an offense. It is the People that enacts these laws and made, under a clear statutory reading, knowing weight an element of these drug possessory offenses. It is the People (through the will of their legislators, should they so choose) who will modify this clearly stated statutory requirements.

44. A Note on Misdemeanor Criminal Trespass

The crime of trespass is one of the most frequent and common property offenses in the Penal Code of this state. The shades of possible trespass violations upon real property are encompassed by four sections of the Penal Code.

P.L Sec. 140.05, entitled, simply, Criminal Trespass, states, in language of summary import, that a person is guilty of trespass when he knowingly enters in or remains unlawfully upon open premises. PL. Sec. 140.05 is a violation exposing the alleged offender to a maximum of fifteen days incarceration.

If the intruder enters into or remains unlawfully in a building or upon real property which is fenced or otherwise enclosed in a manner to exclude intruders, then the criminal offender is guilty of Criminal Trespass in the Third Degree subjecting him to a possible 90 days incarceration. P.L. Sec. 140.10(a). Sec. 140.10 also encompasses a number of similar subcategories of offenses [P.L. Secs. 140.10(b)—(f)].

Finally the third of the misdemeanor trespasses is found in P.L. Sec. 140.15, Criminal Trespass in the Second Degree, which simply reads that a person is guilty of criminal trespass in the second degree when he knowingly enters or remains unlawfully in a dwelling. The nub of the distinction between P.L. Sec. 140.10, Criminal Trespass in the Third degree, and P.L. Sec. 140.15, Criminal Trespass in the Second Degree, is that the latter envisions a property privacy violation with reference to a dwelling, thus elevating the offense to Class A Misdemeanor status and subjecting the offender to a possible year's incarceration.

There is fourth category of trespass offenses, the Class D Felony offense of Criminal Trespass in the First Degree, P.L. Sec. 140.17, where the offender knowingly enters or remains unlawfully in a building, and, when, in the course of committing such crime, he 1) possesses, or knows that another participant in the crime possesses, an explosive or a deadly weapon; 2) possesses a firearm, rifle, or shotgun, as those terms are defined in Section 265.00, and also possesses or has readily accessible a quantity of ammunition which is capable of being discharged from such firearm, rifle or shotgun; 3) knows that another participant in the crime possesses a firearm, rifle or shotgun under circumstances described in subdivision 2.

It is beyond the scope of this article to analyze the more specific import of Criminal Trespass in the First Degree, as this article concerns misdemeanor criminal trespass. In this regard, the violations of the misdemeanor criminal trespass would appear palpable. However, the law is not so clear as it would appear at first blush.

In pertinent part, P.L. Sec. 140.10, Criminal Trespass in the Third Degree, reads that a person is guilty of criminal trespass when he knowingly enters or remains unlawfully in a building or upon real property which is fenced or otherwise enclosed in a manner designed to exclude intruders. This statutory section would seem a model of brightness and clarity, i.e., entering or remaining upon property designed to exclude intruders and doing so unlawfully. At least in this section the nub of Criminal Trespass in the Third Degree is made out. The case law reveals, however, interpretative ramifications that add elements to the offense that are not entirely made out in its codification.

The *Matter of Martin James A.,* 60 A.D.2d 997, 401 N.Y.S.2d 658 (4th Dept. 1958), presents an interesting analysis of this statute. In this case the respondent appealed from an order adjudicating him a juvenile delinquent because he committed acts, which, if done by an adult, would constitute the crimes of Criminal Trespass in the Third Degree and Criminal Mischief in the Fourth Degree. The facts constituting the alleged offense were that the respondent, in the company of two other boys, entered a hospital during visiting hours and ran through the hall, tearing down Halloween decorations. The Fourth Department reversed. The Appellate Court stated that entering or remaining unlawfully as it applies to a public building is defined in sub. 5 of Sec. 140.00 of the Penal Law. That section the court stated, in pertinent part, states that a person who, regardless of his intent, enters or remains in or upon the premises which are at the time open to the public does so with a license or privilege unless he defies a lawful order not to enter or remain, personally communicated to him by the owner of such premise, or other authorized person. The court held that since the proof elicited did not establish that the respondent defied a lawful order not to enter or remain in this public building, personally communicated to him, he was lawfully upon the premises.

In sum, the Fourth Department, constructing P.L. 140.10 and the definition of "enter or remain unlawfully" in P.L. 140.00 held that in the absence of an order to leave a public building and a refusal of the alleged trespasser to do so, the crime is now made out. See also *People v. Jackson,* 72 Misc.2d 297, 339 N.Y.S.2d 429 (Criminal Court, City of New York, Queens County 1972); *People v. Martinez,* 43 Misc.2d 94, 250 N.Y.S.2d 28 (Criminal Court, New York County 1964).

If there is any doubt as to the proper interpretation of this statutory section, then *People v.* Brown, 75 N.Y.2d 374, 306 N.Y.S.2d 449 (1969), lays the matter to rest.

The facts in *Brown* were that the complainant, an insurance broker, entered his street level office and the defendant had entered the office just before the complainant. The complainant approached the defendant and said, "You are the young man who was here on Tuesday and what do you want now?" The defendant replied that he wanted to speak to him in the back of the office. The complainant then told the defendant that he would talk to him right now but the defendant was insistent on speaking to him in the back; and, at this point, the defendant put his hand on the complainant's chest. The complainant then told the defendant that he could talk to him there or in the street. The defendant replied o.k. and as he tried to leave the office, the complainant took his picture. There ensued a verbal exchange between the defendant with the complainant on the sidewalk.

The defendant was arrested and charged with criminal trespass in the second degree (P.L. Sec. 140.10) and menacing (P.L. Sec. 120.15). At trial, the complainant testified to the above facts and his wife also testified substantially the same. Moreover, on cross-examination, she testified that the office was open for business at the time the defendant entered.

At the conclusion of the People's prima facie case, the defendant moved to dismiss but the motion was denied. The defendant then rested and moved for an acquittal on the ground that his guilt had not been proved beyond a reasonable doubt and this motion was also denied. The defendant was convicted of criminal trespass in the second degree and the judgment of conviction was affirmed by the Appellate Term, First Department. The defendant then appealed by permission to the Court of Appeals. The Court of Appeals reversed the judgment of conviction and dismissed the complaint on the basis that the People had failed to establish a prima facie case,

The Court in its decision first recited the language of P.L. Sec. 140.10, Criminal Trespass in the Second Degree and the definitional language of P.L. Sec, 140.00 sub. 5. Applying these companion statutes, the court opined that, since the defendant claimed he had legally entered the building, a crucial element of the crime was required to be established by the People, namely that he had entered or remained unlawfully.

Analyzing the conduct of the defendant in light of these two statutory sections, the court held that the prosecution's own witness established that the office was open to the public, that the defendant was therefore licensed or privileged to enter and that his conviction might only be predicated upon an unlawful entry and defiance of a lawful order not to enter, which was not given here.

The court held that since it was clear that the defendant a fully entered the premises, a conviction could only be had here if the prosecution established that 1) a lawful order not to remain was personally communicated to the defendant and that 2) he defied such order. The court held there was no evidence in the record to establish that such order was personally given and communicated to the defendant or that the defendant defied it.

The holding of *Brown* is clearly the proper interpretation of P.L. Sec. 140.10 and P.L Sec. 140.00. sub. 5. which, taken together, mandate the rule that when a person enters a public building, he does so with a privilege and license, and may not be convicted of the crime of Criminal Trespass in the Second Degree without proof that an order to leave was personally communicated to the defendant and he defied such order.

These above factors, in short, are essential elements of the People's prima facie case under this statute, and without such proof, the People must fail in their prima facie case. See also *People v. De Clemente,* 110 Misc.2d 762, 442 N.Y.S.2d 931 (Criminal Court, City of New York, 1981).

45. A Recent Rosario Decision

C.P.L. Sec. 240.44 applies the Rule of *Rosario* to Pretrial Hearings. The Section states, in pertinent part, that at a Pretrial Hearing held in a criminal court at which a witness is called to testify, each party at the conclusion of the direct examination of each of its witnesses, must, upon request of the other party, make available to the requesting party any written or recorded statement, including testimony before a Grand Jury, made by such witness other than the defendant which relates to the subject matter of the witness' testimony (Sub. 1).

Sub. 2 states that a record of a judgment of conviction of such witness must also be provided if known to the prosecution or the defendant.

Finally, Sub. 3 holds that the existence of any pending criminal action against such witness, if known to the prosecutor or defendant, must be revealed.

This section, in its entirety, is eminently clear in its structure and is regularly applied to the most common Pretrial Hearings: the Wade, Huntley and Mapp Hearings. The section has also, in addition, been held applicable to preliminary hearings pursuant to C.P.L. Sec. 180.60. See *Butts v. Justices of the Court of Special Sessions,* 37 A.D.2d 607, 323 N.Y.S.2d 699 (2d Dept. 1971); app. dism. 29 N.Y.2d 707, 385 N.Y.S.2d 747, 275 N.E.2d 331 (1970).

The question arises, and is of interesting import, to what Pretrial Hearings, if any, does this statutory scheme extend? Does it extend, for example, to a Speedy Trial Hearing?

People v. Robin McPhee, 161 M.2d 660, 614 N.Y.S.2d 884 (1994), (S. Ct. Queens County) (Kohm, J.) sheds light on this very issue.

The issue before the *McPhee* court was whether the *Rosario* doctrine is applicable to C.P.L. Sec. 730 Competency Hearing. In *McPhee,* in the course of a court ordered Competency Hearing, three psychiatrists testified. Each doctor submitted a report. Defense counsel was provided with the handwritten notes which formed the basis of the two doctors' reports but not the third. The defendant maintained that he had a right under *Rosario* to see these notes. Ultimately the notes were turned over in the interest of discovery but the People objected to the use of *Rosario* material in a Competency Hearing and argued that the doctrine applies only to the issues of guilt or innocence and only to an evidentiary hearing.

Initially the court reviewed the history and development of the *Rosario* doctrine in the State of New York. The court then proceeded to analyze the nature, structure and criteria of the Competency Hearing under Sec. 730 of the Criminal Procedure Law.

The court then proceeded to consider whether under Sec. 240.44 of the C.P.L. the *Rosario* doctrine applies to a Competency Hearing. The defendant maintained under both the case law construing statute, specifically *People v. Malinsky*, 15 N.Y.S.2d 86, and *People v. Banch*, 80 N.Y.S.2d 610, 615, as well as the structure of C.P.L. Sec. 240.44 itself that *Rosario* must be applied to any and all Pretrial Hearings including a competency hearing. The People argued that the Hearings referred to in both *Malinsky* and *Banch* were evidentiary in nature and concerned suppression matters and had an immediate bearing on guilt or innocence. In sum, then, the People argued that *Rosario* should be limited to evidentiary hearings. The People also argued that C.P.L. Sec. 240.44 refers to pretrial motions pursuant to Article 255 of the Criminal Procedure Law and that only a suppression hearing pursuant to C.P.L. Sec. 255.10 is applicable to *Rosario*. The court concluded that the language of the statute itself, C.P.L. Sec. 240.44, refers to any and all pretrial hearings and that the psychiatrist's handwritten notes constituted *Rosario* material since these notes were later transmitted into the doctor's formal reports and referred to the witness' testimony and therefore constituted *Rosario* material. The court noted that laboratory report notes and doctor's notes both have been regarded as *Rosario* material and that also the notes taken by an officer relating to his efforts to locate an absent defendant have been held to constitute *Rosario* material and should be introduced at a pretrial Speedy Trial hearing pursuant to C.P.L. Sec. 240.4.

The court, in sum, held on this reasoning that the handwritten notes of the three examining psychiatrists constituted *Rosario* material.

McPhee is an interesting and fruitful decision under C.P.L. Sec. 240.44. The *McPhee* court, in the view of this writer, correctly concluded that the rule of *Rosario* applies to any and all pretrial hearings and not just, as it has been generally applied, to the most common species of suppression hearing. The language of the statute is clear. To limit *Rosario* to the most frequently encountered pretrial suppression hearings is to conclude that because it is most frequently encountered and applied in the context of suppression hearings that the statutory language is to be delimited. *Rosario* is largely a rule of quasi-constitutional fairness and due process. The section applies, most clearly, to all pretrial hearings, whatever their character, nature, or thrust. *McPhee* correctly holds that the codified statutory language, so clear, is to be interpreted clearly and not limited because it is applied only to the most frequent and common types of pretrial hearings and the most common scene, scenario and set of facts.

Codified legislation is in effect the will of the People who spoke through their legislators, and until the legislature otherwise legislates, a statute is to be interpreted not at the whim or wish of the court but as the statute itself clearly mandates and indicates. Thus *McPhee* is a correct and consistent interpretation of C.P.L. Sec. 240.44 as it stands and not as anyone would wish.

46. A Recent Development in New York State Criminal Motion Practice

C.P.L. Sec. 710.6.0, entitled Motion to Suppress Evidence, Procedure, states (sub. I) that a motion to suppress made before trial must be made in writing and upon reasonable notice to the People and with opportunity to be heard. This subdivision further states that the motion papers must state the ground or grounds of the motion and must contain sworn allegations of fact whether of the defendant or of another person or persons. Such allegations may be based upon personal knowledge of the deponent or upon information and belief, provided that in the latter event, the sources of such information and the grounds of such belief are stated. Sub. 3 of this section states that the court may summarily deny the motion if (a) the motion papers do not allege a ground constituting a legal basis for the motion or (b) the sworn allegations of fact do not as a matter of law support the ground alleged; except that this paragraph does not apply where the motion is based upon the ground specified in Sub. 3 of C.P.L. Sec. 710.20.

C.P.L. Sec. 710.60, Secs. 1 and 3, taken together, establish in pertinent part that a suppression motion in this state must first contain sworn allegations of fact and second that this requirement of sworn factual allegations whether based upon personal knowledge or upon information and belief is only applicable to Mapp Motions to suppress tangible property allegedly recovered from the person of the defendant and not to Wade Motions to suppress improper previous identification or a Huntley Motion to suppress involuntary or unconstitutionally obtained statements (C.P.L. Sec. 710.20, 3,6).

What may constitute under New York State law sufficient sworn factual allegations to obtain a Mapp Hearing by the defendant in this state has not been totally made clear.

Thus, most recently in *People v. Kitchen*, 12 A.D.2d 178, 556 N.Y.S.2d 311 (lst Dept. 1994), the First Department held that the defendant's pretrial motion to suppress physical evidence was properly denied without a hearing since his motion papers failed to allege sufficient showing that the property sought to be suppressed had been improperly obtained by the prosecution precluding its admission at trial. The Court went on to state that the defendant's totally conclusory claims failed to set forth factual allegations with respect to his or the police officer's conduct and did not conform to the requirements of the Criminal Procedure Law.

Again, the Second Department held in *People v. Gill*, 138 A.D.2d 738, 526 N.Y.S.2d 552 (2d Dept. 1988), that the defendant failed to set forth sworn allegations of fact pursuant to C.P.L. Sec. 710.60(1) and the People's affirmation in opposition stated that the trooper saw the marijuana in plain view, so giving him the requisite probable cause. The Second Department concluded that the court properly denied suppression of the contraband. See also *People v. Pavesi*, 144 A.D.2d 392, 533 N.Y.S.2d 784 (2d Dept. 1988) (Held: Defendant's motion to suppress was inadequate where the supporting affirmation set forth no allegations in support of the motion and the allegations only made reference to the request for a bill of particulars and other discovery demands which stated in apparently conclusory terms that the property was recovered from the defendant's possession without his consent or any probable cause after he was stopped while a passenger in a car bearing livery plates after having committed no violation of law.) See also *People v. Hernandez*, 124 Misc.2d 840, 479 N.Y.S.2d 105 (S. Ct., Kings County 1984).

The cases on what constitute sufficient sworn factual allegations needful to obtain a Mapp Hearing are legion, and it is clear that actual facts are necessary and not mere legal conclusory allegations as to the lack of probable cause for the arrest or the allegation of unlawful or unconstitutional police conduct. These continue to be insufficient to obtain a Mapp Hearing under C.P.L. Sec. 710.0.

A recent case, however, of the Court of Appeals, *People v. Mendoza et al*, 82 N.Y.2d 415, 609 N.Y.S.2d 922, sheds light on what factual allegations are necessary to obtain a Mapp Hearing,

Mendoza consisted of four appeals from affirmances of the Appellate Division, First Department. The first, *People v. Mendoza,* was an appeal from a plea of guilty of criminal possession of stolen property in the fourth degree. The Appellate Division, First Department affirmed. In the second, *People v. Martinez*, the defendant appealed from a plea of guilty of criminal possession of a weapon in the third degree. The First Department affirmed. In the third, *People v. Coleman,* the defendant appealed from a plea of guilty of criminal sale of a controlled substance in the third degree and endangering the welfare of a child. The First Department affirmed. In the fourth, a juvenile was adjudged to be a juvenile delinquent by the Family Court of Queen's County. The Appellate Division, Second Department, affirmed and the juvenile appealed.

With reference to these appeals, the Court of Appeals initially stated the requirement that a motion to suppress must contain sworn allegations of fact under C.P.L. Sec. 710.60. In each case, the Court of Appeals stated that the trial court denied the suppression motion and the Appellate Division affirmed because the motion did not satisfy the statutory requirement.

The Court of Appeals then proceeded to analyze the structure of C.P.L. Sec. 710.60, the governing statute on the requirement for a legally sufficient motion to suppress, and concluded that hearings are not automatic or available for the asking by boiler-plate allegations but that factual sufficiency should be determined by the face of the pleadings, the context of the motion, and the defendant's access to information, and the court's discretion.

The Court of Appeals then analyzed the facts and character of the motion papers in these cases, in particular, the factual allegation in support of the defendants' motion to suppress. The court then set forth a three-pronged test to sift and analyze what constitutes sufficient suppression motions papers on 1) the fact of the pleadings, 2) the context of the motion, 3) defendant's access to information, 4) the Court's discretion.

By the face of the pleadings, the Court of Appeals apparently meant the defendant's motion and supporting affirmation. The Court of Appeals analyzed what might clearly constitute sufficient factual allegations and whether what can be deemed sufficient can be found in both legal and factual terms. The essential conclusion here was that even if the pleading is partially founded in such legal terms as probable cause or reasonable basis, nevertheless, sufficient facts and not conclusions must be alleged.

The Court of Appeals then proceeded to analyze and define its second criterion, i.e., the context of the motion stating that whether a defendant has raised factual issues requiring a hearing can be determined with reference to the People's contentions. The court noted in this regard that prior to the defendant's actual motion to suppress, a defendant may have received a C.P.L. Sec. 710.30 notice; a VDF, a bill of particulars and supporting depositions and so the defendant is able to specifically deny this information, but if he fails to do so, it may be deemed a concession and may render a hearing unnecessary.

The Court then proceeded to state that the manner in which to measure the sufficiency of the factual averments can be seen in two typical street-crime situations, i.e., the buy and bust operation and the "suspicious" defendant. The court stated that in the former situation probable cause is generated by the drug transaction and it is not enough to say that the defendant was merely standing on the street at the time. He must also deny participation in the drug transaction. The Court of Appeals, with reference to the other scenario, where there is a police allegation that the defendant was acting suspiciously, stated that the defendant could have a factual issue by alleging he was standing in the street when the police approached and searched him.

The court then went on to define and analyze the third criterion to measure a factually sufficient allegation, namely, the degree to which the pleadings may be expected to be precise in view of the information available to the defendant.

Finally, the court stated that C.P.L. Sec. 710.60 does not mandate summary denial of the defendant's motion, although otherwise to some extent factually insufficient, and suggested that if the court orders a Huntley or Wade Hearing and the defendant's Mapp motion is grounded on the same facts, including the same police witnesses, the court may consider it appropriate in the exercise of its discretion to grant the Mapp motion despite a perceived pleading deficiency. The Court of Appeals then proceeded to apply these four criteria to the cases before it and affirmed, except for *Mendoza* which resulted in a modification.

Analysis of this decision of the Court of Appeals and application of the suggested criteria leads one to the first and most important conclusion that facts, and not legal conclusions, must first and foremost be alleged. What is not clear is what, on a case by case basis, will constitute sufficient factual allegations to pass muster under this decision.

Second, the Court suggests that what may constitute sufficient facts is to be measured and filtered by the defendant's pleadings themselves; defendant's motion in context, i.e., whether he has notice; a VDF, or a bill of particulars; information available to the defendant; and the court's discretion where it has granted Wade or Huntley applications.

In sum, the Court suggests that the more information available to the defendant, the more specifically the defendant factually avers and clearly denies, although the court has the discretion if, in the context of the entire omnibus motion, a Wade and/or Huntley Hearing is granted stemming from the same nexus of facts.

Mendoza is a thought-provoking decision, since it establishes the clear necessity for factual allegation for the defendant to obtain a Mapp Hearing and then shows how the courts in the future will measure the sufficiency of those allegations and how they will be judged.

In short, facts, not conclusions, must be alleged in light of the defendant's affirmation, the context of the motion, the defendant's access to information, and whether the Mapp motion is accompanied by a Wade or Huntley application arising from the same transactional facts.

What will follow from the tests established from *Mendoza* remains to be seen and will be fleshed out and made whole by the trial and appellate court decisions on this issue in the future.

47. Batson II

In a previous article in *The Suffolk Lawyer,* entitled "Recent *Batson* Developments," this writer, analyzing two recent Court of Appeals cases, *People v. Kern*, 75 N.Y.2d 638 (1990), and *People v. Bolling and Steele*, N.Y.L.J., 4/8/92, p. 25, col. 1, concluded, based on authoritative language in these cases, that any peremptory strike of a member of the jury panel by the prosecution of any member of a cognizable and protected racial or gender group can give rise to a facial claim by the defense of a *Batson* violation, and it is of no moment that the jury, nevertheless, contains a token member of that racial or gender-protected group. In short, under *Bolling* and *Jenkins*, it is the view of this writer that the former law that a pattern of discriminatory strikes need be established to sustain this violation is no longer good law. See *People v. Jenkins*, *supra*, at 559; *People v. Bolling*, *supra*, at 25.

Indeed, in the more recent case of *People v. Chambers*, decided along with *People v. Mitchell* and *People v. Casiano*, N.Y.L.J. 12/18/92, p.11, col. 1, which held the *Antommarchi* rule not to be retroactive, the Court of Appeals again reiterated the language of *People v. Bolling* that the exclusion of even a single juror on racial grounds is constitutionally forbidden and, on this basis, the Court of Appeals held that the defendant had sustained his *Batson* claim and a new trial was ordered.

The *Childress* Decision: Some Confusing Elements

Most recently, again citing *Jenkins*, the Court of Appeals has broken into a new vista of law on the proper interpretation of *Batson: People v. Childress*, N.Y.L.J., 2/26/93, p. 22, col. 1. *Childress* was an appeal involving the application of *Batson* and, as initially defined by the Court of Appeals, concerned the minimum showing that must be made to establish a prima facie case of unlawful discrimination in the use of peremptory challenges under *Batson*. Also at issue was whether the minutes of the voir dire must be furnished to the appellate court to obtain relief on appeal in a *Batson* claim.

The facts in *Childress* were that the defendant, an African-American, was charged with burglarizing an apartment in Freeport, Long Island. During the jury selection, defense counsel asserted that the prosecutor was using his peremptory challenges to exclude African-American jurors. Specifically in the colloquy on this application, defense counsel indicated that the District Attorney had excluded black jurors on the panel, felt their questioning was proper, pointed out that they indicated no reasons why they could not serve fairly on the jury panel, and since there must be some racially motivated reason on the use of these peremptory challenges, asked the court to exclude those challenges.

The court stated that it did not notice anything and the prosecutor responded that there were three black jurors on the particular panel and that he had in fact accepted one black juror and so was not excluding black jurors because of their race.

Subsequently a 12 person jury was empanelled and the defendant was tried and convicted of burglary in the second degree and possession of burglar's tools.

On appeal from the judgment of conviction, the defendant argued that the trial court had erred in refusing to require the prosecution to furnish a race-neutral explanation for his use of the peremptory challenges to exclude the African-American jurors. The Appellate Division rejected this argument, holding on the basis that the voir dire proceedings had not been made available as part of the record on appeal.

The defendant appealed by permission to the Court of Appeals and that Court affirmed.

Three Important Elements of *Batson*

The Court initially held, again citing *Jenkins* and *Bolling,* that to the extent the trial court based its ruling on any alleged right of the prosecutor to be permitted to make peremptory challenges, regardless of their racial basis, the court clearly misstated the law. The Court went on to state that the Supreme Court in *Batson* and its progeny held that the racially motivated exercise of peremptory challenges violates the Equal Protection Clause of the 14th Amendment. The court then went on to state the three bases for the defense to assert under *Batson* and present a prima facie *Batson* claim.

These, the Court stated, must include a showing that the accused is a member of the cognizable racial group; that the prosecutor excluded one or more members of that race from the venire; and that there exist facts and other relevant circumstances sufficient to raise an inference that the prosecution used his peremptory challenges to exclude potential jurors because of their race.

The Court went on to state that once a prima facie showing has been made, the burden shifts to the prosecution to come forward with a race-neutral explanation for the use of its peremptory challenges. The court then stated the first two elements of a *Batson* claim that the defendant is a member of a cognizable racial group and that the prosecution had used its peremptory strikes to exclude jurors from that same racial group is seldom problematic. The Court, however, stated that the more difficult aspect of a prima facie *Batson* claim is the third element—namely, a showing of facts and other circumstances that would support an inference of impermissible discrimination.

The Court stated that although there were no fixed rules for determining what evidence gives rise to a showing by the defense of the third element, the court noted the third element may be established in other ways: by a pattern of strikes; by questions or statements made during voir dire; by a showing that members of the defendant's racial group were excluded while others with the same relevant characteristics were not; by a showing that the prosecution had stricken members of the defendant's racial group who because of their background and experience might otherwise be expected to be favorably disposed to the prosecution. The court further noted that the third element should also take into consideration the fact that the mere existence of a system of peremptory challenges may serve as a vehicle for discrimination by those with racially-motivated inclinations.

The Court then stated the fact, although rarely dispositive, that a disproportionate number of strikes have been used against members of the defendant's racial group may be indicative of a racially discriminatory motive. Conversely, the mere inclusion of some members of the defendant's ethnic group will not defeat an otherwise meritorious *Batson* motion; the inclusion of token members of a racial group is not an acceptable substitute for a jury selection by racially neutral criteria; and the exclusion of even one member of a group for racial reasons is abhorrent to the fair system of justice.

The Court held, after this analysis, that the defense counsel's sketchy assertion during the colloquy did not establish a basis for relief. The Court stated that while the prosecution admitted that he had exercised his peremptories to strike two of the three African-American jurors, that fact alone is not sufficient to establish a pattern of exclusion sufficient to raise an inference of discrimination. The court rejected the defendant's argument that the burden of proving a pattern of purposeful exclusion should be lessened when the size of the defendant's racial group in a given community is so small as to make statistical evidence unreliable, and the court also rejected the defendant's other assertion that during the *Batson* colloquy, the questioning of the jury was proper and the jurors indicated no reason why they could not serve. The court stated that the latter assertion may serve to show that the stricken jurors demonstrated no biases that would disqualify them for service or support a challenge for cause and that the former assertion was simply too broad and could not support the inference of a discriminatory motive.

The Court noted that in order to give the trial court a proper factual basis for a *Batson* claim and to ensure an adequate record for appellate review, a party asserting a *Batson* claim should articulate and develop all of the grounds supporting the claim, both factual and legal, during the colloquy; and where counsel has perceived something suggesting a discriminatory motive in the questioning of the prospective juror or in answers the juror has given, the specifics underlying defense counsel's concerns should be fully articulated. The court ruled that in this case defense counsel did not satisfy his obligation to state a sound factual basis for his *Batson* claim during the colloquy and that statement in support of his application did not establish the existence of acts and other relevant circumstances sufficient to raise an inference that the prosecutor had used his peremptory challenges to exclude individuals because of race and so affirmed the Appellate Division.

The Importance of the *Childress* Decision

Childress is an important decision on two counts. The first is that the court cites *Jenkins* and *Bolling* with approval. *Jenkins* is cited no less than four times, as is *Bolling*. These cases contain the language, again cited in *Chambers*, that the exclusion of anyone member of a racial- or gender-protected group establishes a prima facie *Batson* claim. It would appear, therefore, that the Court of Appeals may sustain a *Batson* claim based on the exclusion of even one member of a racially or gender protected group.

The second ground on which *Childress* is relevant, and confusing if not actually disturbing, is its focus on the third element that the defendant must establish to sustain a *Batson* claim, i.e., a showing of facts and other relevant circumstances that would support an inference of impermissible discrimination. The Court suggests a number of potential bases to support this third element, including

1. a pattern of strikes or questions and statements made during the voir dire;
2. a showing that members of the defendant's racial group were excluded, while others with the same relevant characteristics were not;
3. a situation where the prosecution has stricken members of the defendant's racial group who because of their background and experience might otherwise be expected to be favorably disposed to the prosecution; and finally,

4. the fact that the mere existence of a system of peremptory challenges may serve as a vehicle for discrimination by those with racially motivated inclinations.

The *Childress* court concluded that the defendant in this case had not made out the third element of a prima facie *Batson* claim, despite his assertion that three African-American jurors were stricken peremptorily, a clear pattern, and that the questioning of these jurors during voir dire indicated their willingness to serve.

General Conclusions

In short, while suggesting that one strike is sufficient to establish a *Batson* claim, the *Childress* court is essentially suggesting that something more is needed and that would seem to be the old pattern law. Thus, while the court states that a pattern is not needed, it suggests in its analysis, nothing more and nothing less. Or, at least, this is the effect of the decision.

Thus, while citing *Bolling*, *Jenkins* and *Chambers* that one racially impermissible strike is sufficient to state a *Batson* violation, the court's analysis of what the defense must show to make out the claim with particular emphasis on the third element mentioned above, effectively results in overruling the language of these cases. and making the showing of a pattern totally necessary.

It remains to be fleshed out how the lower trial and appellate courts will interpret and apply this decision and what will be the final outcome in this area of the law.

Copyright 1994, Andrew J. Schatkin. Reprinted with permission of The Suffolk Bar Association and the <u>Suffolk Lawyer</u>, which disclaim any responsibility for the content.

48. The Confirmatory Identification: A Way to a Hearing

It is the law that where there is a hint of suggestive police arranged identification of the defendant by showup or lineup, the defendant, under *U.S. v. Wade,* 388 U.S. 218 (1967), is entitled to a so-called Wade Hearing. In fact, the showup, the most common form of police arranged identification, is the most suggestive procedure available. *Stovall v. Denno,* 388 U.S. 293 (1967); *People v. Adams,* 53 N.Y.2d 241 (1981). An apparent exception, under New York Law, to the rule of law wherein a Wade Hearing is usually granted, is the confirmatory identification. Simply put, a confirmatory identification is nothing more than an identification by a police officer to other law enforcement officials or an official, that the right man has been nabbed. The context is, in general, where an undercover officer has seen a narcotics sale to the defendant, radios the description of the alleged perpetrator to the backup team, and, in a subsequent driveby or other form of identification, indicates to the backup team that the defendant, who allegedly made the sale to him, is the right man, thereby effectuating the eventual arrest of the defendant. The Courts of the State of New York, have, for the most part, held that this confirmatory identification is not subject to the granting of a Wade Hearing since what is involved is nothing more than good police procedural work in the course of effecting the arrest of the defendant.

The leading case articulating this rule is *People v. Morales,* 37 N.Y.2d 262, 372 N.Y.S.2d 5 (1975). The facts of *Morales* were that in September of 1970 an undercover officer purchased 15 glassine envelopes from the defendant. The officer then informed the backup team, by prearranged signal, that he had completed the drug purchase. The undercover officer then rendezvoused with the backup team where he vouchered the purchase in police property envelopes and wrote a detailed description of *Morales* on the envelope. The detective then cruised the neighborhood until he saw Morales again and then radioed the backup team, directing them to arrest Morales, the man he had described and whom he had seen earlier. Six hours after the arrest, the undercover officer went to the precinct where Morales was being held and viewed and identified the prisoner through a two-way mirror, through which he could see and identify the defendant without being seen.

At trial, the undercover officer, over objection of the defendant, testified to his stationhouse observation of the defendant. The defendant was convicted of criminally selling a dangerous drug. The Appellate Division, however, reversed, holding in part that the defendant's due process rights had been violated by the admission into evidence of the police officer's testimony of that stationhouse identification of the defendant.

The Court of Appeals held that the stationhouse viewing was confirmatory only and that the trial court was correct. The Court of Appeals distinguished a police officer's identification from that of the ordinary citizen, stating it was consonant with good police work. The court noted, particularly, that the identifying officer had been trained for such a role and could be expected to be careful. The courts of this state, trial and appellate, have interpreted *Morales,* for the most part, to mandate denial of a Wade Hearing under the circumstances of a confirmatory identification. See *People v. Leftwich,* 82 Misc.2d 993, 372 N.Y.S.2d 888 (S.Ct. New York County 1975); *People v. Laurain,* 84 Misc.2d 970, 378 N.Y.S.2d 599 (S.Ct. New York County 1976); *People v. Stanton,* 108 A.D.2d 688, 485 N.Y.S.2d 998 (1st Dept. 1985); *People v. Smith,* 103 Misc.2d 513, 426 N.Y.S.2d 420 (Westchester County Court 1980); *People v. Marrero,* 110 A.D.2d 785, 487 N.Y.S.2d 853 (2nd Dept. 1985).

A number of trial and appellate courts, however, have, depending on the circumstances, taken exception to the *Morales* rule of law. *People v. Rubio,* A.D.2d 879, 500 N.Y.S.2d 366 (2d Dept. 1986), is apropos. *Rubio* was an appeal from a judgment of conviction of Criminal Sale of a Controlled Substance in the Third Degree and Criminal Possession of a Controlled Substance in the Third and Seventh Degrees. The matter was remitted by the Second Department for a Wade Hearing.

The case, in essence, arose out of an undercover sale in which the defendant acted as intermediary between the seller and the undercover officer. No arrest was made at the time of the transaction and when the police returned several hours later the suspects could not be located. Twenty-seven days later the informant spotted the defendant in the area of the location of the sale, the police were notified and the defendant was arrested and brought to the station house where he was identified by the undercover officer through a two-way mirror.

The defendant's pretrial motion to suppress the undercover's stationhouse identification was denied by the trial court and, at trial, the officer testified regarding his observation and identification of the defendant at the precinct. The Second Department held that the question whether the station house identification should be regarded as merely confirmatory of the previous identification, or improper, should have been determined by a Wade Hearing. The Appellate Court noted that *Morales* should not be viewed or read as having dispensed with a Wade Hearing invariably under all these circumstances and that the particular facts in hand may suggest that a reasonable possibility exists that the officer's identification of the defendant might be the product of the stationhouse viewing rather than the observations made during the commission of the crime.

See also *People v. Williams,* 79 A.D.2d 929, (1st Dept. 1981); *People v. Lugo,* 62 A.D.2d 1024, 403 N.Y.S.2d 550 (2d Dept. 1978); *People v. Boyle,* 134 Misc.2d 338, 510 N.Y.S.2d 987 (S.Ct. Kings County 1987); *People v. Wright,* 47 A.D.2d 894 (1st Dept. 1975).

It is clear that although the general rule of law in this state is that a Wade Hearing will be denied where there is apparently a confirmatory identification only, it is also clear that, depending on the discrete facts alleged, particularly if there is a gap of time between the initial observations of the undercover officer and the confirmatory identification, a Wade Hearing may be granted.

Hence, it is essential that defense counsel, if he would gain a Wade Hearing in the context of a confirmatory identification must, contrary to the specific requirement of law and practice under the Criminal Procedure Law, allege specific facts to establish a time gap between the initial observations of the undercover officer and the confirmatory identification. This may be difficult since, in point of fact and truth, a legally sufficient *Rubio* time gap may not in fact exist.

What then, if any, is the method whereby a Wade Hearing may be granted absent a specific time gap where the identification is confirmatory as so far defined in this article?

People v. Acevedo, 575 N.Y.S.2d 288 (1st Dept. 1991), provides an answer. *Acevedo* was an appeal from a judgment of the Supreme Court, New York County, convicting the defendant, upon a jury verdict, of Criminal Sale of a Controlled Substance in the Third Degree and sentencing him, as a second felony offender, to an indeterminate term of imprisonment of four and one-half to nine years in prison. In *Acevedo,* the defendant was indicted for Criminal Sale of a Controlled Substance in the Third Degree and, thereafter, moved to suppress any physical evidence and identification testimony. In the portion of his motion papers seeking to suppress physical evidence, defense counsel alleged that the defendant was grabbed and searched immediately after exiting a building where he had been visiting a friend. The defendant maintained that since his search and seizure was not based upon probable cause, any property recovered must be suppressed and also argued that the so-called confirmatory identification by the undercover officer must as well be suppressed, since that occurred after the defendant was arrested without probable cause. In response to the defendant's motion to suppress, the People stated they would not introduce the physical evidence against him at trial and opposed the motion to suppress the identification, stating that the identification was merely confirmatory in character, was not therefore suggestive, was not obtained in violation of the defendant's right to counsel and was obtained after the defendant's arrest which, the people argued, was supported by probable cause.

The Supreme Court denied the defendant's motion to suppress the physical evidence as "moot" and summarily his request for a Wade/Dunaway Hearing. The First Department held most succinctly and in no uncertain terms, that, since the defendant in his motion papers alleged facts challenging the constitutionality of his arrest and further alleged that the identification was the fruit of the allegedly illegal activity, it was error to deny his request for a hearing. The Court noted in conclusion that the People's response merely created issues of facts which would be resolved by a hearing.

The holding of *Acevedo* is clear, namely, that where sufficient facts are alleged by the defendant challenging the constitutionality of the arrest and the ordinarily considered confirmatory identification as the fruit of the illegal arrest lacking probable cause, the basic rule of law that such confirmatory identification does not entitle the defendant to a Hearing, absent a proper allegation under *Rubio* and the cases following it of the time gap between the undercover officer's initial observations and the confirmatory identification, does not hold and a Wade Hearing under this second method based on facts alleging lack of probable cause for the arrest may be had. That the People say otherwise, the First Department stated, merely creates an issue of fact which could only be resolved by a Hearing.

See also *People v. Antonio Vasquez*, N.Y.L.J., 1/19/91 p. 26, col. 5 (Criminal Court New York County); *People v. Sellers*, N.Y.L.J. p. 28, col. 5 (2d Dept. 1990).

It is significant that the First Department in the *Acevedo* decision cited two First Department decisions, *People v. Mosley*, 136 A.D.2d 500, 523 N.Y.S.2d 820 (1st Dept. 1988), and *People v.* Marte, 149 A.D.2d 335, 539 N.Y.S.2d 912 1st Dept. 1989). In *Mosley,* the First Department considered the rule of law that, where the People allege the complainant and defendant know each other, the defense is not entitled to a Wade Hearing, since once again the identification is considered confirmatory. See *People v. Tas,* 151 N.Y.2d 915, 434 N.Y.S.2d 978, 415 N.E.2d 967 (1980); *People v. Gissendanner,* 48 N.Y.2d 543, 423 N.Y.S.2d 893, 319 N.E.2d 925 (1979).

Mosley was an appeal from a judgment of the Supreme Court of New York County, convicting the defendant of Robbery in the First Degree and sentencing him to a term of 10-20 years incarceration. On appeal, the issue was the trial court's denial of the defense motion to suppress identification evidence. In *Mosley* the defendant was arrested and charged with Robbery in the First and Second Degree. After the arraignment on the indictment, the defendant moved to suppress, alleging a suggestive show-up and denying ever having seen the complainant. The prosecutor who opposed the motion alleged the identification procedure used in the case was a confirmatory show-up and that the complainant knew the defendant from the building. Thereafter the trial court denied the defense counsel application for a Wade Hearing on the ground that the identification procedure used was not at issue, based solely on the People's assertion that the parties knew each other.

At trial, identification was an issue before the jury. The complainant testified that his familiarity with the defendant arose from his allegedly having seen him through a peephole passing in the hall and once allegedly having passed him on the stairs.

The court reasoned that the allegations made in support of the defendant's motion would, if contradicted, have been sufficient to warrant suppression and that the People's response did no more than raise an issue of fact which could be resolved only upon a hearing. In short, the court held that where the motion papers submitted by the defense raise an issue of fact, a Wade Hearing is appropriate and necessary. Thus, the Appellate Division, First Department, remanded to the Supreme Court for a hearing on the defendant's motion to suppress the identification evidence.

Mosley, in essence, held that where, despite the People's denomination of the identification as confirmatory due to the parties' prior familiarity with each other, the defense in its motion papers raises an issue of fact as to the extent of the defendant's and complainant's acquaintanceship with each other or whether they actually knew each other, a Wade Hearing is mandated. See also *People v. Marte,* 49 A.D.2d 335, 539 N.Y.S.2d 912 (1st Dept. 1989), where, citing *Mosley*, the First Department held this time in the context of the defense application for a Mapp Hearing, that where the defense counsel's affirmation in support of his motion for Mapp relief was sufficient to place in issue the lawfulness of the defendant's arrest and the reply affirmation of the Assistant District Attorney did not resolve the issue, a hearing should be granted.

It would appear that the First Department has been moving to a rule that where an issue of fact is raised in the defendant's motion papers, be it an application for Wade or Mapp relief, a hearing is appropriate if, in fact, the factual assertions of the People are contradicted by the defense.

Thus, in light of *Acevedo* and *Mosley*, where there is what the People label a "confirmatory identification," it is imperative that the proper allegations are made challenging the confirmatory identification, either, as in the case of an undercover sale, by alleging the arrest lacked probable cause, or, in the context where the People allege the parties know each other, then by challenging the degree of their intimacy. Under such circumstances, a Wade Hearing may be obtained, in spite of the line of case law holding against granting such a hearing.

Copyright 1994 by the New York State Association of Criminal Defense Lawyers. Reprinted with permission.

49. A Note on Sentencing

After a plea is taken in a criminal case or after a conviction following trial, if the defendant is out on bail or released on his own recognizance, there is always the danger, despite the requisite warnings to return having been given by the court, that the defendant will not return· to court on the date of sentencing, and, having failed to appear in court on the date of sentencing, that a warrant will be issued for his arrest.

If the defendant be returned to court on the outstanding warrant, whether voluntarily or involuntarily, defense counsel and his client are faced with the possibility of the sentence, whether promised after the plea or after conviction, being substantially increased.

It is true that a presentence report can be submitted by defense counsel in mitigation of the sentence pursuant to C.P.L. Sec. 390.20.

The question arises, however, and it is the subject of this article, whether anything else can be done in mitigation of this negative scenario.

The answer is contained in Sec. 380.30 of the Criminal Procedure Law and the cases construing it. That Section states under Sub. 1 that in general the sentence must be pronounced without unreasonable delay. The leading case interpreting this section is *People v. Drake,* 61 N.Y.2d 359, 474 N.Y.S.2d 276, 462 N.E.2d 376 (1984). In *Drake,* the defendant was convicted in the Supreme Court of Albany County of Grand Larceny in the Third Degree and appealed. The Appellate Division, Third Department, affirmed. The facts were that the defendant was employed as a supervisor for the New York State Department of Taxation and Finance and, in May of 1976, was called for jury duty at a term of the Albany County Court. The prosecution claimed that the defendant stole portions of two salary checks by presenting a false time card which indicated that he was on jury duty on specified days when, in fact, he was not. Following a jury trial the defendant was found guilty of Grand Larceny in the Third Degree. He was sentenced 39 months later to a conditional discharge.

The defendant contended on appeal that the judgment must be vacated and the indictment dismissed because of the court's unreasonable delay in sentencing him. Citing in particular *People ex rel. Harty,* 10 N.Y.2d 374, 223 N.Y.S.2d 468, 199 N.E.2d 483, and other pertinent case law, the Court of Appeals reversed and remitted to the trial court for a hearing to determine whether the unreasonable delay was excusable. The court held that once a person has been criminally charged and prosecuted, a burden rests on the prosecutor and the court to conclude the proceeding with reasonable promptness and that the failure to do so may result in loss of jurisdiction.

The court stated that it is no excuse that the delay may have been occasioned by extended pleas for leniency and held that the delay of 39 months in this case was unreasonable, with nothing to excuse it, and that the indictment must be dismissed. The court fashioned a rule that whether dismissal is warranted depends upon the length of the delay and reasons for it, and that generally where the delay is long and unexplained, that the court will hold it unreasonable. Conversely, where the delay is not protracted and plausible reasons are offered to explain, the delay will not be held unreasonable. The court went on to state that where there has been an extended delay and there are plausible reasons for it the various factors must be balanced. The court then stated that the New York rule assumes the defendant to have been prejudiced by the unreasonable delay; that he need not prove it; that he is not required to take affirmative measures and demand that the court sentence him; and that the burden rests on the State and its agents. The Court of Appeals concluded that the delay of 39 months was unreasonable and, as unexcused, resulted in the loss of jurisdiction requiring dismissal of the indictment.

Similarly, in the earlier case of *People ex rel. Harty, supra,* cited in *Drake* as controlling, the Court of Appeals held that the trial court had lost its jurisdiction where the sentence for robbery was delayed for six years after the entry of a guilty plea; the matter was earlier called to the attention of the prosecutor, and the sentence was therefore void and the defendant was therefore entitled to a writ of habeas corpus. See also *People ex rel. Acurso v. McMann* (3rd Dept. 1965); *People v. Valdes,* 121 Misc.2d 201 (Criminal Court, New York County 1983).

It is clear that under the foregoing analysis of the case law, that where, for one reason or another there is in fact a delay in sentencing due to the defendant having warranted, or for some other reason, that all is not lost for the defense. Under *Drake,* the controlling Court of Appeals decision and the cases following it under Sec. 380.30 of the Criminal Procedure Law, the defendant is entitled to a prompt sentencing after conviction and depending upon the length of the delay and the reasons for it, the court upon motion of the defense under C.P.L. Sec. 380.30 may lose jurisdiction and obtain that the indictment will be dismissed. It is the responsibility of the State to sentence the defendant and an extended delay without excuse may under this rule of law result in dismissal of the indictment.

Thus, where the defendant has warranted at the time of sentencing, applying the rule of law enunciated in *Drake* and *Harty,* defense counsel may, nevertheless, salvage an otherwise apparently impossible scenario and, so to speak, obtain victory from the jaws of defeat, by making a *"Drake"* Motion, so possibly obtaining dismissal of the indictment.

50. Why I Am Opposed to the Death Penalty

The Death Penalty spells an end to life. The argument is that the full measure of vengeance by the People comes upon another who has taken a life and deters other societal miscreants from doing the same.

Admittedly, homicide is the most heinous of crimes. Yet, not only as a criminal defense lawyer, but as a citizen and a whole person, I oppose it. I do so, not because I believe that it does not truly deter future murders—as I do—and not because I believe that mistakes are made in the criminal justice process and thus the death penalty may be wrongly imposed—as I do—but because every man or woman, be he or she among the handicapped, the elderly, mentally disabled, and yes, the children, all have value. Value is to be accorded to all, not due to their apparent superior intellect or talents, not because of their superior financial status, and not because they are the ruling or dominant class, sex, or race. Those who think themselves so much better are so due to environment, opportunity or the current fashion. The baseball player or rock star is paid millions. Mother Teresa earns nothing for all her service to the outcasts: unwanted, underprivileged, poor. She sees value in all, not because of what they have but because of what they are.

Jesus, a great teacher, forgave the criminals beside him at the moment of his death. He points the way to the truth. It is the way of civilization, the way of all the great religions and teachers, the way of Tao, Buddha, Confucius, and the Talmud. However disheveled, unattractive and apparently abominable, there is value in all.

A society that sees no value in life itself—even in the murderers—falls short of that respect and devotion to life in all its forms that must govern any enlightened society. It is not the outside of a man or woman I see, but the inside, the inner light. This inner light may be found in all, even the weak and the seemingly unattractive. Any civilization or society that chooses to exterminate any of its members for facial reasons of justice, vengeance and deterrence falls short of the measure of an enlightened civilization. Five thousand years have passed since the Code of Hammurabi. If we have not grown up from it, let us at least grow away from it. The English common law once executed pickpockets. That is no longer so. If we are to avoid the stigma of barbarism, let us once and for all cease what amounts to no less than murder in the name of justice. Let us acknowledge that we do not raise ourselves by ending the lives of others. I oppose the Death Penalty, for no other reason than we devalue ourselves and our society by placing no value on a life. This is the way beyond the Holocaust, beyond the Cambodia Genocide and beyond Genghis Khan. Let us take that step.

This article is being reprinted from The Summation, *a publication of the Criminal Courts Bar Association of the County of Queens. That association is no longer in existence.*

51. Some Cases on Alias

The reference to a fictitious name or alias if used by the defendant, whether by the prosecutor on his direct case or through impeaching cross-examination should the defendant take the stand, if permitted by the trial court, can have a potentially disastrous effect on the outcome of a criminal trial for the defense. This is because the jury, although faced with a limiting instruction by the trial judge on this issue, may well draw the inference that where there is smoke there is fire and that the defendant must be guilty, having been engaged in prior criminal, illegal, unlawful, or immoral activity.

Two recent cases, one decided by the Court of Appeals and the other by the Appellate Division, Second Department, reveal the developing law on the reference to defendant's use of an alias or fictitious name, whether by the prosecutor on his direct case or on impeaching cross-examination.

The first, and more significant, case is *People v. Walker*, 83 N.Y.2d 455 (1994). In *Walker*, the defendant was charged with the crimes of Criminal Sale and Possession of a Controlled Substance in the Third Degree. The trial court conducted a Sandoval Hearing with reference both to the defendant's prior convictions and the defendant's use of aliases and other false pedigree information. The People stated that the defendant had used 14 different names and given five different dates of birth and the prosecutor asked to be permitted to cross-examine the defendant on the latter should the defendant choose to take the stand.

Defense counsel offered various explanations for the use of these aliases. After the hearing argument, the court ruled that the People would be permitted to question the defendant about his use of aliases and various dates of birth.

The defendant was subsequently convicted, after a jury trial, of Criminal Sale of a Controlled Substance in the Third Degree and was sentenced to an indeterminate term of imprisonment of 6–12 years. The Appellate Division affirmed. The defendant went on to testify at trial. On appeal to the Court of Appeals, the defendant argued that his use of aliases on prior occasions unrelated to the case on trial was not a proper subject for impeachment and that there should be a special preliminary inquest into the underlying facts whenever the People seek to use alias evidence for impeachment purposes.

The court initially noted that the only present question of law before it was whether the trial court erred as a matter of law in rejecting defense counsel's assertions for limiting cross-examination with regard to the defendant's use of aliases.

The court went on to state that impeachment by cross-examination not only involves an inquiry of the witness that he has been guilty of prior immoral, vicious, or criminal conduct, but also that the elucidation of such facts may demonstrate an untruthful character or reveal a willingness or disposition of the defendant to place his advancement or his self-interest ahead of the interests of society, for the purpose of discrediting the witness or to persuade the trier of fact that the witness is not being truthful.

The court went on, further, to state that a suspect's use of a false name is an indication of dishonesty and shows a willingness to place his individual self-interest ahead of society. The court noted that such evidence is relevant and material to the credibility and honesty of the witness, and so a proper subject for cross-examination. The court went on to state that potentially innocent explanations for the defendant's use of aliases are not a sufficient basis to treat alias evidence differently or to carve out an exception to the general rule that the nature and extent of cross-examination are matters entrusted to the sound discretion of the trial court and that the trier of fact may be entrusted to determine the probative worth of this evidence.

Thus the court concluded that there was no need for a special rule to govern use of alias evidence for impeachment since no undue prejudice would follow but the expected negative impact that naturally flows from evidence elicited for the purpose of impeachment.

Applying these principles, the Court of Appeals held that defense counsel's innocent explanation for the defendant's use of false names and birth dates was highly speculative and did not suggest a legal reason to mandate preclusion. The court in sum stated that the trial court did not exceed or abuse its discretion over the nature and extent of cross-examination when it determined that the People could cross-examine the defendant regarding his prior use of aliases and other false pedigree information.

It should be noted that in a footnote at the end of this decision, the Court of Appeals added that although a Sandoval Hearing on this issue was not mandatory, it would be a practical vehicle, stating that the defendant's use of aliases could be correlated with his prior convictions to ensure that only aliases associated with admissible prior crimes would be used for impeachment purposes and that such procedure would minimize the surprise factor and enable the defendant to make an informed choice as to whether to testify.

Walker is both a provocative and disturbing decision. In essence, the Court of Appeals allows—although it suggested the use of a Sandoval procedure to determine this issue—the total impeachment of the defendant should he choose to testify. To be sure, the court adds that in fact prior convictions are to be correlated with the use of the defendant's aliases and suggested a Sandoval Hearing. The net effect here is to allow the defendant to be made out as a renegade and antisocial individual. For who else but a criminal uses one or more fictitious names? A jury that hears such evidence will draw the inevitable conclusion that "where there is smoke, there is fire," or, at least, that the defendant has been up to no good.

People v. Miller, 123 A.D.2d 721, 507 N.Y.S.2d 409 (2d Dept. 1988), is equally distressing for the defense on this issue. In *Miller* the Second Department held that the trial court properly admitted into evidence testimony regarding the defendant's use of an alias, stating that such testimony is evidence of his consciousness of guilt and noting that the court gave a limiting instruction regarding the probative value of that evidence. The Second Department also held that the People were not required to serve the defendant with notice of their intent to offer into evidence testimony that the defendant gave a fictitious name to the arresting officer, since such information is of a pedigree nature and so not subject to a motion to suppress.

Miller precedes *Walker* but is equally thought-provoking and disturbing from the defense perspective. *Miller* not only allows testimony regarding the defendant's use of aliases as evidence of guilt, but does not even afford the defendant the opportunity of notice by the People of this inquiry.

Thus, both *Miller* and *Walker* allow both on direct and cross-examination for the People to effectively "convict" the defendant in the eyes of the jury. Under this line of case law, the defendant may be caught by surprise on the People's direct case and impeached on cross-examination should he choose to testify.

This is nothing more nor less than total discreditation in the eyes of the citizen jury, who will conclude that the man who lies about who he is must be of a criminal cast who has or must have something to hide.

Allowing the revelation to the jury of an alias will inevitably lead the jury to believe that this man is a criminal or at least of an unsavory character. In many ways, to permit the People to discredit the defendant by this evidence is to allow the defendant to be convicted by uncharged crimes. In this sense, both *Walker* and *Miller* ignore the obvious *Molineaux* issue and so must be regarded as unfair and wrong as painting the picture of a man of questionable past and character when, in fact, all the trier of fact need to be concerned with are the facts of the case before him or her. In a way, these two cases permit a form of conviction by libel or slander serving to allow the impeachment of the defendant's character when all the trier of fact need be concerned with are the facts of the case before him and that justice be done from a full and fair perspective.

It is to be hoped that *Walker* and *Miller* will not be forever and that future and fairer case law will be made in this field.

52. Mental Competency and the Grand Jury

C.P.L. Sec. 60.20, entitled *Rules of Evidence; testimonial capacity; evidence given by children*, states, in pertinent part, that any person may be a witness in a criminal proceeding unless the court finds that by reason of infancy or mental disease or defect that person does not possess sufficient intelligence or capacity to justify the reception of this evidence. C.P.L. Sec. 60.20(1), Subdivision 2, of this statute further states:

2. Every witness more than twelve years old may testify only under oath unless
the court is satisfied that such witness cannot, as a result of mental disease or
defect, understand the nature of an oath. A child less than twelve years old may
not testify under oath unless the court is satisfied that he understands the nature
of an oath. If the court is not so satisfied, such child or such witness over
twelve years old who cannot, as a result of mental disease or defect, understand
the nature of an oath may nevertheless be permitted to give unsworn evidence
if the court is satisfied that the witness possesses sufficient intelligence and capacity to justify the reception thereof.

It is clear from the language of this statute that if there is a question of the
mental competency of a witness over 12 years of age, the statute envisions that
there must be a determination by the trial judge that the witness understands the
nature of an oath or his testimony may be excluded. It should be noted that Subdivision 2 of the statute permits the witness to give unsworn evidence, even
though the witness may not, as a result of his mental incapacity, understand the
nature of an oath, *so long as the court is so satisfied* that the witness possesses
sufficient intelligence and capacity to justify the reception of such testimony. At
the same time, Subdivision 3 of this same statute adds that a defendant may not
be convicted of an offense solely upon unsworn evidence given pursuant to
Subdivision 2.

In short, as regards the purported mental incompetent, the statute apparently
mandates a proceeding whereby the trial judge must inquire and determine
whether the witness possesses sufficient evidence of, or capacity to, justify the
reception of his evidence (C.P.L. Sec. 60.20, Sub. 1); whether he understands
the nature of an oath; and whether, if he does not, he may be permitted to give
unsworn evidence pursuant to C.P.L. Sec. 60.20, Sub. 2.

People v. Chan, 110 A.D.2d 158, 493 N.Y.S.2d 778 (2d Dept. 1985), is an
example of the procedure whereby, under C.P.L. Sec. 60.20, a court determined
and ruled on the mental competency of a witness over 12 years of age. *Chan* was
an appeal from a judgment of conviction of the Supreme Court of Queens
County, in which the defendant was convicted of Kidnapping in the First Degree, Robbery in the First Degree, and Grand Larceny in the First Degree. The
facts were these: on January 12, 1982, a certain Mr. Cheng and his son were
leaving their family residence when they were forced back inside the house at
gunpoint by two men and a woman. Mrs. Cheng and her daughter were home at
the time. The family safe was opened and $7,000 and an amount of jewelry were
taken by the intruders. Tung Cheng, the son, was removed from the premises
and he was returned later that day after Mr. and Mrs. Cheng, accompanied by
two of their captors, withdrew $100,000 from a bank and surrendered the money
for the safe return of their son.

On the first day of trial, Mrs. Cheng recounted the events of January 12,
1982, and identified the defendant, Chan, as one of the three people who had invaded her home. On the second day of trial, Mrs. Cheng was asked if she were a
prisoner and she stated her husband had threatened her in order to appear. She
also asked if she could avoid appearing if she felt ill. At a subsequent discussion

in the Judge's chambers, Mrs. Cheng stated that she had been threatened by gangsters from Hong Kong and was asked questions about her allegation that her husband was protecting an illegal person. Mrs. Cheng also expressed a reluctance to testify if she was not protected from the people who had threatened her.

Defense counsel alleged that Mrs. Cheng had a history of suicide attempts and had been previously diagnosed as a schizophrenic. Mrs. Cheng, however, stated that she could proceed, that she was not taking medication for a mental condition and that she had been falsely accused of being mentally ill. The court also spoke for fifteen minutes with an attorney who had represented Mrs. Cheng on a matrimonial matter and the attorney opined that she could proceed.

At this point, defense counsel moved for a mistrial based on Mrs. Cheng's alleged mental condition and her stated desire to avoid questioning. The court granted the motion pursuant to C.P.L. Sec. 280.10. At this point, for reasons of strategy, the defense counsel withdrew his mistrial motion and the trial proceeded. Prior to resumption of Mrs. Cheng's testimony, defense counsel requested that her testimony be stricken or that she be examined by a psychiatrist with regard to her testimony. The court ruled that it would allow her to testify and subsequently Mrs. Cheng's testimony was beneficial and exculpatory to the defense.

The issue before the appellate court, was, in point and essence, whether the trial court had made an informed determination of Mrs. Cheng's competency to testify and thus did not abuse its discretion in so allowing her to testify despite her admitted history of mental illness. The court noted that a person who is able to understand the nature of an oath and who is able to give a reasonably accurate account of what she has seen and heard with regard to the matters in issue may testify despite a history of mental illness. The court held it is within the discretion of the trial judge to determine whether a person has the mental capacity to testify since he or she has the opportunity to observe the witness's manner and demeanor and make the necessary inquiry concerning the mental capacity of the witness.

The court held that here the trial court did not abuse its discretion in ruling on Mrs. Cheng's capacity to testify and in allowing her to do so. The court noted that the record showed that Mrs. Cheng understood the nature of an oath prior to testifying; that her testimony was clear and lucid; that there was an extensive inquiry by the court into Mrs. Cheng's mental state, during which she asserted that she was not mentally ill and denied being on medication; and that her attorney opined that she was competent to testify.

It is clear, under *Chan* as an example, that, in short, the matter of the mental competency of a witness is within the discretion of the trial judge and, given the sufficiency of the inquiry and determination by the latter, is not to be overturned on appeal.

In sum, in *Chan*, there was, on the record, pursuant to C.P.L. Sec. 60.20, the requisite inquiry by the trial court and the resulting decision by the trial court on the issue of mental competency. See also *People v. Berardicurti*, 167 A.D.2d 840, 561 N.Y.S.2d 949 (4th Dept. 1990).

The question arises, then, if there is an issue of the mental competency of a witness for the People before the Grand Jury, should the issue of the mental capacity of the witness be cast into question or the People be made aware of it, does the trial court have the same and equal responsibility, as at trial, to make the necessary inquiry?

The answer is contained in C.P.L. Sec. 190.30, Sub. 1, which states that ". . . except as provided in this section, the provisions of Article 60 governing rules of evidence and related matters with respect to criminal proceedings in general, are, where appropriate, applicable to Grand Jury proceedings."

At first blush, under the above section, it would seem the trial judge has the responsibility to make the necessary inquiry as to the mental competence of a Grand Jury witness.

This, however, is apparently contradicted by C.P.L. Sec. 190.30, Sub. 6, which states that wherever it is provided in Article 60 that the court must rule upon the competence of a witness to testify or upon the admissibility of evidence, such ruling may in an equivalent situation be made by the Grand Jury Assistant District Attorney. It seems, under this statutory section, that if the People in the Grand Jury are aware or made aware of the issue of the mental competence of a witness that there must be a concomitant determination by the District Attorney in the matter of the witness's competency.

The case law supports this view. *People v. Gorgone*, 47 A.D.2d 347, 366 N.Y.S.2d 647 (1st Dept. 1975), was an appeal from a plea of guilty of Criminal Contempt in the First Degree. In *Gorgone*, the defendant was called as a witness before a New York County Grand Jury investigating the murder of Joseph Gallo. The defendant appeared before the Grand Jury on three separate occasions in the Fall of 1972. On his first appearance before the Grand Jury, the District Attorney advised Mr. Gorgone that he had been granted immunity and attempted, apparently unsuccessfully, to explain the meaning of this terminology. Mr. Gorgone protested that he did not understand and that the questions tended to irritate him and that he was dizzy and nervous.

On his second appearance before the Grand Jury, he told the Assistant District Attorney that he was very sick and presented a letter from the Medical Director of St. Vincent's Hospital clinic stating he had been a clinic patient there since 1964, following a construction accident which had produced considerable cerebral damage.

The defendant was then taken before the court for a direction to answer questions and on a subsequent date he appeared with assigned counsel who informed the court that the defendant had been under psychiatric treatment for many years following a head injury and that his client did not understand the questions. Counsel then requested that Gorgone be sent to the court's psychiatric clinic to determine his mental competency. The request was denied.

At another appearance before the Grand Jury, the defendant answered questions he had previously refused to answer but had great difficulty in answering them. Prior to trial, on defense counsel's motion, Mr. Gorgone was examined by two court-appointed psychiatrists who found that the defendant was not mentally competent. Upon filing this report, defendant moved for dismissal of the indictment. This application was denied. The prosecutor then moved for defendant's mandatory commitment to a state institution pursuant to C.P.L Sec. 730.50. Following a hearing on the report, the court refused to order commitment without a more recent report on defendant's present condition and ordered another examination for such purpose. Subsequently, the defendant pled guilty and was sentenced to five years' probation.

The Appellate Court held the defendant's motion to dismiss the indictment was improperly denied by the trial court. What is most significant is that the court specifically held, quoting C.P.L. Sec. 190.30, that it is mandatory in such a case as this that the question of witness competency be resolved by the District Attorney in the same way that a court would resolve it.

See also *People v. Groff,* 71 N.Y.2d 101, 524 N.Y.S.2d 13, 518 N.E.2d 190 (1987); *People v. Zigles,* 119 Misc.2d 417, (Suffolk County Court, 1983).

It is clear, under the controlling weight of authority, that where in the Grand Jury proceeding there is a question of the mental competency of a witness over 12 years of age, there must be a thorough inquiry by the Assistant District Attorney in the Grand Jury as to the matter of the witness's competency.

It is also the law that this inquiry must appear on the record and if it does not, then reversal and dismissal of the indictment is the result. This is illustrated by *People v. Rivera,* 141 Misc.2d 14, 532 N.Y.S.2d 660 (S. Ct. Kings County, 1988); *aff'd.* 151 A.D.2d 518, 542 N.Y.S.2d 366. In *Rivera,* the defendant was indicted for sodomy based on Grand Jury testimony of a child witness under 12 years of age.

There was, however, no record in the Grand Jury minutes of any determination or allocution by the District Attorney or of a judge that the child was competent to testify as a sworn witness. The District Attorney informed the court that, without making a record, she had in fact conducted such an inquiry and made a determination as to the child's competency.

Noting the obligation of the court under C.PL. Sec. 60.20 to determine the competency of a child witness and the equal obligation of the People under C.PL. Sec. 190.30 to do so, the court opined that upon a motion to inspect and dismiss to determine the sufficiency of the evidence under these circumstances, the procedure whereby the District Attorney determined whether the child should be sworn was critical to the court's evaluation of the sufficiency of the evidence and that without a record of that proceeding, the court was unable to review a critical ruling by the Assistant District Attorney in the Grand Jury. In short, the court held there must be a stenographic record of this inquiry, or a videotape, and that the court should not have to rely on a reconstruction of the preliminary examination made later. The court, therefore, dismissed the indictment. It is clear, by analogy, that this ruling as to the necessity of a transcript for determining the competency of a witness under 12 applies in equal force to the mental incompetent over 12 years of age.

It is, however, not only the law that, by preference, the court should make such inquiry and the Assistant District Attorney in the Grand Jury is mandated to do so, but also the Grand Jury itself should be so informed if the question of competency exists and be given an opportunity to inquire and to determine the issue of the witness's competency.

People v. Gerber, 44 Misc.2d 125, 253 N.Y.S.2d 212 (Onondaga County Court, 1964), speaks to this issue. *Gerber* concerned a motion to dismiss two indictments on the ground that evidence presented to the Grand Jury was insufficient. The witnesses in the Grand Jury were children, both eight years of age, and the father of one of the girls. The father's testimony was used solely to establish the fact that the defendant was over 21 years of age. There was no corroborative evidence, either direct or circumstantial, with regard to the crime charged, which included counts of Sodomy, Assault and Impairing the Morals of a Child.

The People defined the question to be whether a Grand Jury can return an indictment on the uncorroborated testimony of a child under 12 years of age—where that body has determined that the child possesses testimonial capacity. The court noted that in pursuit of his brief the Assistant District correctly stated the Grand Jury is an independent tribunal with the power to determine the qualifications of witnesses who may testify before it, and it is within the Grand Jury's province to determine whether or not the child should be sworn.

It is true that this statement of the law was *in dicta* since the court ultimately dismissed the indictment as resting on the uncorroborated testimony of two child witnesses.

The language of *Gerber,* however, is clear that the Grand Jury has both the right and responsibility to rule on the question of competency, whether that of an underage child or the mental competency, by analogy, of a person over 12 years of age.

See also *People v. Gallia,* 192 N.Y.S.2d 43 (Erie County Court 1959).

Conclusion

This brief review of the statue and case law on the issue of competency in the Grand Jury reveals that the Assistant District Attorney has absolute responsibility to rule on the question, should he be made aware of the question of the competency of a witness; that that inquiry must be transcribed; and finally, that the Grand Jury itself should be made aware of the issue of the competency of a witness and be allowed to make the final determination.

Reprinted with permission from the New York State Bar Journal, December 1994, Vol. 66. No. 8, published by the New York State Bar Association, One Elk Street, Albany, New York 12207.

53. The Forty-Five Day Rule

Sec. 255.20 of the Criminal Procedure Law, entitled Pretrial Motion Procedure, states in pertinent part, in terse and summary form, that where the defendant is represented by counsel or elects to proceed pro se, all pretrial motions shall be served or filed within forty-five days after arraignment and before the commencement of trial, or within such additional time as the court may fix upon application of the defendant. Sub. 3 of C.P.L. Sec. 255.20 adds that despite the provisions of subsections one and two the court must entertain and decide on its merits, at any time before the end of the trial, any appropriate pretrial motion based upon grounds of which the defendant could not, with due diligence, have been previously aware or which for good cause could not reasonably have been raised within the period specified in subdivision one of this section or included with the single set of motion papers as required by sub. 2. This subsection goes on to state that any other pretrial motion made after the forty-five day period may be summarily denied, but the court, in the interests of justice and for good cause shown, may in its discretion, at any time before sentence, entertain and dispose of the motion on its merits.

These subsections (1–3) taken together state a tripartite rule that all pretrial motions in a criminal case in this state must, in general, be made in forty-five days; that the court must entertain and decide on its merits any appropriate pretrial motion based on grounds of which the defendant could not with due diligence have been previously aware; and that the court may extend this time in the exercise of its discretion if good cause is shown and in the interests of justice.

As stated, the statutory provisions would appear clear. It is the subject of this article under what criteria of good cause and the interests of justice, the court may extend this apparently set forty-five days rule.

The discretion of the court upon analysis of the case law is wide both to extend and to limit the 45 days rule.

People v. Frigenti, 91 Misc.2d 139, 397 N.Y.S.2d 313 (S. Ct. Kings County 1977), is illustrative. In *Frigenti* the defendant moved for re-argument of an earlier court order denying as untimely his motion to suppress court authorized electronic surveillance evidence where the motion was made more than one year after arraignment. Upon re-argument the court granted the motion stating that the discovery portion of the defendant's pretrial motion sought discovery of all orders made in connection with the eavesdropping evidence and this demand for discovery was refused by the People and the refusal ratified by the Judge. The court noted the motion here was made promptly after the defendant was supplied with copies of the sealing order. The court concluded that here the defendant had diligently sought by means of his discovery motion the information necessary to support the grounds for his suppression motion and when he was refused this information the suppression motion herein fell out of the discretionary category and into the mandatory category.

Thus, in *Frigenti* the court extended the defendant's motion for stated good cause and in the interests of justice for one year beyond the actual arraignment.

On the other hand, in *People v. Broome,* 78 A.D.2d 718, 432 N.Y.S.2d 558 (3rd Dept. 1980), in a proceeding in which the defendant was convicted of First Degree Robbery and Second Degree Murder, the Third Department held that limiting the defendant to 18 days to make his pretrial motion was not an abuse of discretion, in light of the expeditious disclosure by the prosecution and in view of the prosecutor's express fear that certain witnesses would return to their home state if a speedy trial was not held.

See also *People v. Peligen,* 81 A.D.2d 951, 439 N.Y.S.2d 692 (Third Dept. 1981); (Held: Defendant properly denied permission to file suppression motion where permission was not sought until some 72 months after the defendant's arraignment and four months after his engaging new counsel.; aff. 55 N.Y.2d 529, 450 N.Y.S.2d 244, 435 N.E.2d 699); *People v. Melillo,* 112 Misc.2d 1004, 448 N.Y.S.2d 108 (S. Ct. New York County 1982); (Where defendant's motion to suppress wiretap evidence on the ground that the tapes were not timely sealed was not timely, the court nevertheless considered the merits of the motion in view of the fact that the delay was caused by the voluminous discovery material provided by the People and the long period of time taken to dispose of the preliminary motions); *People v. Hinson,* 110 Misc.2d 541, 441 N.Y.S.2d 882 (District Court, Nassau County 1981); (Held: Good cause for delay in bringing pretrial motion for bill of particulars, discovery and suppression of evidence in prosecution for possession of controlled substance in the seventh degree where SBI report with regard to charge was not available within 45 days of commencement of prosecution); *People v. Bostic,* 47 Misc.2d 1039, 412 N.Y.S.2d 948 (District Court, Nassau County 1978); (Held: Delay in furnishing specifics of defendant's statement intended to be offered into evidence was sufficient good cause for failure of the defendant to move within forty-five days for suppression hearing.)

It is clear that this brief review and analysis of the case law interpreting this statute reveals that the discretion of the court to limit or extend the time for making pretrial motions is wide, and that what may constitute good cause has been decided on an ad hoc, case by case basis, depending on the discrete facts of the case and the ground for extension offered by defendant.

One final point should be noted and that is that there may be a special and particularized rule where the extension for good cause involves discovery.

People v. Wyssling, 82 Misc.2d 708, N.Y.S.2d 142 (Suffolk County Court 1975), is an example. In *Wyssling* the defendant was charged with eight counts of perjury and moved for discovery of the notes relating to a preindictment interview he voluntarily gave at the Office of the District Attorney. The People opposed the motion as untimely under C.P.L. Sec. 255.20. The court held that the discovery of a defendant's statement is mandatory; that the notes were not exempt property; that discovery by the defendant of his own statement is not limited to custodial statements; that law enforcement officers may not limit the mandatory rights of the defendant merely by placing discovery material and other matters into a report which is then characterized as exempt; and that the defendant was entitled to discovery of the notes.

Most importantly, in significant dicta, the court stated that discovery as a category is an essential aid to trial preparation and in delineating the issues to be litigated and there is judicial discretion in granting an extension of time for discovery. *Wyssling* thus apparently articulated a quasi-rule that discovery as a category is subject to special scrutiny and the proper exercise of discretion by the court.

It is hoped that this brief review of the case law will serve to define and refine for defense counsel under what conditions and criteria the court may exercise its discretion to grant, limit, or extend the time for making pretrial criminal motions in the courts of this state in a criminal case; what constitutes good cause and the interests of justice; and that there is an indication that there is a special rule of discretion to extend the time for defense moving for discovery.

Copyright 1995 by the Queens County Bar Association and the Queens Bar Bulletin. Reprinted with permission.

54. Three Recent Ryan Cases

In the most significant case of *People v. Ryan*, N.Y.L.J., 12/20/93, p. 25 col. 1, the Court of Appeals in essence held that scienter of knowledge of the weight for the controlled substance by the defendant is an essential element of any drug possessory crime, in this state. The court suggested ways in which knowledge of the weight could be circumstantially proved including evidence of negotiations concerning weight, potency or price. For controlled substances measured by aggregate the court stated that knowledge of the weight could be inferred from the defendant's handling of the material.[1]

As to substances measured by pure weight the court suggested that the critical knowledge of the weight under these circumstances could be satisfied with evidence that the pure weight of the controlled substance possessed by the defendant is typical for the particular form in which the drug appears. *Ryan* was decided by the Court of Appeals in December of 1993.

This article proposes to analyze three recent trial court decisions which have had occasion to apply the principles set forth in *Ryan*.

The first is *People v. Juan Cabrera and Ramon Latique*, N.Y.L.J., 5/2/94, p.29 col. 1 (New York County, Criminal Term, Justice Rothwax).

In *Cabrera* the defendants were indicted for the crimes of possession of a weapon in the Third Degree and criminal use of drug paraphernalia. The court stated that the evidence before the Grand Jury established that in April of 1993 the police went to the upstairs at 150th Street, knocked on the apartment door, and identified themselves as police officers. As these police officers waited by the apartment door, other officers who were behind the building saw a large gym bag thrown from the apartment window and saw thereafter the defendants climbing down a wire. In the gym bag the officers found, among other things, two bags of a substance containing in the aggregate more than four and 3/4 ounces of a controlled substance. The officers proceeded to arrest the defendant and later found inside the apartment a loaded 22 caliber gun and also a home-made 22 caliber device.

The court ruled, in pertinent part, that although there was no legally suffi-cient basis to establish that the defendant actually knew the cocaine preparation possessed weighed in excess of four ounces, knowledge under these particular circumstances could be inferred under the *Ryan* principle that for controlled sub-stance measured by an aggregate weight, knowledge could be inferred from the defendant's handling of the material. The court went on to state that the nature of the trade in illicit cocaine was such that the weight of the substance deter-mines its value and that it is reasonable to infer that a person who has recently purchased narcotics or is prepared to sell knows the weight. The court concluded that although there was no indication in this case that the bags of drugs were re-cently purchased or prepared for resale it is also reasonable to infer where the amount possessed significantly exceeds the statutory limit defining the offense, that the defendant knows that the quantity possessed significantly exceeds the statutory limit defining the offense. The court concluded in this case that the fact that the defendant possessed 3/4 more than the statutory amount was a reason-able basis on which the Grand Jury could infer justifiably that the defendants knowingly possessed more than two ounces of cocaine.

Applying the *Ryan* criteria, the *Cabrera* court reasoned that when the weight of the controlled substance possessed sufficiently is in excess of the statutory limit then knowledge may be inferred.

Then followed the two cases of *People v. Nelson Lopez*, N.Y.L.J., 5/31/94, p. 29 col. 1 (Bronx S. Ct. J. Davidowitz); and *People v. Robin Santana*, N.Y.L.J., p. 29 col. 1 (Bronx S. Ct. J. Sheindlin).

In *Lopez* the defendant was charged with criminal possession of a controlled substance in the First and Third Degrees. The defendant requested the court to reinspect the Grand Jury Minutes and reduce these charges to criminal posses-sion of a controlled substance in the Third Degree, in accord with the rule of *Ryan*.

The court noted that the evidence before the Grand Jury disclosed that the police saw the defendant smoking a marijuana cigarette in the passenger seat in a livery cab stopped in traffic. The police left the car and approached the cab at which time the defendant then tried to swallow the cigarette, bent down, and handed a large paper bag to the codefendant seated next to him who then tried to throw the bag from the car window which was partially open. The bag struck the window and dropped to the floor. The police recovered the bag which contained cocaine and arrested the defendant who stated that he was delivering the cocaine to someone at Fordham Road and Webster Avenue.

A laboratory analysis showed that the bag contained eight and three-quarter ounces or more than one-half pound of cocaine.

Like the *Cabrera* court, the *Lopez* court noted that the weight of the cocaine was considerably greater than the statutory minimum. Further the court noted that other evidence in the record raised a reasonable and justifiable inference that the defendant knew the weight of the cocaine, including the fact that the defendant tried to dispose of it by handing it to the codefendant and tried to escape responsibility by swallowing the marijuana cigarette he was smoking when the police approached. The court concluded that these facts, together with the defendant's admission that he was going to deliver the cocaine to someone else and was presumably in the livery cab for that purpose, were evidence that the cocaine weighed at least as much as the minimum amount defined in the statute.

The third case to be considered here is *People v. Santana, supra.*

In *Santana* the defendant was indicted for a violation of P.L. Sec. 220.16, Criminal Possession of a Controlled Substance in the Third Degree, and moved for inspection of the Grand Jury Minutes and dismissal of the indictment claiming the evidence before the Grand Jury was legally insufficient to establish the violation of this statute under *Ryan.*

The court initially analyzed the import of the *Ryan* rule that knowledge of the aggregate weight may be inferred from the defendant's handling of the material and cited recent case law construing and interpreting the *Ryan* rule. The court went on to note that the evidence presented to the Grand Jury in the instant case established that the defendant possessed 753 decks of heroin in his pockets when he was arrested and that the weight of the drugs in his pockets caused his pockets to bulge to such an extent that his pockets could not be closed. The officer testified that he could actually see the bundles inside his pockets. The court then noted that the laboratory report indicated that the weight of the drugs was well over half an ounce. The court thus held that under this factual scenario the defendant's knowledge of the weight of the drugs could be inferred.

This brief review of three recent cases interpreting the holding, rule and language of *Ryan* show that in interpreting the *Ryan* rule that scienter of aggregate weight will be inferred from the defendant's handling of the material, the court often narrows or rather seems to stretch or expand the rather clear language of *Ryan.*

In *Lopez*, it was the fact that the weight of the drugs was beyond the statutory minimum, a criterion present in all these cases; that the defendant tried to dispose of the drugs; that he tried to escape responsibility by swallowing a marijuana cigarette and that he admitted he was going to deliver it to someone else.

In *Santana*, again, it was the fact that the weight of the drugs was over the statutory minimum and that bulge in the defendant's pockets was caused by the presence of drugs.

Again in *Cabrera*, it was that the weight of the drugs possessed exceeded the statutory minimum.

If any conclusion can be drawn from these three cases it is that the very specific rules of *Ryan* are not strictly being applied.

These trial courts focus on the amount of the weight as it exceeds the statutory amount to infer scienter.

Whether this is a proper interpretation of the aggregate weight inferential rule of *Ryan* remains to be seen. It would almost appear that these three trial courts are merely seeking to escape the *Ryan* rules by inferring knowledge of weight alone.

What *Ryan* will bring forth in the trial court, whether they will seek to escape its steep strictures or adhere to its letter, remains to be seen and will ultimately be resolved on a case by case basis.

55. Three More Pretrial Hearings

In my May 1994 *Bar Bulletin* article, three lesser known but nevertheless important pre-trial hearings were discussed and analyzed, to wit: The *Gomberg* Hearing, which involves an inquiry by the court directed both to the defendants and their counsel as to the propriety and potential risk of joint representation by the same attorney; the *Isaacson* Hearing, which is an inquiry by the Court as to whether, under the principles of due process and fundamental fairness, the defendant's rights have been violated by prosecutorial or police misconduct; and finally, the *Alfinito* Hearing, again, an inquiry by the court as to whether the affiant's statements in a search warrant were perjurious.

In this article, three more little known but nevertheless significant Pretrial Hearings will be considered and analyzed. The first is the *Rivera* Hearing, so named after *People v. Rivera*, 39 N.Y.2d 519; 384 N.Y.S.2d 726 (1976). In *Rivera*, the defendant was convicted in the Supreme Court of Kings County of the Sale of Marihuana. At that time he was not informed of his right of appeal. The defendant first learned of this valuable right years later when, on the occasion of a second conviction, he was sentenced to ten to fifteen years in prison. The defendant then applied for a writ of *Coram obis* and succeeded in obtaining a judicial determination that he had never been advised of his right to appeal his 1953 conviction and so now was entitled to be resentenced *nunc pro tunc* so as to permit his time to appeal to run anew. It was found thereafter that no transcript of the minutes of his trial or sentencing could be found. After a series of motions, the Appellate Division reversed and ordered a new trial. The People appealed to the Court of Appeals. In essence the court held that the right of the indigent defendant to appeal and have a stenographic transcript provided, if he is unable to afford one, is a fundamental right both of due process and fundamental fairness. If it should develop that a stenographic transcript is unavailable, then the court may order a judicial hearing to determine the availability of means other than a transcript for the presentation of the appealable and reviewable issues and such a hearing may be directed as to the adequacy of substitute means and the presence of the issues themselves.

Based on the inability of the court to reconstruct the trial proceedings, including the defendant's limited knowledge of English; his amnesia due to the administration of shock therapy in prison; the prosecutor at trial having subsequently suffered a paralytic stroke; the fact that Rivera's attorney had been disbarred and could not be located; and also the fact that the trial judge was deceased: all this impelled the Appellate Division to hold that, in the absence of a transcript, the proceedings could not be reconstructed, and the Court of Appeals affirmed. The court finally noted, in conclusion, that in the absence of the transcript, it was impossible in this case to establish either that there were or were not appealable issues, or, if there were, to present such issues properly on appeal.

The second Pretrial Hearing to be considered is the *Montgomery* Hearing so named after *People v. Montgomery*, 24 N.Y.S. 130, 299 N.Y.S.2d 158 (1969). In *Montgomery*, the defendant was convicted upon trial of Murder in the Second Degree and was sentenced to 25 years to life in state prison. A notice of appeal was not filed on behalf of the defendant by his attorney, and the defendant thereafter applied for a writ of *coram nobis,* alleging that because of his indigency, ignorance and infancy at the time of his conviction, he was precluded from seeking appellate review. He also alleged that neither his court-appointed counsel nor anyone else had informed him of his absolute right of appeal from his judgment of conviction. The defendant sought to be resentenced in order that an appeal might be taken from his judgment of conviction. The Supreme Court denied the defendant's application and the Appellate Division, First Department, affirmed.

The Court of Appeals held that because temporal reference of the time to appeal and its value as a right, that the defendant must be accorded a hearing to determine whether in fact he was informed of his right to appeal. The court stated that if at the hearing, it was determined that the defendant was not told of his rights, then clearly he was denied the equal protection of the law, and if the allegation should prove meritorious, then he should be resentenced so that his time to appeal should run anew.

The final Pretrial Hearing to be considered is the *Tunstall* Hearing, so named after *People v. Tunstall*, 63 N.Y.2d 1, 468 N.E.2d 30, 479 N.Y.S.2d 192 (1984).

In *Tunstall*, the defendant was convicted of Rape in the First Degree, Two Counts of Sodomy in the Second Degree, and Grand Larceny in the Third Degree, and he appealed. The Appellate Division reversed and ordered a new trial and the People appealed. The victim initially identified the defendant after viewing a series of lineups. She then made a statement to the Assistant District Attorney that was videotaped. Immediately thereafter, she was hypnotized in an effort to refresh her recollection as to any details of the crime which she might have forgotten. The only information elicited was that the defendant was wearing certain clothing. The victim never testified to those details at trial, and the People made no attempt to introduce them by other means. The Court of Appeals modified the holding of the Appellate Division, and, while not ordering a new trial, did hold that a pretrial hearing must be had to determine what effect, if any, the hypnosis had on the victim's recollection and if the defense's ability to cross-examine the victim was impaired by the hypnosis.

Conclusion

In this article, three little known but nevertheless important pretrial hearings have been considered and analyzed: to wit, the *Rivera* Hearing, the *Montgomery* Hearing, and the *Tunstall* Hearing. All may at one time or another occur in the course of criminal litigation in this state, and it is to be hoped that this article will alert the criminal practitioner to their existence, their possibilities, and their import for any current cases.

56. *A Recent Case on Presence*

The right of the criminally accused to be present at all stages of the criminal proceeding is a subject that has lately tested the interest of the Appellate Courts of this State. It can be generally stated that the defendant has a constitutional right to be present at all critical stages of the criminal litigation.

Thus, the defendant has the right to appear and testify before the Grand Jury. That right, however, can be waived and, under certain discrete circumstances due to the action or lack of action of the prosecutor, can result in dismissal of the indictment. C.P.L. Sec. 190.50(5); C.P.L. Sec. 210.20.

Under certain classes of accusatory instruments, such as the Simplified Information or a summons or desk appearance ticket, the defendant's appearance may be waived by counsel. C.P.L. Sec. 170.10(a)(b).

It is also the law that a defendant may choose not to appear at a pre-trial hearing. By the same token, under C.P.L. Sec. 260.20 the defendant may, by his disruptive conduct, cause his removal from the trial or he may under C.P.L. Sec. 340.50, by filing a written and subscribed statement, waive his right to be personally present. It is beyond the scope of this article, however, to examine in complete depth and complexity when, how, and under what circumstances the defendant's presence at any and every stage of the criminal litigation may be required or, as a matter of law, be waived.

A number of recent appellate decisions of this state have considered the scope and extent to which the defendant's presence is required at the many and various stages of criminal litigation. For example in *People v. Velasco*, 77 N.Y.2d 469, 568 N.Y.S.2d 721 (1991), the Court of Appeals, citing *People v.*

Mullen, 44 N.Y.2d 1, 403 N.Y.S.2d 740, 374 N.E.2d 369; and *Snyder v. Mass.* 241 U.S. 97, 108, 54 S. Ct. 330, 333, 78 L.ED.2d 674; and C.P.L. Sec. 260.20, rejected the defendant's contentions that he had the right to be present at the pre-charge conference and side bar conferences concerning the possible qualification or disqualification of jurors; and a conference in which defense counsel advised the court of his challenges for cause and his peremptory challenges. The Court of Appeals rejected these arguments and affirmed the defendant's conviction.

Similarly in *People v. Lowe,* 117 A.D.2d 755 (2d Dept. 1986), the Appellate Division, Second Department, denied the defendant's contentions on appeal that he was denied due process of law because he was not present at all in camera and side bar proceedings in which his attorney appeared on his behalf.

On the other hand in *People v. Turaine,* 78 N.Y.2d 871 (1991), the Court of Appeals held it was error to exclude the defendant from a hearing during trial outside the presence of the jury to determine if a witness would be permitted to testify whether the defendant threatened the witness to prevent him from testifying.

More recently in *People v. Antommarchi,* 80 N.Y.2d 247, 590 N.Y.S.2d 33, 604 N.E.2d 95 (1992), the Court of Appeals ruled that the defendant was denied his constitutional and statutory right to be present during a material stage of the proceeding when he was not present when the court questioned jurors about their ability to weigh evidence objectively, to hear testimony impartially, questions intended to search for a prospective juror's bias or predisposition to believe or discredit the testimony of potential witnesses. The Court distinguished this from the scenario where it held the defendant's presence is not required where the side bar discussions with the prospective juror relate to the juror's qualifications such as physical impairments, family obligations and work commitments.

A Recent Case

The law has continued to develop apace in this area of when and where in a criminal trial that the defendant's presence is required or mandated as a matter of due process and statutory right.

People v. Williams, 611 N.Y.S.2d 849 (1st Dept. 1944), illustrates the developing law and trend in this area.

In *Williams* the defendant was convicted in the Supreme Court of Bronx County of Robbery in the Second Degree and sentenced as a persistent felony offender to an indeterminate term of imprisonment of eight years to life. He was also in the Supreme Court of Bronx County convicted of Robbery in the First Degree and Robbery in the Third Degree and upon his plea of guilty was sentenced as a persistent violent felony offender to concurrent indeterminate terms of imprisonment of from ten years to life on the First Degree Robbery Count and to three and one-half to seven years on the Third Degree Robbery Count to run consecutively to an indeterminate term of imprisonment from one and one-half to three years on the Attempted Escape Count.

The facts in this case were that in October of 1988, J. Vitale directed that examinations be conducted pursuant to Article 730 of the C.P.L. to determine the defendant's capacity to stand trial. At the time he appeared before J. Vitale, the defendant was a patient at the Mid-Hudson Psychiatric Center following an Art. 730 1988 determination by the County Court Westchester that he was an incapacitated person. Two prior psychiatric reports in July of 1988 prepared in connection with the Westchester County prosecution concluded that the defendant lacked the capacity to understand the proceedings against him or to assist in his own defense based on his substance abuse problem, prior psychiatric hospitalizations, and the diagnosis of schizophrenia and paranoia with a guarded prognosis.

In accordance with J. Vitale's order, the defendant was examined by two staff psychiatrists at Bronx Lebanon Hospital who suggested that he should receive long-term evaluation at Bellevue Hospital. In a report dated February of 1989, two Bellevue psychiatrists concluded that the defendant was fit to proceed to trial. At the defendant's next court appearance defense counsel moved to controvert the Bellevue reports and requested permission to have the defendant be examined by a defense psychiatrist pursuant to C.P.L. Sec. 730. Subsequently, defense counsel withdrew his motion to controvert the Bellevue Reports on the ground that after speaking to his psychiatrist he concluded that the defendant was in fact fit and competent to stand trial.

The prosecutor and defense counsel moved to confirm the reports but waived the defendant's appearance. Defense counsel told the court that he would go to the basement directly to inform his client of what had occurred. The defendant then proceeded to trial on two of the indictments and was convicted. He pled guilty to Attempted Escape in the Third Degree in satisfaction of the third indictment.

The issue before the court was whether the defendant was deprived of his right to be present at the proceedings against him where the court confirmed the Bellevue 730 reports in his absence and deemed him fit to proceed.

Initially, the Court of Appeals analyzed both federal and state law on the matter of the defendant's right to be present. Distinguishing the defendant's right to be present at trial from ancillary proceedings including voir dire of prospective jurors, pre-trial hearings, and hearings conducted during trial, the court concluded that while the defendant has an absolute right to attend trial he has only a qualified right to be present at all ancillary proceedings.

The court concluded that, while the competency proceeding in question was ancillary, the defendant had a right to be present since the proceeding involved factual matters, and while the defendant may not have specific knowledge that would be useful in advancing his or her position or countering the People's position, a proper determination as to the defendant's competency could not be reached without his presence in which the court would have been enabled to assess his demeanor. The court also noted that the defendant, if allowed to be present, would have been able to correct any misimpressions or misstatements of fact contained in the psychiatric reports or to voice any objections to the conclusions reached by the examiners.

Thus the court concluded that, under all the circumstances, the defendant's judgment of conviction must be vacated and the matter remitted for further proceedings including findings concerning his fitness to proceed.

Williams is a correct and astute decision. The determination as to competency must not only involve court and counsel but, as the court observed, the defendant also. The defendant must be present, as the court observed, so that his demeanor may be observed and analyzed and also that he may correct and counter any psychiatric reports. It is clear in this case, where the defendant was found competent and forced to trial and convicted, that the defendant, if he had been present, might have brought about a different outcome.

It is the insight of *Williams'* reasoning that the determination of competency is a critical stage and a material stage of the criminal proceedings at which the defendant is entitled to be present both for observation of his demeanor itself and the opportunity he may have to shed light on the truth.

Like *Antommarchi, Turaine* and *People v. Dokes,* 79 N.Y.2d 656, 584 N.Y.S.2d 761, 595 N.E.2d 836 (1992) (Defendant's presence required at *Sandoval* proceeding), *Williams* is one more step on the expanding and developing case law in the issue of when and where the defendant must be present at a criminal trial.

Copyright 1995 by the New York State Association of Criminal Defense Lawyers. Reprinted with permission.

57. Failure to Pay a Fine: Incarceration or Not

Section 420.10 of the Criminal Procedure Law, entitled Collection of Fines, Restitution or Reparation, provides the mechanism in this state for the collection, payment and possible penalties for nonpayment of fines, restitution or reparation imposed in accord with sentence.

In pertinent part, this section provides that the court may, as a sentencing mandate, direct the payment of a fine to be paid either at the time sentence is pronounced, at some later date, or at periodic intervals. (C.P.L. Sec. 420.10 1[a] {I, I, II}). The Section also provides that the payment of a fine may be made a condition of a probationary sentence (C.P.L. Sec. 1[c]) and that the fine sentence may provide that if the defendant fails to pay the fine, restitution or reparation, the defendant may be imprisoned until the fine is satisfied. C.P.L. Sec. 420.10 also provides that where the fine is imposed for a felony, the period of incarceration may not exceed one year; where it is imposed for a misdemeanor the period may not exceed one-third of the maximum authorized term of imprisonment and where it is imposed for a petty offense the period of incarceration may not exceed fifteen days (C.P.L. Sec. 420.103.4). C.P.L. Sec. 420.10 also states that where, apparently due to indigency, the defendant is unable to pay the fine imposed by the court, he may apply for the court for resentencing and if the court finds that, in fact, the defendant is unable to pay the fine, the court, upon resentencing, must either adjust the terms of the payment, lower the amount of the fine, or revoke the entire sentence imposed and, upon such resentence, the court may impose any sentence it originally could have imposed (C.PL. Sec. 420.10, 5).

It would appear that the statute provides an incarceratory alternative where the defendant is able to but did not pay the fine (C.P.L. Sec. 420.10[3]) but if the defendant was unable to pay the fine due to indigency, the court has a number of alternatives, pursuant to an indigency hearing and resentencing, including adjusting the terms of payment, lowering the amount of the fine and resentencing to the maximum of the incarceratory sentence the court could have imposed.

Under this statute, it is clear that if it turns out, after the fine was imposed and the defendant did not pay, albeit due to indigency, incarceration is a very real alternative. Indeed it is ironic that the indigent defendant, who may be resentenced after an indigency hearing, may be subject to a lengthier period of imprisonment than the defendant who simply was able but did not pay the fine. (Cf. C.PL. Sec. 420.10[4, 5]). In sum, under this statutory scheme, it would appear that the indigent defendant may be imprisoned by reason of his very poverty or indigency. Hence, the palpable unfairness of the statute, at first blush, is evident and obvious and calls to mind no less than the debtors prisons painted in such vivid colors in Charles Dicken's *Little Dorrit.*

The question then is whether, under the New York case law, a person may, in fact, be imprisoned for debt. The case law makes distinctions and provides a solution. Two United States Supreme Court cases have spoken on this issue: *Beardon v. Georgia,* 461 U.S. 660, 103 S. Ct. 2064, 76 L.Ed.2d 221 (1978); and *Tate v. Short,* 401 U.S. 395, 28 L.Ed.2d 130, 91 S. Ct. 668 (1971).

First *Tate.* In *Tate* the petitioner was convicted of nine traffic offenses, punishable by fines only and was fined $425.00. He was unable to pay the fines because of his indigency and pursuant to Texas statute was imprisoned for 85 days, each day of imprisonment serving as a substitute for $5.00 of fines. The Petitioner's Writ of Habeas Corpus was denied by the County Criminal Court of Harris County and the Texas Court of Criminal Appeals affirmed, citing *Williams v. Illinois,* 399 U.S. 235, 26 L.Ed.2d 586, 90 S. Ct. 2018 (1970), where the defendant was given one year's imprisonment for the theft and a $500 fine; and the defendant, upon failure to pay the fine, was incarcerated for the length of time to satisfy the fine at the rate of $5 per day. The Supreme Court held, as applicable to the case before it, the decision in *Williams* that the Illinois statute invoked an invidious discrimination, based on the defendant's poverty and so violated the Equal Protection Clause. The court likened the case before it to *Williams,* since the defendant was discriminatorily imprisoned for debt because of indigency. The court noted that for the indigent defendant unable to pay a fine the state should provide alternatives to incarceration, although imprisonment is not precluded as a last resort, and that, in fact, there was no constitutional infirmity in imprisonment of a defendant with the means to pay the fine but who refuses or neglects to do so.

The holding of *Tate* is clear. For the defendant unable to pay a fine due to his indigency, imprisonment is not appropriate except as a last resort when all other alternatives are neither possible nor appropriate.

Bearden follows *Tate*. In *Bearden* the petitioner was indicted for the felonies of burglary and theft by receiving stolen property. He pleaded guilty and was sentenced to concurrent terms of probation. As a condition of probation, the trial court ordered the petitioner to pay a $500 fine, $100 to be paid that day, $100 the next day and the balance within four months. The Petitioner borrowed money from his parents and paid the first $200. A month later he was laid off from his employment, sought work, was unable to find any, and had no income or assets during this period.

Shortly before the balance of fine and restitution came due in February 1981, the petitioner notified the probation office that he was going to be late with his payment because he could not find a job. Thereafter, in May 1981, a petition was filed in the trial court to revoke the petitioner's probation due to his nonpayment of the fine. After an evidentiary hearing, the petitioner's probation was revoked for failure to pay the balance of this fine, a conviction was entered, and the petitioner was resentenced to the remainder of his probationary term in prison.

The Georgia Court of Appeals rejected the petitioner's claim that imprisoning him for inability to pay the fine violated the Equal Protection Clause of the Fourteenth Amendment and the Georgia Supreme Court denied the review.

The Supreme Court of the United States, citing *Williams* and *Tate*, and applying the two-pronged Equal Protection and Due Process analysis, defined the issue to be whether a sentencing court can revoke a defendant's probation for failure to pay an imposed fine or restitution absent evidence that the defendant was personally responsible for non-payment of the fine, or that alternative forms of punishment were inadequate.

The court initially held to the rule of *Williams* and *Tate*—that a state, upon imposing a fine as a sentence, cannot automatically convert it to a prison term because the defendant is indigent and unable to pay. The court further stated that imprisonment is not precluded where there is an affirmative refusal to pay the fine, even to the extent of failing of seeking employment or borrowing money. The court held, however, that where the probationer has made all reasonable efforts to pay the fine or restitution and cannot do so through no fault of his own, it is fundamentally unfair to revoke probation and resentence him to incarceration without considering whether alternative forms of penalty are available. In short, the court held that in revoking probation for failure to pay a fine the court must inquire into the reasons for non-payment. If it is found that the defendant refused willingly to pay, the defendant can be resentenced to incarceration and probation revoked. If, however, the probationer could not pay due to his indigency, the court must consider alternative means of punishment, such as reduction of the fine, rescheduling the payments, or a period of community service, with incarceration as a last resort.

Bearden follows *Tate* establishing a rule, as it were, that where a defendant has failed to pay a fine, absent evidence that his failure to pay was willful and deliberate thereby allowing imprisonment, the full panoply of nonincarceratory alternatives should be considered, with imprisonment as the last resort, where it is established that the failure to pay was due to indigency.

The New York State courts have followed the lead of *Tate* and *Bearden*. *People v. Montero,* 124 Misc.2d 1020 480 N.Y.S.2d 70 (2d Dept. 1984), is an example. *Montero* was an appeal from a judgment imposing concurrent sentences of 90 days and 10 days for failure to pay fines imposed on convictions of menacing and disorderly conduct. The facts in *Montero* were that the defendant pleaded guilty to menacing and was sentenced to a conditional discharge and a fine of $100, or 10 days incarceration.

The defendant, as the result of his failure to pay the fine, was resentenced without further inquiry or an evidentiary hearing to concurrent terms of 90 days and 10 days. Citing *Bearden* and *Tate,* the court held the sentencing procedure there improper. The court held initially that there must be an evidentiary hearing to determine the defendant's claimed inability to pay the fine due to his indigency. Such a hearing being held, the court held the court should resentence the defendant to incarceration only if it was found that the defendant was genuinely indigent and this accounted for his failure to pay the fine; and that only when all other alternatives (such as a period of community service, reduction of the fine, or rescheduling the fine) were explored and rejected as inappropriate should incarceration be considered. It is noteworthy that the court found that C.P.L. Sec. 420.10(5) was not unconstitutional as permitting incarceration of the defendant who is financially unable to pay the fine inasmuch as under *Bearden,* sub. 5 of C.P.L. Sec. 420.10 permits the court to consider all available sentencing alternatives and does not mandate imprisonment.

See also *People v. McArdle,* 55 N.Y.2d 639, 446 N.Y.S.2d 256, 430 N.E.2d 1309 (1981); *People v. Goddard,* 108 Misc.2d 742, 39 N.Y.S.2d 71 (Criminal Court Kings County, 1981).

In sum, it is clear that *Tate, Bearden, Montero* and *McArdle* and *Goddard* all essentially hold that C.P.L. 420.10(5), to the extent it provides for resentencing to the maximum term of imprisonment the court could originally have imposed upon non-payment of a fine due to poverty and inability to pay, is to be sparingly used and then only after an evidentiary hearing has established that the defendant was, is and continues to be genuinely indigent. Indeed incarceration is only a last resort absent the unavailability of other alternatives.

This is right and fair. Imprisonment for debt and debtors prison, whether for failure to pay a fine or where non-support of children is involved, is a relic of the propertied and Victorian era when Equal Protection was not offered and prescribed for all regardless of their financial status in society. The trial courts, at their peril, may resentence the indigent to incarceration solely by reason of his poverty.

58. Rosario Material: A New Category

The rule of *People v. Rosario,* 9 N.Y.2d 286, 212 N.Y.S.2d 448 (1969), simply states, as codified in section 240.45 of the Criminal Procedure Law, that, after the jury has been sworn and before the prosecutor's opening address, or, in the case of a bench trial after commencement and before submission of the evidence, the prosecutor must, subject to a protective order, make available to the defendant any prosecution witness' prior statement, written or recorded, including any testimony before the Grand Jury and an examination videotaped pursuant to Section 190.32, which relates to the subject matter of the witness' testimony.

In 1965, the *Rosario* rule was extended in *People v. Malinsky,* 15 N.Y.2d 86, 262 N.Y.S.2d 65 (1965), to the suppression hearing and *Malinsky* was codified under C.P.L. Sec. 2J0.4J.

Failure to produce *Rosario* material at trial results in per se reversal of the judgment of conviction. *People v. Ranghelle,* 69 N.Y.2d 56, 511 N.Y.S.2d 580 (1980). See also, *People v. Jones,* 79 N.Y.2d 547, 523 N.Y.S.2d 53 (1987).

If *Rosario* material is lost or destroyed due to the People's failure to exercise due and adequate care to preserve it and the defendant is prejudiced by that mistake, the court must impose an appropriate sanction, including preclusion, striking the witness' testimony, or an adverse inference instruction to the jury. *People v. Martinez,* 71 N.Y.2d 437, 528 N.Y.S.2d 813 (1988). What may be said to constitute *Rosario* material is varied and has been said to include such material as a police officer's memo book (*People v. Buster,* 69 N.Y.2d 56, 511 N.Y.S.2d 580 [1976]); notes of investigating officers (*People v. Gilligan,* 34 N.Y.2d 769, 384 N.Y.S.2d 778 [1976]); a prosecutor's handwritten notes (*People v. Consolazio,* 40 N.Y.2d 446, 387 N.Y.S.2d 62 [1976]); and a ballistics report, (*People v. Dawson,* 157 A.D.2d 606, 550 N.Y.S.2d 625 [1st Dept. 1989]).

The issue this article proposes to consider is whether under the current status of the New York law, the hospital record of a complaining witness has been considered *Rosario* material and whether the failure to produce it at trial is a per se violation or constitutes loss or destroyed material requiring sanctions.

In fact, whether the People are required to produce as *Rosario* material the hospital record of the complaining witness may be critical in a criminal case such as a Murder or Attempted Murder. The degree of injuries as revealed in the hospital records of the complaining witness may bear on the issue of intent. This is also true of a Robbery in the Second Degree where it is alleged that a person

forcibly steals property and causes physical injury to a third person not a participant in the transactional event. The hospital record may bear on the intent to
cause physical injury.

Again, in the Penal Law section 140.30, Burglary in the First Degree, where
it is alleged that a person knowingly enters or remains unlawfully in a dwelling
with intent to commit a crime therein and when, in effecting entry or while in
the dwelling or in immediate flight therefrom, he or another participant in the
crime (P.L. SS 140.30[2]) causes physical injury to any person who is not a participant in the crime, the injuries, as revealed in the hospital record, may again
bear upon the question of intent to cause injury.

Finally, an element of a Robbery in the First Degree (P.L. SS 160.15[1]) is
serious physical injury. The hospital record, if provided, will reveal the serious
character of the physical injury.

It is clear that the hospital record of a complaining witness' injuries therefore is most relevant and in the case of a Murder, Attempted Murder, Robbery I,
Robbery II or Burglary I, where there is an issue of whether there is a true injury, serious injury or the requisite intent to cause the injury in the case. It is also
clear that, under the rule of *People v. Rosario* as codified under C.P.L. Sec.
240.45, this record may well constitute an explicit pretrial statement under
Rosario. It is the view of this writer that the hospital record of a complaining
witness is nothing more nor less than true *Rosario* material, the lack of which, if
not provided by the People prior to trial, is a per se violation mandating eventual
reversal on appeal or, if the record is lost or destroyed, then requiring the imposition of an appropriate sanction under *Martinez*.

There is, however, little case law supporting this view. The sole case this
writer has been able to unearth that the hospital record of a complaining witness
is *Rosario* material is *In the Matter of Raphael M.,* 111 Misc.2d 192, 443
N.Y.S.2d 819 (Fam. Ct. N.Y. County 1981). In *Raphael,* a Juvenile was charged
in a delinquency petition with committing acts which if committed by an adult
would have constituted the crimes of Robbery in the First Degree and Robbery
in the Second Degree. The issue in the case, pursuant to motion, was to what extent the respondent is entitled to pretrial disclosure of witness' statements to law
enforcement officers; their criminal records; and police and hospital records.

The court initially analyzed the motion in accord with C.P.L. Sec. 240.20.
Respondent contended that C.P.L. Sec. 240.20 authorized the pretrial discovery
of police and medical records, the criminal records of the complainant as well as
witness' pretrial statements before the commencement of trial. The court then
proceeded to further analyze the issue here in terms of the right of a defendant to
obtain pretrial statements of prosecution witnesses and permits the respondent to
examine such statements after direct examination of the witness has been concluded. The court went on to state that C.P.L. Sec. 240.45 codifies the *Rosario*
rule and that this statutory provision allows the respondent to obtain written or
recorded statements of persons the prosecution intends to call as witnesses before the prosecution presents its case in chief rather than at the close of its direct
case as mandated in the *Rosario* decision.

The court then proceeded to analyze the issue of when the prosecution is mandated to turn over medical records, criminal records, witness statements and hospital and police reports under the rubric of C.P.L. Sec. 240.20, but under the codification of *Rosario* under C.P.L. Sec. 240.45, and held, in summary, that that section governs when these records must be turned over by the prosecution to the defense, holding that it must await the day of trial and not before.

The court rejected the respondent's contention that the failure to turn over such materials well before trial will cause excessive delay, holding that C.P.L. Sec. 240.20 was intended by the legislature to expedite criminal proceedings by insuring that these materials, including the hospital records of the complaining witness, be made available to the respondent prior to the witness' testimony and that the respondent has not the necessary showing of reasonableness and materiality to invoke the discretionary provisions of C.P.L. Sec. 240.20.

It is clear that *Raphael* supports the view that relevant hospital records of a complaining witness must be analyzed not only under C.P.L. Sec. 240.20 but more specifically under C.P.L. Sec. 240.45. The *Raphael* court concludes in its analysis that the hospital records of a complainant as well as police reports and conviction records are *Rosario* material and subject to the mandates and strictures of the *Rosario* rule.

There is one question however that it leaves unanswered, or rather fails to analyze. That is the question of control. It could be argued that hospital records are not under the sole control of the People as required by *Rosario* and can easily be obtained by defense subpoena. The answer is contained in the seminal language of *People v. Ranghelle,* 69 N.Y.2d 56, 511 N.Y.S.2d 580 (1986), where the Court of Appeals, per Mr. Justice Simons, specifically rejected, in no uncertain terms, the People's argument that *Rosario* should not be applied where the prior statement is not in the sole custody of the People. Thus *Ranghelle,* the case which governs ultimately all *Rosario* issues and application, specifically held that whether the material is under the sole control of the People or equally obtainable by defense subpoena is irrelevant.

Finally, one point must be noted. In addition to the hospital records in the view of this writer being *Rosario* material, whether regarded as an explicit or implicit statement of injury, it is also *Brady* material since it is clearly material to guilt or punishment and may be favorable to the defendant. See, *Brady v. Maryland,* 373 U.S.33, 83 S.Ct. 1053 (1963); *People v. Ahmen,* 20 N.Y.2d 958, 286 N.Y.S.2d 850 (1967).

Indeed *Brady* material has been held to include not only evidence which may actually disprove the People's case but also evidence which may tend to impeach the People's witnesses.

In conclusion, *Raphael,* though a trial court decision, clearly regards the hospital record of the complaining witness under the rubric of *Rosario* material.

The record, it should be noted, can also be equally viewed as *Brady* material subject to discovery under C.P.L. 240.20(h) or as a report of a physical or mental examination under C.P.L. Sec. 240.20(c). Request should be made by defense counsel under all these statutory sections to assure the production of the hospital record and that proper use may be made of it by defense counsel.

Copyright 1995 by the New York State Association of Criminal Defense Lawyers. Reprinted with permission.

59. A Novel Motion in Limine

One of the most troubling and difficult categories of crimes encountered by the criminal lawyer is the sex abuse case.[1] In general, although not uniformly, under the Penal statutory section covering the various levels of sexual abuse, this Penal Law area, other than where the subsections are directed to some form of generalized incapacity, often revolves around the underage child.[2]

For this reason the sex abuse case, whether felony or misdemeanor, presents peculiar difficulties since children are often influenced by adult authority figures such as police, school teachers, principals, parents, siblings, other blood relatives and investigators.

In the face of these "influences" the child may be swayed emotionally not to intentionally lie, but to conform to the wishes of particular adults to whom the child is subject to influence. Story begets story, authority begets conformity, and the result is potential wholesale fabrication on the part of the child.

A recent case on this very scenario suggests that a pretrial hearing may be necessary where these facts are present in a sex abuse case involving a child complainant. That case is *People v. Hudy*.[3]

The facts in *Hudy* were amid reports of unwanted fondling of students by a male teacher in an elementary school. The defendant, following a police investigation, was indicted on twenty-three counts of first degree sexual abuse and nine counts of endangering the welfare of a child. Although the Court of Appeals considered a number of legal issues, the seminal issue before the Court was the trial court's denial of the defendant's request to call two investigators who had originally interviewed the young victims. Defense counsel argued, unsuccessfully, that he should be permitted to question the officers about the interviews in order that he could elicit that the boys' testimony had been influenced by police suggestion. Defense counsel pointed to evidence that at least one of the boys had first denied that any improper touching had occurred and then changed his mind after an investigator told him that the police had two witnesses who had seen such touching occur. Defense counsel also represented, based upon the examination of police reports, the possibility of a number of similar incidents. The trial court concluded that the proposed questioning was only relevant to credibility and was therefore collateral. Thus, the trial court excluded all questioning of the investigating officers.

The defendant was subsequently convicted of all charges, and the Appellate Division affirmed, thereby rejecting the defendant's argument that the trial court had erred in restricting the defendant's right to question the investigating officers.

The Court of Appeals reversed on this issue. The Court stated that extrinsic proof tending to establish a reason to fabricate is never collateral since the proposed line of questioning did not merely involve the issue of credibility but went to a possible reason for fabrication by the young witnesses; i.e., the investigators' suggestive comments.

Hudy brings to light an issue the door to which should long have been opened. Children may be swayed by their dependence on adult authority. Children in their innocence and their dependence on the adults above and around them, and influenced also by group and peer pressure, may be led if not to exaggerate then to create and ultimately, albeit innocently, to fabricate.

The result may be the creation of a story out of whole cloth. It is not so much an intentional fabrication, but the result of a child in his dependence on adults and the group unable to think and sift independently, so the final result is a deviation from total truth that the child is unaware of. A story evolves that is not seen by the child as a fabrication but has come about in the child's unawareness by the undue influence of those above and around them.

Hudy rules that for a trial court not to permit the exploration of this area of truth is erroneous. Based on the ground of what a child is, and what his or her nature may be, the decision is a logical, coherent, and correct response to what and how nature functions in the underage individual.

Since undue or suggestive influences are at work in the reasoning of the decision, it is clear that some sort of motion in limine or pretrial hearing is necessary in this category of case should defense counsel be aware of the potential for undue influence of investigatory officers or police in the case. It is in the nature of a Wade Hearing,[4] the purpose of which is the determination and removal of the potential taint of suggestiveness and undue influence. In this sense, the pretrial hearing would be akin to a Wade or Rodriguez Hearing, to assure the eradication of any suggestive impropriety.

In short, in any sex abuse case where the complainant is an underage child, it is incumbent upon defense counsel to move at some point before trial for a hearing of this issue whereby the investigating officers and child, if necessary, may be examined so that there is an assurance that if suggestiveness or undue influence are at work, the tainted evidence may be excluded or other appropriate remedial measures may be fashioned by the court.

In this way the door to total truth may be opened and assured in this most sensitive and slippery category of cases in the New York Penal Law.

60. The Voluntariness Hearing in Criminal Law

It is settled law of New York that evidence of a statement, admission or confession made by the defendant may be suppressed by the court where shown to have been involuntarily made (Criminal Procedure Law [C.P.L.] §710:20 [3]; see also, C.P.L. 60.45). C.P.L. Section 710.30 provides that notice of the People's intention to offer evidence of a such statement must be served upon the defendant within 15 days of arraignment and the defendant, upon service of such notice may move, pursuant to C.P.L. 710.30 (within the period specified under C.P.L. Sec. 255.20) to suppress such evidence. The court may summarily grant or deny the motion or, if it does neither, conduct a hearing on the issue (see C.P.L. Sec. 710.60).

C.P.L. Article 710, which prescribes the method by which defense counsel may seek to suppress a statement, admission or confession as either involuntarily made or unconstitutionally obtained, not only affords defense counsel the opportunity to bar the use of such evidence by the People on their direct case, but also, even if the motion to suppress is lost, allows defense counsel, through cross examination of the police witness or other party to whom the statement was made, valuable insight, information, and discovery of the People's case in chief.

C.P.L. Section 60.45, which codifies the categories of statements which are subject to suppression, states that a statement, confession or admission is involuntarily made when physical force is used or threatened, or improper conduct or undue pressure is used, which impairs the defendant's physical or mental condition to the extent of undermining his ability to make a choice whether or not to make a statement. Under this rubric, the confession, statement, or admission may have been obtained though physical or psychological coercion by any party, private or public (C.P.L. §60.45[2][a]).

The section also provides that a statement, admission or confession is involuntary when obtained by a public servant engaged in law enforcement, or person acting under his direction or cooperation, by means of a promise or statement of fact which creates a substantial risk that the defendant might falsely incriminate himself (C.P.L. §60.45[2][b][i]).

Finally, the statute provides that a statement is considered involuntary when obtained in violation of the defendant's state or federal constitutional rights (C.P.L. §60.45 [2][b][i]).

It is clear, then, that the statutory definition includes involuntary statements made to persons in law enforcement and private parties, if such statements are the product of classic coercion; statements obtained by a deceptive promise by a public servant engaged in law enforcement or one acting under his cooperation or direction; and a statement, confession or admission obtained by a person engaged in law enforcement, or one acting under his cooperation or direction, in violation of, *inter alia, Miranda v. Arizona,* 384 U.S. 436, 86 S.Ct. 1602, 16 L.Ed.2d 694 (1966), reh. den. 385 U.S. 890, 87 S.Ct. 11, 17 L.Ed.2d 121.

The People, given their knowledge of a possible "involuntary statement," have the option of either not giving notice of the statement at all, or of withdrawing the notice if previously given. The effect of this strategic decision is for the People to give up their right to use the statement on their direct case, because they will be subject to preclusion if they attempt to do so. However, the People will still be permitted to use the alleged statement as a means of impeaching the defendant, should he choose to testify, as a prior inconsistent statement

The Issue

Defense counsel in countering either possible withdrawal by the prosecution of a C.P.L. Section 710.30 notice of intention to use the defendant's statement on its direct case at trial or, or no notice of intention to use the statement at all, is faced with the dilemma that the statement not only will be used to discredit and impeach his client's testimony, but also that he will be deprived of the suppression hearing that he would otherwise have been entitled to had he received notice of the statement, or had it not been withdrawn.

Defense counsel, however, has an additional weapon in his arsenal. He may, under the law, move to obtain a hearing under these circumstances, concerning the voluntariness of the alleged statement. Obtaining this hearing is useful for two reasons: the statement may yet be suppressed on the basis that it is involuntary, thereby preventing its use as an impeachment device; and the hearing will open a window into the People's case.

The leading case to address this issue is *People v. Maerling*, 64 N.Y.2d 134, 485 N.Y.S.2d 23, 474 N.E.2d 231 (1984). In *Maerling*, the defendant appealed from a judgment convicting him of felony murder and first degree robbery. The charges arose out of a 1972 entry into the home of one Jerry LoBosso, a reputed bookmaker, during which LoBosso was killed, his wife injured, and jewels and cash stolen. On the night of the defendant's arrest, he signed a three-page confession in which he stated that he and codefendant Ragonese entered the LoBosso house while a third codefendant, Franciatti, remained in the car. The defendant admitted accidentally wounding Mrs. LoBosso and stealing property from her home.

The defendant stated that before he left the house, he heard a gunshot in another room and later, upon leaving, saw Mr. LoBosso on the floor. Defendant took the stand and alleged his written confession was false and the product of threats and beatings. The defendant also denied, on cross-examination, making any statements to the Suffolk County Police and the Assistant District Attorney. In rebuttal two Suffolk County police officers and the Assistant District Attorney testified that they met with the defendant and that he made inculpatory statements. The court allowed the testimony, but instructed the jury that it was only to be considered on the issue of the defendant's credibility. The defendant asserted that this rebuttal evidence was obtained in violation of his constitutional rights. However, the court held that because the defendant did not contend that his statements were involuntary, they were admissible for impeachment purposes.

The clear import of the holding in *Maerling* is that absent an assertion by the defendant that his statement was involuntary, it may be used for impeachment purposes.

The appellate courts of this state have consistently followed *Maerling* on this issue. See *People v. Knights,* 109 A.D.2d 910 (3d Dept. 1985); *People v. Walker,* 110 A.D.2d 730 (2d Dept. 1985); *People v. Padron,* 134 A.D.2d 625 (2d Dept. 1987); *People v. Herman D. Neu,* 145 A.D.2d 784 (3d Dept. 1988); *People v. Halts,* 76 N.Y.2d 190 (1990); *People v. Quick,* 160 A.D.2d 820 (2d Dept. 1990).

If there is an assertion by the defendant that his statement was classically the product of coercion and involuntary, a hearing on the issue of voluntariness must be conducted before the statement may be used by the People at trial.

People v. Ames, 119 A.D.2d 755 (2d Dept. 1986), clearly articulates this principle. In *Ames,* the defendant appealed from convictions of robbery in the second degree under three separate indictments. The charges arose out of an incident in which it was alleged the defendant entered the offices of the complainant, a dentist, displayed a gun, stole money from the dentist and locked him in a closet. Prior to trial, the defendant requested that the People disclose any statements made by the defendant to any individual so that the voluntariness of the statements could be determined before the People used them as direct evidence or for impeachment purposes. The People claimed that there were no statements discoverable under C.P.L. Section 240.20 and the case proceeded to trial. Both the defendant and the dentist testified at trial, the defendant presenting an entirely different version of the incident. On cross-examination of the defendant, the District Attorney impeached the defendant through the use of a statement he had made to his parole officer. The defendant objected to the use of this statement, stating it had not been tested for voluntariness. The court overruled the defendant's objection and permitted impeachment of the defendant's testimony through the use of the prior inconsistent statement. The defendant argued to the appellate court that the use of the statement for impeachment purposes constituted reversible error. The Second Department held that the People's nondisclosure of the defendant's statement to his parole officer, a person engaged in law enforcement activity, deprived the defendant of an opportunity to challenge the voluntariness of it, and the trial court erred in denying the defendant's request for a hearing on that issue. See also, *People v. Wendel,* 123 A.D.2d 410 (2d Dept. 1988); *People v. Mitchell,* 143 A.D.2d 147 (2d Dept. 1988).

It is clear that the case law following *Maerling* envisions a finding by way of pretrial hearing on the issue of voluntariness, should the statement be sought to be used for impeachment of the defendant, although not used in the People's direct case.

One final point should be noted. *Maerling* and the cases following it also hold that even though a statement is obtained in violation of the defendant's *Miranda* rights or his right to counsel, nevertheless the statement may be used to impeach, provided it has been found to have been voluntary after a challenge on that issue by defense counsel. *People v. Maerling, supra,* at 25; *People v. Chrazanowski,* 147 A.D.2d 652 (2d Dept. 1989); *People v. Neu, supra; People v. Woods,* 144 A.D.2d 512 (2d Dept. 1988); *People v. Pardon, supra; People v. Ames, supra; People v. Granger,* 114 A.D.2d 285 (2d Dept. 1986); *People v. Walker,* 110 A.D.2d 730 (2d Dept. 1985); *People v. Knights, supra.*

It is somewhat ironic that under New York law, a statement obtained in violation of *Miranda* and the defendant's right to counsel may nevertheless, unless found to be the product of classical coercion, be used for purposes of impeachment by the People of the defendant should he choose to take the stand. See *People v. Harris,* 25 N.Y.2d 175, 303 N.Y.S.2d 71, 250 N.E.2d 349, aff'd., *Harris v. New York,* 401 U.S. 22~ (1971).

Conclusion

In sum, unless defense counsel has been given notice of a statement and the notice is withdrawn, defense counsel may be in the dark as to the existence of a statement which the People may, as it were, be holding in reserve to discredit the defendant should he choose to testify. Therefore, defense counsel must, by way of the C.P.L. Section 240.20 or oral request, seek to determine if the statement exists and thereby obtain the hearing he is entitled to under the law. If he asks, he may either obtain the hearing if the People concede the existence of the statement, or seek its preclusion should they, having failed to accede to the defendant's request, seek to use it to impeach. Even if preclusion is not obtained. the defense is nevertheless entitled to the hearing, in this writer's view, even at the brink of or in the midst of trial, should it be sought to be used by the People against the defendant

61. The Station House Identification

In general, it may be said that of all forms of pretrial identifications, whether lineup, showup, or photographic identification, the showup which occurs at the station house, due to its obviously highly suggestive character, is most disfavored. The presence of the defendant in contact and confrontation with the complainant in the highly charged suggestive environment of the police precinct will most obviously produce such an overwhelming suggestive taint as to compel a positive identification that might not otherwise occur.

The rule concerning the propriety of station house identifications is set forth in the companion cases of *People v. Riley,* and *People v. Rodriguez,* 70 N.Y.2d

523, 522 N.Y.S.2d 842. (1987). The Court of Appeals, in those cases, enunciated the general rule at page 529:

> Showup identifications, by their nature suggestive, are strongly disfavored but are permissible if exigent circumstances require immediate identification (*People v. Rivera,* 22 N.Y.2d 453), or if the suspects are captured at or near the crime scene and can be viewed by the witness immediately (*People v. Love,* 57 N.Y.2d 1023). Generally, a showup identification will be inadmissible when "there was no effort to make the least provision for a reliable identification and the combined result of the procedures employed" establish that the showup was unduly suggestive (*People v. Adams,* 53 N.Y.2d 241, 249).
>
> Unreliability of the most extreme kind infects showup identifications of arrested persons held at police stations, and the evidence will be inadmissible as a matter of law unless exigency warrants otherwise.

In the two cases before it the Court concluded that the station house identifications were unfair and unduly suggestive where in one case the stolen property and gun were set on a table near the suspects and in the other case the defendant was handcuffed at the time of showup. The court specifically found that the fact that in one case the station house was undergoing a renovation and in the other that the station house identification occurred in order to minimize the length of the suspect's detention were not acceptable exigent factors or circumstances to excuse the failure to conduct the more preferred and fairer line-up procedure rather than the showup identification .

A good example of the application of the *Riley – Rodriguez* rule is *People v. Gildersleeve,* 143 A.D.2d 361, 532 N.Y.S.2d 418 (2d Dept. 1988). *Gildersleeve* was an appeal from a judgment of conviction convicting the defendant of Robbery in the Second Degree. The court held, citing *Riley,* that the second showup at the police precinct was unduly suggestive, noting the absence of exigent circumstances and the fact that the complainant had already identified the defendant in a showup that evening. See also, *People v. Duvon,* 77 N.Y.2d 541, 569 N.Y.S.2d 346. N.E.2d 654 (1991); *People v. Sturdwick,* 170 A.D.2d 969, 565 N.Y.S.2d 944 (4th Dept. 1991): *People v. Cox,* 164 A.D.2d 779, 559 N.Y.S.2d 878 (1st Dept. 1990); *People v. Tillman,* 147 A.D.2d 599, 537 N.Y.S.2d 894 (2d Dept. 1989); *People v. Ferraro,* 144 A.D.2d 976, 534 N.Y.S.2d 279, (4th Dept. 1988); *People v. Guillermo,* 137 A.D.2d 832, 525 N.Y.S.2d 295 (2d Dept. 1989); *People v. Joy,* 494 N.Y.S.2d 420,114 A.D.2d 517 (2d Dept. 1985); *People v. Chandler,* 153 Misc.2d 332, 581 N.Y.S.2d 530 (S. Ct. Queens County 1991); *People v. Ptah,* 149 Misc.2d 488, 565 N.Y.S.2d 397 (S. Ct. Bronx County 1990).

An application of the exception to the general *Riley* rule is articulated in *People v. Burden,* 131 A.D.2d 494, 516 N.Y.S.2d 109 (2d Dept. 1987). In *Burden,* the Second Department held that the hearing court properly declined to suppress the complainant's identification testimony since the evidence established that the defendant and the complainant were known to each other, and the station house identification was more in the nature of a confirmatory than a true identification and so there was no issue, the court held, of suggestiveness. See also, *People v. Marrero*, 167 A.D.2d 559, 562 N.Y.S.2d 230 (2d Dept. 1990); *People v. Johnson*, 124 A.D.2d 748, 508 N.Y.S.2d 249 (2d Dept. 1986); *People v. Charles*, 111 A.D.2d 405, 489 N.Y.S.2d 370 (2d Dept. 1985).

A station house identification may also be viewed as confirmatory where it is seen as the proper completion of integral police procedures. Under these circumstances the general rule is inapplicable and the identification will not be suppressed as unduly suggestive. Thus, in *People v. Maxwell*, 184 A.D.2d 661, 584 N.Y.S.2d 868 (2d Dept. 1992), the Second Department ruled that the defendant's contention that the undercover officer's station house showup identification of him on the night of his arrest was unduly suggestive was without merit, since the showup constituted the proper completion of an integral police procedure.

A sub-category of the confirmatory station house identification is where the station house identification follows promptly on the heels of a prior identification on the street. Thus, in *People v. Fulmore*, 133 A.D.2d 169, 518 N.Y.S.2d 831 (2d Dept. 1987), the Second Department held the station house identification of the defendant by the complainant was proper since it served merely as a prompt confirmation of the prior identification made on the street. See also, *People v. Forestier*, 171 A.D.2d 630, 567 N.Y.S.2d 471 (1st Dept. 1991); *People v. Griffin*, 161 A.D.2d 799, 556 N.Y.S.2d 131 (2d Dept. 1990).

Another exception to the general rule of *Riley* is where the showup at the precinct is accidental. These showups at the precinct are not seen as unduly suggestive since due to a happenstance the identification is unavoidable and not attributable to any misconduct on the part of the police. Under this scenario, *Riley* will not govern and the accidental showup at the precinct will not be suppressed. Thus in *People v. Sims*, 150 A.D.2d 402, 504 N.Y.S.2d 834 (2d Dept. 1980), the Second Department held that where bar patrons observed the defendant in the holding cell precinct, the showup was not the result of any improper police activity but was accidental or unarranged and so not impermissibly suggestive. On this see also, *People v. Magee*, 192 A.D.2d 559, 596 N.Y.S.2d 104 (2d Dept. 1993); *People v. Maddox*, 139 A.D.2d 597, 527 N.Y.S.2d 89 (2d Dept. 1988); *People v. Hampton*, 129 A.D.2d 736, 514 N.Y.S.2d 496 (2d Dept. 1987); *People v. Whitaker*, 126 A.D. 688, 511 N.Y.S.2d 112 (2d Dept. 1987).

Finally, the general *Riley* rule will also apply where although no on-the-scene confirmatory identification has occurred, the undercover police officer is shown a single suspect at the station house several hours after the alleged drug buy. Thus, in *People v. Hill*, 136 Misc.2d 670, 510 N.Y.S.2d 166 (Sup.Ct. Queens County 1987), Justice Friedman, now a member of the Appellate Division, Second Department, held:

> There was no on-the-scene showup here. (See, *People v. Martinez*, 79 A.D.2d 661, 662; *People v. Morales, supra.*) The only confirmation of selection took place at the station house. That showup was conducted some seven hours after the street purchase. This court holds that showup was improper and suggestive

and, therefore, constitutionally impermissible (compare with *People v. Adams*, 53 N.Y.2d 241, *supra*).

Conclusion

The station house identification under the *Riley – Rodriguez* rule and developed New York State case law is strongly disfavored as being unduly and impermissibly suggestive and will generally be suppressed in the absence of some showing of exigent circumstances to justify its use in place of the preferred line-up procedure. There are, however, recognized exceptions to the general *Riley* rule which can be summarized as follows:

1. the confirmatory identification where the parties are previously known to each other
2. the confirmatory identification the result of essentially prompt police identification at the station house which follows promptly on the street identification
3. the identification at the station house which is unavoidable or accidental and not the result of improper police activity.

These categories of cases are not subject to the strictures of the *Riley* rule and generally suppression will not result.

If the criminal law practitioner is familiar with the general *Riley* rule but alert to the possible application of the exceptions to the rule, the handling of station house identification issues will be less burdensome. It is hoped that this discussion has contributed to that goal.

Copyright 1995 by <u>New York Criminal Law News</u>. Reprinted with permission.

62. The Rape Shield Law: A Recent Case

C.P.L. Sec. 60.42, entitled *Rules of Evidence; admissibility of evidence of victim's sexual conduct in sex offense cases,* commonly known as the "Rape Shield Law," defines the limitations and conditions whereby evidence of a victim's general sexual conduct may be admitted into evidence in a sex offense prosecution. The basic purpose of the statute is to prevent harassment of victims and to prevent prejudicial matter, which is essentially irrelevant to guilt or innocence, from being considered by the jury as evidence. This statute is subdivided into five sections which codify exceptions to the general introductory rule that evidence of a victim's sexual conduct may not be admitted into evidence in a prosecution under Sec. 130.00 et al. of the Penal Law.

The first exception under sub. 1 states that such evidence may be admitted where it proves or tends to prove specific instances of the victim's prior sexual conduct with the accused. The second, under sub. 2, is where it proves or tends to prove that the victim has been convicted of an offense under Sec. 230.00 of the Penal Law within three years prior to the sex offense which is the subject of the prosecution. The third, sub. 3, is where such evidence rebuts evidence introduced by the People of the victim's failure to engage in sexual intercourse, deviate sexual intercourse or sexual contact during a given period of time. The fourth, sub. 4, is where such evidence rebuts evidence introduced by the People which proves or tends to prove that the accused is the cause of pregnancy or disease of the victim or the source of semen found in the victim. The fifth, sub. 5, is where it is determined by the court, after an offer of proof by the accused outside the hearing of the jury or such hearing as the court may require and a statement by the court of its findings of fact essential to its determination, to be relevant and admissible in the interests of justice. This fifth subsection, in its language and operation, is of particular interest. It may be denominated as the interest of justice exception of the general statutory prohibition against the admission of evidence of a victim's prior sexual conduct in a sex offense case. The state proves that such evidence may be admitted into evidence after an offer of proof by the accused outside of the jury's presence, or some sort of hearing. The court must make findings of fact that the evidence is relevant and admissible in the interests of justice.

A recent case, *People v. Williams, et. al.,* 81 N.Y.2d 303, 598 N.Y.S.2d 167 (1993), illustrates how the court may consider to choose to apply this fifth catchall exceptional section. In *Williams,* the defendants were convicted of multiple counts of and rape and sodomy in the first degree. The facts in *Williams* were that a New Jersey woman alleged the defendants forced her into their car outside a Manhattan dance club, took her to a Brooklyn apartment and there raped and sodomized her. The defendant, Williams, the only one to take the stand, essentially testified that the entire sexual encounter was consensual. The defendant challenged the trial court's application of the Rape Shield Law, wherein the court denied their application to introduce evidence showing the complainant had previously engaged in group sex. Specifically, at trial, the defendant Faeroe's defense counsel asked the court to admit evidence showing the complainant, who was white, had previously engaged in consensual group sex with black males. The defendant made an offer of proof, arguing the evidence would be relevant with regard to the complainant's motivation in terms of testifying against the defendants. After a colloquy with both prosecution and defense counsel, the court ruled against admission of the evidence.

The defendants asserted on appeal that the procedure adopted by the trial court denied them the minimal right to make an adequate offer of proof and that the proceedings were so limited as to deny them due process and their federal constitutional right to present evidence and cross-examine witnesses in their defense.

The court initially proceeded to analyze the Rape Shield statute, its legislative purpose and history by way of a review of the relevant case law, in light of the requirements of due process and the right of the defense to confront the prosecution's witnesses and to present a defense. The court went on to state that the accused's right to cross-examine witnesses and present a defense is not absolute and that evidentiary restrictions are to be voided only if they are arbitrary and disproportionate to the purpose they are intended to serve.

The court went on to state that the Supreme Court has recognized that the Rape Shield laws express the State's legitimate interest in preventing harassment of victims and the prevention of surprise at trial. The court held that the procedural requirements of the statute were met here, stating that defense counsel was allowed to describe the proposed evidence. The court held that the trial court had satisfied its obligation to hear the offer of proof that evidence of prior group sex with black males could be relevant to motivation and consent. Defense counsel, the court noted, was given an opportunity to summarize the evidence and explain its relevance. The trial court's findings of fact, the court held, were also adequate. The court also stated that reversal was also not required on the basis of a constitutional violation, since the court did not refuse to hear the offer of proof to defense. The court went on to state that to require the accused to make a threshold showing of relevance under Sec. 604.2 is a minimal demand of the adversarial system and the court did not err in refusing to proceed to a full hearing. The court noted that defense counsel made no effort to explain how prior sexual conduct would be probative of motivation to testify and did not suggest the evidence might be relevant to consent. In sum, the Court of Appeals held the trial court had acted reasonably.

Williams is a significant decision in that it makes clear that the procedure of sub. 5 of the Rape Shield Law will be minimally applied by the Court of Appeals. As long as defense counsel is given some opportunity to make his argument, the statutory requirement is satisfied. In *Williams*, in spite of the obvious relevance of the proffered evidence in this case, the Court of Appeals upheld the trial court's rejection of its being heard.

Surely, it can be argued the evidence in this case, to wit, the prior sexual conduct of the victim in this case was probative and relevant. To prevent the unearthing of this evidence in this rape case is to unduly protect the victim's feelings and reputation. It is surely relevant evidence that the victim has entered into consensual group sex in the past and now claims rape. The complainant who initiates a prosecution and takes the stand palpably puts her character and reputation on the line. The defendant, in a Sandoval Hearing, is not completely protected from his prior bad acts and offenses should he choose to take the stand. Nor, in the same way, should the complainant be protected. Such evidence as was proffered in this case, is relevant and the court is unduly limiting the application of the interests of justice section of the Rape Shield to prevent its reception into evidence.

For better or worse, we are all victims of our past and the sum total of our experiences and actions. Sandoval ensures fairness to the defendant should he choose to testify. The Rape Shield Law does the same for the complainant. Neither should serve to fully shield, but rather exists to ensure fairness. Excluding such evidence as was offered in *Williams* fails in its result to ensure that total fairness and total truth will be reached and, as *Williams* concluded, to say that such evidence is irrelevant is begging the question.

63. The Motion for a Mistrial in a Criminal Case

C.P.L. §280.10, entitled "Motion for Mistrial," states in pertinent part (sub. 1) that at any time during trial the court must declare a mistrial and order a new trial of an indictment upon motion of the defendant when there occurs during the trial an error or legal defect which is prejudicial and deprives him of a fair trial. This subsection further states that when such an error occurs in a multiple defendant trial, the court must declare a mistrial only as to the defendant or defendants making or joining in the motion.

Subd. 2 of C.P.L. §280.10 states that the People may make the motion when there occurs during the trial, inside or outside the courtroom, gross misconduct by the defendant or some person acting on his behalf or by a juror, resulting in substantial and irreparable prejudice to the People's case. This subsection, mirroring sub. 1, states that when such misconduct occurs during a joint trial of two or more defendants and when the court is satisfied that it did not result in substantial prejudice to the People's case as against a particular defendant and that such defendant was in no way responsible for the misconduct, it may not declare a mistrial with respect to such defendant but must proceed with the trial as to him.

Sub. 3, the final subsection of this overall statutory section, states that upon motion of either party a mistrial motion may be granted, or on the court's own motion when it is physically impossible to proceed with the trial in conformity with law.

Thus, C.P.L. §280.10 defines the criteria and bases for the granting of a mistrial when made on application of the defendant (subs. 1, 3), the People (subs. 2, 3) or the court (sub. 3).

This article proposes to consider the proper criteria and analyze the relevant case law as to when a mistrial motion made by the defendant will be granted by the court and by what methodology the People or the Court sua sponte may successfully move for a mistrial when the defense objects or does not consent.

First it should be noted that granting a mistrial when the defendant requests it rests in the sound discretion of the court. See *People v. Collins,* 72 A.D.2d 431, 424 N.Y.S.2d 954 (4th Dept. 1980); *People v. Portalatin,* 105 Misc.2d 725, 433 N.Y.S.2d 57 (Sup. Ct., Queens County 1980). Motions by the defense are frequently made but seldom granted and generally the purported prejudicial defect or error is cured not by the court's granting the defendant's application for a mistrial, but by a curative cautionary instruction by the Court directed to the jury.

Thus in *People v. Santiago,* 52 N.Y.2d 865 (1981), the Court of Appeals affirmed the trial court's denial of the defendant's mistrial application holding that any prejudice resulting from the brief mention at the defendant's trial of uncharged criminal activity was cured when the court took curative action. Similarly, in *People v. Reed*, 176 A.D.2d 972 (2nd Dept. 1991), the Appellate Division held that any prejudice resulting from the police officer's inadvertent reference to a gun found near the defendant which had previously been ruled inadmissible was negated by a curative instruction. See also *People v. Richardson*, 175 A.D.2d 143 (2nd Dept. 1991); *People v. Mosley*, 170 A.D.2d 990 (4th Dept. 1991); *People v. Foster*, 164 A.D.2d 894 (2nd Dept. 1990).

There are times however when upon application of the defendant a mistrial will be granted. The error must be sufficiently egregious and prejudicial such that the taint may not be cured by a mere cautionary instruction by the court.

Some examples will suffice to illustrate. *People v. Barranco*, 174 A.D.2d 343, 570 N.Y.S.2d 555 (1st Dept. 1991), was an appeal from a jury verdict where the defendant was convicted in the Supreme Court of Bronx County of Criminal Sale of a Controlled Substance in the Third Degree. The First Department held that the defendant was properly entitled to a mistrial when, after the prosecutor and defense counsel had agreed that vials of cocaine found in the search of the lobby where the defendant had allegedly sold cocaine to an undercover officer should not have been offered into evidence or referred to, the arresting officer referred to eleven vials when asked whether he had recovered anything of an evidentiary nature.

Again, in *People v. Copeland*, 127 A.D.2d 846, 511 N.Y.S.2d 949 (2nd Dept. 1987), the Second Department sustained the trial court's granting of the defendant's mistrial application, when the prosecutor made repeated references to the defendant's three and one quarter hours of silence following arrest, despite instructions by the court that evidence of the defendant's silence was inadmissible for impeachment purposes. See also *People v. Cardinale*, 35 A.D.2d 1073, 316 N.Y.S.2d 369 (4th Dept. 1970); *People v. Ramos*, 141 Misc. 2d 930, 525 N.Y.S.2d 662 (S. Ct. New York County 1988).

Thus, although a mistrial application engendered by the defendant is rarely granted, defense counsel may be successful in the application where he can convince the court, primarily though the use of creative legal argument, that the prejudice and taint are too great to be cured by a mere court instruction to the jury. It is of value. to the defendant to have the application granted since he has already gained a major insight into the People's case, and the prosecution is locked into the testimony of its witnesses. The defendant may thus be in a better position to prevail in a retrial, or in the alternative, obtain a favorable disposition since, for reasons of scarce resources and judicial economy or the unavailability of prosecution witnesses, the People may be disinclined to proceed to a retrial.

Of course, the other side of the coin must be considered that, if defense is successful in a mistrial application, he runs the risk of not obtaining an acquittal which might have been obtained in the absence of the making of the application and its granting. Also, like defense counsel, the prosecution will have gained an opportunity to retry the case and an opportunity to avoid past mistakes with an equally clear insight into the defendant's case.

In short, apart from considerations of preserving the record, the making of a mistrial application is always a gamble and defense counsel must tread carefully in this sensitive aspect of a criminal case.

With respect to the People's application for a mistrial, the statutory basis for such a motion is set forth in C.P.L. §280.10 subs. 2, 3. Under these subdivisions there must be gross misconduct during a trial by the defendant or by a person acting on his behalf or by a juror; or a claim that it is physically impossible to proceed to trial in conformity with the law.

The overall basis for a mistrial obtained by the court's or prosecutor's application where the defendant does not consent or where he objects is stated in *Enright v. Siedlecki,* 59 N.Y.2d 195, 464 N.Y.S.2d 418 (1983), which is the classic New York case on "manifest necessity" and its particular application. *Enright* was an Article 78 proceeding brought to prohibit further criminal proceedings following the declaration of a mistrial. The Appellate Division granted the relief sought and appeals were taken by permission of the Court of Appeals. The Court of Appeals initially stated that when a mistrial is declared without the consent or over the objection of the defendant, retrial is precluded unless there is manifest necessity for the mistrial. The court cited several U.S. Supreme Court and New York State Court of Appeals decisions. The court then analyzed the Appellate Division's determination to grant the Article 78 petitions therein on the ground that the trial judge had abused his discretion in granting the mistrial application. In short, the issue before the Court of Appeals was whether such manifest necessity existed so that retrial would be permitted.

The Court held that manifest necessity existed for the declaration of a mistrial when an essential defense witness became unavailable in the companion case of *Huntzinge,* and also in *Enright* when, after opening statements referring to a confession by a defendant had been made, the prosecutor discovered a Miranda warning statement indicating that the defendant had requested counsel and the confession was suppressed.

The implementation of the manifest necessity criterion has been variously interpreted by the appellate courts of this state. Thus, in *Matter of Cardin,* 53 A.D.2d 253, 385 N.Y.S.2d 667 (4th Dept 1976), where, after the court forbade inquiry into pending sales charges in a criminal drug possession case pursuant to its ruling in a pretrial Sandoval hearing, the court's ruling was violated by two successive police witnesses, the Fourth Department held that the court improvidently exercised its discretion when it declared a mistrial over the defendant's objection, finding that no manifest necessity existed. Similarly, in *People ex rei. Brinkman v. Barr,* 248 N.Y. 126, 168 N.E. 444 (1928), the Court of Appeals found that manifest necessity existed when the trial was interrupted by the illness of the judge.

Familiarity with the nuances of when a mistrial motion is proper is essential to the skills of a practicing criminal law attorney and it is hoped that this article has shed some informative light on the subject.

64. Possession with Intent to Sell: A Matter of Sufficiency

P.L. Sec. 220.16(1), entitled Criminal Possession of a Controlled Substance in the Third Degree, is one of the most common of possessory drug crimes. The charge often occurs in conjunction with the charge of P.L. Sec. 220.39, Criminal Sale of a Controlled Substance in the Third Degree. In pragmatic terms, the charge of Criminal Possession of a Controlled Substance in the Third Degree is often founded where the defendant has been arrested for an undercover or observation sale, or has been seen making sales, and drugs are recovered from his person in the search incident to his arrest or seized from the area of his curtilage.

This article proposes to analyze what type of proof may be sufficient to sustain this charge and, in particular, whether the possession of drugs alone can sustain the charge.

The case law falls into certain discrete categories. The most common category is where a sale has been made or has been seen to have been made and drugs are subsequently recovered from the person of the defendant or within his purview. *People v. Lemonious,* 168 A.D.2d 636, 563 N.Y.S.2d 470 (2d Dept. 1990), is a good example. *Lemonious* was an appeal from a judgment of the Supreme Court of Kings County convicting the defendant of Criminal Possession of a Controlled Substance in the Third Degree and Criminal Possession of a Weapon in the Third Degree. The facts were that an undercover officer purchased a tinfoil packet of cocaine through a slot in a steel door in an abandoned apartment building in Brooklyn. A few minutes later, a backup team arrived and battered down the door. On entering the apartment, the police found the defendant standing within two feet of a rifle and handgun. More significantly, the police found several tinfoil packets of cocaine, drug paraphernalia, and a pile of loose cocaine in plain view.

The appellate court sustained the conviction.

It is clear that the element of "intent to sell" was found in the prior sale through that same apartment door where the defendant, drugs, and drug paraphernalia were also found. A classical example is found in *People v. Torres,* 168 A.D.2d 363, 562 N.Y.S.2d 697 (1st Dept. 1990), where the First Department affirmed a conviction for both Criminal Sale and Criminal Possession of a Controlled Substance in the Third Degree. In this case, after the defendant transacted a sale to an undercover officer and upon a subsequent search, the defendant was found with prerecorded "buy" money and two additional glassine envelopes of cocaine in his pants pocket. Again the fact of the sale clearly resulted in the affirmance of the charge of P.L. Sec. 220.16. despite the fact that only two units of cocaine were subsequently recovered from the defendant's person. See also *People v. Hansen,* 158 A.D.2d 542, 551 N.Y.S.2d 311 (2d Dept. 1990).

People v. Randolph, 157 A.D.2d 866, 550 N.Y.S.2d 741 (2d Dept. 1990), represents another factual variation or play, so to speak, on this category. In

Randolph, an officer in an area known for its high incidence of narcotics trafficking thought he observed the defendant exchanging several small plastic bags of U.S. currency. The defendant went to an establishment nearby known as the Blue Room where the defendant was observed throwing away small plastic bags toward the bar area, which, when they were retrieved by the police, were found to contain cocaine. The Appellate Division again sustained the conviction. Once again, the fact that the defendant was observed making an earlier sale was the primary fact leading the Appellate Division in sustaining this conviction for Possession With Intent to Sell. See also *People v. McKinnon,* 176 A.D.2d 193, 574 N.Y.S.2d 201 (lst Dept. 1990).

A second category of cases where such convictions will be sustained by an appellate court is where, in addition to drugs, a substantial amount of cash is recovered from the person of the defendant. Thus, in *People v. Wells,* 159 A.D.2d 799, 552 N.Y.S.2d 688 (3rd Dept. 1990), the Third Department affirmed a P.L. Sec. 220.16 conviction, where a search of the defendant's person, after an arrest for Aggravated Unlicensed Operation of a Motor Vehicle, revealed that he was carrying $800 to $900 in cash, and a subsequent search of the defendant's vehicle revealed the presence of drug paraphernalia and a substantial amount of cocaine. Clearly, in this case, the amount of cash coupled with the amount of drugs led the appellate court to sustain this conviction.

Similarly, in *People v. Ortiz,* 170 A.D.2d 396, 566 N.Y.S.2d 285 (1st Dept. 1991), the First Department sustained the conviction where there was not only an offer to sell made to the undercover officer by the defendant, but he was found in possession of $88.00 in cash and eight glassine envelopes of heroin. In this case, the presence not only of an offer to sell, but the cash and drugs found on the defendant, led the Appellate Court to sustain this conviction. See also *People v. Walton,* 184 A.D.2d 675, 584 N.Y.S.2d 879 (2d Dept. 1992) – Defendant observed making sales and found in possession of 86 vials of cocaine and $701.00 in cash at the time of his arrest. See also *People v. Rivera,* 177 A.D.2d 664, 576 N.Y.S.2d 365 (2d Dept. 1991).

People v. Calada, 154 A.D.2d 700, 546 N.Y.S.2d 681 (2d Dept. 1991), introduces the additional factor of a beeper being found on the defendant and also a sum of cash. These factors led the Appellate Division, Second Department, to sustain the P.L. Sec. 220.16 conviction.

The third category where a conviction of P.L. Sec. 220.16 will be sustained by an appellate court of this state is where a large amount of drugs are recovered from the defendant's person. Thus, the Second Department in *People v. Blue,* 173 A.D.2d 836, 570 N.Y.S.2d 659 (2d Dept. 1991), sustained a P.L. Sec. 220.16 conviction where 50 vials of cocaine were recovered from the vehicle the defendant occupied. See also *People v. Vailes,* 150 A.D.2d 406, 540 N.Y.S.2d 837 (2d Dept. 1989) – 48 bags of marijuana and 21 packets of cocaine.

This review of the pertinent case law reveals that to establish the requisite mental culpability to infer the "intent to sell" under P.L. Sec. 220.16, the defendant must have either made a sale and, upon search of his person, drugs are found on him; or have been observed making a sale or sales; be found with a substantial amount or cash, drugs, or a beeper; or be found with such a large amount of drugs as to lead to the conclusion that the requisite "intent to sell" is proved.

If one can conclude anything from this brief review of the case law, it is that to infer the "intent to sell" element of this drug possession charge—unless a large amount of drugs are recovered from the defendant's person—there must be other facts present, such as a sale, a large amount of cash or a beeper recovered from the defendant's person. One can conclude the presence of a small amount of drugs recovered from the defendant's person without some other coupling factor or nexus will not lead an appellate court of this state to sustain this charge.

65. A Note on the Scope of Criminal Discovery in New York

The insanity defense can be one of the most potent tools of the attorney for the defense. An effective array of psychiatrists and their reports can overwhelm the jurors. An indigent defendant, however, can ill afford a private psychiatric examination and may request the court to provide one. Assuming an indigent criminal defendant is granted his motion for a psychiatric examination and report, the question arises whether the District Attorney can obtain these reports prior to trial and call these doctors to testify, regardless of the favorable or unfavorable character of the reports. Is reception of these reports by the People and the testimony of psychiatrists based thereon violative of defendant's right against self-incrimination or the physician-patient privilege? Consideration of these questions requires some understanding of the nature and scope of criminal discovery in the State of New York.[1]

The Competency Statute

C.C.P. 658–662 provided a procedure whereby a defendant's fitness to proceed to trial could be determined through the use of a court-ordered psychiatric examination. Sec. 662 strictly prohibited the admission of this report into evidence.[2]

The Criminal Procedure Law replaced the old Code of Criminal Procedure in 1970. Sec. 730.20, *Fitness to proceed; generally,* replaced C.C.P. 662. Subdivision 6 of section 730.20 is new and provides:

> 6. When a defendant is subjected to examination pursuant to an order issued by a criminal court in accordance with this article, any statement made by him for the purpose of the examination or treatment shall be inadmissible in evidence against him in any criminal action on any issue other than that of his mental

condition, but such statement is admissible upon that issue whether or not it would otherwise be deemed a privileged communication.

The new statute represents an extension of C.C.P. Sec. 662 under which a psychiatric report was always inadmissible. Under Sec. 730.20(6) a defendant's statements, in the course of such examination, are admissible solely on the issue of his mental condition, regardless of their privileged character. Moreover, in *People v. Wise* (47 A.D. 2d 969), the court rejected defendant's contention that testimony based upon an examination conducted under Sec. 730.20 of the Criminal Procedure Law should not be admitted into evidence at trial on the issue of defendant's sanity. This is but one step from admitting the report itself into evidence and, indeed, may establish a precedent for admitting the report.[3]

The 730.20 schema refers only to a report issuing during a competency hearing. The statute and its interpretation under *Wise* are, however, indicative of a liberalized trend to the discovery and admissibility of the psychiatric report in a criminal trial.

Criminal Discovery: An Overview

Criminal discovery in the State of New York traces its origin to case law, not statute, and was originally limited in scope and solely the prerogative of the defendant. Thus, in *People ex rei. Lemon v. Supreme Court*, 245 N.Y. 24, Judge Cardozo rejected the defendant's request for disclosure, in advance of trial, of notes and memoranda prepared by the prosecutor's office. Judge Cardozo refused however to rule out criminal discovery altogether and, in dicta, left leeway for the courts, in their discretion, to extend the scope of criminal discovery on an ad hoc, case by case, basis through an inherent supervisory jurisdiction to grant disclosure in the appropriate circumstances. *People ex rei. Lemon v. Supreme Court, supra*, at 32-33.

Subsequent cases extended the scope of criminal discovery to the following documents and evidence: photostatic copy of memorandum of agreement (*People v. Radeloff*, 140 Misc. 690); incriminating letters (*People v. Wargo*, 149 Misc. 461); hospital records (*People v. Preston*, 13 Misc.2d 802); admissions (*People v. Stokes*, 24 Misc.2d 755); civil service examination papers allegedly forged by defendant (*People v. Calandrillo*, 29 Misc.2d 491).[4]

This extension in the scope of criminal discovery culminated with the enactment of C.P.L. 240.20, the discovery provision. This statute not only codifies prior case law in this area, but broadens the subject of discovery and provides, under certain conditions, for reciprocal discovery by the People (*People v. Collins*, 75 Misc.2d 535). The following is the statutory scheme for reciprocal discovery under Sec. 240.20:

1. a prior defense motion for discovery with respect to property specified in Sec. 240.20(2,3)
2. a timely motion by the People to condition defendant's order of discovery upon discovery by the People (C.P.L. 240.20[4])

3. The property sought to be discovered must be material to the preparation of the People's case, and the request must be reasonable. (C.P.L. 240.20[4]).

4. The property sought to be discovered must be of the same kind or character as that authorized to be discovered by the defendant, must be within the possession, custody, or control of the defendant, and must be property he intends to, or is likely to, produce at trial (C.P.L. 240.20[4])

5. The statute also provides for a hearing in opposition to the motion and for a number of protective devices (C.P.L. 240.20[5]).

Thus, in our given hypothetical case, at such time as the defendant is granted a motion for discovery of a comparable mental examination under C.P.L. 240.20(2), the People, upon a showing of materiality and reasonableness, may move to condition this order of discovery upon discovery of defendant's psychiatric report if it is (a) in the possession, custody, or control of the defendant and (b) if defendant intends to or is likely to produce it at trial.[5]

This statutory scheme is preemptive of any prior case law and is given strict adherence under the applicable cases (Physical examination discoverable, while the observations of the arresting officer are not, since the latter constitutes work product and so is exempt property under the statute) (*People v. Lawrence,* 74 Misc.2d 1019); (Defendant's omnibus motion for discovery not granted since discovery is limited to the items specifically listed in Sec. 240.20 under the conditions set forth therein) (*People v. Spencer,* 79 Misc.2d 72); (People could not discover scientific reports in defendant's possession since [1] People's motion was untimely because two prior motions for discovery by defendant were granted by the court without any condition and the orders were complied with, [2] People failed to show materiality and reasonableness, [3] People did not specify the property as of the same kind as that discovered by the defendant). (*People v. Rexhouse,* 77 Misc.2d 386).

Thus, if the statutory scheme is strictly complied with, the People may discover defendant's psychiatric report unless production would violate a constitutional or statutory privilege. *People v. Sumpter,* (75 Misc.2d 55).[6]

The issue, then, is whether the Fifth Amendment privilege against self-incrimination or the physician-patient privilege prevent the People from obtaining defendant's psychiatric report under Sec. 240.20, using the report at trial, and calling the psychiatrist who prepared the report to testify.[7]

The Privilege Against Self-Incrimination

The privilege against self-incrimination is waived with respect to psychiatric testimony when defendant pleads an insanity defense. In *Lee v. County Court of Erie County,* 27 N.Y.2d 432, *cert. den.* 404 U.S. 823, the People moved for a psychiatric examination of defendant pursuant to C.C.P. Sec. 658. Defendant pleaded not guilty by reason of insanity and refused to submit to an examination which the court had ordered him to undergo prior to this, on the ground of a violation of his Fifth Amendment privilege. The Court of Appeals held, initially, that the privilege does, in fact, obtain during a pretrial psychiatric examination since, under *Schmerber v. California,* 384 U.S. 757, such a pre-trial examination concerning defendant's mental state at the time of the commission of the crime constituted evidence of a testimonial or communicative nature and so was protected by the Fifth Amendment. The court further held, however, that in raising the defense of insanity, defendant voluntarily waived the self-incrimination privilege. The physician is competent to testify only as to those facts which form the basis of his medical opinion with respect to defendant's state of mind at the time of the alleged commission of the crime; he does not, because of this waiver, become a competent witness on all matters concerning the commission of the crime. The District Attorney cannot use the psychiatric examination as evidence on the issue of guilt, nor can an admission as to the crime in question be considered by the jury in determining whether the defendant committed the crime charged (*Lee v. County Court, supra*).

The narrow holding of *Lee* is that a defendant, in interposing an insanity defense, waives his privilege against self-incrimination which existed at the pretrial stage, and so has no constitutional right to refuse to submit to a psychiatric examination. Once the privilege is waived by interposing the insanity defense, the examining psychiatrist is free to testify as to the facts which form the basis of his medical opinion with respect to defendant's sanity.

Lee also holds that it is irrelevant which party requests the examination since it is the plea of not guilty by reason of insanity which is the basis of the psychiatrist's competency to testify at trial, thus broadening the holding of an earlier case (*People v. Di Piazza,* 24 N.Y.2d 342). The *Lee* court held where defendant requests a mental examination, he cannot complain that his privilege against self-incrimination was violated. *People v. Di Piazza, supra* at 352.[8]

Lee, did not however apply this waiver rule where discovery of the psychiatric report is sought.

In *People v. Gliewe, supra,* defendant served upon the People, pursuant to C.P.L. 250.10, notice of his intent to rely on the defense of mental disease. The People moved for an order directing the defendant to submit to a psychiatric examination to be conducted for the purpose of adducing testimony for trial on the issue of defendant's mental disease or defect at the time of the alleged murder. On oral argument of the motion, defense counsel requested a copy of the mental examination report which would be provided to the District Attorney by his psychiatrist while the People sought, pursuant to C.P.L. 240.20, copies of any mental examination report which might be provided to defense counsel by his privately selected psychiatrist. Defense counsel objected to this, asserting the report of defendant's psychiatrist may not be the subject matter of discovery under C.P.L. Sec. 240.20. The court reasoned that to require the District Attorney to provide a copy of the mental report to defense counsel and allow the defendant nondisclosure of his mental reports would violate the underlying rule of fairness required in *Lee.*

People v. Gliewe supra, is a somewhat anomalous holding. The court bases its decision that People must furnish a copy of the mental examination report to defendant, and defendant a copy of his psychiatric report to the People, on a purported rule of underlying fairness in *Lee.* C.P.L. 240.20, however, is preemptive of the case law in this area, is given strict adherence, and provides a scheme similar to *Gliewe,* whereby defendant could discover the report of the People and the People under this reciprocal discovery statute, could discover defendant's psychiatric report.[9]

The question is whether C.P.L. 240.20(4) and *Lee,* as construed by *Gliewe,*[10] can coexist as two equally valid modes of reciprocal discovery or is the statute preemptive so that while under *Lee,* the People must provide the defendant with a copy of the psychiatric examination report conducted by People's psychiatrist, the defense, by not moving for disclosure, under C.P.L. 240.20(2) may prevent disclosure of the report of defendant to People.

People v. Blacknall, 82 Misc.2d 646, suggests an answer to these and other questions. The court notes, first, that the rule of fairness in *Lee* was in the context of the issue of the presence of counsel at the psychiatric examination reports. Second, the court concluded that to provide for a definite procedure and reconcile the *Lee-Gliewe* holdings with the requirements of C.P.L. 240.20, ". . . the requirement for the People to provide defendant with a copy of the People's psychiatric report is equivalent to the defendant actually having made application pursuant to C.P.L. Sec. 240.20 (subd. 2)." (*People v. Blacknall, supra,* at 649). *Blacknall* is a County Court decision and hence there is no real resolution of the question as to whether two modes of reciprocal discovery coexist under New York law, or whether C.P.L. preempts *Lee.*

The Physician-Patient Privilege

Neither the report nor psychiatric testimony based thereon is subject to the physician-patient privilege. The privilege exists at the pretrial state of litigation.[11]

The physician-patient privilege in New York is codified in C.P.L.R. 4504 and made applicable to criminal actions by C.P.L. 60.10. The statute provides that unless the patient waives the privilege, a physician shall not be allowed to disclose information which he acquired while attending a patient in a professional capacity and which was necessary to enable him to act in that capacity. Hence, in order that the privilege may be claimed under the statute, the cases hold that three elements must exist:

1. The relationship of physician and patient must exist. This relationship exists when a physician is present for the purpose of treatment. *People v. Decina*, 1 A.D.2d 592, aff'd 2 N.Y.2d 133.
2. The information alleged to be privileged must have been acquired while the physician was attending the patient in a professional capacity. *People v. Cook,* 25 Misc.2d 722.

3. The allegedly privileged information must be necessary for treatment. *People v. Decina*, 2 N.Y.2d at 143.

The subject matter of this article is not within the ambit of the statute and its construing case law. There is not a relationship of physician and patient but of expert witness and criminal defendant. The defendant in *People v. Austin*, 199 N.Y. 446, was indicted for first degree murder. On arraignment he pleaded not guilty on the grounds of insanity. Prior to trial, defense counsel, upon an affidavit asserting that defendant was without means with which to procure the services of a physician to examine him as to his sanity and so render testimony at trial, asked that a physician be appointed by the court for this purpose. The order was made and a doctor was appointed to examine the defendant. He did so but he was not called on behalf of defendant as a witness at trial. After testimony as to defendant's sanity was offered by defendant, the People called this psychiatrist in rebuttal. Defense counsel objected that any information with respect to this examination was privileged. The court held that it was clear from the statute that if the physician never attended the defendant in a professional capacity and never obtained information from him to enable him to prescribe in a professional capacity, he can testify the same as any other person. The court concluded that where, as in this case, a physician is sent to jail by the District Attorney on defendant's motion, to make an examination of the prisoner's mental and physical condition, the relation of physician and patient, as contemplated by the statute, does not exist. *People v. Austin, supra*, at 452-53.

One final point should be noted. The People may have no occasion to call the psychiatrist and if the examination shows the defendant to be sane at the time of the commission of the crime, the latter certainly would not call him. Although the prosecution has the burden of proof on the matter of defendant's sanity, there is a presumption of sanity, the effect of which is to enable the prosecution to establish a prima facie case and satisfy its burden without introducing further evidence of defendant's sanity unless the defendant offers evidence on this issue.[12]

Even assuming arguendo, that part, or all, of the psychiatrist's testimony is subject to the physician-patient privilege, i.e. the privilege can still be waived.

In *People v. Al-Kanani*, 33 N.Y.2d 260 cert. den. 417 U.S. 916, appellant sought reversal of a murder conviction, contending that the physician-patient privilege was violated when the prosecution produced a psychiatrist who had treated defendant at a state hospital and who testified that defendant was sane at the time of the slaying. The court held that the psychiatrist's testimony was not privileged since defendant had previously offered the testimony of a psychiatrist who had examined him shortly after the murder, and who stated that, in his opinion, defendant was insane at the time the crime was committed. The court stated that where insanity is asserted as a defense and the defendant offers evidence in support of his plea, the defendant waives his physician-patient privilege and the People may call psychiatric experts to testify regarding his sanity, although they may have treated him. (*People v. Al-Kanani, supra*, at 264). Thus, in our hypothetical case, the physician-patient privilege, if it exists, is waived when defendant pleads an insanity defense and offers evidence in support thereof.[13]

The effect of *Al-Kanani* is not clear. In a later case, *State of Florida v. Axelson*, 80 Misc.2d 419, the court claims to give *Al-Kanani* precedential effect, yet states that the *Al-Kanani* court held that the physician-patient privilege is waived by a defendant who asserts the insanity defense and so affirmatively puts his mental condition in controversy. (*State of Florida v. Axelson, supra*). The court makes no mention of offering evidence in support thereof, an element of the *Al-Kanani* rule for an effective waiver of the physician-patient privilege. In support of this rule this court cites, along with *Al-Kanani*, an earlier case, *People v. Buthy*, 38 A.D. 10. In *People v. Buthy, supra*, two of the People's psychiatrists had previously treated defendant as a private patient. The court rejected defendant's contention that the information thus obtained was privileged since defendant introduced evidence to prove his insanity and so waived the privilege accorded him by C.P.L.R. 4504(a). The court went on to say that, as a general rule, the privilege is waived when the issue has been put in controversy. (*People v. Buthy, supra*, at 13).

The criterion for an effective waiver in *Buthy* is not clear. First the *Buthy* court states that the privilege was waived, in that case, when defendant introduced evidence to prove his insanity and cites a number of decisions in support thereof. The court then cites *Koump v. Smith*, 25 N.Y.2d 287, for the general proposition that waiver of the privilege results when the issue has been put in controversy. The *Koump* court states that a defendant's mental or physical condition is put in controversy when it is affirmatively put in issue.

> We do not hold that the privilege is waived whenever a party defends an action in which his mental or physical condition is in controversy. The rule laid down today is limited to cases in which a defendant affirmatively asserts the condition either by way of counterclaim or to excuse the conduct complained of by plaintiff. *Koump v. Smith, (supra*, at 294).

Under *Koump*, it would appear the pleadings determine whether a mental or physical condition has been put in controversy so that a waiver of the physician-patient privilege occurs. Hence, *Axelson* may not be in accord with *Al-Kanani* on the criterion for an effective waiver of the physician-patient privilege, since *Axelson* holds that a waiver of the privilege occurs when defendant asserts an insanity defense and cites *Buthy* and *Al-Kanani* for the "put in controversy" test. *Buthy*, in turn, refers to *Koump* for this test. The latter case holds that a mental condition is put in controversy when put in issue by the pleadings, whether by counterclaim or otherwise. Hence, *Axelson* apparently establishes a rule for waiver of the physician-patient privilege similar to the *Lee* rule for waiver of the privilege against self-incrimination—when raised in the pleadings the privilege is waived—and erroneously cites *Al-Kanani* as authority for this differing rule. *Axelson*, however, may be interpreted as following *Al-Kanani* since the court states the privilege is waived when the defendant asserts the insanity defense. A possible interpretation of "assertion" may include the offering of evidence in support of said defense, the *Al-Kanani* rule. Moreover, the *Axelson* court cites *Al-Kanani* as precedent but also cites *Buthy* wherein the latter case states that a waiver occurs when the defendant introduces evidence to prove his insanity.

Conclusion

It is clear that under C.P.L. 240.20 the psychiatric report on a defendant and the testimony based thereon is discoverable by the People and admissible provided the statute is strictly complied with. Once the defense of insanity is noticed under C.P.L. 250.10, the self-incrimination privilege is waived under *Lee v. County Court, supra*, at 432. The physician-patient privilege is not applicable to the present situation since there is no relationship of physician and patient. In any case, the privilege may be waived by pleading the defense of insanity and submitting evidence in support thereof, *People v. Al-Kanani, supra*. Although certain problems remain reconciling the holdings of *Lee* and *Gliewe* with the statute (C.P.L. 240.20) and properly interpreting *Axelson* in light of *Al-Kanani* and *Buthy*, the law of discovery in this area is relatively clear.

66. Three Final Pretrial Hearings

In two previous articles published by the *Queens Bar Bulletin,* various little known but nevertheless significant Pretrial Hearings were considered and analyzed, in addition to the most common Huntley, Wade, Mapp and Rodriguez Hearings. In this final trio of three articles, three equally uncommon but potentially significant Pretrial Hearings will be considered, defined, and analyzed.

The first is the *Argentine* Hearing, so named after the case *People v. Argentine*, 67 A.D.2d 180, 414 N.Y.S.2d 732 (1979). In *Argentine*, the defendant was arrested for the charge of Forgery in the Second Degree. The defendant claimed that he spoke with two Nassau County Detectives and an Assistant District Attorney of Nassau County who, the defendant claimed, obtained his cooperation in a homicide investigation and promised that in return for his cooperation that the felony charge would be dropped to a Misdemeanor; that the violation of his parole charges would be held in abeyance; and that he would be restored to parole.

The defendant was then arraigned and released on his own custody. The record, the court stated, was unclear as to whether the defendant had performed any services on behalf of the police and District Attorney regarding the homicide investigation.

The defendant testified before the Grand Jury, was indicted and moved to dismiss both indictments alleging prosecutorial misconduct in failing to honor the promise made at the time of his arrest. These motions were denied.

Thereafter the defendant pled guilty to the crime of Attempted Criminal Possession of a Forged Instrument in the Second Degree in satisfaction of both indictments. The defendant contended on appeal that his motion to dismiss on the ground of prosecutorial misconduct, i.e., that the People had failed to honor their promise of leniency in return for the defendant's promise of cooperation, was improperly denied.

The court held that where the defendant showed in his motion papers by affidavits of the Assistant District Attorney and Detective that a promise of leniency had been made to the defendant for his cooperation in the investigation of a homicide offense and the People merely asserted that no promise had been made, a Hearing should be held to determine whether a promise was made, its nature and scope, and whether the defendant had performed services in reliance on the promise.

If these factors at the hearing should be found to exist, the court held, in essence, that the bargain should be enforced in favor of the defendant even though these efforts may have been found to have been unsuccessful.

The second Hearing to be considered is the *Hellenbrand* Hearing so named after the case *Matter of Holtzman v. Hellenbrand*, 92 A.D.2d 405, 460 N.Y.S.2d 591 (2d Dept. 1983). *Hellenbrand* emanated from an Article 78 Proceeding wherein the District Attorney sought a Writ of Mandamus directing the trial judge to conduct a Hearing to determine whether the defendant's misconduct had induced a state's witness to refuse to testify. In this case, the defendant Neil Sirois was charged with Murder in the Second Degree. The defendant's wife was a witness and testified before the Grand Jury against her husband. Subsequently she advised an Assistant District Attorney that she wished to recant her testimony and reconcile with the defendant. She then fled the jurisdiction. Therefore, Adele Sirois, the wife, was arrested pursuant to a Material Witness Order in Brooklyn where she was residing with the defendant under an assumed name. When this matter came to trial Mrs. Sirois refused to testify and was adjudged in contempt of court and sentenced to serve 30 days in jail and to pay a fine of $250.00. When the People's request for an Adjournment of 30 days was denied, the People moved for a Hearing on the authority of *U.S. v. Mastrangelo*, 693 E.2d 269 (2d Cir, 1982), to determine whether the defendant by his misconduct had induced his wife to unlawfully refuse to testify at trial and if so to find that Mrs. Sirois' Grand Jury testimony should be admitted as direct evidence at her husband's Murder Trial. The trial court denied the People's request for such a Hearing and the people then filed the instant Article 78 Proceeding. The court then proceeded to deny the Writ of Mandamus but stated that where the People allege specific facts which demonstrate a distinct possibility that a criminal defendant's misconduct has induced a witness to unlawfully refuse to testify, a Hearing must be held in which the People shall have the opportunity to prove misconduct by clear and convincing evidence and upon an affirmative finding of prosecutorial misconduct the People can introduce the witness' prior Grand Jury testimony and such testimony may be admitted as direct evidence at trial.

The final Hearing, in the trio of Hearings to be considered, is the *Townsend* or *Singer* Hearing so named after *People v. Townsend*, 38 A.D.2d 669, 328 N.Y.S.2d 333 (2d Dept. 1971); *People v. Singer* 44 N.Y.2d 241, 405 N.Y.S.2d 17 (1978).

Both these cases held that a Hearing must be held for the People to establish that a preindictment or prearrest delay was reasonable and had good cause. In *Singer* there was a 42-month delay in arresting the defendant. In *Townsend* there was a delay of one year.

It is hoped that this third and final article on the subject of not widely known but nevertheless important pretrial Hearings, taken together with the Hearings analyzed in the two prior articles, will serve as a guide to criminal defense counsel whereby a way may be found amid the labyrinth of continually developing and expanding Pretrial Hearings in the criminal law of this State.

67. *Constructive Possession: An Overview*

The concept of possession and, in particular of constructive possession, is an important one in the criminal law since if actual possession of the property, whether a gun, controlled substance, or car, cannot be proved then the notion of constructive possession comes into play, a concept and burden the People, under the case law, may not be able to sustain. Thus, the client may be faced with a charge of gun possession, P.L. Sec. 265.01, a Class A Misdemeanor; or P.L. Sec. 265.02, a Class D Felony; one of many possessory controlled substance crimes such as P.L. Sec. 220.03, Criminal Possession of a Controlled Substance in the 7th Degree, P.L. Sec. 165.40, a Class A Misdemeanor; Criminal Possession of Stolen Property in the Fourth Degree, P.L. Sec. 165.45, a Class E. Felony; or Criminal Possession of Stolen Property in the Third Degree, P.L. Sec. 165.50, a Class D Felony.

Whatever the possessory charge, the client who comes to consult you who is charged with one of these classes of crimes, whether it be, specifically, possession of a stolen car, stolen jewelry, a stolen purse, controlled substance, or weapon, often has not been found in actual physical possession of the article in question. He may be a passenger in the car and the gun may have been found in the back seat. He may be visiting someone's apartment and the controlled substance may have been found lying on the kitchen table. Notwithstanding these facts, your client may be charged with a possessory crime based on the theory of constructive possession, i.e., that the defendant had dominion and control over the tangible property despite his lack of actual physical possession.[1]

What constitutes dominion and control, however, over the property in question is significant since if the People cannot prove dominion and control over the property, the case may be won for the defense. The purpose of this article, therefore, is, to some extent, to survey past and recent case law on this subject so that the criminal law practitioner may have some guide to making the determination whether dominion and control can be proved by the People. If it cannot, as a matter of law, the case may be won for the defense on this ground.

First, some recent cases. *People v. Milton Davis*, N.Y.L.J., p. 25, col. 5, 3/29/89 (2d Dept.), is instructive. *Davis* was an appeal from a 1985 conviction of Criminal Sale of a Controlled Substance in the Third Degree and Criminal Possession of a Controlled Substance in the Third Degree. *Davis* arose out of a buy and bust operation in which an undercover officer purchased cocaine through a steel slot in a building in exchange for prerecorded buy money. When the transaction was completed, the backup team moved in, broke into the apartment, proceeded to the second floor, and discovered two men in the apartment, one of whom was the defendant. Both men had fluorescent powder on their hands, a substance with which the prerecorded buy money had been treated. A search of the building revealed cocaine on the first floor, cocaine on the third floor and a jacket containing defendant's identification on the first floor. The defendant's uncle testified at trial that the defendant was in the house for the purpose of letting his children in when they arrived from school and that he gave the defendant a key to the apartment when he arrived that morning. The defendant corroborated his uncle's testimony. The jury found the defendant guilty of Criminal Sale of a Controlled Substance in the Third Degree, P.L. Sec. 220.39, and Criminal Possession of a Controlled Substance in the Third Degree, P.L. Sec. 220.16.

The Appellate Division, Second Department, sustained the sale conviction, but reversed the possession conviction. The Appellate Division held there was no evidence linking the defendant to the cocaine found on the third floor except his presence in the building or showing that the defendant exercised dominion and control over the drugs found on the first floor since his presence alone was insufficient to establish constructive possession of the drugs found there.

Finally, the Court held that the defendant's presence in a bedroom on the second floor combined with his possession of a key to the second floor apartment was insufficient to establish his constructive possession of the cocaine found in another bedroom of the second floor apartment.

Davis is most helpful to a defendant faced with a drug possession charge who merely happens to be in a particular place at a particular time where drugs are found. It is significant that the Appellate Division reversed the possession charge even though the defendant was admitted to the apartment that day by his uncle, had a key, and knew a drug ring was being operated from the apartment, though he denied involvement. The Appellate Division reversed the possession conviction although, in addition to the above facts, a jacket containing the defendant's identification was found on the first floor where drugs were found.

Despite all this, the Appellate Court found that the defendant did not constructively possess the drugs recovered beyond a reasonable doubt.

People v. Royster, N.Y.L.J., p. 23 col. 2 1/5/90 (2d Dept.), follows *Davis* in time, in reasoning, and in result. *Royster* was an appeal from a judgment of the Supreme Court of Kings County, rendered in January of 1988, convicting the defendant of Criminal Sale of a Controlled Substance in the Third Degree, P.L. Sec. 220.39, Criminal Possession of a Controlled Substance in the Third Degree, P.L. Sec. 220.16, and Criminal Possession of a Controlled Substance in the 7th Degree, P.L. 220.03. The Appellate Division reversed the possession convictions. *Royster* like *Davis*, involved a buy and bust operation through the slot of an apartment door. The backup team, on completion of the sale, gained entrance to the apartment, a social club. Defendant and a co-defendant were present in the apartment and the police recovered $850.00 from the defendant's pants pocket, including the prerecorded buy money. A search of the premises revealed three hundred and twelve vials of cocaine concealed between the apartment door and a steel plate welded onto the inside of the door. The Court held, however, that the defendant's mere presence at the social club, albeit the situs of the sale and the place where the prerecorded buy money was found, was insufficient to establish the defendant's dominion and control over the drugs found concealed in the door, on the basis of lack of constructive possession.

Once again, the proximity of the sale was insufficient to establish dominion and control and was insufficient to establish dominion and control over the premises the defendant was found in and from which he conducted the sale.

See also *People vs. Mario Garcia,* N.Y.L.J. p. 23, col. 4, 1/5/90 (2d Dept), where in response to a call that an armed individual was observed entering an apartment building, the defendant was discovered in the bathroom of one of the apartments. Drugs were found in the main room of the apartment, while a weapon was found under a mattress in the bedroom of the apartment. The Second Department sustained the narcotics conviction under the statutory presumption of P.L. Sec. 220.25 (2), but reversed the weapons conviction on a theory of lack of dominion and control, or on the theory of lack of constructive possession.

Other cases, both recent and older, argue the view that mere presence and proximity to the drugs, guns, or even car is not enough to sustain a criminal possession charge on the theory of constructive possession. For example in *People v. Ortiz,* 126 A.D.2d 677, 510 N.Y.S.2d 909 (2d Dept. 1987), agents of the Immigration and Naturalization Service went to an apartment in Queens County to investigate the report of an illegal alien at that location. The defendant opened the door of the apartment and, subsequently, one of the agents recovered two plastic bags containing a white powder which later analysis revealed to be cocaine. Testimony at trial revealed the defendant did not lease the apartment, nor was he observed near the bedroom from which the cocaine was recovered, although his passport was found in a kitchen drawer. The Appellate Division held that the evidence failed to establish the defendant exercised any dominion and control over the area where the cocaine was found, reversed the defendant's possession conviction and dismissed the indictment.

Compare, however, *People v. Angel Torres,* 68 N.Y.2D 677, 505 N.Y.S.2d 595, 496 N.E.2d 684 (1986), where following the seizure of narcotics, a gun, and narcotics paraphernalia from an apartment leased by defendant and his girlfriend, the defendant was convicted, after a jury trial, of Criminal Possession of a Controlled Substance in the 1st and 7th Degrees, Criminal Use of Drug Paraphernalia in the 2nd Degree and Criminal Possession of a Weapon in the 4th Degree. The Court of Appeals affirmed the Appellate Division, holding that dominion and control was established by the People beyond a reasonable doubt since the defendant leased the apartment, had keys, left the apartment the morning of the drug seizure with a suitcase, leaving behind his gun and other effects, was seen twenty-five to thirty times by the doorman in the month of the seizure, gave the apartment as his address when he arrived in Puerto Rico, and called the doorman from Puerto Rico to ask if the marshal, who was executing eviction warrant, had found anything.

See also on the criteria of constructive possession and sufficient dominion and control *People v. Olivo,* 120 A.D.2d 466, 502 N.Y.S.2d 739 (1st Dept. 1986) (A search of the defendant's automobile repair shop incidental to his drug arrest revealed a shotgun in plain view in back of a car. Held: insufficient dominion and control); *People v. Leandro Perez,* 125 A.D.2d 236, 504 N.Y.S. 330 (1st Dept. 1986) (Where co-defendant tossed gun out of window, into the courtyard the Appellate Division, 1st Department, held evidence could not sustain the defendant's constructive possession of that gun under P.L. 10.00, 8). But compare *People vs. Patel,* 132 A.D.2d 498, 518 N.Y.S.2d 384 (1st Dept. 1987) where the co-defendant who tossed the gun out of the window was found to have sufficient dominion and control over the weapon; *People v. Garcia,* 133 A.D.2d 123, 518 N.Y.S.2d 659 (2d Dept. 1987) (Mere presence in the apartment in which cocaine was found in the area of the bedroom closet is insufficient to conclude the defendant exercised dominion and control over the area); *People v. Hylton,* 125 A.D.2d 409, 509 N.Y.S.2d 128 (2d Dept. 1986) (Held: No dominion and control over loaded revolver found in plain view in poolroom, examined pursuant to search warrant.); *People v. Lucas,* 84 A.D.2d 582, 443 N.Y.S.2d 422 (2d Dept. 1981) (No constructive possession where defendant displayed a gun to an undercover officer, paid part of the price of the gun, and gave it to a friend, who gave it to the undercover officer); *People v. Russell,* 34 N.Y.2d 261, 357 N.Y.S.2d 415, 313 N.E.2d 732 (1974); *People v. Bentley,* 112 A.D.2d 109, 492 N.Y.S.2d 909 (2d Dept. 1987); *People v. Cicero,* 106 A.D.2d 901, 483 N.Y.S.2d 545 (4th Dept. 1987); *People v. Guzman,* 51 A.D.2d 1045, 381 N.Y.S.2d 286 (2d Dept. 1976); *People v. Harris,* 47 A.D.2d 385, 366 N.Y.S.2d 697 (4th Dept. 1975); *People v. Jefferson,* 43 A.D.2d 112, 350 N.Y.S.2d 3 (1st Dept. 1973); *People v. Patello,* 41 A.D.2d 954, 344 N.Y.S.2d 33 (2d Dept. 1973); *People v. Sanabria,* 73 A.D. 696, 523 N.Y.S.2d 223 (2d Dept. 1979); *People v. Headley,* 143 A.D.2d 937, 533 N.Y.S.2d 562 (2d Dept. 1988); *People v. Vastada,* 70 A.D.2d 918, 417 N.Y.S.2d 287 (2d Dept. 1979).

It is clear, in light of the case law here cited and examined, that where a possessory crime is charged and the basis of the indictment or information is not actual physical possession, but constructive possession of the car, controlled substance, or stolen property, a motion to dismiss the indictment may be in order, depending upon the discrete facts alleged under C.P.L. Sec. 210.20(b), on the ground the evidence before the Grand Jury was not legally sufficient to establish the offense charged or any lesser included offense.

If a misdemeanor possessory crime is charged in an information, a similar motion may be made under C.P.L. Sec. 170.35, based on factual insufficiency.

It is imperative for defense counsel, therefore, where a case based on constructive possession is alleged, to thoroughly investigate the matter in preparation for a motion to dismiss based on the law and the facts.

A final note should be added. If a technical motion to dismiss should not lie, all hope is not lost, for counsel may still file and possibly be successful on a Clayton motion or a motion to dismiss in the interest of justice under either Section 210.40 of the C.P.L, if the defendant is indicated on a felony charge, or, if the charge is a misdemeanor, under Section 170.40 of the C.P.L.

This writer recently was successful in dismissing a controlled substance offense on this ground in the Queens County Supreme Court, citing a number of cases referred to in this article. In this case, the defendant was charged and indicted under P.L. 220.09, Criminal Possession a Controlled Substance in the Fourth Degree, a Class C Felony. She had no prior criminal record and faced a maximum between five and fifteen years in prison. The facts were that the defendant was working as a barmaid and there occurred an undercover sale outside of the premises. The perpetrator in the undercover sale fled into the bar and hid the drugs she had in her possession behind the bar. Some moments later, the police came into the bar, found the drugs some twenty feet from the defendant and arrested the defendant and charged her under P.L. Sec. 220.09. In a Clayton motion to dismiss in the interest of justice, the facts of the case were reported in detail, the defendant's exemplary character given as background, the witnesses prepared to testify in the case cited, including character witnesses and a witness to all the actual events, and a number of constructive possession cases included. The People, on their own motion, dismissed.

Hence, counsel, where he is faced with a possessory based on the theory of constructive possession, should not only move to dismiss based on the case law, but would do well, if unsuccessful in the latter endeavor, to file a Clayton motion to dismiss in the interest of justice. Release of the Grand Jury Minutes should also be sought to determine if the People gave the proper instructions to the Grand Jury on the law of constructive possession.

If all these attempts are unsuccessful, counsel may yet win on the law and facts at trial or be successful on appeal, as the Appellate decisions cited indicate.

This article previously appeared in an edition of The Nassau Lawyer, a publication of the Nassau County Bar Association, and is being reprinted here with the permission of The Nassau County Bar Association.

68. Dismissal of an Indictment under Sec. 190.50 of the Criminal Procedure Law (Part I)

The right of a defendant, arraigned upon a felony complaint to testify before the Grand Jury, if he so chooses, is a substantial statutory right, enshrined and codified in Sec. 190.50(a) of the Criminal Procedure Law. The right is substantial and a specious, unwarranted or weak prosecution may, as it were, be stopped in its tracks, should the Grand Jury choose to credit the defendant or discredit the People's prosecution.

Since the right of the defendant to testify is so critical, the abrogation of that right by the People may result in dismissal of the indictment under Sec. 190.50(5)(c) of the Criminal Procedure Law. The motion to dismiss must, however, be made within 5 days of arraignment upon the indictment or it is waived. If the prosecution is not re-presented to the Grand Jury within 45 days after dismissal under Sec. 190.50(c), the defendant, if incarcerated, will be paroled. In any event, the matter will be marked off the court calendar. The People, however, do have a full 6 months to re-present the matter to the Grand Jury if they choose or are able to do so.

The deprivation of the defendant's right to testify before the Grand Jury, by the People, is a substantial error. Hence, it is the purpose of this article to examine the law and criteria whereby an indictment may be dismissed, upon application of the defendant under Sec. 190.50(c) of the Criminal Procedure Law, since the defense attorney, if successful in a 190.50 motion, may not only be able to dismiss the indictment for a time, but, what is equally important, if his client is incarcerated, obtain his release.

There are four common contexts, scenarios, or situations in which a defendant is effectively deprived of his right to testify by the People. First, under C.P.L. Sec. 190.50(5)(a), the District Attorney must afford the defendant a reasonable time in which to exercise his right to appear as a witness. One day's written notice has been held by the courts of this state to be inherently unreasonable.

The leading case stating the law on this subject is *People v. Gini*, 72 A.D.2d 752, 421 N.Y.S.2d 269 (2d Dept. 1979). In *Gini* the defendant was convicted in the Supreme Court of Kings County of First-Degree Manslaughter and Criminal Possession of a Weapon in the Third Degree. The appeal to the Second Department brought up for review the denial of the defendant's motion to dismiss the indictment on the ground he was not afforded an opportunity to appear before the Grand Jury. The Appellate Division, Second Department, reversed and dismissed the indictment. The facts were that on September 10, 1977, the defendant was arraigned on a felony in the Criminal Court. The matter was adjourned to September 12th. On that date defense counsel orally informed the People of the defendant's desire to appear before the Grand Jury and also, on that day, served written notice on the People of the defendant's desire to testify before the Grand Jury.

The People's case on September 12 was presented immediately to the Grand Jury, without the defendant being given a chance to appear, and, on September 13th, an indictment was voted and filed.

The Appellate Division, Second Department, citing C.P.L. Sec. 190.50 5 (a) held the one day notice by the People to be inadequate, concluding that ". . . it is apparent that the defendant was not given a reasonable time to exercise his right to appear. . . ." *People v. Gini,* 72 A.D.2d 752, 421 N.Y.S.2d 270 (2d Dept. 1979). See also *People v. Eiffel,* 139 Misc. 2d 340, 527 N.Y.S.2d 347 (Supreme Court, Queens County, 1988); *People v. Singh,* 131 Misc.2d 1094, 503 N.Y.S.2d 228 (Supreme Court, Queens County, 1986); *People v. George Neilson,* N.Y.L.J., 10/23/89, p. 28, col. 4, (Supreme Court, Queens County); *People v. Yafim Pinis,* N.Y.L.J., 11/30/89, p. 30, col. 1, (Supreme Court, Queens County).

The second common basis on which an indictment may be dismissed is, if the defendant is incarcerated, the failure of the Department of Correction to produce the defendant in time before the presentment of the case by the People to the Grand Jury. This failure is, so to speak, to be charged or attributed to the People and the decision of the prosecution to present the case to the Grand Jury, in the absence of the defendant and not awaiting his production when Sec. 190.50 notice has been served upon the People by the defense, constitutes an effectual if not actual deprivation of his right to testify before the Grand Jury. *People v. Winslow,* 140 Misc.2d 210, 530, N.Y.S.2d 749 (Supreme Court, Queens County, 1988), is on point. In *Winslow* the defendant, charged in the indictment with Criminal Possession of a Weapon in the Third Degree, moved for an order dismissing the indictment pursuant to C.P.L. Sec. 190.50 on the ground he was denied his right to testify before the Grand Jury that indicted him.

The facts were that on February 22, 1988, the defendant was arrested and arraigned on the felony complaint in the Criminal Court. At arraignment the defendant served the People with written notice of his intention to testify before the Grand Jury and the matter was adjourned to February 26, 1988. On February 24, 1988, the People served the defense counsel with written notice of their intention to hold the Grand Jury proceeding an February 26, 1988. On February 26, 1988, the defendant was not produced in Part A.P. 6, and an indictment was vacated and filed with the court in the absence of the defendant.

The court held that the failure of the Department of Correction to produce the defendant would be attributed to the People. The court noted that, although there were no cases on point on the subject, the courts of the State of New York have consistently held that the failure of the Department of Correction to produce the defendant is to be attributed to the prosecutor insofar as the indictment must be dismissed under Sec. 30.30 of the Criminal Procedure Law if that failure has prevented the People from answering ready for trial within the period prescribed by Sec. 30.30. The court analogized that rule to the issue before it, namely, that the defendant should be released from pre-trial detention if that failure prevented the defendant from testifying before the Grand Jury. The court further noted that the People had other alternatives available to them under Sec.

180.80 of the C.P.L. including requesting a preliminary hearing, obtaining the defendant's consent, or showing good cause why an order of release should not be issued. Accordingly, the indictment was dismissed under C.P.L. Sec. 190.50 with leave to resubmit. See also *People v. George Neilson*, N.Y.L.J, 10/23/89 p. 28, col. 4, (Supreme Court, Queens County).

The third frequent basis for dismissal of the indictment under Sec. 190.50 of the C.P.L. due to the deprivation of the defendant's right to testify is the unavailability of defense counsel to be present on the date or dates of presentment.

People v. Young, 137 M.2d 400, 520 N.Y.S.2d 924 (Supreme Court, Nassau County, 1987), is apropos. In *Young*, defense counsel duly notified the People by written notice concerning his desire to testify before the Grand Jury. The defendant requested an adjournment of three weeks because of the unavailability of his retained attorney who was going out of the country. The Assistant District Attorney refused to schedule the Grand Jury presentation for a date after the attorney's return. The court held that the refusal to delay the presentment caused undue prejudice to the defendant since the People would not have been prejudiced by rescheduling the presentment. The court concluded that the refusal of the Assistant District Attorney to adjourn the presentment abrogated the defendant's right to be represented by counsel of his choice thus depriving the defendant of his statutory right to testify under C.P.L. Sec. 190.50. The court granted the defendant's motion to dismiss the indictment with leave for the People to represent within 45 days.

See also *People v. Bizzell,* 144 M.2d 1000, 545 N.Y.S.2d 528 (Supreme Court, Queens County, 1989), where the court granted a conditional dismissal of the indictment under Sec. 190.50 based on counsel's unavailability to be present at the presentment of the case to the Grand Jury and *People v. Stevens,* 151 A.D.2d 704, 542 N.Y.S.2d 754 (2d Dept. 1989).

The fourth and final general area whereby the law has often mandated dismissal of the indictment under Sec. 190.50 of the C.P.L. due to deprivation of the defendant's right to testify is where the prosecutor has acted unfairly in his presentation of the case to the Grand Jury. The unfairness of misconduct may be manifested by excessive cross-examination of the defendant, inflammatory comments, and excessive inquiry into the defendant's post-conviction record or the facts underlying them. *People v. Miller*, 144 A.D.2d 94, 537 N.Y.S.2d 318 (3rd Dept. 1989), is a good example. In *Miller* the defendant appealed from a judgment of conviction of Criminal Possession of a Forged Instrument in the Second Degree and Criminal Possession of Stolen Property in the Third Degree. The court reviewed in part the alleged prosecutorial misconduct before the Grand Jury. The court held that where the defendant chooses to exercise his right to testify before the Grand Jury he must be afforded an opportunity to give his version of the events prior to being examined by the People. Here, the court stated, the defendant had barely started his narrative when he was interrupted and persistently questioned by the prosecutor without being given a meaningful opportunity to continue his narrative. On this ground the court dismissed the indictment with leave to re-present to the Grand Jury. See also *People v. Lerman,* 116

A.D.2d 665, 497 N.Y.S.2d 733 (2d Dept. 1986); *People v. Davis*, 119 M.2d
1013, 465 N.Y.S.2d 404 (Supreme Court, Queens County 1983) (Improper and
prejudicial to question the defendant as to his place of birth, to infer he was
prone to violence due to his environment, and inquire whether he even struck
anyone in his life, and to repeat this inquiry, despite his denial of the same).

See also *People v. Thomas Barbaccia*, N.Y.L.J. 12/29/89, p. 27, col. 5 (Supreme Court, Kings County) (Indictment dismissed where the Assistant District
Attorney improperly cross-examined the defendant about his prior arrest and
drug use and failed to instruct the Grand Jurors about the limited use of such testimony); *People v. Rueben Mendez*, N.Y.L.J. 12/21/89, p. 26, col. 3 (Supreme
Court, New York County) (Indictment dismissed where the Grand Jury voted
not to call an alibi witness after Assistant District Attorney's comment pointing
out the lateness of the hour).

Given the vagaries of human conduct, the types of improper conduct by the
prosecutor are as varied as the infinitude of human nature. Suffice to say that the
cases cited herein afford some examples and guidance to defense counsel who
wishes to move to dismiss an indictment on this ground under Sec. 190.50 of the
C.P.L.

In conclusion there are perhaps other grounds for dismissal of an indictment
under Sec. 190.50 of the C.P.L. The grounds set forth in this article, however,
are, in the opinion of this writer, the most common and it is to be hoped that this
short overview will afford some guidance to counsel who believes he has
grounds to dismiss an indictment under Sec. 190.50 of the C.P.L.

69. The Speedy Trial Consequences of an Unavailable Prosecution Witness

C.P.L. § 30.30 sets forth the specific time frames in which the People must be
ready for trial, whether on a felony, misdemeanor or violation. The statute defines the criteria to be applied and designates certain situations or events in
which the People will be chargeable with any delay which occurred or whether
an "excludable" period will be applicable. The statute is complex and has been
subject to extensive interpretation by trial and appellate courts and only recently
was also the subject of some legislative modification to overcome the Court of
Appeals holding in *People v. Bolden*, 81 N.Y.2d 146 (1984).

One issue which attempts to be addressed by C.P.L. § 30.30 is whether and
to what extent the unavailability of an essential prosecution witness will result in
chargeable delay and possible dismissal of the accusatory instrument. C.P.L. §
30.30(3)(b) provides with respect to this situation that

a motion made pursuant to subdivisions one or two upon expiration of the specified period may be denied where the people are not ready for trial if the people were ready for trial prior to the expiration of the specified period and their present unreadiness is due to some exceptional fact or circumstance, including, but not limited to, the sudden unavailability of evidence material to the people's case, when the district attorney has exercised due diligence to obtain such evidence and there are reasonable grounds to believe that such evidence will become available in a reasonable period.

The two key criteria within the statutory provision which have been stressed by appellate courts in order to exclude prosecutorial delay have been actual proof of "unavailability" and the exercise of "due diligence." Thus in the leading case of *People v. Zirpola*, 57 N.Y.2d 706 (1982), the Court of Appeals in remitting the matter back to the trial court for a hearing stressed at page 708, that

> the "exceptional circumstances" which may justify a delay in prosecution are explicitly "not limited to" cases where a continuance has been granted. The unavailability of a prosecution witness may be a sufficient justification for delay (cf. *People v. Goodman*, 41 N.Y.2d 888), provided that the People attempted with due diligence to make the witness available.

On both of the elements of "unavailability" and "due diligence," the People have the burden of proof. See *People v. Berkowitz*, 50 N.Y.2d 333 (1981).

Appellate courts in applying the dictates of *People v. Zirpola, supra*, have continually stressed the People's burden to establish both elements. Thus in *People v. Holmes*, 105 A.D.2d 803 (2d Dept. 1981), the Second Department ordered the granting of a defendant's speedy trial motion where, although the People established unavailability, they failed, to the court's satisfaction, to establish that they "exercised due diligence in their attempts to locate the witness."[1]

The First Department in *People v. Drayton*, 226 A.D.2d 171 (1st Dept. 1996), has also recently injected a third criteria into the analysis, to wit, whether any prejudice has occurred to the defendant because of the delay in question.[2]

Whether unavailability and due diligence have been established is basically a factual issue to be determined on a case by case basis. Criminal law practitioners should be aware however that both criteria must be established in order to exclude any prosecutorial delay from the speedy trial time clock. Whether in light of both recent statutory and case law efforts to ease the due diligence burden on prosecutors with respect to the other portions of the speedy trial statute[3] will cause a concomitant change with respect to subdivision 3(b) analysis, remains to be seen.

Copyright 1997 by <u>New York Criminal Law News</u>. Reprinted with permission.

70. Defendant's Presence at Trial: Recent Developments

The right of the criminally accused to be present at all stages of the criminal proceeding is a subject that has lately tested the interest of the appellate courts of this state. It can be generally stated that the defendant has a constitutional right to be present at all critical stages of the criminal litigation.

Thus, the defendant has the right to appear and testify before the Grand Jury. That right, however, may be waived and, under certain discrete circumstances, due to the action or lack of action of the prosecutor, may result in dismissal of the indictment (C.P.L. § 190.50[5]; C.P.L. § 210.20).

Under certain classes of accusatory instruments, such as the simplified information or a summons or desk appearance ticket, the defendant's appearance may be waived by counsel (C.P.L. § 170.1[0][a], [b]).

It is also the law that a defendant may choose not to appear at a pre-trial hearing. By the same token, under C.P.L. Section 260.20 the defendant may, by his disruptive conduct, cause his removal from the trial or he may, under C.P.L. 340.50, by filing a written and subscribed statement, waive his right to be personally present. It is beyond the scope of this article, however, to examine in complete depth and complexity when, how, and under what circumstances the defendant's presence at any and every stage of the criminal litigation may be required or, as a matter of law, be waived.

The Problem

Specifically, this article will consider the distinct problem as to the circumstances, under the present state of the case law, when a defendant's presence, as a matter of due process and statute is required at a certain stage of the criminal proceeding. The area of case law development to be considered, under this rubric, is under what circumstances the presence of the defendant is required as a matter of due process when the jury requests instructions, read-back or clarification of certain facts or procedure. It can be generally stated to be the law that at any point in the trial when a deliberating jury requests instructions of the court, the court must, upon notice to counsel and in the presence of the defendant, give the requested information or instructions.

People v. Mehemedi, 69 N.Y.2d 759 (1978), is illustrative of this general rule. In *Mehemedi*, the defendant was indicted and tried on charges of weapons possession as a result of driving a car in which two loaded unlicensed guns were found pursuant to a lawful stop and search by the police. The police officer testified that the search for the guns was predicated upon his observation of bullets in the console compartment between the front seats which were exposed to his view when the defendant opened the console to look for the auto's registration. The defendant denied he opened the console and claimed that he had no knowledge that the guns were in the car, which belonged to his brother. After the jury began deliberations, the court received an inquiry from the jury to the effect of who opened the console during the search for the papers? In the presence of the attorneys, but in the absence of the jury and the defendant, and upon consultation with counsel, but over defense counsel's objection, the court forwarded a written note to the jury stating that the police officer said the defendant did, which the defendant denied. Defense counsel did not object to the failure to return the jury to the courtroom or to the defendant's absence from the proceeding. On appeal, the Appellate Division reversed and ordered a new trial because the court issued instructions to the jury in absence of the defendant. The Court of Appeals affirmed. The court, interpreting C.P.L. Section 310.30, held that the defendant has an absolute and unequivocal right to be present during any instruction to the jury and in this case he was, contrary to the requirement of statute, absent from a material part of the trial. Hence the court held that the harmless analysis was inappropriate, holding that the defendant must be present when the request and supplemental instruction involve questions of fact or questions of law.

In similar fashion in *People v. Bonamassa*, 160 A.D.2d 888 (2d Dept. 1990), on appeal by the defendant from a judgment of the County Court of Nassau convicting him of Attempted Grand Larceny in the Third Degree and Attempted Grand Larceny in the Fourth Degree upon a jury verdict, the facts were that during their deliberations, the jurors sent a note inquiring whether it was their duty to arrive at a verdict with respect to both of the counts submitted to them, the Attempted Grand Larceny in the Third Degree and the Attempted Grand Larceny in the Fourth Degree. The court issued its response to this question of law, in the absence of the defendant, and the Second Department held that under C.P.L. Section 310.30, the defendant's presence was required in response to an inquiry from a deliberating jury. The court held that the error was not harmless inasmuch as the court's failure to comply with the provisions of C.P.L. Section 310.30 was not harmless because the issuance of the court's instructions was not a purely ministerial act.

It is clear, therefore, under *Mehemedi* and *Bonamassa*, that any supplemental instruction on the facts or in explanation of the law to the jury requires the defendant's presence under C.P.L. Section 310.30. The question arises, however, whether every comment from the jury and every response from the court requires the presence of the defendant under C.P.L Section 310.30.

In *People v. Bonaparte,* 78 N.Y.2d 26 (1991), the court considered that very issue. Bonaparte was convicted of two counts of Murder in the Second Degree after a jury trial. The jury was sequestered after 5:00 P.M and reached a verdict the following morning. Defense counsel contended that the court should have instructed the jurors to stop their deliberations before sequestration. The court asked the court officer to state on the record what he said to the jurors prior to their sequestration and the officer said he told the jurors to cease all deliberations and informed them that they were going to be taken to dinner and sequestered for the evening. The court officer stated that jurors had not discussed the case during dinner or breakfast, the jurors had had no opportunity for joint deliberations, and that all jury supplies had been secured in the courtroom before the jury left for the evening. Based on the court officer's information, the court found no indication that the jurors had deliberated during the sequestration period.

On appeal, the Appellate Division held that there had been no violation in this case since the court officer, at the court's direction, simply told the jurors that they should stop deliberating because they were going to be taken to dinner and sequestered for the evening, communications that were simply ministerial under C.P.L. Section 310.30, because the officer did not convey instructions to the jury. The Appellate Division, however, held that the issue that the court should have given certain proper instructions upon sequestration was not preserved for review. The court added, however, that the better practice would have been for the court, in the presence of the defendant and his counsel, to have notified the jurors of their sequestration and instructed them on their duties and obligations concerning their duty to refrain from discussing the case amongst themselves.

The holding of *Bonaparte* is clear, namely that where the communication, in this case for the jury to adjourn for dinner and sequestration for the evening, is merely ministerial and no actual instructions on the law or facts are given, the presence of the defendant is not required; however, the court held that the better practice would be for the jurors to receive their instructions about their duties upon sequestration by the court in the presence of counsel and the defendant.

See also *People v. Nacey*, 78 N.Y.2d (1991), where the Court of Appeals held that it was within the administerial duties of the court officer to tell the jurors that they should stop deliberating and should start deliberating when they return to court in the morning. Similarly, the court held that although the defendant's right to be present at a critical stage of the trial was not violated, the better practice would be for the court to notify the jurors they were going to be sequestered for the evening and to instruct them on their duties and obligations, including their duty to refrain from discussing the case among themselves, in the presence of counsel and the defendant.

Again, in *People v. Harris*, 76 N.Y.2d 810 (1990), the Court of Appeals held that where the deliberating jury sent the judge a note asking for a read-back of the trial testimony, the judge and both counselors went to the jury room and requested clarification of the read-back request. Thereafter, in the presence of the jury and the defendant, the court clarified the request to hear the read-back of the complainant's testimony. The Court of Appeals held that the court's communication to the jurors seeking clarification of their request was not a violation of C.P.L. Section 310.30; the ministerial communication was wholly unrelated to the substantive legal or factual issues at trial.

Finally, in *People v. Bartlett*, 160 A.D.2d 245 (lst Dept. 1990), the First Department held that where the judge directed the court officer to return to the jury room to inquire if the jurors wanted the elements of the crime upon receiving a note from the jury asking for an interpretation of charges, and five minutes later the court received a second note requesting that the elements of the charge be reread, there was no violation of the defendant's right to be present during a critical and material stage of the trial because in asking whether the jury wished the elements of the crime reread, the court officer was acting as messenger to deliver the question. Upon the jury's request to have the elements reread, the court immediately directed the jury to be returned to the courtroom and the jurors were given the requested instruction in the presence of the defendant. In sum, the court held that no violation took place, since the court officer was functioning solely as a messenger for a ministerial act.

It is clear, from this review of when and where the defendant's presence is required, that in cases where a jury make some sort of request of the court requiring an answer, depending on whether under C.P.L. Section 310.30 the appellate courts of this state interpret the request as a request for an instruction on the evidence of law under *Mehemedi* and *Bonamassa*, or as a request for a clarification or communication that essentially involves a ministerial act as in *Harris*, *Bonaparte, Nacey,* and *Bartlett*, the nub of the distinction is what actually occurs and if it is sufficiently substantive to require the presence of the defendant under C.P.L. Section 310.30.

If the request is of sufficient substance to the extent that it seeks an instruction somehow related to the evidence of the law, the defendant's presence will be required. If the action is perceived as mere ministerial, then the defendant's presence will not be mandated.

Whether this is a distinction without real difference or, to some degree, a play on words is elusive. Certainly, the courts of the state suggest the better practice that would assure total fairness would be for the defendant to be present at all times whatever the request of the court officer. When any action is taken by the court in response to a jury inquiry, whether labeled ministerial or not and whether or not the action is taken by a court officer, the direction of the court is that the better safer practice would be for the defendant to be present thus affording the defendant the full latitude and allowance of his right to be present.

71. DNA Admissibility in New York State Criminal Cases

Deoxyribonucleic Acid, or DNA, is a substance found in the organism of living cells. It consists of chromosomes within the nucleus and provides the genetic code which determines a person's individual characteristics. This article will discuss the leading and most recent decisions on the admissibility of DNA evidence in New York criminal trials.

The most significant New York State Court of Appeals case to reach this issue is *People v. Wesley,* 83 N.Y.2d 417, 611 N.Y.S.2d 97, 633 N.E.2d 451 (1994). *Wesley* was an appeal by permission of an Associate Judge of the Court of Appeals from an Order of the Appellate Division, Third Department, affirming a judgment of the Albany County Court convicting the defendant of Murder in the Second Degree, Rape in the First Degree, Attempted Sodomy in the First Degree and Burglary in the Second Degree. The primary issue on appeal was the introduction of the DNA profiling evidence. In this case a DNA analysis was made of a blood stain taken from the defendant's T-shirt, hair follicles taken from the deceased, and blood drawn from the defendant. The court concluded that the DNA print pattern on the defendant's T-shirt matched the DNA print pattern from the deceased and that the DNA print pattern from the blood of the defendant was different from that of the decedent.

The Court of Appeals, after an extensive analysis of the facts of the case, the testimony at the Frye Hearing, and the scientific basis for reliability, held the DNA evidence was properly admissible since it was now accepted as reliable by the relevant scientific community.[1]

More recently two cases have added ramifications to the scientific reliability and admissibility of DNA evidence. Thus in *People v. Anthony Palumbo*, 162 Misc.2d 650 (Sup. Ct., Kings Cty. 1994), Judge Kreindler, of the Kings County Supreme Court, held that DNA evidence derived from a test known as the polymerase chain reaction method or PCR had been admitted in other states and held that such evidence has been generally accepted as reliable and so could be admitted at a pending murder trial. Judge Kreindler specifically observed at pgs. 655, 656:

> Expert testimony relating to scientific evidence can only be admitted if it is "generally accepted as reliable" within the relevant scientific community (*People v. Wesley*, 83 N.Y.2d 417, 422-23; *People v. Middleton*, 54 N.Y.2d 42, 49). There is no real dispute within the scientific community regarding the general theory underlying DNA identification (*People v. Golub*, 96 A.D.2d 637, 637-38; *People v. Wesley*, 183 A.D.2d 75, 78, aff'd 83 N.Y.2d 417). In addition, the Court of Appeals has found that DNA profiling, using the restriction fragment length polymorphism (RFLP) technique as reliable by the relevant scientific community (*People v. Wesley, supra*, 83 N.Y.2d at 425).
>
> . . .
>
> This case involves the polymerase chain reaction (PCR) test. The PCR procedure can test much smaller samples than the RFLP procedure. However, its ability to identify a particular individual to the exclusion of others is much lower (Annotation, *Admissibility of DNA Identification Evidence*, 84 A.L.R.4th 313, 323). Although the initial step of extracting the DNA from a sample is similar to the first step of the RFLP test, the other steps in the PCR procedure involve different lab procedures (*Spencer v. Commonwealth*, 240 Va. 78, 393 S.E.2d 609, 620, cert denied 498 U.S. 908).
>
> There are no published opinions in New York on whether the PCR technique has been generally accepted as reliable. Several courts in other States have allowed admission of PCR test results. . . .
>
> A court may find scientific tests reliable based on legal writings and judicial opinions (citation omitted). In such a case, a hearing is not required for the admission of novel scientific evidence (citations omitted).

> Defendant has raised no question as to the reliability of PCR tests in his papers. In light of this failure, and in light of the acceptance of the test in other jurisdiction, this court finds that the PCR test has been generally accepted as reliable in the scientific community.

Similarly, in *People v. Robert Morales,* 227 A.D.2d 648 (2d Dept. 1996), the Appellate Division, Second Department, affirmed a trial judge's ruling in a Murder case that the type of DNA testing known as the polymerase reaction method or PCR had acceptance and reliability in the scientific community and that therefore the results of such tests were admissible during the trial.

Citing Judge Kreindler's decision in *People v. Palumbo, supra,* the Second Department noted that there had been an overwhelming acceptance of the PCR methodology in other states, many of which apply the Frye standard of reliability. The Appellate Division thus concluded at 227 A.D.2d 648, 649 that

> we agree with the court that the hearing evidence sufficiently established that the reliability of the PCR method had gained general acceptance in the relevant scientific community so as to permit the submission of evidence obtained by that method to a jury.

It is clear that DNA evidence is now admissible in New York trial courts as having general and accepted scientific reliability. Since the results of scientific tests such as DNA testing are quite persuasive to a jury, criminal law practitioners should carefully consider the weight that a jury could give to such test results and the instructions which should be required from a trial court with respect to a jury's consideration of such evidence. In this way the use of DNA evidence can be integrated into the ultimate goal of insuring that the true facts be established and that a defendant be granted a fair trial.

72. Readiness and Relation Back

C.P.L. § 30.30, the statutory speedy trial provision of the State of New York, applicable to all criminal prosecutions, provides in pertinent part that the People in a criminal prosecution must answer ready within six months of the commencement of a criminal action where the defendant is accused of one or more offenses, at least one of which is a felony. If the People have not answered ready, the indictment may be subject to dismissal by motion of the defense. § 30.30 (4) further adds that certain periods of time are to be excluded from this statutory readiness rule.

The question arises, however, and it has lately teased and captivated the interest of the trial and appellate courts of this State, where a superseding indictment issues does the indictment relate back for the purpose of computing excludable time under C.P.L. § 30.30 (4).

In *People v. Sinistaj*, 67 N.Y.2d 236 (1986), the Court of Appeals considered this very issue. The facts in *Sinistaj* were that the defendant was originally indicted for Criminal Possession of a Weapon in the Third Degree under P.L. § 265.02(4) and other related crimes. Several months later, the People obtained a second indictment charging the defendant with another subdivision of this statute—P.L. § 265.02(4). The second indictment was obtained because the defendant had been mistakenly indicted under a provision of the Penal Law excluding possession in a place of business. The second indictment, although charging the defendant with a crime under the same Penal Law Section based on the same criminal transaction and involving possession of a weapon, included an additional element, namely that the defendant had been convicted of a felony previously. Thereafter, the Supreme Court, pursuant to the defendant's C.P.L. § 30.30 motion, granted his motion to dismiss. The Appellate Division modified the Supreme Court's Order by reinstating the first indictment and affirming the dismissal of the second, holding that certain excludable periods of time, applicable to the first indictment, were simply inapplicable to the second indictment inasmuch as that indictment had not even been filed within six months of the original felony complaint.

The Court of Appeals held that the new indictment obtained after the original one had been dismissed should be related back to the commencement of the criminal proceeding for purposes of the six months readiness rule under C.P.L. § 30.30(1)(a). The court held that a subsequent indictment should be related back to the commencement of the proceeding for the purpose of computing the time to be excluded from that limitation.

The Court initially reasoned that C.P.L. § 30.30 should be read together in all its sections and that therefore the interpretation afforded under C.P.L. § 30.30 (1)(a) should be applied to C.P.L § 30.30(4).

The Court further held that to hold otherwise would result in not permitting the People a new indictment, contrary to the legislative history and intent of the statute permitting the People to obtain a superseding indictment in the same criminal action.

Based on this reading of the statute and case law, the Court of Appeals reversed the Appellate Division order granting the defendant's motion to dismiss. *Sinistaj* thus effectually holds excludable time is to be related back from the second to the first indictment where even though defendant is charged under a different subsection of the same Penal Section and is defined as a prior felony offender in the second indictment, elements which were not present in the first indictment, as long as the second indictment relates back in its essential facts and arises from the same criminal transaction.

People v. Rodriguez, 150 A.D.2d 265 (1st Dept., 1989), under a different set of facts reaches a different result. *Rodriguez* was an appeal from a judgment of conviction convicting the defendant after a jury trial of Attempted Assault in the First Degree; Assault in the Second Degree; Criminal Possession of a Weapon in the Second and Third Degrees and sentencing him as a persistent violent felony offender to a concurrent indeterminate term of imprisonment from 10 years to life.

The charge arose from a shooting in New York County in 1984. The defendant was originally charged with the crime of Criminal Possession of a Weapon in the Second and Third Degrees based on the police officer's testimony that he had pointed a loaded revolver at him. The charges resulted in a mistrial and thereafter the People filed a superseding indictment which, in addition to the weapons charges, charged the defendant with the attempted murder of the complainant; Robbery in the First and Second Degrees; Attempted Assault in the First Degree and Assault in the Second Degree. A second trial resulted in the defendant's conviction on the weapons and assault charges.

The court held at the conclusion of the opinion, that although under C.P.L § 30.30 there is continuity between the original and superseding indictment as to the original charges, such continuity does not extend to the additional charges and so the defense motion to dismiss the superseding indictment on speedy trial grounds should have been granted.

Rodriguez must be distinguished from the relation back rule of *Sinistaj* and must be viewed as carving out an exception to the *Sinistaj* rule where entirely new charges, unrelated to the charge in the first indictment, are filed in the superseder.

People v. Cintron, N.Y.L.J. 6/24/94 p. 26, col. 6 (Sup. Ct., New York County), follows the rule of *Rodriguez*. In *Cintron*, the defendant was indicted for Robbery in the Second Degree and Grand Larceny in the Fourth Degree, although the original felony complaint charged him with Criminal Possession of a Controlled Substance in the Third Degree, based on the fact that the defendant at the time of his regularly scheduled appointment with his parole officer was seen carrying seven glassines of heroin and admitted to his parole officer that he intended to sell.

When it became apparent to the District Attorney that he would not be able to prosecute under the Robbery charge, due to witness unavailability, a new indictment was voted, charging the defendant with Criminal Possession of a Controlled Substance in the Third Degree.

The Court granted the defendant's § 30.30 motion declining to apply the *Sinistaj* rule. Citing *Rodriguez*, the Court held that the relation back doctrine of *Sinistaj* was inapplicable to the case where entirely new charges, based on an entirely distinct criminal transaction, are filed.

The impact of these three cases is clear—namely that where there is a second indictment involving an entirely separate and distinct charge arising from a separate criminal transaction, the relation back rule of *Sinistaj* is inapplicable and the People must suffer a successful § 30.30 motion by defense counsel.

This rule is logical and correct. The People should, where in a superseding indictment a new crime is added arising from the context of a separate transactional analysis, not have, so to speak, the benefit of a *Sinistaj* analysis. *Cintron* and *Rodriguez* simply hold that a new charge in a superseding indictment is not old wine in new bottles but a new vintage to be accorded separate treatment.

73. C.P.L. 30.30: A Kind of Delay

C.P.L. Sec. 30.30, the statutory speed trial statute of the State of New York, codifies the various time frames within which the People must be ready for trial, whether on a felony—6 months; a Class A Misdemeanor—90 days; a Class B Misdemeanor—60 days; or a violation—30 days. If the People are not ready for trial within the appropriate time reference, then the accusatory instrument must be dismissed. Time is calculated depending on whether or not the time must be charged to the People or excluded.

This article proposes to consider the question whether a delay in the transcription of the Grand Jury minutes will be charged to the People, with the result that the accusatory instrument will be dismissed pursuant to C.P.L. Sec. 30.30.

It may be said that the general rule is that a sufficiently lengthy delay in the transcription of the Grand Jury minutes will result in dismissal of the accusatory instrument. *People v. Barrah*, 29 A.D.2d 816, 287 N.Y.S.2d 494 (3d Dept. 1968), is exemplary. *Barrah* was an appeal from a judgment of the County Court upon a verdict convicting the defendant of Grand Larceny in the Second Degree; Petit Larceny; and two counts of Unlawful Entry. The court held the trial court was incorrect in denying the defendant's speedy trial motion. The appellate court held that, although the People had established "good cause" with respect to the delay occasioned by the prosecutor having been engaged in a two-month murder trial and because a change of counsel was necessary, the delay was occasioned by reason of the failure to move the case for trial at the opening of the October term and that the inability of the District Attorney to have the minutes of the Grand Jury proceeding transcribed must be charged to the People and the indictment dismissed.

Similarly in *People v. Cruz*, 123 Misc.2d 316, 473 N.Y.S.2d 307 (S. Ct. New York County 1989), aff'd. 111 A.D.2d 725, 401 N.Y.S.2d 330 (ld Dept. 1985), the Supreme Court of New York County held in pertinent part that the

> 1.) Sixteen day delay caused by the People's failure or inability to transcribe the Grand Jury minutes for a superseding indictment following the defendant's request for court inspection was chargeable to the People.[1]

The case law is clear that it is the responsibility of the People to obtain within timely fashion a proper transaction of the Grand Jury minutes and that dismissal of the accusatory instrument may result, even if the delay is due to outside factors beyond the People's control such as occurred in *Saunders*, i.e. congestion in the stenographer's office.

On the other hand there is a line of cases that appear to establish a differing rule. Thus in *People v. Allen*, 108 A.D.2d 601, 489 N.Y.S.2d 831 (1st Dept. 1985), the First Department held that since Grand Jury Minutes constitute

Rosario material and there is no requirement that the People furnish *Rosario* material prior to trial after the jury has been sworn and before the prosecutor's opening address, the court reasoned that the unavailability of the Grand Jury Minutes in no way impeded or impaired the People's ability to proceed to trial and that the trial court erred in charging the People with this delay.

In the same way, in *People v. Corporan*, 122 A.D.2d 152, 504 N.Y.S.2d 531 (2d Dept. 1986), the Appellate Division Second Department held the delay in providing the defendant with a transcript of the Grand Jury Minutes of the defendant and alibi witness did not impede the People's or the defendant's ability to prepare for trial since, like *Brady* and *Rosario* material, this may be provided at any time prior to the time the trial commences and so was not chargeable to the People. It is interesting to note that the court held that the minutes in this case were not required for the court's decision on the defendant's omnibus motion.

It can be seen that there are, in the State of New York, two lines of cases with differing rules as to whether a delay in the transcription of the Grand Jury Minutes will be charged to the People, resulting in dismissal of the indictment. One line of cases holds that as long as the delay does not impede the People's or the defendant's ability to prepare for trial, since Grand Jury Minutes are *Rosario* or *Brady* material, this material need be provided only prior to trial and after the jury has been sworn and before the prosecutor's opening address in the case of a jury trial. Prior to this point in the litigation, this line of cases holds the failure to provide the Grand Jury Minutes to defense counsel will not be charged to the People and no speedy trial dismissal will result.

Under a second and differing line of cases, a delay in the transcription and provision of the Grand Jury Minutes will be charged to the People for speedy trial purposes, even when the delay is due to factors beyond the People's control such as congestion in the stenographer's office.

The distinction in these two rules must be understood in the need or necessity for the minutes. If the minutes are necessary and connected with trial then they are *Rosario* material or *Brady* material and as long as they are provided to defense counsel in accord with those rules, i.e. prior to trial, the time will not be charged to the People.

If, however, the minutes are needed for decisions on a defense omnibus motion, i.e., inspection of Grand Jury Minutes, then the delay will be charged to the People. *People v. Cruz, supra*; *People v. Saunders, supra*.

It is somewhat unclear how *People v. Barrah, supra*, is to be interpreted since it is opaque in that decision whether the minutes were required in response to a defense omnibus motion to inspect the Grand Jury Minutes or in light of trial preparation. The opinion appears to hold that the People cannot answer ready for trial in the absence of a transcription of the Grand Jury Minutes and that the time will be charged to the People.

The determinative act would seem to be whether the case is in trial posture or in omnibus motion stage. If it is at trial the *Rosario* rule of time is to be applied and no speedy trial dismissal will result. If at omnibus motion stage then the delay may result in a statutory speedy trial dismissal.

74. A Case of Interplay

C.P.L. Section 190.50 grants the defendant the right to testify before the Grand Jury provided that timely notice is given to the accused. On the other hand, C.P.L. Section 180.80 mandates the release of the defendant being held in pretrial detention pending action of the Grand Jury after one hundred and twenty or one hundred and forty-four hours, unless an indictment has been voted.

A significant case, *People v. Evans* et al., 79 N.Y.2d 407, 583 N.Y.S.2d 358, 592 N.E.2d 1362 (1992), illustrates the interconnection and interplay of these statutes and reaches an interesting result. *Evans* included three separate appeals from three separate arrests and felony complaints.

The day after their respective arrests, the People served the defendants with notice under C.P.L. Section 190.50(a) that criminal charges would be presented to the Grand Jury, and the defendants responded with written notice of their intention to testify before the Grand Jury. The defendants were held in pretrial detention and their cases were adjourned to a scheduled date and time for presentment before the Grand Jury and their appearance to testify before that body.

On the scheduled dates, the last day of the C.P.L. Section 180.80 period, despite court orders for their production before the Grand Jury, two of the defendants were not produced until after the indictments were already voted while the third defendant was produced but due to lack of security was returned to detention before being given the opportunity to testify.

According to the prosecutor's affirmations, the Assistant District Attorneys presented the cases to the Grand Jury and obtained indictments to avoid the consequences of C.P.L. Section 180.80.

Defense counsel objected to the voting of the indictments in the face of the defendants' nonproduction and nonappearance and the People, in response, offered to delay filing the indictments and offered to reopen the Grand Jury proceeding to allow the defendants to testify before the Grand Jury that had already voted to indict them. Defense counsel rejected this suggestion and the indictments were filed.

When the defendants were arraigned on the indictments they moved to dismiss pursuant to C.P.L. Section 190.50(5)(c) on the ground that the defendants had been deprived of the opportunity to testify before the Grand Jury.

The People argued that a reopened presentment would satisfy C.P.L. Section 190.50(5); that the defendants would suffer no prejudice by this procedure; and, that the People should not be bound by the failure of the New York City

Department of Corrections to produce the defendants,b because the District Attorney does not control that Department. The People argued that C.P.L. Section 190.50(5) merely requires a defendant's appearance any time prior to the filing the indictment and that in any event they should not be required to delay the Grand Jury presentation where such a delay would result in the release of the defendant under C.P.L. Section 180.80.

The Supreme Court of Queens County dismissed each indictment. The Appellate Division affirmed and the People obtained leave to appeal to the Court of Appeals.

The Court of Appeals initially analyzed the history and structure of C.P.L. Section 190.50(5)(c), noting that the defendants must be informed of a pending Grand Jury proceeding against them but that the statute also allows the defendant to serve notice of his intent to testify at any time prior to the filing of the indictment.

The Court further analyzed that the statute is silent and does not resolve the issue when the defendant gives timely notice prior to the Grand Jury presentment and vote, whether they must be given preindictment right to testify.

The Court went on to state, upon consideration of C.P.L. Section 190.50(5) together with its history and purpose, that the legislature intended that individuals who give timely notice prior to the prosecutor's presentment of evidence to the Grand Jury and prior to the voting of the indictment are entitled to testify before that vote. The Court stated that this interpretation effectuated that statutory purpose allowing the defendant to appear and to testify before the Grand Jury so that the defendant's testimony would and could affect the Grand Jury's ultimate decision.

The Court further held that the failure of the Department of Corrections to produce the defendant was no excuse for the People's failure to enforce the defendant's right to testify under C.P.L. Section 190.50 and that the practical difficulty the prosecution may encounter has no bearing on the effectuation of the defendant's right to testify.

In sum, the Court of Appeals stated that it agreed with the Appellate Division that the right to testify prior to the vote of the Grand Jury is quantitatively different from and more advantageous to the defense than the opportunity to testify before a reopened presentment after the Grand Jury has voted based on the People's ex parte presentment of the evidence.

Evans is a significant decision on three counts. First is that the defendant should be allowed to testify within the full meaning and import of C.P.L. Section 190.50 and before a vote of the Grand Jury, an unfettered and uneviscerated right. Second, that any failure to produce the defendant by the Department of Corrections does not excuse the People's obligation under C.P.L. Section 190.50 and in that sense is charged to their responsibility. Third, that the determination to hold the defendant in light of his possible release under C.P.L. Section 180.80 has no bearing on the defendant's right to testify under C.P.L. Section 190.50.

In short, the *Evans* decision rightly establishes that should a defendant choose to exercise his right to testify before a Grand Jury the People must give free and full meaning to that right.

That right will not be enforced and satisfied by a past vote and subsequent reopening of the Grand Jury proceeding before what in effect is a tainted and affected and improper Grand Jury that has already reached a determination that ultimately can only be overturned by a motion to dismiss or on appeal.

The defendant's right to testify under C.P.L. Section 190.50, according to the *Evans* decision, will not be affected by the fact that the defendant may be released under C.P. Section 180.80, and it will not be excused by the failure of the Department of Corrections to produce the defendant with the result that he will be entitled to release under C.P.L. Section 180.80.

Evans gives the required impact and significance to the defendant's right to testify before an untainted Grand Jury and does not allow that right to be eviscerated by the possibility of the release under C.P.L. Section 180.80. *Evans* gives the defendant's right to testify before the Grand Jury the teeth it deserves, holding that no other statute or consideration should affect the defendant's right to testify at this most critical stage of the criminal proceeding. For *Evans* the right and exercise by the defendant of testifying before the Grand Jury is of paramount importance, and *Evans* gives that right the significance it deserves, leaving it unaffected and unfettered by statute, considerations of judicial economy, or the practicalities of the criminal justice system.

75. The Batson Hearing

In *People v. Batson*, 107 S.Ct. 1712, 476 U.S. 79, 90 L.Ed.2d 69 (1986), the United States Supreme Court held, upon equal protection grounds, that where the prosecutor exercises a series of peremptory challenges against jurors of the same race as the defendant, an inference of discrimination arises, and the prosecutor is required to offer a plausible racially neutral explanation for the use of these challenges. In the absence of a plausible explanation those jurors may be stricken.

Batson has been extended from its original holding that the stricken jurors be of the same race as the defendant, to where the jurors are of a different race. See *Powers v. Ohio*, U.S., 111 S.Ct.. 1364, 113 L.Ed.2d 411 (1991).

It is no moment that it is the defendant rather than the state that exercises the challenges. See *Georgia v. McCollum*, U.S, 112 S.Ct. 2348, 120 L.Ed.2d 33 (1992).

Although *Batson* and its progeny are and have been subject to continuing developments, the question arises, and it is the subject of this article, whether, when the defendant does make a *Batson* challenge and the prosecutor fails to come forth with a race neutral explanation, the defendant is entitled to some sort of hearing. The answer would appear to be in the affirmative. *People v. Lavon,* 166 D.2d 670, 561 N.Y.S.2d 259 (2d Dept. 1990), speaks to this issue. In *Lavon,* the defendant was convicted in the Supreme Court of Kings County of Burglary in the Third Degree and appealed. The Second Department held that once the defendant has established a prima facie case of purposeful discrimination in jury selection by the prosecutor it then becomes necessary for the prosecutor to come forward with a race neutral explanation for the use of his peremptory challenges. In the absence of such explanation, the court held that an evidentiary hearing was necessary to determine the propriety of the prosecutor's exercise of the peremptory challenges and the Appellate Division remitted for a hearing and report on that question.

Again in *People v. Epps,* 163 A.D.2d 325, 557 N.Y.S.2d 449 (2d Dept. 1990), the Second Department again held that where the defendant had established a prima facie case of purposeful discrimination in jury selection by the prosecutor and the prosecutor failed to provide racially neutral explanations for the exclusion of these individuals, the Appellate Division held there must be an evidentiary hearing on that issue and remitted for such hearing and ordered the appeal held in abeyance. On this see also *People v. Graham,* 181 A.D.2d 504, 580 N.Y.S.2d 773 (1st Dept. 1992); *People v. Jackson,* 154 A.D.2d 48, 546 N.Y.S.2d 28 (2d Dept. 1989).

This hearing appears to have its genesis and meaning in whether a *Batson* violation has occurred and has been referred to as a *Batson* Reconstruction hearing. Thus in *People v. Lincoln,* 145 A.D.2d 924, 536 N.Y.S.2d 609 (4th Dept. 1988), in an appeal from a judgment convicting the defendant of Burglary in the Second Degree and Possession of Burglar's Tools, where the defendant raised objections before the trial court on the prosecutor's alleged misuse of his peremptory challenges to exclude three black venire men and the objections elicited no response, the Fourth Department held that the defendant had raised a sufficient question to require a response and ordered a "Reconstruction" hearing on the issue, with an order to the trial court to make specific findings of fact and conclusions of law. On this see also *People v. Bryant* 159 A.D.2d 962, 552 N.Y.S.2d 779 (4th Dept. 1990).

Conclusion

This brief review of the pertinent law reveals that where a *Batson* challenge is made and elicits no adequate response from the prosecution and the issue is preserved, the appellate court will order a hearing to determine whether a *Batson* violation has occurred, denominated "Reconstruction" or otherwise.

76. Withdrawal of the Guilty Plea under the Federal Rules of Criminal Procedure: An Analysis

Rule 32(d) of the Federal Rules of Criminal Procedure governs the basis and method of withdrawal of a guilty plea under the Federal Rules of Criminal Procedure.

The Rule states that a motion to withdraw a plea of guilty or *nolo contendere* may be made only before sentence is imposed or imposition of sentence is suspended. The statutory section goes on to state, however, that to correct a "manifest injustice" the court, after sentence, may set aside the judgment of conviction and permit the defendant to withdraw his plea.

The section thus sets forth two conditions whereby a guilty plea may be withdrawn: first, in general before sentence is imposed or suspended, and, second, after sentence is imposed, to correct a manifest injustice.

This article proposes to analyze the rules and grounds governing withdrawal of a guilty plea under Rule 32(d) of the Federal Rules of Criminal Procedure before sentence is imposed. A subsequent article will consider what may be said to constitute "manifest injustice" such as to allow withdrawal of a guilty plea after sentence is imposed under Rule 32(d).

In general it may be said that, under Rule 32(d) of the Federal Rules of Criminal Procedure, the withdrawal of a plea before sentence should be freely allowed. *United States v. Stayton*[1] states the rule well. In *Stayton* the Appellant and his wife were indicted for conspiracy to alter and possess counterfeit bills. The Appellant originally pled not guilty and then changed his plea to guilty. Thereafter the Appellant Mr. Stayton filed a motion to withdraw his guilty plea. After a hearing, the motion was denied and the appellant subsequently received a sentence of a fine and imprisonment. The Appellant appealed from the refusal of trial court to allow him to withdraw his plea of guilty. U.S. Court of Appeals for the Third Circuit stated very specifically on passing on this issue that the motion to withdraw a guilty plea protects the right of the accused to trial. Therefore, the court held, such requests made before sentencing shall be construed liberally in favor of the accused by the trial courts.[2]

In *United States v. Hancock*[3] the U.S. Court of Appeals for the Tenth Circuit further stated and even refined this of Rule of "liberality" stating that although a criminal defendant does not have an absolute right to withdraw a plea of guilty, a request to withdraw such a plea should be considered carefully and with liberality.[4]

It is true that there is no absolute right to withdraw a plea of guilty. The decision to allow withdrawal is committed to the sound discretion of the trial court. Thus in *United States v. Abdul*[5] the U.S. Court of Appeals for the Seventh Circuit held in 1996 that the decision to permit a plea withdrawal rests within the sound discretion of the District Court and will be reversed only upon a showing of an abuse of discretion.

More recently in 1997 the U.S. Court of Appeals for the Second Circuit held in *United States v. Maher,*[6] in defining what may be said to constitute the District Court's discretion in this regard, that a defendant has in fact no automatic entitlement to have a motion to withdraw granted since the People have a strong interest in the finality of guilty pleas and, second, allowing withdrawal of pleas may undermine confidence in the integrity of judicial procedures; increase the volume of judicial work; and delay and impair the orderly administration of justice, citing *United States v. Sweeney.*[7]

In *United States v. Moore*[8] the U.S. Court of Appeals for the Fifth Circuit stated a broad rule that the District Court may permit a defendant to withdraw a guilty plea prior to sentencing upon a showing of a "fair and just" reason.

Indeed in *United States v. Pressley*[9] the U.S. Court of Appeals for the Fifth Circuit, citing *Kercheval v. United States,*[10] held that if there appears to be any reason in the exercise of the court's discretion to allow withdrawal of a guilty plea prior to sentencing, leave should be freely granted.

Again the U.S. Court of Appeals for the Third Circuit, in *United States v. Cavalcante*[11] reiterated the rule set forth in *Moore* that the court's discretion in this regard is most wide and favors the withdrawal of the guilty plea for any fair and just reason, should such reason be shown.

The question arises then what the Federal Courts have held to be a "fair and just reason" to permit withdrawal of a guilty plea.

There are, in the view of this writer, three seminal bases to justify the District Court allowing withdrawal of a guilty plea. The first is a claim of innocence. In *United States v. Barker*[12] the U.S. Court of Appeals for the District of Colombia Circuit held, by way of interpreting the term "fair and just," that whether the movant has asserted his legal innocence is an important factor to be weighed. The court went on to state that, where the movant asserts or claims his legal innocence, plea withdrawal should be freely allowed.

The law, however, is that the claim of innocence must be credible, and a mere claim of innocence per se is insufficient to justify allowing the presentence withdrawal of a guilty plea.[13]

The claim of ineffective assistance of counsel is an additional basis to allow the withdrawal of a guilty plea. Thus in *Gawartka v. United States,*[14] the U.S. Court of Appeals for the Third Circuit held that, in the absence of an allegation that defense counsel was not acting competently and adequately, the defendant would not be entitled to withdraw his plea of guilty.

Finally the claim of coercion, like the claim of innocence and the claim of ineffective assistance of counsel, is also a basis for the withdrawal of a guilty plea. *United States v. Conner*[15] is illustrative. In *Conner* the defendant moved to withdraw his guilty plea. On review of the case law in this field, the court held that defendant had not presented a fair and just reason for withdrawal of his guilty plea. The court noted that the defendant did not maintain his innocence; it was not alleged that the defendant was coerced by his attorney to plead guilty or that he did not have time to review the plea agreement.

It should be noted that it has been held that the application to withdraw a guilty plea will not be granted when the government has been prejudiced by reliance on the guilty plea. Thus in *United States v. Roberts*[16] the California District Court held that when the government will suffer any prejudice by the granting of the defendant's motion to withdraw his guilty plea the courts will usually exercise their discretion to deny withdrawal of the guilty plea but where such prejudice is absent or minimal, withdrawal is routinely permitted.

Conclusion

This brief review of the case law governing withdrawal of a guilty plea before sentence is imposed under Rule 32(d) of the Federal Rules of Criminal Procedure reveals a basic rule of liberality and discretion governing the trial court's determination whether to grant the application to withdraw or not. The analysis here also shows the seminal and basic criteria bearing on the decision by the court to allow withdrawal of a guilty plea: 1) the defendant's credible maintenance of his innocence, 2) coercion, and 3) ineffective assistance of counsel. Overarching these three basic criteria or rules is the broad rule that if any fair or just reason is alleged then there is a policy favoring withdrawal of the plea.

Finally, whether the government will be prejudiced or not by the withdrawal of the plea is a background factor bearing on the trial court's decision to permit withdrawal of the defendant's plea of guilty.

Reprinted with permission of the Criminal Justice Journal, Vol. 70, No. 2, Winter 1999, published by the New York State Bar Association, 1 Elk Street, Albany, NY 12207.

77. Probable Cause and Pretrial Hearings

Wade, Huntley and *Mapp* pretrial hearings are an important part of New York State criminal trial practice. The *Wade* hearing concerns the suggestiveness of the pretrial identification procedure-showup or lineup. The *Huntley* hearing concerns voluntariness of a pretrial statement or confession, oral or written. The *Mapp* hearing has as its subject the constitutionality or lawfulness of a search or seizure.

While the subject of these hearings, it would appear, is clear, the question arises whether there may be an added component of these hearings, i.e., the *Dunaway* or probable cause issue. This article proposes to consider whether an essential aspect of these three hearings is the *Dunaway* or probable cause issue, and if this is so, is probable cause part of the People's burden of going forward at each of the hearings.

The law is clear that on a motion to suppress, whether tangible property, a statement or witness identification, the People have the initial burden of establishing the reasonableness of the police conduct. Once that burden is met, the burden shifts to the defendant to prove that the pretrial identification was unduly suggestive, the statement involuntary or in violation of the defendant's Fifth Amendment or *Miranda* rights, or the search or seizure constitutionally invalid.

Thus, in *People v. Geames*,[1] the Appellate Division, Second Department, held that in an identification hearing the People have the initial burden of going forward to demonstrate the reasonableness of the police conduct.[2] In similar fashion, in *People v. White*,[3] the Appellate Department, Second Department, held, with respect to the burden of the People where the defendant moves to suppress evidence as the fruit of unlawful police conduct and arrest, that the burden is cast upon the prosecution to come forward in the first instance with evidence establishing probable cause for the arrest.

Also, at the *Huntley* hearings the prosecutor has the initial burden of establishing that the defendant's statement was voluntary. Thus, in the *Huntley* hearing the prosecution must establish the legality of the police conduct and the defendant's waiver of his rights.[4]

It is clear that the weight of authority holds that probable cause, or the *Dunaway* issue, is an integral and required aspect of all pre-trial criminal hearings, including the *Wade, Mapp,* and *Huntley* hearings.[5] There are illustrative cases. In *People v. Pejacinovic*,[6] the Appellate Division, First Department, held that where the defendant's arrest for assault was unsupported by probable cause, any evidence derived from the subsequent lineup should have been suppressed as the product of the illegal arrest.

People v. Dodt[7] is particularly apropos. In *Dodt*, the Court of Appeals held that when the police act on the basis of a teletype or radio bulletin, the prosecution's burden on the issue of probable cause for the arrest in the context of a pretrial hearing to suppress a lineup identification as the fruit of an unlawful arrest is not discharged absent proof regarding the contents of the communication received. The Court of Appeals held that the information conveyed must be proved. The court went on to state that when a suppression motion is filed the content of the bulletin upon which the police acted must be proved at the hearing. The court stated further that in the case at bar the prosecutor offered no evidence of the description contained in the teletype on the basis of which the judge could reach a conclusion that there was probable cause. The court concluded that since the lineup identification followed from the illegal arrest of the defendant without probable cause it was error to admit evidence of that evidence at trial.

The court went on to state that since the victim's identification had been the primary evidence against the defendant at trial and that the identification had been bolstered by evidence regarding the lineup, the admission of the lineup identification could not be deemed harmless and that, therefore, there must be a new trial because of the admission of testimony concerning the lineup identification.

Again, in *People v. Castor*[8] the Appellate Division, First Department, held that at the *Mapp* hearing where the detective did not provide the contents of particulars of the radioed description of the individuals involved in the drug transaction, there were insufficient facts to establish the reasonable suspicion or probable cause necessary to justify the police action taken against the defendant and that the identification should have been suppressed.

People v. Sanchez[9] is also relevant. In *Sanchez*, the defendant was arrested after he was purportedly observed discarding a bag that was found to contain cocaine. The defendant subsequently moved to suppress the evidence. At the conclusion of the *Mapp* hearing, the court denied the motion to suppress, finding that the bag of cocaine was legally retrieved by the police and that the money taken from the defendant's pocket was seized in a search incident to an arrest. The defendant was convicted after a jury trial.

The First Department held that the People bear the burden of coming forward to justify police activity once it is challenged by the defendant, and it is incumbent upon the suppression court to permit a thorough inquiry into the propriety of the police conduct. The court went on to state that in those cases where the defendant was denied an opportunity at the suppression hearing to examine the full circumstances surrounding the arrest, the matter should be remanded for a hearing to fully determine all events leading up to the arrest.

The court concluded that in view of the evidence before it the case should be remanded for a full exploration of the legality of the defendant's arrest.

In conclusion, this brief survey of the pertinent case law reveals a clear rule that in all pretrial hearings probable cause, or the *Dunaway* component, is an integral aspect to all the hearings and a part of the People's burden of going forward.

There is a caveat, however. In the pretrial motion papers requesting the hearing, whether *Mapp*, *Huntley*, or *Wade*, there must be factual allegations raising or putting into issue probable cause or, in essence, requesting the *Dunaway* hearing. Thus, in *People v. Covington*,[10] the Appellate Division, First Department, held that a defendant is entitled to a suppression hearing on the issue of probable cause only after he first meets the statutory burden of alleging facts showing that the property sought to be suppressed was obtained by the prosecution under circumstances precluding its admission in a criminal prosecution.

Again, the Appellate Division, First Department, held in *People v. McBrydell* that it was proper to deny the defense motion to suppress identification testimony on the ground of an unlawful seizure where the defendant does not make factual allegations

In short, probable cause, or the *Dunaway* component, is part of all pretrial hearings, but, in some minimal fashion, facts must be alleged in the defense motion papers injecting the probable cause issue into the litigation mix, even though it might appear from the cases cited in this article, which make no explicit mention of that requirement, that probable cause is an issue in the hearing, whether put into issue or not in the defense counsel motion papers.

78. *Extending the Time for Taking an Appeal in a Criminal Case*

In general, it may be said that an appeal as of right in a civil case, must be taken within thirty (30) days after service upon the appellant of a copy of the judgment or order appealed from and written notice of its entry. If a civil appeal requires permission, as it may under the relevant statutory section of the C.P.L.R., then a motion for permission to perfect an appeal must be made, from the date of service upon the party seeking permission, of a copy of the judgment or order to be appealed from and written notice of its entry. An appeal of course is taken by serving on the adverse party a notice of appeal and filing it in the office where the judgment or order of the court of original instance is entered.

A similar structure, with variants, governs appeals taken from judgments of convictions in criminal cases. Specifically, C.P.L.R. Sec. 460.10 mandates, in pertinent part, that a party seeking to appeal from a judgment or sentence must, within 30 days of the imposition of sentence, file with the clerk of the criminal court in which sentence was imposed, a notice of appeal in duplicate.

At least, and most assuredly in a civil case, the time within which to appeal is rigid and, if not attended to in a timely fashion, results in forfeiture of the right to appeal. Not even a stipulation may extend or modify this set time frame.

Although the time within which to file a notice of appeal or to move for permission to appeal is most rigid and fixed in New York Civil Practice, the Criminal Procedure Law provides, as it were, "a window out" in this respect. The relevant governing provision of the Criminal Procedure Law (hereinafter C.P.L.) Sec. 460.30 entitled "Extension of Time for Taking Appeal" states four grounds upon which an extension may be granted. They are (1) improper conduct of a public servant; (2) improper conduct of the defendant's attorney; (3) death or disability of the defendant's attorney; (4) inability of the defendant and his attorney to have communicated in person or by mail concerning whether an appeal should be taken prior to the expiration of the time within which to take an appeal through no lack of due diligence or fault of the attorney or the defendant due to defendant's incarceration in an institution.

This section concludes with the advisement that the motion must be made with due diligence after the time for the taking of such appeal has expired and in any case not more than one year thereafter.

This section exists, in the view of this writer, to allow the criminally accused some escape and leeway from the otherwise rigid appellate time frame. The section functions as a modification of the otherwise rigid rule allowing the defendant the benefit of the doubt in perfecting his appeal under certain circumstances and having his rights, if not enforced, then not lost. In short, the statute permits the defendant to have his day in the appellate court when mistakes have occurred that in civil practice would not provide the same basis for granting an extension of the time to appeal.

This article proposes to consider, based upon an analysis of case law in the field, what may be said to constitute: (1) improper conduct of counsel; (2) improper conduct of a public servant. The article will also consider the case law interpreting the one year time frame for making this motion and will conclude with an analysis of cases that state a more general construction of this statutory section.

Conduct of Counsel

The leading case on what constitutes improper conduct of counsel under Sec. 460.30 is *People v. Corso*. In *People v. Corso*, the Court of Appeals stated that a failure to advise the defendant of his right to appeal may be deemed improper conduct within the meaning of this section.

Similarly, in *People v. Nunez*, the Appellate Division, Fourth Department, held that defense counsel was guilty of improper conduct in failing to provide the defendant, upon sentencing, with written notice of his right to appeal, the time limitations involved, the manner of instituting the appeal, and the right to apply for leave to appeal as a poor person.

More to the point, in *People v. Buchner* the Appellate Division, Third Department, held that where the notice of appeal was filed with the County Clerk some ten months after the defendant's conviction and it appeared that trial counsel had not informed the defendant of his right to appeal *in forma pauperis*, the motion to file a late notice of appeal would be granted.

In sum, the case law strongly indicates that the form of improper conduct of defense counsel under the statutory section is the failure to advise the defendant, preferably in writing, of his appellate rights.

Conduct of Public Servant

The leading case on improper conduct of a public servant under this statutory section is *People v. Johnson*. In *Johnson*, the Court of Appeals held that the defendant would be allowed to appeal a 23-year old conviction where the defendant had made diligent pro se efforts to obtain review of the conviction and defendant's effort had been thwarted by the State.

In the same way in *People v. Thomas*, again the Court of Appeals held that the People were stopped from asserting the one year limit to defeat defendant's motion for an extension of time to appeal his criminal conviction where omissions on the part of the prosecutor in failing to supply to the Appellate Division requested information concerning when notice of appeal had been filed frustrated the good faith exercise of the defendant's right to a remedy.

The Court of Appeals would seem to hold that where in any form the servant of the state seeks to thwart or prevent the defendant from exercising his appellate rights this is enough to grant the motion for an extension under C.P.L. Sec. 460.30.

Time

The case law uniformly holds that the time frame for the making of this motion, i.e., one year, is set and cannot be modified. Thus, the Court of Appeals held in *People v. Corso* that a motion to take an appeal under this section must be made with due diligence and in any event not more than one year after the time for taking an appeal has expired.

The law is clear that the one year time limitation to bring the motion under this statutory section is fixed and cannot be varied with the caveat that the motion must be brought with due diligence, thus allowing denial of the motion if due diligence is not shown even though the motion be brought within the one year time frame.

In General

In 1974 the Court of Appeals in *People v. Sher* stated a more general rule. In *Sher*, the court of Appeals stated the factors for consideration in determining an application for an extension of the time for filing and service of the notice of appeal after the certificate granting leave has been issued including an acceptable excuse on the part of the appellant for noncompliance; prejudice suffered by the respondent in consequence of such noncompliance; and the existence of persisting substantial grounds for review on the merits.

Conclusion

This brief review of the case law interpreting C.P.L. Sec. 460.30 reveals
1. that the seminal and essential improper conduct of defense counsel in the section is the failure to advise, preferably in written form, of the right to appeal;
2. that the improper conduct of a public servant in thwarting or preventing the defendant from filing, perfecting and/or pursuing his appellate rights;
3. that the one year time limit to bring this motion is fixed and the court may find less time if the requisite "due diligence" is not shown; and finally;
4. that there is one more general rule in *People v. Sher* that the motion will be granted if the movant provides an excuse; there is a lack of prejudice on respondent; and there is a substantial ground for review on the merits.

79. *The Criminal Defense Interview*

Proper and exact Criminal Practice and Procedure, whether in the Federal or State Courts, has been and continues to be the subject of many books and articles. The subject is of broad interest and impact both to the practicing criminal bar, the bench, and the Academic community, since the issues argued and fleshed out at trial, and on appeal, often present matters of constitutional dimension that in their resolution by the trial and appellate courts have wide impact on the public, whose concern is the continued safety of their families and community, and to the bench, bar, and academic community, whose equally pressing concern is for the continued assurance of fair trials, Due Process and Equal Protection for the accused, and the continued overall vitality of our democratic and constitutional system of government.

As a practicing criminal defense lawyer, my concerns are practical, i.e., providing a fair trial for the accused and hopefully attaining or rather unearthing some truth with a view to vindication of the accused.

The initial encounter of the criminal defense lawyer with the accused is surely the most important and critical stage of the criminal proceedings. The interview often occurs after the client has been arrested and booked and is incarcerated. The potential client is approached under the most stressful of conditions, held in a correctional facility, often awaiting arraignment for many hours before he has had the opportunity to see a lawyer. Defense counsel, if he is lucky, often will have spoken with friends, relatives, a wife, or girlfriend, of the accused, also upset, concerned, and also under stress. Defense counsel is confronted with a client whom he has only had the opportunity to speak to and then briefly, who is excited and in the dark as to what is going on, if understood at all. It is wise first to reassure family and friends of the accused and to take time to explain what is occurring at the arraignment, and the possibility of making or not making bail, and the range wherein bail will be set. The charges should be explained to the family, copies of the felony complaint given to them, and the range of incarceratory exposure explained. The family should know that this is only the beginning, the first stage of the criminal case, and there is much to happen and to be done between arraignment and plea or trial. If time allows, it should be explained to the family what arraignment and bail is; how it works; and, in brief, how the criminal justice system operates, particularly explaining the difference between plea and trial.

Then occurs the interview with the accused. As stated, particularly if the case is a serious one such as rape or murder, the accused will likely be incarcerated and will have been waiting in prison under stress and unsure as to what is happening. Defense counsel should first explain that he is his lawyer and give him his card. It is most important that the accused be reassured. He should not be subjected to some sort of verbal face-off or spoken to with condescension, but at all times spoken to with equality, kindness, and understanding for his predicament, never with the implication that he is in an inferior position, but rather is a person with a problem the attorney has come to address.

In sum, the lawyer should immediately establish a relationship with the accused. He is there to help both as a friend and as a professional and not there to criticize and upbraid. Defense counsel should ask the client how long he has lived in the area. Inquiry should be made of his citizenship status. If he is not a citizen it should be determined whether he is a resident alien or illegal. His current and prior addresses should be found and the length of time he has lived in those places. Further inquiry should be made whether he is married, legally or at common law, and the number, ages, and sex of his children, if any. His prior employment history should be established, both the positions he has held in the past, his present position if any, the nature of these positions, and his current or prior salary history.

His age may be determined either from his NYSSID sheet or from direct questioning of him. His NYSSID sheet should be carefully examined to determine any prior convictions and the nature of the convictions and the sentences he has received. The client should be questioned whether those convictions were the result of plea or trial and the underlying facts, or rather his version of the facts, that led to these arrests and convictions.

The client should be questioned as to any open cases. It will probably be too early to determine the exact status of those cases although immediate telephone inquiry is a possibility. It is probably unwise to defer completely or depend on the accused's statements as to the status of his open cases since the defendant will always be unclear in his own mind as to what exactly is occurring in these cases and will often claim they are or are about to be dismissed, an explanation often not borne out by reality.

All these inquiries as to employment, age, family, citizenship, and prior and current residences, are obviously directed to establishing community ties, to the end that the court may be convinced that this is a stable individual bound and likely to return to the court if released.

The purpose of determining prior convictions, sentences, the facts underlying those convictions, and open cases is to minimize if possible to the court, not the fact, but the quality of these convictions and cases so that the court may be convinced at arraignment that the defendant's prior conviction history and his open cases are not so serious as at first blush they were thought or supposed to be, or as would appear upon reading them in print without the benefit of all the surrounding facts.

By far the most significant part of the interview is the confrontation of the accused with the charges against him. If possible, just as the family waiting in court were given copies of the charges, so the accused should be given a copy of the felony complaint. He should be given time to read the complaint. The charges should also be read out to him and any legal or difficult terminology or words explained to him in layman's terms. He should be told that this is the State's version of the events. It should be emphasized that these are only charges or accusations and that as far as the attorney is concerned his client is innocent and credible.

After the charges have been read and explained the defendant should not be asked if they are true since this calls forth a simple denial with no opportunity given to the client to explain the facts. Rather, he should be asked just what happened. Counsel thus should give his client the full opportunity to explain himself. If the case is a drug case, or any other case, the client may say he was there and the police rounded him up. Here he should be asked where he was going to and coming from with a view to fleshing out how the arrest happened and what events preceded it.

In all cases, including the sale of drugs, the names and addresses of any person he says he was previously with or going to meet should, if possible, be established. Who he was with at the time of the crime should be established.

All and any potential witnesses at the scene or arrest should be found out: names, addresses, and phone numbers. If the defendant has an alibi, or alibi witnesses, their, names, addresses, and phone numbers should be obtained. This is most important should the defendant wish to testify before the Grand Jury and should he wish to bring witnesses to the Grand Jury. Alibi witnesses' names, addresses, phone numbers, and other pertinent information, must be determined, since within 8 days of arraignment Alibi notices must be served. All witnesses must be immediately contacted for the obvious purpose of testifying at the Grand Jury as well as bearing on the immediacy of the bail application and in preparation for trial. It must be emphasized that this interview is aimed not only at the arraignment and Grand Jury but also at trial. The initial client interview, as well as any further discussion with the defendant, must always occur with the overriding consideration of preparation for and victory at trial.

The time between the purported criminal transaction and the arrest should be known as well as the location of the arrest as opposed to the location of the violation.

Much time may have passed between the time of the incident and the arrest as well as differences in blocks or even miles between the scene and the place of arrest. These facts, if accessed, analyzed, and made use, of may well succeed in weakening the People's position at arraignment and even may result in successfully obtaining the release of the defendant.

If the client has suffered injuries at the hands of the police, the nature of the injuries, and where and how he was treated and by whom, and if he was hospitalized, and where, should also be found out.

It is wise for the lawyer to bring to the arraignment a Polaroid camera and take photos of the injured accused both in terms of possible preparation for trial and as a factor in obtaining the release of the defendant or in favor of setting a low bail and for a possible U.S.C. 42 Sec. 1983 litigation against the City, County, Town or Village.

What the accused is wearing at arraignment should be noted since what he is wearing at arraignment may contrast with what he was wearing at the time of arrest or at the time of the incident. Examination of the arrest photo is useful to see if there has been a change and also with a view to establishing a possible identification defense for trial or even as a fact in argument for release.

It should also be determined if the accused knows the complainant or the police who arrested him. The complainant's address and phone number should be elicited if the accused claims to know him. If the case is a burglary it is likely that the complainant's name and address will have been set forth in the felony complaint. This reasoning equally applies to the robbery of a store. In this way the complainant's residence or work location can be immediately determined since in preparation for trial, defense counsel will wish to interview him. All these inquiries, as has been stated, are directed always with a view to preparation for trial, successfully obtaining the release of the defendant at arraignment, or the setting of a low bail. In short the initial client interview often occurring, from the perspective of the accused, under the most stressful conditions is an essential and significant event that may determine not only the outcome of the arraignment, but even the outcome of trial, since the case at this juncture is hot and the facts fresher than they will ever be as months, and even years, pass before the case is tried. If the initial interview brings about the release of the defendant then the scales tip to the defendant, who is no longer in the position of being in jail awaiting a favorable plea offer to avoid the harsher consequences of trial. Rather, he can proceed to trial posture without this Sword of Damocles of endless incarceration hanging over him before his day in court arrives. In sum, a successful bail application is largely based on this initial client interview. The outcome can significantly affect the outcome of the case. Hence the client interview cannot be sufficiently thorough since if the defendant is released he not only occupies a superior strategic position but a much superior feeling of psychological well being, which also can contribute to the outcome of the case.

It is hoped that this short article on the initial client interview will point the way to the criminal defense lawyer on how the first client interview should be conducted and what should be done and said at this stage of the proceeding. Preparation not only for bail argument, arraignment, but also for Grand Jury and Trial, is always in the foreground. It is the beginning of a fruitful and confidential relationship between equals. It prepares the way, one may hope, to the client's release, to a successful disposition, or to acquittal or success on appeal.

The client should be allayed but he should not be misled that he will somehow in some way be released on facts that must inevitably militate against him such as the undercover sale where buy money was recovered from the person of the defendant as well as drugs. In this scenario release or even a low bail may be unlikely unless the defendant is an adolescent. In this case, i.e. where the defendant is under the age of 21, if the parents of the accused are not available, then some relative of the accused should be contacted and requested to appear at the bail setting arraignment since at that age the argument can be made that the age of the defendant and the presence of his parents or relatives in the courtroom can serve to support the argument that the defendant is a good risk to return to the court on subsequent dates if he is released into the custody of his parents or relatives who will guarantee the court that the defendant will return at all times to the court when required.

The defendant is never to be lied to. If release is not in the offing, or unlikely, he should be told that. He should be informed of his possible exposure at trial and that trial exposure is not case exposure, and the difference and distinction between trial by jury and plea before the court. If he asks the question what are my chances, the answer is always it is too early to tell without much added information and investigation. He should not be told he will win based on his present bold assertions of innocence but equally should be told that his version of the facts that he may say in the course of the case and at trial have as much weight and are to be given as much credit as the State, the complainant, and the police. If he asserts his innocence, it is the obligation of defense counsel to accept that claim knowing that at all times the accused is presumed innocent throughout the proceeding. Defense counsel does not sit in judgment. He is an advocate. It is the jury who finds the facts, not defense counsel. Hence, at any time, for defense counsel to disbelieve the accused is not only unfair and improper but simply incorrect and erroneous since the facts have not yet been found and remain to be discovered. A careful, caring, and thorough initial client interview paves the way for victory at some point that might not otherwise have been possible. This interview is not only the interview of a client with his lawyer, but is the encounter of each man or woman who aim in our life contests and relationships for equal treatment of all those around us as equal citizens under the law. This brief article not merely shows or may show the way to a successful arraignment, trial or appeal, but most importantly, points the way for all of us to be more caring and of service in our professional and personal relationships, both as lawyers and as persons, to those whom we are assigned in our lives at some point to serve.

80. Is It a Dwelling or Building? A Significant Factor in Determining the Type of Criminal Conduct

Penal Law § 140.25, entitled Burglary in the Second Degree, states in pertinent part in subdivision 2 that a person is guilty of Burglary in the Second Degree when he knowingly enters or remains unlawfully in a building with the intent to commit a crime therein when the building is a dwelling. The statutory wording would appear to be eminently clear. The issue arises, however, and it is the subject of this article, what in fact constitutes "dwelling" for the purposes of this crime as defined in the statue. For example, is a house a dwelling when it is not lived in and unkempt, for the purposes of this statute? Is a mischievous youngster still guilty of burglary when he chances to remove a chest of drawers from this "abandoned" building? The answer lies in the case law defining "dwelling" for the purpose of this statue. The law is varied.

In *People v. Sheirod*, 124 A.D.2d 14, 510 N.Y.S.2d 945 (4th Dept 1987), the Appellate Division reached a close definition of what constitutes a "dwelling" for the purpose of P.L. § 140.25 (2) when the house is apparently unoccupied. In *Sheirod*, the complainant moved from New York to Colorado and left his New York residence completely furnished; the utilities remained operable and his neighbors were hired to check the house daily for break-ins or weather damage. A year later the complainant's house was burglarized and the defendant was subsequently apprehended and, after a jury trial, convicted of Burglary in the Second Degree; Attempted Petit Larceny; and criminal mischief.

The defendant contended on appeal that the trial court erred by refusing to charge Burglary in the Third Degree and Criminal Trespass in the Third Degree as lesser included offenses. Initially the court noted that for conviction of burglary in the second degree proof is required that the residence is a dwelling, which is statutorily defined as a building which is usually occupied by a person lodging therein at night (P.L. §140.00[3]). The defendant argued that since the residence had not been occupied for a year the residence was therefore a "building" not a "dwelling" and the submission of the lesser included offenses was warranted. The court then noted that prior to 1967 proof of actual presence by a person was an essential element of Burglary in the Second Degree, but now actual presence is not required and the element of a "usual occupancy" in the definition of "dwelling" is satisfied even though the residence is temporarily unoccupied at the time of the Burglary.

The court defined the issue here as whether absence for a year may be considered temporary. The court went on to state that there are a number of factors relevant in considering whether absence is merely temporary:

1. The nature of the structure, i.e., its adaptation to occupancy by a person at the time of the burglary;
2. The intent of the owner to return; and
3. The issue of whether, on the date of the burglary, a person could have occupied the structure overnight.

The court held that on consideration of these factors there should be a ruling of temporary absence since the structure had been used as a family residence for 13 years and was adapted for overnight accommodation; it was furnished; and the necessary utilities were connected. The owner intended to return and did return two weeks after the burglary. In fact, at the time of the burglary the complainants had left Colorado and were on route to their home. The court noted the complainant's personal belongings and valuables had been received at the residence and were being stored in the garage. The court therefore concluded that the absence of the occupants was temporary and that the residence was "usually" occupied within the meaning of P.L. § 140.00(3). The court concluded that the trial court correctly refused to charge the lesser included offense to the jury.

More recently in *People v. Santospargo*, 198 A.D.2d 313, 603 N.Y.S.2d 551 (2nd Dept 1993), the court held that even though the house lacked a certificate of occupancy, the house was nevertheless a dwelling since the house had been continuously lived in for two months; was supplied with water, heat, electric and phone services; was fully equipped with kitchen appliances and with such items as a bed, T.V., videocassette recorder and living room furniture; and the had a closet with clothes in it. Once again, like the Fourth Department in *Sheirod*, the Second Department in *Santospargo* employed a factual analysis in the determination of whether livability is present so as to make the building a "dwelling" for statutory purposes.[1]

In sum, this brief examination of the case law interpreting the definition of a dwelling or building under P.L. §§ 140.25 and 140.00 reveals that the Appellate Departments of this state employ a multi-factual analysis, sifting through a number of categories, rubrics or rules to determine whether an apparently perhaps unoccupied residence remains nevertheless a dwelling under P.L. § 140.25. In this way, the court, in essence, holds that a seemingly abandoned house is no more than temporarily unoccupied and so may still be the subject of a P.L. § 140.25 burglary though no person may be actually present at the time of the criminal transaction.

Copyright 1996 by New York Criminal Law News. Reprinted with permission.

81. Good Cause under C.P.L. Sec. 180.80: An Analysis

Section 180.80 of the Criminal Procedure Law, entitled Proceedings upon felony complaint, release of defendant from custody upon failure of timely disposition, states in pertinent part that upon application of a defendant against whom a felony complaint has been filed with a local criminal court and who since his arrest, or subsequent thereto, has been held in custody pending disposition of such felony complaint for a period of more than one hundred and twenty hours or in the event that a Saturday, Sunday or legal holiday occurs during such custody, one hundred forty-four hours, without either a disposition of the felony complaint or commencement of a hearing thereon, that defendant must be released on his own recognizance, unless the court is satisfied that the People have shown good cause why such order of release should not be issued and that such good cause must consist of some compelling fact or circumstance which precluded disposition of the felony complaint within the prescribed period or rendered such action against the interest of justice.

This article proposes to consider what, under the case law, constitutes the requisite good cause as defined under C.P.L. Sec. 180.80(3), i.e. some compelling fact or circumstances which precludes disposition of the felony complaint or renders such action against the interest of justice.

The most obvious basis for the granting of a "good cause" application by the People pursuant to C.P.L. Sec. 180.80(3) is where the complainant is in the hospital in critical condition (See Practice Commentary).

Other bases are not so obvious and the case law must be consulted. For example, in *People v. Sweeney*, 143 Misc.2d 175, 539 N.Y.S.2d 77 (N.Y. Criminal Court 1989) the trial court granted a good cause adjournment sought by the People for a few hours where the prosecutor was able to state that Grand Jury action would take place shortly and the basis for the adjournment was court congestion.

On the other hand, in *People v. Smith*, 143 Misc.2d 100, 539 N.Y.S.2d 663 (N.Y. Criminal Court, 1989), the court held good cause could not be found to exist on the ground that they did not have the results of a court-ordered examination of the defendant's competency to stand trial, rejecting the People's argument on this particular ground.

There are few cases defining what does or does not constitute good cause as defined in C.P.L. Sec. 180.80(3). In general, it must be said that in any particular case, it will be for the court to say whether the application falls within the ambit of C.P.L.. Sec. 180(3). *People ex. rel. Barna v. Malcom*, 85 A.D.2d 383, 448 N.Y.S.2d 176 (1st Dept. 1982).

In sum, the judgment of what constitutes good cause under C.P.L. Sec. 180.80(3) involves the consideration of largely practical considerations and an assessment of the factual nexus before the court. It is only then that the court will be enabled, albeit on an ad hoc case by case basis, to find whether good cause exists or no.

82. The Motion for Severance in New York Criminal Law

C.P.L. Sec. 200.40 states, in pertinent part, that two or more defendants may be jointly charged in a single indictment provided that all such defendants are jointly charged with every offense alleged therein. The section goes on to state that even in this case the court, upon motion of the defendant or the people made within the 45 day period provided by C.P.L. Sec. 255.20 for good cause shown, can order in its discretion that any defendant be tried separately from the other defendant or defendants.

This article proposes to consider what constitutes good cause for the granting of a severance under this statutory section. In general, it may be said that a motion for a severance or separate trial is a matter directed to the sound discretion of the trial court and subject to review by a court having jurisdiction over the facts, the criterion for review and possible reversal being whether an abuse of discretion has occurred. *People v. Bornholdt*, 33 N.Y.2d 75, 350 N.Y.S.2d 369, 305 N.E.2d 461 (1973); cert. 94, S.Ct. 1609, 416 U.S. 905, 401 L.Ed.2d 1109; *People v. Fisher*, 249 N.Y. 419, 164 N.E.2d 336 (1928); *People v. Diaz*, 10 A.D.2d 80, 198 N.Y.S.2d 278, 170 N.E.2d 411 (1st Dept. 1960); *People v. Schwarz*, 10 A.D.2d 17, 196 N.Y.S.2d 472 (1st Dept. 1960).

The cases run the gamut as to what constitutes a proper showing of good cause whereby a severance may be granted and the criteria and limits of the court's discretion. For example, upon a proper showing by the movant of the need for a codefendant's testimony it may be an abuse of discretion to deny a severance. *People v. Owens*, 22 N.Y.2d 93, 291 N.Y.2d 313, 238 N.E.2d 715 (1968). Under this rule, the *Owens* court stated that the defendant must clearly show what the co-defendant would testify to and that such testimony would tend to exculpate the defendant. The court went on to state that the court is not required to sever where the possibility of the co-defendant's testifying is merely colorable or speculative.

Applying these rules the Court of Appeals in *People v. Bornholdt, supra*, stated that the trial court did not abuse its discretion in denying the defendant's motion for a severance where the moving defendant never offered proof as to what co-defendant's testimony would be save for a conclusory statement, did not show how the purported statement would aid his defense, or that the co-defendant would, in fact, testify.

Thus, *Owens* and *Bornholdt*, taken together, establish the criteria for granting of a severance where the need for a codefendant's testimony is made out. See, also *People v. Matonti*, 53 A.D.2d 1022, 385 N.Y.S.2d 992 (4th Dept. 1976).

The second common basis for the exercise of the court's discretion to grant a severance is the so-called *Bruton-Cruz Rule* so named after the seminal U.S. Supreme Court cases *Bruton v. United States*, 391 U.S. 123, 20 L. Ed 476, 88 S. Ct. 1620 (1968); and *Cruz v. New York*, 481 U.S. 186, 95 L.Ed.2d 162, 107 S. Ct. 1714 (1987). *Bruton* enunciated the rule that a nontestifying co-defendant's confession that implicates another may not be introduced at the joint trial even if the jury is warned not to consider the confession against the second defendant. The Supreme Court in *Bruton* held further that a limiting instruction is simply ineffective when such evidence is presented. Hence, in the *Bruton* scenario, the granting of a severance is most appropriate. The Supreme Court in *Cruz v. New York, supra*, held that the interlocking or corroborative character of a confession given by a defendant does not create an exception to the *Bruton* rule which would appear to mandate a severance under these conditions although the Supreme Court in *Richardson v. March*, 481 U.S. 200, 95 L. Ed. 176, 107 S. Ct. 1702 (1987), held that reduction of the non testifying co-defendant's confession to eliminate all references to the defendant's existence is a sufficient remedy so long as the jury is instructed not to consider that confession against the defendant. Thus, *Bruton-Cruz* and *Richardson* establish the rule that a severance is proper when a non-testifying co-defendant's confession, interlocking or no, is sought to be used, although redaction and a court limiting instruction may be a sufficient remedy. On this, see also *People v. Cavanaugh*, 48 A.D.2d 949, 369 N.Y.S.2d 211 (1975); *People v. Payne*, 35 N.Y.2d 22, 358 N.Y.S.2d 701, 315 N.E.2d 762 (1974).

People v. Boyling, 84 A.D.2d 892, 444 N.Y.S.2d 760 (3rd Dept. 1981), represents something of an exception. In *Boyling*, the Third Department, in a prosecution for burglary, held that the trial court did not abuse its discretion in denying the defendant's motion for a severance based on a mutually inculpatory statement of the co-defendant. The court reasoned that the statement was relevant to prove the state of mind or intent of the defendants.

Boyling, this writer would opine, appears to stretch and even ignore *Bruton-Cruz* in admitting a non-testifying defendant's inculpatory statement against the defendant. See also *People v. Marcus*, 220 App. Div. 697, 222 N.Y.S. 456 (2d Dept. 1927), aff'd. 246 N.Y. 637, 159 N.E. 682.

In sum, the *Owens* and *Bruton* rules, glossed by *Bornholdt* and *Cruz*, serve to enumerate two essential bases whereby the defendant in a multiple defendant criminal case may apply 200.40.

Other grounds and bases may exist and be created by future case law. In the view of this writer, these are the most basic, common and essential grounds upon which a motion for a severance may be successfully attained by defense counsel.

83. Stay of Judgment and Bail Pending Appeal
by Andrew Schatkin and Spiros Tsimbinos

After a defendant is convicted and sentenced to an incarceratory term, the immediate issue of concern to defense counsel is whether, if the defendant is going to appeal his conviction, he is entitled to bail pending appeal. The procedures for obtaining a stay of judgment pending appeal are covered in C.P.L. § 460.50 and § 460.60 and the companion provisions relating to bail pending appeal are covered in C.P.L..§ 530.45 and § 530.50.

C.P.L. § 460.50 provides that for an appeal to the Appellate Division, any justice of the Appellate Division may issue a stay of judgment, or in the alternative, if the judgment is of the Supreme Court, any justice of the Supreme Court of the judicial district embracing the County in which the judgment was entered may also do so. If the judgment involved is from a County Court, stay may also be obtained from a Supreme Court justice of the judicial district embracing the County in which the judgment was entered or a judge of such County Court.

If the appeal is to an Appellate Term, then a stay may only be granted by a Supreme Court justice of the judicial department embracing the County in which the judgment was entered. C.P.L. § 460.50 thus provides defense counsel with a variety of options or judges before whom the stay application can be made.

An important word of warning, however, is that pursuant to C.P.L. § 450.50(3) only one application can be made. For example, if an application is made to the trial court who sentenced the defendant and is denied, no further application to an appellate judge will be entertained. This restriction regarding only one application is qualified, however, by the requirement that the Notice of Appeal must have actually been filed before the initial application was made. Otherwise, any application made prior to the filing of the Notice of Appeal will be considered a nullity, thereby clearing the way for a subsequent motion to be considered. See *Matter of Morgenthau v. Rosenberger*, 86 N.Y.2d 626 (1995).

A further word of caution is that if a stay and bail application are granted the defendant is obligated to perfect his appeal within 120 days unless otherwise extended by the Appellate Court. Failure to so perfect results in the automatic termination of the stay and subjects the defendant to immediate surrender and incarceration.

C.P.L. § 460.60 deals with a stay while a matter is pending in the Court of Appeals. This section authorizes a judge who is considering an application for leave to appeal to the Court of Appeals to continue the stay and bail pending appeal during the determination of the leave application and, if granted, while a further appeal through the Court of Appeals is being considered.

C.P.L. § 530.50 authorizes the fixing of bail pending appeal for all convictions except a Class A felony sentence.[1]

A unique situation authorizing bail pending appeal is also covered by C.P.L. § 530.45. This is the case where the defendant is remanded after verdict but before sentence. Under § 530.45 an Appellate Division Justice may grant bail if the action was pending in the Supreme Court or County Court. If the action was pending in a local criminal court, the application must be made to a Judge of the Supreme Court holding a term thereof in the County in which the conviction was entered. If bail is granted under Section 530.45, the defendant must also comply with the Notice of Appeal and the 120 day perfection requirements.

Since C.P.L. § 460.50 and § 460.60 do not specifically set forth the criteria to be considered in granting a stay of judgment, but instead specifically refer to the bail provisions in C.P.L. Article 530, the criteria set forth in the bail provisions are the main factors to be considered in determining whether to grant the application in question. In addition, consideration should be given to the possible merits of the defendant's appeal, but the chance of ultimate success on appeal is not totally determinative of whether bail pending appeal should be granted.

Thus, courts in the various judicial departments have specifically addressed this issue. In *People v. Surretsky*, 67 Misc.2d 966 (Sup. Ct. N.Y. Cty. 1971), Justice Fein, now of the Appellate Division, First Department, specifically stated on page 967:

> Under the prior statute (Code Crim. Pro., §§ 527 and 529), on an application for a certificate of reasonable doubt, the issue was not whether "there will be a reversal on appeal, but rather . . . whether . . . there is presented an arguable substantial question as to claimed error which, injustice, should be decided by the Appellate Tribunal. (*People v. Brod*, 203 N.Y.S.2d 947, 948; *People v. Von Cseh*, 9 Misc.2d 718; *People v. Hines*, 12 N.Y.S.2d 454).

The new Criminal Procedure Law does not change this rule; it shifts the emphasis to the question of bail.

As indicated in Professor Denier's Practice Commentary, § 460.50 of the C.P.L. does not postulate any criteria for issuance of stay. It "cursorily provides for discretionary stay orders accompanied by discretionary orders of bail." (C.P.L. 460.50, McKinney's Cons. Laws of N.Y., Book 11A Part 2, p. 429). As noted in the Commentary, the criteria for bail are set forth in paragraph (b) of subdivision 2 of section 510.30 of the C.P.L.: "Where the principal is a defendant-appellant in a pending appeal from a judgment of conviction, the court must also consider the likelihood of ultimate reversal of the judgment. A determination that the appeal is palpably without merit alone justifies, but does not require, a denial of the application, regardless of any determination made with respect to the factors specified in paragraph (a)."

The factors specified in paragraph (a) are the factors to be considered on any bail application.

In *People v. McNair,* 78 Misc 2d 341 (Sup.Ct. Monroe Cty. 3d Dept. 1974), the Court also made the following observation:

> [R]eferring to the practice commentary to CPL 460.50, a Judge is authorized to refuse to fix bail solely upon the ground "that appellate reversal is highly improbable." That seems to be the situation in the case before me. I cannot say on the generalized attack on the sufficiency of the evidence in the papers submitted even that there is a "reasonable possibility of reversal on appeal."

In *People v. Kern,* 137 A.D.2nd 862 (2d Dept. 1988), Justice Brown outlined the relevant considerations for bail pending appeal as follows:

> When an order pursuant to CPL 460.50 is sought as a matter of judicial discretion, the concern of the Judge or Justice to whom the application is made is to insure that the defendant will remain amenable to the order of the court determining the appeal (see CPL 460.50). The criteria upon which such an application is to be decided are set forth in CPL 510.30 (2) (a) and (b). Those criteria include the defendant's character, reputation, habits and mental condition; his employment and financial resources; his family ties and the length of his residence in the community; his previous criminal record, if any; his previous record, if any, in responding to court appearances when required or with respect to flight to avoid criminal prosecution; and the merit or lack of merit of the appeal and the sentence which has been imposed (CPL 510.30 [2] [a] [i]-[iii]). Also to be considered is the likelihood of ultimate reversal of the judgment (see CPL 510.30 [2] [b]).While a determination that the appeal is palpably without merit alone justifies a denial of the application, it does not, in and of itself, require such denial (CPL 510.30 [2] [b]). Even though the statute recognizes that a convicted defendant is in a different position than one awaiting trial, the issue—regardless of whether recognizance or bail is sought in an ongoing criminal action or pending appeal from a judgment of conviction therein—is that of securing the defendant's future court attendance when required (see *People v. Surretsky,* 67 Misc. 2d 966; *People v. Holder,* 70 Misc. 2d 819, *affd* 45 A.D.2d

820; Bellacosa, Practice Commentary, McKinney's Cons Laws of NY, Book 11A, CPL 510.30, at 22).

Another important factor which is considered when determining whether to grant bail pending appeal, and which should be advanced vigorously by defense counsel if it is applicable, is whether all or a substantial portion of the sentence will be served before the appeal is decided. This been viewed by the courts to be in the nature of an "interest of justice" consideration. Thus Justice Fein in *People v. Surretsky supra* at page 968, observed:

> Even if I believed the appeal to be without merit, there would still be a manifest danger of injustice to the defendant if I were to deny the application. All or a substantial portion of the sentence may be served, before the Appellate Division has an opportunity to review my decision and order denying suppression.

After conviction there is no constitutional right to bail, and the only right to bail pending appeal in New York State Courts is that granted by the statutory provisions discussed herein. The statutory provisions and their judicial interpretation call for a consideration of the factors relevant on the general question of bail, an examination of the possible merits of the appeal and the potential for manifest injustice. The exercise of the judge's discretion after consideration of all these factors will serve to determine whether an application for bail pending appeal will be granted. It is hoped that this review of the basic principles and criteria relevant to the issue of stays of judgment and bail pending appeal will assist the practitioner in properly representing his client in this specialized area of practice.

Copyright 1996 by <u>New York Criminal Law News</u>. *Reprinted with permission.*

84. Withdrawing The Guilty Plea

It may occur, in the course of criminal litigation, that the defendant, both for the fact of it and also for reasons of practicality and prudence, makes the decision to plead guilty rather than risk the potentiality of the heavy consequences of a loss at trial. It also may happen that this same defendant may at a later point in time, and before or on the day of sentencing, decide that he wishes to withdraw his guilty plea, perceiving perhaps that he was the victim of a misunderstanding on his part of what his admission entailed or meant or was the victim of some sort of fraud or even coercion. Under these circumstances, the defendant may, as has been stated, wish to begin the process anew and seek to obtain some sort of vacation of his plea. Analyzing both statutory provisions and case law applications, this article will consider the criteria and circumstances under which a defendant may be permitted to withdraw his plea.

C.P.L. § 220.60 entitled "Plea; Change of Plea" sets forth the statutory requirements as follows:

1. A defendant who has entered a plea of not guilty to an indictment may as a
   matter of right withdraw such plea at any time before rendition of a verdict
   and enter a plea of guilty to the entire indictment, pursuant to subdivision
   two, but subject to the limitation in subdivision five of section 220.10.
2. A defendant who has entered a plea of not guilty to an indictment may,
   with both the permission of the court and the consent of the People, withdraw such plea at any time before the rendition of a verdict and enter: (a) a
   plea of guilty to part of the indictment pursuant to subdivision four but subject to the limitation in subdivision five of section 220.10, or (b) a plea of
   not responsible by reason of mental disease or defect to the indictment pursuant to section 220.15 of this chapter.
3. At any time before the imposition of sentence, the court in its discretion
   may permit a defendant who has entered a plea of guilty to the entire indictment or to part of the indictment, or a plea of not responsible by reason
   of mental disease or defect, to withdraw such plea, and in such event the
   entire indictment, as it existed at the time of such plea, is restored.

The withdrawal of a plea is not within the power of the prosecutor but rests
solely within the discretion of the court.[1] The motion must be made in writing
with an accompanying supporting affidavit by the defendant setting forth the
factual matters supporting his claim of innocence.[2] The defendant has the burden
of establishing the grounds which would justify the withdrawal of his plea of
guilty.[3] The trial court cannot, without the defendant's consent in the absence of
fraud, new evidence, or gross error, vacate a plea of guilty.[4] Likewise the trial
court may not sua sponte authorize withdrawal of a guilty plea without the consent of the prosecutor.[5] Where the defendant's contentions are fully set forth in
his motion papers and the plea minutes or record provide a substantial basis for
rejection of the defendant's contentions, the trial court in its discretion may
deny, without a hearing, the defendant's motion to withdraw his guilty plea.

The defendant is not entitled to withdraw his plea where his application to
withdraw his plea is supported by nothing more than vague conclusory allegations of innocence, ineffective assistance of counsel, or some vague undefined
physical illness.[6] Thus, the Appellate Division, Second Department, held in *People v. D'Orio,* that the defendant was not entitled to withdraw his plea of guilty
to the charge of Attempted Robbery where the defendant's approach to withdraw his plea application was supported by nothing more than vague conclusory
allegations and insubstantial claims alleging ineffective assistance of counsel
and the defendant's claim of an unspecified physical illness.[7]

It may be said that where the defendant, at the time of the sentencing,
makes statements which include allegations of innocence, the trial court should
not impose sentence without holding a hearing on the issue.[8] Of course, it is in
the discretion of the trial court to determine whether to hold a hearing or not.[9]
The trial court not only has the discretionary power to permit a withdrawal of a
plea of guilty before the institution of judgment, but afterwards.[10]

There are a number of grounds upon which the defendant will be allowed to
withdraw his plea of guilty. The first and most common ground is where the de-

fendant claims he is not guilty. With respect to such a contention, the court can either grant an application to allow the plea to be withdrawn or conduct a hearing.[11] A second ground for the basis of withdrawal of a guilty plea or the granting of a hearing is where defense counsel claims he has new unascertained evidence supplying a defense.[12] In addition to the claim of innocence and newly discovered evidence, a third ground for withdrawal of a guilty plea or at least the granting of a hearing is a claim by the defendant of fraud or mistake in inducing the plea.[13] Another ground for the withdrawal of a guilty plea or the granting of a hearing is a claim of ineffective assistance of counsel.[14] A final ground for withdrawal of a plea of guilty or a granting of a hearing on the issue is a claim of coercion or duress in the plea process.[15]

Coercion on the part of a co-defendant, if shown, can result in withdrawal of a plea of guilty. The claim of coercion can also result from the purported improper action or advice of the defendant's attorney. This too can result in a withdrawal of a plea of guilty or a hearing on the issue.[16] It is also the law, as a sub-category of coercion, that misleading comments of the court can result in the withdrawal of a guilty plea or a hearing on the issue.[17] A second sub-category of coercion where the court will allow the defendant to withdraw his guilty plea is where the prosecutor has coerced him by threats or deceit to enter into the plea.[18] A guilty plea may also be withdrawn where the plea of guilty has been entered into by mistake or misunderstanding.[19]

It is hoped that this brief survey on the method and procedure whereby a plea may be withdrawn will assist criminal law practitioners in dealing with this issue.

Copyright 1998 by New York Criminal Law News. *Reprinted with permission.*

85. Duplicative Counts: An Analysis

P.L. 200.30, entitled "Indictment, duplicitous counts prohibited," states, in pertinent part, that each count of an indictment may charge one offense only (sub 1). The section adds in sub(2) that a statutory provision which provides in different subdivisions of a paragraph different ways in which such offense may be committed defines a separate offense in each such subdivision or paragraph. The section then states that a count of an indictment charging such named offense without specifying or clearly indicating the particular subdivision or paragraph of the statutory provision charges more than one offense if facts are alleged which could support a conviction under more than one such subdivision or paragraph. As stated in its two subsections, the language of the statute appears clear.

The remedy for duplicitous or multiple counts is dismissal of that count of the indictment. *People v. Seabrooke.*[1]

There is authority, however, for the proposition that a duplicitous or multiple count indictment may be remedied by an election of counts by the prosecution or by corrective instructions given by the court.[2] The question that arises, however, and that is the subject of this article, is what the case law has held to be a duplicitous count requiring dismissal of that count or counts of the indictment.

People v. Materse is illustrative.[3] *Materse* was an appeal from a conviction of two counts of Burglary in the Third Degree and Grand Larceny in the Third Degree. The facts were that a witness saw the defendant enter an apartment through a window and exit later, carrying a television set. After the defendant returned, he entered by way of the window and later exited with a canvas bag full of unknown property. The facts and theory upon which the question of Grand Larceny was submitted to the jury suggested that there was one illegal scheme and that the two entries were performed in pursuance of that scheme. The Appellate Division First Department held the conviction for the count of Burglary was required to be reversed on the ground of duplicity. Here duplicity was found in the fact of the one illegal scheme and that the two entries were performed in pursuit of that scheme.

On the other hand, in *People v. Barhan*[4] the New York County Criminal Court held the information charging the defendant with aggravated harassment was not duplicitous even though it grouped a number of calls from the defendant to the complainant in a single count. The court held the offense could be established either by a single telephone call or by a number of calls to the same person repeated over a period of time. In *Barhan*, the court based its analysis of duplicity, or not, under its reading and understanding of the offense allowing repetitive acts of the same character to establish the offense. In *People v. Cintron*[5] the Supreme Court held that the Indictment charging the defendant with soliciting, accepting, and agreeing to accept approximately $98,000 in bribes over a three-year period was not duplicitous where it was clear the Indictment charged only one illegal agreement pursuant to which money was accepted over a three-year period. In turn, like *Materse*, *Barhan* has as the basis of its reasoning, an agreement or common scheme or plan.

In sum, it would appear to be a basic rule that if the multiple acts are sufficiently distinct and separate, the Indictment may be dismissed as duplicitous, unless there can be shown the existence of a common scheme or agreement or if the statute itself permits, in its interpretation, a repetition or multiplicity of acts.

Continuous Acts or Conduct

It has been held that where a count alleges the commission of a particular offense occurring repeatedly during a designated period of time, this constitutes more than one offense and is duplicitous. *People v. Keindl.*[6]

Exemplary is *People v. Corrado*[7] where the Appellate Division, Second Department, held that the first and second counts of the Indictment were properly dismissed as duplicitous where a review of the Grand Jury minutes revealed that each count was premised upon multiple acts of sexual abuse.[8]

In like fashion, in *People v. Pries,* the Appellate Division, Fourth Department, held that accepting specific dates from a rape victim in an in camera examination in satisfaction of a statutory indictment required reversal. The Appellate Division held the rule was violated that each count of the Indictment may charge only one offense, and so, the count was defective for duplicity. The court held that multiple rapes of the same victim did not constitute a continuing offense but rather each act of intercourse is separate and distinct.[9]

Multiple Offenses

Multiple Offenses may not be charged in the same count of the Indictment and the count will be dismissed as duplicitous. Thus, in *People v. Hartwell*[10] the Court of Appeals held that an Indictment was properly dismissed as duplicitous where a single count charged, on its face, the commission of more than one crime.

Conclusion

This short review of some case law interpreting and concerning possible dismissal on the ground of duplicity or multiplicity under C.P.L 200.30 results in a threefold analysis:

1. where a conviction on two counts occurs and there was shown a common scheme or plan or course of conduct, then the conviction on such separate criminal counts is proper and the Indictment is not subject to dismissal on the ground of duplicity.[11]
2. Where the acts are multiple in character, such as repeated acts of sexual abuse committed during a period of time, then the Indictment may be dismissed as duplicitous, unless the acts occurred pursuant to some sort of agreement or were allowable as one offense under the statutory scheme.[12]
3. Finally, multiple offenses charged in the same count are always subject to dismissal.[13]

86. Section 450.50 Appeal by the People from an Order of Suppression: An Overview

Introduction

Section 450.50 of the Criminal Procedure Law (C.P.L.) defines and sets forth the circumstances and process by which the People are allowed to appeal from an Order Suppressing Evidence in a criminal case in the state of New York.

Subsection 1 states that, in taking an appeal from an order granting suppression pursuant to subsection 8 of C.P.L. 450.50, the People must file, in addition to a Notice of Appeal, an Affidavit of Errors, a statement asserting that the deprivation of the use of the evidence ordered suppressed has rendered the sum of the proof available to the People with respect to the criminal charge which has been filed in court either (a) insufficient as a matter of law or (b) so weak in its entirety that any reasonable possibility of prosecuting such charge to a conviction has been effectively destroyed.

The Necessity of the Statement

It has been said that the purpose of the section allowing the People to appeal from the Suppression Order is the feeling that where the effect of the order is to leave the prosecution with insufficient evidence, the order is for the most practical purposes final, and an appeal should be permitted. The Appellate Term, in *People v. Midgett*,[1] so stated.

This statutory guarantee of finality, as enunciated in C.P.L. 450.50, the Affidavit of Errors and the filing of statement in the appellate court is unnecessary where the indictment itself is also dismissed simultaneously with the Suppression Order.

Thus in *People v. Townsend*,[2] where the count of an indictment charging Bribery in the First Degree was dismissed and the defendant's statements relating back thereto were suppressed by order of the Supreme Court of New York County, the Appellate Division, First Department, held that an appeal from the suppression of the defendant's statements was properly taken. The court held that C.P.L. 450.50 was designed to limit interlocutory appeals by the People from suppression orders so that dismissal of the indictment, simultaneously with the suppression of statements, guarantees finality and renders the filing of a statement pursuant to C.P.L. 450.50(1) unnecessary.

Section 2 of the same statute specifically states that appeal from the suppression order constitutes a bar to the presentation of the accusatory instrument involving the evidence ordered suppressed unless and until such suppression order is reversed on appeal and vacated.

There is a caveat and limit to this restriction, however. Where the appeal is withdrawn with the permission of the court, this relieves the People from the bar to further presentation of and prosecution under the accusatory instrument. Hence in *People v. McIntosh*[3] the Court of Appeals held that withdrawal with the permission of the appeals court makes the appeal a nullity. Under these particular and peculiar circumstances, the court held that there is no bar to further prosecution within the meaning of C.P.L. 450.50(2). Of course, if the appeal under the statement is unsuccessful, any further prosecution of the defendant for the charges contained in the accusatory instrument is totally barred. If the appeal is successful it is obvious that the prosecution may proceed.[4]

The Statement

This statutory section specifically states that the statement filed with an appellate court must allege that the deprivation of the use of the evidence order suppressed has rendered the sum of the proof available to the People with respect to a criminal charge, which has been filed in court either (a) insufficient as a matter of law, or (b) so weak in its entirety that any reasonable possibility of prosecuting such charge to a conviction has been effectively destroyed.

Again, there is a gloss here. Thus, in *People v. Casadei*,[5] the Appellate Division, Fourth Department, held that the People were not precluded from introducing the contested blood test evidence at trial with respect to a Penal Law charge where the People had prevailed on a suppression appeal. They so held even though the People had not indicated the Penal Law charge against the defendant in their statement in support of their appeal from the suppression order and their statement only discussed the charge under the VTL count. The clear thrust of the *Casadei* holding is that success on appeal cures any deficiency in the statement that may have lacked a full explanation of the charges. Under *Casadei*, any error in the statement is mooted.

Another twist on some supposed deficiency in the statement under C.P.L. 450.50 is set forth in *People v. Brooks*.[6]

In *Brooks*, the Appellate Division, Fourth Department, held that the prosecution's failure to file the statement asserting the deprivation of evidence suppressed by the trial court nullified any possibility of conviction and did not preclude the People's appeal from the trial court's order dismissing the indictment. The Court reasoned that since the appeal was from an order of full indictment dismissal, and not merely and solely from an order granting suppression, that statement was not required in the case in which, as in *Brooks*, the trial court had suppressed the evidence and had also dismissed the indictment.

In similar fashion in *People v. Midgett*,[7] the defendant appealed from an order granting the defendant's motion to suppress physical evidence and a subsequent order dismissing the information because the People were unable to proceed to trial without the suppressed evidence. The appellate court held that where there has already been a judicial determination that the People were unable to proceed without the suppressed evidence, a statement by the People to that effect is superfluous.

Specifically, the court held that the requirements of C.P.L. 450.50 are satisfied where the court dismisses the information on the ground that the People are left with insufficient evidence to proceed with the prosecution, and so the filing of the statement under those circumstances is not required.[8]

A final point should be noted. The statute here, C.P.L. 450.50, prohibits any further prosecution of the accusatory instrument under this limited type of appeal. Further, if the prosecution seeks to continue the matter by obtaining a superseding indictment which contains the same charges set forth in the original indictment, the newly indicted charges may also be dismissed. The Court held in

Forte v. Supreme Court[9] that where all the evidence which suppressed both the original and superseding indictment was known to the prosecutor, the prosecution cannot avoid the statutory bar by obtaining a superseding indictment alleging the same offense, unless there is a showing of newly discovered evidence.

Conclusion

This review of the import and meaning and ramifications of C.P.L. 450.50 reveals a number of threads. First, the purpose of the statute and its requirements is to preclude appeal from a non-final order and to preserve finality.[10] Second, where the indictment has been dismissed, the rule and its necessity is rendered unnecessary.[11]

Third, where the appeal is successful, under the statutory section any minor deficiency or deficiencies in the statement will be cured.[12] Fourth, where the appeal is withdrawn with the permission of the court this allows, or rather removes any bar to, further prosecution within the meaning of C.P.L. 450.50, which would be otherwise operative during the appellate process.[13]

In the same way, when the appeal is from dismissal of the full indictment, the failure to file the statement is rendered harmless. The statement is also not required where the trial court has dismissed the indictment.[14] Again, if the appeal is unsuccessful any further prosecution will be barred.[15]

Finally, and in conclusion, the People cannot evade the affirmation of the suppression order and continue the prosecution by filing a superseding indictment unless the indictment alleges newly discovered evidence.

Reprinted with permission from New York Criminal Law *Newsletter, Spring 2005, Vol. 3, No. 2, published by the New York State Bar Association, One Elk Street, Albany, New York 12207.*

87. The Pen Register: A Constitutional Excursus

The pen register may be defined as a device that serves to record on its installation, all numbers dialed from a specific telephone line. Pen registers are not listening devices. They record no sound or conversations. On its face, it would appear that the installation of a pen register may be in some sense a violation of a person's Fourth Amendment Constitutional Right to be free from this unreasonable search and seizure.[1]

The Fourth Amendment of the United. States Constitution sets forth the parameters on the reach and ability of the government to search for evidence without a warrant. If the search is warrantless, as a pen register would be, the criterion for this sort of warrantless search is that the government's intrusion—in this case the installation of a pen register—does not violate the person's "reasonable expectation of privacy." What constitutes and defines what may be considered a reasonable expectation of privacy is set forth in the seminal and significant

United States Supreme Court Case, *Katz v. United States*.[2] In *Katz*, the Government placed an electronic listening device on the outside of a telephone booth where Katz made his call from, for the purpose of eavesdropping. Katz argued that he had a reasonable expectation of privacy as to his seized conversations.

The Court ruled that listening to and recording Katz's phone conversations with an electronic listening device attached to the outside of a phone booth constituted a "search and seizure" subject to Fourth Amendment protection. In *Katz*, the court devised a two pronged "test:" whether the individual's conduct reflected a subjective expectation of privacy, and whether the subjective expectation is one society is prepared to recognize as reasonable.

The Court ruled that a search is constitutional if it does not violate a person's "reasonable" or "legitimate" expectation of privacy. In the case of Katz, the Court held Katz had a reasonable expectation of privacy. When Katz shut the door to the telephone booth, the Court held that he expected his telephone conversation to be private and that the police violated his privacy by attaching an electronic listening device to the telephone booth. In short, the Court held that listening to and recording telephone conversations was a "search and seizure" subject to Fourth Amendment protection.

On the other hand, pen registers record all numbers dialed from a specific telephone line, but do not record conversations. Because pen registers do not overhear oral communications, they have received different treatment by some courts than other electronic surveillance instruments such as wiretaps. *Smith v. Maryland*, 442 U.S. 735 (1979), states the current view in this area of law. In *Smith*, the court held that the installation and use of a pen register was not a search within the meaning of the Fourth Amendment and, hence, no warrant was required. In applying the *Katz* analysis to the case, the Court concluded that because pen registers do not hear sound and do not record conversation, they do not infringe on Fourth Amendment rights in the same fashion a wiretap or other recording devices do. Moreover, all dialed calls already transmit information to a third party, that is, to the telephone company, and so the Court observed, under this factual scenario, no ground for a reasonable expectation of privacy existed.

Both Mr. Justice Marshall and Mr. Justice Stewart dissented from the majority opinion of Mr. Justice Blackmun, who held that once the individual conveyed numeric information to the telephone company and to its equipment somehow, he assumed the risk that the company would reveal the information to the police or others.[3]

A better and more forward view on this emerging issue is expressed by the Supreme Court in *Kyllo v. U.S.*,[4] where the Supreme Court had occasion to address, as a Fourth Amendment issue, the issue of the use of technology and electronic surveillance and its use by law enforcement.

Mr. Justice Scalia noted in this opinion that where the search of the interior of a home is involved, there exists under that particular circumstance a minimal expectation of privacy, which we all acknowledge to be reasonable, and the Fourth Amendment privacy guaranteed is present there.[5]

Conclusion

This very brief note on the use of pen registers reveals that at present, their installation and use, whether in a home or office, is not a violation of the Fourth Amendment guarantee of privacy.

Kyllo represents a more enlightened and informed view of the use of technology to reach or, if you will, intrude, on a person and his affairs. In the opinion of this writer, it could be stated that *Kyllo*'s fine distinction of an intrusion into one's home is a distinction without a difference. The reasoning of *Smith* that one's privacy rights are lost when they are revealed to and given access to the telephone company and so to the public, government, and police is a mistaken view. When one places a call, overheard or not, in one's home or office, one assumes privacy and restriction of the event. It is no argument and it is fallacious to say that making the call represents some sort of assumption of the risk. One has no reason to suspect, and this is a reasonable expectation, that the numbers will be taken and disseminated to the authorities. *Smith* is the wrong view. There is intrusion and invasion here and saying numbers are different from sound begs the question. The expectation of privacy is the same in both and the Fourth Amendment guarantee should be afforded in both.[6]

88. Waiver of the Right to Appeal

It is established law that, provided that certain elements are present, a defendant may effectively waive his right to appeal. The leading case establishing the proper criteria for an effective waiver of the right to appeal is *People v. Seaberg*.[1] In *Seaberg*, one defendant pled guilty to Attempted Criminal Possession of a Weapon in the Second Degree and Robbery in the First Degree and agreed to waive his right to appeal as part of the bargain. He was sentenced and then appealed. The Appellate Division dismissed the appeal. A second defendant was convicted of Driving While Impaired and Driving While Intoxicated and agreed to waive his right to appeal in exchange for a particular sentence and then appealed. The Appellate Division dismissed that appeal.

The Court of Appeals engaged in an extensive analysis of what was necessary for a defendant to effectively waive his right to appeal and concluded that for a waiver to be enforceable it must be voluntary, knowing, and intelligent. The Court of Appeals went on to state that the trial court determines if those requirements are met by considering all the relevant facts and circumstances surrounding the waiver, including the nature and terms of the agreement and the age, experience, and background of the accused. The Court of Appeals also stated that the court must consider, in overseeing this process, the reasonableness and appropriateness of the bargain and its effect on "the integrity of the

Criminal Justice System" before accepting it. The Court finally noted that, as with plea and sentence bargains generally, the terms and conditions of the agreement and the defendant's understanding of them should be placed on the record to facilitate Appellate Review. The Court concluded in the case before it that, despite the fact that defendant *Seaberg* did not personally enter into the Court's discussion with his lawyer when the details of the bargain were stated, there was ample evidence in the record. The Court concluded that the defendant agreed to the bargain and did so voluntarily with an "appreciation of the consequences."

Seaberg is the landmark case establishing the validity of waivers of appeal and what is necessary for them to pass legal muster. Cases following this have reiterated the factors that must be considered by the Appellate Court to determine if a waiver is legally valid.[2]

There have been many cases interpreting and applying the criteria of *Seaberg. People v. Robinson*[3] is relevant. In *Robinson*, the Court specifically asked defense counsel if he had spoken to the defendant about the appeal issue, i.e., the waiver of the right to appeal as part of the plea agreement, and the defense counsel replied that it was not a problem. Later the defendant acknowledged that he had had ample time to consult with this attorney before deciding to plead guilty and that he discussed all aspects of the case with his attorney. In the course of the plea allocution the Court asked the defendant if he was willing to sign a waiver of the right to appeal and the defendant answered yes to this question. Thereafter, the defense counsel expressly stated that he had advised the defendant of his right to appeal and the defendant told him that he did not want to appeal. The Court also read the waiver of the right to appeal form aloud to the defendant and the defendant and his attorney executed the waiver form in the presence of the Court. Under these circumstances and facts, the Court held that it was clear that the defendant's waiver of his right to appeal was knowing, intelligent, and voluntary.

Robinson is an excellent example of an exhaustive waiver process. The defendant stated that he had consulted with his attorney about it; defense counsel expressly stated he had advised the defendant of his right to appeal and the defendant told him he did not want to appeal; and, most significant, the Court read the waiver form aloud to the defendant, and the defendant and his attorney executed the waiver form in the presence of the Court.[4]

The cases are legion that interpret and explain what may constitute a valid waiver. For example, in *People v. Moissett,*[5] counsel for the defendant made it clear that his client was waiving his right to appeal and the Court thereafter questioned the defendant as to his understanding of his lawyer's statements and whether he had any questions concerning the statements.[6]

Another excellent case interpreting the waiver criteria is *People v. DeLuna,*[7] where the Appellate Division First Department found an appeal waiver knowing and voluntary where the Court informed the defendant of the waiver and the defendant was given time to discuss this condition with his lawyer and said he understood the waiver.

Again, *People v. Ciatto*[8] is an excellent example of what has been held to be an effective waiver. In that case, it is significant that the defendant was given a waiver to execute, and defense counsel determined that it was appropriate to sign the waiver. In addition, the Court stated that the client could read it as well as sign it and asked the defendant if he did sign the waiver of right to appeal to which the defendant answered, "Yes, Sir." Defense counsel, the record showed, discussed the waiver with his client. The Court concluded that these facts and circumstances and specifically the colloquy on the record supported the enforcement of the defendant's waiver of his right to appeal as knowing, voluntary, and intelligent.[9]

There can be no doubt as to the state of the law on this matter, namely that a waiver is valid if found by the Court to be knowing, intelligent, and voluntary. The question arises, however, whether a waiver forecloses all chance of appeal. It is clear under *Seaberg* that it does not waive, for example, speedy trial claims or the issue of the defendant's competency to stand trial. Nor, *Seaberg* held, does the waiver interfere with the interest of justice jurisdiction of the Appellate Division. More important, however, *Seaberg* states that a defendant may not waive the right to challenge the legality of his sentence. This article proposes to examine what is encompassed and meant by the inability or unacceptability, legally, of waiving the issue of the legality of a sentence.

It does not include the excessiveness of the sentence, that much is clear from *Seaberg*, and that is not what is meant by the legality of the sentence. *People v. Mack*[10] is relevant on what is meant by the legality of a sentence. In that case, the defendant contended that the sentences imposed must run concurrently and were therefore illegal. The Appellate Division Second Department held that this claim survived the defendant's waiver to his right to appeal citing *People v. Callahan*[11] and *People v. Seaberg*.[12]

Again, *People v. Frazier*[13] is of import. In *Frazier,* the Supreme Court, New York County, convicted the defendant, upon his plea of guilty, of Manslaughter in the First Degree and Criminal Possession of a Weapon in the Third Degree and sentenced him to consecutive terms of 8 1/3 to 25 years and 2 1/3 to 7 years respectively. The Appellate Division First Department specifically stated that the defendant's challenge to the legality of his sentences survived his guilty plea and his waiver of right to appeal, but found that the consecutive sentences were lawful. The Court noted that it was clear that the defendant's possession of a weapon, which was complete several hours prior to the shooting and in subsequent use, were separate, successive acts. It is interesting to note that the Appellate Division First Department specifically stated that the defendant's waiver of his right to appeal barred his challenge to the sentences on the grounds of excessiveness.

People v. Rozo[14] bears careful examination. In *Rozo*, the defendant was convicted of Attempted Criminal Possession of a Controlled Substance upon a plea of guilt and she appealed. As part of the negotiated plea it was agreed that the defendant would plead guilty to a class A-II felony and receive an indeterminate term of 4 years to life imprisonment. The defendant, however, pled guilty to the crime of Attempted Criminal Possession of a Controlled Substance in the First Degree, a class A-I felony. The Court noted that the sentence of an indeterminate term of 4 years to life imprisonment constituted an illegally low sentence for an A-I felony. The Court went on to state that, at the plea proceeding, the parties were under the mistaken impression that the crime of Attempted Criminal Possession of a Controlled Substance in the First Degree was a class A-II felony, which would permit the imposition of the agreed upon sentence. On appeal, defendant argued that her conviction should be reduced to a class A-II felony and that the people consent to that reduction. Under these circumstances, the Court concluded that the conviction of attempted Criminal Possession of a Controlled Substance in the First Degree should be reduced to the lesser included offense of Attempted Criminal Possession of a Controlled Substance in the Second Degree to better effectuate the clear purpose and intent of the plea agreement.[15]

People v. Bourne[16] represents another aspect or play on what constitutes a valid waiver and whether an appeal may be had despite a waiver. In *Bourne*, the Appellate Division First Department held that the defendant's waiver of his right to appeal a criminal conviction, entered as a condition to a negotiated plea, did not bar the defendant from invoking the unique, historically recognized, and constitutionalized power of the Appellate Division to review his sentence as a matter of discretion and in the interest of justice.[17]

Conclusion

This brief review of the law of appellate waiver and its exceptions reveal that the waiver will be upheld as long as in the totality of the circumstances given, the nature of the case, the terms of the agreement, and the age and background of the accused, along with the reasonableness and appropriateness of the bargain, the waiver is knowing, intelligent, and voluntary. The case law following *Seaberg* and *Callahan* shows that the defendants preferably should be included in the discussion about the waiver; they should be given an opportunity to express assent or views to the Court and the lawyer; the lawyer should discuss the matter with the client; and preferably a written waiver should be executed on the record and read out and explained to the defendant.

This analysis also shows that there are exceptions to the total effectiveness of the waiver. *Seaberg* and the cases following it establish that where there is an issue about the legality of the sentence, that is to say that the sentence is somehow legally improper under statute or case law, that issue is appealable and survives the waiver as do the issues of competency of the defendant and speedy trial. Finally, as an afterthought and addition, the Appellate Division always retains its interest of justice jurisdiction to review the sentence and even the plea.

Reprinted with permission from: <u>*New York Criminal Law*</u> *Newsletter, Spring 2006, Vol. 4, No. 2, published by the New York State Bar Association, One Elk Street, Albany, New York 12207*

89. *The Motion to Set Aside a Sentence: The Criteria and Bases*

The motion to set aside a sentence is codified in the New York State Criminal Procedure Law under C.P.L. §440.20. That Section states, in pertinent part, that at any time after the entry of a judgment, the Court in which the judgment was entered may, upon the motion of the defendant, set aside the sentence upon the ground it was unauthorized, illegally imposed, or otherwise invalid as a matter of law.[1] This article will consider, upon analysis and interpretation of the pertinent case law, the criteria for granting or denying a motion to set aside the sentence by the defendant under this statutory section.

The statute itself defines three grounds for granting the motion: it was unauthorized, illegally imposed, or otherwise invalid as a matter of law.[2]

The case law is varied in its interpretation of what constitutes an illegal sentence. Thus, in *People v.   ,*[3] the Appellate Division, Second Department held an indeterminate sentence of ten to 20 years imprisonment for attempted murder in the second degree was illegal and had to be vacated. In *People v. Bligen,*[4] the Appellate Division, First Department reached a similar result. In *Bligen,* the sentencing court informed the defendant unless the probation report indicated any prior felony convictions or important new information, the defendant would receive a sentence of an indeterminate term of imprisonment of not more than four years. But the sentencing court also warned if the defendant failed to appear for sentencing, a sentence of not more than seven years would be imposed. The defendant failed to appear and was sentenced to an indeterminate sentence with a maximum of seven years, without a hearing to determine whether his failure to appear was intentional. The First Department held the sentencing court did not abuse its discretion when, upon recognizing the sentence was possibly illegal, it vacated the seven year sentence on defendant's motion and resentenced the defendant to an indeterminate term of imprisonment not to exceed four years.[5]

On additional "legal" sentences, see *People v. Henriquez*[6] and *People v. Ekinici.*[7] It has been held where there :has been a change in the law, this motion can be granted. Thus, in *People v. Main,*[8] the Appellate Division, Fourth Department, held where the defendant was resentenced on the ground he was not a second felony offender and thus his first sentence was improper and where the resentencing took place after an ameliorative amendment pertaining to the possession of stolen property had redefined his offense as a class A misdemeanor, he was entitled to the benefit of the amendment.[9]

It has been further held a cruel and unusual sentence, or even a harsh or excessive sentence, can be a basis for setting aside a sentence. The case law seems to hold and indicate these bases are difficult to apply in accord with this statutory section. In *People v. Peterson*[10] the Appellate Division, First Department held confusion over the defendant's sentencing on state and federal drug charges, which caused the defendant to remain incarcerated eight months beyond his good behavior conditional release date, did not amount to cruel and unusual punishment since he was not incarcerated beyond the maximum term of a statutorily valid sentence. On the other hand, in *People v. Sehn*[11] the Appellate Division, Third Department, held the modification of a sentence of 45–90 years of imprisonment, for a defendant convicted of rape, sexual abuse, and endangering the welfare of a child, was not warranted given the nature of the crimes, the ages of the child victims, defendant's exploitation of his trusted relationship with them, and the absence of extraordinary circumstances.

In general, the harshness or excessiveness of a sentence as a ground for the granting of this motion under C.P.L. 440.20 presents a difficult challenge and task. Thus, for example, in *People v. Allah*[12] the Appellate Division, Second Department, held the fact the sentence imposed was greater than that which the defendant would have received had he accepted a plea offer did not establish the defendant was entitled to a lesser sentence or that the sentence imposed was excessive.[13]

As an aside, it should be noted in subsection 2 of C.P.L. 440.20, the statute states specifically this motion must be denied where the ground or issue raised thereon was previously determined on the merits upon an appeal from the judgment or sentence, unless, since the time of such appellate determination, there has been a retroactive change in the law controlling the issue.[14]

An additional ground for granting this motion is possible judicial misconduct or improper comments or remarks of the judge at sentencing. In *People v. Cappolla*[15] the Appellate Division, First Department, held the possibility that the sentencing judge was influenced by the prosecution's ex parte revelation to the judge of the existence of a plot to bribe him required the sentence be vacated in a *Coram Nobis* proceeding and the matter be set down for resentencing.

Another ground for setting aside a sentence is where the issue concerns the defendant's appellate rights. In *People v. Melton*[16] the Court of Appeals held where the defendant makes a substantial showing he was not advised by counsel of his right to appeal, he is entitled to a hearing on this claim and, if there is merit on the claim, he is entitled to resentencing for the purpose of taking an appeal. Similarly, in *People v. Zirconium*[17] the Appellate Division, Second Department, held where the defendant was not informed of his right to appeal from his conviction for second-degree murder, and did not in fact know of such right, and would have appealed if he knew of such right, he was entitled to resentencing so his time to appeal would run anew.[18]

Ineffective assistance of counsel is also a ground for setting aside a sentence under this statutory section. Thus, in *People v. Morris*[19] it was held to be ineffective assistance of counsel where the defendant, 18 years of age, not previously convicted of a crime, and with a limited education, waived counsel at the time of his plea and it appeared from incomplete records the court intended the defendant to be represented by counsel at the time of sentencing, but the attorney did not in fact appear, defendant's application for vacation of the sentence on application for writ of error *Coram Nobis* would be granted and the defendant directed to appear for the imposing of a new sentence.

Another ground for setting aside a sentence under this statutory section is prosecutorial misconduct. Under this doctrine in *People v. Catti*,[20] the Appellate Division, Second Department, held where there was sufficient evidence at the postconviction hearing to justify the conclusion the defendant could, and did, reasonably rely on the prosecutor's representations made during plea bargaining negotiations regarding sentence recommendations, and there was no indication the prosecutor would, contrary to the general policy of not making any sentence recommendations, recommend the maximum sentence, the sentence imposed on defendant, who pled guilty to attempted possession of a dangerous drug in the first degree, would be vacated for resentencing, which should be made without any recommendation by the prosecutor.[21]

An additional ground for setting aside a sentence under this section is where there is a mistake as to prior or predicate convictions at the time of sentencing. In *People v. Perron*[22] the Appellate Division, Third Department, held a postconviction petitioner was entitled to a hearing on his motion to set aside a sentence, where the state did not contest the petitioner's predicate conviction for second-felony offender sentencing purposes, which had been an out-of-state sexual assault conviction that would not have been considered a felony in New York, and where petitioner's trial counsel submitted an affidavit that she failed to investigate this issue and never contested petitioner's status as a prior felony offender.

Another case illustrative of this doctrine is *People v. Bigio*.[23] In *Bigio*, the Appellate Division, Third Department, held resentencing was required where defendant, convicted of a felony, was dealt with as having been previously convicted of another felony, but a predicate felony statement was not filed or provided to him, and defendant neither acknowledged legitimacy of any prior felony conviction, nor was asked to controvert it, and no hearing to determine the propriety of any such conviction was conducted.[24]

Finally, it has been held this statutory section and a motion under it can be entertained where a defendant challenges the power of the court to impose sentence in the absence of a proper psychiatric report.[25]

Conclusion

This brief review of the criteria, which the appellate and trial courts have held to govern the motion to set aside a sentence reveals where the sentence is illegal in some fashion the motion may be granted, or where the sentence is harsh or excessive this too can be a basis for setting aside a sentence, although in general this does not occur with great frequency. Additional grounds for granting this motion are ineffective assistance of counsel, failure to inform of appellate rights, possible prosecutorial or judicial misconduct or improper comments or remarks by the judge at sentencing, a mistake as to the predicate status or non-status of the defendant at sentencing, and the absence of a proper psychiatric report as required at the time of sentencing. Although this article is a cursory and bare overview of this field and the rules governing this statutory section, it hopefully provides some background as to the bases for granting or not granting this motion under C.P.L. §440.20.

This article previously appeared in an edition of The Nassau Lawyer, a publication of the Nassau County Bar Association, and is being reprinted here with the permission of The Nassau County Bar Association.

90. Peremptory Challenges Under Attack

The Peremptory Challenge may be defined as a challenge to a prospective Juror for which no reason need be given or cause assigned. The exercise of a peremptory challenge, by and large, allows a party to excuse a juror without offering a reason. Peremptory challenges and their allowance have no constitutional basis but are creatures of statute. The theory behind peremptory challenges is to achieve, as much as possible, a completely impartial jury. The attorney examining the prospective juror thus has to determine if the juror or jurors, by reason of their background and their answers to his questions, are somehow biased or adverse to his client or, as it were, unsympathetic. If the examining attorney reaches this conclusion or determination, he or she may exercise a peremptory challenge to eliminate the adverse or unsympathetic juror from the panel deciding his case.

Peremptory challenges are available in both Civil and Criminal cases. In a Civil case, the plaintiff or plaintiffs are entitled to a combined total of three peremptory challenges plus one peremptory challenge for every two alternate jurors. A Defendant or Defendants are entitled to a combined total of three peremptory challenges plus one peremptory challenge for every two alternate jurors.[1]

The Peremptory challenges are equally available in criminal matter.[2] In the highest Criminal charge, or a Class A felony, twenty peremptory challenges are allowed and two for each alternate juror.[3] If the highest charge is a Class B felony or Class C felony, fifteen peremptory challenges are permitted and two for each alternate juror.[4] In all other Felony cases, ten peremptory challenges are allowed for regular jurors and two for each alternate juror.[5] In a Criminal Court Proceeding on a Misdemeanor, three are allowed for regular jurors and one for the alternate juror or jurors.[6]

The use or exercise of a peremptory challenge will result in the exclusion of the juror from further service. The only exception is when the challenge can be shown to be used to exclude a juror from service based on an improper consideration such as race or gender.[7]

Since Colonial times the allowance and use of a peremptory challenge has been a fixture in our jury trial system. Of late, however, their existence and use have been under question and scrutiny, if not attack, not only by some of the Judiciary but by many in both City and State Government.

The Argument is that they are unnecessary since the Trial Judge is presumed to be well able, as in the Federal System, to select a fair and impartial jury. It is said the use of peremptory challenges unduly delays the trial process and is an unfair tool of Counsel to weed out a person or persons on the jury he or she perceives, subjectively, to be unfair to his case or unsympathetic.

The arguments misunderstand the trial and litigation process and, most importantly, fail to understand human nature.

Trials are by their nature a drawn out, lengthy, and somewhat cumbersome process. Their purpose is past occurrence and event reconstruction, to attain shots and types of truth. The method of obtaining an approach to what may have happened is by testimonial evidence, and the production and showing of relevant documents, photos, and records, if available.

Trials, as has been stated, are time consuming and can be seen at times as cumbersome. The issues, however, they determine and resolve—liability and damages, or guilt or innocence—are of great import. The critical end of the trial process can be death itself. To say that the allowance and use of peremptory challenges add time to this already time consuming process begs the question.

Where the end be death itself or life incarceration, or an award of damages that may permit a severely injured person to have and continue with a quality of life, should we make as our model rushed efficiency and computerization? The question carries its own answer. The rule for the resolution of the issues at any trial, civil or criminal, is not less but more time.

As to the second argument that the allowance and use of peremptory challenge by Counsel is a tool to eliminate otherwise fair and impartial jurors that Counsel may perceive as unfavorable for no good or articulable reason other than his subjective perception of bias, this must also fail. The codification of peremptory challenges is long standing and their existence and use recognizes what human beings may seek to hide but what is not far beneath their cool translucent surface: their prejudices, their lies, and their hates.

Can a member of an exclusive private club that bars or has no Blacks or Hispanics or Women be permitted to sit as a Juror when he blithely and cleverly answers the Judge's question that he can truly be fair to this Black defendant charged with Rape?

Can an Anti-Abortion activist who devotes much of his time to the Right to Life Movement be fair to an unchaste woman in a Paternity case?

Peremptory challenges recognize that the accurate determination of partiality or impartiality must be obtained by probing, intuitive, and creative questioning that reveals the slight glimpse beneath the facade that the court and counsel desperately need to discover the depths and truth about ourselves that we carefully and craftily hide from those about us in our daily lives and encounters.

Peremptory challenges, properly and astutely exercised, reveal the naked-ness of us all, not what we may choose to present to the world. Peremptory chal-lenges, as it were, reveal not the sycophantic compliments of our neighbors and coworkers but their unflattering and unfavorable tittering behind our backs.

Peremptory challenges, if abolished, leave us with the conclusion that we should be satisfied with who these persons say they are and that we should credit them to be so. We are left with the carnage and genocide of this past century to account for.

Copyright 2005 by the Queens County Bar Association and the Queens Bar Bulletin. *Re-printed with permission.*

91. Motion to Dismiss an Indictment under C.P.L. 190.50: Time-barred? Maybe Not

The five most common contexts wherein a defendant may be effectively de-prived of his/her right to testify before the Grand Jury, warranting dismissal un-der Section 190.50 of the Criminal Procedure Law (C.P.L.) are

1. the failure of the District Attorney to afford the defendant a reasonable time in which to appear as a witness (one day's written notice has been held inherently unreasonable);
2. the failure of the Corrections Department to timely produce the defendant before the Grand Jury;
3. the unavailability of defense counsel on the date(s) of presentment;
4. unfairness or misconduct by the prosecutor in presentation of the case to the Grand Jury manifested by excessive cross-examination of the defen-dant, inflammatory comments, or profuse inquiry into the defendant's conviction record or the facts underlying it; and
5. the situation where the felony upon which the defendant is arraigned, given notice of charges, and bases the decision whether to testify varies materially from the crimes for which he/she is eventually indicted.

This article will consider the requirement under C.P.L. 190.50(5)(c) that a motion based upon the above-noted grounds be made within five days of the de-fendant's arraignment on the indictment, and if not so asserted is waived, and the indictment or prosecutor's information may not thereafter be challenged upon such ground.

The Rule

Generally, the case law adheres to the apparent statutory mandate that the motion be made within five days after the defendant is arraigned on the indict-ment. For example, in *People v. Maldonado,* 176 A.D.2d 586, 574 N.Y.S.2d 749 (1st Dept. 1991), the defendant appealed from a judgment convicting him of

Criminal Possession of a Weapon in the Third Degree and sentencing him to three and one-half to seven years imprisonment. On appeal, the defendant contended that he was deprived of his right to testify before the Grand Jury under C.P.L.190.50. The court flatly rejected that argument, stating—in no uncertain terms—that the defendant had not moved to dismiss the indictment within five days of arraignment.

Similarly, in *People v. Brown,* 176 A.D.2d 641, 575 N.Y.S.2d 293 (1st Dept. 1991), the First Department restated the seemingly mandatory rule, holding that the trial court did not err in denying the defendant's C.P.L. 190.50 motion to dismiss on the ground that he was denied his right to testify before the Grand Jury, since the motion was made well beyond the statutory time limit of five days after arraignment on the indictment (in this case, eleven months).

In short, the general rule is that an untimely motion to dismiss pursuant to C.P.L. 190.50 waives the defendant's right to so challenge the indictment and, if violated, is a complete bar.

The Exception

There is a line of case law, however, that represents an exception to this otherwise inviolate rule. *People v. Stevens,* 151 A.D.2d 704, 542 N.Y.S.2d 754 (2nd Dept.), was an appeal from a judgment convicting the defendant of Criminal Sale of a Controlled Substance in the Fifth Degree (upon a plea of guilty) and imposing sentence. The Second Department held that the trial court erred in denying the defendant's pro se C.P.L. 190.50 motion based on the ground that he had been deprived of his statutory right to testify before the Grand Jury due to the absence of counsel during those proceedings.

The *Stevens* court reasoned that, although the motion was made more than five days after arraignment on the indictment, the facts were that, at the time of his post-arrest arraignment, the defendant was represented by a Legal Aid attorney and notified the prosecution that he intended to testify before the Grand Jury. The defendant, however, was not represented by counsel at the Grand Jury proceedings, did not testify, and there was no explanation why his Legal Aid attorney did not appear at the Grand Jury presentment.

Following the defendant's arraignment on the indictment, the matter was adjourned to assign an attorney to represent him. Shortly before counsel was assigned, the defendant moved pro se to dismiss the indictment pursuant to C.P.L.190.50. The Second Department concluded that, because the defendant was without counsel at the time of his pro se motion, the five day rule should not be strictly applied.

Likewise, in *People v. Prest,* 145 A.D.2d 1078, 482 N.Y.S.2d 172 (4th Dept. 1984), the Fourth Department held that, where a public defender was assigned for arraignment on the indictment only, the defendant was told that another attorney would be appointed to represent her, and some time after being assigned new counsel, moved to dismiss pursuant to C.P.L. 190.50, the defendant was deprived of her right to testify before the Grand Jury and strict application of the five day rule was inapplicable, since once finally assigned, counsel moved promptly to dismiss the indictment.

See also *People v. Hooker,* 113 Misc.2d 159, 448 N.Y.S.2d 363 (S. Ct. Kings Co, 1982) (five day rule held inapplicable where defendant made timely request to testify, request was bona fide, delay in motion was only 27 days and People not prejudiced); *People v. Carter,* 73 Misc.2d 1040, 343 N.Y.S.2d 431 (S. Ct., New York Co. 1973) (C.P.L, 190.50 motion granted despite untimeliness where felony charges reduced to misdemeanors by agreement, and the Grand Jury returned indictment without defendant's receiving notice).

Conclusion

Thus, although the five day limitation under C.P.L. 190.50 is usually strictly enforced, there has developed a "rule of special circumstances" wherein exception may be made when the motion is untimely. It is also clear that allowance will be made particularly where the defendant is proceeding pro se or is represented by assigned counsel. The lack of counsel, or the absence or even presence of assigned counsel, would appear to be the salient consideration for not applying the five day statutory time limit, as witness *Stevens* and *Prest.*

The mandatory restriction may even be ignored as in *Hooker,* where the delay is short and the People are not prejudiced; or as in *Carter,* where due to some form of misfeasance, the defendant received no notice. Hence, the rule is not set in stone and defense counsel whose time has passed to make the motion would nonetheless be well advised to do so upon the showing of some special circumstance.

This article previously appeared in an edition of The Nassau Lawyer, a publication of the Nassau County Bar Association, and is being reprinted here with the permission of The Nassau County Bar Association.

92. *A Note on Criminal Appellate Practice*

Criminal Appellate Practice and Procedure, whether in the State or Federal Courts, has been the subject of many books and articles. The subject is of broad interest and impact both to the bar and to the general public since criminal appeals often present issues of constitutional dimension that in their resolution by the appellate courts often have wide and imminent impact both on the community whose concern is always the continued safety of their community and families, as well as the bench and bar whose perhaps more pressing concern is the continual assurance of fair trials for all accused and the continued viability of our constitutional and democratic system of government.

Criminal appellate practice and procedure is governed by sections 450, 460, and 470 of the Criminal Procedure Law.

The proper preparation and perfection of a criminal appeal is complex. Every criminal appeal presents issues requiring research, analysis, and the proper formulation of effective written argument. Although every case is sui generis, nevertheless certain issues may and often do recur. One error constant is whether physical evidence subsequent to a Mapp Hearing on the unconstitutional character of the search was rightly suppressed; whether a statement or confession when the defense argues that the statement is the product of classical physical or psychological coercion, or that the statement was taken in violation of the defense's Fifth Amendment Rights under the *Miranda* decision, was correctly suppressed; and finally whether a showup, where the defense has maintained the identification was unduly suggestive under Wade, was legally suppressed. If the trial court incorrectly denied suppression, most certainly this decision and order will substantially impact the defense trial case and will present an equally compelling issue for appeal.

Thus, the decision on the defense pretrial motions and the decision and order subsequent to these hearings can have telling impact and the issue will almost always be raised on appeal.

This article will consider one procedural aspect of this legal area, i.e., whether in the brief of the defendant when he argues the erroneous character of the granting of suppression the legal argument in the brief can be solely based on this issue as it was raised and occurred at trial or whether reference must be solely and only to the testimony at the Pretrial Hearing itself.

The answer that the weight of authority in this state holds is that the issue must be argued from the Pretrial Hearing testimony itself and it is incorrect and improper to argue this issue with reference solely to the trial testimony.

People v. Brathwaite[1] is relevant. *Brathwaite* was an appeal from a judgment of the Supreme Court of Kings County convicting him of Criminal Possession of a Weapon in the Third Degree. The appeal brought for review the denial, after a hearing, of the defendant's motion to suppress physical evidence and statements made by him to law enforcement authorities. The facts, as adduced at the suppression hearing, were that the two officers were patrolling an area in Brooklyn known for drug trafficking. There was a group of men walking in the street and two men, on seeing the officers, turned away and began walking away fast. The officers followed in their car and one officer then exited the car and told the men he wanted to speak to them. The defendant walked toward him, turned around, reached into his waistband and dropped a gun. When the officer approached him the defendant ran away, the gun was recovered, and the defendant was then arrested. The Appellate Division, Second Department, held the stop reasonable and legitimate and stated that the defendant's conduct in discarding the gun was an abandonment. Most important, however, the Second Department held that in so far as the defendant sought to use testimony adduced at trial to establish the unlawful police conduct the court held it was well settled that the trial testimony could not be considered in reviewing the hearing court's denial of the defendant's motion to suppress evidence.

More recently, in 1995 the Appellate Division, Second Department, held again in *People v. Davis*[2] that the trial testimony may not be considered in reviewing a hearing court's denial of the defendant's motion to suppress evidence and that in the particular case because the defendant relied solely on the trial testimony in support of his claim that the cocaine was seized from his car and should have been suppressed, this claim was not properly before the court for review.[3]

Conclusion

The rule that reference must be had solely to the hearing itself rather than the trial to argue the point of improper denial of the suppression or some other error that may have occurred at the hearing makes good sense. The trial testimony may vary from, and even be inaccurate as to, what had happened that led to the denial of suppression. If error at a particular point in the litigation is raised, that point must be argued and no other. If the hearing is the issue, then that issue must be addressed also. There is another perspective. The rule, if applied to blind the appellate court to the improper denial of suppression because the argument was made with trial rather than hearing testimony, could be seen as unduly harsh. If the issue should be heard, the court and counsel could easily have recourse to the minutes since it is ultimately the minutes rather than the argument, however framed in the defense of People's brief, that must inevitably determine all issues in the case. The minutes are the arbiter. The rule here, if strictly applied, could prevent the court from hearing an issue that should be heard and could be determinative solely due to a moment of procedural inadvertence on the part of defense counsel or his failure to know all the niceties of criminal appellate practice. All criminal practice, whether at the trial or appellate level, should be conducted with a view to assuring a fair trial or a fair shake in the appellate court. The rule here is sensible but, as happens all too often, represents an insensitivity to the goal of fairness. The legitimacies of criminal practice should never bar a court from hearing what should be heard. The proper and exact adherence to the rules of procedure, at least in criminal practice, must give way to the realization that each time we bar an issue from being heard in a criminal trial or appeal due to some alleged violation we diminish not the defendant who may suffer some loss but ourselves as lawyers and judges whose pressing concern in every criminal case is hearing everything that can be heard so some glimmer of truth may be grasped, thus preserving our constitutional system which values not highly exact procedure but overall due process.

Notes

7. Conspiracy: The Necessity of an Overt Act

1. A person is guilty of conspiracy in the sixth degree when, with intent that conduct constituting a crime be performed, he agrees with one or more persons to engage in or cause the performance of such conduct.

2. A person is guilty of conspiracy in the fifth degree when, with intent that conduct constituting:
    1. a felony be performed, he agrees with one or more persons to engage in or cause the performance of such conduct; or
    2. a crime be performed, he, being over eighteen years of age, agrees with one or more persons under sixteen years of age to engage in or cause the performance of such conduct.

3. A person is guilty of conspiracy in the fourth degree when, with intent that conduct constituting:
    1. a class B or class C felony be performed, he or she agrees with one or more persons to engage in or cause the performance of such conduct; or
    2. a felony be performed, he or she, being over eighteen years of age, agrees with one or more persons under sixteen years of age to engage in or cause the performance of such conduct; or
    3. the felony of money laundering in the third degree as defined in section 470.10 of this chapter, be performed, he or she agrees with one or more persons to engage in or cause the performance of such conduct.

4. A person is guilty of conspiracy in the third degree when, with intent that conduct constituting a class B or a class C felony be performed, he, being over eighteen years of age, agrees with one or more persons under sixteen years of age to engage in or cause the performance of such conduct.

5. A person is guilty of conspiracy in the second degree when, with intent that conduct constituting a class A felony be performed, he agrees with one or more persons to engage in or cause the performance of such conduct.

6. A person is guilty of conspiracy in the first degree when, with intent that conduct constituting a class A felony be performed, he, being over eighteen years of age, agrees with one or more persons under sixteen years of age to engage in or cause the performance of such conduct.

7. A person shall not be convicted of conspiracy unless an overt act is alleged and proved to have been committed by one of the conspirators in furtherance of the conspiracy
8. 50 N.Y. 2d 333, 428 N.Y.S. 2d 927, 406 N.E. 2d 783 (1980).
9. 93 N.Y. 2d 990, 695 N.Y.S. 537, 717 N.E. 2d 783 (1980).
10. 268 A.D.2d 699, 704 N.Y.S. 151 (3rd Dept. 2000).
11. 259 A.D.2d 990, 686 N.Y.S. 392 (1st Dept. 1999).
12. 100 A.D.2d 6, 473 N.Y.S. 288 (4th Dept. 1984) See also on the law that all overt acts performed by any of the co-conspirators become the legal act of any other conspirator, *People v. Adams*, 2 Misc. 3d 166, 766 N.Y.S. 765 (County Court, Niagra County 2003).

13. 156 Misc. 2d 904, 595 N.Y.S. 1011 (S. Ct. N.Y. County 1993).

14. 53 Misc. 2d 109, 277 N.Y.S. 697 (S. Ct. Nassau County 1966).

15. See also on the requirements of conspiracy *People v. McGee*, 49 N.Y. 2d 48, 424 N.Y.S. 157 (1979).

16. *People v. Menache*, 98 A.D.2d 335, 470 N.Y.S. 171 (2nd Dept. 1983).

17. 182 A.D.2d 418, 582 N.Y.S. 152 (1st Dept. 1992).

18. On telephone conversations being "overt acts" in furtherance of a conspiracy see *People v. Weaver*, 157 A.D.2d 983, 550 N.Y.S. 467 (3rd Dept. 1990) (Held: Telephone conversations between co-conspirators were overt acts in furtherance of a conspiracy to obtain cocaine in Florida for distribution; co-conspirators sought to arrange for delivery of cocaine and the conversation led to the co-conspirators' flight to Florida to obtain cocaine.) See also on this *People v. Kellerman*, 102 A.D.2d 629, 479 N.Y.S. 815 (3rd Dept. 1984) (Held: Phone calls of government informant to defendant from county to arrange delivery of cocaine constituted an overt act in furtherance of the conspiracy.) See also on this *People v. Menache, id.*; cf. *People v. Bavisotto*, 120 A.D.2d 985, 502 N.Y.S. 867 (4th Dept. 1986) where the Appellate Division Fourth Department held that the evidence was insufficient to support convictions for conspiracy in the Second and Fourth Degrees where nothing in the telephone conversations which constituted the conspiracy established an agreement to sell cocaine or marijuana.

19. 125 A.D.2d 351, 509 N.Y.S. 76 (2nd Dept. 1986).

20. On this, see also *People v. Kiszenik*, 113 Misc. 2d 462, 449 N.Y.S. 414 (S. Ct. N.Y. County 1982).

21. 38 N.Y. 2d 481, 381 N.Y.S. 438, 344 N.E. 2d 370 (1976).

22. 68 Misc. 2d 917, 329 N.Y.S. 2 (Greene County Court 1972).

23. Compare *People v. Gross*, 51 A.D.2d 191, 379 N.Y.S. 885 (4th Dept. 1976) (Held: not Necessary that there be direct evidence of a meeting at which defendants mapped out a detailed strategy to defraud the town.).

24. 69 N.Y.2d 892, 515 N.Y.S. 227, 507 N.E.2d 1083 (1987).

25. 116 A.D.2d 164, 500 N.Y.S.2d 532 (2nd Dept. 1986).

26. 100 A.D.2d 6, 473 N.Y.S. 288 (4th Dept. 1984).

27. 62 A.D.2d 1158, 404 N.Y.S. 210 (4th Dept. 1978).

28. *Id.*

29. Cf. *People v. Bauer*, 32 A.D.2d 463, 305 N.Y.S. 42 (4th Dept. 1969); *People v. Wolff*, 24 A.D.2d 828, 264 N.Y.S. 40 (4th Dept. 1965).

30. *Id.*

31. 136 Misc. 2d 758, 519 N.Y.S. 491 (S. Ct. New York County 1987).

32. See also *People v. Monday*, 309 A.D.2d 977, 765 N.Y.S. 705 (3rd Dept. 2003); *People v. Rodriguez*, 274 A.D.2d 826, 711 N.Y.S. 865 (3rd Dept. 2000); *People v. Jewsbury*, 115 A.D.2d 341, 496 N.Y.S. 164 (4th Dept. 1985); *People v. Burton*, 104 A.D.2d 655, 480 N.Y.S. 32 (2nd Dept. 1984). Cf. *People v. Macklowitz*, 135 Misc. 2d 232, 514 N.Y.S. 883 (S. Ct. N.Y. County 1987).

33. On this see *People v. Walker*, 116 A.D.2d 948, 498 N.Y.S. 521 (3rd Dept. 1986); *People v. DiDominick*, 94 Misc. 2d 392, 406 N.Y.S. 420 (S. Ct. Kings Co. 1978). Cf. however, *People v. Wisan*, 132 Misc. 2d 691, 505 N.Y.S. 361 (S. Ct. Richmond Co. 1986) where the trial court held that where the co-conspirators drove from the scene of the crime to New Jersey; dropped the murder weapon into a sewer; received money from the defendant; and divided the money between them, all of which allegedly occurred on the day following the murder, did not allege overt acts in furtherance of the conspiracy and would be stricken from the indictment.

34. Acknowledgement is made to the Practice Commentary interpreting Article 105 in McKinney's Consolidated Laws, published by the West Publishing Company.

13. Notice and the Confirmatory Identification

1. On this subject see also the dicta in *People v. Rodriquez,* N.Y.L.J. 5/12/92, p. 22, col. 1 where the Court of Appeals noted that Article 710.30 of the C.P.L. requires the People to inform the defendant that they intend to offer identification testimony at trial.

23. The Confirmatory Identification

1. (See that article for the cases cited herein for this general proposition.) For further cases on the general rule denying a hearing where the identification is labeled confirmatory, see *People v. Richardson,* 173 A.D.2d 846, 525 N.Y.S.2d 310 (2d Dept. 1989); *People v. Kearn,* 118 A.D.2d 871, 500 N.Y.S.2d 357 (2d Dept. 1986); *People v. Carolina,* 112 A.D.2d 244, 491 N.Y.S.2d 459 (2d Dept. 1985); *People v. Wharton,* 74 N.Y.2d 921, 550 N.Y.S.2d 260, 549 N.E.2d 462 (1984).

35. Residue of Cocaine

1. See also, *People v. Hicks,* 7 A.D.2d 829 161 N.Y. Supp.2d 835 (1st Dept. 1957) (Trace of narcotic in wad of cotton insufficient to support finding of possession of narcotic drug). Cf. *People v. Baker,* Appellate Division 2nd 707, 179 N.Y. Supp.2d 892 (1st Dept. 1958). (Six hypodermic needles and substantial amount of solution containing a narcotic drug found near the couch occupied by the defendant constituted ample proof to sustain a finding of possession by the defendant of the narcotic drug and its instruments.)

43. A Question of Weight

1. See P.L. Sec. 220.03, Criminal Possession of a Controlled Substance in the Seventh Degree; P.L. Sec. 220.06, Criminal Possession of a Controlled Substance in the Fifth Degree; P.L. Sec. 220.09, Criminal Possession of a Controlled Substance in the Fourth Degree; P.L. Sec. 220.16, Criminal Possession of a Controlled Substance in the Third Degree; P.L. Sec. 220.18, Criminal Possession of a Controlled Substance in the Second Degree, P.L. Sec. 220.21, Criminal Possession of a Controlled Substance in the First Degree.

54. Three Recent Ryan Cases

1. It should be noted that there is a bill pending in the New York State Legislature to overturn the *Ryan* holding.

59. A Novel Motion in Limine

1. See Penal Law §130.55, Sexual Abuse in the Third Degree; Penal Law §130.60, Sexual Abuse in the Second Degree; Penal Law §130.65, Sexual Abuse in the First Degree; and, Penal Law §130.70, Aggravated Sexual Abuse.

2. See Penal Law §130.55(2) (less than 11 years of age); Penal Law §130.65 (less than 11 years of age); Penal Law §130.60 (less than 14 years of age); and, Penal Law §130.70 (less than 14 years of age).

3. 47 N.Y.2d 40 (1988).

4. *U.S. v. Wade*, 388 U.S. 218 (1967); see also *People v. Adams*, 53 N.Y.2d 241.

65. A Note on the Scope of Criminal Discovery in New York

1. On this area in general, see Annot. 96 ALR2d 1224; Annot. 7 ALR 3rd 8; Annot., 5 ALR 3rd 819; 23 Am. Jur.2d, Depositions and Discovery, §§ 307-323 Louisell, CRIMINAL DISCOVERY: DILEMMA REAL OR APPARENT, 49 CAL. L. REV. 56; Robert L. Fletcher, PRE-TRIAL DISCOVERY IN STATE CRIMINAL CASES, 12 STANFORD L. REV. 293; PRETRIAL DISCLOSURE IN CRIMINAL CASES, 60 YALE L. J. 626.

2. See *People v. Draper*, (278 App. Div. 298, aff'd 303 N.Y. 653); *People v. Butchino*, (13 A.D.2d 183); *People v. Colavecchio*, (11 A.D.2d 161); *People v. Roth*, (11 N.Y.2d 80); *People v. Szwalla*, (31 A.D.2d 979, aff'd 26 N.Y.2d 655, cert. den. 408 U.S. 926); *People v. Lund*, (15 A.D.2d 582).

3. *Contra, People v. Colavecchio, (supra)* where District Attorney, by psychiatrist-witness over defendant's objection, established that, from examination, he was of opinion defendant was able to understand the charge against him and prepare and make his defense. The court by its questioning of the witness ascertained that a report containing similar findings and conclusions had been submitted to court. The court concluded that "of course, section 662 of the Code of Criminal Procedure provides that such report shall not be received in evidence upon the trial. It may not be circumvented by having the examining psychiatrist testify to the contents thereof." *(supra,* at 164).

4. See also *People v. Matera*, (52 Misc.2d 674); *People v. Quarles*, (44 Misc.2d 955); *People v. D'Andrea*, (20 Misc.2d 1070).

5. For analysis of this statute, its legislative history and construing case law, see C.L.S. Criminal Procedure Law § 240.20.

6. See also *People v. Norman*, (76 Misc.2d 644); *People v. Royster*, (73 Misc.2d 89); *People v. Gilmour*, (78 Misc.2d 383); *People v. Player*, (80 Misc.2d 177); Traynor, GROUND LOST AND FOUND IN CRIMINAL DISCOVERY, 39 N.Y.U.L. REV. 228 (1964).

7. The Sec. 240.20 scheme and the problems of "privilege" attendant on discovery of defendant's psychiatric report and by psychiatrist's testimony must be distinguished from the competency status (C.P.L. 730.20) and the interpretation thereof in *People v. Wise, supra*.

8. For cases following *Lee*, see *People v. Traver*, (70 Misc.2d 162); *People v. Gliewe*, (76 Misc.2d 696); *People v. Sullivan*, (48 A.D.2d 398, aff'd 39 N.Y.2d 903); *Antinore v. State*, (49 A.D.2d 6); *People v. Green*, (83 Misc.2d 583). See also 38 BROOKLYN LAW REVIEW (1972); COMMENT, THE SELF-INCRIMINATION PRIVILEGE: BARRIER TO CRIMINAL DISCOVERY, 51 CALIF. L. REV; 135; 76 HARV. L. REV. 838.

9. See this article *supra* and the analysis in *People v. Traver, supra*, at 164.

10. It must be emphasized that it is only the *Lee* holding—that People must provide a copy of mental report to defense counsel—which is binding. *Gliewe* is a trial court decision and so merely persuasive in its view that defendant is bound to disclose his psychiatric report on an alleged rule of underlying fairness, implicit in *Lee*. On this fairness rule and the self-incrimination privilege, see the Advisory Committee's Notes concerning the comparable clause of the Federal Rule of Criminal Procedure, Rule 16 (subd. e) cited by C.L.S. Sec. 240.20.

While the government normally has resources adequate to secure information necessary for trial, there are some situations in which mutual disclosure would appear necessary to prevent the defendant from obtaining an unfair advantage.

For example, in cases where both prosecution and defense have employed experts to make psychiatric examinations, it seems as important for the government to study the opinions of the experts to be called by the defendant in order to prepare for trial as it does for the defendant to study those of the government's witnesses. Or in cases . . . in which the defendant is well represented and well financed, mutual disclosure so far as consistent with the privilege against self-incrimination would seem as appropriate as in civil cases. State cases have indicated that a requirement that the defendant disclose, in advance of trial, materials which he intends to use on his own behalf at the trial is not a violation of the privilege against self incrimination.

11. *Hughes v. Kackas,* (3 A.D.2d 402); *Racioppa v. Hanson,* (30 Misc.2d 565); *Padovani v. Ligget & Meyers Tobacco Co.* (23 F.R.D. 255).

12. RICHARDSON ON EVIDENCE at p. 41 (Prince ed. 1964)

13. For cases following *People v. Al-Kanani, supra,* see *People v. Edney,* (39 N.Y.2d 620), (defendant, charged with kidnapping and manslaughter, interposed insanity defense. Prosecution called psychiatrist who had originally examined defendant, at defendant's attorney's request, and testified that, in his opinion, at the time of the murder, defendant knew and appreciated the nature of his conduct and knew that such conduct was wrong. Held: where insanity is asserted as a defense and evidence is offered in support thereof, a complete waiver is effected and prosecution may call psychiatric experts to testify regarding defendant's sanity, even though they may have treated defendant.) See also *U.S. ex rei. Edney V. Smith,* (425 F. Supp. 1038).

67. Constructive Possession, An Overview

1. See P.L. 10.00, 8, Definition of "possess"; *People v. Sierra,* 45 N.Y.2d 56, 407 N.Y.S.2d 669, 379 N.E.2d 196 (1978); *People v. Diaz,* 41 A.D.2d 382, 343, N.Y.S.2d 474 (1st Dept. 1973), aff'd. 34 N.Y.2d 689, 356 N.Y.S.2d 295, 312 N.E.2d 478 (1974).

71. DNA Admissibility in New York State Criminal Cases

1. Cf. however, *People v. Castro,* 144 Misc.2d 956, 545 N.Y.S.2d 985 (Sup. Ct. Bronx Cty. 1989), where Justice Shendlin held wherein a prosecution for Second Degree Murder the People sought to introduce DNA identification evidence, the Court held the *Frye* standard of admissibility was satisfied in that there was a general scientific acceptance of the theory underlying DNA identification and that DNA forensic identification techniques and experiments are generally accepted in the scientific community. The Court held, however, that pretrial hearing on this issue of whether the DNA evidence was admissible was a question of fact for the jury. The Court held, however, that the evidence here was deemed inadmissible since this testing laboratory failed in major respects to use the generally accepted scientific techniques and experiments for obtaining reliable results with a reasonable degree of scientific certainty. It would appear that *Castro* is overruled in its result and reasoning by the Court of Appeals in *Wesley* and that *Wesley* was, is and remains good authority on this issue. See also *People v. Roberto Rivera,* N.Y.L.J. 6/19/92, p.26, col. 1 (Cty. Ct. Suffolk Cty.); *People v. Lopez,* N.Y.L.J. 1/6/89 p. 29, col. 6 (Sup. Ct. Queens County); *Dabbs v. Vergari,* 149 Misc.2d 844, 570 N.Y.S.2d 765 (Sup. Ct. West. Cty. 1990); *U.S. v. Randolph Jakobetz,* 955 F.2d 786 (2d Cir. 1992); *People v. Moore,* 194 A.D.2d 32, 604 N.Y.S.2d 976 (3rd Dept. 1993); *People v. Jimmie Lee Barnes,* N.Y.L.J. 7/1/91, p. 30, col. 6 (Sup. Ct Queens Cty.); *People v. Keene,* 156 Misc.2d 108, 591 N.Y.S.2d 733 (Sup. Ct. Queens Cty. 1992). .

73. C.P.L 30.30: A Kind of Delay

1. On this see also *People v. Saunders* 84 Misc.2d 467, 376 N.Y.S.2d 879 (Crim. Ct. City of New York, New York County, 1975), where the Criminal Court of the City of New York held the defendant was denied his right to a speedy trial, as prescribed by statute within 90 days, where due to the congestion in the Grand Jury stenographer's office delay resulted in receipt of the Grand Jury Minutes for use in connection with the motion.

76. Withdrawal of the Guilty Plea under the Federal Rules of Criminal Procedure: An Analysis

1. 408 F.2d 559 (3d Cir. 1969).

2. See also on this *Kadweller v. U.S.*, 315 F.2d 667 (9th Cir. 1963), where the Ninth Circuit, in the most exact language, stated that leave to withdraw a guilty plea should be freely granted and allowed prior to sentencing; *United States v. Young*, 424 F.2d 1276 (3d Cir. 1970); *Gearhart v. United States*, 272 F.2d 499 (D.C. Cir. 1959); *Kirshberger v. United States*, 392 F.2d 782 (5th Cir. 1968); *Poole v. United States*, 250 F.2d 396, 400 (D.C. Cir. 1957).

3. 607 F.2d 337 (10th Cir. 1979).

4. See also on this *United States v. Barker*, 579 F.2d 1219 (10th Cir. 1978).

5. 75 F.2d 327 (7th Cir. 1996). See also on this *United States v. Ranum*, 96 F.3d 1020 (7th Cir. 1995); *United States v. Bushert*, 997 F.2d 1343 (11th Cir. 1993); *United States v. Williams*, 23 F.3d 629 (2d Cir. 1994).

6. 108 F.3d 1513 (2d Cir. 1997).

7. 878 F.2d 168 (2d Cir. 1989).

8. 37 F.3d 169 (5th Cir. 1994). See also on this *United States v. McMillan*, 914 F. Supp. 1387 (E.D. La. 1996); *United States v. Doyle*, 981 F.2d 591 (1st Cir. 1992); *United States v. Strauss*, 563 F.2d 127 (4th Cir. 1977); *United States v. Bradin*, 535 F.2d 1039 (8th Cir. 1976); *United States v. Stayton, id.*

9. 602 F.2d 709 (5th Cir. 1979).

10. 274 U.S. 220, 475 S. Ct. 582, 71 L.Ed. 1009 (1927).

11. 449 F.2d 139 (3d Cir. 1971). See also on this *United States v. Saft*, 558 F.2d 1073 (2d Cir. 1979); *United States v. Moore*, 290 F.2d 501 (2d Cir. 1961); *United States v. Napolitano*, 212 F. Supp. 743 (SDNY 1963).

12. 514 F.2d 208 (DC Cir. 1975); See also on this *United States v. Young, id.; Poole v. United States, id.; Gearhart v. United States, id.*

13. *United States v. Smith*, 818 F. Supp. 123 (W.D. Pa. 1993), aff'd, 14 F.3d 50; cert. den., 114 S. Ct. 1235, 510 U.S. 1184, 127 L.Ed.2d 579; *United States v. Allen*, 668 F. Supp. 969, (W.D. Pa. 1987), aff'd, 845 F.2d 1016 (W.D. Pa. 1987); *United States v. Clark*, 429 F. Supp. 89 (W.D. Okla. 1976).

14. 327 F.2d 129 (3d Cir. 1964). On this see also *United States v. Craig*, 985 F.2d 175 (4th Cir. 1993); *United States v. Pitino*, 887 F.2d 42 (4th Cir. 1989); *United States v. Martinez*, 785 F.2d 111 (3d Cir. 1986).

15. 906 F. Supp. 436 (S.D. Ohio 1995). On this see also *United States v. Leung*, 783 F. Supp. 357, (N.D. Ill. 1991); *United States v. Diaz*, 770 F. Supp. 840 (S.D. NY 1991), aff'd 756 F.2d 1166; *United States v. Allen*, 668 F. Supp. 969 (W.D. Pa. 1987); *United States v. Killingworth*, 117 F.3d 1159 (10th Cir. 1997).

16. 570 2d 570 F.2d 999, 187 U.S. App. D.C. 90 (CADC. 1977); *United States v. Savage*, 561 F.2d 554 (4th Cir. 1977); *United States v. Saft, id.; United States v. Brown,* 617 F.2d 54 (4th Cir. 1980).

77. Probable Cause and Pretrial Hearings

1. 157 A.D.2d 744 (2d Dept. 1990)
2. See also *People v. Kennedy*, 151 A.D.2d 830 (3rd Dept. 1989); *People v. Stephens*, 143 A.D.2d 692 (2d Dept., 1988); *People v. Jackson*, 108 A.D.2d 357, 484 N.Y.S.2d 913 (2d Dept. 1985); *People v. Chipp*, 75 N.Y.2d 437, 553 N.Y.S.2d 77 (1990)
3. 117 A.D.2d 127 (2d Dept. 1986)
4. *People v. Chavis*, 147 A.D.2d 582, 537 N.Y.S.2d 875 (2d Dept. 1989)
5. *People v. Berrios*, 28 N.Y. 361 (1971); *People v. Jones*, 124 A.D.2d 1024 (4th Dept. 1986)
6. 174 A.D.2d 461, 571 N.Y.S.2d 245 (1st Dept 1991)
7. 61 N.Y.2d 408, 474 N.Y.S.2d 441 (1984)
8. 206 A.D.2d 333, 615 N.Y.S.2d 18 (1st Dept 1994)
9. 236 A.D.2d 243 (1st Dept. 1997)
10. 144 A.D.2d 238 (1st Dept. 1998)
11. 223 A.D.2d 425 (1st Dept. 1996)

78. Extending the Time for Taking an Appeal in a Criminal Case

1. See also *People v. Spadafora*, 131 A.D.2d 40, 519 N.Y.S.2d 979 (1st Dept. 1987); *People v. Daniel P.*, 94 A.D.2d 83, 463 N.Y.S.2d 838 (2d Dept. 1982); *People v. White*, 81 A.D.2d 486, 442 N.Y.S.2d 300 (4th Dept. 1981); cert. den. 102 S.Ct 1619, 455 U.S. 992, 71 L.Ed 853. *People v. Khan*, 146 A.D.2d 806, 537 N.Y.S.2d 284, app. den. 73 N.Y.2d 1021, 541 N.Y.S 776, 539 N.E.2d 604 (2d Dept. 1989), is also instructive. In *Khan*, it was held by the Appellate Division, Second Department that the People had exercised due diligence in attempting to secure the presence of their key witness where, upon learning that the witness was living in Florida and that he was reluctant to testify, the People immediately prepared a material witness order, had it signed and forwarded it to the office of the Florida State Attorney. The Second Department held under these facts that the People had exercised due diligence. Cf., however, *People v. Meyers*, 114 A.D.2d 861, 494 N.Y.S.2d 897 (2d Dept. 1985), where the Second Department held that the record failed to demonstrate that the People had attempted with due diligence to make the reluctant witness available. The court stated that the People had failed to demonstrate the type of credible vigorous activity necessary to enable the People to invoke the exceptional circumstances statutory exception where they never subpoenaed the witness to testify before the Grand Jury or ever called or contacted the witness thereafter.

See also *People v. Robbins*, 223 A.D.2d 735, 637 N.Y.S.2d 208 (2d Dept. 1996); *People v. Capers*, 117 A.D.2d 992, 578 N.Y.S.2d 14 (4th Dept. 1991); *People v. Mims*, 155 Misc.2d 103, 587 N.Y.S.2d 536 (Supreme Court New York County 1992). In *Mims*, the trial court held that the vacation period of the prosecution witness did not render the witness "unavailable" so as to justify exclusion on the ground of "exceptional circumstances" where the People had not shown that they attempted to subpoena policy witnesses, attempted to inquire from their command as to their precise whereabouts, or had taken appropriate measures to ensure their appearance at hearings or trial.

2. On the issue of prejudice see also *People v. Thomas*, 210 A.D.2d 736, 620 N.Y.S.2d 555 (3rd Dept. 1994); *People v. Quiroz*, 192 A.D.2d 730, 597 N.Y.S.2d 106 (2d Dept. 1993); *People v. Carpenito*, 194 A.D.2d 522, 606 N.Y.S.2d 24 (2d Dept. 1993).

3. See C.P.L. § 30.30(4)(c) and *People v. Sigismundi*, N.Y.2d, decided March 27, 1997 (N.Y.L.J. pg. 27, 3/28/97).

80. Is it a Dwelling or Building? A Significant Factor in Determining the Type of Criminal Conduct

1. See also *People v. Lewoc*, 101 A.D.2d 927, 475 N.Y.S.2d 933 (3rd Dept. 1984), where the Appellate Division Third Department held that a two and one half year absence constituted a temporary absence, and so the building was a dwelling for the purpose of the statute and sustained the burglary conviction under P.L. § 140.25.

83. Stay of Judgment and Bail Pending Appeal

1. See *Rogers v. Leff*, 45 A.D.2d 630 (1st Dept. 1974); *People v. McGuire*, 101 A.D.2d 914 (3d Dept 1984); *Gold v. Shapiro*, 62 A.D.2d 62 (2nd Dept 1978).

84. Withdrawing the Guilty Plea

1. *People v. Selikoff*, 35 N.Y.2d 227 (1974); *People v. Stubbs*, 110 A.D.2d 725 (2d Dept.); *People v. Sloan*, 228 A.D.2d 974 (3rd Dept. 1996); *Van Leer-Greenberg on Behalf of Morris v. Massaro*, 87 N.Y.2d 996 (1996).

2. *People v. McDermott*, 146 A.D.2d 874 (3rd Dept. 1989).

3. *U.S. ex rel Rivera v. Follette*, 395 F.2d 450 (2d Cir. 1968); *People v. Sanchez*, 75 A.D.2d 918 (3rd Dept. 1980).

4. *Randolph v. Leff*, 220 A.D.2d 281 (1st Dept. 1995); *Crooms v. Corriero*, 206 A.D.2d (Dept. 1994); *People v. Ifill*, 108 A.D.2d 202 (2d Dept. 1985); *People v. Grant*, 99 A.D.2d 536 (2d Dept. 1984).

5. *People v. Vaughn*, 119 A.D.2d 779 (2d Dept. 1986); *People v. Evans*, 18 A.D.2d 1018 (2d Dept. 1963).

6. *People v. Stone*, 193 A.D.2d 838 (3rd Dept. 1993); *People v. Aiken*, 186 A.D.2d 897 (3rd Dept. 1992).

7. 210 A.D.2d 424 (2d Dept. 1994); see also *People v. Lee*, 132 A.D.2d 625 (2d Dept. 1987); *People v. Grady*, 110 A.D.2d 780 (2d Dept. 1985).

8. *People v. Hall*, 56 A.D.2d 893 (2d Dept. 1977); *People v. Ehlers*, 99 Misc.2d 764 (Dist. Ct., Suffolk Cty. 1979); *People v. Artis*, 74 A.D.2d 644 (2d Dept. 1980); *People v. McKennion*, 27 N.Y.2d 671 (1970).

9. *People v. Miller*, 42 N.Y.2d 946 (1977); *People v. Roder*, 32 A.D.2d 641 (2d Dept. 1969); *People v. Guerra*, 157 A.D.2d 500 (1st Dept. 1990); *People v. McCaskell*, 206 A.D.2d 547 (2d Dept. 1994).

10. *People v. Weissman*, 34 Misc.2d 670 (Sup. Ct., N.Y. Cty. 1962); *People v. Brim*, Misc.2d 335 (N.Y. Gen. Sess. 1960).

11. *People v. Artis*, 74 A.D.2d 644 (2d Dept. 1980); *People v. Derrick*, 188 A.D.2d 486 (2d Dept. 1992). It shall be noted that a challenge to a guilty plea, raised for the first time on appeal, is not preserved for appellate review. On this, see *People v. Fernandez*, 110 A.D.2d 657 (2d Dept. 1985), aff'd, 67 N.Y.2d 686 (1986); *People v. Paulk*, 142

A.D.2d 754 (3rd Dept. 1988); *People v. Vignera*, 29 A.D.2d 657 (2d Dept. 1968); *People v. McKennion*, 27 N.Y.2d 671 (1970).

12. *People v. Sanders*, 36 A.D.2d 619 (2d Dept. 1971).

13. *People v. Cance*, 155 A.D.2d 764 (3rd Dept. 1989); *People v. Bryan DD*, 76 A.D.2d 963 (3rd Dept. 1980); *People v. Randolph*, 78 A.D.2d 566 (3rd Dept. 1980).

14. *People v. Stephens*, 175 A.D.2d 272 (2d Dept. 1991); *People v. Hamilton*, 192 A.D.2d 738 (3rd Dept. 1993); *People v. Black*, 170 A.D.2d 383 (1st Dept. 1991); *People v. Boans*, 93 A.D.2d 1000 (4th Dept. 1983); *People v. Simons*, 158 A.D.2d 728 (2d Dept. 1990).

15. *Chaipis v. State Liquor Authority*, 44 N.Y.2d 57 (1978); *People v. Collins*, 186 A.D.2d 298 (3rd Dept. 1992); *People v. Lisbon*, 187 A.D.2d 457 (2d Dept. 1992); *People v. Harris*, 118 A.D.2d 583 (2d Dept. 1986), aff'd, 69 N.Y.2d 850 (1987); *People v. Colon*, 75 A.D.2d 771 (1st Dept. 1980).

16. *People v. Rodriguez*, 79 Misc.2d 1002 (Sup.Ct., Bx. Cty, 1974); *People v. Gonzalez*, 171 A.D.2d 413 (1st Dept. 1991); *People v. Salsman*, 185 A.D.2d 469 (3rd Dept. 1992); *People v. Lewis*, 170 A.D.2d 538 (2d Dept. 1991).

17. *People v. Martinez*, 162 A.D.2d 274 (1st Dept. 1990); *People v. Goldfadden*, 145 A.D.2d 959 (4th Dept. 1988); *People v. Christian*, 139 A.D.2d 896 (4th Dept. 1988); *People v. Fanini*, 222 A.D.2d 1111 (4th Dept. 1995); *People v. Joy*, 114 A.D.2d 517 (2d Dept. 1985); *People v. Griffith*, 80 A.D.2d 590 (2d Dept. 1981).

18. *People v. Jones*, 44 N.Y.2d 76 (1978); *People v. Muncey*, 214 A.D.2d 432 (1st Dept. 1995),

19. *People v. Englese*, 7 N.Y.2d 83 (1959); *People v. Walters*, 176 A.D.2d 277 (2d Dept. 1991). It should be noted here that where the court is unwilling or unable to sentence the defendant in accord with the plea agreement, the defendant must be given an opportunity to withdraw his plea. On this, see *People v. Rosenberg*, 148 A.D.2d 346 (1st Dept. 1989); *People v. Powell*, 105 A.D.2d 761 (2d Dept. 1984); *People v. Brown*, 198 A.D.2d 901 (4th Dept. 1993); *People v. Danise*, 208 A.D.2d 555 (2d Dept. 1994); *People v. Zimmer*, 112 A.D.2d 500 (3rd Dept. 1985); *People v. Cohen*, 176 A.D.2d 596 (1st Dept. 1991).

85. Duplicative Counts: An Analysis

1. 152 A.D.2d 760, 544 N.Y.S.2d 379 (3rd Dept. 1989).

2. *People v. Horne* 121 Misc.2d 389, 468 N.Y.S.2d 433 (S. Ct. Kings Co. 1983).

3. 57 A.D.2d 765, 394 N.Y.S.2d 643 (1st Dept. 1977).

4. 147 Misc.2d 253, 556 N.Y.S.2d 441 (Crim. Ct. N.Y. Co. 1990).

5. 134 Misc.2d 453, 511 N.Y.S.2d 480 (S. Ct. N.Y. Co. 1987).

6. 68 N.Y.2d 410, 509 N.Y.S.2d 790 (1986).

7. 161 A.D.2d 6598, 556 N.Y.S.2d 95 (2d Dept. 1990).

8. 81 A.D.2d 1039 (4th Dept. 1981).

9. See also *People v. Algarin* 166 A.D.2d 287, 560 N.Y.S.2d 771 (1st Dept. 1990) (Held: Indictment fatally duplicitous where although the Indictment charged only one offense per count the bill of particulars alleged as to each count that the defendant engaged in a continuing course of conduct over a period of time rendering it impossible to determine which of the multiple acts alleged was the basis of the defendant's conviction on the given counts.)

10. 166 N.Y. 361, 59 N.E. 929 (1901).

11. *People v. Materse id.*; *People v. Burton id.*; *People v. Cintron, id.*

12. *People v. Keindl id.*; *People v. Corrado, id.*

13. *People v. Hartwell, id.*

86. *Section 450.50 Appeal by the People from an Order of Suppression: An Overview*

1. *People v. Midgett*, 86 Misc.2d 3, 383 N.Y.S.2d 784 (S. Ct. App. Term 1976).
2. *People v. Townsend*, 127 A.D.2d 505, 511 N.Y.S.2d 858 (1st Dept. 1987).
3. 80 N.Y.2d 87, 587 N.Y.S.2d 568 (1992).
4. *People v. Felton*, 171 A.D.2d 1034, 568 N.Y.S.2d 988 (4th Dept. 1991).
5. *People v. Casadei*, 106 A.D.2d 885, 483 N.Y.S.2d 875 (4th Dept. 1989).
6. 54 A.D.2d 333, 388 N.Y.S.2d 450 (4th Dept. 1976).
7. *Id.*
8. *Id.*
9. *Forte v. Supreme Court*, 62 A.D.2d 704, 406 N.Y.S.2d 854 (2nd Dept. 1978), aff'd, 48 N.Y.2d 179, 422 N.Y.S.2d 26 (1979).
10. *People v. Midgett*, 86 Misc.2d 3, 383 N.Y.S.2d 784 (S. Ct. App. Term 1976).
11. *Brooks*, 54 A.D.2d 333.
12. *People v. Casadei*, 106 A.D.2d 885, 483 N.Y.S.2d 875 (4th Dept. 1989).
13. *People v. McIntosh*, 80 N.Y.2d 87, 587 N.Y.S.2d 568 (1992).
14. *Brooks*, 54 A.D.2d 333.
15. *Forte v. Supreme Court*, 462 A.D.2d 704, 406 N.Y.S.2d 854 Dept. 1978), aff'd, 48 N.Y.2d 179, 422 N.Y.S.2d 26 (1979).

87. *The Pen Register: A Constitutional Excursus*

1. AMENDMENT IV [1971] U.S. CONSTITUTION

The right of the people to be secure in their persons, houses, papers, and effects, against unreasonable searches and seizures, shall not be violated, and no warrants shall issue, but upon probable cause, supported by oath and affirmation, and particularly describing the place to be searched, and the persons or things to be seized.

AMENDMENT XIV [1868] U.S. CONSTITUTION

Section 1. All persons born or naturalized in the United States, and subject to the jurisdiction thereof, are citizens of the United States and of the State wherein they reside. No State shall make or enforce any law which shall abridge the privileges or immunities of citizens of the United States; nor shall any State deprive any person of life, liberty, or property, without, due process of law; nor deny to any person within its jurisdiction the equal protection of the laws.

2. *Katz v. United States*, 389 U.S. 347 (1967)
3. *Smith v. Maryland*, 44 U.S. 735 (1979)
4. *Kyllo v. United States*, 533 U.S. 27 (2001)
5. Justice Marshall wrote in his dissent in *Smith* that one is entitled, when one dials a number from his home, that it will be recorded solely for phone company business purposes and held that law enforcement must and should obtain a warrant to make use of a Pen Register.

Similarly, Mr. Justice Stewart stated that numbers dialed from a private telephone are subject to constitutional protection and that the information obtained from a Pen Register is information in which the telephone subscriber, whether in home or office, has a legitimate expectation of privacy. *Smith* v. *Maryland, id.*

6. On this see *Commonwealth v. Beauford*, 475 A.2d 783 (Pa. Super. 1984). The Pennsylvania Court held that the use of a Pen Register constituted an intrusion of a person's legitimate expectation of privacy and was protected by the state constitution and required some sort of Judicial Order.

88. Waiver of the Right to Appeal

1. 74 N.Y.2d 1, 543 N.Y.S.2d 968 (1989).

2. See *People v. Stack*, 140 A.D.2d 389, 527 N.Y.S.2d 569 (2d Dept. 1988); *People v. De Long*, 134 A.D.2d 199 (1st Dept. 1987); *People v. Allen*, 82 N.Y.S.2d 761, 603 N.Y.S.2d 820 (1993). See also *People v. Veaudry*, 133 A.D.2d 524, 519 N.Y.S.2d 895 (4th Dept. 1987).

3. 188 A.D.2d 622, 591 N.Y.S.2d 74 (2d Dept. 1992).

4. Compare *People v. Cance*, 155 A.D.2d 764, 547 N.Y.S.2d 702 (3d Dept. 1989), where the Appellate Division, Third Department, found the defendant's waiver of appeal invalid where there was no indication that the County Court had specifically discussed the waiver of a right to appeal with him or that he understood the nature, terms and effect upon him. On this see also *People v. Simmons*, 167 A.D.2d 924, 562 N.Y.S.2d 593 (4th Dept. 1990), where the Court held that "understanding and acceptance" of the purported waiver had not been demonstrated.

5. 76 N.Y.2d 909, 563 N.Y.S.2d 43 (1990).

6. *People v. Callahan*, 80 N.Y.2d 273, 590 N.Y.S.2d 46 (1992), explains fully what is required for an effective waiver in light of the decision of the Court of Appeals in *Seaberg.*

7. 193 A.D.2d 466, 597 N.Y.S.2d 691 (1st Dept. 1993).

8. 290 A.D.2d 560, 737 N.Y.S.2d 104 (2d Dept. 2002).

9. On this see also *People v. Scott*, 215 A.D.2d 787, 627 N.Y.S.2d 718 (2d Dept. 1995).

10. 242 A.D.2d 543, 661 N.Y.S.2d 674 (2d Dept. 1997).

11. *Id.*

12. *Id.*

13. 228 A.D.2d 171, 644 N.Y.S.2d 172 (1st Dept. 1996).

14. 196 A.D.2d 514, 600 N.Y.S.2d 752 (2d Dept. 1993).

15. On this see also *People v. Dukes*, 14 A.D.3d 732, 788 N.Y.S.2d 229 (3d Dept. 2005), where the Third Department held that the issue of whether the defendant was improperly sentenced as a second felony offender was a challenge to the legality of the sentence and survived despite a waiver of the right to appeal.

16. 139 A.D.2d 210, 531 N.Y.S.2d 899 (1st Dept. 1988).

17. On this see also *People v. Meredith*, 256 A.D.2d 641, 682 N.Y.S.2d 250 (3d Dept. 1998); *People v. Marziale*, 182 A.D.2d 1035, 583 N.Y.S.2d 36 (3d Dept. 1992) (Held: Waiver of a criminal defendant's right to appeal operates to foreclose all appellate review except in instances involving the legality of the sentence.); *People v. Taylor*, 242 A.D.2d 925, 662 N.Y.S.2d 894 (4th Dept. 1997) (Held: Defendant's waiver of right to appeal did not encompass challenge to the legality of the Court imposed sentence.).

89. The Motion to Set Aside a Sentence: The Criteria and Bases

1. The Section continues

Where the judgment includes a sentence of death, the court may also set aside the sentence upon any of the grounds set forth in paragraph (b), (c), (f), (g), or (h) of subdivision one of §440.10 as applied to a separate sentencing proceeding under §400.27, provided, however, that to the extent the ground or grounds asserted include one or more of the aforesaid paragraphs of subdivision one of §440.10, the court must also apply subdivisions two and three of §440.10, other than paragraph (d) of subdivision two of such section, in determining the motion. In the event the court enters an order granting a motion to set aside a sentence of death under this section, the court must either direct a new sentencing proceeding in accordance with §400.27 or, to the extent that the defendant cannot be resentenced to death consistent with the laws of this state or the constitution of this state or of the United States, resentence the defendant to life imprisonment without parole or to a sentence of imprisonment for the class A-I felony of murder in the first degree other than a sentence of life imprisonment without parole. Upon granting the motion upon any of the grounds set forth in the aforesaid paragraphs of subdivision one of §440.10 and setting aside the sentence, the court must afford the people a reasonable period of time, which shall not be less than ten days, to determine whether to take an appeal from the order setting aside the sentence of death. The taking of an appeal by the people stays the effectiveness of that portion of the court's order that directs new sentencing proceeding.

2. Notwithstanding the .provisions of subdivision one, the court must deny such a motion when the ground or issue raised thereupon was previously determined on the merits upon an appeal from the judgment or sentence, unless since the time of such appellate determination there has been a retroactively effective change in the law controlling such issue.

3. Notwithstanding the provisions of subdivision one, the court may deny such a motion when the ground or issue raised thereupon was previously determined on the merits upon a prior motion or proceeding in a court of this state, other than an appeal from the judgment, or upon a prior motion or proceeding in a federal court, unless since the time of such determination there has been a retroactively effective change in the law controlling such issue. Despite such determination, however, the court, in the interest of justice and for good cause shown, may in its discretion grant the motion if it is otherwise meritorious.

4. An order setting aside a sentence pursuant to this section does not affect the validity or status of the underlying conviction, and after entering such an order the court must resentence the defendant in accordance with the law.

2. *People v. Corso,* 40 N.Y.2d 578, 338 N.Y.2d 886, 357 N.E.2d 357 (1976); *People v. Strong,* 93 Misc.2d 170, 402 N.Y.S.2d 508 (S. Ct. Monroe Co. 1977).

3. 119 A.D.2d 692, 501 N.Y.S.2d 116 (2nd Dept. 1986).

4. 72 A.D.2d 678, 421 N.Y.S. 212 (1st Dept. 1979).

5. Cf. however *People v. Banks,* 242 A.D.2d 726, 663 N.Y.S. 46 (2nd Dept. 1997) (Held: discrepancy between court reporter's transcript showing 3-6 year sentence following conviction for assault and extract of clerk's minutes of those proceedings showing the

sentence of 3-7 years did not effect the validity of the sentence.) See also *People v. Myers*, 241 A.D.2d 705, 660 N.Y.S. 456 (3rd Dept. 1997) (Held: while sentence imposed for violation of probation should be set aside as illegal if individual was not subject to enforceable probation terms, summary denial of motion to set aside sentence on those grounds is warranted where factual allegations of illegality are made solely by the defendant and are unsupported by any other affidavit or evidence).

6. 2005 WL 53633.

7. 191 Misc.2d 510, 743 N.Y.S.2d 651 (S. Ct. Kings Co. 2002).

8. 195 A.D.2d 1025, 600 N.Y.S.2d 523 (4th Dept. 1993).

9. Cf. however *People v. Wilson*, 177 Misc.2d 340, 678 N.Y.S.2d 441 (West Co. Ct. 1998), and *People v. Stampler*, 115 Misc.2d 547, 454 N.Y.S.2d 411 (1982) (Held: retroactive application does not create illegality).

10. 264 A.D.2d 574, 695 N.Y.S.2d 550 (1st Dept. 1999).

11. 295 A.D.2d 749, 744 N.Y.S.2d 526 (3rd Dept. 2002).

12. 283 A.D.2d 436, 725 N.Y.S.2d 659 (2nd Dept. 2001).

13. For additional cases on this ground see *People v. Cook*, 287 A.D.2d 884, 731 N.Y.S.2d 552 (3rd Dept. 2001) (Held: Indeterminate sentence of one and a third to four years for criminal mischief in the third degree was not excessive in the light of the defendant's lengthy criminal history.); *People v. Yusca*, 222 A.D.2d 928, 635 N.Y.S.2d 766 (3rd Dept. 1995); *People v. McIntire*, 287 A.D.2d 890, 731 N.Y.S.2d 547 (3rd Dept. 2001). Cf. however *People v. Bellamy*, 160 A.D.2d 886, 554 N.Y.S.2d 320 (2nd Dept. 1990), where the Appellate Division Second Department held that while the judge had authority to vacate minimum permissible sentence he had imposed on the defendant for second-degree murder, the defendant's right to due process was violated when the judge thereafter imposed a maximum permissible sentence without offering any justification for doing so. On sentences not being harsh or excessive see also *People v. Schelling*, 107 A.D.2d 847, 484 N.Y.S.286 (3rd Dept. 1985); *People v. Rawlins*, 105 A.D.2d 552, 481 N.Y.S.2d 500 (3rd Dept. 1984). It should be noted that there is some authority for the proposition that the mere excessiveness or harshness of the sentence is not a ground for *Coram Nobis* relief; see *People v. Coe*, 36 Misc.2d 181, 232 N.Y.S.2d 944 (Oneida Co. Ct. 1962).

14. See on this *People v. Bronksy*, 21 A.D.2d 981, 244 N.Y.S.2d 677 (2nd Dept. 1963). On further authority following *People v. Bronksy* see *People v. Grimaldi*, 24 Misc.2d 43, 203 N.Y.S.2d 397 (Kings Co. Ct. 1960).

15. 34 A.D.2d 764, 310 N.Y.S.2d 539 (1st Dept. 1970).

16. 35 N.Y.2d 327, 361 N.Y.S.2d 877, 320 N.E.2d 622 (1974).

17. 36 A.D.2d 619, 318 N.Y.S.2d 950 (2nd Dept. 1971).

18. See also *People v. Bell*, 36 A.D.2d 617, 318 N.Y.S.2d 803 (2nd Dept. 1971); *People v. Stroud*, 66 Misc. 2d 306, 320 N.Y.S.2d 661 (Tioga Co. Ct. 1971) (Held: Where, at hearing in *Coram Nobis* proceeding, the petitioner and his counsel were unable to say that notice of right to appeal was not given following a 1945 conviction. Resentencing was not warranted). See also *People v. Thomas*, 48 Misc.2d 100, 264 N.Y.S.2d 299 (S.Ct. Erie Co. 1965). On this, see also *People v. Floyd*, 39 A.D.2d 588, 331 N.Y.S.2d. 738 (2nd Dept. 1972), where the Appellate Division Second Department held that where a defendant who has been misled as to his right to appeal, or has been induced by reason of representation by counsel that an appeal would be taken to allow his appeal time to expire, should be resentenced *nunc pro tunc* on his previous finding of guilt.

19. 18 Misc.2d 203, 193 N.Y.S.2d 123 (Niagara Co. Ct. 1959).

20. 43 A.D.2d 958, 352 N.Y.S.2d 40 (2nd Dept. 1974).

21. Cf. *People v. Royster*, 104 A.D.2d 1011, 481 N.Y.S.2d 7 (2nd Dept. 1984) (Held: No evidence of broken promises of the District Attorney, nor any prosecutorial misconduct during plea negotiations sufficient to warrant vacatur of sentence under this section).

22. 273 A.D.2d 549, 710 N.Y.S.2d 134 (3rd Dept. 2000).

23. 124 A.D.2d 907, 508 N.Y.S.2d 662 (3rd Dept. 1986).

24. On this rule see also *People v. Creekmore*, 105 A.D.2d 260, 482 N.Y.S.2d 278 (1st Dept. 1984) (Held: defendant's sentence upon his conviction of first-degree manslaughter was predicated upon his status as an armed felony offender, whereas first-degree manslaughter is not an armed felony offense, sentence would be vacated under this section and matter remanded for predicate felony hearing.) See also on this *People v. Cappucci*, 94 A.D.2d 746, 462 N.Y.S.2d 507 (2nd Dept. 1983); *People v. Lawrence*, 37 A.D.2d 872, 325 N.Y.S.2d 219 (3rd Dept. 1971); *People v. Smith*, 37 A.D.2d 863, 327 N.Y.S.2d 63 (2nd Dept. 1971).

25. *People v. Kearse*, 28 A.D.2d 910, 282 N.Y.S.2d 136 (2nd Dept. 1967); see also *People v. Fuller*, 27 A.D.2d 982, 278 N.Y.S.2d 701 (4th Dept. 1967); *People v. Smith*, 22 A.D.2d 333, 256 N.Y.S.2d 292 (4th Dept. 1965); *People v. Mills*, 18 A.D.2d 960, 238 N.Y.S.2d 115 (4th Dept. 1963). It should be noted it is not a ground for setting aside a sentence where defendant claims a theory that the court denied him an opportunity to controvert a probation report (*People v. O'Dell*, 34 A.D.2d 702, 309 N.Y.S.2d 716 (3rd Dept. 1970). Nor, it has been held, is rehabilitation a ground for setting aside a sentence, where the defendant acknowledged he had repeatedly sold drugs on the university campus, expressed no remorse for the offense, and rehabilitated himself after his escape from prison. See *Richardson v. State*, 182 Misc.2d 895, 700 N.Y.S.2d 378 (Co. Ct. Monroe Co. 1999).

90. *Peremptory Challenges Under Attack*

1. C.P.L.R. Sec. 4109.

2. C.P.L. Sec. 270.25.

3. C.P.L. 270.25(2)(a).

4. C.P.L. 270.25(2)(b).

5. C.P.L. 270.25(2) c).

6. C.P.L. Sec. 360.30(2).

7. *Batson v. Kentucky*, 476 U.S. 79, 106 S.Ct. 1712, 90 L.Ed.2d 69 (1986). For this entire section, see 73A N.Y. Jur.2d Jur. Secs. 98-100; 33 N.Y. Jur.2d Criminal Law Secs. 2288, 2290, 2291, 2292.

92. *A Note on Criminal Appellate Practice*

1. 172 A.D.2d 548 (2nd Dept. 1991).

2. 220 A.D.2d 445, 631 N.Y.S.2d 896 (A.D.2d Dept. 1995).

3. On this see also *People v. Anderson*, 127 A.D.2d 77d (2d Dept. 1987); *People v. Malone*, 121 A.D.2d 656 (2d Dept. 1986); *People v. Rivers*, 71 N.Y.2d 705 (1988); *People v. Johnson*, 73 A.D.2d (2d Dept. 1989).

Introduction to Evidence Reprinted Articles

These articles on Evidence primarily touch upon the admissibility of polygraph evidence, or rather, its present status in the New York Courts of inadmissibility, and the admissibility of DNA evidence. Both of these evidentiary subjects are of pressing interest, since these types of scientific evidence will ultimately play a much greater role in our legal system. Also included is an article on the more general subject of circumstantial evidence.

Chapter 2
Evidence Reprinted Articles

1. Polygraph Evidence: Admissibility in Civil and Criminal Cases

In two prior articles[1] this writer considered the question of the admissibility of polygraph evidence in the State of New York. In this article, it is proposed to, once again, present an overview of the current state of the law in this field and, most particularly, to consider the case law, pro and con, in the field since 1985.

The lie detector or polygraph is a device whereby certain physiological phenomena—blood pressure, respiration, pulse, and galvanic skin reflex—are recorded on a chart by means of sensors connected to the person being questioned. The examiner, on the theory that lying or deception involves stress which reveals itself by changes from the norm in particular bodily phenomena, may infer from the chart that records these phenomena, whether the examined believes he is lying or telling the truth.

Polygraph evidence has not, historically, been admissible in evidence in the State of New York, with the exception of some few trial court decisions.[2] Thus, in *Stenzel A. v. B.*, 71 Misc. 2d 719, 336 N.Y. Supp. 2d 839 (Family Court, Niagra County, 1972), the trial court held polygraph evidence to be admissible when one or more parties testifies in a paternity proceeding on the issue, solely, of credibility. In a similar fashion in *Walther v. O'Connell,* 72 Misc. 2d 316, 339 N.Y. Supp. 2d 386 (Civil Court of the City of New York, Queens County, 1972), where the plaintiff sued for the balance of a partially unpaid loan, and the issue was perjury, or the credibility of one of the parties, the trial court once again ordered the parties to submit to a polygraph test and then admitted the results of the test into evidence, likening the polygraph result to the testimony of an expert witness, entitled to such weight as the court would find the expert's qualifications in his field warranted.

The state of case law, both trial and appellate, between 1978 and 1985, has continued to reject, for the most part, the admissibility of polygraph evidence in the courts of this state. *People v. Tarsia*, 67 A.D. 2d 210, 415 N.Y. Supp. 2d 120 (3rd Dept. 1979); *People v. Smith*, 61 A.D. 2d 91, 401 N.Y. Supp. 2d 353 (4th Dept 1978); *People v. Frank*, 101 Misc. 2d 736, 422 N.Y. Supp. 2d 317 (Nassau County Court, 1979); *People v. Vinson*, 104 Misc. 2d 664, 428 N.Y. Supp. 2d 832 (Supreme Court, Westchester County, 1980); *People v. Leonard*, 59 A.D. 2d 1, 397 N.Y.S. Supp. 2d 386 (2nd Dept. 1977); *People v. Jones*, 118 Misc. 2d 687 (County Court, Albany County, 1983); *People v. Hughes*, 88 A.D. 2d 17 (4th Dept. 1982).

Between 1978 and 1985 three New York Courts, two trial and one appellate, have admitted the results of the polygraph test into evidence.[3]

In *May v. Shaw*, 79 A.D. 2d 970, 434 N.Y.S.2d 285 (2d Dept. 1981), the Second Department held that it was proper to admit into evidence the results of the polygraph in a proceeding pursuant to Article 78. In *People v. Vernon*, 89 Misc. 2d 472, 391 N.Y.S.2d 959 (S. Ct., New York County 1977), the New York County Supreme Court granted the preliminary application of the defendant to receive in evidence the results of polygraph examinations to which the accused submitted, in the context of a Clayton Hearing.

Finally, in *People v. Daniels*, 422 N.Y.S.2d 832 (S. Ct., Westchester County 1979), the Court held that the proper standard for the admissibility of polygraph evidence should not be general acceptance in the scientific community but, rather, whether the evidence is probative and relevant and does not endanger the defendant's rights, prejudice the jury, or mislead the proper administration of justice. The court went on to allow the reception of the test results in evidence and also the testimony of the polygrapher, given certain procedural safeguards.

It is clear that the weight of the case law authority in this state, at least up until 1985, ruled against the admissibility into evidence of polygraph results and that the exceptional cases in which the courts ruled in favor of admissibility of polygraph results were limited in their holdings. Thus, in *Stenzel A. v. B. supra*, and *Walther v. O'Connell*, *supra*, the evidence was admitted on the issue of credibility only. *May v. Shaw*, *supra*, held polygraph evidence admissible in an Article 78 proceeding and *Vernon* ruled only on the issue of the evidence's admission in the context of a Clayton Hearing. Until 1985 the only Supreme Court of this state to allow the use of polygraph results in an actual trial as evidence in chief was the *Daniels* court which permitted its admission into evidence with certain specific procedural safeguards.

The State of the Law Since 1985

The case law since 1985, with some few exceptions to be analyzed at a later point in this article, continues to reject the admission of polygraph results into evidence.

Thus, in *People v. Johnson*, 112 M.2d 590, 447 N.Y.S.2d 341 (S. Ct., New York County), the trial court, in ruling that the defendant's statements were to be suppressed as involuntary and also because the defendant's arrest and detention was without probable cause, noted that the polygraph had no evidentiary standing in the criminal law. *People v. Johnson, supra*, at 345. See also, *People v. Davis*, 94 A.D. 2d 610, 462 N.Y.S.2d 7 (1st Dept. 1983) (See Dissenting Opinion); *People v. Frank*, 101 M.2d 736, 422 N.Y.S.2d 317 (Nassau County Court 1979), Mfd. 83 A.D. 2d 642, 441 N.Y.S.2d 1002 (2d Dept. 1981) (Polygraph results not admissible for use in Grand Jury proceeding upon testimonial offering of the defendant). (But note the dissent in *People v. Frank, supra*, at 1004, where Mr. Justice Hopkins voted to reverse the judgment and dismiss the indictment with leave to the People to apply for an order permitting resubmission to another Grand Jury and opined that the new Grand Jury should have the right to consider in the exercise of its discretion whether polygraph evidence might be submitted to it;) See also *People v. Shedrick*, 104 A.D. 2d 263, 482 N.Y. S. 2d 439 (4th Dept. 1984), affd. 66 N.Y.2d 1015, 484 N.E.2d 1290, 499 N.Y.S.2d 388 (1985), where the Fourth Department specifically rejected the *Daniels* holding; *In the Matter of Michelle B.*, 133 Misc. 2d 89, 506 N.Y.S.2d 634 (Family Court, Lewis County 1986) (Polygraph evidence excluded in child abuse proceeding as lacking in general scientific reliability); *Matter of Dona D.*, 141 Misc. 2d 46, 532 N.Y.S.2d 696 (Family Court, Richmond County 1988) (Polygraph results inadmissible in child protective proceedings); *Matter of Aryeh-Levi K.*, 134 A.D. 2d 426, 521 N.Y.S.2d 49 (2d Dept 1987).

Some Recent Cases

In the years since 1985, some few trial courts have, in fact, ruled in favor, albeit at times with limitation, on the admissibility of polygraph evidence as evidence in chief at trial. *In the Matter of Meyer*, 132 M.2d 415, 504 N.Y.S.2d 358 (Family Court, Kings County, 1986), is of interest. In this case the facts were that an estranged husband was accused of sexually abusing his two young daughters during his visitations with them. The children were unable to testify and their hearsay statements were admitted under the hearsay exception of the Family Court Act Sec. 1046(a)(vi). The testimony was adequately corroborated. The respondent father in this child protective proceeding moved for the admission into evidence of expert testimony regarding certain polygraph examinations. The court first noted that, in New York, polygraph evidence has generally been excluded with certain exceptions: *Matter of Stenzel, supra*; *People v. Daniels, supra*; *Zinn v. Bernic Construction. Inc.*, 99 M.2d 510, 416 N.Y.S.2d 725 (S. Ct., Queens County 1979) (admission pursuant to stipulation of parties permitted). The court went on to reason first that the exclusionary rule for polygraph evidence evolved in criminal cases where the standard of proof, beyond a reasonable doubt, differs from the standard in child protective proceedings where the case against the respondent need only be proved by a preponderance of the evidence and the traditional rules of evidence are significantly relaxed.

Second, the court noted that criminal cases involve jury trials while child protective proceedings are tried without a jury. The court then went on to state that, unlike hearsay, which is clearly inadmissible, polygraph evidence is not inadmissible per se. The court stated that the admission of expert testimony, without specific statutory or appellate proscription, is left to the discretion of the trial court. The court further stated that the relevant statutes and case law disclosed no prohibition to the admission of polygraph evidence in child protective proceedings and that the Court of Appeals in *People v. Leone*, 25 N.Y.2d 511, 307 N.Y.S.2d 430, 255 N.E. 2d 696 (1969), specifically limited and applied its ruling to the area of criminal law.

The court concluded, thus, after considering the factual material pursuant to stipulation, including the affidavits of the two polygraphers, an article on the subject and the discussion of the science of polygraphy in certain case law authority, that the polygraph experts would be able to testify with accuracy as to the results of the polygraph examinations. The court noted that polygraph evidence appears no less reliable than the psychiatric and psychological validation evidence finding acceptance in child protective proceedings. The court concluded that given the unique nature of child protective proceedings due process and fundamental fairness required the admission of expert polygraph testimony.

In the Matter of Smith, 133 M.2d 115, 509 N.Y.S.2d 962 (Family Court, Queens County 1986), the Family Court reached a slightly different result. *Smith* was also a child abuse proceeding brought by the Dept. of Social Services, alleging sexual abuse by the respondent father against the child. In *Smith*, prior to resting, the respondent orally moved to have the results of a polygraph examination admitted into evidence. The respondent's offer of proof consisted of representations that the polygraph test was administered to him at his request by an examiner of his choosing, without stipulation between the parties and that the results were favorable to the respondent. The court denied the respondent's application, citing the New York general rule against admissibility of this species of evidence, on the ground that the polygraph lacked the necessary proven scientific reliability. The *Smith* court rejected the holding in *Meyer*, stating that validation evidence may not be equated with the polygraph in terms of the requisite scientific consensus as to reliability and efficacy and that the danger of undue weight being given to the polygraph test where the fact finder is the court rather than the jury did not obviate the danger.

In short, the court initially held the polygraph evidence unreliable, even in a child protective proceeding as opposed to a criminal proceeding, thereby differing on this issue from the *Meyer* court. The court reasoned that a lie detector cannot be cross-examined, although the expert who administered the test may, that undue reliance may be placed upon it as a tool of science, and that an expert presenting psychological or psychiatric evidence is subject to cross-examination. The court, however, did say that polygraph evidence may be admitted where the circumstances heighten its reliability to such a degree as to warrant its admission into evidence, such as where it is obtained pursuant to court order or on stipulation of the parties and is admitted in conjunction with a psychological or psychiatric profile of the respondent. The court held that since the polygraph evidence was admitted without the requisite procedural safeguards, and, in particular, without a psychological or psychiatric profile of the respondent, it was therefore inadmissible.

It is significant that the *Smith* decision was affirmed by the Appellate Division, Second Department, *In Matter of Smith*, 128 A.D. 2d 784, 513 N.Y.S.2d 483 (2d Dept. 1987), although the Appellate Division made no mention of the reasoning or conclusion or holding of the *Smith* trial court on the issue of the criteria for the admission of polygraph results into evidence in a child protective proceeding. See also *Matter of Jazmin M.*, 139 M.2d 731, 528 N.Y.S.2d 771 (Fam. Ct., Queens County, 1988), where the court, although rejecting the use of polygraph results in a child abuse proceeding, stated that, in the court's discretion, it may be admitted into evidence where the procedural safeguards set forth in *Matter of Smith, supra*, are adhered, although the *Smith* criteria were lacking in the instant case.

Meyer, Smith and *Jazmin* are noteworthy decisions since in *Meyer* the trial court adopted a "blanket" approach with regard to the admissibility of polygraph evidence in a child protective proceeding and in *Smith* and *Jazmin* the Family. Court forged a rule allowing admission of this evidence given the fulfillment of certain procedural safeguards. In short, along with *May v. Shaw, supra*; *People v. Daniels, supra*; *People v. Vernon, supra*; *Walther v. O'Connell. supra*; *Stenzel A. v. B., supra*; and *Smith, Meyer* and *Jazmin* it would appear that the trial and appellate courts of this state are reaching toward a rule of limited admissibility of polygraph results under certain classes of cases, including administrative proceedings, child protective proceedings, Clayton Hearings, paternity cases, at least on the issue of credibility, and even in criminal cases, at trial, given certain procedural safeguards. It is clear, however, that the courts of this State are most concerned with, given its admission into evidence, its effect on a jury. Hence, for the most part, with the exception of *Daniels*, where courts have permitted its admission into evidence, it has been in nonjury hearings or trials.

Conclusion

This brief review of some recent developments and case law on the subject of the admissibility of polygraph evidence evidences a continuing and inching trend toward total admissibility into evidence in the courts of this state. Perhaps someday, much as ballistics, blood tests and the DNA tests have been admitted as evidence in chief, so too, the results of the polygraph test will be admitted into evidence as scientifically reliable, whereby the trier of fact may indeed weave a spotless robe of truth with which to clothe the figure of justice, even from such "poor material as this" *Stenzel A. v. B., supra*, at 719.[4]

2. Admissibility of Polygraph Evidence in the State of New York

This article proposes to trace the history and current status of the admissibility of lie detector or polygraph evidence in the State of New York.[1]

The lie detector or polygraph is a device whereby certain physiological phenomena—blood pressure, respiration, pulse, and galvinic skin reflex are recorded on a chart by means of sensors connected to the person being questioned. The theory behind the process is that lying or deception involves stress which manifests itself by changes from the norm in these particular bodily phenomena. The examiner may infer from the chart that records these phenomena or polygraphs, whether the examined believes he is lying or telling the truth. The results may also be inconclusive. Polygraphs must be interpreted by a qualified examiner. Some states have licensing statutes; New York does not!

Polygraph evidence, until recently, was not admissible in any jurisdiction, except upon stipulation of the parties. *Frye v. U. S.*, 293 F 1013 (D. C. Cir. 1923), was the first Appellate Court to rule on the admissibility of lie detector evidence and articulated the standard which has since been followed. The Circuit Court affirmed the trial Court's refusal to admit the results of a systolic blood pressure deception test appellant had taken, holding that in order for expert testimony based on a scientific principle to be admissible, said principle, in this case the connection between the act of deception and changes in blood pressure, must have gained general acceptance in the particular field to which it belongs. The Court concluded that the test had not gained such standing and scientific recognition among experts in the fields of physiology and psychology as to warrant its admission into evidence. *Frye v. U. S., supra* at 1014. Subsequent federal and state decisions have excluded polygraph evidence, citing this standard.[2]

Recently, however, a number of federal and state trial courts have admitted polygraph evidence for various purposes, having concluded that the device is scientifically reliable, on the basis of the *Frye* criterion of general acceptance in the field. It would appear that polygraph evidence will no longer be automatically excluded as lacking a true scientific basis.[3]

The State of New York does not admit the results of a polygraph test into evidence.[4]

In *People v. Forte*, 279 N.Y. 204, 18 N.E.2d 31, 119 A.L.R. 1198, rearg. den. 279 N.Y. 788, 18 N.E.2d 870, the New York Court of Appeals affirmed the trial Court's refusal to sustain defendant's request to be tested on a pathometer, stating that "the record was devoid of evidence tending to show a general scientific recognition that the pathometer possesses efficacy." 279 N.Y. at 206.

Subsequent cases have, with the exception of some few trial court decisions to be discussed in this article, adhered to the *Frye-Forte* standard. See *People v. Dobler*, 29 Misc. 2d 481, 215 N.Y.S.2d 313 (Suffolk County Court, 1961); *People v. Brownsky*, 35 Misc. 2d 134, 228 N.Y.S. 476, 23 A.L.R. 2d 1306 (Court of General Sessions, New York County, 1962); *Matter of Sowa v. Looney*, 23

N.Y.2d 329, 296 N.Y.S.2d 760, 244 N.E.2d 243 (1968); *People v. Leone,* 25 N.Y.2d 511, 307 N.Y.S.2d 430 (1969); *Tree v. Ralston,* 62 Misc. 2d 582, 309 N.Y.S.2d 229 (Family Court, New York County, 1970); *People v. Dodge,* 72 Misc. 2d 345, 338 N.Y.S.2d 690 (Nassau County Court, 1972); *People v. Jacobson,* 71 Misc. 2d 1040, 337 N.Y.S.2d 616 (Supreme Court Queens County, 1972); *People v. Parish,*[5] 70 Misc.2d 577, 333 N.Y.S.2d 631 (Nassau County Court, 1972). *People v. McCain,* 42 A.D.2d 866, 347, N.Y.S.2d 72 (2d Dept. 1973); *Dolan v. Kelly,* 76 Misc. 2d 151, 348 N.Y.S.2d 483 (Supreme Court, Suffolk County, 1973); *People v. Hargrove,* 80 Misc. 2d 317, 363 N.Y.S.2d 241 (Supreme Court, Westchester County, 1975); *In the Matter of Lillie Anonymous v. Robert Anonymous,* 75 Misc. 2d 823, 348 N.Y.S.2d 938 (Family Court, Rockland County 1973); *People v. Guerir,* 47 A.D.2d 788, 366 N.Y.S.2d 61 (3rd Dept. 1975); *People v. Black,* 86 Misc.2d 909, 382 N.Y.S.2d 944 (Supreme Court, Kings County, 1976).

To this date, polygraph results and expert examiner's opinion and interpretation thereof remain inadmissible in the State of New York.

Effect of Reference to fact polygraph examination was conducted or accused's willingness or refusal to take the test

In general most appellate courts have held it improper to admit into evidence the fact a polygraph examination was conducted, accused's willingness or refusal to take a Lie Detector test, or reference to the latter by court or counsel. Whether evidence of or comment on the Latter results in prejudicial and so reversible error depends on the appellate court's assessment of the totality of the circumstances.[6]

New York is no exception in this respect. In *People v. McCain, supra* at 72, the County Court of Nassau County, in a prosecution for rape and sexual abuse, permitted the People to call their polygraph-expert witness. Although the State did not question him with respect to the polygraph examination, defense counsel, on cross-examination, elicited from witness the fact that he had voluntarily submitted to taking a polygraph examination. Subsequently, the People were permitted to put into evidence graphs, the witness' explanation thereof, and his opinion as to whether defendant was telling the truth when he denied having committed the crime with which he was charged. The People argued, in support of affirmance, that by admitting into evidence the fact of defendant's voluntary submission to the polygraph examination an inference was created in the minds of the jury that the results were favorable to defendant's case and that the People were hiding them. Hence, the People argued, evidence of the results of the examination should be admitted into evidence to rebut such inference. The court held that, while it agreed with this point of view urged by the People, it thought the County Court had permitted them too much latitude in this respect and allowing the witness to offer his opinion as to defendant's veracity during the examination was so prejudicial as to require that defendant be given a new trial at which such evidence would not be permitted. The court added, by way of Caveat, "that defense counsel should not have been permitted to question the witness with regard to the polygraph test in the first instance." *People v. McCain, supra* at 74.

The Court holds, first, by way of dicta, that questions with respect to a polygraph test, in this case elicitation of the fact of defendant's voluntary submission to the polygraph examination are improper. Clearly, this holding would cover questions not only as to accused willingness or refusal to submit to the examination, but even to the fact thereof.[7]

Second, the Court held, once the fact, albeit prohibited, of defendant's voluntary submission to a polygraph examination is admitted into evidence, so creating an inference that defendant had passed, the People have a limited right to rebut this favorable inference. Thus, the People, in *People v. McCain, supra,* were permitted to put the graphs resulting from the examination and witness' explanation thereof into evidence, but not witness' opinion as to defendant's veracity during the examination, since the latter was too prejudicial. It is not clear whether this limited right of rebuttal invariably excludes expert evidence. The *McCain* Court appears to regard the error of the trial court as an excess allowance of latitude, to be interpreted, perhaps, as an abuse of discretion so prejudicial as to compel a new trial.[8]

Admissibility based upon agreement and stipulation between opposing attorneys prior to the examination

The Courts are divided as to the effect of a stipulation among the parties as to the admissibility of lie detector evidence. Some states hold the results of a polygraph test are always admissible, others always inadmissible, while the rest hold their admissibility to be dependent on the fulfillment of certain conditions.[9]

New York will admit polygraph evidence, but only on specific stipulation between the parties to admit the results into evidence. In *Pereira v. Pereira,* 35 N.Y.2d 301, 361 N.Y.S.2d 148, 319 N.E.2d 413 (1974), plaintiff instituted this proceeding against defendant to enforce the terms of a judgment of divorce, wherein custody of her two children was awarded her, and sought to hold defendant in contempt of court for refusing to comply therewith. Subsequently, counsel for plaintiff and for defendant stipulated that defendant and his mother would submit to a polygraph examination. The stipulation, however, contained no provision for the use of the test results. The trial court, over objection of defendant, received into evidence the results of the polygraph test and examiner's opinion that defendant was lying with respect to one critical issue. The trial court found defendant in contempt of court. The Appellate Division modified and affirmed. The Court of Appeals considered at some length the admissibility of the results of polygraph tests in light of a stipulation of the parties. The court concluded that the question of the admissibility of stipulatory evidence need not be reached under these circumstances since the stipulation herein was a limited one insofar as it did not provide for the use of the polygraph tests in court. It was not established, the court concluded, that the tests were to be used for other than investigatory purposes. Thus, the Court of Appeals in *Pereira*, declined to consider the issue of the admissibility of stipulated to polygraph results, but implied that if a stipulation is specifically evidentiary then, at least, the issue is ripe for judicial consideration.

Kresnicka v. Kresnicka, 48 A.D.2d 929, 369 N.Y.S.2d 522 (2nd Dept. 1975), extends the *Pereira* holding. The court holds, citing *Pereira*, that the results of certain polygraph examinations taken by the parties are not admissible, since their use as evidence was never agreed to. This statement would seem to imply that once their use in evidence is, in fact, agreed to, polygraph tests are admissible. Hence, this writer suggests that the position of the State of New York with respect to this issue is that stipulatory polygraph results are admissible into evidence so long as the stipulation is sufficiently specific, i.e., *agreed to as to their use in evidence. Kresnicka, supra* at 929.

A third case confirms this view. In *People v. Prado*, 81 Misc. 2d 710, 365 NYS 2d 943 (Supreme Court, Bronx County 1975), defendant was indicted for homicide. In a written stipulation between prosecution and defense, defendant voluntarily agreed to submit to a polygraph examination regarding his guilt or innocence of the charges in the indictment. Parties agreed that, on the one hand, should the results of the examination indicate defendant was telling the truth in denying his culpability, the prosecutor would recommend defendant's discharge on his own recognizance; on the other hand, if the results indicated defendant was not telling the truth, the results would be admissible at trial. After defendant subsequently took and passed the examination, the District Attorney refused to honor the stipulation and release defendant. The court confirmed the validity and effect of the stipulation, holding that such stipulation, to have moral and ethical significance, cannot be treated lightly, affecting, as it does, the rights and obligations of the parties. Attorneys, the court stated, should be able to rely and depend on a stipulation and the District Attorney is no less bound by the terms of a stipulation to which he is a party. The court concluded that "the stipulation between the parties is a binding agreement, a contract between the District Attorney and counsel for defendant as well as the defendant whose terms must be enforced." *Prado, supra* at 712. The case was dismissed since the state did not abide by the bargained-for stipulation.

To be sure, this is a Supreme Court decision and so persuasive and not binding. It does not cite *Pereira*, a decision of the Court of Appeals. *Kresnicka*, of course, is a later Appellate Division decision (June 30, 1975). *Prado*, however, is on all fours with both *Pereira* and *Kresnicka*. The stipulation therein was held to bind both parties—the District Attorney should the results be exculpatory, no less than the defendant should the results be inculpatory and so admissible under the terms of the agreement. The stipulation, in accord with the *Pereira* and *Kresnicka* rule, provided for admissibility and use at trial should it be determined defendant was not telling the truth or should defendant admit his guilt in the course of the examination.[10]

The polygraph confession

Under New York law a polygraph test may vitiate, in the totality of the circumstances, a confession, rendering it inadmissible as coerced. There are two New York cases on this issue. In *People v. Zimmer,* 68 Misc.2d 1067, 329 N.Y.S.2d 17, aff'd. 40 A.D.2d 955, 339 N.Y.S.2d 671 (4th Dept. 1972) (Wayne County Court 1972), defendant and her husband agreed to submit to a polygraph test concerning the death of her adoptive daughter. Defendant was taken to a small room where she remained alone with the polygraph examiner for two and one-half hours. She was given a four page journal to read explaining the operation of the instrument, duties of the operator and general application of polygraph tests. After reading the pamphlet, defendant was shown a plastic heart in reference to which investigator explained to defendant the physical reaction of the heart, during the test, if her answers were not truthful. At the conclusion of the polygraph examination, examiner left the room, returned shortly and told defendant she had been lying. Examiner told defendant at least three times she had not told the truth. Shortly thereafter, defendant made oral and written confession with respect to her culpability in the infant's death. Defendant moved to suppress these statements. The court noted that, at the conclusion of the test, defendant was told several times she was lying.

She was alone, bewildered, with no one to advise her, except the investigator, who insisted she lied. The interview with the investigator lasted almost three hours. The court held that, under all the circumstances set forth, the statement made by defendant was not her free and voluntary act, but was coerced through the use of the polygraph. The court laid particular stress on the fact that, for all defendant knew, the examination could be used against her to show she was lying, since she was not told that such results could under no circumstances be used against her. *People v. Zimmer, supra* at 1073. In sum, the court held that the totality of the circumstances under which the polygraph test was given was such as to effectively coerce the contested statements and so render them inadmissible.

On the other hand, in *People v. Wilson,* 78 Misc.2d 468, 354 N.Y.S.2d 296 (Nassau County Court, 1974), defendant, in a criminal prosecution, moved to suppress evidence of a record describing a statement made by him to a public servant on the ground that the statement was coerced through the use of a polygraph device. Defendant herein was twice given his Miranda warnings and so informed of his constitutional rights; twice cautioned not to take the test if he intended to lie; informed of the theory and functioning of the machine and the questions the examiner would ask; twice given the test and twice told he had lied. Defendant subsequently made oral confession. The court stated that the polygraph examination is but one factor to be considered in determining whether or not a confession was coerced and cited *People v. Zimmer, supra,* where "the subject's state of mental derangement, the implication that polygraph results could be used in evidence, the technique of the examination and its length were all considered as factors which, taken together, amounted to coercion." *People v. Wilson, supra* at 475.

The *Wilson* court held defendant's statement admissible and not subject to suppression as coerced through the use of a polygraph on three grounds. First, the techniques used were truth-fostering and so the court deemed the confession trustworthy and so worthy of reception into evidence. Second, the court held the statement voluntary in the due process sense since evidence was lacking that the behavior of the police was tyrannical and calculated to overbear defendant's will to resist. Third, defendant 5th Amendment privilege against self-incrimination was not violated since defendant Wilson, though neither suspect nor in custody, was twice informed of his constitutional rights before the test, and twice warned not to take the test if he intended to lie. He knowingly and intelligently waived his rights to silence and counsel and voluntarily chose to speak and confess.

The courts in *People v. Zimmer, supra* at 1067, and *People v. Wilson, supra* at 468, appear to use differing analyses to reach dissimilar results. The *Zimmer* court used a totality of the circumstances test—are the circumstances surrounding the test so coercive as to vitiate any statement or admission obtained therefrom, rendering it inadmissible. The *Wilson* court analyzed the possible inadmissibility of the polygraph procured confession through three legal principles: the evidentiary principle that a coerced confession is an inherently untrustworthy one; the 14th Amendment due process principle which focuses on whether the behavior of law-enforcement officials was such as to overcame defendant's freewill and so produce an involuntary confession; and the 5th Amendment self-incrimination privilege. The court sifted the facts through these legal rubrics and held the confession passed evidentiary and constitutional muster.

This writer would suggest that the approaches of these courts are not so far removed. *Wilson* cites *Zimmer* as authoritative precedent. *People v. Wilson, supra* at 474. In addition the *Wilson* court states that, as a general proposition, the inadmissibility of coerced confessions rests on these three principles and proceeds to consider the facts of the case under these headings. The *Wilson* court is not altering the *Zimmer* totality of the circumstances test but analyzing the totality of the circumstances through these principles. In a word, the court in *Wilson* simply sifts and arranges the facts in parallel columns to determine whether all taken they vitiate an admission. The *Zimmer* court prefers to consider them as one. The analysis may differ but the rule remains the same.

Recent Admissibility Trends in the State of New York[12]

Three recent trial court decisions have admitted polygraph results into evidence. In *Stenzel A. v. B.,* 71 Misc.2d 719, 336 N.Y.S.2d 839 (Family Court, Niagra County, 1972), the Family Court, in a paternity proceeding, for the first time admitted into evidence the results of a pre-trial polygraph examination of a petitioner-mother, wherein, contrary to her testimony at trial, not only did the graphs from her test indicate she was telling the truth when she stated to the examiner that she, in fact, had sexual relations with other men during the period of conception and that one of them could be father, but she also subsequently admitted to the examiner that she had had relations with another man during the critical period.

The court conceded that lie detector results had never been allowed in evidence in the New York courts, but pointed out its widespread use in business and law enforcement and concluded the time had come for its use, not as a substitute for judge and jury, but as a help and guide to truth. The court stated that the polygraph is particularly appropriate in matters of disputed paternity, since the court, in these proceedings, is often called upon to, as it were, spin the web of truth from the proof of none other than two conflicting stories, only one of which can be true. As additional factors arguing for admissibility, the court further observed that when a lie detector test is given by pre-trial order, it may induce quick settlement, respondent gains protection when petitioner takes the test and, in the case at bar, petitioner's case was weak since, by her own admission, she had had sexual relations with men since she was sixteen, had a previous illegitimate child, could not actually pinpoint who the father was and never approached respondent on the parentage of the child.

This holding is limited: polygraph evidence is admissible when one or more parties testify in a paternity proceeding on the issue of credibility. *Stenzel A. v. B., supra* at 722, 723, 724.

In *Walther v. O'Connell*, 72 Misc. 2d 316, 339 N.Y.S.2d 386 (Civil Court of the City of New York, Queens County, 1972), plaintiff alleged he loaned defendant a sum of money which defendant only partially repaid, and sued for the balance. Defendant denied having asked for or received the money. The issue was perjury—one of the parties was lying. The court ordered the parties to submit to a polygraph test on the ground that the case presented an ideal situation for the test since the testimony was directly opposed and so one of the parties was lying. The examiner found plaintiff a truth teller and defendant to have symptoms such as are associated with persons anxious about guilt being revealed. The court admitted the results of the polygraph tests as the testimony of an expert witness not controlling but entitled to such weight as the court finds the expert's qualifications in his field warrant.[13]

The court distinguished this case from *People v. Leone, supra* at 511. There the Court of Appeals, although it held the results of polygraph tests inadmissible, allegedly cited the inexperience of the operator of the machine as a major reason for its decision, whereas, in the case at bar, the evidence was rightly admitted as expert testimony since a competent and certified expert operated the machine and interpreted the results.

Finally, the court stated that the admission of polygraph results administered by an expert has precedent in *U.S. v. Ridling, supra* at 90, which also held the result of a lie detector test can be admitted as evidence at a perjury trial. The *Ridling* court observed that a perjury case is the best case for testing the admissibility of polygraph testimony and stated that experts agree that the polygraph is aimed at exactly this aspect of truth and that the polygraph is now scientifically reliable. Hence, previous opinions excluding polygraph evidence on this basis are not persuasive.

Walther v. O'Connell, supra, is a ground breaking decision. First, the court does not analyze the issue of the admissibility of polygraph results as a special species of scientific evidence, the peculiar principle of which, in the words of the *Frye-Forte* standard, must have gained general acceptance in the scientific community before appropriate for judicial consideration, a standard which for some fifty years has effectively barred the polygraph from the courtroom. The courts hold that, once the operator of the machine and interpreter of the poly-graphs is qualified as an expert in lie detection techniques, the results of the tests are admissible solely and simply as the testimony of an expert witness. This ex-pert opinion evidence, of course, is not controlling and can be totally rejected should the court deem other evidence so warrants. Simply stated, the Civil Court tells us that once the expert's qualifications are established, polygraph results are admissible.

Second, although it is not clear whether the court may be limiting its deci-sion to the issue of perjury where it must be determined who is lying and who is not, this writer would suggest the decisional language does not compel so nar-row a construction. The court says, first, the case presents an ideal situation for the use of the tests. Second, it holds that its action in admitting the results of a polygraph test administered by an expert in a case involving perjury is not with-out precedent, citing Judge Joiner's statement in *Ridling* that a perjury case is the best case for testing the admissibility of the polygraph examination. The fact that this case is ideal for the introduction of polygraph evidence does not mean that the holdings of the Civil Court may not be brought to bear upon less than the best. The court does not imply this interpretation, much less compel it. Thus, we have a Civil Court case which in no way limits or conditions the reception of polygraph evidence. It is admitted as evidence in chief, not for the limited pur-pose of impeachment or the measurement of credibility.[14]

Finally, in a case only reported in the New York Law Journal, *Saletros v. Saletros,* 171 (77) N.Y.L.J. (4/22/74) 20, Col. 6F (Supreme Court, Suffolk Co.), the results of a polygraph test offered by defendant as evidence of his credibility were admitted in this divorce action as "mechanical evidence of psychological and physiological reactions of a person to which some weight may be given by the observer."

Conclusion

The State of New York, unlike the Federal Courts of late and some state courts, has traditionally been wary of and, indeed, most loath to and conserva-tive of admitting polygraph results into evidence absent stipulation. The law of the State of New York on this subject remains *People v. Forte, supra* at 204, and the standard that of general scientific recognition within the field such that rea-sonable certainly can follow from the results. Three New York trial courts have, however, admitted polygraph results into evidence, for the limited purpose of credibility only, at least this writer would conclude, as evidence in chief. These cases, to be sure, are persuasive, not authoritative. But they are indicative of a trend. If so, then, perhaps much as blood tests were initially opposed and at length accepted as competent evidence, albeit with limitations and conditions in some instances, so too the polygraph test will take its place as one means, whereby the trier of fact may, indeed, weave a spotless robe of truth with which to clothe the figure of justice, even from such "poor material as this."[15]

This article previously appeared in an edition of The Nassau Lawyer, a publication of the Nassau County Bar Association, and is being reprinted here with the permission of The Nassau County Bar Association.

3. The DNA Test: the Mechanism

Deoxyribonucleic Acid or DNA is a substance found in the organism of living cells. It consists of chromosomes within the nucleus and provides the genetic code which determines a person's individual characteristics. DNA testing has been approved in the State of New York in both civil and criminal cases, and in both the State and Federal courts. See *Matter of S.L.B. v. K.A. a/k/a K.D.,* 588 N.Y.S.2d 710 (F. Ct., New York County, 1992); *Matter of L.I. v. E.T.R., a/k/a T.,* 588 N.Y.S.2d 65; *Matter of S.L.B. a/k/a K.D.,* 153 Misc.2d 47, 579 N.Y.S.2d 964 (F. Ct., New York County, 1992); *People v. Castro,* 144 Misc. 2d 956, 545 N.Y.S.2d 985 (S. Ct., Bronx County, 1989); *People v. Wesley,* 83 N.Y.2d 417 (1994).

The statutory mechanism whereby the state trial court can order a DNA test upon motion of the People is C.P.L. Sec. 240.40 2(b)(v). That section states that, upon motion of the prosecutor, the court in which an indictment, superior court information, prosecutor's information, information, or simply an information charging a misdemeanor is pending may order the defendant to provide non-testimonial evidence and that the order may, among other things, require the defendant to have samples of blood, hair, or other materials taken from his body in a manner not involving an unreasonable intrusion thereof or a risk of serious physical injury thereto.

It is clear, in this section, that the court in its discretion may order, upon application of the prosecutor, a DNA test. It should be noted that has long been the law under *Schmerber v. California,* 389 U.S. 757, 8 S. Ct. 1826, that the defendant has no right under these circumstances to assert a Fifth Amendment privilege. It is also clear, under this statutory section, that the section is discretionary.

The question arises, then, and it is of interest to bench and bar, as to whether there are any limits, criteria or guidance with respect to the exercise of that discretion. The leading case is *Matter of Abe A.,* 56 N.Y.S. 2d, 298 (1982). In *Abe A.,* the People with reference to a suspect in a homicide investigation, sought that he be compelled, pursuant to court order, to supply the People with a blood sample for scientific analysis. The court held that the People must establish probable cause to believe the suspect has committed the crime; a clear indication that relevant and material evidence will be found; and that the method used to secure the sample must be safe and reliable; impose no undue physical discomfort than is reasonably necessary and that when the body is invaded, the procedure should be carried out by a qualified physician in accordance with accepted medical standards. The court further stated that the court must consider if there are alternative means or methods for obtaining the evidence. Applying these rules and criteria, the Court of Appeals reversed the order of the Appellate Division, First Department, which had reversed the order of the trial court in New York County, holding the respondent in contempt of court for failure to comply with a prior order directing the taking of blood samples from his body, thus allowing blood testing of the suspect.

The criteria and rules for allowing the taking of a DNA test at the behest of the prosecutor have since been allowed by the lower courts of this state. See *People v. Handley,* 105 Misc. 2d 215 (St. Ct. Monroe County 1980); *In the Matter of David M. v. Dwyer.* 107 A.D. 2d 884 (3rd Dept. 1985). It is clear that, upon application, should the People propose a DNA test, they must be put to the burden to establish the criteria and requirements of *Abe A.* and the cases following it.

Of course, the outcome of a DNA test is always problematic and presents a risk both to the prosecutor and the defense counsel.

Nevertheless, it is most wise for the defense to oppose the test and insist on total fulfillment of the criteria laid out in *Abe A.* In this way, a potentially disastrous scientific result may be possibly avoided or help the defense to be victorious on appeal.

4. *The Polygraph Confession*

The lie detector or polygraph is a device whereby certain physical phenomena—blood pressure, respiration, pulse, and galvanic skin reflexes—are recorded on a chart by means of sensors connected to the person being questioned. The theory behind the process is that lying or deception involves stress which manifests itself by changes from the norm in these particular bodily phenomena. The examiner may infer from the chart that records these phenomena or polygraphs whether the examined believes he is lying or telling the truth. The results may also be inconclusive. A polygraph must be interpreted by a qualified examiner. Some states have licensing statutes; New York does not.

This article does not propose to consider the current status of the admissibility of polygraph evidence in the State of New York, a subject considered in previous articles by this writer.[1]

What will be analyzed in this article are the circumstances under past and current case law whereby a polygraph test may vitiate, in the totality of the circumstances, a confession, rendering it inadmissible as coerced. There are two older New York cases on this issue.

In *People v. Zimmer*, 68 Misc.2d 1067, 329 N.Y.S.2d 17, affd, 40 A.D.2d 955, 339 N.Y.S.2d 671 (4th Dept. 1972) (Wayne County Court, 1972), defendant and her husband agreed to submit to a polygraph test concerning the death of her adoptive daughter. Defendant was taken to a small room where she remained alone with the polygraph examiner for two and one-half hours. She was given a four page journal to read explaining the operation of the instrument, duties of the operator and general application of polygraph tests. After reading the pamphlet, defendant was shown a plastic heart in reference to which investigator explained to defendant the physical reaction of the heart, during the test, if her answers were not truthful. At the conclusion of the polygraph examination, the examiner left the room, returned shortly and told defendant she had been lying. The examiner told defendant at least three times she had not told the truth. Shortly thereafter, defendant made oral and written confession with respect to her culpability in the infant's death. Defendant moved to suppress these statements. The court noted that at the conclusion of the test defendant was told several times she was lying.

She was alone, bewildered, with no one to advise her except the investigator, who insisted she lied. The interview with the investigator lasted almost three hours. The court held that, under all the circumstances set forth, the statement made by the defendant was not her free and voluntary act, but was coerced through the use of the polygraph. The court laid particular stress on the fact that, for all defendant knew, the examination could be used against her to show she was lying, since she was not told that such results could under no circumstances be used against her. *People v. Zimmer, supra*, at 1073, 329 N.Y.S.2d at 24. In sum, the court held that the totality of the circumstances under which the polygraph test was given was such as to effectively coerce the contested statements and so render them inadmissible.

On the other hand, in *People v. Wilson*, 78 Misc.2d 468, 354 N.Y.S.2d 296 (Nassau County Court, 1974), defendant, in a criminal prosecution, moved to suppress evidence of a record describing a statement made by him to a public servant on the ground that the statement was coerced through the use of a polygraph device. Defendant herein was twice given his Miranda warnings and so informed of his constitutional rights; twice cautioned not to take the test if he intended to lie; informed of the theory and functioning of the machine and the questions the examiner would ask; twice given the test and twice told he had lied. Defendant subsequently made an oral confession. The court stated that the polygraph examination is but one factor to be considered in determining whether or not a confession was coerced and cited *People v. Zimmer, supra*, where "the subject's state of mental derangement, the implication that polygraph results could be used in evidence, the technique of the examination and its length were all considered as factors amounting to coercion." *People v. Wilson, supra*, at 475, 354 N.Y.S.2d at 304.

The *Wilson* court held defendant's statement admissible and not subject to suppression as coerced through the use of a polygraph on three grounds. First, the techniques used were truth-fostering and so the court deemed the confession trustworthy and so worthy of reception into evidence. Second, the court held the statement voluntary in the due process sense since evidence was lacking that the behavior of the police was tyrannical and calculated to overbear defendant's will to resist. Third, defendant's 5th Amendment privilege against self-incrimination was not violated since defendant Wilson, though neither suspect nor in custody, was twice informed of his constitutional rights before the test and twice warned not to take the test if he intended to lie. He knowingly and intelligently waived his rights to silence and counsel and voluntarily chose to speak and confess.

The courts in *People v. Zimmer, supra*, at 1067, 329 N.Y.S.2d at 17 and *People v. Wilson, supra*, at 468, 354 N.Y.S.2d at 296, appear to use differing analyses to reach dissimilar results. The *Zimmer* court used a totality of the circumstances test—are the circumstances surrounding the test so coercive as to vitiate any statement or admission obtained therefrom, rendering it inadmissible. The *Wilson* court analyzed the possible inadmissibility of the polygraph procured confession through three legal principles: the evidentiary principle that a coerced confession is an inherently untrustworthy one; the 14th Amendment due process principle which focuses on whether the behavior of law-enforcement officials was such as to overcome defendant's free will and so produce an involuntary confession; and the 5th Amendment self-incrimination privilege. The court sifted the facts through these legal rubrics and held the confession passed evidentiary and constitutional muster.

This writer would suggest that the approaches of these courts are not so far removed. *Wilson* cites *Zimmer* as authoritative precedent. *People v. Wilson, supra*, at 474, 354 N.Y.S.2d at 304. In addition, the *Wilson* court states that, as a general proposition, the inadmissibility of coerced confessions rests on these three principles and proceeds to consider the facts of the case under these headings. The *Wilson* court is not altering the *Zimmer* totality of the circumstances test, but analyzing the totality of the circumstances through these principles. In a word, the court in *Wilson* simply sifts and arranges the facts in parallel columns to determine whether all taken in, they vitiate an admission. The *Zimmer* court prefers to consider them as one. The analysis may differ but the rule remains the same.

The older case law, prior to and up to 1985, consistently follows the totality of the circumstances test as defined in *Wilson* and *Zimmer*. [2]

Since 1980 the cases have also, without dissent, followed the rule that there must be a finding under the totality of circumstances that the results of a polygraph test will be deemed involuntary and inadmissible as the product of coercion. What these particular facts and circumstances are or will be depends upon the seminal facts surrounding the taking of the polygraph test including evidence of the defendant's mental and psychological condition at the time and prior to the test, the use of deceptive verbal practices by the polygraph examiner, and any evidence of physical coercion.

People v. Sohn, 148 A.D.2d 553, 539 N.Y.S.2d 29 (2d Dept. 1989), is illustrative. *Sohn* was an appeal by the defendant from a judgment of the County Court of Rockland County convicting her of murder in the second degree (two counts); robbery in the first degree (two counts); and grand larceny in the second degree upon a jury verdict and sentencing. The issue on appeal was the denial, after a hearing, of that portion of the defendant's omnibus motion to suppress statements made to law enforcement authorities. The court considered the issue of the voluntariness of the defendant's confession in light of the use of a polygraph test. The court stated the use of a polygraph will not in and of itself render a confession inadmissible as the product of coercion but that its use or misuse, is, however, a factor to be considered in determining whether coercion was involved. The court, although stating that a measure of guile was employed by the polygraph examiner when he told the defendant that in his opinion she was not being completely truthful without explaining to her that the test results were inconclusive, said the deception was not so fundamentally unfair as to deny due process.[3]

It is clear that this review of the case law on the subject of the polygraph induced confession reveals that the facts of the case will create the hinge upon which it is determined whether or not the statement taken when a polygraph has been used will be deemed inadmissible. A slightly deceptive or coercive practice is not enough under *Sohn*. There must be a substantial pattern of guile and coercion, it would appear, taking into account all the criteria of the defendant's age, physical condition and psychological state at the time of the taking of the test. It is only, in short, when the totality of the circumstances mandate, that a statement will be suppressed through the use of and following a polygraph test.

5. A Note on Circumstantial Evidence

Circumstantial evidence is one of the most common forms of evidence to be used at a trial. It is, or can be, one of the most compelling and convincing types of evidence. In essence, the notion behind circumstantial evidence is that the witness testifies not directly to the fact to be established based on his own personal knowledge but, rather, to a fact brought to light by witnesses which, taken with others, leads by the process of inference to the direct fact in issue.

In short, circumstantial evidence is proof of collateral facts from which the fact or facts in issue may be inferred. In the case of direct evidence, the witness testifies based on his own personal knowledge of the fact in issue while in the case of circumstantial evidence the witness testifies to the facts or circumstances from which the trier of fact may infer facts which may reasonably follow.[1]

Ridings v. Vaccarello[2] is an example.

Ridings was an Article 78 proceeding brought to review a sanitation commissioner's determination made after a hearing, dismissing the petitioner from his position as a sanitation worker. The Supreme Court, Appellate Division, held that the commissioner's determination that the petitioner was subject to dismissal because he aided and abetted a fellow employee in assaulting a foreman and failed to come to the foreman's aid was not supported by substantial evidence since the commissioner drew inferences mostly unfavorable to the petitioner from circumstances wholly innocuous. In holding that the respondent's determination was without evidentiary support, the court said,

> to prove a fact by circumstances there must be positive proof of some fact which does not itself directly establish the fact in dispute, but which affords a reasonable inference of its existence. The fact upon which it is sought to base an inference must be shown and not let to rest on conjecture. If and when the fact is shown it must then appear that the inference drawn is the only one that is fair and reasonable.[3]

People v. Millan[4] is also illustrative of how the courts of this state have sought to define the circumstantial evidence rule. In *Millan*, the People presented testimony that the defendant was observed earlier in the day in possession of a handgun that prior to the shooting the defendant had been involved in a dispute between the victim and an associate of the defendant; that the defendant was observed by several witnesses walking purposefully toward the victim shortly before the fatal shot was fired; that the man identified by several witnesses as the defendant was observed walking directly behind the victim, producing a handgun and firing it at the victim; and that the fatal wound was inflicted by an individual shorter than the defendant. The Appellate Division, First Department, concluded on the facts that the trial court's instructions on reasonable doubt and circumstantial evidence were proper.

Both *Ridings* and *Millan* establish a clear rule as to what constitutes circumstantial evidence: evidence is circumstantial, and not direct, as long as the fact is or can be drawn by inference and not direct observation or personal knowledge on the part of the witness.

The circumstantial evidence charge, however, is required to be given to the jury only where the evidence is "wholly" circumstantial, that is, where no element of the offense is established by direct evidence. Whenever a case relies wholly on circumstantial evidence to establish all the elements of the crime the jury should be instructed that the ultimate inference to be drawn must be established to a moral certainty. However, where a crime is supported by both circumstantial and direct evidence, the court need not so charge the jury.[5]

There are, however, two subrules, or glosses, on this rule. In *People v. Trail*,[6] the defendant appealed from a conviction, after a jury trial, of murder in the second degree and criminal possession of a weapon in the second degree. In ruling on the defendant's claim that the trial court erred in not giving a circumstantial evidence charge, the Appellate Division held that the claim was meritless since "the People's primary witness offered direct testimony concerning the circumstances of the shooting and as inferences to be drawn were clear, strong and logical, a circumstantial evidence charge was not required."[7]

The rule, or rather subrule, of *Trail* appears to be that where there is sufficient direct testimony and there are inferences in addition where the inferences to be drawn are strong enough, a circumstantial evidence charge is not only unnecessary but not required.

A second subrule in this area of law is stated in *People v. Rumble.*[8] The Court of Appeals held there that the defendant's statement to his brother that "I'm not responsible for what I did," if interpreted by the fact finder as a relevant admission of guilt, destroyed the notion that the case was based wholly on circumstantial evidence and so the circumstantial charge was not required or applicable. *Rumble* seems to hold that where the evidence at trial includes a statement by the defendant which may reasonably be interpreted as a confession of the crime, that is in itself enough to render unnecessary any instruction to the jury on circumstantial evidence.[9]

Conclusion

What emerges in this short analysis of what constitutes circumstantial evidence and when the circumstantial evidence charge must be given is an overall basic rule and some subrules.

First, where inferences are drawn, the evidence is circumstantial and the charge on circumstantial evidence is appropriate. Second, the evidence must be wholly circumstantial. If it is in part direct, the circumstantial evidence charge "to a moral certainty" is neither necessary nor required. Third, even if the evidence is circumstantial, if the inferences are strong and logical the circumstantial evidence charge is not needed .

6. Three Cases on Laboratory and Ballistics Reports

In two recent Court of Appeals cases, in the *Matter of Rodney J.,* 83 N.Y.2d 503 (1994), and *Matter of Wesley M.,* 83 N.Y.2d 898 (1994), the Court of Appeals concluded, respectively, that if a ballistics or laboratory report do not certify that they are signed by the original tester of the weapon or controlled substance and is therefore not based on full and personal knowledge of the tester, this constitutes, at least in Family Court petitions, a fatal defect in the accusatory instrument, mandating dismissal of the petition.

It would appear that *Wesley M.* and *Rodney* may also be applied to felony indictments or misdemeanor information where a gun or controlled substance is alleged. That is to say the laboratory or ballistics report presented to C.P.L. section 190.30(2) is not a statement sworn to by the original tester, or the laboratory or ballistics report necessary to convert a misdemeanor complaint to an information does not contain an affidavit by the original tester of the controlled substance or weapon, the indictment or information may be subject to dismissal.

The question arises, however, how and in what manner, *Wesley M., supra,* and *Rodney J., supra,* will be applied by the lower courts of this state.

Three recent trial court decisions have addressed this same issue. They are *People v. Wheeler,* N.Y.L.J. pg 27 col. 2 (Oct. 7, 1994) (Bronx County Criminal Court Pt. Ap 10; *People v. Green,* N.Y.L.J. pg. 34 col. 26 (Oct. 7, 1994) (Kings County Criminal Court Pt. Ap 2); and *People v. Dominguez,* N.Y.L.J. p. 35 col. 2 (Oct. 7, 1994) (S. Ct. County of Queens Pt. K-10).

In *Wheeler,* the codefendants were charged with criminal possession of a weapon in the fourth degree. In each case the People filed a ballistics report that stated that the gun and ammunition tested were operable. The reports were signed, respectively, by a Detective and police officer with an accompanying certification that the report was a true and full copy of the original report.

The defendant moved to dismiss on the ground of facial insufficiency, arguing that the requirements of *Rodney J., supra,* were not complied with.

The court held that, upon analysis and application of the holding in *Rodney J.,* that the reports filed in these cases purported to be only copies of the original reports and that although the ballistics reports did contain a statement that the gun was tested, where there was nothing to indicate that the officers who signed the certification were in fact the ones who performed the tests or that the original reports were signed by anyone at all, the information was insufficient as a matter of law.

The trial court thus concluded that the requirements of the Court of Appeals set forth in *Rodney J., supra,* were not complied with since the certification was not based on personal knowledge, but purported to be only a copy of the original report. The court held, as an addendum, that in order to meet the requirements of *Rodney J.,* the certification would have to state that "I tested the gun and ammunition and that the foregoing reports are a full and true copy of the of the original report."

Different results were reached in *Green* and *Dominguez.* In *Dominguez,* the defendant moved orally for reargument of the denial of his original motions to dismiss the indictments. The court noted that the Court of Appeals held, in *Rodney J.,* that the petition and supporting documents were jurisdictionally defective on their face since the papers failed to contain a non-hearsay allegation as to the weapon's operability in that the ballistics reports purported to be a copy of the reports, but did not indicate that it was signed by the person who tested the gun and prepared the original report.

The court went on to state that the defendant contended that the laboratory reports in the cases before it were hearsay as not complying with C.P.L. section 190.30 The court held the certification sufficient since it stated that the foregoing reports were a true and full copy of the original reports made by me indicating the original reports were prepared by the certifiers.

The court further noted that the Police Laboratory Controlled Substance Reports introduced into evidence before the Grand Jury and the Requests for Laboratory Examination Controlled Substance/Marihuana, read together, clearly stated on their faces that the chemists who signed the reports were the same chemists who prepared and signed the original analysis reports. The court found therefore in this case that the requirements in *Rodney J.* had been met.

Green reached a decision similar to the *Dominguez* court. In *Green*, the defendant moved to dismiss the charge of P. L. section 220.03 in that the insufficiency of the laboratory report rendered the information jurisdictionally defective. The defendant argued, in the alternative, that the laboratory reports were insufficient to convert the complaint to an information. The defendant also moved to dismiss on C.P.L. section 30.30 grounds.

The Court initially held that the language of the complaint itself rendered it jurisdictionally sufficient on its face.

The court went on to consider the defendant's argument that the laboratory reports were not sufficient in that the person who signed the report did not certify that he was the person who actually performed the test in accordance with the *Wesley* and *Rodney J.* rule that a laboratory report must sufficiently detail whether the person who signed the report was the same person who conducted the testing.

The court noted that, in the present case, the laboratory report presented by the District Attorney to convert the complaint to an information was signed by one S. Ansam, contained a certification that the report was a true and full copy of the original report that was lacking any language which would establish that the signer of the document was the person who tested the material recovered from the defendant.

The court held that although this was a pleading defect for a Family Court Petition this was not so for a criminal court instrument. Hence the court denied the defendant's motion.

Those three cases, whose facts and holdings have been analyzed herein, reach, if only in one case, different results from the others, but also reason disparately as to the applicability of *Rodney J.* and *Wesley*.

The *Wheeler* court held, applying *Rodney J.*, that the copy of the original ballistics report, with no indication that it was signed by the person who tested the gun and prepared the original report, was insufficient under *Rodney*. *Wheeler* held that the certification should have stated, to pass legal muster, that the preparer tested the ammunition and the gun and that the copy of the report submitted was a true and full copy of the original report prepared by me.

The *Green* court, although not in that the laboratory report merely stated that it was a true copy of the original report, lacking any language which would establish that the signer of the document was the person who tested the material, nevertheless concluded that although the report was defective for Family Court purposes, it was not defective as a Criminal Court accusatory instrument.

Dominquez found the laboratory certification sufficient under *Wesley* and *Rodney J.*, since it stated it was a true and full copy of the original report made by me.

Dominguez and *Wheeler* agree in their reasoning, but reach different decisional conclusions: *Wheeler* finds the certification insufficient, *Dominguez* finds it sufficient. Both agree that the proper certification under *Rodney J.* and *Wesley* must indicate that the copy of the report submitted is a true copy of the original report by the original tester or preparer.

Green, although it finds, albeit impliedly, that the report is insufficient under *Rodney J.*, and *Wesley* in lacking language to establish that the signer of the document was the person who tested the controlled substance recovered from the defendant, concluded that this was not a pleading defect as far as a Criminal Court Complaint is concerned.

The better reasoning is that *Wheeler* and *Dominguez* both conclude that a proper certification must contain a statement that the report, although a copy, was prepared by the original tester thus establishing the nonhearsay character of the submission.

The rule in *Dominguez* and *Wheeler* establishes essential compliance with the Court to appeals in *Rodney J.* and *Wesley* that a ballistics report or laboratory report submitted by the People must contain the assurance that the person who tested the gun or drugs is the same person who is now submitting the report.

Green evades, in the view of this writer, the issue, finding the report defective under *Wesley* and *Rodney J.*, but finding if not a pleading or jurisdictional defect, thus in effect, ignoring the obvious requirements for these Court to appeals cases.

It is the court, in *Dominguez* and *Wheeler*, who rightly apply the Court of Appeals' holding in *Rodney J.* and *Wesley*, insisting that a laboratory or ballistics report, whether in support of an indictment or information, must show that the person who prepared the reports is the one who submitted the report to the court in support of the charges, thus assuring that these sort of criminal charges are truly supported by the original evidence of a nonhearsay character.

Notes

1. Polygraph Evidence: Admissibility in Civil and Criminal Cases

1. "Admissibility of Polygraph Evidence in the State of New York" by Andrew J. Schatkin, *Article of Special Interest, Advance Sheet, New York Supplement*, Feb. 28, 1979;

"Polygraph Evidence: Admissibility in Civil and Criminal Cases," *Brooklyn Barrister,* March 1985.

2. For cases rejecting the use of polygraph and the admissibility of polygraph results into evidence, see *People v. Dobler,* 29 Misc.2d 481, 215 N.Y. Supp. 2d 313 (Suffolk County Court, 1961); *People v. Brownsky,* 35 Misc.2d 134, 228 N.Y.Supp. 2d 746 (Court of General Sessions, N.Y. County 1962); *Matter of Sowa v. Looney,* 23 N.Y.2d 329, 296 N.Y.Supp. 2d 760 (1968); *People v. Leone,* 25 N.Y.2d 511, 307 N.Y. Supp. 430 (1969); *Tree v. Ralston,* 62 Misc.2d 282, 309 N.Y.Supp. 229 (Family Court, N.Y. County, 1970); *People v. Dodge,* 72 Misc. 2d 345, 338 N.Y. Supp. 2d, 690 (Nassau County Court, 1972); *People v. Jacobson,* 71 Misc.2d 1040, 337 N.Y. Supp. 2d 616 (Supreme Court, Queens County, 1972); *People v. Parish,* 17 Misc. 2d 577, 333 N.Y. Supp. 2d 631 (Nassau County Court, 1972); *People v. McCain,* 42 A.D.2d 866, 347 (N.Y. Supp. 2d 72) (2nd Dept. 1973); *People v. Hargrove,* 80 Misc.2d 317, 363 N.Y. Supp. 241 (Supreme Court, Westchester County, 1975); *In the Matter of Lillie Anonymous v. Robert Anonymous,* 75 Misc.2d 823, 348 N.Y. Supp.2d 938 (Family Court, Rockland County, 1973); *People v. Guerin,* 47 A.D.2d 788, 366 N.Y. Supp.2d 61 (3rd Dept. 1975); *People v. Black,* 86 Misc.2d 909, 382 N.Y. Supp.2d 944 (Supreme Court Kings County, 1976).

3. These cases were examined and analyzed at some length and in detail in "Polygraph Evidence: Admissibility in Civil and Criminal Cases," *supra*

4. It should be noted that it continues to be the law of this State that the results of polygraph tests will be admitted into evidence on the basis of a stipulation between the parties to admit these results. See *Pereira v. Pereira,* 35 N.Y.2d 301, 361 N.Y.S.2d 148 (1974); *Kresnicka v. Kresnicka,* 48 A.D.2d 929, 369 N.Y.S.2d , 522 (2d Dept. 1975); *People v. Prado,* 81 M.2d 710, 365 N.Y.S.2d 943 (S. Ct. Bronx County 1975); *Zinn v. Bernic Construction,* 99 Misc. 2d 510, 416 N.Y.S.2d 725 (S.Ct. Queens County 1979); "Admissibility of Polygraph Evidence in the State of New York," *Advance Sheet, New York Supplement* 2/28/79, p. 31-33; "Polygraph Evidence: Admissibility in Civil and Criminal Cases," *Brooklyn Barrister,* March 1985, p. 128.

2. Admissibility of Polygraph Evidence in the State of New York

1. On the theory, use, operation, scientific basis and effectiveness of the lie detector see among the many books and articles, J. REID, F. INBAU, TRUTH AND DECEPTION (1966); Skalnick, SCIENTIFIC THEORY AND SCIENTIFIC EVIDENCE: AN ANALYSIS OF LIE DETECTION, 70 YALE L. J. 694 (1961); E. McCORMICK, EVIDENCE § 207 (2d ed. 1972); WIGMARE, EVIDENCE § 999.

2. See REID AND INBAU, *supra* at 238; Note: PINOCCHIO'S NEW NOSE, 48 N.Y.U. L.REV. 341(1973); for exhaustive list of cases rejecting polygraph evidence in accord with this standard see Annot. 23 ALR 2d 1306 (1952) LATER CASE SERVICE, Vol. 19-24 ALR 2d 1970 and SUPP. June 1977; 29 AM. JUR. 2d, EVIDENCE §831 (1967).

3. See *U. S. v. De Betham,* 470 F. 2d 1367 (9th Cir. 1972); *U. S. v. Zeiger,* 350 F. Supp. 685 (D. D. C. 1972), rev'd. without opinion 475 F.2d 1280 (D. C. Cir. 1972); *U. S. v. Ridling,* 350 F. Supp. 90 (E. D. Mich. 1972); *U. S. v. Dioguardi,* No. 72 Cr. 1102 (E. D. N.Y. Record of Nov. 30, 1972); *U. S. v. Hart,* 344 F.Supp. 522 (E. D. N.Y. 1971); *People v. Cutter,* 12 Crim. L. Rptr. 2133 (Cal. Super. Ct. Nov. 6, 1972); *State v. Dorsey,* 88 N. M. 184, 539 P.2d 204 (Supreme Court 1975); *State v. Watson,* 115 N. J. Super. 213, 278 A.2d 543 (Hudson County Ct. 1971). For discussion of these and other cases, see Note, PINOCCHIO'S NEW NOSE, *supra* at 342; U. S. v. RIDLING: THE POLYGRAPH BREAKS THE "TWILIGHT ZONE." 23 CATHOLIC U. L.REV. 101 (1974); Tarlow, ADMISSIBILITY OF POLYGRAPH EVIDENCE IN 1975: AN AID IN DETERMINING CREDIBILITY

IN A PERJURY-PLAGUED SYSTEM, 26 HASTINGS LAW J aumal 917 (1975); CRIMINAL LAW—UNSTIPULATED POLYGRAPH EVIDENCE ADMISSIBLE UNDER CERTAIN CONDITIONS IN CRIMINAL TRIALS. COMMONWEALTH V. A. JUVENILE (NO. 1) 313 N.E.2D 120 (MASS. 1974) CATHOLIC U. L. REV. (1975).

4. In *People v. Kenny*, 167 Misc. 51 3 N.Y.S.2d 348 (County Court, Queens County, 1938), a case decided at nearly the same time as *Forte*, over objection of the prosecutor the trial court permitted evidence of the lie detector. The court was apparently swayed by the examiner's claim of and supporting statistics concerning the reliability and accuracy of the instrument. *Forte* would appear to overrule *Kenny*, although no reference is made in *Forte* to the decision of the trial court in *Kenny;* on *People v. Kenny, supra,* see Reid & Inbau, *supra* at 238-239. One commentator has suggested that *Kenny* and *Forte* are distinguishable on the ground that in *Kenny* a proper foundation was laid for the Lie Detector evidence, while in *Forte* none was laid. See ADMISSIBILITY OF LIE DETECTOR TESTS, 4 THE JOHN MARSHALL JOURNAL OF PRACTICE AND PROCEDURE, 233, 251, (1971); POLYGRAPH EVIDENCE: THE CASE FOR ADMISSIBILITY UPON STIPULATION OF THE PARTIES, 9 TULSA LAW JOURNAL 253 (1973).

5. The author acknowledges the format of this article and, in particular, the introductory readings, to REID & INBAU, *supra* 237-256.

6. See REID & INBAU, *supra* at 244; Annat. 95 ALR 2d 811 (1964); LATER CASE SERVICE, Vol. 92-100 ALR 2d pp 246-248 (1976); 29 AM. JUR. 2d EVIDENCE, § 296, § 831, 22 A.C.J.S., CRIMINAL LAW, § 645 (2) (1967).

7. See LATER CASE SERVICE, Vols. 2 92-100 ALR 2d at 246, where *People v. McCain, supra* at 866, is cited, amid a wealth of other cases from various jurisdictions, as recognizing the impropriety of evidence tending to establish that accused had been willing or unwilling to take the lie detector test. See also *People v. Johnson,* 51 A.D.2d 851, 380 N.Y.S.2d 775 (3rd Dept. 1976), where, in the course of defendant's cross-examination of a prosecution witness, in response to a proper question, the witness answered that he asked defendant if he would take a lie detector test. Citing *People v. McCain, supra,* as authority, the Court held that since evidence of one's submission to such test should not be elicited, the trial court was correct in precluding defense counsel from pursuing this line of inquiry and instructing the jury to disregard the matter.

But, see *Fifty States Management Corp. v. Public Service Mutual Insurance Co.,* 67 Misc. 2d 778, 324 N.Y.S.2d 345 (Supreme Court, Erie County, 1971), where the Court stated, quoting from *Terpstra v. Niagra Fire Ins. Co.,* 26 N.Y.2d 70, 308 N.Y.S.2d 378 (1970), that plaintiff's refusal to take a polygraph test is per se meaningless "but the jury may consider all of the conversations relating to the polygraph test insofar as that has a bearing upon alleged admissions or other statements made by him." *Fifty States Management v. Public Service Mutual Insurance, supra* at 787.

The Court concluded that here Fifty's president refused to take a polygraph test and it was not error to receive this refusal into evidence with the appropriate charge that was given the jury that the reliability of the lie detector has not been sufficiently established such as to warrant admission into evidence.

It is not clear, from the language of this decision, whether a refusal to take a lie detector test is admissible if accompanied by the appropriate charge to the jury on the inherent evidentiary unreliability of lie detector results. If so, then the decision is contra *People v. McCain, supra* at 866, and *People v. Johnson, supra* at 851, which prohibit absolutely such to be admitted into evidence and is implicitly overruled by these later Appellate Division cases.

On the other hand, this language, i.e., that a refusal to take a lie detector test may be admitted into evidence with the appropriate charge to the jury, may be read in the context of the preceding paragraph, which holds that all statements with respect to the polygraph test are admissible as relevant to statements or admissions examined. If this is so, the decision remains relevant and persuasive.

8. But see *People v. Daley,* 54 A.D.2d 1007, 388 N.Y.S.2d 359 (3rd Dept. 1976), where, as in *People v. McCain, supra,* defendant testified he had voluntarily submitted to a lie detector test and failed to state the result, thereby creating an inference he had passed. On cross examination by the prosecutor, defendant denied he had been told by the polygraph examiner that he had failed the test. The issue on appeal was whether prosecutor could rebut the favorable inference by the introduction of evidence to the contrary. Citing *People v. McCain, supra,* the Court held the People had a limited right to rebut the favorable inference created by defendant's voluntary submission, but declared that since the expert was not permitted to give evidence as to the test result, it was unnecessary to determine if the People's right of rebuttal should include the opinion evidence of the expert that defendant had failed the test. It would seem that the 3rd Dept. in *People v. Daley, supra,* considers the issue of whether the *McCain* right of rebuttal extends to the reception of examiner's opinion to be open, yet to be decided, while the 2nd Dept., in the earlier *People v. McCain, supra,* regards the matter as closed.

9. On this issue, see ADMISSIBILITY OF LIE DETECTOR TEST TAKEN UPON STIPULATION THAT THE RESULT WILL BE ADMISSIBLE IN EVIDENCE, 53 A.L.R. 3rd 1005; ENFORCEABILITY OF AGREEMENT BY STATE OFFICIALS TO DROP PROSECUTION IF ACCUSED SUCCESSFULLY PASSES POLYGRAPH TEST. 36 A.L.R. 3rd 1280; REID & INBAU, *supra* 247-252; among numerous articles see EVIDENCE—LIE DETECTOR TESTS—EFFECT OF PRIOR STIPULATION OF ADMISSIBILITY, 46 IA. L. REV. 651 (1961), EVIDENCE—LIE DETECTOR—ADMISSIBILITY UNDER PRETRIAL STIPULATION, 15 ALA. L. REV. 248 (1963); EVIDENCE—LIE DETECTOR TESTS—PRIOR STIPULATION OF ADMISSIBILITY, 2 NATURAL RESOURCES J. 162 (1962); CRIMINAL LAW—PRETRIAL IMMUNITY AGREEMENT—BINDING BOTH SIDES TO RESULTS OF POLYGRAPH TEST UPHELD AS A PLEDGE OF PUBLIC FAITH, 16 N.Y.L.F. 646 (1970).

10. *Contra People v. Hargrove,* 80 Misc.2d 317, 363 N.Y.S.2d 241 (Supreme Court, Westchester County, 1975), where the court stated that the polygraph test, in the present state of the law in N.Y., is inadmissible, even if the People and defendant were to stipulate that the tests be so utilized.

11. On this see SMITH, THE LAW OF CONFESSIONS AND SCIENTIFIC EVIDENCE, 205 (1963); REID & INBAU, *supra* at 252; Brasch, POLYGRAPH CONFESSION, 9 WILLAMETTE LJ 54 (1973), STATE V. GREEN, THE POLYGRAPH PROCURED CONFESSION—OREGON DECLINES TO ADMIT LIE DETECTION EVIDENCE IN CRIMINAL TRIALS, 11 WILLAMETTE LJ 459, (1975).

12. On recent cases and trends in this area see EVIDENCE—THE ADMISSIBILITY OF POLYGRAPH TEST RESULTS IN PATERNITY CASES, 76 W. VA. L. REV. 76 (1973); EVIDENCE—HOW SAME COURTS HAVE LEARNED TO STOP WORRYING AND LOVE THE POLYGRAPH, 51 N. C. L. REV. 900 (1973); EMERGENCE OF THE POLYGRAPH AT TRIAL, 73 COLUM. L. REV. 1120 (1973); Nate, EVIDENCE: LIE DETECTORS: DISCUSSIONS AND PROPOSALS, 29 CORNELL L.Q. 535 (1944); Note, EVIDENCE—POLYGRAPH TESTIMONY—POLYGRAPH TEST RESULTS ADMISSIBLE UNDER CERTAIN CONDITIONS. COMMONWEALTH V. A. JUVENILE (No. 1) 55 B.U.L. L. REV. 302 (1975); EVIDENCE—VOLUNTARY POLYGRAPH EXAMINATION RESULTS ADMISSIBLE AS EXPERT TESTIMONY, 44 MISS. L. J. 800 (1973); Arther, THE JOURNAL OF POLYGRAPH STUDIES, Vol. II, No. 1, July-August, 1967.

13. The manner in which the court distinguishes away *People v. Leone, supra* is at the least, somewhat tenuous. The court states that *Leone* cited the inexperience of the operator as one of the major reasons for its decision. *Walther v. O'Connell, supra* at 318. This is not so. *People v. Leone, supra,* in the context of listing the arguments pro and con with respect to the admissibility of polygraph tests states that "opponents of the machine . . . contend that polygraph tests are unreliable because the people administering them are inadequately trained." *People v. Leone, supra* at 516. This is in no way the basis for the decision which is the failure of the polygraph principle to have gained general acceptance in the particular field to which it belongs. *People v. Leone, supra* at 517.

14. Two recent Appellate Division cases are also relevant and indicative of a trend to admissibility. *Habersham v. Grimaldi,* 18 A.D.2d 615, 234 N.Y.S. 2d 599 (1st Dept. 1962) (Denial of defendant's motion for "Galvanic Skin Response Test" reversed since no indication submission to the test will unduly burden plaintiff or subject him to danger); *Carpinelli v. Manhattan Battling Corporation,* 21 A.D.2d 792, 250 N.Y.S.2d 756 (2d Dept. 1964) (Order of Supreme Court denying motion for leave to renew a prior motion to direct examination of infant plaintiff by psychogalvanic skin reaction tests reversed and defendant's renewed motion to examine granted on condition that admissibility in evidence at trial of finding and results of tests rest in discretion of trial judge and exercise of discretion be dependent on reasonable certitude of findings and results. The court held original denial of tests improvident since they are of some value, at least for research purposes and have, citing *Habersham,* received previous judicial approval.) It is interesting to note that both these decisions compel submission to the polygraph test. For analysis of these cases see Merker, POLYGRAPH FOR THE DEFENSE, 40 N.Y.S. B. J. 569 (1968).

15. *Stenzel A. v. B., supra* at 719.

4. The Polygraph Confession

1. See "Admissibility of Polygraph Evidence in the State of New York," *Nassau Lawyer,* April 1978; Reprinted in Feb. 1979 *Advance Sheet of the New York Supplement;* "Polygraph Evidence: Admissibility in Civil and Criminal Cases," *Brooklyn Barrister,* March 1985; "Polygraph Evidence: Admissibility in Civil and Criminal Cases," *The Queens Bar Bulletin,* Oct. 1993.

2. See *People v. Leonard,* 59 A.D.2d 1,397 N.Y.S.2d 386 (2d Dept. 1977); *People v. Tarsia,* 50 N.Y.2d 1, 405 N.E.2d 188, 427 N.Y.S.2d 944 (1980); *People v. LaBelle,* 44 Misc.2d 327, 253 N.Y.S.2d. 901 (Rensselaer Co. Ct. 1964); *People v. Brown,* 408 N.Y.S.2d 1007 (Tompkins Co. Ct. 1978); *People v. Rhodes,* 102 Misc.2d 377, 423 N.Y.S.2d 437 (S. Ct. Monroe County, 1980).

3. See also *People v. Knighton,* 91 A.D.2d 1077, 458 N.Y.S.2d 320 (3rd Dept. 1983); *People v. Hopkins,* 96 A.D.2d 957, 46 N.Y.S.2d 857 (3rd Dept. 1983); *People v. Bullock,* 122 A.D.2d 302, 504 N.Y.S.2d 272 (3rd Dept. 1986); *People v. Harris,* 128 A.D.2d 891, 513 N.Y.S.2d 817 (2d Dept. 1987); *People v. Madison,* 135 A.D.2d 55, 522 N.Y.S.2d 230 (2d Dept. 1987).

5. A Note on Circumstantial Evidence

1. 57 N.Y. JUR2d EVIDENCE AND WITNESSES Sec. 194 pp. 421-424; RICHARDSON ON EVIDENCE (10th Ed. Princeton), Sec. 145; *People v. Bretagna,* 298 N.Y. 323 (1948); *Markel v. Spencer,* S AD. 2d 400, 171 N.Y.S. 2d 770 (4th Dept. 1958); *Sherman v. Concourse Realty Corp.,* 47 AD. 2d 134, 365 N.Y.S. 2d 239 (2d Dept. 1975); *People v.*

Mitchell, 64 AD. 2d 119, 408 N.Y.S. 2d 513 (2d Dept. 1978); *People v. Gibson,* 65 AD. 2d 235, 411 N.Y.S. 2d 71 (4th Dept. 1978); *People v. Daley,* 47 N.Y.2d 916, 419 N.Y.S. 2d 485 (1979)

2. *Ridings v. Vaccarello,* 55 AD. 2d AD. 650,390 N.Y.S.2d 152 (2d Dept. 1976)

3. *Ridings v. Vaccarello, supra,* 55 AD. 2d at 651

4. *People v. Millan,* 216 AD. 2d 93,628 N.Y.S.2d 90 (1st Dept. 1995)

5. *People v. Daddona,* 81 N.Y.2d 990, 991 (1993); *People v. Silva,* 69 N.Y.2d 858, 859 (1987); *People v. Ruiz,* 52 N.Y.2d 929, 931 (1981)

6. *People v. Trail,* 172 AD. 2d 320 (1st Dept. 1991)

7. *People v. Trail supra,* 172 A.D.2d at 321

8. *People v. Rumble,* 45 N.Y.2d 879, 881 (1978)

9. On this, see, also, *People v. Stern,* 226 A.D. 2d 238 (1st Dept. 1996) (The defendant's statement to the informant that "no one else knows" that defendant and informant killed the victim was an 'admission that constituted direct evidence, so that the circumstantial evidence charge was not required.) *People v. Guidice,* 83 N.Y.2d 630 (1994); *People v. Alexander,* 153 AD. 2d 507 (1st Dept. 1989); *People v. Jones,* 153 AD. 2d 590 (2d Dept. 1981)

Introduction to Civil Procedure Reprinted Articles

These articles cover the gamut of procedural issues in the Courts of the State of New York. They include such areas as the Notice of Claim; Mistrials; the Note of Issue; Conflicts Law; the interpretation of the General Obligations Law; Amending the Pleadings in connection with the filing of the Notice of Claim; Appellate Practice; Conforming the Pleadings to the Proof; the Ad Damnum Clause; and an examination of bifurcated trials. Also included here is an article on the compromise verdict, as well as a more general examination of what I call the art of cross-examination. The reader here will gain an overview, both in a specific and more general sense, of a broad range of procedural issues.

Chapter 3
Civil Procedure Reprinted Articles

1. A Note on the Notice of Claim

General Municipal Law, §§ 50-e and 50-i, the notice of claim statute, governs the commencement of all tort actions against municipal corporations and provides that no tort claim may be maintained against a municipal corporation for personal injury to real or personal property alleged to have been sustained by reason of the negligence or wrongful act of the municipality, unless a notice of claim is served upon the municipal corporation within ninety days after the claim arises.

Failure to file a notice of claim within the ninety day statutory period is fatal to the prospective plaintiff's action unless timely application is made to file a late notice of claim and it is accepted by the court.

The statute is clear in its requirements and mandatory in character. Simply stated, the thrust of the law is that when a plaintiff sues a municipality for a tort, a notice of claim must be filed. Thus, where the lawsuit is for false arrest or medical malpractice, the notice of claim requirement is obvious. But how far does the statute extend?

The question arises, and it is the subject of this article, whether a notice of claim must be filed where a claim is brought against a Municipality pursuant to Title 32, Section 1983 of the United States Code.

The 1983 action is one of the most common actions today, found both in the federal and state courts, and is brought to redress the alleged deprivation of a citizen's civil rights by one acting under color of law of a statute or custom of a state or territory.[1]

The action is brought under Title 42, Section 1983 of the United States Code and, though as brought under Section 1983, it is an action to redress the purported violation of a citizen's civil rights, it is often, in its root and essence, little more than a tort claim for false arrest, false imprisonment, assault and/or battery.

Thus for example, when a citizen has allegedly been falsely arrested, and thereafter assaulted with excessive force, and imprisoned by the police officer or officers of a municipality, whether employed or acting on behalf of a Town, Village, City or County, and the complaint or charges brought against our offended citizen by the District Attorney are withdrawn or dismissed, this citizen will often bring his damage suit in the form of a civil rights action in federal court under 42 U.S.C. Section 1983, rather than a simple tort action in state court. It should be noted that, under the doctrine of pendent jurisdiction set forth by the United States Supreme Court in *United Mine Workers of America v. Gibbs*, 383 U.S. 715, 86 S.Ct. 1130, 16 L.Ed.2d 218 (1966), the plaintiff in a Civil Rights Action under Section 1983 may include the related or pendent tort claims of false arrest, assault, battery and the intentional infliction of mental distress, provided that it is shown to the District Court that both the Federal Civil Rights claim and the pendent state tort claims arose from a common nucleus of operative fact.

Our Civil Rights plaintiff moreover in his pleading, if sufficiently inclusive and properly framed, will sue not only the individual police officer or officers who supposedly falsely arrested, attacked and imprisoned him, but also the Police Department and Municipality that employed these officers.

In short the civil rights actions under Section 1983, in this day and age of the assertion of the individual rights, has become a frequent, if not omnipresent, denizen of our courts.

It is of prime importance therefore to examine the question whether a notice of claim filed pursuant to Sec. 50(e) of the General Municipal Law is mandated when a Title 42 Sec. 1983 action is sought to be brought against a municipality, since if it is in fact required and not served, the action may be barred.

It was apparently formerly the law in the State of New York that a notice of claim need not be filed as a proper condition precedent to the commencement of a Civil Rights Action under Title 42 Sec. 1983.

Cooper v. Morin, 50 A.D.2d 32, 375 N.Y.S.2d 928 (4th Dept. 1975), is illustrative. *Cooper* was a class action commenced by six named female plaintiffs, inmates of the Monroe County jail, on behalf of themselves and others similarly situated, alleging a violation of their civil rights in that the defendants failed to provide adequate medical treatment to them during the period of their incarceration in the facility. Plaintiffs pleaded their causes of action under Title 42 Sec. 1983 of the United States Code, the U.S. Constitution and the New York State Constitution. The named defendant DiMarisco, the official physician of the Monroe County jail, moved for summary judgment on the ground that the plaintiffs failed to file a notice of claim required under Sec. 50(e) of the General Municipal Law. Special Term granted summary judgment dismissing the claim against defendant DiMarisco stating that, inasmuch as the action was a medical malpractice action under the guise of a 1983 action, the failure to file a notice of claim was a fatal defect in the complaint against the named defendant Di-Marisco.

The Fourth Department held, however, that since the relief sought was primarily equitable, affirmative and injunctive in character and the monetary relief sought incidental to the equitable relief, the notice of claim provision of the General Municipal Law did not apply. It is to be noted that although the *Cooper* court held the Notice of Claim requirement inapplicable to a 1983 action, nevertheless the door was, as it were, left open where solely monetary damages might be sought under the rubric of a Sec. 1983 action. Nevertheless the Third Department as recently as 1988 in *Zarat v. Town of Stockport,* 142 A.D.2d 1, 534 N.Y.S.2d 777 (3rd Dept. 1988), held the notice of claim requirement inapplicable to an action commenced under Title 42 Sec. 1983 of the United States Code.

In 1983, the Court of Appeals in *Mills v. County of Monroe,* 59 N.Y.2d 307, 451 N.E.2d 456, 464 N.Y.S.2d 709 (1983), reached a different result.

In *Mills,* the plaintiff's employment as a keypunch operator for the County of Monroe was terminated. Plaintiff then commenced a Sec. 1983 action alleging the County had terminated her employment on the basis of her race and national origin, thereby utilizing Sec. 1981 Title 42 of the United States Code. The plaintiff did not file a notice of claim and the County unsuccessfully moved for summary judgment and dismissal of the complaint based on this fact. The Appellate Division reversed and dismissed the complaint. The Court of Appeals affirmed. The plaintiff contended, on appeal, that Sec. 52 of the County Law, the exact analog to Sec. 50(e) of the General Municipal Law, did not apply to her Federal or State civil rights claims. The Court of Appeals, held, however, the state notice of claim requirement was not antithetical to the policy underlying the civil rights law, despite the fact that Federal District Courts of the State of New York have not applied the notice of claim statute in civil rights claims arising under Title 42 Sec. 1981.

The court distinguished, however, the situation where a civil rights action is brought to vindicate the public interest from where it is brought to vindicate a private right. In the former case, the court held, the notice of claim requirement is inapplicable. Thus, the court concluded that since the plaintiff alleged that the County engaged in unlawfully discriminatory practices against her and alleged her termination as a result of this, seeking money damages for losses of her wages and damages to her reputation, the action was brought to vindicate a private as opposed to a public right to vindicate the rights of others. Under this reasoning the court held the notice of claim requirement applicable and affirmed the Order of the Appellate Division dismissing the complaint on this basis.

The holding of the Court of Appeals in *Mills,* namely, that where a Civil Rights Action has been brought to enforce a private right as opposed to vindicating the public interests, the notice of claim statute is applicable to the action, has been consistently followed by the trial and appellate courts of this state. See for example, *423 South Salina Street Inc. v. City of Syracuse,* 68 N.Y.2d 474, 503

N.E.2d 63, 510 N.Y.S.2d 507 (1986); *Benjamin v. County of Warren,* 128 A.D.2d 973, 513 N.Y.S.2d 288, 290 (3rd Dept. 1987).

Although the rule of law established in *Mills* is binding on 1983 actions commenced in the New York State Court, the District Courts of this state have, for the most part, held the notice of claim requirement inapplicable to action commenced against municipalities or their subdivisions in the federal District Courts of this state pursuant to Title 42 Sec. 1983 of the United States Code.

Glover v. City of New York, 401 F. Supp. 632 (E.D.N.Y. 1975), is a good example. In *Glover,* a 1983 action was brought by the mother as administratrix, and stepfather against the City of New York and two former police officers for the fatal shooting of their ten-year-old son, The defendant officers moved to dismiss for failure to commence the action within one year and 90 days. The court held most specifically that "it is well settled that the notice of claim requirement is inapplicable to 1983 actions." *Glover v. City of New York, supra* at 635.

See also *Brandon v. Board of Education of Guilderland Central School District,* 487 F. Supp. 1219 (N.D.N.Y. 1980); *Brown v. United States of America,* U.S. Court of Appeals, District of Columbia Circuit, 1984); *Paschall v. Mayone,* 454 F. Supp. 1289 (S.D.N.Y. 1978); *Davis v. Krauss,* 478 F. Supp. 823 (E.D.N.Y. 1979); *Burroughs v. The Holiday Inn,* 621 F. Supp. 351 (W.D.N.Y. 1985); *Cardo v. Lakeland Central School District of Shrub Oak, N.Y.,* 592 F. Supp. 765 (S.D. N.Y. 1984) where the Southern District held that the Notice of Claim requirement applicable to actions commenced against municipalities or their subdivisions under 42 U.S.C. 1983.

In sum, under *Mills,* if counsel wishes to commence a timely and effectual 1983 action against a municipality in the New York State Courts, he should file a notice of claim within 90 days lest he face dismissal for failure to do so. He should be wise also, given the slight difference of opinion in the District Courts of this state and the total failure of the Circuit Courts of the State to rule upon the issue to do the same in the federal courts of this state, although the weight of opinion would seem to indicate that he will not face dismissal of a 1983 action for failure to do so.

2. Some Points on the Writing of an Appellate Brief

The writing of an effective appellate brief is both an art and a science. It is an art because it calls upon the practitioner to persuade the appellate court through the use of language and creative legal thought. It is a science because the written rhetoric and creativity must be disciplined and informed by the proper rules of law. The composition of a compelling appellate brief is no different from any other form of persuasive expository writing. The difference in the particular subject matter, in this case law, is not to be distinguished from any other form of written work. Whether the subject matter is the John Gotti case, the proper rule of law, or the Persian Gulf War, the rules and standards of good English prose hold true.

What follows here are what this writer feels are some pointers on the composition of a successful appellate brief.

First, the record must be read, reread, and reflected upon. This can be a daunting task. In a civil appeal where the trial has often been lengthy and complicated and there have been various forms of pleading and motion practice, this is no mean task. It cannot, however, be avoided. It is essential that the trial record, pleadings and prior motions be read and thoroughly digested at least twice through. Copious notes should be taken and a detailed summary of the entire record should be made.

Ideas concerning possible trial court error should be noted. This period of reading and reflection allows the mind of the appellate practitioner time to ferment. Notions of error and the possible means of reversing the trial court judgment come to the appellate lawyer as he reads, considers and thinks upon the record before him. Points of reversible error come to the lawyer who troubles to take upon himself this tedious task.

Thus, it is that after the record has been digested and thought upon and the nascent points of the brief been formulated in the mind of the appellate practitioner, that the task of legal research begins.

It is beyond the scope of this article to render advice on the methodology of legal research. Suffice to say, however, that legal research, in the context of writing an appellate brief, has no purpose and no end absent the ideas that can only come to mind after reading and reflecting at length upon the entire record. Second comes the actual composition of the brief. This includes a Table of Contents, the Statement Pursuant to C.P.L.R. 5531, the Questions Presented Pursuant to C.P.L.R. 5528(a), the Statement of Facts Pursuant to C.P.L.R. 5528(a), the Points in the Brief and the Conclusion. It is difficult to tell any appellate practitioner how to write an appellate brief since every person and lawyer thinks differently, writes differently, and will present his case differently. Some general pointers, however, are appropriate and advisable. The appellate writer must remember that he has at his disposal one of the great languages of world culture and civilization. The English language is not solely the language of the *Daily News* and the *West Headnotes*. It is the language of Shakespeare, the Authorized Version of the Bible, Milton, Spenser, Keats, Shelly, Dickens, Thackeray and Donne. The English speaker has at his command the heritage of one of the great literatures of world civilization with a vocabulary of over a million words deriving from a rich admixture of many languages, including German, French, Latin, and Greek. Thus, a brief, it cannot be overemphasized must, most important of all, be in good, clear, expository, declarative English prose. The brief writer, if he is to be good, must be well read. He must come to his task with a love of the English language and its possibilities. If the sole diet of the brief writer has heretofore solely been the daily newspaper, he will not produce a convincing specimen of English prose.

Thus, the brief writer must set about to write a work of art and beauty. He must seek to persuade by all the resources of the language at his command. He must be terse and he must be sharp. His writing should fall upon the appellate court like waves upon the rocky shore, crashing, compelling, and convincing. There is, in the opinion of this writer no more effective model of English style than the Authorized Version of the Bible. Here the reader is convinced not by any prolixity or complications of language, but by simple declarative sentences of ultimate beauty. Excessive complications of points and paragraphs and even sentences are to be avoided. Let us remember that the Twenty-Third Psalm, as a piece of English poetry, has stirred more hearts and minds than the lengthiest work of history or biography or law to be found in any library.

In conclusion, the "brief" advice given amounts to no more than this point: that the thoughtful reflection on the record combined with good writing in a great language are the essential elements in the creation of a good appellate brief addressed to any appellate court.

3. Appealing the Mistrial Order

The Background

The motion for a mistrial whereby, on the application of a party to the litigation, a trial may be aborted and a new trial granted, or the original trial itself merely continued or adjourned to proceed at a later date before the self-same jury, is governed by C.P.L.R. Section 4402. This section states that

> at any time during the trial, the court the motion, of any party, may order a continuance or a new trial in the interest of justice on such terms as may be just.

The thrust of the mistrial procedure and motion is to remedy certain prejudicial effects that may occur in the course of a trial either by the granting, as was stated, of a new trial outright or an adjournment. The determination of whether or not to grant or declare a mistrial is within the discretion of the trial court. *Dunbar v. Ingraham*, 275 A.D. 898, 89 N.Y.S.2d 841 (4th Dept. 1949); *Sincock v. Boehme*, 9 A.D.2d 579, 189 N.Y.S.2d 571 (3rd Dept. 1959); *Concord Oil Corp. v. York Heat Service, Inc.*, 262 A.D. 758, 27 N.Y.S.2d 738 (2nd Dept. 1941); *Ismail v. City of New York*, 18 Misc.2d 818, 181 N.Y.S.2d 848 (Supreme Court, Kings County, 1959); *Landberg v. Fowler*, 278 A.D. 661, 102 N.Y.S.2d 548 (2nd Dept. 1951); *Dombrowski v. Somers*, 51 A.D.2d 636, 378 N.Y.S.2d

825 (3rd Dept. 1976); rev'd on other gds., 41 N.Y.2d 858, 393 N.Y.S.2d 706 (1977)].

The discretion of the trial court, however, to grant or not grant a mistrial, though wide, is not unlimited. *Murphy v. City of New York*, 273 App. Div. 492, 78 N.Y.S. 2d 191 (1st Dept. 1948), is illustrative of the limits of the trial court's discretion under C.P.L.R. Section 4402. *Murphy* was a personal injury action for injuries sustained by the plaintiff, while a passenger in an automobile, when involved in a collision with a streetcar. The trial began, and two physicians were slated to give testimony on the nature and extent of the plaintiff's injuries, respectively, at 1:00 p.m. and 2:00 p.m. on December 10, 1947. The plaintiff rested at noon that day, subject to the calling of these physicians, and the court stated that if these doctors did not appear at the time the defendant's case was concluded, it would continue without the benefit of their testimony. When the defendant's evidence was completed and the doctors did not arrive, the plaintiff requested a 25 minute adjournment to await the arrival of the first two physicians. The court denied this application and ordered counsel to sum up without the benefit of medical testimony. The plaintiff then requested a mistrial which the court refused to grant. The plaintiff elected to discontinue his action; however, at a later date he made application to withdraw his motion to discontinue and to declare a mistrial. The lower court denied the motion for a mistrial. The First Department noted initially, that although the trial court has wide discretion with respect to an application for a mistrial, that discretion is not unlimited and the facts of a particular case may be such that a refusal to declare a mistrial would constitute reversible error and may be corrected upon appeal. The Appellate Court held that the court below should have allowed the postponement requested by the plaintiff to await the arrival of the two important witnesses and the plaintiff's motion for a mistrial should have been granted.

Thus, the discretion of the trial court to grant or not grant a mistrial, though wide, is not without bounds and fences. Its limits are defined by the grounds for the application, and whether those grounds are legally valid under the case law construing C.P.L.R. Section 4402.

Under the case law interpreting C.P.L.R. Section 4402, the mistrial provision, the grounds for a mistrial are discrete but varied. Thus, a mistrial motion will be granted where the plaintiff attempts to show that the defendant is covered by insurance. [*Luther v. Jacobs*, 282 A.D. 809, 122 N.Y.S.2d 518 (3rd Dept. 1953); *Ismail v. City of New York, supra*; *Rendo v. Shermerhorn*, 24 A.D.2d 773, 263 N.Y.S.2d 743 (3rd Dept. 1965)].

A mistrial may also be granted by reason of the misconduct of counsel, of a juror, or even of the judge himself. [*Kopp v. Hoffman*, 280 A.D. 954, 160 N.Y.S.2d 194 (2nd Dept. 1952); *Campbell v. Towber*, 46 Misc.2d 891, 261 N.Y.S.2d 458 (Supreme Court, Kings County, 1965); *Habenicht v. R. K. O. Theaters, Inc.*, 23 A.D.2d 378, 260 N.Y.S.2d 890 (1st Dept. 1965)]. A mistrial may also be granted where an attorney is taken ill and can no longer proceed, or where a witness falls ill, or is late, and, arriving at the time of summation, is not permitted to testify. *Flanzer v. Annette Manor Realty Corp.*, 228 A.D. 606, 238 N.Y.S. 300 (2nd Dept. 1929); *Castro v. Beekman Downtown Hospital,* 43 A.D.2d 537, 349 N.Y.S.2d 683 (1st Dept. 1973); see also Weinstein-Korn-Miller, N.Y. Civ. Prac., Sections 4402.02, 4402.03; Siegel, N.Y. Prac. Section 403]. Finally, as an epilogue or addendum to this introductory overview of the mistrial scheme of the C.P.L.R., the statutory section, C.P.L.R. Section 4402, states and mandates that the court may grant a mistrial only on application of a party. The statutory mistrial scheme of C.P.L.R. 4402, apparently, does not state, imply, or envision, that the court, sua sponte, may take the burden of declaring a mistrial without the benefit of either party's formal application.

It should be noted, however, that there have been instances in which the lower courts, sua sponte, have, in fact declared a mistrial, without the application of a party to the litigation. An example is *Jaworski v. New Cassel Fuel Corp.,* [251 N.Y.S. 2d 929 (2nd Dept. 1964)]. *Jaworski* was an action for personal injury sustained by the plaintiff. The defendant appealed from the order of a trial court wherein the court, on its own motion, after the opening of the case to the jury, declared a mistrial. The Second Department affirmed the order of the lower court and granted other related relief, without opinion. Thus, in *Jaworski*, the Second Department, it would appear, dealt with a sua sponte declaration of a mistrial by the court without application of the parties. The Second Department, however, in its opinion in *Jaworski*, made no mention of the action of the trial court in this respect and merely affirmed without opinion. Hence, *Jaworski*, does not effectively represent the Second Department's seal of approval on this, at least unorthodox and in fact under the statute erroneous, method of declaring a mistrial. Indeed, *Jaworski* must be regarded as, if not an eccentric holding, then, at least, a sport in the case law construing C.P.L.R. Section 4402, and to be, therefore, totally disregarded as lacking true authority, the great weight of which, in this State, supports the statutory scheme of C.P.L.R. Section 4402 which mandates that for a trial court to declare a mistrial, there must be an application on the part of a party.

The Issue

In light of the frequency and importance of the mistrial motion, the result of which, in the course of an ongoing trial, can be not merely an adjournment but a cancellation of the trial outright, the trial to begin, as it were, de novo with a new jury and possibly a new judge, and with both plaintiff and defendant having obtained a greater or lesser insight, as the case may be, into the case of one or the other, the question arises whether, in New York Practice, the granting of an order of mistrial may be appealed at that point in the litigation, whether as of right or by motion or leave of the Trial or Appellate Court. The question is seminal since, given the radical character of the mistrial remedy, it would seem appropriate that, at the stage of its initial granting, immediate appellate review be allowed and encouraged, rather than, in the manner of a ruling in the course of trial, the possible erroneous and prejudicial character of the mistrial order, await resolution and determination in appellate review of the final judgment in the case, where all possible prejudicial error would be considered.

The Current Law

The current law, is, with a limited exception to be considered later in this article, that the order granting a mistrial is not appealable. The leading case in *Graney Development Corp. v. Taksen,* [66 A.D.2d 1008, 411 N.Y.S.2d 757 (4th Dept. 1978). In *Graney* the plaintiff sought to review on appeal certain rulings of the trial court which were embodied, in part, in an order entered on plaintiffs' motion granting a mistrial pursuant to Section 4402 of the C.P.L.R. The court stated, the following in terse form, assuming and even presuming the holy and hallowed and hoary rule, that

> an order granting a mistrial motion and rulings made by the court during trial are not appealable. " *Graney Development Corp. v. Taksen, supra* at 757.

Thus, in *Graney,* the court held that even though the order granting a mistrial has been signed and entered and does not exist merely in the oral form of its occurrence at trial, it is, notwithstanding, not appealable since, analogizing the order to a ruling at trial, on that ground and basis it is not appealable.[1]

It is clear that the weight of authority in this State prohibits an interlocutory appeal from the order granting a mistrial. In the midst of this quandary, however, certain appellate departments at least suggest an alternative solution. The Fourth Department, in its wisdom, has suggested that although an appeal does not lie directly from an order granting a mistrial, the proper procedure to defeat such an order of mistrial is to move to vacate the order: [*Matter of Taylor,* 271 App. Div. 947, 67 N.Y.S.2d 823 (4th Dept. 1947)]. The First Department of this State also, in *Fine v. Cummins, supra,* states that although there is no appeal, once again, from an order of mistrial, whether embodied in a written order or not, and such appeal should be dismissed, nevertheless, the plaintiff should be given leave to move to vacate the mistrial order so as to be relieved from any liability from costs granted upon the mistrial. *Fine v. Cummins, supra* at 572.

The Conclusion

Under the present status of the law no interlocutory appeal lies from the order of mistrial. There is a suggestion, however, by the First and Fourth Departments that the proper procedure in the manner of seeking relief from a default judgment is to move to vacate, or be relieved of, the order of mistrial. Neither the First nor the Fourth Department states whether an appeal in fact lies from a denial of this motion to vacate. There would be, however, no reason why such appeal could not lie and be prosecuted and perfected from such a denial of a motion to vacate the mistrial order, Since the similar denial of a motion to vacate a judgment of default is not only most often appealed, but, indeed, is the only method wherein a judgment of default may be appealed since, as has been stated so often, no appeal as of right lies from a judgment of default. The default judgment must first be vacated and, if such motion is denied, then appealed.

Hence, the reasonable implication of the holdings of the Fourth and First Departments in *Taylor* and *Fine* is that the proper procedure to attack a mistrial order is not an interlocutory appeal as of right, which is prohibited, but a motion to vacate the order, and then, if this is denied, appealing the denial of the motion. There would seem to be no other way to immediate appellate review of the mistrial order since, in the absence of the motion to vacate the mistrial order and its granting or denial, the appellant must await appellate review of the final judgment which may take up to a year or more. By means of a motion to vacate the mistrial order and an appeal, if it so happens, of the denial of the motion, speedy appellate review is afforded the party against whom the mistrial order has been granted, which is surely desirable and appropriate.

In sum, if one wishes to obtain a speedy trial and/or appellate review of the mistrial order, the safest and surest method to proceed is to move to vacate the order and then, if this is denied, to appeal the order of denial since under the present law the Appellate Courts of this State unanimously bar interlocutory appeal from the mistrial order as such.

The Epilogue

The order of mistrial, in its starkest form, aborts and ends an ongoing trial. The motion may be granted at any stage of the trial whether at the point of opening statements, in the midst of the plaintiff's or defendant's case, or at the close of trial. Once granted, either or both parties to the litigation have gained insights and advantages into their opponent's case. Hence, the granting of the motion can effectively wreak great prejudice upon the party against whom it is ordered. In a sense, the order granting mistrial circumvents or even nullifies the rules of res judicata and collateral estoppel since, in essence, the issues that have already been litigated, must be and will be litigated again. It is fair, just, and appropriate, in the view of this writer, that appeal be permitted directly from the order of mistrial. The granting of such an order is nothing less than volcanic and the prejudice palpable. To say that the granting of the order of mistrial in the midst of a trial, as the Appellate Courts of this State have said, is nothing more than a ruling, and so not appealable, is technically true. Surely, however, a ruling barring the admission of testimonial or demonstrative evidence must be distinguished, for interlocutory appellate purposes, from an order aborting a trial and compelling its beginning anew.

Perhaps the solution and answer to the law of this State that no direct appeal lies from the order of mistrial might be found in a requirement that if the application for a mistrial is made on notice and papers, the order, then, as granted, may be appealed. By this method, the order will be removed from the rubric and denomination of a ruling in the course of trial and transferred to the more legitimate nomenclature of an appeal from an order emanating from a motion on notice, most varieties and kinds of which are, in this State, allowed appellate review. C.P.L.R. Section 5701(a)(2). Indeed the Third Department in *Richardson v. Weingatz,* [33 A.D.2d 947 (3rd Dept. 1970)] stated, in dicta, that although the denials of the appellant's oral motions to dismiss were not appealable since they were rulings in the course of trial, the result might have been otherwise if the motions had been made upon notice. *Richardson v. Weingatz, supra* at 947. By way of analogy to the holding in *Richardson,* and extension of that holding, it is suggested that where the order of mistrial emanates from a motion on notice, it could well be appealable under C.P.L.R. Section 5701.

In conclusion, if the practitioner in this State wishes appellate review of an order of mistrial which may be entered against him, he should first insist that the order be made upon notice, and then, if the motion is granted, appeal from that order or, in the alternative, if the mistrial order does not stem from a motion on notice, he should have the oral order embodied in a signed order and move to vacate the order; if his motion to vacate the order of mistrial is denied, appeal would most assuredly lie from the intermediate order. By the above mentioned procedures, the prohibition of direct appeal from the order of mistrial may be defeated and the victim of the mistrial order may gain speedy and immediate appellate review of the order of mistrial against him.

4. Confirming the Pleadings to the Proof

The determination of whether to grant a motion to conform the pleadings to the proof pursuant to C.P.L.R. section 3025(c)[1] is within the discretion of the trial court.[2] In this article, the criteria used by the court in this regard will be discussed and the bases under which a motion pursuant to this section must be granted will be analyzed.

The Criteria for the Motion

As noted above, the determination of a motion to conform the pleadings to the proof pursuant to section 3025(c) of the C.P.L.R. is within the discretion of the trial court. A motion pursuant to that section may be granted to amend the plaintiff's complaint to reflect a new theory of recovery or to substitute a new cause of action which was proven at trial. The motion may be granted by the trial court either during or after trial or even after judgment. Thus, in *Diemer v. Diemer,*[3] a husband's separation complaint had pleaded cruel and inhuman treatment as its ground. The Court of Appeals granted the separation on the ground of abandonment, stating that the pleadings and testimony of the parties had established that the wife's refusal to have sexual relations constituted abandonment as a matter of law and supported the husband's cause of action for separation, notwithstanding that the specific ground of abandonment had not been pleaded in the complaint.[4]

The motion may also be granted under section 3025(c) to add an affirmative defense to the defendant's answer.[5] In *Murray v. City of New York,*[6] decedent's family brought a wrongful death action against decedent's employer, the City of New York. The municipal defendant failed to plead the Worker's Compensation Exclusivity defense in its answer. After plaintiff rested at trial, defendant formally moved to interpose this defense. The motion was granted and upheld on appeal on the ground that decedent's employment with the city was known to all parties throughout the proceedings and, thus, the raising of the defense resulted in no prejudice or surprise to the adverse party.[7]

The trial court's discretion to permit amendment of the pleadings to conform to the proof as adduced at trial is circumscribed by whether the adverse party will be surprised by the motion and prejudiced by its granting.[8] The issue, then, becomes: Under what criteria must the motion be granted?

A Hypothetical Case

Assume the following facts: Plaintiff, P, detects a lump in her right breast. She consults a physician who, in the course of a manual examination, fails to detect a lump and diagnoses P's problem as muscle tension. P conducts manual self-examinations of her breasts on a weekly basis for six months, notes the continued existence and growth of the lump in her right breast and finally goes to another doctor, who x-rays her chest and performs a biopsy, revealing a malignant tumor in her right breast. P subsequently undergoes a mastectomy. One year late, P's localized cancer is found to have metastasized.

P sues the physician, D, who originally examined her and failed to detect the cancer in her right breast, claiming that the doctor's failure to detect the cancer at the time of the initial examination led to the growth and spread of the cancer and her resulting shortened life span. In his answer to P's complaint, D fails to plead the affirmative defense of P's culpable conduct. At the conclusion of P's prima facie case, D applies to the court to amend his answer under C.P.L.R. section 3025(c) to include the defense of P's culpable conduct, thereby conforming his pleadings to the proof presented at trial.

The rationale for D's motion is that there would be no surprise or prejudice suffered by P should the motion be granted. P was aware of the technique and method of manual breast examination prior to the performance of his tests, as P testified to both during the EBT and at trial. Further, D would contend that from the time P was examined by him to the time of her visit to the physician who discovered the malignancy in her breast, P continued to note the size, location and growth of the lump and, in spite of this, failed to seek any form of medical assistance. In short, although aware of her dangerous and deteriorating condition, P failed to timely seek out appropriate medical help to avert the pain and suffering, as well as her shortened life span, that ultimately followed.

It is the view of this writer that, based upon P's testimony both before and at trial, D's motion must be granted.

The First Ground

First, the evidence of the matter which constitutes the basis of the application to conform the pleadings to the proof was unobjected to at trial.

In *DiRosse v. Wein*,[9] a physician was sued for personal injuries sustained by the patient, the resulting medical expenses and the loss of services by her husband. The defendant appealed from a judgment of the trial court upon a jury verdict. The Appellate Division, Second Department, affirmed, holding that the defendant's assertion, that the evidence of the failure to disclose the dangers in the treatment, was not within the allegations of the pleadings and had no force since there was no objection to the evidence on that ground at trial.[10] Therefore, the pleadings could be amended to conform to the proof.[11]

The Second Ground

The second basis which compels the granting of the motion to conform in our case is that the plaintiff testified to the same culpable conduct both at the examination before trial and at trial. Thus, the party opposing the motion to conform had notice, at the EBT, of the new claim or additional affirmative defense sought to be added and cannot now claim surprise or prejudice. In *Di Benedetto v. Lasker-Goldman Corp.*,[12] plaintiff filed a negligence action to recover damages for personal injuries. Following a ruling during trial dismissing the complaint, plaintiff appealed. The Appellate Division, Second Department, reversed on the law and in the interests of justice, granted a new trial and permitted the plaintiff to serve an amended complaint and bill of particulars as to the issue of liability. The court noted that the plaintiff's trial testimony concerning the accident was at variance with the allegations contained in his complaint and bill of particulars. In addition, the court held, respondent had notice of the new claims sought to be added because of plaintiff's testimony at the EBT. It was determined, therefore, that the trial court's denial of the plaintiff's application to amend his pleadings a second time and its subsequent dismissal of the complaint was in error. The court ruled

> the C.P.L.R. mandates liberality in the construction and amendment of pleadings (C.P.L.R. 3025, 3026). As respondents were apprised of the theory upon which plaintiff was proceeding and claimed no surprise, plaintiff should have been permitted to amend his pleadings to conform to the proof.

Under our facts, P created, injected and indeed admitted her partial culpability. It follows, then, that when D seeks to amend his answer to reflect this fact, P cannot raise the hue and cry of surprise and prejudice to defeat this motion.[13]

The Third Ground

Finally, the fact that all issues had been fully litigated without objection by both parties leads to the last ground: consent. In *Garone v. Robberts Trade School,*[14] plaintiff brought an action against a school in which an accident had occurred resulting in the loss of his eye. Among the named defendants to the action was the physician who treated plaintiff. The Supreme Court dismissed the patient's complaint. The Appellate Division, First Department, reversed, holding that a factual issue was presented as to whether the physician was responsible for his failure to obtain informed consent for the operation. The court noted that the fact that the pleadings did not state the cause of action of informed consent did not preclude consideration of the issue by the court since the action based on lack of informed consent had been litigated The pleadings were, therefore, deemed to be conformed to the proof.[15]

P's statements, unobjected to trial testimony and consent are three factors which usually favor a court's granting of a party's motion to conform the pleadings to the proof.

Conclusion

If this article has a final word for the practitioner, it is this: If you do not wish a motion to conform to be granted pursuant to C.P.L.R. section 3025(c), do not permit the new matter to be introduced at an examination before trial. In the event of a second attempt to do the same at trial, the testimony must be objected to, lest defeat be snatched from the jaws of victory.

5. Rule for Lex Loci Has Received New Impetus in Conflicts Cases

For some time now, courts in New York faced with multi-state tort cases involving a conflict of laws have applied the law of the jurisdiction with the most significant contacts. This approach, termed "interest analysis" or "center of gravity," was first set forth by the Court of Appeals in *Babcock v. Jackson,* 12 N.Y.2d 473, 240 N.Y.S.2d 743 (1963). The court rejected the older rule of *lex loci,* under which the law of the place of the tort or accident governs the litigation, and replaced it with the new rule of "interest analysis." There has been, however, a recent trend in which the rule of *lex loci* has received a new impetus.

The first hint of this trend appeared in *Neumeier v. Kuehner,* 31 N.Y.2d 121, 335 N.Y.S.2d 64 (1972), in which Judge Breitel noted in his concurring opinion that *lex loci* is the normal rule of conflicts in multi-state tort cases, to be rejected only when the situs of the accident is the least of several factors or influences to which the accident may be attributed.

Subsequently, in *Rakaric v. Croatian Cultural Club*, 76 A.D.2d 619, 430 N.Y.S.2d 829 (2nd Dept. 1980), the Appellate Division held that *lex loci* is to be displaced only upon a showing of special or extraordinary circumstances.

It can now be said that the rule of *lex loci* will govern in the absence of special circumstances. As a corollary, the law of the state in which a plaintiff accepts workmen's compensation benefits will govern and determine the rights of the parties when a party brings a plenary action in a state other than where the workmen's compensation benefits were accepted.

The leading case is *In Re O'Connor's Estate*, 21 A.D.2d 333, N.Y.S.2d., (2d Dept. 1964). In *O'Connor*, the petitioner's husband died in a plane crash in Oklahoma during the course of his employment with a New York corporation. Pursuant to the terms of an insurance policy issued to the employer, the carrier commenced the payment of workmen's compensation benefits to the surviving widow and son which ultimately totaled over $12,000.

Thereafter, the petitioner widow commenced a third party action in Oklahoma against the United States Government which resulted in a compromise settlement of $90,000. The carrier asserted a lien against this fund under New York law.

Under the law of Oklahoma, no such right of subrogation exists so the Surrogate Court applied the Oklahoma law and disallowed the lien.

The court addressed the question of whether the carrier was entitled to reimbursement out of the proceeds of the third-party action for the compensation payments it made to the petitioner under New York law. The court held, in spite of *Babcock*, that since the accident occurred in Oklahoma and the action was commenced and settled there, that state's tort law determined the rights of the parties in the third party action. While the death statutes and workmen's compensation benefits of Oklahoma were intended to complement each other, petitioner did not invoke that state's compensation law, but chose to proceed under the Workmen's Compensation Law of New York. The rights of parties are governed by the law under which workmen's compensation benefits are accepted. Thus the petitioner, by invoking the provisions of the New York statute and accepting and retaining benefits under it, made the New York law applicable. The liability of the carrier was established under such law, and its right to subrogation arose under it. Hence, the carrier was entitled to a lien to the extent of the obligations paid or incurred by it.

Foti v. Stone & Webster, Inc. (Sup. Ct. Queens Co., 3/28/80) closely followed and applied the holding in *O'Connor*. In *Foti* the plaintiff, a New York resident and a member of a New York union, was employed by a subcontractor of the defendant in connection with construction work in Virginia. Defendant had contracted with a Virginia corporation to furnish materials and erect a scaffold in connection with this work and had hired the plaintiff in New York from the union for that purpose. The plaintiff was injured at the job site, returned to New York and received workmen's compensation benefits under the Virginia Workmen's Compensation Law during the period of his disability. He instituted a third-party suit against the defendant general contractor, which was permitted under Section 29(1) of the New York Workers' Compensation Law, but barred under the Virginia Workers' Compensation Law.

The court held that the Virginia law should apply. The court concluded that under the "most significant contacts test" enunciated by the Court of Appeals in *Babcock*, Virginia had the most contacts: the plaintiff was hired in Virginia; was employed in Virginia by a Virginia corporation; worked in Virginia five days a week, returning home to New York only on the weekends; sought and obtained workmen's compensation benefits under the Workmen's Compensation Act of the State of Virginia; and the defendant expected that its operations would be governed by Virginia's Workmen's Compensation Law because the insurance was obtained from Virginia. The fact that the plaintiff was hired through a union local in New York was not considered to be important.

The court also noted that Virginia would have the primary public interest in industrial accidents happening within the state. In addition, the plaintiff consciously elected and freely chose with advice of counsel to seek Virginia's workmen's compensation benefits. Hence, in so choosing, the plaintiff was deemed to have acquiesced in the totality of the Workmen's Compensation Act of the State of Virginia. The rule which evolved in *O'Connor* and *Foti* is a new application of *lex loci*. Consequently, once one accepts a state's workmen's compensation benefits, he is bound by the law of that state.

The rule in *O'Connor* and *Foti* might be contrary to *lex loci* since, in both these cases, the law of the situs state was not the law of the state which was applied—the law of the state where the worker's compensation benefits were accepted. Furthermore, one might conclude that the rule of the *lex loci* is inapplicable where the law of worker's compensation is involved since the state where worker's compensation benefits are accepted may or may not be the state of the situs of the tort. However, worker's compensation is sui generis. The state where worker's compensation benefits are accepted is the "situs" for the purpose of conflict of law determinations and is the preeminent and paramount contact with the state. Acceptance of benefits is equivalent of a situs since it establishes that presence in the state which outweighs and overshadows all others. In conclusion, then, *lex loci* and the rule of acceptance of benefits are not contrary, but rather parallel each other.

This article previously appeared in an edition of The Nassau Lawyer, a publication of the Nassau County Bar Association, and is being reprinted here with the permission of The Nassau County Bar Association.

6. A Note on the Note of Issue

The Background

It is the law of this state, as mandated in the Rules of the Appellate Division, Second Department, that when the Note of Issue and Statement of Readiness are filed by the plaintiff with the court and served on opposing counsel, there must be an allegation, in the Statement of Readiness, that all discovery proceedings have been completed.[1]

When, in fact, all discovery has not been completed, the proper remedy for the party seeking further discovery, whether plaintiff or defendant, is to move within twenty (20) days of service of the Statement of Readiness to strike the action from the Trial Calendar.[2]

The legal consequence of the failure to move to strike the Note of Issue prematurely filed or, in the alternative, withdraw if within twenty (20) days of service of the Note of Issue upon the defendant, is a waiver, by all parties, of further pre-trial disclosure.

Thus, in *Warren v. Vick Chem. Co.,* 37 A.D.2d 913, 325 N.Y.S.2d 495 (4th Dept. 1971), the Appellate Division, Fourth Department, held that

> since neither party moved within the 20 day period following the filing of the Note of Issue and Statement of Readiness, there is a waiver of their rights to conduct any further pretrial procedures.

Thus, when neither the plaintiff nor the defendant moves to strike the note of issue for failure to complete discovery, or the plaintiff, sua sponte, fails to withdraw the Note, the plaintiff is deemed, under the law, to have waived any further examination of the defendant, and the defendant is held to have waived any further examination of the plaintiff.

There is a rub, however, to this rule of waiver. The plaintiff or defendant may move, under certain conditions, for a further examination. Thus, although it is true that it is the law that the failure of either party to move to strike the Note of Issue within twenty (20) days of its filing constitutes a waiver of further pre-trial discovery, as a corollary of this rule, it is also the law that further pre-trial discovery may be obtained after the Note of Issue has been filed and after the mandatory 20-day period within which to strike the Note of Issue has passed, upon a convincing and specific showing of unusual, special, unanticipated, or unexpected circumstances that may be said to necessitate further disclosure.

In *Kirk v. Blum,* 79 A.D.2d 700, 434 N.Y.S.2d 269 (2nd Dept. 1980), the Second Department states this rule of "special circumstances" well. In *Kirk*, the plaintiff-appellant, in a negligence action for personal injuries, appealed from an order of the Supreme Court of the County of Nassau, which, upon defendants' motion for discovery and plaintiff's cross motion for a protective order, directed the plaintiff to appear for an examination before trial and to provide certain medical authorizations and personal or income tax records. This Appellate Divi-

sion reversed, stating that the record failed to indicate any unusual or unanticipated circumstances that would permit the conducting of further discovery 9
months after the case had been placed on the trial calendar. See also for this rule,
Niagara Falls Etc. v. Pomeroy Real Estate, 74 A.D. 2d 734, 425 N.Y.S.2d 701
(4th Dept. 1980); *Doll v. Kleinklaus,* 66 A.D.2d 1003, 411 N.Y.S.2d 761 (4th
Dept. 1978); *Schuster v. Constantine,* 56 A.D.2d 737, 392 N.Y.S.2d 745 (4th
Dept. 1977); *Alter v. O'Hare,* 54 A.D.2d 888, 388 N.Y.S.2d 14 (2nd Dept.
1976); *Burnett Process, Inc. v. Richlar Industries, supra*; *Marchitelli v. Greco
Sales Service, Inc., supra*; *Wayne E. Edwards Corp. v. Romas, supra*; *Giddens v.
Moultrie,* 66 A.D.2d 993, 411 N.Y.S.2d 774 (4th Dept. 1978).

This, to coin a phrase, rule of "special circumstances" is embodied in Rule
675.7 of the Rules of the Appellate Division, Second Department. This rule
states that after an action has been placed on the Trial Calendar

> no pre-trial examination or other preliminary proceedings may be had unless
> unusual and unanticipated conditions subsequently develop which make it nec-
> essary that further pre-trial examinations or further preliminary proceedings be
> had, and if without them the moving party would be unduly prejudiced. In such
> case, the court may make an order granting permission to conduct such exami-
> nation or to take such proceedings and prescribing the time therefor. Such an
> order may be made only upon motion showing in detail by affidavit the facts
> claimed to entitle the moving party to relief under this section.

What constitutes those unusual, or special circumstances whereby, after the
Note of Issue has been filed and the 20 day period within which to strike the
Note of Issue for failure to complete pre-trial discovery has passed, further discovery may be had by order of the Court, is, for the most part, left to the discretion of the trial court.

Hence for example, in *Schneph v. New York Times Co.,* 22 A.D.2d 641, 252
N.Y.S.2d 934 (1st Dept. 1964), the Appellate Division, First Department, held
that the fact that the Statement of Readiness had been filed did not deprive the
plaintiff of the right to examine the defendant with respect to a new third affirmative defense, where the issue of malice on which further examination was
sought, though present in the case before insertion of the new third defense, was
not present in the formal manner raised by the new third defense, and the new
third defense shifted the burden of proof.

Similarly in *Szarf v. Blumenfeld,* 5 A.D.2d 887, 172 N.Y.S.2d 984 (2d Dept.
1958), the Second Department held that the proposed amendment of the answer
to include foreign statutes as part of the defendant's defense was such an unanticipated circumstance as to permit the plaintiff, despite having filed the Statement of Readiness, to take such procedural steps before trial as he would deem
advisable.

On the other hand, in *Riggle v. Buffalo General Hospital,* 52 A.D.2d 751,
382 N.Y.S.2d 204 (4th Dept. 1976), the Fourth Department held the fact that the
plaintiff sought to depose its primary witness, who was out of state, the importance of whose testimony was long known, and who was unable to participate in

the trial, did not constitute "those special circumstances" as set forth in the Rule.[4] Although the determination whether the requisite special or exceptional circumstances are present appears to vary from case to case, it is clear from a cursory review of the case law construing this rule, that there must be a proper and compelling showing that new matter has somehow, of late, been thrust into the litigation, requiring a fleshing out, as it were, by the devices of discovery, notwithstanding that the Note of Issue has long since been filed and the 20 day statutory period has passed. The new matter may be a new defense *(Schneph)* or foreign statutes *(Szarf)*.

It is not enough that the defendant has changed his attorney *(Baranyk)* or a party has requested a long adjournment on the eve of trial *(Wozznicki)*. There must, so to speak, be a showing of "newness" in the litigation, requiring the investigative devices of pre-trial discovery.

The Problem

Let us assume the plaintiff has filed the Note of Issue and Statement of Readiness, indicating thereon that all discovery has been completed. In fact, the plaintiff has not examined the defendant, fails to strike or withdraw the Note of Issue within 20 days of its filing and makes no motion to compel examination of the defendant, since the plaintiff can show to the court no unusual or exceptional circumstances to justify examination of the defendant, which he has quite simply overlooked, in perfect "law office failure" fashion. The plaintiff, however, believes that in this litigation he has another option and he unilaterally removes or marks the case off the calendar and proceeds to notice the defendant for examination and indeed does so.

The question arises and, in the view of this writer, it is a procedural issue of great import to the bar and bench of this state, whether, when the Note of Issue has been filed with the allegation thereon that all discovery has been completed, when the 20 days within which to strike the Note of Issue has passed and when no motion has been made to compel further discovery, the plaintiff may by simply removing the case from the calendar, obtain the unlimited discovery he would otherwise be barred from.

The Current Law

The present law would appear to permit the plaintiff to employ the device of marking a case off the calendar to obtain the further discovery he would otherwise under the law be denied but for a motion to strike the Note of Issue within 20 days of its filing, or a compelling showing of "special circumstances.

The leading case is *Pezzella v. Catholic Medical Center of Brooklyn and Queens, Inc.,* 50 A.D.2d 867, 377 N.Y.S.2d 144 (2d Dept. 1975).

In *Pezzella* the defendant Medical Center, in a malpractice action, appealed from an order of the Supreme Court granting the plaintiff leave to conduct examinations before trial, although the Statement of Readiness had been filed. The Court held that

> in this malpractice action involving serious and permanent physical injuries and large special damages, plaintiffs shall not be deprived of a meaningful day in court because of the dereliction of their counsel. . . . Furthermore, since the action has been marked off the trial calendar and a third party claim has since been asserted by appellant, there will be no trial delay of the kind sought to be avoided by Section 675.1 and 675.6 of the Rules of this Court. *Pezzella v. Catholic Medical Center of Brooklyn and Queens, supra,* at 145.

The holding of *Pezzella* is clear: where a matter is unilaterally and voluntarily marked off the trial calendar and involves serious injuries and substantial special damages, the plaintiff will be granted leave to conduct examinations before trial, despite the dereliction of his counsel.

Grigorian v. Poluszek, 22 A.D.2d 704, 253 N.Y.S.2d 804 (2d Dept. 1964), is also relevant on this issue. In *Grigorian,* an action for breach of warranty, the plaintiff moved to direct the defendant-Poluszek to make disclosure or, in the alternative, to strike his answer for failure to appear for a pre-trial examination. The trial court denied the motion and the plaintiff appealed. The Appellate Division reversed directing the defendant to appear for examination. The court noted initially that the basis for the trial court's order denying the plaintiff's motion to compel disclosure by the defendant was that the plaintiff's prior attorney had filed a Note of Issue without having sought or conducted a pre-trial examination of the defendant. The court noted, however, that on another defendant's motion, the action had been struck from the trial calendar for non-readiness. The court concluded that

> it follows therefore that the rights of the parties with respect to disclosure procedures have been restored and are now the same as though the abortive, premature note of issue and statement of readiness had never been filed. *Grigorian v. Poluszek, supra,* at 805.

Grigorian, at first glance, is susceptible of one interpretation and follows the holding of *Pezzella*: that where an action is taken off the calendar, the rights of the parties are restored and discovery may proceed anew. *Grigorian,* however, must be distinguished from *Pezzella* since, in *Grigorian,* a co-defendant struck the matter from the calendar while in *Pezzella* the primary and sole defendant unilaterally marked the case off.

Moreover, in *Grigorian,* the court made no mention of the *Pezzella* requirement of a serious injury to the plaintiff and substantial special damages.[5]

The Appellate Division has most recently spoken on this issue in *Colville v. King,* 90 A.D.2d 492, 454 N.Y.S.2d 492, 454 N.Y.S.2d 757 (2d Dept. 1982), and in that case, adheres completely to the *Pezzella* rule. In *Colville,* a negligence action, the plaintiff appealed from an order denying his motion to strike the defendant's answer for his failure to appear for pre-trial examination or, in the alternative, to direct the defendants to appear. The Appellate Division reversed, directing the defendant to appear for pre-trial examinations. The court noted, first, that the complaint and bill of particulars alleged serious and permanent physical injuries and large special damages. The court went on to state that, after the defendants conducted their examination before trial of the plaintiff, the plaintiff's attorney, through claimed "clerical error," filed a note of issue and statement of readiness, although neither of the defendants were produced for oral deposition in response to the plaintiff's demand.

Special Term, then, denied the plaintiff's motion shortly before trial to conduct examinations of the defendant, while retaining the action on the trial calendar, since the plaintiff had had more than adequate time to depose the defendants, had waived his right to such further depositions, and had not shown such unusual and unanticipated conditions as to warrant this deposition. Thereafter, the plaintiff's attorney reluctantly marked this case off the calendar on the ground he was not ready for trial and retired the defendant for an Examination Before Trial, which the defendant refused. The plaintiff then made a motion to strike the answer or compel the examination before trial of the defendants.

The court held, citing *Pezzella* and *Grigorian*, that

> under the circumstances, plaintiff's motion should have been granted, to the extent of directing defendants to appear for pre-trial examinations.

Colville is an echo, if not a facsimile, of *Pezzella*. That is to say, if substantial special damages are alleged and serious injuries in dispute, where a matter has unilaterally been marked off the calendar although a Note of Issue and Statement of Readiness has been filed, discovery may, nevertheless, be had.

Conclusion

The trend and theory of *Pezzella* and *Colville* are clear: if large special damages and serious injuries are in the case, and if a matter has then *sua sponte* by the plaintiff been removed from the calendar, discovery and examinations may proceed, although the Note of Issue has been filed stating that discovery has been completed, there has been no motion to strike the Note within 20 days of its filing, and no special circumstances have been shown to justify further discovery.

Grigorian is a slight variation on the theme of *Pezzella* and *Colville* but the thrust is the same: where the action is off the calendar, albeit stricken by the motion of a co-defendant, the rights of all parties are restored with respect to disclosure procedures.

Roberson, something of a sport, merely states that where there are serious and permanent injuries and no prejudice to the plaintiff, a physical examination of the latter will be permitted, although the Note of Issue has been filed asserting the completion of discovery and no motions to strike the Note, within 20 days of its filing or to compel further discovery, have been made.

Indeed, the *Roberson* court appears to base its decision solely on an interest of justice criterion citing the plaintiff's serious injuries and the lack of prejudice to the plaintiff in granting the motion.

This writer thinks the trend of *Pezzella* and *Colville* a disturbing one since the Second Department seems to hold, in these decisions, that if a party wishes to continue discovery he has failed to properly pursue and has announced for all the world that it is finished, all he need do is unilaterally take the matter off the calendar and the pre-trial phase of the action may proceed de novo, and, as it were, at his pleasure, despite his having failed or been unable to avail himself of the remedies provided by statute and the decisional law.

It is not too much to say that the requirement that a Note of Issue be stricken within 20 days of its filing if discovery is incomplete or, beyond this, that special circumstances be shown to justify the continuance of discovery is, if not weakened, then almost nullified, since all a party need do is mark his case off the court calendar, so solving his problem in this facile manner.

The holdings of *Pezzella, Grigorian* and *Colville,* read with *Roberson,* may be said to go further, since all speak of the necessity of a serious injury as one criterion whereby discovery may continue, and, in *Roberson,* this is the sole and compelling consideration.

Perhaps the appellate courts of this state are moving toward a rule that the unusual or special circumstances, under which discovery may continue when the Note of Issue has been filed and 20 days have passed, are fulfilled with a showing of serious injury and nothing more, since in *Roberson* the Court granted the defendant's motion for a physical examination of the plaintiff on this basis alone.

7. Non Sui Juris: An Overview of the Current New York Law

Introduction

Non Sui Juris may be defined as that age at which a child, whether as a matter of law, or as a matter of fact, will not be held liable, as party plaintiff, for its contributory negligence. This article proposes to trace the history of the concept under the law of this state, within specific categories, and consider the current status of the law.

Non Sui Juris as a Matter of Law

It is established law in the State of New York that a child under 4 years of age will be conclusively presumed incapable of contributory negligence, as a matter of law, and the jury will be charged as such. The matter thus is removed from their fact finding function.

The landmark case is *Verni v. Johnson,* 295 N.Y. 436, 68 N. 431 (1946). *Verni* was an action for the wrongful death of a child by reason of the defendant's alleged negligent operation of his automobile. The trial judge submitted to the jury the issue as to the contributory negligence of the plaintiff's intestate, an infant 3 years and 2 months at the time of the accident. The plaintiff's counsel requested a charge that a child 3 years 2 months of age is, as a matter of law, Non Sui Juris and so incapable of contributory negligence. This request was refused and the Court of Appeals granted leave to appeal on the correctness of this rule.

The Court held, that under the great weight of authority of state, and, indeed throughout the United States, a 3-year-old child is conclusively presumed to be incapable of contributory negligence. Moreover, the Court stated that a child under 4 years of age is Non Juris as a matter of law. The Court of Appeals stated that this rule, which refuses to allow such young children to be penalized for potential fault, had been followed by the Court since 1868 and there appeared no reason for changing what was a just rule of law. Court of Appeals hence reversed and granted a new trial.

Subsequent cases, both appellate and trial, have followed the rule set forth in *Verni* and have extended it. See *Novak v. State,* 99 N.Y.S., 2d 962, 965 (Court of Claims, 1950) (infant 2-½ years old struck by State operated vehicle held Non Sui Juris as a matter of law); *Sr. v. State,* 117 N.Y.S.2d 163, 166 (Court of Claims, 1952) (in claim death of 3½-year-old infant, drowned in unguarded pool maintained at State Fish Hatchery, infant Non Sui Juris as a matter of law); *Glick v. Barbara Lickver Ltd.,* 39 A.D.2d 547, 331 N.Y.S.2d 692 (2d I 1972) (action to recover from dress store for injuries customer sustained when mirror fell from wall and shattered. Customer entitled to recover from dress store even if accident was caused by the combined negligence of the store owner and the customer's 2-1/2 year old son, since the latter was Non Sui Juris under the law); *Popkin v. Sharker,* 36 Misc. 2d 242, 232 N.Y.S.2d 574 (Supreme Court, Nassau County, 1962); *Beekman Estate v. Midanick,* 44 Misc. 2d 11, 252 N.Y.S.2d 885 (Supreme Court, New York County, 1964); *Calara v. Smith,* 273 App. Div. 927, 77 N.Y.S.2d 621 (3d Dept. 1948); *Logan v. Jackson,* 1 A.D.2d 146, 148 N.Y.S.2d 466, 467 (1st Dept. 1956); *Chandler v. Keene,* 5 A.D.2d 42, 168 N.Y.S.2d 788, 791 (3d Dept. 1957); *Masone v. Gianotti,* 54 A.D.2d 269, 388 N.Y.S.2d 322, 327 (2nd Dept. 1976).

There can be no doubt but that *Verni v. Johnson, supra,* is the law of this state and remains so.

Some few cases, however, have extended to children over 4 years of age the rule that a child under 4 years of age will be deemed Non Sui Juris and so incapable of contributory negligence. *Romanchuk v. County of Westchester,* 40 A.D.2d 887, 337 N.Y.S.2d 926 (2nd Dept. 1972), is instructive. *Romanchuk* was a negligence action to recover for injuries sustained by an infant as the result of an accident which occurred while he was sleigh riding in a park owned and maintained by the defendant County and for a loss of services. Judgment was in favor of the defendant County upon a jury verdict. The Appellate Division held that the trial court erred in submitting the issue of contributory negligence of the infant plaintiff to the jury. The Court stated that the infant, several days short of his 5th birthday, was sleigh riding in an area of the park where such activities were permitted and under the supervision of his father. The Court concluded that under these circumstances the infant must, as a matter of law, be deemed free of contributory negligence. The Court added that

> although no exception was taken to the charge, a new trial should be granted in the interests of justice. *Romanchuk v. County of Westchester, supra,* at 927, 928.

In similar fashion, in an earlier case, *Ehrlich v. Marra,* 32 A.D.2d 638, 300 N.Y.S.2d 81 (2nd Dept. 1969), the Second Department again held that a child 4 years 10 months of age was Non Sui Juris as a matter of law.

On the other hand, two courts, one trial and one appellate, have held that a child between 3 and 4 years of age is not Non Sui Juris as a matter of law, and the issue of his contributory negligence is a question of fact for the jury. *Goldstein v. Dry Dock, E. & B.R. Ca.,* 35 Misc. Rep. 200 71 N.Y.S. 477, 479 (City Court, 1901); *Hine v. Air-Dan Ca.,* 232 App. Div. 359, 250 N.Y.S. 75 (3rd Dept. 1931).

These cases extending the conclusive presumption of Non Sui Juris beyond 4 years of age (*Romanchuk* and *Ehrlich*) and the two cases which hold that the contributory negligence of the child under 4 years of age is a fact question for the jury (*Goldstein* and *Hine*) must be regarded as sports on this issue. The law in this state must be regarded as firmly set, under *Verni* and its progeny, that a child 4 years of age or below be deemed incapable of contributory negligence, and so Non Sui Juris.[1]

The Older Cases

Where a child is beyond 4 years of age, there is an older line of cases that hold that a rebuttable presumption exists that a child under 12 years of age is Non Sui Juris, while a child over 12 is presumed Sui Juris. The leading case is *Ramirez v. Perlman,* 284 App. Div. 130 N.Y.S. 398 (1st Dept. 1954). *Ramirez* was an action for injuries sustained when a 9-year-old boy was run over by the defendant's automobile. The jury found for the defendant and the issue on appeal was the Court's charge in respect to the applicable law of contributory negligence. The Trial Court had charged that the 9-year-old infant, running out into highway while playing, was guilty of contributory negligence as a matter of law. The Appellate Division held that a child under 12 years of age is presumed by the law to be Non Sui Juris and that a child of 9 may be charged with responsibility for his own acts to the extent commensurate with what is to be expected of one of his comparable age, years, experience and intelligence, and that the consideration of the child's contributory negligence is a matter for the jury. The Court concluded that

> to advise the jury that it must, on a given set of facts find contributory negligence by a child of 9 without considering the mental development of the child, takes away from the jury a function which must be left to it. *Ramirez v. Perlman, supra,* at 400.

Ramirez is clear in its holding that a child under 12 will be presumed Non Sui Juris, to be rebutted by evidence of its mental capacity by the defendant. A number of other courts have followed this rule of presumption articulated in *Ramirez.* Thus in *Gerber v. Boorstein,* 113 App. Div. 808, 99 N.Y.S. 1091 (2nd Dept. 1906), where a 9-year-old boy was crossing the street and was injured by a streetcar, the court noted that the law presumed an infant of 12 Sui Juris, but the contrary may be proved and found as a fact by the side asserting it, the defendant, while a child under 12 is not presumed Sui Juris, but whether he is so a question of fact, again to be raised by the side asserting it, the defendant. *Gerber v. Boorstein, supra,* at 1092. See also *Batchelor v. Degnon Realty and Terminal Imp. Co.,* 131 App. Div. 136, 115 N.Y.S. 93 (2nd Dept. 1909); *Jacobs v. H. J. Koehler Sporting Goods Co.,* 208 N.Y. 416, 102 N.E. 519 (1913); 41 N.Y. Jur. *Negligence* § 67; See also cases cited in *Camarda v. New York State Rwys.,* 247 N.Y. 111, 159 N.E. 880 (1928); 57 Am. Jur. 2d *Negligence* §§ 364-366; Harper & James, *supra* at 926; Restatement Torts, ibid; For cases in other jurisdictions adopting this Rule of Presumptions, see 77 A.L.R.2d pp. 9255930 and Later Case Service pp. 122-123.[2]

It is the current law that where an infant is beyond 4 years of age, the issue of the child's contributory negligence is for the jury to determine based on the evidence adduced at trial. Only where the facts, as they develop at trial, admit the sole inference that the child, because of his lack of capacity, is inherently incapable of negligence, may the court decide, as a matter of law, that the child may not be found guilty of contributory negligence, as Non Sui Juris, and so charge the jury.

The leading case is *Camarda v. New York State Railways,* 247 N.Y. 111 (1927). In *Camarda,* the infant plaintiff, 4 years 10 months old at the time of the accident, was struck by a streetcar operated by the defendant and sustained serious injuries. The trial judge submitted to the jury the issue of the infant plaintiff's freedom from contributory negligence and the defendant's negligence. The jury found for the defendant. The plaintiff asserted, on appeal, that the trial judge erred in submitting to the jury the question of the plaintiff's freedom from contributory negligence. The court noted that a child may be of such tender years as to be incapable of contributory negligence and, so, Non Sui Juris. The court held, however, that where the child is not of such age as to be considered Non Sui Juris as a matter of law, the issue is one of fact for the jury. Specifically, the court stated that where conflicting inferences may be drawn as to whether the child has failed to exercise that degree of care as the law requires and so proved his freedom from contributory negligence, the question is one of fact for the jury. On the other hand, where, based on the evidence, only one inference may be drawn, that the child was, as a matter of law, capable of exercising due care, or, given the child's capacities, was not, the matter is reserved to the court to determine, to be appropriately charged to the jury. The court went on to state that

> the determination whether under the particular circumstances in each case, reasonable men might differ as to the inferences that can be drawn, is decisive of whether, upon the evidence, a question of fact or law is presented. . . . Only where the circumstances admit of only one inference, may the court decide as a matter of law what inference shall drawn. *Camardo* v. *New York State Railways,* SUI at 117, 118.

The court concluded that the question of the degree of care which can be expected of children is based upon factors which the jury is fully competent to weigh in the light of their experience. Only in cases, the court stated, where the judge can readily decide that reasonable juries will arrive at the same determination, is the issue to be left to the court. In all other circumstances, the question of a child's capacity to take care of itself, the court held, should be left to the jury.

It should be noted that the court, in *Camardo*, distinguished cases concerning presumptions of age on this issue, with the caveat that the rule is more accurately stated to be that under certain circumstances in the absence of evidence of the capacity of a particular child, except age, an inference may be drawn as to the child's ability to apprehend and avoid the danger which resulted in his injury.

The holding in *Camarda* is clear, that although there is a certain age below which an infant will be deemed Non Sui Juris as a matter law (4 years of age), beyond that age the question is one for the jury in the absence of an inference, drawn by the court from the evidence as developed at trial, that the child was inherently incapable of exercising care, or was inherently able to do so.

New York law has consistently followed the holding in *Camardo* to this day and has rejected the former rule concerning presumption (*Manikas v. Carswell,* 283 App. Div. 1003, 130 N.Y.S.2d 602 (4th Dept. 1954); *Mark v. State,* 197 N.Y.S.2d 92, 21 Misc.2d 63 (Court of Claims 1959); *Sierra v. Georgiu,* 236 N.Y.S.2d 773 (Supreme Court, Nassau County, 1962); *Jacobs v. Leader,* 255 App. Div. 954, 8 N.Y.S.2d 129 (1st Dept. 1938); *Stanley v. Surface Transit Inc.,* 26 A.D.2d 336, 274, N.Y.S.2d 524, 527-8 (1st Dept. 1966); *Finkelstein v. Brooklyn Heights Railway Co.,* 51 App. Div. 287, 64 N.Y.S. 915 (2nd Dept. 1900);[3] *Radford v. Sample,* 30 A.D.2d 558, 290 N.Y.S.2d 30 (3rd Dept. 1968); *Kennedy v. Cromer,* 34 A.D.2d 559, 310 N.Y.S.2d 794 (3rd Dept. 1970); *Eagle v. Janoff,* 12 A.D.2d 638, 208 N.Y.S.2d 579 (2nd Dept. 1960); *Busby v. Levy,* 101 N.Y.S.2d 946 (Supreme Court Kings County, 1951); *Mitchell v. State,* 20 Misc.2d 381. 195 N.Y.S.2d 511 (Court of Claims, 1959); *Gonzalez v. Medina,* 69 A.D.2d 14, 470, N.Y.S.2d 953 (1st Dept. 1979); *Van Gasbeck v. Webatuck*

Cent. Sch. D. No. 1, 21 N.Y.2d 239, 287 N.Y.S.2d 77, 83 (1967); *Coleman v. Brooklyn and Queens Transit Corp.,* 252 App. Div. 215, 298 N.Y.S. 513 (2nd Dept. 1937); *Willis v. Young Men's Christian Association of Amsterdam,* 34 A.D.2d 583, 307 N.Y.S.2d 583 (3rd Dept. 1970); *Giordano v. Sheridan Maintenance Corp.,* 38 A.D.2d 552, 328 N.Y.S.2d 241 (2nd Dept. 1971); *Searles v. Dardani,* 75 Misc.2d 279, 347 N.Y.S. 2d 662 (Supreme Court, Albany County, 1973) (4½-year-old infant struck by defendant's automobile brought suit to recover for injuries. Held: While there is some authority that a child of that age is Non Sui Juris as a matter of law, that question may be passed upon by the justice presiding at trial); *Collazzo v. Manhattan and Bronx Surf. Trans. Op. Auth.,* 339 N.Y.S.2d 809 (Supreme Court, Bronx County, 1972) (action for injuries sustained by 5½-year-old child struck by bus owned and operated by the defendants. The court noted that the question of whether a child of 5-1/2 years of age, as plaintiff, is Sui Juris and capable of contributory negligence, is not free from doubt, citing *Verni* and *Camardo*); *McLoughlin, et al. v. Bonpark Realty Corp.,* 260 App. Div. 471, 23 N.Y.S.2d 156 (1st Dept. 1940); *Fron v. Wolski,* 232, N.Y.S. 747 (4th Dept. 1929); *Gloshinsky v. Bergen Milk Transp. Co.,* 279 N.Y. 58, 117 N.E.2d 766 (1938); *Trudell v. N.Y. Rapid Transit Corp.,* 281 N.Y. 82, 22 N.E.2d 244 (1939); *Touris v. Fairmont Creamery Co.,* 228 App. Div. 569, 240 N.Y.S. 225 (4th Dept. 1930); *Nugent v. Jungaldi Bldg. & Construction Co., Inc.,* 249 N Y.S. 315 (City Court, New York County 1931); *Culvert v. Deckert,* 239 N.Y.2 923 (4th Dept. 1930); *Decker v. Dundee Central Sch. Dist.,* 4 N.Y.2d 462, 176 N.Y.S.2d 307 (1958); *Betancourt v. Wilson,* 3 A.D.2d 465, 162 N.Y.S. 2d 115 (1st Dept. 1957):

Two Appellate decisions are particularly representative of the continuing force of *Verni* and *Camardo* and the death of the older rule of presumptions. *Logan v. Jackson,* 148 N.Y.S.2d 466 (1st Dept. 1956) and *Yun Jeong Koo v. St. Bernard,* 89 Misc. 2d 775, 392, N.Y.S.2d 815 (Supreme Court, Queens County, 1977). *Logan v. Jackson, supra,* was an action by an 8½-year-old infant by his guardian *ad litem* and parent for injuries sustained by the infant. The Supreme Court rendered judgment for the infant and parent and the defendant appealed. The First Department held that the charge of the trial court on the contributory negligence of the infant plaintiff was so confusing to the jury as to require reversal. The court stated, in its opinion, that since the child was 8-1/2 years of age, the rule of a conclusive presumption with respect to the incapacity of a child between 3 and 4 years of age did not apply, and, moreover, that the rule that a certain presumption exists, stated in the older cases, that an infant was Sui or Non Sui Juris depending on whether the child was 4 or less than 12 years old, no longer had validity in the light of *Camardo,*

Yung Jeong Koo, supra, is particularly instructive. *Yun Jeong Koo* was an action brought to recover personal injuries sustained by a child 4 years 10 months old, due to the defendant's negligent operation of his automobile. The defendant asserted the affirmative defense of contributory negligence and the plaintiff moved to dismiss the defense on the ground that the infant plaintiff, as a matter of law, could not be contributorily negligent, under *Ehrlich v. Marra, supra*. The Supreme Court held the affirmative defense viable and that it was incumbent upon the defendant to plead and prove that the infant was of such insufficient maturity to appreciate the danger facing him and take steps to avoid it. The court noted that where a child is under 4 years of age, a conclusive presumption exists with respect to its incapacity, but held, that, despite the decision in *Ehrlich* extending this conclusive presumption to 4 years 10 months of age, an infant of this age is unprotected by "any presumption" and that it was incumbent upon the defendant to plead and prove that the infant had the capacity to appreciate and avoid the danger facing him and that it was for the jury, upon a proper charge, to determine the standard for an infant of this age and experience. The court concluded that

> it would therefore appear that the *Camardo* case, though decided in 1928, would be even more applicable in today's world and more pertinent to advancing technology. *Yun Jeong Koo v. St. Bernard, supra*, at 818.

It is the view of this writer, upon review of the case law both preceding and following *Camarda*, that where an infant is beyond 4 years of age, the courts of this state will refer the issue of his contributory negligence and the accompanying issue of whether the infant is St Non Sui Juris to the jury, except under the unusual circumstances when the facts mandate the court removing the matter from the hands of jury and directing a finding that the infant is inherently or not inherently capable of contributory negligence.

Violation of Statute

Whether an infant plaintiff is Sui or Non Sui Juris is a question of fact for the jury unless exceptional circumstances present themselves. Following this rule, where an infant plaintiff is charged with contributory negligence by reason of a violation of statute, this also is a fact question for the jury, based on evidence of the infant's age, experience, intelligence, and development in thereby understanding the meaning import of the statute. Only under these circumstances may an infant plaintiff be charged with negligence for statutory violation.

A recent case articulating this standard is *Quinn v. Count Sullivan,* 48 A.D.2d 965, 369 N.Y.S.2d 551 (3rd Dept. 1975). *Quinn*, the administrator of the estate of a 14-year-old infant pedestrian plaintiff brought an action against the county and motorist for the death of the infant-pedestrian. The Supreme Court rendered judgment in favor of the motorist-defendant, and, after reducing the verdict in favor of the administrator against the County, the County-defendant appealed. The Appellate Division held that the County was negligent in failing in its duty to clear the sidewalk of snow, thereby forcing the infant pedestrian to walk in the highway. The court held that this was a question for the jury. The court further held that the infant plaintiff's contributory negligence was a question for the jury. The court stated that the fact that the infant was walking with traffic instead of against it, as required by Sub.(b) of § 1156 of the Vehicle and Traffic Law, did not constitute negligence as a matter of law and that the court properly charged the jury that it could take into consideration the age, experience, and intelligence of the infant-decedent in determining whether he had or lacked the mental capacity to comprehend the statute; the court held that this also was a fact question for the jury. See also *Chandler v. Keene,* 5 A.D.2d 42, 168 N.Y.S.2d 788 (3rd Dept. 1957) (Infant 4 years, 11 months of age; violation of Sub. 4 Sec. 85 of the Vehicle and Traffic Law requiring pedestrians to yield right of way to vehicles upon highway between intersections and crossings); *Trippy v. Basile,* 44 A.D.2d 759, 354 NY.S. 235 (4th Dept. 1974) (5½-year-old infant, infant plaintiff not crossing at crosswalk); *Coloro v. Smith,* 273 App. Div. 927, 77 N.Y.S.2d 621 (3rd Dept. 1948); *Locklin v. Fisher,* 264 App. Div. 452, 36 N.Y.S.2d 16 (3rd Dept. 1942); PJI 2:49, Contributory Negligence—Persons Under Disability—Violation of Statute; 41 N.Y. Jur. § 67, Negligence.

It should be noted that there is some authority for the proposition that an infant plaintiff is not to be charged with the duty to observe certain portions of the Vehicle and Traffic Law. See *Schaffner v. Rockmacher,* 38 A.D.2d 835, 329 N.Y.S.2d 630 (2nd Dept. 1972); *Rubin v. O'Donnell,* 37 A.D.2d 858, 326 N.Y.S.2d 25 (2nd Dept. 1971); PJI: 49 *supra.*

Parent and Child

Where a child is Non Sui Juris as a matter of law, the issue arises whether the negligence of a parent, guardian, or sibling, for alleged failure to supervise the child, or otherwise act in a negligent manner with respect to the child, such as to partially bring about the accident and injury in the case, may be imputed to the incapable child and thus bar his recovery where he has been so injured by a tortious defendant. The law, in this respect, has undergone a metamorphosis.

It was formerly the law of this state, prior to 1929 and the enactment of § 73 of the Domestic Relations Law, that where a child is Non Sui Juris, the negligence of a parent or guardian contributing to an injury to the child would be imputed to the child and thus bar his recovery. *Novak v. State,* 99 N.Y.S.2d 962 (Court of Claims, 1950).

The enactment of § 73 of the Domestic Relations Law in 1935, which was subsequently repealed and re-enacted with § 3-111 of the General Obligations Law, changed this rule of law. This section states that

in an action brought by an infant to recover damages for personal injuries the contributory negligence of the infant's parent or other custodian shall not be imputed to the infant.

The cases construing this law have interpreted it literally. *Brennan v. Union Free School District,* 228 N.Y.S.2d 134 (2nd Dept. 1962), was an action against the school district for injuries suffered by a school pupil when he was playing and jumping over a bicycle rack in a schoolyard. The Supreme Court, Appellate Division, Second Department, very specifically held that it was error to charge that the contributory negligence of the parent could be imputed to the infant plaintiff. See also *Collazo v. Manhattan & Bronx Surface Transit Operating Auth., supra; Searles v. Dardani, supra; Kowalski v. McHsenin,* 38 A.D.2d 274, 329 N.Y.S.2d 37 (2nd Dept. 1972); *Klein v. Eichen,* 310 N.Y.S.2d 611 (Supreme Court, Bronx County 1970); *Rubin v. Olympic Resort, Inc.,* 198 N.Y.S.2d 408 (Supreme Court, Nassau County, 1960); *Holodook v. Spencer,* 364 N.Y.S.2d 859 (1974); *Yun Jeong Koo v. St. Bernard, supra; Hairston v. Broadwater,* 73 Misc.2d 523, 342 N.Y.S.2d 787 (Supreme Court, Nassau County, 1973); *Bullis v. Schuyler Heights,* 226 App. Div. 630, 97 N.Y.S.2d 242 (3rd Dept. 1950); *Meyer v. Inguaggiato,* 258 App. Div. 331, 60 N.Y.S.2d 672, App. Den. 258 App. Div. 1055, 17 N.Y.S.2d 1021 (2nd Dept. 1940); *Corveduu v. Blumner,* 10 A.D.2d 712, 199 N.Y.S.2d 72 (2nd Dept. 1960).

It should be noted, however, that this section and the cases interpreting it, do not preclude the recovery of contribution, in the form of a counterclaim or cross-claim, by the defendant against a parent, where the parent's conduct toward his child would be a tort if done by one ordinary person to another, but does preclude contribution where the parent's failure to provide adequate supervision would result in diminishment of the child's recovery against a third party. See *Hollodook v. Spencer, supra; Yun Jeong Koo v. St. Bernard, supra; Hairston v. Broadwater, supra.*[4]

Conclusion

Beyond the age of 4, it is clear that the issue of whether a child is Sui or Non Sui Juris, and therefore capable or incapable of contributory negligence, is, under the law of this state, a fact question for the jury unless the court determines that the evidence permits of the conclusion that the inference may be drawn that the child, as a matter of law, is Sui or Non Sui Juris. Under the age of 4, there is a conclusive presumption in this state that the child is, as a matter of law, Non Sui Juris. In addition, where there is a question of statutory violation, it is also for the jury to determine that the child has sufficient capacity to comprehend the nature of the statute and so be held responsible for its violation.

Thus, it is the conclusion of this writer that the determination of whether a child beyond the age of 4 is Sui or Non Sui Juris will be a fact question for the jury with the possibility that the trial judge may remove the issue from the jury, based on the evidence of the child's obvious capacity or incapacity to be held culpable.

8. The Law of Conflicts: A Recent Trend

It has, for some time, been the law of the State of New York that, in multi-state tort cases, where there is a conflict of laws as between the laws of two or more states, the court should apply the law of the jurisdiction with the most significant contacts and concerns with the specific issue or issues raised in the litigation, by reason of its relationship to the occurrence or parties. This rule of so-called "interest analysis" or the theory of conflicts of laws known as the "center of gravity" or "grouping of contacts," was first fully stated by the Court of Appeals of this State in *Babcock v. Jackson*, 12 N.Y. 2d 473, 240 N.Y.S. 2d 743, 95 A.L.R. 2d 1 (1963), on remand 40 Misc. 2d 756, 243 N.Y.S. 2d 715 (1963). *Babcock* was a personal injury action wherein a guest, a resident of the State of New York, sued for injuries sustained by reason of the alleged negligence of her driver host, while the latter was driving from New York to Ontario, Canada. The accident occurred in Ontario where there was in force a "guest statute" providing that the owner or driver of a motor vehicle, other than a vehicle operated in the business of carrying passengers for compensation, is not liable for any loss or damage from bodily injury to, or the death of, any person being carried in the motor vehicle, although no such bar was recognized under the law of torts of the State of New York. The defendant moved to dismiss on the ground that the law of the place where the accident or tort occurred, or the *lex loci*, which, until that time, was the rule of law of conflicts in multi-state tort cases, governed the litigation, and so that Ontario's guest statute barred recovery. The trial court granted the motion to dismiss of the defendant and the Appellate Division affirmed.

The Court of Appeals held that the question before it was whether the law of the place of the tort, i.e., where the injury occurred and the wrong causing the injury occurred, should invariably govern the availability of relief for the tort, or whether the applicable choice of law rule should reflect a consideration of other relevant factors. The court noted that, heretofore, the traditional choice of law rule in multi-state tort cases had been that the substantive rights and liabilities arising out of a tortious occurrence were determinable by the law of the place of the tort and that this rule had its conceptual foundation in the vested rights doctrine, namely, that a right to recover for a foreign tort owes its creation to the law of the jurisdiction where the injury occurred.

The court went on to state that the rule of the *lex loci*, however, ignores the interest which jurisdictions other than the situs of the wrong may have in the resolution of particular issues, noting that the Court of Appeals itself, in the area of contract law and wrongful death, had applied the "center of gravity" or "grouping of contacts" theory of conflict of laws, applying the law of the place which had the most significant contact with the matter in dispute. The court concluded that the "center of gravity" or "grouping of contacts" doctrine, adopted by the court in contract litigation, was the most appropriate approach for determining the application of competing interests in multi-state tort cases with multi-state contacts, and the best practical result

> may be achieved by giving controlling effect to the law of jurisdiction which, because of its relationship or contact with the occurrence or the parties has the greatest concern with the specific issue raised in the litigation. *Babcock v. Jackson, supra,* at 749.

The court went on to state that the significance of the relationship or contacts of the respective jurisdictions were to be evaluated in light of the issues in the case, the character of the tort, and the relevant purposes of the tort rules involved. The court held, applying the theory of "interest analysis" to the case before it, that, upon analysis of the relevant contacts and interests of New York and Ontario in the litigation and upon analysis of the issues presented—whether to apply the Ontario guest statute or not—that the state of New York had the greatest concern in applying its law, which did not bar recovery by a guest against a host driver, since the action involved injuries sustained by a New York guest in the operation of an automobile by a New York host, garaged, licensed, and insured in New York, in the course of a weekend journey which was to begin and end in New York; that Ontario's sole relationship with the occurrence was the purely fortuitous circumstance that the accident occurred there; that New York's policy of requiring a tort-feasor to compensate his guest for injuries caused by his host was undoubted; that the New York courts had no reason to depart from the policy simply because the accident, only affecting New York residents only arising out of the operation of a New York based automobile, happened beyond its borders; and that Ontario had no interest in denying a remedy to a New York guest against a New York host for injuries suffered in Ontario since the object of Ontario's guest statute was to prevent the fraudulent assert of claims by passengers, in collusion with drivers, against insurance companies. The court further stated that the fraudulent claims intended to be prevented by the statute were those asserted against Ontario defendants and their insurance carriers and not New York defendants and their insurance carriers, a policy inapplicable to the present context where New York defendants and insurers were involved.

The court concluded, however, with the admonition that where the issues involve standards of conduct, the law of the place of the tort should govern, and the disposition of all other issues must turn on the law of the jurisdiction which has the strongest interest in the resolution of the particular issue presented.

This rule of "interest analysis" or the conflicts theory of "grouping of contacts" or "center of gravity," whereby, in multi-state tort cases, the law of the jurisdiction with the strongest interest in the resolution of the issue raised, as measured by its contact with the occurrence or parties, in light of the policy behind the application of each jurisdiction's particular law, has since been followed by the courts of this State with little variation in multi-state tort cases, effectively replacing the older rule that, in these cases, the rule of the place of the tort must govern all the issues in multi-state tort litigation. See *Macey v. Roz-bicki,* 18 N.Y. 2d 289, 274 N.Y.S. 2d 591 (1966); *Tooker v. Lopez,* 24 N.Y. 2d 569, 301 N.Y.S. 2d 519 (1969); *Dym v. Gordon,* 22 A.D. 2d 702, 253 N.Y.S. 2d 802 (2d Dept. 1964), aff'd 16 N.Y. 2d 120, 262 N.Y.S. 2d 463 (1965); *Thomas v. United Airlines, Inc.,* 30 A.D. 2d 32, 290 N.Y.S. 2d 753 (1st Dept. 1968), rev'd. on other grounds, 24 N.Y. 2d 714, 302 N.Y.S. 2d 973, 39 A.L.R. 3rd 197 (1969), cert. den. 396 U.S. 991, 24 L.Ed. 2d 453, 90 St. Ct. 484 (1969); *Martin v. Julius Diereck Equipment Co.,* 52 A.D. 2d 463, 384 N.Y.S. 2d 479 (2d Dept. 1976), affd. 43 N.Y. 2d 583, 403 N.Y.S. 2d 185 (1978); *Bray v. Cox,* 39 A.D. 2d 299, 333 N.Y.S. 2d 783 (4th Dept. 1972), mot. den. 33 N.Y. 2d 789, 350 N.Y.S. 2d 653 (1973).[1]

The law, then, heretofore, as it was stated in *Babcock* and has been followed in its progeny, is clear that, in multi-state tort cases, the law of the state with the most significant contacts with respect to the issue presented will apply, except where the issue involves the standard of care or conduct, in which instance, the law of the *lex loci* will apply.

The conflicts rule, denominated "interest analysis," has not only been accepted by the state judicial system of the State of New York, but has also been adopted by the federal courts of this State in diversity litigation as the law of conflicts in multi-state tort cases, displacing the rule of *lex loci,* since the federal courts in diversity cases must utilize the choice of law rules of the forum state, to determine the law that governs a party's claim.[2]

Thus, the federal courts have been extensively adhered to and have applied the conflicts rule of interest analysis in multi-state tort cases.[3]

Indeed, the federal courts of this State have even adopted that part of the *Babcock* ruling which states that the rule of interest analysis is to be applied in all aspects of multi-state tort cases, except where the issue is the standard care or conduct, in which event the law of the *lex loci* applies.[4]

A Recent Trend

It would appear that the conflicts theory of "interest analysis" has conquered the field and holds the day in multi-state tort cases, if not replacing, then at least displacing, the older rule of the *lex loci,* or situs of the tort. If we, it seems, have not grown above the rule of the *lex loci,* then, at least, we have grown away from it. Recent cases, however, both state and federal, have been reaching to, if not displacing, the rule of interest analysis in *Babcock,* then at least providing a companion to it which, as it were, sings a new and different song from the tune of *Babcock,* reaching back to the rule of *lex loci* for its focus.

The first hint of this rule was stated by the Court of Appeals in *Neumeir v. Kuehner,* 31 N.Y. 2d 121, 335 N.Y.S. 2d 64 (1972). *Neumeier* was a death action against a Canadian Railroad Corporation and a New York resident, brought by the estate of a domiciliary of Ontario, Canada, killed when the automobile he was riding in, owned and operated by a New York resident, collided with a train in Ontario. The issue in the appeal was whether, in the action brought by the Ontario passenger's estate, the New York defendant should be permitted to apply Ontario law and its guest statute which provides that the owner and driver of a motor vehicle is not liable for damages or injury to his guest unless he was guilty of gross negligence.

After reviewing the relevant contacts of Canada and the State of New York with respect to a specific issue raised in the case—the applicability of Ontario guest statute—and after considering the Court of Appeals' decision in *Tooker v. Lopez, supra,* the court held that the State of New York's connection with the controversy was insufficient to justify displacing the rule of *lex loci delictus. Neumeier v. Kuehner, supra,* at 71. Judge Breitel noted in his concurring opinion that

> it is still true, however, that *lex loci delictus* is the normal rule, . . . to be rejected only when it is evident that the situs of the accident is the least of the several factors or influences to which the accident may be attributed. *Neumeier v. Kuehner, supra,* at 72.

It would appear that the Court of Appeals in *Neumeier* is moving to a doctrine that, in multi-state tort cases, *lex loci delictus* is still the normal rule in the absence of a strong showing of special factors, influences or circumstances showing that it must be displaced.

In *Rakaric v. Croatian Cultural Club,* 76 A.D. 2d 619, 430 N.Y.S. 2d 829 (2d Dept. 1980), the Second Department takes up the cudgel of *Neumeier* and further refines and defines the rule stated there. *Rakaric* was a personal injury action brought against a charitable corporation organized under New Jersey Law for injuries sustained by the infant plaintiff while engaged in a volunteer project, clearing the defendant corporation's property. The defendant alleged, as an affirmative defense, that, under the statute law of New Jersey, it was immune from liability as a charitable corporation. The question for resolution on appeal was the applicability of this statutory immunity under New Jersey Law to the defendant, thereby applying the rule of *lex loci delictus.*

The Second Department proceeded to review the cases which had theretofore established the conflicts rule of "most significant contacts" and which, apparently, displaced the old rule of *lex loci delictus.* The court defined the question as whether the rule in *Babcock* or the rule of *lex loci delictus* should prevail, because the accident happened in New Jersey. The court, after extensive review of the case law of the State of New York, the Second Circuit, and that of other jurisdictions concerning this doctrine of charitable immunity and its application in choice of law situations, noted that the doctrine had been rejected by the Court of Appeals of the State of New York in *Bing v. Thunig,* 2 N.Y. 2d 656, 163 N.Y.S. 2d 3 (1957), and had been displaced by 31 other states as well.

The Appellate Division reversed the order of the trial court and dismissed the defense of charitable immunity, holding that defense of charitable immunity, holding that under the present state of our law, as stated in *Neumeier v. Kuehner, supra, . . .* the doctrine of *lex loci delicti* remains the general rule in tort cases to be displaced only in extraordinary circumstances. . . . This case presents a factual situation which impels the conclusion that such "extraordinary circumstances" do exist, and, thus, the case warrants a departure from that rule since a resident of the State of New York is involved in this case, whose rights will be impaired by a doctrine of charitable immunity from liability for tort, which has not only been completely rejected by this State in *Bing v. Thunig,* 2 N.Y. 2d 656, 163 N.Y.S. 2d 3 (1959) . . . , but, likewise, in other jurisdictions. *Rakaric v. Croation Cultural Club, supra,* at 835.

The thrust in *Rakaric* is obvious that the rule of *lex loci delictus* must hold in the absence of extraordinary circumstances.

The First Department of this state has also adopted the new rule of "special circumstances" in multistate tort cases where choice of law situations are present. *Grancaris v. J.I. Hass Co.,* 79 A.D. 2d 551, 434 N.Y.S.2d 19 (1st Dept. 1980), is apropos. *Grancaris* was a personal injury action brought by painters for injuries when a bridge painting scaffold collapsed while the painters were working on it, in the course of the repair of the bridge spanning Chesapeake Bay in Maryland. Suit was also brought against the painting subcontractor (J.I. Hass Co., Inc.), a New Jersey corporation, the supplier of equipment (J.I. Hass Equipment Co., Inc.), also a New Jersey corporation, and the general contractor, U.S. Steel. Hass Equipment asserted cross-claims against the remaining defendants, and the defendants asserted cross-claims against Hass and Equipment. Hass moved to dismiss the complaint against it and also the various cross-claims against it. The court granted the motion to dismiss the plaintiff's complaint against Hass and Equipment since the trial court felt that *Dole* might be applicable to them. Reargument was sought and granted and the original determination was adhered to on the theory that Hass and Equipment subjected themselves to New York Law by doing business in New York, hiring the plaintiffs there, and directing them to Maryland to work there. Hass Equipment appealed from this determination.

The court's holding was two-fold. First, the Appellate Division noted the complaint against Equipment stated that Equipment was the plaintiff's employer and that it failed to provide the plaintiffs with a safe place to work in violation of the law of Maryland and Federal law. The court held it was clear from the complaint that the plaintiffs were relying on Maryland law, and that the law barred the action, and Special Term erred in holding otherwise. *Grancaris v. J.I. Hass & Co., supra,* at 21.

The court concluded, however, that Maryland law applied to the cross-claims since tort cases, though transitory, still remained subject, in choice of law matters, to the rule of *lex loci delictus,* except in rare instances. *Grancaris v. J.I. Hass & Co., supra,* at 21.

The holding in *Grancaris* is of great importance. That clearly follows the Second Department view in *Rakaric* that the rule of *lex loci delicti* must govern in choice of law matters except in rare instances or special circumstances. Numerous cases have seen fit to adopt this new reiteration in *Grancaris* and *Rakaric* of the primacy of the rule of *lex loci*. See *Belisaro v. Manhattan Motor Rental, Inc.*, 48 A.D. 2d 477, 370 N.Y.S. 2d 574 (1st Dept. 1975); *Cousins v. Instrument Flyers*, 44 N.Y. 2d 698, 699, 405 N.Y.S. 2d 441, 442 (1978); *Rogers v. U-Haul Co.*, 41 A.D. 2d 158, 342 N.Y.S. 2d 158 (2d Dept. 1973); *Towley v. King Arthur Rings, Inc.*, 49 A.D. 2d 555, 370 N.Y.S. 2d 595 (1st Dept. 1975).

Indeed, even the Federal District Courts of this State and, in particular, the Eastern District Court of the State of New York, have, to some degree, adopted this revival, as it were, of the rule of the *lex loci*. An example is *Cameron v. G and H Steel Serve, Inc.*, 494 F. Supp. 171 (E.D.N.Y. 1980). In *Cameron*, the plaintiff, in a diversity action, while working on the premises of DuPont, in New Jersey, was injured by an explosion. The plaintiff also sued defendant, G and H Steel Service, a sub-contractor on the job, who brought a third-party action for contribution against Pre-Load Co., the plaintiff's employer, and the general contractor, and against Don Cameron, also an employee of Pre-Load Co.

Pre-Load and Don Cameron, third-party defendants, moved from summary judgment to dismiss the third-party complaint against them. The Court defined the initial issue as whose state's law should apply. The Court initially notes that the law of the situs of the accident, New Jersey, was the State whose law should apply and govern the litigation and that, where negligence in that state caused the injury in that State, the law of the situs jurisdiction should apply. The Court went on to state that New York's contacts with the third-party defendant, Pre-Load, as the State of its incorporation and principal place of business were not of significance where the action arose out of alleged negligence in the State of New Jersey and that where all the significant events concerning the accident occurred in New Jersey, the situs. The Court when on to state that New York did not have a compelling interest in that litigation and in the application of its law

merely by virtue of the fact that the plaintiff resides in New York. *Hottling v. Smith, supra.* See *Bray v. Cox*, 39 A.D. 299, 333 N.Y.S. 2d 783 (4th Dept. 1972), app. dismd. 38 A.D. 299, 333 N.Y.S. 2d 783 (4th Dept. 1972), app. dismd. 38 N.Y. 2d 350, 379 N.Y.S. 2d 803, 342 N.E. 2D 575 (1976). It is clear then that New Jersey law will apply due to a determination of the rights and obligations arising out of this New Jersey accident. *Cameron v. G. & H. Steel Service, Inc., supra*, at 174.[5]

Conclusion

It is still the trend in the law of conflicts in multi-state tort cases in the State of New York, that the theory of interest analysis commands the day. A review, however, of recent case law in this field reveals that there is an emerging rule of conflicts in multi-state tort cases, first articulated by the Court of Appeals in *Neumeier v. Kuehner, supra,* and since (to some extent followed by both the State and Federal courts of this State, that the rule of the *lex loci*, or of the place where the tort occurred, including both the place of the injury and the place of civil wrong, must govern multi-state litigation in the absence of special or exceptional circumstances. The recent case law in this area does not precisely reveal what those unique circumstances are or must be, and it would seem that what constitutes exceptional factors, such that the rule of *lex loci* will not apply in multi-state tort cases, will be decided and determined on an ad hoc case-by-case basis.

This article previously appeared in an edition of The Nassau Lawyer, a publication of the Nassau County Bar Association, and is being reprinted here with the permission of The Nassau County Bar Association.

9. Settlements Under Section 15-108 of the General Obligations Law: Two Means to the End

Section 15-108 of the General Obligations Law, entitled "Release or Covenant Not to Sue," defines the effect to be given to a prior settlement by one or more joint tortfeasors with the plaintiff. The statute, in brief, states that where a release or covenant not to sue is given to one or more persons liable, or claimed to be such, for the same injury or wrongful death, it does not discharge any of the other tortfeasors from liability for the injury or death, unless its terms so provide. It does, however, release the claim of the plaintiff-releasor against the other tortfeasors to the extent stipulated in the release or covenant, the amount of consideration paid for it, or the amount of the released tortfeasor's equitable share of the damages under Article 14 of the C.P.L.R., whichever is greater.

The statute, on its face, is clear: A prior settlement by one or more tortfeasors releases the plaintiff's claim against the remaining tortfeasors by either the amount stipulated in the instrument of settlement, the consideration paid for the instrument, or that tortfeasor's equitable share of the damages, whichever is largest.

The question arises, however, as to the manner or method whereby this settlement must be taken into account, inasmuch as the statute merely says that the claim of the releasor against the releasee is reduced by the amount of stipulated settlement, the amount of consideration paid for it, or the amount of the released tort-feasor's equitable share of the damages under Article 14 of the C.P.L.R., whichever is greatest, but does not precisely reveal how this is to be accomplished.

It is this question that this article proposes to examine. Let us assume, in this article, a hypothetical case. Prior to the trial of a common law negligence action, one of two joint or concurrent tortfeasors settles his suit against the plaintiff for $50,000.00. The case goes to trial and the plaintiff obtains a verdict of $100,000.00 against the remaining tortfeasor. How, then, is this prior settlement to be taken into consideration, whether by Court or jury?

The Law

There are under the law of this State two methods to reduce the verdict pursuant to Section 15-108 of the General Obligations Law. The first is set forth in Rule 4533-b of the C.P.L.R. entitled "Proof of Payment by Joint Tort-feasor." This statute states that

> in an action for personal injury, injury to property or for wrongful death any proof as to payment by settlement with another joint tort-feasor, offered by a defendant in mitigation of damages, shall be taken out of the hearing of the jury. The court shall deduct the proper amount, as determined pursuant to section 15-108 of the General Obligations Law, from the award made by the jury.

In simple terms, under this statute, where proof of settlement by the plaintiff with one joint tortfeasor is offered, the court must deduct the proper amount in accord with Section 15-108 of the General Obligations Law. In our hypothetical case, then, it would appear that the court, upon being offered proof of payment, must deduct $50,000.00 from the total award of $100,000.00 rendered by the jury. A cursory reading of this statute reveals that this constitutes a mandatory method. The court must reduce from the total verdict the settlement amount or consideration paid therefor, entered into by one joint tortfeasor and the plaintiff prior to trial. The reduction or deduction from the verdict is an act of the court: the jury having and playing no part. The statute leaves no discretion in this respect on the part of the court.

The case law construing this statute interprets it strictly in accord with its precise wording. The leading case is *Mulligan v. Wetchler,* 39 A.D. 2d 102, 332 N.Y.S. 2d 68, app. dism. 30 N.Y. 2d 951, 335 N.Y.S. 2d 701 (1st Dept., 1972). *Mulligan* was a medical malpractice and death action against the City of New York, various hospitals and Dr. Bernard Wetchler, the plaintiff's private treating physician. During the trial, Dr. Wetchler, a joint tortfeasor defendant, paid the plaintiff $75,000.00 in settlement. The jury determined, in accord with the court's instructions, the full compensatory amount of damages for the plaintiff without diminution of the $75,000.00 paid by Dr. Wetchler. The court held that the defendant, City of New York, was entitled to be credited with that sum in partial satisfaction of the damages, and the jury should have been so instructed. The court concluded

> the recently subsequently enacted C.P.L.R. 4533-b effective September 1, 1971, [indicated] that where there has been payment by a joint tort-feasor, the court should subtract the amount of the payment from the award made by the jury. *Mulligan* v. *Wetchler, supra,* at 72.

It is true that the court, in *Mulligan,* held that the City of New York was entitled to be credited with the sum of the settlement and the jury so instructed. The court noted, however, the effect of C.P.L.R. §4533-b, stating that the court itself under this statute should subtract the amount of the payment from the award made by the jury. Cases subsequent to *Mulligan* have followed its lead in strictly interpreting C.P.L.R. §4533-b. See *Hager v. Hutchins*, 91 Misc. 2d 402, 398 N.Y.S. 2d 316 (Sup. Ct., Orange Co., 1977); *Lowenstein v. City of New York*, 50 A.D. 2d 585, 374 N.Y.S. 2d 673 (2d Dept. 1975); *Killen v. Reinhardt*, 71 A.D. 2d 851, 419 N.Y.S. 2d 175 (2d Dept. 1979); *Abernathy v. Azzoni*, 358 N.Y.S. 2d 264, 78 Misc. 2d 832 (Sup. Ct., Suffolk Co., 1974); *Purcell v. Doherty*, 102 Misc. 2d 1049, 424 N.Y.S. 2d 991 (Sup. Ct., Bronx Co., 1980).

The second and earlier rule or method by which a settlement of a joint tortfeasor may be taken into consideration by the court or jury is defined in the case law and is not a matter of statute. Under this rule, the remaining co-defendants, or rather remaining tortfeasors, may choose to prove the degree or amount of the settling tortfeasors' liability. The jury is then instructed by the Court to apportion the proportionate percentage of liability to be ascribed to the settling tortfeasor. The remaining co-defendants may put in such proof of the joint tortfeasor's liability as they deem fitting and proper. *Driscoll v. New York City Transit Authority*, 53 A.D. 2d 391, 385 N.Y.S. 2d 540 (1st Dept. 1976), is relevant. In *Driscoll*, an infant plaintiff brought a personal injury action for injury sustained while the minor plaintiff tripped while roller skating and was thereafter hit by a bus. The lawsuit was commenced against the New York City Transit Authority and the Consolidated Edison Company. The initial settlement with the defendants was vacated and, before trial, the plaintiff settled this lawsuit against the New York City Transit Authority. The trial court then granted the plaintiff's motion to sever his action against the New York City Transit Authority and, thereupon, Consolidated Edison served a third-party complaint upon the New York City Transit Authority seeking indemnification from the latter. During the course of trial, the Trial Judge refused Consolidated Edison's repeated request to apply General Obligations Law, §15-108, and stated that the case was proceeding not on a theory of joint tortfeasors, but on the theory that Consolidated Edison was completely responsible for the accident and resulting injury. At the conclusion of the trial, the court denied Consolidated Edison's request to charge on the theory of *Dole v. Dow* apportionment as regards the New York City Transit Authority's liability. Consolidated Edison excepted to this refusal of the trial court. (*Dole v. Dow*, 30 N.Y.2D 143, 331 N.Y.S.2d 382 [1972]). The First Department held that the trial court erred in refusing to allow the City Transit Authority's culpability to be a factor in the course of the trial and in refusing to instruct the jury as to apportionment between joint tortfeasors. *Driscoll v. New York City Transit Authority, supra.* In sum, the *Driscoll* court held that, where a joint tortfeasor has settled his case, the remaining tortfeasor or tort-feasors are entitled to present the issue of the culpability of the settling defendant to the jury and to receive an instruction on apportionment. See also *Madaffari v. Wilmod Co., Inc.*, 96 Misc. 2d 729, 409 N.Y.S. 2d 587 (Sup. Ct., N.Y. Co., 1978); *Meleo v. Rochester Gas & Electric Corp.*, 72 A.D. 2d 83, 432 N.Y.S. 343 (4th Dept. 1979).

The jury then, under *Driscoll*, may apportion the fault with respect to settling tortfeasor and once this percentage apportionment is calculated, verdict of the plaintiff against the remaining defendant or defendants may be reduced by the amount of that percentage as applied to the total verdict. Thus, if the jury, in our hypothetical case, apportions 40 percent of the liability to the settling tortfeasor, the verdict will thereby be reduced by 40 percent of $100.000.00 or $40,000.00.

These alternative methods, however, of taking into account a private settlement are not mutually exclusive; nor do they operate independently of one another, in satellite worlds as it were. The key to their interrelationship is to be found in Section 15-108 itself. This statute reads that in the event of a prior settlement with one joint tortfeasor, the total verdict of the plaintiff against the remaining tortfeasor-defendants may be reduced by the amount of the settlement or the settling tortfeasor's equitable share of the damages under Article 14 of the C.P.L.R., whichever turns out to be greater. Hence, the non-settling defendant may put in evidence the settling tortfeasor's purported liability, subpoena witnesses for that purpose, and request the court to charge an apportionment with respect to the settling tort-feasor's liability. The jury, if it so chooses, may apportion a percentage of liability to the settling tortfeasor, and the total verdict against the remaining defendants may be reduced by the percentage apportioned share of the liability assigned by the jury to the settling defendant, as applied to the total verdict gained by the plaintiff. On the other hand, if the amount of the settlement with the joint tortfeasor turns out to be greater than that tortfeasor's percentage apportioned share of the liability, as determined by the jury and as applied to the total damage award, the verdict under Section 15-108 will be reduced by the settlement amount, pursuant to Section 15-108 and C.P.L.R. §4533-b. In this case, it is the court and not the jury that reduces the verdict.

Section 15-108 and C.P.L.R. 4533-b provide, ineluctably, two methods whereby a settling joint tortfeasor's liability may be considered by the court and jury. *Purcell v. Doherty, supra*, well displays the operation of the statute. *Purcell* was a personal injury action wherein the plaintiff suffered injuries as the result of an automobile accident while a passenger in an automobile operated by the defendant Doherty and owned by the Gelco Corporation. The plaintiff, while a passenger in the Doherty vehicle when it became stuck in the snow, exited the vehicle and was struck in the left leg while in the rear of the Doherty vehicle, by a vehicle owned by the defendant Delgado. Shortly thereafter, a vehicle owned by the defendant Ehner and driven by the defendant McKay, struck the Ehner vehicle, causing the Delgado vehicle to strike the plaintiff again. Two defendants, during trial, settled with the plaintiff for $50,000.00 and $100,000.00, respectively. Stipulations of discontinuance and general releases were given in exchange for this settlement agreement. Counsel for the settling tortfeasors withdrew from the action, and no mention was made to the jury concerning their absence. The jury was instructed not to draw any inferences concerning their absence, and they were to consider these defendants as still in the case and determine their liability, if any. The jury returned a verdict against the defendants Doherty, Gelco Corporation, and Delgado for $775,000.00 and apportioned 65 percent of the liability to the Delgado vehicle and 35 percent to the Doherty/

Gelco vehicle. A motion was made to reduce the verdict by the amount of the settlement, which the court denied with leave to renew upon proper papers and memoranda of law.

The plaintiff contended initially that the moving defendant wrongdoers were successive, not joint tortfeasors, and that, in order to be entitled to offset the amount of the settlement against the verdict, there must be a finding that the settling defendants were in some way negligent, or a windfall would result to the non-settling defendants. The court rejected this first argument, stating that C.P.L.R. §4533-b must be held to apply to successive as well as joint tortfeasors. With respect to the second argument, the court, after reviewing C.P.L.R. §4533-b, Section 15-108 of the General Obligations Law, and the relevant case law, held that

> the amount of the released tortfeasor's . . . equitable share of the damages, as determined by the jury, was zero; the amount of the released tortfeasor's settlement was $150,000.00; thus plaintiff's claims against the remaining tortfeasors should be reduced by the greater of the two amounts (that is, $150,000.00). *Purcell v. Doherty, supra,* at 995.

The court went on to conclude that for the non-settling tortfeasor to benefit from C.P.L.R. §4533-b and General Obligations Law 15-108, the settling defendants need only be claimed to be liable in tort for the same injury, implying that it need not be found that said settling defendants were, in fact, determined to be liable to the plaintiff. *Werner v. Our Lady of Lourdes,* 60 A.D. 2d 791, 400 N.Y.S. 2d 659 (4th Dept. 1977), is also apropos. In *Werner,* the plaintiff, who was injured in a school gymnasium, sued the school and the student who struck the plaintiff. The plaintiff, at trial, settled her claims against the defendant-student. The jury returned a verdict against the school for $3,000.00, but held that there was no cause of action by the plaintiff against the defendant-student. The Supreme Court, Monroe County, reduced the judgment by the amount paid by the student in settlement of the plaintiff's claims, and the Fourth Department affirmed. In similar fashion, in *Bellamy v. Prime,* 25 A.D. 2d 923, 270 N.Y.S. 2d 93 (3rd Dept. 1966), the plaintiffs, while passengers, were injured in an automobile accident and sued the driver of the car they were in as well as the driver of the other automobile involved in the accident. Prior to trial, the plaintiffs settled with the driver of the second car for $7,500.00. The jury later awarded a verdict of $10,000.00 in favor of the plaintiffs against the driver of the automobile in which the plaintiffs were passengers, exonerating the driver who settled with the plaintiffs. The Third Department affirmed the lower court's reduction of the judgment by the amount of the prior settlement.

Epilogue

Section 15-108 of the General Obligations Law, together with C.P.L.R. §4533-b, provide two procedures to take into account settling tortfeasors' liability. The total verdict may be reduced by the amount of the settlement or the percentage of the liability that the jury finds should attach to the settling defendants, upon all the evidence adduced at trial. Section 15-108, however, upon careful reading, contains within it a statement of these same two procedures, stating that the verdict must be reduced by the settlement amount or the settling tortfeasor's equitable share of the damages, as found under Article 14 of the C.P.L.R., whichever is greater. The question arises—why C.P.L.R. §4533-b at all? The answer is articulated in *Aberathy v. Azzoni, supra.*

This article previously appeared in an edition of The Nassau Lawyer, a publication of the Nassau County Bar Association, and is being reprinted here with the permission of The Nassau County Bar Association.

10. Section 50-e: The Importance of Filing a Notice of Claim

Introductory

General Municipal Law, §§ 50-e and 50-i, the notice of claim statute, governs the commencement of all tort actions against municipal corporations and provides that no tort claim may be maintained against a municipal corporation for personal injury to real or personal property alleged to have been sustained by reason of the negligence or wrongful act of the municipality, unless a notice of claim is served upon the municipal corporation within ninety days after the claim arises.

Failure to file a notice of claim within the ninety day statutory period is fatal to the prospective plaintiff's action unless timely application is made to file a late notice of claim and it is accepted by the court.[1]

The statute is clear in its requirements and mandatory in character. Simply stated, the thrust of the law is that when a plaintiff sues a municipality for a tort, a notice of claim must be filed. Thus, where the lawsuit is for false arrest or medical malpractice, the notice of claim requirement is obvious. But how far does the statute extend? If money or property are seized by the police of a municipality pursuant to a valid search warrant and the plaintiff wishes to get his property back, must he file a notice of claim? It is this question that this article will examine.

The Law

The leading cases on this issue are *Boyle v. Kelley,*[2] and *Abramowitz v. Guido.*[3] In *Boyle*, $14,960.35 was seized from the apartment of the plaintiff, Donald J. Boyle, in December 1973. The plaintiff was arrested, along with his brother, and charged with various gambling offenses. A motion to vacate the search and suppress the evidence was granted in June 1974 as to Donald Boyle. Boyle's request for the return of the property was denied on the ground that it was not established whether such property constituted the fruits of a crime.

Thereafter, the People moved to dismiss the indictment against Boyle on the ground that, since the evidence had been suppressed, they would not be able to present a prima facie case. Prior to the hearing of this motion, Donald Boyle died. On June 18, 1974, the motion was granted and the indictment was dismissed.

On August 30, 1974, a demand was made upon the Suffolk County Police Commissioner, by motion, for the return of the money. The motion was withdrawn pending the appointment of an administrator for Boyle's estate. An administrator was appointed on July 30, 1975, but no subsequent demand was made nor a notice of claim filed. In September of 1975, a summons and complaint were served upon the Suffolk County Police Commissioner by the administrator of the Boyle estate, stating that the retention of the money was wrong in light of the dismissal of the charges against Mr. Boyle and the fact that more than thirty days had passed and no appeal was taken by the People. The complaint demanded the return of the money to the plaintiff as administrator of the estate. The plaintiff moved for summary judgment while the defendant crossmoved to dismiss for failure to state a cause of action because a notice of claim had not been served. Special Term granted the plaintiff's motion. The court reasoned, citing C.P.L. ~ 710.70, subd:1, that plaintiff's title or right to possession of the money had been adequately asserted and, since it had been established that the property taken did not constitute the fruits of a crime, it should be returned.[4]

On appeal, the Second Department affirmed. The court held that the service of a notice of claim pursuant to Section 50-e of the General Municipal Law was not required in this context. The court stated that the case before it was an action for moneys had and wrongfully received, or for unjust enrichment. The court then defined the case before it as equitable in character, thereby obviating the need for compliance with Section 50-e since where an action sounds in equity only, no notice of claim is required because it is not truly a tort action.[5]

Second, the court cited two cases to further support its position that the filing of a notice of claim was not required in this case: *Caggiano v. Frank*[6] and *McClendon v. Rosetti.*[7]

Caggiano involved a claim against the Police Commissioner of Nassau County for the return of money seized from the petitioner in connection with a gambling arrest. The court in *Caggiano* held that the subsequent dismissal of the criminal charges cast a duty upon the authorities to return the money to the petitioner upon demand. *McClendon* involved claims for the return of personal property seized by the police in connection with criminal arrests where the property was not returned after the criminal matters had been resolved. In *McClendon*, the court held that, absent evidence of criminal misconduct, personal property may not be forfeited to the state. The Appellate Division, in *Boyle*, reasoned from *Caggiano* and *McClendon* that, as a matter of justice and fairness, the money should be returned and that, apparently, the notice of claim requirement was irrelevant.[8]

The reasoning of the Appellate Division in *Boyle* is faulty. It is true that the action for unjust enrichment is equitable in character and so, as a technical matter of law, a notice of claim need not be filed. In fact, however, the so-called action for unjust enrichment is largely tortious in character. The action grew out of assumpsit. It was held that where a debt existed, the law would supply a promise to pay. Moreover, the debt and the promise are implied where a person had received or used something which justice required that he compensate another for. The assumpsit action was held to lie where defendant had converted and sold the plaintiff's goods and where money or property was obtained by misrepresentation. The plaintiff was permitted to rescind the transaction and recover the value of what he had parted with. The action was finally held to allow the plaintiff to maintain a claim for replevin or conversion for goods which he had surrendered to the defendant.

It is true that this remedy, which grew out of assumpsit and acquired the name of Quasi-contract, restitution or unjust enrichment, was essentially an equitable remedy. However, the leading authority on the law of torts concluded his analysis of the history of actions for unjust enrichment with the following caveat:[9]

> Out of this common law procedure there has developed the doctrine that where the commission of a tort results in the unjust enrichment of the defendant at the plaintiff's expense, the plaintiff, may disregard, or "waive" the tort action, and sue instead on a theoretical and fictitious contract for restitution of the benefits which the defendant has so received. "Waiver" of the tort is an unfortunate term, since the quasi-contract action itself is still based on the tort, and there is merely an election between alternative, co-existing remedies, and the unsuccessful pursuit of the "implied" contract will not bar a later action for the tort itself.

The action for unjust enrichment or restitution is no more than a secondary remedy to the enforcement and redress of a civil wrong. If this is so then the notice of claim is still required where the claim is in reality tortious in character although the remedy to redress the wrong be historically equitable.

The Appellate Division's citation of *Caggiano* and *McClendon* to support its holding that a notice of claim need not be filed also misses the mark. *Caggiano* sets forth the principle that the dismissal of the criminal charges against a potential plaintiff raises a duty upon the authorities to return money upon the demand of the petitioner. It states that arbitrary refusal to return that money upon demand may be reviewed in an Article 78 proceeding. *McClendon* states that without evidence of unlawful conduct, criminal sanctions may not be imposed nor property forfeited. The fact that the courts, in *McClendon* and *Caggiano*, held that money and property should, by some general rule of fairness and justice, be returned when taken by the police and no longer needed in light of the dismissal of criminal charges against the prospective plaintiff, does not bear upon the issue whether a notice of claim must be filed by the plaintiff to obtain the return of the money or property.

The Court of Appeals, upon review of the Appellate Division's decision in *Boyle*, rejected the arguments of the intermediate appellate court and reversed.[10]

The court stated that the Appellate Division's reliance on the supposed equitable nature of the claim as the ground for not requiring service of a notice of claim, was misplaced. The Court argued that equity will not entertain jurisdiction where there is an adequate remedy at law—in this case, an action for replevin or an Article 78 proceeding. Second, the court held that the specific language of County Law ~ 52 (1)[11] would still require a notice of claim.

The second of these arguments would appear to be of limited application inasmuch as County Law § 52 applies only to counties and so excludes all other forms of public corporations such as villages, fire districts and cities. The Court of Appeals in *Boyle* did not base its decision on General Municipal Law § 50-e which applies not only to counties, but also to cities, towns, villages and school districts.

In a sense, then, the Court of Appeals' decision in *Boyle* is somewhat openended. Since although County Law ~ 52 requires the filing of a notice of claim, whether the action be legal or equitable, that statute is limited to counties alone. The Court of Appeals, in *Boyle*, also holds that where there is an adequate remedy at law, the filing of a notice of claim is required. Implicit in that holding is the notion that, where there is no adequate remedy at law and a solely equitable remedy exists to redress the civil wrong, then no notice of claim must be filed.

If there was any confusion as to the proper application and interpretation of the Court of Appeals' holding in *Boyle*, the Second Department made its position clear in *Abramowitz v. Guido*.[12] *Abramowitz* was an article 78 proceeding to compel the Police Commissioner of Nassau County to return to the petitioner money taken from his possession by the Nassau County Police upon his arrest for criminal possession of a dangerous drug. The Second Department held that

> the holding in *Boyle v. Kelley*, . . . is all-embracing as to the requirement that a notice of claim be timely filed where the gravamen is the wrongful retention by a municipality of money or property after the dismissal of a criminal action in the course of which the money or property had been seized. The requirement may not be evaded by resort to a CPLR article 78 proceeding instead of an action in tort for conversion, or by an action upon the equitable principle of unjust enrichment (see County Law, § 52; General Municipal Law, § 50-e).

The *Abramowitz* case enunciates the same rule as the Court of Appeals set forth in *Boyle*—that a notice of claim must be filed where the action is for the wrongful retention of money or property by a municipality after the dismissal of the criminal action in which the money or property had been seized. The reasoning in *Abramowitz*, however, is broader and more inclusive. The Second Department is heading towards a doctrine, in *Abramowitz*, that it is not the form of action used, whether Article 78, a conversion action, or an action upon the principle of unjust enrichment, that is determinative of whether a notice of claim must be filed. The important fact is that a civil wrong—the wrongful detention of money or property by a municipality—exists for which the plaintiff seeks to be made whole. Therefore, a Section 50-e notice of claim requirement still remains.[13]

The results reached by the Court of Appeals in *Boyle* and by the Appellate Division in *Abramowitz* are correct. The retention of property by a municipality, obtained pursuant to a search or arrest and retained after criminal charges have been dismissed against the plaintiff, clearly constitutes an alleged tort. Hence, in order to regain possession of this money or property, purportedly wrongfully withheld, the plaintiff, in order to commence a valid lawsuit, must, as in all cases where a municipality is sued in tort, file a notice of claim under Section 50-e.

The Court of Appeals in *Boyle* and the Appellate Division, Second Department, in *Abramowitz* have given force and teeth to Section 50-e where, in some instances, intermediate appellate courts have sought to limit its true meaning and effect. As long as the statute remains as a law of this state, any plaintiff who wishes to sue a municipality for an alleged wrongful act must comply with the notice of claim requirement.

Counsel who seeks the return of his client's money or property from the Police Property Clerk, whether he commences his lawsuit as an Article 78 proceeding, a conversion action, a replevin action, or an action for restitution, must take care to fulfill the strict mandates of Section 50-e of the General Municipal Law or the municipality will be rewarded with an unanticipated windfall.[14]

11. Amendment of the Pleadings and the Notice of Claim

The Issue Defined

The notice of claim statute, sections 50-e and 50-i of the General Municipal Law, is the bridge that must first be crossed for the plaintiff's attorney who wishes to prosecute a tort action against a municipality. This statute governs the commencement of all actions against municipal corporations and provides that no tort claim may be maintained against a municipal corporation unless a Notice of Claim is served upon the municipality within ninety (90) days after the claim arises.[1]

Section 50-e(5) of the statute provides a mechanism whereby the court may, upon application by the plaintiff, grant leave to file a late notice of claim based on a number of relevant considerations.[2] Section 50-e(6) of the statute states that a bona fide mistake on omission in the notice of claim may be rectified by the Court providing that the other party was not prejudiced.[3] Section 50-i of the General Municipal Law provides that no action can be maintained against a municipality for injury to real or personal property alleged to have been sustained by reason of the negligence or wrongful act of the municipality unless a Notice of Claim is served in compliance with Section 50-e. The requirements of Sections 50-e and 50-i of the General Municipal Law that a Notice of Claim be served upon a municipality within ninety (90) days after the claim arises have been and continue to be strictly construed and applied by the courts of this state.[4] Failure to file a notice of claim within the statutory period is fatal to the prospective plaintiff's action unless timely application is made by the plaintiff to file a Notice of Claim and it is accepted by the court. The plaintiff's attorney then must be wary of the pitfalls of the statute and careful to comply with its strictures. There can be no doubt but that the statute requires that the tort action must be, as it were, pleaded in the Notice of Claim as a condition precedent to the prosecution of the action and that failure to do so is death to the plaintiff's lawsuit. Or is it? C.P.L.R. § 3025(b) provides that a party may amend his pleading and supplement it at any time by leave of the court or by stipulation of the parties and that leave shall be freely given by the court. Section 203(e) provides that a claim asserted in an amended pleading is deemed to have been interposed at the time the claims in the original pleading are interposed if the original pleading gives notice of the transactions, occurrences, or series of transactions or occurrences to be proved pursuant to the amended pleading.[5] Under these statutes, it would appear that if the court determines that the original pleadings gave notice of a new claim which the plaintiff seeks to add to his complaint by way of amendment, the complaint may be amended under C.P.L.R. §§ 203(e) and 3025(b) to include a new claim even though that claim may not have been specifically pleaded in the original notice of claim. Thus, for example, if the plaintiff pleads the constituent elements of an assault action in his Notice of Claim and complaint, and some years later, on the eve of trial, the court grants his application to amend his complaint pursuant to C.P.L.R. §§ 3025(b) and 203(e) to add a cause of action for negligence on the theory that this new claim relates back to the original assault claim, which provided, in theory, adequate notice of the new cause of action, the plaintiff has effectually commenced an additional tort action and so escaped the proscription of Sections 50-e and 50-i of the General Municipal Law since the new claim was not included in the original notice of claim nor was application made under Section 50-e(5) to add this new claim. Whether a plaintiff may, by this method, so evade filing a notice of claim or making application to file a late Notice of Claim with respect to the new tort action he has now included in his amended complaint, is the question this article proposes to examine

The Law

There are two lines of appellate cases on the issue whether a complaint may be amended to add a new tort action which was not pleaded in the notice of claim. *Kieninger v. City of New York,* 53 A.D.2d 602, 384 N.Y.S.2d 11 (2d Dept. 1976), was an action to recover damages for false imprisonment, malicious prosecution, and assault. The defendant, City of New York, appealed from a judgment of the Supreme Court in favor of the plaintiff upon a jury verdict. The Second Department reversed and dismissed the assault cause of action and granted a new trial on damages only.

The court held that because the plaintiff failed to state his assault cause of action in his Notice of Claim, the defendant City's trial motion to dismiss this cause of action for failure to adequately comply with the notice requirements of Section 50-e should have been granted to the extent of dismissing the assault claim.

The Court noted, however, that

> although the malicious prosecution cause of action was also not stated in the notice of claim, that cause of action was properly not dismissed since it had not accrued at the time the notice of claim was served and, moreover, within 90 days after it did accrue (the time limitation for the service of a notice of claim), plaintiff commenced the instant action (see *Quintero v. Long Is. R.R.,* 31 A.D.2d 844 [298 N.Y.S.2d 109]). *Kieninger v. City of New York, supra,* at 602, 384 N.Y.S.2d 11.

The holding in *Kieninger*, at first glance, is clear and not susceptible of more than one interpretation: simply that failure *to state* a cause of action for assault in the notice of claim required dismissal of this cause of action. Two additional points should be noted, however. First, the *Kieninger* court stated that the defendant's motion to dismiss should have been granted as to the assault "*for failure to adequately comply with the notice requirements* of section 50-e of the General Municipal Law." Second, the court refused to dismiss the malicious prosecution for the reason that within 90 days of its accrual, the plaintiff commenced the instant action, citing *Quintero*. In *Quintero*, the Supreme Court granted the plaintiff's motion for leave to serve an amended complaint and amended notice of claim. The court held that because the summons and complaint contained all the information necessary to comply with the statutory requirements with respect to a notice of claim, it would be deemed a notice of claim. The *Kieninger* court, in the opinion of this writer, is hinting that if somehow proper notice is provided in the complaint to the defendant as to the claim sought to be added, the strict pleading requirements of the notice of claim statute may be waived.

In a similar case, *Colena v. City of New York,* 68 A.D.2d 898, 414 N.Y.S.2d 220 (2d Dept. 1979), the appellate court again faced the same issue. *Colena* was an action to recover damages for assault, false arrest and malicious prosecution. The defendant, City of New York, appealed from an order which denied its cross motion to dismiss the plaintiff's complaint and granted the plaintiff's motion to strike certain affirmative defenses. The Appellate Division reversed and granted the defendant City's motion to dismiss. In *Colena*, the plaintiff was allegedly assaulted on October 24, 1970, by an off-duty New York City policeman, the defendant, Morris H. Maduro. The plaintiff was arrested and released the following day. The criminal proceeding was terminated in his favor on April 27, 1971, six months after the alleged assault. On March 9, 1971, one hundred

and thirty-six days after the event of October 24, 1970, the plaintiff served a notice of claim against the City of New York for personal injuries. The notice
stated that the claim arose "as a result of a violent and unprovoked assault by
Sergeant Morris Maduro."

The summons and complaint were served on or about April 30, 1974. The
complaint set forth three causes of action. The first was for assault against the
defendant, Morris Maduro. The second was for false imprisonment against the
City of New York and defendant Maduro and also reasserted the assault claim
by incorporation. The third was against defendant Maduro alone, seeking punitive damages for alleged actual malice in arresting and bringing criminal charges
against the plaintiff.

The answer of the City of New York asserted non-compliance with Section
50-e of the General Municipal Law. The plaintiff moved on November 30, 1976,
more than six years after the alleged assault, to strike this affirmative defense.
The City of New York cross moved to dismiss the complaint against it, alleging
untimely service of the notice of claim. The court first dismissed the assault
claim against the City on the ground that no notice of claim was filed nor was
application made to file a late notice of claim within one year of the accrual of
the event upon which the claim was based. More importantly, the court further
held that

> the cause of action for *false imprisonment* (which is the only explicit cause of
> action in the complaint against the City of New York) suffers the impediment
> that it was not mentioned, directly or indirectly, in the notice of claim. There-
> fore, the notice of claim could not alert the City of New York to the fact that
> plaintiff was seeking a recovery for anything more than personal injuries for the
> "violent and unprovoked *assault*" (emphasis supplied) by the defendant police
> officer on October 24, 1970. *Colena v. City of New York, supra*, at 900, 414
> N.Y.S.2d 220.

Colena is of great import. The court held that the cause of action for false
imprisonment must be specifically mentioned in the notice of claim. It is interesting to note that the court set off the words "false imprisonment" in italics, indicating that these very words must appear in the notice of claim for the claim to
pass muster under section 50-e.

Finally, there is *Alaxanian v. City of Troy*, 69 A.D.2d 937, 415 N.Y.S.2d
293 (3rd Dept. 1979). *Alaxanian* was an appeal from an order of the Supreme
Court, Special Term, which granted defendants' motion to dismiss the complaint
for failure to state a cause of action and denied plaintiff's cross motion to re-
plead. *Alaxanian* was an action arising from the arrest of plaintiff by individual
defendants, members of the Troy Police Department, and the subsequent dismissal of the charges. The amended complaint alleged five causes of action including one for violation of the plaintiff's civil rights. Citing *Kieninger v. City of
New York, supra*, the court ruled that

the record reveals that the notice of claim did not set forth any cause of action for a violation of civil rights. Special Term, therefore, properly dismissed said cause of action since there was a failure to comply with section 50-e of the General Municipal Law. *Alaxanian* v. *City at Troy, supra* 937, 415 N.Y.S.2d 293.

There can be only one interpretation of *Kieninger, Colena* and *Alaxanian*—that unless the original notice of claim specifically states the cause of action claimed against the municipality, whether for civil rights (*Alaxanian*), false imprisonment (*Colena*), or assault (*Kieninger*), that action must fall. In short, these cases establish a rule of law that where the plaintiff fails to allege a cause of action in his notice of claim and then attempts to do so by way of amending his pleadings, such a cause of action must be dismissed.

There is another line of cases that sing a new and different song. These cases hold, apparently, that if the plaintiff seeks to amend his complaint to add a new cause of action not stated in his original notice of claim, such amendment will be sustained by the appellate court if it can be shown first that notice of this new claim is provided in the original notice of claim and complaint, and second if it can also be proved that no prejudice will fall upon the municipality should the amendment be granted. *Watso* v. *City of New York,* 39 A.D.2d 960, 333, N.Y.S.2d 492 (2d Dept. 1972), was an action to recover damages for wrongful death and conscious pain and suffering. The Supreme Court of Kings County denied the plaintiff's motion to add a third cause of action for assault. The Second Department reversed stating

> the notice of claim served on the defendant City of New York set forth that plaintiff's decedent was shot through the negligence and improper conduct of a police officer and the original complaint was framed in negligence. Although the proposed amended complaint is framed in assault as well as in negligence, all the causes relate to the same state of facts and therefore the addition of the assault causes does not prejudice defendant. *Watso* v. *City of New York, supra,* at 961, 333 N.Y.S.2d 492.

A more recent decision on this issue is *Carlisle* v. *County of Nassau,* 75 A.D.2d 593, 426 N.Y.S.2d 815 (2d Dept. 1980). *Carlisle* was an action for assault and false arrest. The plaintiff moved to amend his complaint to add a cause of action alleging negligence, and the trial court denied the motion. The Appellate Division reversed, reasoning that

> the original complaint put the defendant on "notice of the transactions, occurrences, or series of transactions or occurrences to be proved pursuant to the amended pleading" (C.P.L.R. 203, subd. [e]). The same transaction which gave rise to the original claim of assault, the confrontation between the plaintiff and the defendant's employee, a police officer, is at the base of the amended claim alleging negligence. The defendant was given sufficient notice, at the time of the original complaint, of the acts of which the plaintiff is now complaining (see *Watso* v. *City of New York,* 39 A.D.2d 960, 333 N.Y.S.2d 492).

Both *Watso* and *Carlisle* are tort actions against municipalities. In both cases, the Second Department ignored the salient fact that the cause of action which the plaintiff sought to add to his complaint was not specifically set forth in his notice of claim, which was the entire basis of the holdings in *Kieninger*, *Colena* and *Alaxanian*. In both *Watso* and *Carlisle*, the Appellate Court based its decision on the ground that, under C.P.L.R. § 203 (e), the same facts lay at the base of both the original claim set forth in the complaint and that claim sought to be added. Hence, the court reasoned in *Watso* and *Carlisle* that, since the defendant theoretically had notice at the time of the original complaint of the facts supposedly underlying both the original claim and the new claim, there was notice to the municipality of the additional claim and *ipso facto* no prejudice to the municipality in the addition of a claim not mentioned in the original notice of claim or complaint.

Amendment of the Notice of Claim under Section 50-e(6)

Section 50-e(6) of the General Municipal Law sets forth a procedure whereby notice of claim may, at any time at or before trial of the action, be amended to correct, supply, or disregard a mistake, omission, irregularity, or defect in the notice of claim made in good faith. The question comes to mind, in light of Section 50-e(6), that perhaps the notice of claim may be amended to add a new cause of action not originally stated in the notice of claim, thereby rectifying the plaintiff's failure to plead this new cause of action in his original notice and so, under Section 50-8(6), correcting his mistake. The cases interpreting Section 50-e(6), however, uniformly hold that a notice of claim may not be amended to state a new cause of action under that section.

Dale v. Half Hollow Hills School District, 37 A.D.2d 778, 325 N.Y.S.2d 267 (2d Dept. 1971), was an appeal from an order of the Supreme Court which denied plaintiffs' cross-motion to amend their notice of claim. The Second Department denied plaintiffs-parents' application to amend their notice of claim to add a claim for pain and suffering resulting from the wrongful death of their daughter. The court held the amendment to be substantive in nature and so not within the purview of Section 50-e(6) of the General Municipal Law since it would be the interposition of a new cause of action subsequent to the time limited by statute. In *Kinard v. City of New York,* 26 A.D. 2d 821, 273 N.Y.S.2d 775 (2d Dept. 1966), the Second Department again refused to permit the amendment of the notice of claim to add a cause of action for malicious prosecution in addition to the cause of action asserted in the notice of claim on the same ground asserted in *Dale*—that the amendment would constitute the addition of a new cause of action and so was not within the ambit of Section 50-e(6) of the General Municipal Law.

Grant v. City of Rochester, 68 Misc.2d 358, 326 N.Y.S.2d 691 (Sup. Ct., Monroe Co. 1971), is highly instructive. *Grant* was a claim against the City of Rochester and its police department for assault and false imprisonment arising from incidents which occurred on April 28, 1968. The notice of claim was timely filed on July 1, 1968, and in February of 1969 the plaintiff commenced an action for assault and false imprisonment. The plaintiff, in 1971, sought to amend his notice of claim and complaint to add a cause of action for malicious prosecution. The plaintiff argued that Section 50-e(6) of the General Municipal Law permitted such amendment because, through inadvertence or oversight, the charge of malicious prosecution was not included in the original notice of claim. The court reasoned first that C.P.L.R. § 3025(b) freely allows amendment of the pleadings and that, under C.P.L.R. § 203(e), a claim in an amended pleading is deemed to have been interposed at the time that the claim in the original pleadings were interposed, unless the original pleading does not give notice of the transactions or occurrences sought to be proved pursuant to the amended pleading. The court concluded that, if the proposed amendment were to be allowed in the complaint, the one year statute of limitations for a malicious prosecution action would not be a bar (C.P.L.R. § 215). The court, upon analysis of the particular case confronting it, held that the notice of claim did not give reasonable notice of a possible claim of malicious prosecution in connection with the false arrest and false imprisonment causes of action.

> False arrest or imprisonment and malicious prosecution are totally different substantive torts. Malicious prosecution is a judicial proceeding, begun in malice, without probable cause, which finally ends in failure. False imprisonment is the intentional and unlawful detention of another against his will. Malice is not an element of false arrest (see 2 N.Y. PJI 600). Plaintiff may not amend his claim to now include a cause of action for malicious prosecution. Such amendment would be of a substantive nature and not contemplated by the General Municipal Law (§ 50-e, subd. 6) (see *Matter of Kinard v. City of New York*, 26 A.D.2d 821 [273 N.Y.S.2d 775]; *La Rocco v. City of New York*, 37 A.D.2d 529 [322 N.Y.S.2d 163], affd. 29 N.Y.2d 687 [325 N.Y.S.2d 418, 274 N.E.2d 751]).
>
> The motion is denied. *Grant v. City of Rochester, supra*, 326 N.Y.S.2d at 693.

The holding in *Grant* is of great significance. The court holds that, on the one hand, a notice of claim may be amended to add a new cause of action if the original notice of claim provides what it deems to be reasonable notice of the new claim under C.P.L.R. § 203(e). The court seems to say that a notice of claim may be amended in the manner of a pleading under C.P.L.R. §§ 3025(b) and 203(e) where notice of the sought for amendment may be found in the language of the original notice of claim. *Grant* also states that the addition of a new cause of action such as malicious prosecution, with its additional element of malice, to a false arrest claim inherently cannot be "noticed" by the original false arrest claim inasmuch as false arrest and malicious prosecution are totally different substantive torts with differing elements.[6]

The cases construing Section 50-e(6) of the General Municipal Law all hold that a notice of claim may not be amended to add a new substantive cause of action, be it a new claim for pain and suffering in addition to one for wrongful death (*Dale*), malicious prosecution in addition to false arrest and assault (*Grant*), assault in addition to negligence (*Oliveras*), or personal injuries in addition to property damages (*La Rocco*). It is true that *Grant* appears to hold that, if the original cause of action stated in the notice of claim provides reasonable notice under C.P.L.R. § 203(e) of the new claim, then the notice of claim may be amended to add that new claim. *Grant*, as has been noted, refused to permit such amendment when a new substantive claim was sought to be added by the plaintiff, reasoning that where the claim to be added is neither more nor less than a different substantive tort, introducing new elements to be proved, there cannot be, per se, adequate notice under Section 203(e) of the Civil Practice Law and Rules, and so there cannot be an amendment of the notice of claim in this fashion.

Thus, the cases interpreting Section 50-e(6) of the General Municipal Law do not permit the notice of claim to be amended to add a new tort claim. In this writer's opinion, as a matter of logic and common sense, if the General Municipal Law itself does not permit such amendment, as interpreted without dissent by the courts of this State, then to permit the amendment of the pleadings to add a new claim, not stated in the notice of claim, is to debase and, in fact, evade the entire scheme of the General Municipal Law, and Section 50-e(6) in particular.

Conclusion

The appellate courts of this State are divided on the issue whether a new claim, unstated in the notice of claim, may be added by amending the pleadings pursuant to C.P.L.R. §§ 3025(b) and 203(e). *Colena, Kieninger,* and *Alaxanian* all bar amendment of the complaint to add a new cause of action, where that claim is not stated in the original notice. *Kieninger* hints that, if the notice of claim provides "notice" of the new cause of action, the complaint may be successfully amended to add a new claim and so escape the letter, so to speak, of Section 50-e(6), which bars amendment of the notice of claim itself to add this new claim.

Watso takes up the cudgel of *Kieninger* and holds that a complaint framed first in negligence only may be amended to add a claim sounding in assault if the facts set forth in the notice of claim provide notice under C.P.L.R. § 203(e) of the assault claim as well as the original claim.

Carlisle makes no mention of the notice of claim or Section 50-e of the General Municipal Law and gives its imprimatur to the addition of the negligence claim to the assault claim on pure notice grounds alone.

It is clear that the appellate courts of the State of New York are moving to a doctrine that, where the facts in the original notice of claim and/or complaint provide, in the judgment and discretion of the court, "adequate notice" of the new claim sought to be added under C.P.L.R. § 203(e), the complaint may be amended on this ground, to add a new cause of action with new constituent elements nowhere stated in the original notice and, in fact, without reference to the notice of claim at all or Section 50-e.

In the opinion of this writer, this trend is a mistaken one and a disturbing one. C.P.L.R §§ 3025(b) and 203(e), which provide the mechanism to, and the method whereby, a pleading may be amended to add a new claim even though that claim may be barred by the statute of limitations, if notice of the new claim can be found by the court in the initial complaint, have reference to the pleadings only. Nowhere in C.P.L.R §§ 3025 and 203(e) does it state, nor do the cases interpreting these statutes hold, that a Section 50-e notice of claim is included under their rubric and so covered under the umbrella of the mechanism of notice pleading.

The notice of claim statute, Sections 50-e and 50-i of the General Municipal Law, is a statute separate and apart from these sections of the C.P.L.R concerned with amendment of the pleadings. Indeed, the General Municipal Law, under Section 50-e(6) has a method for amending the notice of claim and neither that section itself, nor the case law construing it, permit amendment of a notice of claim to add a new cause of action. If the framers of the General Municipal Law wished to permit amendment of the notice of claim through the notice mechanism provided for amendment of the pleadings under C.P.L.R § 203(e), they would doubtless have done so, and if the courts desired to interpret Section 50-e(6) to allow amendment of the notice of claim on this basis and import C.P.L.R § 203(e) into the statute, they, too, would have done so.

Both in *Watso* and *Carlisle*, the courts permitted a party to thrust into the litigation claims, respectively, for assault and negligence, claims not set forth in the notice of claim and complaint. In effect, the court, in these cases, permitted the plaintiffs to write into their lawsuit a new play, with new actors, and a new plot, evading the strict requirements of Section 50-e by adding a second scenario to litigation that was first played upon the municipality in one act.

This writer must argue that to permit a plaintiff to add a new claim, unmentioned in his notice of claim, to his complaint is, if not to effectually eliminate Section 50-e of the General Municipal Law as a statute, then, at least, to emasculate and castrate its force and effect. It is to read the amendment procedure of Section 50-e(6) out of the statute and replace it with C.P.L.R § 203(e) that has no place in the 50-e scheme. If the people of this State are dissatisfied with Section 50-e of the General Municipal Law as a whole, and Section 50-e(6) in particular, then it is for them, acting through their legislators, to repeal or amend the statute, to provide a procedure whereby a notice of claim may be amended to add a new cause of action not heretofore mentioned in the notice of claim or complaint. It is not for the courts, through the methods set forth in the C.P.L.R for amendment of the pleadings (C.P.L.R §§ 3025[b] and 203[e]), to gloss over the patent requirement and intent of Section 50-e that a cause of action must be specifically stated in the notice of claim and that this notice of claim may not thereafter be modified to include a novel cause of action.[7]

Reprinted with permission from New York Supplement (Advance Sheet July 1981) published by Thomson-West, 610 Opperman Drive, St. Paul, MN 55164.

12. Bifurcation and Trifurcation

It has long been the accepted and authorized rule and practice in the State of New York that, in all negligence actions, the issue of liability and damages shall be tried separately and separate verdicts rendered.[1] The rationale for the rule has been variously stated, but the courts have generally cited, as a justification of the policy, the efficient operation of court calendars and the speedier disposition of cases.[2]

Schollmeyer v. Sutter, 151 N.Y.S.2d 795 (S. Ct., Queens Co., 1956), is an excellent summary of the rationale underlying this rule of bifurcation. In *Schollmeyer,* at the opening of the trial of the negligence action, the court directed that the issue of liability be tried first without proof of the plaintiff's injuries. If the verdict on liability were to be in favor of the plaintiff, the relevant medical testimony would then be received and considered by the jury in finding the amount of damages. The procedure was ordered by the court on the authority of Section 443, subd. 3, of the Civil Practice Act which, at that time, read that

> the court, in its discretion, may order one or more issues to be separately tried prior to any trial of the other issues in the case.

The plaintiff's trial counsel in *Schollmeyer* objected to this procedure of bifurcating the liability and damage phases of the action and refused to proceed to trial. The court then dismissed the complaint to permit the issue of his discretion to bifurcate to be fully presented to the appellate court. Plaintiff's counsel then moved for reconsideration by the trial court of the split trial procedure directed therein or, in the alternative, for a stay of judgment pending appeal. The court granted the stay, but denied reargument. The court initially noted that, if the jury verdict therein was for the defendant on the question of liability, it would be unnecessary to consider medical proof, thus,

> saving a day or two of the time of court counsel, jury, medical witnesses and other personnel, as well as the expense to both litigants of bringing medical experts to court. *Schollmeyer v. Suter, supra,* at 796.

The court went on to summarize the reasons for the split trial procedure:

> Even in a comparatively short negligence action, the medical testimony often consumes a full day of the court's time; in longer actions, it may consume two, three or more days. Trying the issue of liability separately will result in a considerable savings of time and expense with no detriment to the litigants.
>
> It was not the court's purpose to exclude from this trial of the question of liability all testimony of the injuries sustained, but only that of the medical experts. The plaintiff, himself, would be permitted to state in layman's language the injuries he suffered, thus enabling the jury to have a fair idea of the importance to the plaintiff of this litigation. More than this a plaintiff cannot ask since the jury is instructed not to base its verdict on either sympathy or bias.

While it is true that a separate trial of one issue in a case has in the past been generally limited to issues which are in the nature of a plea in bar, such as release, res judicata, etc., *Smith v. Western Pacific Railroad Company,* 144 App. Div. 180, 128 N.Y .S. 966, affirmed 203 N.Y. 499, 96 N.E. 1106, 40 L.R.A., N.S., 137, on the other hand it has been the glory of the common law that it is not static but dynamic and capable of adapting itself to changing times and economic conditions. The present calendar congestion appears to present a sufficient reason for the court "in its discretion" to order the separate trial of the issue of liability. Civil Practice Act, 443. *Schollmeyer v. Sutter, supra,* at 796, 797.

The rule then is, apparently, founded upon reasons of judicial economy and convenience to attain a speedier disposition and disposal of negligence trials and the avoidance of calendar congestion. Moreover, the rule, it would seem, derives its power from CPLR § § 603 and 4011.[3]

Taken together, these sections of the Civil Practice Law and Rules lodge within the trial judiciary the right and discretion to sever and separately try discrete factual issues in the order that the court deems appropriate.

The Exception

The rule then of bifurcation in negligence trials is general and of wide application. The appellate courts of this state, however, in their wisdom, have carved out an exception to this rule of bifurcation that, in certain defined circumstances, the trial court may order a full trial on liability and damages in a negligence case. Thus, the cases hold, that where the nature of the plaintiffs injuries has such a bearing and connection with the issue of liability such that proof of injury, medical or otherwise, must be shown in order to prove liability, or where a casual connection must be shown between the acts producing the injuries and the injuries sustained, a bifurcated trial may not be ordered and a full trial must be ordered.[4]

Lowe v. Board of Education of the City of New York, 36 A.D.2d 952, 321 N.Y.S.2d 508 (2d Dept. 1971), was a negligence action for personal injuries sustained by the plaintiff, Judith Lowe, while she was a pupil in a high school gymnasium class. The trial court dismissed the plaintiff's complaint at the close of the plaintiff's case. Upon a jury trial limited to the issue of liability, the Appellate Division reversed and granted a new trial.

The plaintiff, at the trial, claimed she had a physical disability because of a prior injury and stated at the trial that the defendant had notice of her disability by reason of the submission of three notes from her doctor and the fact that, over her protest, her teacher insisted that she do broad jumps as part of the gymnasium exercises. The court stated that this proof constituted the plaintiff's prima facie case provided, the court noted, it could be said that

there was a causal connection between the negligence claimed—compel a disabled pupil to perform physical exercises—and the injury incurred. However, no medical proof was offered by the plaintiffs to show such casual connection. *Lowe v. Board of Education of the City of New York, supra,* at 952.

The court thereupon concluded that

this was a split trial and only the limited issue of liability was tried. In such trials where causal connection is evident the medical proof is reserved for that part of the trial given to assessment of damages. Under the facts of this particular case, the causal connection is of such a nature as to require expert medical opinion.

Under the circumstances discussed, a complete trial, embracing both the liability and damage issues, should now be held, in view of the apparent necessity for medical proof. *Lowe v. Board of Education, supra,* at 952.

The general rule of bifurcation of negligence trials and its exception, as stated, are simple and left, in their application, to the discretion of the trial judiciary on an ad hoc case-by-case basis.

The Codification

In spite of the plethora of case law clearly stating the rule and its exception, the Appellate Division, Second Department, in a rule effective September 21, 1979, codified and expanded the law of this state with respect to bifurcated trials. It is useful to set forth the rule in its entirety:

699.14 Bifurcated trials in negligence actions to recover damages for personal injury.

(a) In all negligence actions to recover damages for personal injury, the issues of liability and damages shall be severed and the issue of liability shall be tried first. In exceptional circumstances, for reasons to be stated in the record, where, in the discretion of the judge presiding over the calendar part, good cause exists as to why such a severance should not be granted, he may order a single trial on the issues of liability and damages.

(b) During the voir dire conducted prior to the liability phase of the trial, counsel may question the prospective jurors with respect to the issue of damages in the same manner as if the trial were not bifurcated.

(c) In opening to the jury on the liability phase of the trial, counsel may not discuss the question of damages. However, if the verdict of the jury shall be in favor of the plaintiff on the liability issue, all parties shall then be afforded an opportunity to address the jury on the question of damages before proof in that regard is presented to them.

(d) In the event of a plaintiff's verdict on the issue of liability, the damage phase of the trial shall be conducted immediately thereafter before the same judge and jury, unless the judge presiding over the trial, for reasons stated in the record finds such procedures to be impracticable.

Rule 699.14 provides an entire schema of the bifurcated trial procedure. The rule mandates that the trial judge, in all personal injury actions, must separately try the issues of liability and damages. The judge presiding over the calendar part, however, in his discretion, upon a showing of good cause and exceptional circumstances, may order a full trial on liability and damages. The rule further states that, in the voir dire, counsel may question the jurors on the question of damages in the same manner as if the trial were full, and that the opening statements of counsel in the liability phase may not address the jury on the question of damages, although they may do so should the trial proceed to the damage phase.

Finally, the rule states that, in the event of a plaintiff's verdict on liability, the damages trial shall be conducted immediately before the same judge and jury, unless the judge presiding over the trial finds such procedure impractical, for reasons stated in the record.

Rule 699.14 is complete. It compels split trial in all personal injury actions unless the calendar judge orders otherwise and, even then, there must be a showing of good cause and exceptional circumstances set forth in the record. The discretion, in effect, heretofore residing in the trial judge to order or not to order split trials in accord with the broad rules set forth in the case law has been removed, and what was once a matter of discretion and custom solely residing in the trial judge has been codified into a rule to be obeyed by the trial judiciary unless the calendar judge orders otherwise. It is interesting to note that Rule 699.14 does not reveal what precisely "exceptional circumstances" are, and the case law has yet to reveal the import of this language. One may strongly suspect that the "exceptional circumstances" of the rule are no more than a codification of the earlier case law which held a full trial to be appropriate in personal injury actions where the medical proof has such a bearing on or connection with the issue of liability, that one cannot be proved without proof of the other. This, however, is only speculation and it will require further construction by the courts.

Trifurcation

If the courts of this state have long given their imprimatur to the bifurcation of personal injury cases and, now, with Rule 699.14, have codified their rulings for such a mandate, then their view of the trifurcation, or the splitting of an action into three separate trial phases, has been jaundiced indeed. The leading case is *Greenberg v. City of Yonkers*, 45 A.D.2d 314, 358 N.Y.S.2d 453 (2d Dept. 1974). *Greenberg* consisted of consolidated wrongful death and personal injury actions, which stemmed from a fire in a building in the City of Yonkers. The architect of the building (Rabineau), the building owner (the Federation of Jewish Philanthropies of Yonkers, Inc., the Yonkers Jewish Community Center), and the supplier of certain materials used in the building (Cyanamid) were sued. The first phase of the trial was on the issue of liability against the building owner, the architect, and the materials supplier (Center, Rabineau, and Cyanamid). The verdict was against the defendants Center and Rabineau and in favor of Cyanamid against the plaintiffs. Thereafter, the Center and Rabineau settled with the plaintiffs without prejudice to proceed on their cross-claims against the defendant, Cyanamid.

In the second phase of the trial, the court submitted to the jury the appointment of responsibility between defendant Center and Rabineau, as well as the cross-claims of these defendants against the defendant, Cyanamid. The jury, under *Dole v. Dow* (30 N.Y.2d 143, 331 N.Y.S.2d 382 [1972]), apportioned the liability of the Center and Rabineau at 30 percent and 70 percent, respectively, and on the cross-claims found that the manufacturer, Cyanamid, was negligent. The third phase of the trial was on the reasonableness of the plaintiffs' settlements with the Center and the architect. Cyanamid refused to concede the reasonableness of the settlement between the plaintiffs and defendants. The defendant, Cyanamid, appealed on the ground that it had been exonerated from liability in the first stage of the proceeding and that it was error under *Dole v. Dow* to compel it to participate in the second stage of the trial. The Appellate Division affirmed the trial court and rejected this argument of Cyanamid, holding that the second stage of the trial was not only an apportionment proceeding, but also a trial of the Center and Rabineau's cross-claim against Cyanamid. *Greenberg v. City of Yonkers, supra*, at 318.

The Court of Appeals affirmed this Appellate Division decision in a memorandum opinion. The court noted, however, that

> our affirmance should not be taken as an approval of the trifurcation procedure utilized here by the trial court. It is preferable, and sometimes essential, that issues of liability be resolved at one stage of the trial. *Greenberg v. City of Yonkers, supra*, at 907.

In a more recent case, *Smerechniak v. County of Nassau, supra*, the Second Department, following the Court of Appeals' dicta in *Greenberg*, voiced disapproval of the trifurcation process. *Smerechniak* was a personal injury action against the County of Nassau brought by five infant plaintiffs as a result of a gas explosion in an underground County water main which these plaintiffs had entered in a course of an "exploring expedition." While they were proceeding through the main, one plaintiff, Guy Smerechniak, raised a lighted candle which ignited a concentration of natural gas in the culvert, causing an explosion and fire, resulting in severe injures to all five plaintiffs. There were two separate actions brought, one by the plaintiff Smerechniak, and the other by the remaining four plaintiffs. The court originally directed that these actions be tried jointly and that the issues of liability and damages be tried in a full procedure. At the opening of trial, the infant plaintiffs in the second action moved to amend their complaint by increasing the *ad damnum* clause. The trial judge, over the objection of the County of Nassau, granted the motion on the condition that the case be adjourned to permit physical examinations of the four plaintiffs in the second action to prevent any prejudice to the defendant. Plaintiff Smerechniak opposed the adjournment of the trial. The trial court, as a solution to this dilemma, ordered a full trial as to the plaintiff Smerechniak on liability and damages and a split trial on liability only with respect to the remaining four infant plaintiffs, both to be heard jointly. The court held that it was error to permit such a trifurcated trial. The jury was permitted to hear and view evidence of gruesome burns of the face, arms and body incurred by plaintiff Guy Smerechniak, while only deciding the issue of liability in the second action. This created undue prejudice as to the county's case in the latter action and precluded it from receiving a fair trial on the liability issue therein. *Smerechniak v. County of Nassau, supra,* at 140, 141.

Hence, it is clear that the highest appellate courts in this State look askance with any effort on the part of the trial courts to further split trial procedure other than under the sections defined in Rule 699.14.

In fact, upon close analysis in *Smerechniak,* we have neither bifurcation, where there was a clear cleavage of damage and liability, nor a trifurcation and trial of separate issues by a full trial as to one plaintiff and separate liability and damage trials for the rest, but a new creation or hybrid, wedding the whole of one plaintiff's action with the liability halves of the rest.

Conclusion

The courts of this State, in case law and code, have made the bifurcation of the personal injury action the virtual *sine qua non* of this most common of cases, absent exceptional circumstances. What these "exceptional circumstances" may be, the future we law will reveal. This rule of bifurcation however will not be extended beyond its limited confines of the negligence action, and the courts have most strongly discountenanced and continue to disapprove of further division of litigation into further phases such as occurred in *Smerechniak* and *Greenberg.*

This article previously appeared in an edition of The Nassau Lawyer, a publication of the Nassau County Bar Association, and is being reprinted here with the permission of The Nassau County Bar Association.

13. The Art of Cross Examination

To the nascent practitioner shortly graduated from law school, Cross-Examination is either regarded as a species of Delphic mystery or as an easy play on words. The law student, whose total knowledge and experience may consist solely of having, to this point, analyzed scores of appellate decisions and having answered law school class and examination hypotheticals and finally, the State Bar Examination, will often approach the daunting task of the first cross-examination with some fear and apprehension, even if she or he has sufficient motivation, knowledge and imagination. For the truth of the matter is that an effective, searching, searing, and probing cross-examination is the heart and soul of the creation of a defense in any criminal case. The defense lawyer may, it is true, have experts, alibi witness and eyewitnesses to establish or buttress his case, or, in turn, be able to effectively discredit the State in a criminal case. Yet, a defense case will most ultimately be won with a pointed cross-examination that will serve to bring forth those sparks of truth that would otherwise remain hidden under the facial truth of the State's case. Cross-Examination, probingly executed, will not only serve to discredit and shake the People's case, but bring about a closeness and nearness to truth that would in the interaction and play of the drama of trial remain elusive.

In short, an effective Cross-Examination is integral to the inauguration and creation of a defense in a criminal case. How, then, can the inexperienced practitioner approach this veiled mystery?

The ever-familiar bromide is total preparation. If the student has fully investigated and prepared his case, locating all witnesses, having gone to the scene, reviewing and rereviewing all police reports, he may anticipate the direct examination of the People's witnesses in a criminal case. If, for example, he has all discovery and subpoenaed material in hand, he may detect the obvious inconsistencies in the People's case, if such exists. For example, if the defendant has, in a Robbery case, an identification defense, relying on inconsistencies of height, weight, bodily or facial characteristics, such as the absence of a beard or scar in one report, and its presence in another, this kind of discrepancy can serve to create doubt. If the arrest was late at night, undoubtedly the police witnesses will describe in sure detail the area as well lighted. In fact, this may not be so. If the defense, in an undercover sale of narcotics, is agency or entrapment, cross-examination can be prepared, in light of this defense, to discredit the people's case and create doubt. A rape charge can be prepared with a defense of consent where an extended common law relationship existed, and so a searching cross-examination can be prepared.

In sum, the wisdom of total and thorough preparation fully applies to cross-examination. There is no easy road whereby a properly perceptive and anticipative cross-examination can be evaded without thorough reflection on and total preparation of the case. Even when the cross-examination is fully prepared, every question written out and artfully delineated, an elusiveness exists as a barrier to an effective and thorough cross-examination that may take years for the inexperienced practitioner to pierce and master. For a trial is a dynamic. Questions inevitably arise and are asked, answers given that the intuitive examiner must be prepared to respond to. Unknown and dazzling doors to facts may come forth in the dynamic and drama of a trial that only the experienced practitioner, with honed and sensitive intuition, can respond to and pursue. Cross-examination, however well prepared, is always and must be an intuitive art. Years of experience are required to master and be alert to those sparks, and flames, of truth and a sensitivity developed such that in split seconds the criminal lawyer can leap to the gap to a possible victory at trial, that—once open—can reveal that fraction of truth and leap of faith leading to doubt and ultimate acquittal.

Finally, in addition to thorough preparation and the ability to respond to the quick and elusive phrase, answer or question, there is another factor in building

the effective cross-examination. That may be termed, for lack of a better alternative, the ability to hammer. Thus, for example, where the charge is assault, and
the injuries possibly minimal, questions directed to the minimal nature of the
medical treatment rendered, the dearth of doctor's visits, the lack of prescrip-
tions, and the unlikelihood of real physical pain and suffering because of these
injuries must be hammered and literally bludgeoned in order to create the doubt
necessary to obtain the sought for acquittal. Question must be followed by question, without stop, hammering, probing and chipping away at the witness's veracity. Nothing should be left for the jury to figure out or infer, but multiple
probing and disconcerting questions following one on the other.

Preparation is the initial basis and groundwork for the searching cross-
examination. Question must be followed by question, answer by successive answer, demolishing the witness and the People's case. But, with it all, in the dynamic of trial and its ongoing drama and play, preparation cannot entirely anticipate the unforeseen word, phrase or question that may serve to open the door
to that most elusive element and ray of truth, however imperfect and however
broken and jagged. It is this ability, the ability to intuitively respond to the flying
sparks at trial, that sets apart the experienced cross-examiner from the novice,
and it is that sensitivity, and intuitive sensibility, that can only be developed
with time and experience. It is this element that makes cross-examination not a
mechanical exercise but an art whereby the cross-examiner may respond and
paint those fragments of truth into a total picture that lights the defense and leads
to ultimate victory.

14. A Note on the Compromise Verdict

It is the law of this state that a civil trial verdict which reveals a compromise by
certain of the jurors as to liability and is unwarranted by the evidence will not be
permitted to stand. 8 Carmody Wait 2d Sec. 588; 4 Weinstein-Korn-Miller, N.Y.
Civil Prac. Par. 4402-2, 3; N.Y. Jur. 2d Appellate Review Sec. 4041.

The question arises as to how the error of a compromise verdict may be
raised by the Appellant at trial or on appeal. What comes to mind is a finding of
judgment of liability in favor of the plaintiff and a concomitant minimal award
of damages. It could be argued that the verdict was the product of compromise
as to liability by some of the jurors in exchange for a minimal award of damages.

In general, however, the law is that inadequacy of damages alone is not sufficient proof that a compromise verdict was reached or that it was to liability.
Thus the Court of Appeals in *Figliomeni v. Board of Education*, 38 N.Y. 2d 178
(1975), held that an $18,000 verdict in favor of the plaintiff was not the product
of compromise where there was considerable proof that the defendant Board of

Education was liable for the injuries suffered when the severely handicapped plaintiff was struck in the head by a hard baseball thrown to him by the teacher who had not read the child's health card and so was not aware of the danger of such activity. Thus, in spite of the fact that the injuries included deformation of the arteries into the left frontal area of the brain, fracture of the frontal bone, and consequent surgery to remove an infected bone which left an area through which the brain could be seen pulsating under a covering of the skin and resulting epileptic seizures, the court concluded that inadequacy of damages alone is not sufficient proof that a compromise verdict was reached and that

> it is only when it can be demonstrated that an inadequate verdict could only have resulted from a compromise on the liability issue that the court must revert to the former rule requiring retrial on all issues. *Figliomeni v. Board of Education, supra* 182.

The law is clear that inadequacy for damages alone is not sufficiently probative to show that a compromise verdict as to liability was reached. *Figliomeni v. Board of Education, supra.* There must be an additional factor in the record, in addition to the patent inadequacy of the damage award, to show that a compromise had been reached on liability, although a number of Courts have held that gross inadequacy of damages is sufficiently evidentiary of a compromise verdict. *Kepner v. Barry,* 24 A.D. 2d 825 (4th Dept. 1965); *Resto v. Metropolitan Distributors,* 1 Misc. 2d 889 (1954); *Honigsberg v. New York Transit Authority,* 43 Misc. 2d 1 (1964). Thus, in *Frozzita v. Inc. Village of Freeport,* 57 A.D. 2d 827 (2nd Dept. 1977), the Court stated that because the damage award was excessive if certain injuries were excluded by reason of the plaintiff's failure to use her seat belt, and inadequate if the plaintiff may recover for such injuries, the award was the result of improper compromise and must be set aside in the interests of justice. Accord, *Parlato v. Semmes Motors, Inc.,* 38 A.D. 2d 844 (2nd Dept. 1972). In *Lallo v. W. T. Grant,* 31 A.D. 2d 941 (2nd Dept. 1969), the Trial Court set aside a damage verdict in favor of the plaintiff and ordered a new trial on damages. This Court reversed and held, at p. 942, that

> on the whole record herein, in our opinion the foregoing sequence of events indicates that the jury would not have resolved liability in favor of plaintiffs if it had not been assured it would be in a position to determine the sums to be awarded in damages. At the same time it is reasonable to assume, from the undisputed fact that the award was grossly inadequate, that at least some of the jurors thought that the injuries merited an evaluation substantially higher than the sum ultimately awarded. In the circumstances, it may be concluded that there was a reciprocal relinquishment of convictions upon liability and damages in order to arrive at a verdict. Such a compromise may not stand. In the circumstances, the interests of justice to all the issues and not (as plaintiffs urge) with respect to the issue of damages only.

McSherry v. City of New York, Supreme Court Bronx Co., N.Y.L.J., 3/5/79, p. 19, col. 4, is an interesting decision. In *McSherry,* the infant plaintiff was injured when a lit kerosene smudge pot exploded. The burning kerosene enveloped the infant and caused him to sustain second and third degree burns over 30% of his body. The resulting scarring was unsightly, permanent and irremediable. The nature and extent of the injury and the costs sustained were uncontroverted at trial. The jury rendered a verdict in favor of the infant plaintiff and his mother, $55,000 and $8,784 respectively. The Trial Court granted the post verdict motion of the defendant, City of New York, to set aside the verdict as the result of a compromise as to liability. The Court stated that a jury verdict must be overturned when it is clear that under no possible theory could a jury have arrived at the amount of damages they found. The court concluded that

> after careful scrutiny and evaluation of the record as a whole, it is the opinion of this court that the award rendered to the infant is so disproportionate in relation to the severities of the injuries sustained, that it should only have been the result of a compromise on the issue of liability.

In sum, one may conclude from this brief review of the case law that although gross inadequacy of damages alone is insufficient to prove that a compromise has been reached on liability, though case law exists to support that proposition, the general rule is that the determination that a verdict is the product of compromise in a civil case must be based on some other and salient and pertinent factors playing into the drama of an eventual civil verdict.

Copyright 1996 by the Queens County Bar Association and the Queens Bar Bulletin. Reprinted with permission.

15. C.P.L.R. 325(d) and the Ad Damnum

C.P.L.R. 325 entitled "Grounds for Removal" sets forth seven grounds by which a court may remove a pending action to another court, in subsections a-e. It is beyond the scope of this article to consider and analyze, in detail, the thrust and meaning of each of the C.P.L.R. 325 statutory subsections. This article proposes to consider an aspect of, or rather point in the proper understanding of, one subsection, C.P.L.R. Sec 325(d), which provides for removal without consent to a court of limited jurisdiction.

More specifically C.P.L.R. Sec 325(d), entitled Grounds for Removal (d) without consent to court of limited jurisdiction, states, in pertinent part, that the Appellate Division, may, by rule, provide that the court in which an action is pending can, in its discretion, remove such action, without consent, to the lower court, where it appears that the amount of damages sustained may be less than demanded. The section, also states, that the lower court must have had jurisdiction but for the amount of damages demanded. If the action is so removed, the section ends, the verdict or judgment shall be subject to the limitation of the monetary jurisdiction of the court in which the action was originally commenced and shall be to the extent of the amount demanded within such limitation. The provision at issue and consideration is obvious. The issue arises, however, and it is the subject of this article, whether the language of the statute that when an action is removed and the verdict is subject to the limitation of the monetary jurisdiction of the court in which the action was originally commenced means and can allow, upon application of the plaintiff, an increase in the *ad damnum*. The question is significant since the statutory language states that the verdict must be within the limitation of the monetary jurisdiction of the court in which the action was originally commenced.

There is only one case dealing precisely with this issue, i.e., *Southwell v. New York City Transit Authority.*[1] *Southwell* was a negligence action brought in Bronx County to recover $100,000 for personal injuries. By order of the Supreme Court pursuant to C.P.L.R. 325(d), the action was transferred to the Civil Court, thus retaining the original *ad damnum* in the Civil Court. Plaintiff moved to increase the *ad damnum* to $500,000, alleging aggravation of a pre-existing arthritic condition and consequent inability to work. The defendant contended that the motion should be denied on the ground that the civil court lacked jurisdiction to determine a motion to increase the *ad damnum*, arguing the Civil Court's jurisdiction was limited by C.P.L.R.325(d) to the monetary jurisdiction of the court in which the action was originally commenced.

The court rejected the defense argument on the ground that, in fact, there was no limitation on the monetary jurisdiction of the Supreme Court and so the statutory language did not limit what could be demanded in the *ad damnum* clause. The court reasoned that since there was no recognized limit on the monetary jurisdiction of the Supreme Court, the transfer under C.P.L.R. 325(d) was of no moment.

The *Southwell* rule and decision makes good sense. Where a transfer is made to a court of more limited monetary jurisdiction, C.P.L.R. 325(d) states the verdict or judgment shall be limited to the monetary jurisdiction of the court in which the action was originally commenced and shall be lawful to the extent of the amount demanded within such limitation.[2]

Since the Supreme Court has no jurisdictional monetary limits, *Southwell* rightly holds that an increase in the *ad damnum* may be requested and granted, despite transfer to a court of more limited monetary jurisdiction and despite the amount originally demanded in the *ad damnum*.

By the same token and logic, where the civil court has jurisdiction of a case beyond its jurisdictional maximum amount, it has been held a motion may be made and granted to reduce the *ad damnum* clause so as to bring the case within its jurisdiction.[3]

Though the point here is small, plaintiff's counsel need have no fear that a 325(d) transfer will bar him from recovering in his case what he wants, seeks, or may ask for.

16. Filing a Late Notice of Claim: One Basis and Analysis

Sec. 50(e) of the general municipal law defines the criteria and basis for filing a Notice of Claim as a condition precedent for the commencement of an action sounding in tort against a municipality. In general, the Notice of Claim for a tort action to be preserved, maintained and properly commenced against a municipality in this State must be filed within 90 days of the occurrence lest the right to sue be lost. Sub. 5 of the statute provides the mechanism, criteria and basis whereby a motion to file a late notice of claim against a municipality may be granted and the late notice filed. Subsection 5 of Sec. 50(e) of the General Municipal Law provides in pertinent part that upon application, the court in its discretion may extend the time to serve the notice of claim beyond the ninety days after the claim arises and the trial court shall consider, in particular, whether the public corporation, its attorney, or insurance carrier acquired actual knowledge of the essential facts constituting the claim within the time specified in Sub. 1 or within a reasonable time thereafter. The statute also states that the court shall also consider all other relevant facts and circumstances including: whether the claimant was an infant, or mentally or physically incapacitated, or died before the time limited for service of the claim; whether the claimant failed to serve the notice of claim by reason of his justifiable reliance upon settlement representations made by an authorized representative of the corporation or its insurance carrier; whether claimant in serving a notice of claim made an excusable error concerning the identity of the public corporation against which the claim should be asserted; or whether the delay in serving the notice of claim substantially prejudiced the public corporation in maintaining its defense on the merits.[1]

Although considerable case law exists concerning the interpretation and construction of the listed factors and criteria set forth in G.M.L. Sec. 50(e) sub. 5 determinative of whether an application by a plaintiff against a public corporation may be permitted by the trial court to file a late notice of claim, this article will consider, most particularly, what in fact has been held by the courts of this state to constitute actual knowledge by the public corporation, its attorney, or its insurance carrier, of the essential facts concerning the claim thereby providing the specific basis for the court to permit the plaintiff to file a late notice of claim.

The leading appellate court decision on this issue is *Hayden v. Village of Hempstead.*[2] In *Hayden*, appeal was taken from an order of the Supreme Court of Nassau County denying his application for leave to file a late notice of claim against the Village of Hempstead. The Appellate Division held that Special Term erred when it found that the village of Hempstead did not have actual knowledge of the essential facts concerning the petitioner's claims. The court reasoned first that the village clerk, as one of the alleged tortfeasors, acquired actual knowledge of the essential facts constituting the intentional torts alleged committed by him and the individual respondents within the statutory ninety day period, noting incidentally that the village clerk is a person designated by law to accept service of a notice of claim on the Village. Second, the court noted that the Village conducted an investigation of the facts surrounding the petitioner's tort claim within three months after expiration of the statutory prescribed period for serving a notice of claim had expired, thus negating any prejudice that might have accrued to the municipality as a result of the delay.

Under *Hayden* the law is clear. If a proper official of the municipality has received actual notice of the claim within the statutorily prescribed period, and no prejudice can be shown, leave to file a late notice of claim will be sustained.[3]

Actual knowledge of the claim may be obtained under the law from a variety of sources. Thus, for example, in *Cicio v. City of New York,*[4] the Second Department held that, on appeal by the City of New York from an order which granted the petitioner's application for leave to serve a late notice of claim, the court held that affirmance was called for since first the delay was minimal; second, the city neither suffered nor claimed prejudice; and third, and most importantly, the city obtained actual knowledge within the ninety day period through the filing of an accident report.[5]

In addition to an accident report, a second source of actual notice is where some officers, employees, or agents of the municipality obtain actual knowledge of the essential facts constituting the claim within the ninety day period. Under this factual scenario, in general, the courts of this state will justify the filing of late notice of claim provided that it can be shown that no prejudice will result.

Thus, in *Mestel v. Board of Education of the City of Yonkers,*[6] the Appellate Division, Second Department, held that leave to serve a late notice of claim was properly granted plaintiff where two supervising employees of the City were present and assisted the plaintiff so that it was clear the defendant had actual knowledge of the essential facts constituting the claim and had not been substantially prejudiced maintaining its defense.[7]

One final point should be noted. It is a matter of some surprise, but it is nevertheless the law, that knowledge of a public officer or officers of a police department cannot be considered actual knowledge of the municipal corporation regarding the essential acts of a claim.[8]

Nevertheless, it is equally significant and true that although knowledge of individual police officers is not held to be knowledge to be imputed to the public corporation, the Fourth Department stated in *Cooper v. City of Rochester*[9] that if a municipal chief of police has timely acquired actual knowledge of the facts constituting the claim against the municipality, this could constitute actual knowledge to be imputed to the municipality and the claimant would be entitled to file a notice of claim.

Conclusion

The cases construing Sec. 50(e)5 of the General Municipal Law, and specifically the ground whereby the municipality has acquired actual notice of the claim against it within the statutory period, fall into two categories and two subcategories. First, if some official of the municipality has acquired knowledge of the facts essentially constituting the claim within the prescribed statutory period, late filing will be permitted. Second, if the municipality has acquired knowledge of the facts constituting the claim within the prescribed statutory period, late filing will be permitted. As a subcategory, although police officers are employees, and in some cases officials, of the municipality, their knowledge concerning the claim will not be imputed to the municipality. There is, however, authority that actual knowledge of the claim by the Chief of Police, will be imputed to the public corporation by reason of his position, being more than a mere police officer.

It is hoped that this brief review of the relevant case law concerning the "actual knowledge" provision of a G.M.L. Sec. 50(e)5 will constitute some guide to the plaintiff's practitioner confronted with a late filing problem and will point the way to successfully filing a late notice of claim, thereby permitting, ultimately, the plaintiff to be made whole and obtain redress for his bodily or emotional loss.

17. A Note on the Workers' Compensation Law

The Workers' Compensation Law[1] is a statutory method and mechanism whereby every employer must provide for the payment of the benefits to its employees for injury or death. The employer may either purchase a Workers' Compensation Insurance Policy, from an agency authorized to provide such coverage by the New York Superintendent of Insurance[2]; purchase a policy from the State Insurance Fund[3]; or offer to self-insure its liability to pay benefits upon proof of financial security and ability to pay benefits when an injury occurs with the permission of the Chair of the Workers' Compensation Board.

The statutory mechanism is operative, regardless of the fault of the employer or employee, but only in a statutory amount dependent upon wages received by the employee.[4] The Workers' Compensation Law, Chapter 67 of the Consolidated Laws, consists of a number of articles which relate to and provide compensation to an employee for injuries or death in the course of employment. In addition, there are subsequent enacted articles, the Disability Benefits Law[5]; and the Workers' Compensation Act for Civil Defense Volunteers.[6]

Many treatises and articles have been written on this complex and comprehensive statute. This particular article will consider one small point: What may be considered to be the case where an injury can be said to occur "in the course of employment"?

The Workers' Compensation Law states that to be compensable an accidental injury must arise out of and in the course of employment.[7] The statute goes on to define as employment a trade or business or occupation, carried on by an employer, for pecuniary gain.[8]

The general rule is that for an injury to be compensable it must arise out of employment as well as in the course thereof.[9] Many are the cases glossing and interpreting the above rule. Thus, in *Burton v. Mallouk*[10] the Appellate Division, Third Department, held that where, at the time of the accident, the employee was moving a piece of furniture which had been given to him, and he had been directed to move it, the Board might legitimately infer that he was acting within the scope of employment until the furniture had been completely and safely set at rest; and that the record sustained a finding that the injury arose out of and in the course of employment.

It has been held that in determining whether an injury arises out of and in the course of employment, each case must be judged on its own facts and the test is whether the activity is a reasonable activity at that place and, if so, only then may the risks inherent in such activity be an incident of employment.[11]

There must be, it has been held, a sufficient nexus to the employment for it to arise out of and in the course of employment. Thus, in *Robinson v. Village of Catskill Police Department*[12] the Appellate Division, Third Department, held that the police officer's injuries which occurred when his wife shot him during a domestic dispute that erupted during their lunch together had no nexus to his employment, and so he was not entitled to benefits, even though his service revolver was involved and he was on duty when shot. The Court held that substantial evidence supported the finding that the wound was intentionally inflicted and arose out of personal differences.

In the same way in *Williams v. Schenectady County Department of Social Services*[13] again, the Appellate Division, Third Department, held that a back injury sustained by the claimant while bending over to tie her shoe during breaks from work did not arise out of or in the course of her primarily sedentary employment and, therefore, did not give rise to Workers' Compensation benefits.

The pattern is so far clear: the injury must arise out of and in the course of employment.[14] The general test is that the activity to be compensable must be reasonable at that place, and only then may the risks inherent in such activity be an incident of employment. Further, a sufficient nexus must exist to the employment to arise out of and in the course of employment.[15]

Let us, however consider a more distinct and defined problem, the exact subject of this article. What of where there is some deviation from employment or duties, or there is a question or allegation that the employee was injured in the course of personal or private business. What are the parameters and definitions set forth by the case law on these issues? How far, for example, may an employee deviate from his "normal and regular duties," incur an injury, and still be covered by Workers' Compensation?

In *Scheper v. Board of Education UFSD No. 2*[16] the Appellate Division held that the school cleaner's trip to the school in order to return a package, which belonged to another and which she had mistakenly taken home after work the previous evening, fell within the Workers' Compensation scheme.

Similarly in *Armstrong v. Aero Mayflower Transit Co.*[17] the Appellate Division stated that in determining whether the employee has deviated from the course of his employment it is irrelevant that the claimant is not taking the best route to his business destination, so long as she is heading in the general direction.[18]

The scene is so far clear: the deviation must arise to the level of an unconnected, personal, virtual abandonment of the employer for the workers' injury under the circumstances not to be covered by Workers' Compensation. In effect, there must be some complete severance for the Workers' Compensation Law to be inoperative.

Thus, in *Commissioner of Taxation and Finance v. Fisher,*[19] the Appellate Division held that evidence in a Workers' Compensation proceeding sustained a finding that the employee had not abandoned his employment at the time he was run over by a bus and that his death resulted from a causally related accident. Stating that where an employee temporarily departs for a brief period of time in an interest other than his employer but directly or indirectly this interest may result in a benefit or advantage to his employer, it is a natural and normal incident of his employment and within the scope of the Workers' Compensation Law.

What does the law say further of what may be considered to be the case when an employee is pursuing his private interests? The general rule is that when an injury was incurred while an employee is pursuing his own private interests on his own time and at a distance from the employer's premises as such, it is not considered in the course of employment.[20] What, it may be asked, is the pursuit of one's private interests, such as to bring the consequent injury out of the statutory scheme?

In *Daly v. Bates*[21] the Court of Appeals held that a laundress injured while using her employer's plant after regular working hours to do her own laundry cannot be regarded as injured in the course of her employment. On the other hand in *Bailey v. Gilbert*[22] the Appellate Division held that the fact that the employee "punched out" and began to leave the employer's premises for lunch did not change the nature of his acts from "employment related" to "personal" so as to remove him from the Workers' Compensation Law.

Similarly, in *Summa v. Westchester County*[23] the Appellate Division held that an accident sustained by the claimant who regularly parked her car in a municipal parking lot located a short distance from where she worked, who several times a day left the office with the employer's permission to deposit money in a parking lot meter, and who was struck in a parking lot on her return to the office after putting money in a meter, happened within the course of her employment.

Even where the purpose of the trip is partly personal, it has been held that there need not be a finding that the decedent's death did not arise out of and in the course of employment for the purpose of determining whether the accident arose out of and in the course of the decedent's employment.[24]

If there is any sense to the case, the rule, as in deviation rule, is that there must be a complete dissociation from the business context to take the injury out of the statute. Thus, in *Joslyn v. Oneida Community*[25] the Court of Appeals held that an employee injured in another building than that in which he was employed while purchasing goods for a friend was not entitled to an award.

Conclusion

This brief analysis and consideration of what may constitute an injury "arising out of and in the course of employment" shows a general rule of reasonableness. Further law states that a sufficient nexus must exist to the employment activity. If the employer maintains that the employee was deviating from the work assignment or hours, or that the employee was acting on solely personal or private business, in either case, there must be a complete break, sufficiently substantial, to take the employee's activities and actions out of this statutory mechanism. Part is not enough if still somehow, or in some way, there is work relation.

Reprinted with permission from: Torts, insurance & Compensation Law Section Journal, Summer 2005, Vol. 34, No 1, published by the New York State Bar Association, One Elk Street, Albany, New York 12207 York

18. Trial by Jury Revisited

In an article in the *Queens Bar Bulletin* entitled "Trial by Jury: Is There a Doubt?"[1] this writer analyzed the impact and import of three recent Supreme Court of the United States Decisions: *Gilmer v. Interstate/Johnson Lane Corporation;*[2] *Circuit City v. Adams;*[3] and *EEOC v. Waffle House, Inc.*[4] and determined and concluded that these Decisions in permitting, if not compelling and making, an employee agree to submit any and all disputes to Arbitration when asked to sign a prospective employment contract had the result of forcing the employee to waive his Constitutional and legal right to a federal jury trial and, effectively, of waiving access to the Courts, along with a waiver of the Rules of Evidence; trial by jury in open court; full Pretrial Discovery; and the right of Appeal. The net effect of making a condition of employment submitting all future disputes to Arbitration was to deny a powerless employee, seeking to survive economically, Constitutional access to the Courts and a jury trial.

The Supreme Court of the United States thereafter decided an even more legally significant and impacting case in *Aetna Health Care, Inc. v. Davila v. Calad*[5]. This case bears careful analysis. In two consolidated cases, two individuals sued their health maintenance organization (HMOs) for their alleged failure to exercise due care in the handling of coverage decisions in a violation of a duty imposed by the Texas Health Care Liability Act (THCLA). The facts were that the Respondent, Mr. Davila, and Ruby Calad were both beneficiaries in ERISA-Regulated Employee Benefit Plans. Their plan sponsors had entered into agreements with petitioners Aetna Health, Inc. and Cigna Healthcare of Texas, Inc. to administer the plans. The Respondents both suffered injuries arising from Aetna's and Cigna's decisions not to provide coverage for certain treatment and services recommended by the Respondents' treating physicians. Specifically, Mr. Davila's treating physician prescribed Vioxx to remedy Mr. Davila's arthritis pain, but Aetna refused to pay for this. Mr. Davila then began taking another drug from which he suffered a severe reaction that required extensive treatment and hospitalization,

Ms. Calad underwent surgery. Although her treating physician recommended an extended hospital stay, a Cigna discharge nurse determined that Ms. Calad did not meet the plan's criteria for a continued hospital stay, and so Cigna denied coverage for the extended hospital stay. Ms. Calad experienced post-surgery complications forcing her to return to the hospital and argued that the complications would not have occurred had Cigna approved coverage for a longer hospital stay.

Originally the Respondents brought separate suits in the Texas State Court against the Petitioners arguing, under THCLA Sec. 88.002(a), that the Petitioners' refusal to cover the requested services violated their "duty to exercise ordinary care when making healthcare treatment decisions," and that these refusals caused their injuries. The Petitioners then removed the case to the Federal District Court arguing that the Respondents' cases were in the scope of, and were therefore completely pre-empted by, ERISA Sec. 502(a). The District Courts agreed and declined to remand the cases to the State Court and because the Respondents refused to amend their complaints to bring ERISA claims, the· District Courts dismissed the complaints.

Both Davila and Calad appealed the refusals to remand to state court, and the United States Court of Appeals for the Fifth Circuit concluded that the Respondents' claim could possibly fall under either ERISA Sec. 502(a) (I)(B), which provides a cause of action for the recovery of wrongfully denied benefits and Sec. 502(a)(2), which permits suit against a plan fiduciary for breaches of the fiduciary duty to the plan. The Fifth Circuit concluded that the claims did not fall within either of these statutory sections concluding they were tort claims and not actions for breach of contract or reimbursement for benefits denied, but rather requests for tort damages arising from an external statutorily imposed duty of care.

The Supreme Court of the United States then proceeded to analyze these ERISA sections as applicable to the cases before them. The Court concluded that the ERISA statute completely pre-empted these particular types of claims. The Court noted that ERISA Sec. 502 (a)(l)(B), which provides that a civil action may be brought —(1) by a participant or beneficiary . . . (B) to recover benefits due to him under the terms of his plan, to enforce his rights under the terms of the plan, or to clarify his rights to future benefits under the terms of the plan.

29 USC Sec. B32(a)(l)(B) simply provided that if a participant of beneficiary believes the benefits promised to him under the plan are not provided he can bring suit seeking provision of those benefits; can enforce his rights under the plan; or clarify any of his rights to future benefits.

It is clear that this Section to which the Court was referring allows a contract action to recover benefits due to him under the plan, whatever they might be; allows some sort of equitable mechanism to enforce his rights under the terms of the plan, possibly by some sort of injunctive relief; or allows the participant to seek what appears to be a Declaratory Judgment to clarify his rights under the plan. The Court concluded that if an individual brings suit as these individuals did, or so the Court analyzed the situation, complaining of a denial of coverage of medical care, where the individual is entitled to such coverage only because of the terms of an ERISA-regulated employee benefit plan, then the lawsuit falls within the scope of this ERISA Section 502(a)(l)(B). The Court concluded that in absence of any other independent legal duty the individual's cause of action is completely pre-empted by ERISA Sec. 502(a)(l)(B).

The Court proceeded to analyze more exactly the Respondents' complaint and the statute on which their claims were based, THCLA. The Court noted that Mr. Davila alleged that Aetna provided health coverage under his employer's plan; that his doctor prescribed Vioxx, which Aetna refused to pay for, and Aetna refused to approve payment for the Vioxx prescription. Similarly, Calad stated that, despite the advice of her treating physician, she was refused coverage for her extended hospital stay. The Court concluded that the Respondents complained only about the denials of coverage promised under the ERISA-Regulated plans and that upon denial of benefits the Respondents could have paid for treatment themselves and then sought reimbursement through ERISA Sec. 502 (a)(l)(B) or sought a preliminary injunction. The Court went on to state that the complaint of these actions alleged violation of legal duties independent of this ERISA Section or the terms of the plan and also alleged that the petitioners violated a duty of care under the THCLA, thereby causing them injuries for which they sought tort relief. The Court concluded, differing from the Respondents, that the duties imposed by the THCLA are not independent of ERISA, but pre-empted by it. The Court opined that if an HMO correctly concludes, under the terms of the relevant plan, that a particular treatment was not covered, the HMO denial of such coverage would not be the cause of any injury arising from the denial, rather the failure of the plan itself to cover the requested treatment would be the cause. The Court noted that the THCLA created no obligation on the part of the health insurance carrier to provide an insured treatment not covered by the healthcare plan of the entity and so an HMO could not be subject to liability under the THCLA if it denied coverage for treatment not covered by the healthcare plan it was administering.

Thus, the Court concluded that the terms of the benefit plans formed an essential part of the THCLA claim and exists here only because of the Petitioners' administration of ERISA-Regulated benefit plans. The Court concluded that the Respondents could only bring suit to rectify a wrongful denial of benefits under an ERISA plan and so fell within the scope of ERISA Sec. 502 (a)(l)(B). In the language of the opinion following the above analysis, the Supreme Court of the United States proceeded to examine the Fifth Circuit's opinion and the law the Circuit relied on. It is beyond the scope of this article to consider fully that part of the Supreme Court's opinion. Suffice to say that the Court concluded ERISA, specifically under Sec. 502(a)(I)(B), completely pre-empted any other form of action to redress the injuries here caused by the denial of coverage and limited any relief to a form of contractual or equitable remedy. Apparently the Court concluded that the duties imposed by the THCLA in these particular cases did not arise independently of ERISA, but were deeply connected to this ERISA Section in some fashion.

Analysis

The Supreme Court of the United States in *Aetna Healthcare* reached a far-reaching and, again, societally impacting conclusion. The Court determined that when a plan denies coverage resulting in serious injury, the Plaintiff will not be permitted access to the Court to seek compensation and to be made whole for the error in judgment that caused these injuries. Once again, the Supreme Court here is denying any suit sounding in a common law tort action; denying effectively access to the Courts to correct and make right serious physical injuries brought about by carelessness, malpractice, mistakes, and errors in judgment that have caused great suffering and grief to Plaintiffs who in these cases sought monetary compensation and relief for these injury-causing errors. Once again, as in *Gilmer,* in *Circuit City*, and in *EEOC v. Waffle House. Inc.*, the Supreme Court of the United States is limiting access to the Courts and the right to trial by jury. The Court's reasoning here is tortured and fails to deal with a harm that has occurred and denies correction, compensation, and redress.

The right to seek relief for an injury caused by inattention, carelessness, indifference, callousness, and possible stupidity is basic to our common law system of Plaintiff's rights. The right of a citizen to seek compensation for an injury is a basic right. It is deeply imbedded in our common law system. It involves not merely the right to seek to be made whole for an injury caused by another, whether an individual, a business or even an international corporation or a government, but the right to have access to the Courts and a trial by jury for every person regardless of their race, their economic status, their social status, their intellect, their sex, their national origin, or their religion.

Once again the Supreme Court in this decision strikes at the basic and seminal right of the individual to gain access to the Courts and to have his rights enforced against the more powerful. The criterion for access to the Courts is not statutory interpretation, however exact, but the more important policy that every injury and every injustice should be allowed to be heard.

Conclusion

Aetna Healthcare in its reach and impact is far reaching. The decision states or implies that an HMO that makes a medically incorrect decision, whether the decision is not to hospitalize or to prescribe a certain medication that causes injury, is insulated and protected from tort suit and liability. The injured Plaintiff is left with a contract and equitable action that will do him little or no good in terms of compensating him for his injury. For this he cannot go to court, so says *Aetna*; he cannot sue for this injury; he is left with relief that does not address his problem and merely gives him a breach of contract action under ERISA Sec. 502(a)(1)(B). The net effect of *Aetna* is to not merely to deny the tort action or the possibility of a tort action, but in a very real sense to deny access to the Courts on this issue and this injury. *Aetna*, like *Gilmer* and *Circuit City*, strikes at the heart of our common law system of jury trials and actions and leaves the helpless injured individual with, in actuality, no recourse. *Aetna*, simply put, denies the injured Plaintiff access to the Court to bring a case for his injury and denies him a jury trial; and denies him the right of Appeal, should he lose, to correct a possible error. *Aetna* pecks away at the right of access to the Court and the right to a jury trial and is one more step to a system of justice that excludes rather than includes and that is limiting rather than welcoming and expansive.

Notes

1. A Note on the Notice of Claim

1. Every person who, under color of any statute, ordinance, regulation, or usage, of any State or Territory, subjects or causes to be subjected, any citizen of the United States or other person within the jurisdiction thereof to the deprivation of any rights, privileges or immunities secured by the Constitution and Laws, shall be liable to the party injured in an action at law, suit in equity, or other proper proceeding for redress.

3. Appealing the Mistrial Order

1. See also *Richardson v. Weingatz*, 33 A.D.2d 947 (3rd Dept. 1970); *Fine v. Cummins*, 260 App. Div. 569 (2nd Dept. 1940); *Landberg v. Fowler*, 278 App. Div. 661 (2d Dept. 1951). In *Fine* the Fourth Department noted that it is improper to enter an order incorporating a ruling in the course of trial, when, as in *Fine*, the ruling embodied a mistrial

order, and then to appeal from it since "we believe that generally an appeal in advance of entry of judgment on questions which may be decided at trial and which may be reviewed upon an appeal from a judgment entered after the trial should be discouraged." *Fine v. Cummins, supra* at 572. Thus, *Fine* is, if not at actual, then at implied variance with *Graney* since in *Graney* the Appellate Court raised no objection to the transformation of the mistrial ruling into a signed and entered order.

4. Conforming the Pleadings to the Proof

1. C.P.L.R. section 3025(c) states that a court may permit pleadings to be amended before or after judgment in order to conform them to the evidence upon such terms as may be just, including the granting of costs and continuances.

2. *Murray v. City of New York*, 43 N.Y.2d 400 (1977); *Dittmar Explosives v. A. E. Ottaviano, Inc.*, 20 N.Y.2d 498 (1967); *Hall & Co. of N. Y. v. Orient Overseas Assoc.*, 65 A.D.2d 424 (1st Dept. 1978), aff'd, 48 N.Y.2d 958 (1979); *D'Antoni v. Goff*, 52 A.D.2d 973 (3d Dept. 1976).

3. 8 N.Y.2d 206 (1960).

4. See also *Nixon Gear and Machine Co., Inc. v. Nixon Gear, Inc.*, A.D.2d 746 (4th Dept. 1982); *Kremer Construction Co., Inc. v. City of Yonkers*, 73 A.D.2d 639 (2d Dept. 1979); *Harbor Associates, Inc. v. Asheroff*, 35 A.D.2d 667 (2d Dept. 1970); *Dampskib-sselskabet v. Thos. Paper*, 26 A.D.2d 347 (1st Dept. 1966).

5. See *Murray v. City of New York. supra* note 2.

6. 43 N.Y.2d 400 (1977).

7. See also *Reich v. Knopf*, 65 A.D.2d 618 (2d Dept 1978); *Family Finance Corp. v. Secchio*, 65 Misc.2d 344 (Civ. Ct. City of N.Y. 1970); WEINSTEIN-KORN-MILLER, N.Y. CIV. PRACTICE, vol. 3, para. 3025.28.

8. *Sharapata v. Town of Islip*, 82 A.D.2d 350 (2d Dept.), aff'd, 56 N.Y.2d 332 (1981); *Rodolitz Realty Corp. v. Cosmopolitan Mutual Ins. Co.*, 71 A.D.2d 975 (1st Dept. 1979); *Rodriguez v. Robert*, 47 A.D.2d 548 (2d Dept. 1975); *Matter of Lipsi*, 50 Misc.2d 289 (S. Ct. West. Co. 1966).

9. 24 A.D.2d 510 (2d Dept. 1965).

10. 24 A.D.2d, 510 (2d Dept. 1965).

11. Similarly, in *Mazella v. City of New York*, 255 A.D. 996 (2d Dept. 1938), the court held that an infant-plaintiff's personal injury action was wrongly dismissed on the merits where there was no claim of surprise and no objection to the evidence of crowding, which allegedly resulted in the plaintiff's injury. See also *Averill v. Atkins*, 32 A.D.2d 738 (4th Dept. 1969); *Hass v. Brown*, 282 A.D. 916 (4th Dept 1953); *Davis v. Title Guarantee & Trust Co.*, 246 A.D. 754 (2d Dept.), aff'd, 272 N.Y. 440 (1935); *Murph and Fritz's v. Loretta*, 112 Misc.2d 554 (46 A. City Ct. of Buffalo 1982).

12. D. 2d at 910.

13. See also *Miller v. Perillo*, 71 A.D.2d 389 (1st Dept. 1979), app. dismissed, 49 N. Y.2d 1044 (1980); *Averill v. Atkins, supra*, note 11.

14. 47 A. D. (1997).

15. See also *K & P Fancy Stitching Machine Co., Inc. v. Weiss*, 3 A.D.2d 826 (1st Dept. 1957); *Dabrowski v. Dabrowski*, 279 A.D. 971 (4th Dept. 1952).

6. A Note on the Note of Issue

1. Rule 675.2, Rules Appellate Division, Second Department.

2. Rules of the Appellate Division, Second Department, Section 675.3, 675.4; Siegel, *N.Y. Practice*, Section 370; WEINSTEIN, KORN & MILLER, NEW YORK CIVIL PRACTICE, Section 3402.12.

3. See also *Williams v. New York City Transit Authority*, 23 A.D.2d 590, 256 N.Y.S.2d 708 (2d Dept. 1965). *Holihan v. The Regina Corp.*, 54 Misc.2d 264, 282 N.Y.S.2d 404, 406 (S. Ct. Onondaga County, 1967); *Marchitelli v. Greco Sales and Service, Inc.*, 52 A.D.2d 746, 382 N.Y.S.2d 197 (4th Dept. 1976); *Pioneer Jewelry Corp. v. All Continent Corp.*, 24 A.D.2d 436, 260 N.Y.S.2d 700 (1st Dept. 1965); *Burnett Process, Inc., v. Richalr Industries*, 47 A.D.2d 994, 366 N.Y.S.2d 704 (4th Dept. 1975); *Wayne E. Edwards Corp. v. Romas*, 36 A.D.2d 789, 319 N.Y.S.2d 84 (3rd Dept. 1971); *Mosca v. Pensky*, 73 Misc.2d 144, 341, N.Y.S.2d 219 (S. Ct. West. Co. 1973); SIEGEL, N.Y. PRAC., Section 370, p. 470; WEINSTEIN, KORN & MILLER, NEW YORK CIVIL PRAC., Section 3402.12.

4. See also *Baranyk v. Baranyk*, 73 A.D.2d 1004, 424 N.Y.S.2d 46 (3rd Dept. 1980) (that defendant had changed attorneys three times since the commencement of the action did not constitute a special circumstance); *Woznicki v. Lynn Terrace Apartments*, 22 A.D.2d 883, 254 N.Y.S.2d 772 (1st Dept. 1964) (Granting of opponent's request for adjournment on the eve of trial not unusual condition); *Williams v. New York City Transit Authority*, 23 A.D.2d 590, 256 N.Y.S.2d 708 (2nd Dept. 1965); *Marchitelli v. Greco Sales and Service, Inc., supra*; *Pioneer Jewelry Corp. v. All Continent Corp., supra*.

5. Cf. *Roberson v. Fordham Rent Car Corp.*, 38 A.D.2d 535, 326 N.Y.S.2d 844 (1st Dept. 1971). In *Roberson* the trial court denied the defendant's motion to obtain a physical examination of the plaintiff and the plaintiff appealed. The First Department reversed stating that although the defendant failed to timely vacate the Statement of Readiness, in view of the serious injuries to the plaintiff and the lack of prejudice to the plaintiff, a physical examination of the plaintiff, in the interests of justice, should be permitted. *Roberson*, it should be noted, did not involve a case being removed from the calendar whether unilaterally, as in *Pezzella*, or by motion to strike, as in *Grigorian*. The court in *Roberson* simply held that if the plaintiff's injuries are serious, even though the Note of the Issue has not been timely stricken or a motion to compel a physical examination been sought, under the indicia of "special circumstances" discovery may be had if serious permanent injuries are claimed and the plaintiff can show no prejudice.

7. Non Sui Juris: An Overview of the New York Law

1. On the matter of the conclusive presumption of a child 4 years of age or under with respect to its potential contributory negligence, see also PROSSER, LAW OF TORTS, § 32 p. 156; 41 N.Y. JUR., *Negligence* § 67 pp. 87-88; for cases in other jurisdictions, concurring in the New York rule and extending it to 8 years of age or older, see 65A C.G.S. NEGLIGENCE § 145; HARPER & JAMES, THE LAW OF TORTS, Vol. 2, § 16.8 p. 925; RESTATEMENT TORTS 2d, , 2 § 283A Children; 57 Am. Jur. 2d *Negligence*, §§ 361-363 (in many jurisdictions the courts presume or consider a child incapable of contributory negligence if he is under 7 or 8 and a conclusive presumption to that effect in some jurisdictions may be established by statute such as in Wisconsin when statute fixes the age at 7; see *Bair v. Stats*, 10 Wisc. 2d 70, 102 N.W. 26. See also 77 A.L.R.2d 908ff. and Later Case Service, Vols. 77-78 A.L.R p. 122.

2. For other New York cases adopting this Rule of Presumptions, see *Buscher v. New York Transportation Co.*, 106 App. Div. 493, 94 N.Y.S. 798 (1st Dept. 1905);

McDonald v. Met. St. Ry Co., 80 App. Div. 233, 80 N.Y.S. 577 (1st Dept. 1903*); Day v. Johnson,* 265 App. Div. 383, 39 N.Y.S.2d 203 (4th Dept. 1943).

3. In *Finkelstein,* a Case preceding the holding in *Camardo,* it is interesting to note that the court held that where an infant plaintiff, 7 years of age, was struck by a car, the question of the plaintiff's contributory negligence, of whether he was Sui Juris or Non Sui Juris, are considered questions for the jury. Similarly, in a 1917 case, also preceding *Camardo,* the Court of Appeals held that where an 8-year-old infant plaintiff was struck by a trolley, the jury was properly instructed to determine whether the plaintiff was Sui or Non Sui Juris. See *Nowakowski v. N.Y. & N.S. Traction* 220 N.Y. 51 (1917).

4. For cases in New York and other jurisdictions adopting the view that, beyond the age of 4 years, et al., the culpability of an infant plaintiff is a fact question for the jury and also cases where violation of a statute is involved, see 41 N.Y. JUR., Negligence §67, pp. 85-88; 65 A.C.G.S. Negligence, §§ 145-148, pp. 177-188; 57 Am. JUR. 2d Negligence §§ 367-376, 382; HARPER & JAMES, THE LAW OF TORTS, Vol. 2, § 16.8; PROSSER, LAW OF TORTS, § 32; RESTATEMENT TORTS 2d Vol. 2 § 283A, Children; 28 N.Y. DIGEST 2d, Negligence § 85,77 A.L.R.2d, CONTRIBUTORY NEGLIGENCE OF CHILDREN, pp. 932, 934; LATER CASE SERVICE, pp. 123-124.

8. *The Law of Conflicts: A Recent Trend*

1. For overview of development of the rule of *lex loci* in multi-state tort cases and history of interest analysis, see 19 N.Y. JUR. 2d, CONFLICT OF LAWS, § 28-41; 16 AM JR. 2d, CONFLICTS OF LAWS, § 98-126.

2. See *Klaxon Co. v. Stentor Electric Mfg. Co.,* 313 U.S. 487, 61 S. Ct. 1020, 85 L. Ed. 1477 (1941); *Rosenthal v. Warren,* 475 F. 2d 438 (2d Cir. 1972, cert. den. 414 U.S. 856; 94 S. Ct. 159, 381. Ed. 2d 106 (1973); *Perdue v. J.C. Penney Co.,* 470 F. Supp. 1234 (S.D.N.Y. 1979).

3. See *Loebig v. Larucci,* 572 F. 2d 81 (2d Cir. 1978); *Delbrueck & Co. v. Manufacturers Hanover Trust Co.,* 404 F. 2d 989 (S.D.N.Y. 1979), affd. 609 F. 2d 1047 (2d Cir. 1979); *Cruise v. Castleton,* 449 F. Supp. 564 (S.D.N.Y. 1978); *Armstrong v. Rangain Corp.,* 493 F. Supp. 390 (S.D.N.Y. 1980); *Rudin v. Dow Jones & Co., Inc.,* 510 F. Supp. 210 (1981); *O'Connor v. Lee Hy Paving Corp.,* 579 F. 2d 194 (2d Cir. 1978), cert. den. 439 U.S. 1034, L.Ed. 696, 99 S. Ct. 638, reh. den. 441 U.S. 918, 60 L.Ed. 2d 392, 99 S. Ct. 2023 & cert. den. 439 U.S. 1034, 58 L.Ed. 2d 696, 99 S. Ct. 639, reh. den. 441 U.S. 918, 60 L.Ed. 2d 392, 99 S. Ct. 2023; *Rosenthal v. Warren, supra.*

4. See *Gordon v. Eastern Airlines, Inc.,* 391 F. Supp. 31 (S.D.N.Y. 1975). In *Gordon,* the widow of a decedent killed in an airline crash in Florida brought a wrongful death action against the airline. The defendant, Eastern Airlines, admitted liability by formal stipulation; the sole issue at trial was damages. The conflicts issue arose whether the Florida law of damages should apply, since the State of Florida was the situs of the tort, or whether the New York law of damages should apply, the State of plaintiff's residence, since the Florida wrongful death statute, unlike the New York statutes, provided for damages for loss of consortium. The defendant airlines moved to strike that portion of the plaintiff's *ad damnum* clause such as demanded compensation for loss of society, love, and affection. The court held that the New York law would apply with respect to the issue of damages, applying the "interest analysis" theory of conflicts whereby the law of the jurisdiction applies, in multi-state tort cases which, because of its relationship with the occurrence or parties has the greatest concern with the specific issue raised in the litigation. The District Court, however, noted, with approval, the entirety of the holding in *Babcock,* stating that

more specifically, the New York Court of Appeals, in *Babcock v. Jackson, supra*, has carefully distinguished between those cases where the defendant's exercise of due care is in issue and those cases where the sole issue is the extent of plaintiff's recovery. In the former situation, the law of the state where the tort occurred controls. *Id.,* 12 N.Y. 2d at 438, 24 N.Y.S. 2d at 750, 191 N.E. 2d at 284. As the Court there observed

> in such a case, it is appropriate to look to the law of the place of the tort so as to give effect to the jurisdiction's interest in regulating conduct within its borders, and it would be almost unthinkable to seek the applicable rule in the law of some other place.

In the latter situation however—where the sole issue at bar is the measure of plaintiff's damages—the court must apply the law of the place which has the dominant contacts with the parties and transaction and the superior claim for application of its law. *Id. Gordon v. Eastern Airlines, supra,* at 33.

5. See, also, *Posen United Technologies Corp.,* 484 F. Supp. 490 (S.D.N.Y. 1980); *Bing v. Halstead,* 495 F. Supp. 517 (S.D.N.Y. 1980); *Patton v. Carnike,* 519 F. Supp. 625 (S.D.N.Y. 1981); *Haehl v. Village of Portchester,* 463 F. Supp. 845 (S.D.N.Y. 1978); *Hausman v. Buckley,* 299 F. 2d 696, 93 ALR 2d 1340, cert. den. 369 U.S. 885, 8 L.Ed. 2d 6, 82 S. Ct. 1157; *Chance v. E.I. DuPont de Nemours & Co.,* 371 F. Supp. 439 (S.D.N.Y. 1974). In 19.N.Y. Jur. 2d, Conflict of Laws, §38, the authors state that the federal courts, in applying the law of conflicts in multi-state tort cases, never fully adopted the theory of interest analysis, but have to some extent continued to adhere to the rule of the *lex loci* to determine the rights and liabilities of the parties in multi-state tort litigation. The authors, however, note the dicta in *O'Connor v. Lee Hy Paving, supra,* where the Second Circuit stated that in the New York choice of law rules, the New York tort plaintiffs will be afforded the benefit of New York law, more favorable than the *lex loci delictus,* whenever there is a fair basis for doing so.

10. Section 50-e. The Importance of Filing a Notice of Claim

1. GEN. MUN. L. § 50-e(5).

2. 53 A.D.2d 457, 385 N.Y.S.2d 791 (2d Dept. 1976), rev'd 42 N.Y.2d 88, 396 N.Y.S.2d 834 (1977).

3. 61 A.D.2d 1045, 403 N.Y.S.2d 120 (2d Dept. 1978).

4. *Boyle v. Kelley,* 53 A.D.2d at 457, 385 N.Y.S.2d at 792.

5. 53 A.D.2d at 461, 385 N.Y.S.2d at 794 citing *Fontana v. Town of Hempstead,* 18 A.D.2d 1084, 239 N.Y.S.2d 512 (2d Dept. 1963); *Lyon v. City of Binghampton,* 256 A.D. 397, 10 N.Y.S.2d 951 (3rd Dept. 1930).

6. 44 A.D.2d 828, 355 N.Y.S.2d 170 (2d Dept. 1974).

7. 460 F. 2d 111 (2d Cir. 1972).

8. 53 A.D.2d at 462, 385 N.Y.S.2d at 794-95.

9. PROSSER. HANDBOOK OF THE LAW OF TORTS, § 94 (4th ed.). See CALAMARI AND PERILLO. THE LAW OF CONTRACTS §§ 15-2 to 1977.

10. 42 N.Y.2d 88, 396 N.Y.S.2d 834.

11. County Law § 52(l) states

> Any claim or notice of claim against a county for damage, injury or death, or for invasion of personal or property rights, of every name and nature, and whether casual or continuing trespass or nuisance and any other claim for dam-

ages arising at law or in equity, alleged to have been caused or sustained in whole or in part by or because of any misfeasance, omission of duty, negligence or wrongful act on the part of the county . . . must be made and served in compliance with section fifty-e of the general municipal law.

12. 61 A.D.2d 1045, 403 N.Y.S.2d 120 (2d Dept. 1978).

13. Subsequent cases, all dealing with counties, have uniformly followed the *Abramowitz* and *Boyle* reasoning. See, *Oakely v. Police Property Clerk of Nassau Co.*, 75 A.D.2d 816, 427 N.Y.S.2d 477 (2d Dept. 1980); *Mealmarkets Inc. v. Dillon*, 77 A.D.2d 897, 430 N.Y.S.2d 687 (2d Dept. 1980), *op. recalled and aff'd on other gds.*, 80 A.D.2d 839, 436 N.Y.S.2d 780 (2d Dept. 1981).

14. If an Article 78 proceeding is used to obtain the return of the money or property from the police property clerk, under CPLR 217, there is a four month statute of limitation which begins to run upon demand to the municipality and its refusal.

11. Amendment of the Pleadings and the Notice of Claim

1. G.M.L. § 50-e(1) When service required; time for service; upon whom service required.

(a) In any case founded upon tort where a notice of claim is required by law as a condition precedent to the commencement of an action or special proceeding; against a public corporation, as defined in the general construction law, or any officer, appointee or employee thereof, the notice of claim shall comply with and be served in accordance with the provisions of this section within ninety days after the claim arises.

2. G.M.L. § 50-e(5) Application for leave to serve a late notice.

Upon application, the court, in its discretion, may extend the time to serve a notice of claim specified in paragraph (a) of subdivision one. The extension shall not exceed the time limited for the commencement of an action by the claimant against the public corporation. In determining whether to grant the extension, the court shall consider, in particular, whether the public corporation or its attorney or its insurance carrier acquired actual knowledge of the essential facts constituting the claim within the time specified in subdivision one or within a reasonable time thereafter. The court shall also consider all other relevant facts and circumstances, including whether the claimant was an infant, or mentally or physically incapacitated, or died before the time limited for service of the notice of claim; whether the claimant failed to serve a timely notice of claim by reason of his justifiable reliance upon settlement representations made by an authorized representative of the public corporation or its insurance carrier; whether the claimant in serving a notice of claim made an excusable error concerning the identity of the public corporation against which the claim should be asserted; and whether the delay in serving the notice of claim substantially prejudiced the public corporation in maintaining its defense on the merits.

An application for leave to serve a late notice shall not be denied on the ground that it was made after commencement of an action against the public corporation.

3. G.M.L. 50-e(6) Mistake, omission, irregularity or defect. At any time after the service of a notice of claim and at any stage of an action or special proceed-

ing to which the provisions of this section are applicable, a mistake, omission, irregularity or defect made in good faith in the notice of claim required to be served by this section, not pertaining to the manner or time of service thereof, may be corrected, supplied or disregarded, as the case may be, in the discretion of the court, provided it shall appear that the other party was not prejudiced thereby.

4. *Chikam v. City of New York*, 10 A.D. 2d 862, 199 N.Y.S.2d 829, appeal den. 11 A.D.2d 688, 205 N.Y.S.2d 850 (2d Dept. 1960); *Camarella v. East Iron-Dequoit School*, 41 A.D.2d 29, 341 N.Y.S.2d 729 (4th Dept. 1973), affd. 34 N.Y.2d 139, 356 N.Y.S.2d 553, 313 N.E.2d 29 (1974); *O'Neill v. Manhattan and Bronx Surface Transit Operating Authority*, 23 A.D.2d 488, 255 N.Y.S.2d 903 (4th Dept. 1965); *Weed v. County of Nassau*, 42 A.D.2d 848, 346 N.Y.S.2d 702 (2d Dept. 1973), affd. 34 N.Y.2d 723, 357 N.Y.S.2d 493, 313 N.E.2d 787 (1964); *Komar v. City of New York*, 24 A.D.2d 941, 265 N.Y.S.2d 331 (1st Dept. 1965); HERBERT WACHTELL, NEW YORK PRACTICE UNDER THE C.P.L.R., 5th Ed., 1976, p. 89.

5. C.P.L.R. § 3025(b), Amendments and Supplemental pleadings by leave. A party may amend his pleading, or supplement it by setting forth additional or subsequent transactions or occurrences, at any time by leave of court or by stipulation of all parties. Leave shall be freely given upon such terms as may be just including the granting of costs and continuances.

C.P.L.R. § 203(e). Claim in amended pleading. A claim asserted in an amended pleading is deemed to have been interposed, at the time the claims in the original pleading were interposed, unless the original pleading does not give notice of the transactions, occurrences, or series of transactions or occurrences, to be proved pursuant to the amended pleading.

6. See also *Oliveras v. New York City Transit Authority*, 27 Misc.2d 711, 207 N.Y.S.2d 313 (Sup. Ct., Kings Co. 1960); *La Rocco v. City of New York*, 37 A.D. 2d 529, 322 N.Y.S.2d 163 (1st Dept. 1971); *Glover v. City of New York*, 401 F. Supp. 632 (E.D.N.Y. 1975).

In *Oliveras*, the first notice of claim alleged that because of certain acts of negligence in the maintenance, operation and supervision of respondent's subway platform and tracks, the plaintiff-infant was injured. Plaintiff moved to amend the notice of claim to allege that his injuries arose from an assault upon him by a conductor of the Transit Authority. The court held that the transformation of the claim from one grounded in negligence to one based upon an intentional assault was substantive in nature and that, under Section 50-e(6), the court had no power to allow an amendment which is substantive in nature "and changes the *theory* of the claim" (Italics supplied). *Oliveras v. New York City Transit Authority, supra*, at 713, 207 N.Y.S.2d 313. In *La Rocco*, the Appellate Division reversed an order of the Supreme Court granting the plaintiff's motion for leave to amend a notice of claim *nunc pro tunc*. The plaintiff here originally commenced an action for property damages and, under Section 50-e(6), sought to add a claim for personal injuries, which the Appellate Division denied.

In *Gordon*, the plaintiff appealed from an order of the Supreme Court, Kings County, which denied his motion to permit a correction of his notice of claim and to strike certain affirmative defenses. The court affirmed the order of the trial court stating that Special Term properly denied the plaintiff's motion under Section 50-e(6) to correct his notice of claim by adding to allegations in the notice of claim of assault and excessive force, further allegations that his damages had been the product of the defendant's negligence. The court held that such an amendment would "have substantially altered the nature of the plaintiff's claim by adding thereto a new *theory of liability* not previously interposed." *Gordon v. City of New York, supra.* The court in *Gordon,* citing *Dale, Colena,* and *Alaxanian,* noted that amendments of a substantive nature to a notice of claim are not within the purview of Section 50-e(6) of the General Municipal Law.

7. Mr. Robert S. Hoshino, the Bureau Chief of the Bureau of Municipal Services in the Office of the County Attorney, County of Nassau, I am advised, will recommend that a bill be submitted to the Legislature in Albany addressed to the issue discussed in this article.

12. Bifurcation and Trifurcation

1. See *Nemeth v. Terminal Cleaning Contractors, Inc.,* 30 A.D.2d 518, 219 N.Y.S 2d 224 (1st Dept. 1968); *Berman v. H.J. Enterprises, Inc.,* 13 A.D.2d 199, 214 N.Y.S.2d 945 (1st Dept. 1961); *Dillenbach v. Bailey,* 32 A.D.2d 735, 301 N.Y.S.2d 900 (4th Dept. 1969); *Garcia v. Herald Tribune Fresh Air Fund, Inc.,* 51 A.D.2d 897, 380 N.Y.S.2d 676 (1st Dept. 1976).

2. See *Mercado v. City of New York,* 25 A.D.2d 75, 265 N.Y.S.2d 834 (1st Dept. 1966).

3. CPLR §603. Severance and separate trials.

In furtherance of convenience or to avoid prejudice the court may order a severance of claims, or may order a separate trial of any claim, or of any separate issue. The court may order the trial of any claim or issue prior to the trial of others.

CPLR. 40 1 Sequence of trial.

The court may determine the sequence in which the issues shall be tried and otherwise regulate the conduct of the trial in order to achieve a speedy and unprejudiced disposition of the matters at issue in a setting of proper decorum.

4. See *Cully v. City of New York,* 25 A.D.2d 519, 267 N.Y.S.2d 282 (1st Dept. 1966); *Castelli v. Regina Center, Inc.,* 54 A.D.2d 954, 388 N.Y.S.2d 632 (2d Dept. 1976); *Williams v. Robert E. Adams,* 46 A.D.2d 952, 362 N.Y.S.2d 68 (3rd Dept. 1974); *Keating v. Eng,* 50 A.D.2d 898, 377 N.Y.S.2d 928 (2nd Dept. 1975); *Williams v. City of New York,* 36 A.D.2d 620, 318 N.Y.S.2d 536 (2nd Dept. 1971); *Matter of Movielab, Inc. v. Mastercraft Record Plating, Inc.,* 39 A.D.2d 691, 332 N.Y.S. 2d 369 (1st Dept. 1972); *Turkel v. I.M.I. Warp Knits, Inc.,* 50 A.D. 543, 375 N.Y.S. 2d 333 (1st Dept. 1975); *Thorne v. Burr,* 41 A.D.2d 662, 340 N.Y.S.2d 677 (2d Dept. 1973); *Smerechniak v. County of Nassau, et al.,* A.D.2d 431 N.Y.S.2d 134 (2d Dept. 1980).

15. CPLR 325(d) and the Ad Damnum

1. 96 Misc. 2d 206, 408 N.Y.2d 869 (Civil Court of the City of New York, Bronx County 1978).

2. C.P.L.R. 325(d).

3. *B&R Textile Corp. v. Empire Bias Binding Co.,* 126 Misc.2d 965, 484 N.Y.S.2d 487 (New York Civil Court 1985). See also *Unterterberg v. Scarsdale Imp. Corp.* 128 Misc.2d 873, 491 N.Y.S.2d 571 (S. Ct. West Co. 1985) (Held: transferee to County Court

under Const. Art 6 Sec 19 automatically effected reduction in *Ad damnum* clause to place case within monetary jurisdictional limits of lower court); *LaPlaca v. Boorstein,* 87 Misc.2d 45 (S. Ct. Queens Co. 1970) (Held: an action may be removed to the Civil Court under C.P.L.R. 325[d] without regard to any statutory or constitutional limitation on the amount of monetary damage which may be awarded by the Court).

16. Filing a Late Notice of Claim: One Basis and Analysis

1. G.M.L. Sec. 50(e)5.
2. 103 A.D. 2d 765, 477 N.Y.S. 2d 392 (2d Dept. 1984).
3. See also *Matter of Darmstedter v. Buffalo Sewer Authority,* 96 A.D. d 1148, 467 N.Y.S. 2d 460 (4th Dept. 1983) where the Appellate Division Fourth Department held that timely service of notice of claim on the Corporation Counsel of City of Buffalo was deemed actual notice to Buffalo Sewer Authority and plaintiff's application to file late notice was granted since the City Corporation Counsel was regularly engaged in representing the Sewer Authority; *King v. City of New York,* 88 A.D. 2d 891, 452 N.Y.S. 2d 607 (1st Dept. 1980). Again in *Law v. Rochester City School District,* 107 A.D. 2d 1089, 486

17. A Note on the Workers' Compensation Law

1. N.Y. Workers' Compensation Law Ch. 67 Consolidated Laws.
2. N.Y. Workers' Compensation Law Art. 4 Sec. 50(2).
3. N.Y. Workers' Compensation Law Art. 6 and Sec. 50(1).
4. 109 N.Y. Jur 2d, Workers' Compensation See. 1, pp. 158, 159.
5. CLS Workers' Compensation Law, Art. 9, which provides for payment of benefits to employees for disabilities resulting from an occupational injury and sickness; Vol. 109 N.Y. Jur 2d, Workers' Compensation, Sec. 4, p. 163.
6. CLS Workers' Compensation Law, Art. 10; Vol. 109 N.Y. Jur 2d, Workers' Compensation, Sec. 4 pp. 163, 164.
7. N.Y. Workers' Compensation Law Sec. 2(7).
8. N.Y. Workers' Compensation Law Sec. 2(5).
9. *Davis v. Newsweek Magazine,* 305 N.Y.20, 110 N.E.2d 406 (1953); *Anadio v. Ideal Leather Furnishers,* 32 A.D.2d 40, 299 N.Y.S.2d 489 (3d Dept. 1969).
10. 268 App. Div. 935, 51 N.Y.S.2d 131 (1944).
11. *Hancock v. Ingersoll-Rand Co.,* 21 A.D.2d 703, 249 N.Y.S.2d 43 (3d Dept. 1964).
12. 209 A.D.2d 748, 617 N.Y.S.2d 475 (3d Dept. 1994).
13. 232 A.D.2d 677, 648 N.Y.S.2d 180 (3d Dept. 1996).
14. *Hancock,* 21 A.D.2d 703.
15. *Robinson,* 209 A.D.2d 748.
16. 27 A.D.2d 612, 275 N.Y.S.2d 627 (3d Dept. 1966).
17. 14 A.D.2d 958, 221 N.Y.S.2d 225 (3d Dept. 1961).
18. See also *Morningstar v. Corning Baking Co.,* 6 A.D.2d 178, 176 N.Y.S.2d 388 (3d Dept. 1958) (Held: wherein the course of employment an employee temporarily departs for a brief period of time in an interest other than his employment, but directly or indirectly his interest may result in a benefit or advantage to his employer, it is a natural and normal incident of employment and within the system of the Workers' Compensation Law); *Rosebrock v. Glen and Mohawk Milk Ass'n Inc.,* 40 A.D.2d 978, 338 N.Y.S.2d 366 (3d Dept. 1972) (Held: negligent operation of motor vehicle, even apparently in violation

of traffic law, prior to fatal accident, while acting pursuant to employer's instruction to call on customer while en route home, did not amount to a deviation from employment and did not bar compensation under Workers' Compensation Laws.)

19. 89 A.D.2d 644, 453 N.Y.S.2d 103 (3d Dept. 1966); Cf., however, *Walter v. Ed Walters, Inc.*, 26 A.D.2d 870, 273 N.Y.S.2d 1006 (3d Dept. 1966) (Held: record supported findings of deviation from employment and that the employee was engaged in personal activity at the time of the injury, which was unconnected with his employment).

20. *Malacarne v. City of Yonkers Parking Authority*, 41 N.Y.2d 189, 391 N.Y.S.2d 402 (1976).

21. 224 N.Y.126, 120 N.E.118 (1918).

22. 76 A.D.2d 955, 428 N.Y.S.2d 737 (3d Dept. 1980).

23. 63 A.D.2d 1114, 406 N.Y.S.2d 392 (3d Dept. 1978).

24. *Wright v. General Electric Co.*, 81 A.D.2d 722,439 N.Y.S.2d 456 (3d Dept. 1981).

25. 256 N.Y. 599, 177 N.E.156 (1931). See also *Hill v. All Seasons Service Inc.*, 255 A.D.2d 680, 674 N.Y.S.2d 456 (3d Dept. 1998); *Knaub v. Real-Time Business-Systems Inc.*, 251 A.D.2d 840, 674 N.Y.S.2d 799 (3d Dept. 1998), N.Y.S. 2d 540 (4th Dept. 1985) the Fourth Department held actual knowledge could be imputed to school districts where the school principal visited accident site. On this also see *Annis v. New York City Transit Authority*, 108 A.D. 2d 643, 485 N.Y.S. 2d 529 (1st Dept. 1985); *Barnes v. County of Onondaga*, 103 A.D. 2d 624, 481 N.Y.S. 2d 539 (4th Dept. 1984); *Matter of Timothy Morris*, 88 A.D. 2d 956, 451 N.Y.S. 2d 448 (92nd Dept. 1982).

4. 98 A.D. 2d 38, 469 N.Y.S. 2d 467 (2d Dept. 1983).

5. *Lucas v. City of New York*, 91 A.D. 2d 637, 456 N.Y.S. 2d 816 (2d Dept. 1982); *Somma v. City of New York*, 81 A.D. 2d 889, 439 N.Y.S. 2d 50 (2d Dept. 1981).

6. 90 A.D. 2d 809, 445 N.Y.S.2d 667(2d Dept. 1982).

7. See also *Van Horn v.Village of New Paltz*, 57 A.D. 2d 642, 393 N.Y.S.2d 219 (3rd Dept. 1977) where the Appellate Division, Third Department, held that the public corporation acquired actual knowledge of the essential facts constituting the claim in light of disciplinary proceedings against the police officer following the claimant's death.

8. *Caselli v. City of New York*, 105 A.D. 2d 251, 483 N.Y.S. 2d 401 (2d Dept. 1984); *Williams v. Town of Trondequoit*, 59 A.D. 2d 1049, 399 N.Y.S. 2d 807 (4th Dept. 1977).

9. *Cooper v. City of Rochester*, 84 A.D. 2d 947, 446 N.Y.S. 2d 644 (4th Dept. 1981).

18. Trial By Jury Revisited

1. *Queens Bar Bulletin*, Vol. 67, No. 6, March 2004.

2. 500 U.S. 20, 114 L. Ed. 2d 26, 111 S. Ct. 1647 (1991).

3. 532 U.S. 105, 121 S. Ct. 1302, 149 L.Ed. 2d 234 (2001).

4. 122 S. Ct. 54 (2002).

5. 42 U.S. 200, 142 S. Ct. 2488, 159 L. Ed. 2d 312, 72 U.S.L.W. 4516 (2004).

Introduction to Family Law Reprinted Articles

These articles are exclusively concerned with the law of Paternity and Child Abuse and Neglect. The two articles on the subject of Artificial Insemination and Paternity represent an examination of an issue that has certainly not yet been resolved and whose outcome the future will certainly hold.

.

Chapter 4
Family Law Reprinted Articles

1. Artificial Insemination and Paternity

The charge of paternity often strikes the man in the prime of life. Faced with the charge of alleged paternity and the concomitant obligation to support the out-of-wedlock child, the charge, if proven, may carry a substantial financial obligation. The Family Court of the State of New York has exclusive jurisdiction over paternity proceedings under Section 500 of the Family Court Act. It is beyond the scope of this article to consider the niceties of paternity proceedings. For this, the practitioner is referred to the authoritative treatise on the subject, "Disputed Paternity Proceedings" by Sidney B. Schatkin.

The subject to be considered here is a most modern problem—namely, where a child is conceived by the process of artificial insemination with the consent of the husband by a third party donor, is the child born of this process the legitimate product of the marriage and, whether this is so or not, does the husband of the artificially inseminated woman have the duty to support the child?

There are few reported cases on the subject and all of them, in this state, are trial court decisions.

The first case to consider the issue in this state was *Strnad v. Strnad.*[1]

In *Strnad*, a custody proceeding, the plaintiff was artificially inseminated with the consent of the defendant. The defendant was held entitled to visitation with the child conceived by this procedure. The court concluded, however, that the child was not a legitimate child, stating the situation was no different from where a child, born out of wedlock, is by law made legitimate upon marriage of the interested parties. The court held, second, that the child was adopted or semi-adopted by the defendant and that the husband of the artificially inseminated woman was entitled to the same rights of visitation as those acquired by a foster parent who has formally adopted the child. The court refused to rule on the morality or propriety of procreation by the process of artificial insemination.

A New York Supreme Court, in *Gursky v. Gursky*,[2] also ruled on these same issues. In *Gursky*, plaintiff alleged causes of action for annulment and separation on the grounds of abandonment and cruel and inhuman treatment. Defendant-wife counterclaimed for separation. The court dismissed the plaintiff's action for annulment for failure of proof. There were no issue of the marriage. The defendant was granted an annulment due to a failure of consummation of the marriage. The evidence indicated that, due to medical infirmities of the plaintiff-husband, the parties agreed, in a written consent agreement, to have the defendant-wife artificially inseminated with the semen of a third party donor. The plaintiff-husband promised to pay all expenses resulting from the procedure. A child was born, and Mr. Gursky was listed as the father on the birth certificate. The court noted first, on review of the prior case law and statutory enactment, that a child begotten through a father who is not the mother's lawful husband, is deemed to be illegitimate and must be held so. The court distinguished *Strnad*, stating that visitation was the sole issue there; the conclusion there that the child was legitimate was supported by no legal precedent and the holding in that case that the child was adopted or semi-adopted could not be legally sustained, since there was no legal adoption proceeding in accord with the Domestic Relations Law (DRL) § 110. The court went on to state that the idea in *Strnad* that the child was semi-adopted was an implicit recognition of the fact that the birth would otherwise be illegitimate. Thus the court here concluded that the child indeed was not the legitimate issue of the husband.

The *Gursky* court, however, concluded that the husband's written consent to the artificial insemination procedure implied a promise to support the offspring. In sum, the court implied a contract, based on the agreement and, in the alternative, held that the doctrine of equitable estoppel was applicable since the wife, based on her husband's consent to the procedure, changed her position and acted in reliance on her husband's wishes. Hence, the court here held the husband liable for the support of the child.

Gursky reaches a slightly different result from *Strnad*. The *Gursky* court, unlike the *Strnad* court, does not conclude that the child is made legitimate through a theory of constructive adoption, so to speak, but does agree with *Strnad* that since the husband in some way consented to the procedure with his wife, he is entitled in *Strnad* to visitation and in *Gursky* therefore incurred the obligation of support.

The next case to be considered, *Anonymous v. Anonymous*,[3] follows *Gursky* insofar as it holds that the husband has a duty to support children conceived by artificial insemination of a third party donor's semen, pursuant to a written agreement between the husband and wife. This case was a motion by plaintiff-wife for temporary alimony, counsel fees and support for herself and her two daughters both conceived by artificial insemination, as a result of a written agreement made by the parties with the specific consent of the husband to the wife's pregnancies. The court held, citing *Gursky*, that the husband had an obligation to support his wife and two children. The court, however, did not reach or consider the issue of the legitimacy of the child.

The case of *In the Matter of Adoption of Anonymous*[4] did

The facts in this case were that the child was born of consensual artificial insemination by a third party donor. The husband was listed as father on the birth certificate. The parties later separated and were divorced. Both the separation agreement and divorce decree declared the child to be the daughter and child of the couple. The wife was granted support, the husband visitation rights. The wife remarried and the new husband petitioned to adopt the child, to which the first husband refused his consent. The petitioner argued, however, that his consent was not required since he was not the true parent of the child. The court noted that DRL § 111, with certain exceptions, requires the consent of the parent of a child born in wedlock, to an adoption. Hence, the court defined the issue to be that, if the husband is, in fact, the parent of the child, citing the statute, and refuses his consent to the adoption, whether the new husband's petition must be dismissed.

On the issue of the legitimacy of the child, the court distinguished the holding in *Gursky*, which held the child illegitimate, noting that the concept and definition of a child born out of wedlock, upon which *Gursky* relied, was developed long before the advent of the practice of artificial insemination; that the child conceived by this process is begotten by an anonymous donor with whom the wife does not have sexual intercourse or commit adultery; that since there is consent, there is no marital infidelity; and the child, therefore, is born in wedlock.

The court concluded, in view of the strong policy of New York State in favor of legitimacy, that a child born as a result of consensual artificial insemination during a valid marriage is a legitimate child entitled to all the rights and privileges of a naturally conceived child of the same marriage.

The most recent case to consider the issue of the legitimacy of a child born by artificial insemination is *Estate of Bernard H. Gordon*.[5] In that case the fiduciary sought to exclude as contingent remaindermen of testamentary trusts two children born during wedlock by artificial insemination of the wife of the decedent's son by a third party donor. The issue before the court was the legitimacy of two children conceived by artificial insemination of the wife by a third party donor.

The court initially noted that, in fact, DRL § 73 provides that "any child born to a married woman by means of artificial insemination performed with the consent in writing of the woman and her husband should be deemed the legitimate natural child of the husband and his wife for all purposes."[6] The court noted, however, that neither this statute, nor any other statute, existed at the time of the death of the decedent or birth of either objectant. The court held that the 1974 statute was not to be applied retroactively, noting that, in any event, the statute was inapplicable to the case before it since here there was no writing as required by statute. The court held, however, citing *Gursky, Strnad* and the other cases considered in this article, that the child conceived by the process of artificial insemination by a third party donor with the husband's consent is the legitimate issue of the husband.[7]

In conclusion, the following points should be noted:

First, DRL § 73 states that any child born as a result of artificial insemination with the written consent of the parties is deemed the legitimate child of the parties. The statute does not cover the situation where the procedure occurs absent a writing, albeit with the consent of the parties, or the scenario where it occurs without the husband's knowledge.

Second, all the courts of this state that have considered the issue, whether they have found the child legitimate as in *Strnad*, or illegitimate as in *Gursky*, have found the married man liable to support the child based on a theory of implied contract or equitable estoppel.

Third, the most recent case to consider the issue, *Estate of Gordon*, (in light of DRL § 73) has held the child legitimate, even in the absence of a written agreement between the husband and wife, as long as there was some sort of consent to the procedure.

It is clear that the trend of the case law, even in the absence of writing, is to deem the child to be the legitimate issue of the husband, as long as there was some consensual agreement, with the concomitant obligation of support and ancillary rights of custody and visitation. What the law is or will be when the procedure occurs with no consent or without the knowledge of the husband is an open question.

Reprinted with permission from: Family Law Review, December 1994, Vol. 26. No. 4, published by the New York State Bar Association, One Elk Street, Albany, New York 12207.

2. Artificial Insemination and Paternity: Part Two

In a previous article (*Queens Bar Bulletin*, November 1992), this writer considered the issue of the legitimacy of a child born as a result of artificial insemination of the wife by a third party donor, with the consent of the husband. It was found that, with some exceptions, the few reported cases in this state supported the view that the child was the legitimate offspring of the marriage, despite impregnation of the wife by a third party, usually, an anonymous donor. In that article it was noted where, in fact, there is a consensual agreement in writing by the parties of the marriage to the procedure, Sec. 73 of the Domestic Relations Law makes the issue of this process the legitimate issue of the marriage.[1]

Suppose, however, that the wife resorts to artificial insemination by a donor other than the husband without the latter's knowledge or consent? This writer has found no reported cases in this state on this fact pattern. Such a bizarre state of facts was presented to the Ontario (Canada) Supreme Court in 1921 in *Orford v. Orford* (58 D.L.R. 251). In *Orford,* the parties were married in Canada and then returned to England. The parties were separated then, the husband returning to Canada, while the wife remained in England. While in England she resorted to artificial insemination without her husband's knowledge or consent. The wife returned to Canada with the child and sued her husband for divorce, alleging his neglect and cruelty had driven her to the act described.

The court held the child to be born as a result of adultery and rejected her claim that the child had been born as a result of artificial insemination. The court noted, however, assuming the truth of the wife's narrative, that her submission to artificial insemination without her husband's knowledge or consent constituted an act of adultery. The court reasoned that the adultery involved was not so much a violation of the moral law, but the wife's surrender of her reproductive powers to another man. Thus the court concluded, at 258-259,

> but can anyone read the Mosaic law against those sins which, whether of adultery or otherwise, in any way affect the sanctity of the reproductive functions of the people of Israel, without being convinced that, had such a thing as "artificial insemination" entered the mind of the lawgiver, it would have been regarded with the utmost horror and detestation as an invasion of the most sacred of the marital rights of the husband and wife, and have been the subject of the severest penalties?

In my judgment, the essence of the offence of adultery consists, not in the moral turpitude of the act of sexual intercourse, but in the voluntary surrender to another person of the reproductive powers of faculties of the guilty person, and any submission of those powers to the service or enjoyment of any person other than the husband of the wife comes within the definition of 'adultery'.

The fact that it has been held that anything short of actual sexual intercourse, no matter how indecent or improper the act may be, does not constitute adultery, really tends to strengthen my view that it is not the moral turpitude that is involved, but the invasion of the reproductive function. So long as nothing takes place which can by any possibility affect that function, there can be no adultery; so that, unless and until there is actual sexual intercourse, there can be no adultery. But to argue from that that adultery necessarily begins and ends there is utterly fallacious. Sexual intercourse is adulterous because in the case of the woman it involves the possibility of introducing into the family of the husband a false strain of blood.

Any act on the part of the wife which does that would, therefore, be adulterous. That such a thing could be accomplished in any other than the natural manner probably never entered the heads of those who considered the question before. Assuming the plaintiff's story to be true, what took place here was the introduction into her body by unusual means of the seed of a man other than her husband. If it were necessary to do so, I would hold that that in itself was "sexual intercourse." It is conceivable that such an act performed upon a woman against her will might constitute rape.

Mr. White was driven, as a result of his argument, to contend that it would not be adultery for a woman living with her husband to provide by artificial insemination a child of which some man other than her husband was the father! A monstrous conclusion surely. If such a thing has never before been declared to be adultery, then, on the grounds of public policy, the court should now declare it so.

Orford is the only court decision this writer has been able to discover concerning the issue of non-consensual Artificial Insemination. The court apparently held that the lack of consent of the husband to the Artificial Insemination Process had the effect of illegitimizing or bastardizing the child and so relieving him of the duty of support. The question, however, will surely remain open in this country until such time as the courts resolve the issue.

3. *Child Abuse and Neglect: A Limit*

Child abuse and neglect in the State of New York and, indeed throughout this country, has increasingly become more and more visible, actual, and of immediate pressing concern to both Government and the individual. Each day, our daily newspaper reveals one more added instance of the abuse and neglect of children, the details of which puzzle and shock the imagination of the reader. Along with the rights of women and other minorities, the rights of children have come to the fore and will not be further denied. The Courts of the State of New York, reflecting the concern of society and providing, at the same time, commendable leadership, increasingly and appropriately will remove children from the home where there is the slightest hint of physical, sexual, or even psychological abuse. Where there can be shown a neglect of the child, be it of his person, his home environment, his education, or his physical and emotional state, the courts of this State have shown that they will act.

It is surely correct that the courts of this State, our elected officials, parents, and indeed all levels and sectors of decent society should protect innocents unable to protect themselves from parents or guardians who use, abuse, and take advantage of the weakness and innocence of our children.

At the same time, however, the power of the courts to remove children from undesirable and inappropriate home environments, though wide, is not without limits. It is one limitation of this power that this article proposes to consider.

Let us assume, for the sake of argument, that under Section Ten of the Family Court Act, a finding of neglect or abuse is made pursuant to a Fact Finding Hearing and the child, thereafter, at the conclusion of a Dispositional Hearing is removed from the custody of his parents and placed in an appropriate agency or in foster care. Let us also assume that the child's parent or parents are not present at the Fact Finding Hearing or the Dispositional Hearing. The question arises whether such a finding of neglect or abuse and the subsequent placement of the child in a setting other than that of the child's parents can be sustained, upheld, and justified. In a word, does this society's concern for the well-being of its children and their removal from a possibly detrimental environment extend to the point that a child may be removed from the custody of its parents without the parents being present at trial to contest the matter and defend their right to love and care for their child. Does society's good purposes for its children and its statutory right to interfere in the child/parent relationship where danger to the life and well-being of the child is at stake extend to the removal of the child from the home, all in the absence of the accused parents.

The answer is found under Section 1042 of the Family Court Act. That Section states,

> If the parent or other person legally responsible for the child's care is not present, the court may proceed to hear a petition under this article only if the child is represented by counsel, a law guardian, or a guardian *ad litem*. If the parent or other person legally responsible for the child's care thereafter moves the court that a resulting disposition be vacated and asks for a rehearing, the court shall grant the motion on an affidavit showing such relationship or responsibility, unless the court finds that the parent or other person willfully refused to appear at the hearing in which case the court may deny the motion.

A clear and unencumbered reading of this statute reveals that, where a parent is absent from hearings under the article and an Order of disposition is entered, the disposition as such has no effect at all, and the Order of Disposition may be vacated upon an affidavit of the parent or parents showing that he or she is in fact the one with such relationship or to whom has been entrusted the responsibility of care for the child. The section is mandatory stating that the court *shall* grant the motion upon a sworn statement of the parent or parents showing the required relationship or responsibility.

The section, however, does state that the court, in the exercise of its discretion, may deny the parent's motion to vacate if the court finds that the parent or other person legally responsible has willfully refused to appear at the hearing. Even then, under the statute, the court need not deny the motion and may, in its discretion, choose to grant it, notwithstanding the fact that the parent or parents willfully failed to appear.

In sum, a cursory reading of this statutory section reveals a policy against the rendering of inquests resulting in the removal of children from their parents under Section Ten of the Family Court Act. The policy is so strong that a mere showing of relationship or responsibility is sufficient to nullify any default judgment entered in the absence of the parents and, even though the parents willfully failed to appear, the court in its discretion may cancel the default.

The pertinent case law supports the above interpretation of this statute and buttresses the policy underlying and defining the statute that children are not to be taken from the custody of parent or guardian on the ground of abuse or neglect in the absence of such parent or guardian and, should this happen, the interests of justice and the sanctity and importance of the parent/child relationship demand cancellation and nullification of the finding of abuse or neglect and resulting disposition and removal. The truth of the finding is not a factor. The demand of due process requires nothing more and nothing less.

The Second Department articulated the policy inherent in Section 1042 of the Family Court Act in *Matter of Ana Maria Q. v. Mirna V.*, 52 AD 2d 607, 382 N.Y.S.2d 107 (2nd Dept. 1976).

In *Mirna*, appeals were taken from two modified orders of disposition of the Family Court of Rockland County, each of which granted custody of the child to the Department of Social Services for one year. The Second Department reversed on the law and remitted the matter to the Family Court for a hearing to determine whether the appellant willfully violated the order of supervision without just cause. The court concluded, stating the general rule that

> absent unusual justifiable circumstances, one's rights should not be terminated without his presence at the hearing. (*In re Cecilia R.*, 36 N.Y. 2d 317, 367 N.Y. Supp. 2d 770, 327 N.E. 2d 812). Petitioner was unjustifiably denied the right to present testimony and cross-examine witnesses before the termination of her custodial rights. *Ana Maria Q. v. Mirna V., supra*, at 108.

In Re Yem, 54 A.D. 2d 73, 388 N.Y. Supp. 2d 7 (1976), a later First Department case, is relevant and adds an interpretive twist to the statute. In *Yem* facts were that on May 21, 1975, an order was entered requiring a psychiatric examination report concerning the appellant and the examination was never held. The Court, however, on July 8, 1975, in the absence of the appellant-parent, proceeded to determine that both children, Hime and Suzanee, had been neglected. The appellant's assigned counsel was not present at the hearing. The appellant applied to the Court to open the default in the Suzanne Yem proceeding on August 5, 1975, stating that the appellant had been given an incorrect date for her appearance in court, that she appeared on July 9 instead of the scheduled date on July 8, and that she thereafter communicated with her attorney for the purpose of having the order entered at the inquest vacated and that she be given an opportunity to contest the matter on the merits. Counsel also submitted an affidavit stating that he had had difficulty in communicating with the appellant because she had been in Bellevue Hospital, that he did not have her correct address to enable him to reach her and that he first saw her on July 30, 1975. An application to open the default in the Hime Yem proceeding was made on September 24, 1975. Thus, the appellant sought to lift two default judgments, one adjudging the child Suzanne a permanently neglected child and the other adjudging her infant brother Hime, a neglected child (Articles 6 and 10 of the SCA). The Appellate Division held

> the failure of the court to ascertain whether appellant's non-appearance was inadvertent or willful was error, in the absence of the psychiatric examination and reports as ordered, and warrants a reversal of the order denying appellant's application to set aside her default. (*Matter of Rivera Children, Angelina Rivera*

(Commissioner of Social Services), 48 A.D. 2d 639, 368 N.Y.S.2d 23. *In Re Yem, supra* at 8.

Yem holds that not only was the inquest and default judgment inappropriate and to be reversed, but the court even went so far as to rule that at the time of the inquests, the Family Court's failure to determine whether the appellant's nonappearance was inadvertent or willful was error since the court did not have the psychiatric report in hand and the report was a necessary ingredient of a proper hearing.

And, finally, this writer recently successfully vacated a default in a parent's non-appearance in a child neglect proceeding, which had resulted in a determination that the child was neglected and in the removal, under an order of disposition, from the custody of the parent to placement in foster care. The mother made a showing in her affidavit in support of the motion to vacate the order of neglect and disposition that she did not know the exact date that she had to appear in court, that she never received a copy of the summons and petition, and that she had insufficient funds for carfare in order to get to court. In addition, she was ill. The court, in its decision, stated that the default of the accused mother was not willful since she had alleged that she was ill at the time that she had to appear in Court and had insufficient funds to get there in any event. The court held that in the interest of justice the accused mother was entitled to a new hearing on the allegations alone.

Both Section 1042 of the Family Court Act and the case law interpreting the statute establish a clear rule that an inquest in a child neglect or abuse proceeding, unless particular and special circumstances be shown, is a highly inappropriate vehicle to achieve the protection of children in our society. The parent/child relationship is the fountain head and source of our society. It is the building block whence family, schools, state, nation and mankind as a whole achieve their being and vitality. Unless the circumstances be exceptional and even compelling, the child/parent relationship must be preserved unless there can be a fair showing with all parties present that it has lost its vital substance.

The protection of our children from neglect and abuse is a pressing societal concern. The law of the State, as reflected in Section 1042 of the Family Court Act and the manner in which Appellate Courts have interpreted this Section, have, however, laid a limit to that concern. The limit is that ultimate limit of due process, and it is that the removal of a child from the parent cannot and should not happen without all the protections and rights that our society affords. It is rightly the law of this State that our children can and should not, in the absence of proof offered and contested by all parties, be removed. It is, then, a tribute to the continued vitality of our common law system and the rights of the individual that though money may be taken and property taken without contest, our children cannot.

4. The Permanently Neglected Child: Certain Criteria

Part I

Section 614 of the Family Court Act (FCA) defines the criteria for the origination of the proceeding for the commitment of the guardianship and custody of a permanently neglected child.

Essentially, there are five listed criteria defined as necessary for the origination of the proceeding. They are

1. that the child is a person under 18 years of age, FCA § 614(1)(a); the child is in the care of an authorized agency, FCA § 614(1)(b);

2. that the authorized agency has made diligent efforts to encourage and strengthen the parental relationship and specifies the efforts made or asserts that such efforts would be detrimental to the best interests of the child and specifying the reasons therefore, FCA § 614(1)(c);

3. that the parent or custodian, notwithstanding the agency's efforts, has failed for a period of more than one year following the date such child came into the care of an authorized agency substantially and continuously or repeatedly to maintain contact with or plan for the future of the child, although physically and financially able to do so, FCA § 614(1)(d);

4. and that the best interests of the child require that the guardianship and custody of the child be committed to an authorized agency to a foster parent authorized to originate this proceeding under section three hundred ninety-two of the social services law or section one thousand fifty-five of this action.

These criteria, as enumerated, would appear to be the model of clarity.

This article will focus on the case law interpreting and construing the meaning and import of FCA § 614(1)(d), which states in part that the parent or custodian for one year following the date the child came into the care of the agency must have failed substantially and continuously or repeatedly to maintain contact with the child although physically and financially able to do so, in order for there to be a finding of permanent neglect under this section of the statute.

In short, the question and issue this article proposes to consider is what, under the case law, constitutes failure to maintain contact such as to sustain a finding of permanent neglect.

It is the law that a finding of either a failure to plan for a period of one year or a failure to maintain contact result, under the law, in a finding of permanent neglect.[1] The case law, however, varies as to what, in fact, constitutes a failure to maintain contact. The Third Department held in *Matter of Kimberly*[2] that permanent neglect had not been proven where there were numerous contacts between the mother and the child during the period of foster care and these contacts could not be considered insubstantial merely because it appeared to the agency caseworker and foster mother that there was little interaction between the natural mother and child. The court held that the natural mother had taken substantial strides to provide adequate shelter and a stable home for the child.

On the other hand, in the *Matter of Orlando F.*[3] the First Department held that where the period of lack of contact was only eight months, it was insufficient to terminate the parent's custody of the child.[4]

Conclusion

This brief review of the case on this subject reveals the following:

First: There must be a failure to maintain contact for one year.[5]

Second: The actuality of contact will not be measured by any subjective assessment of the quality of the contacts or interaction on the part of the mother.[6]

Third: Nor will contact be measured by any subjective assessment of the background of the natural mother.[7]

Fourth: Even if the parent is incarcerated, contact will be measured by the opportunity to maintain telephone or written contact.[8]

This review, albeit brief, of the case concerning failure to maintain contact under FCA § 614(1)(d) reveals, if anything, that it is the actual contact by the parent, not to be subjectively interpreted, that controls how the action will be interpreted and that the contact will be sustained even if only by phone or letter.

Part II

In Part I, this writer considered what, under the New York State Family Court Act § 614(d), constitutes the failure of the parent or custodian to maintain contact with the child who has come into the care of an authorized agency, despite being physically and financially able to do so, for a period of one year while the child is under the care of the state agency.

Part II of this article will consider the import and meaning of the second prong of FCA § 614(d), which states that the failure of the parent or custodian to plan for the future of the child for a period of one year while the child is under the care of an authorized state agency can result in adjudication of permanent neglect and the child being eventually adopted, the natural parental rights being terminated.

The weight of authority in this state holds that the trial court's finding of a failure to plan for the future of the child, for a period of one year while the child is in the temporary care of a state foster care agency, suffices to support a determination of permanent neglect, if it is found that the parents are financially and physically able to do so.[9]

Of course, it is equally true that a finding of either a failure to plan or to maintain contact, can, equally, function to support a finding of permanent neglect.[10]

The issue this article proposes to consider, namely what may be said to constitute a failure to plan under the case law interpreting FCA § 614(d), is significant since the effect of a finding of permanent neglect is to end the natural parental custodial rights with respect to the child—in essence severing the biological natural relationship of parent and child.

The leading case on what constitutes "failure to plan" is *Matter of Leon R.R.*[11] In *Leon*, the Court of Appeals held that the failure to plan requires that the parents formulate a feasible plan both for themselves and the future of the child and that this presupposes at a minimum that the parents take steps to correct the conditions which led to the removal of the child from their home and that the parents project a future course of action taking into account how the child will be supported financially, physically and emotionally and that the adequacy of the parents' plan must not be evaluated with reference to unrealistically high standards.

In *Matter of Roxann Joyce*,[12] the Second Department held that the father's plan for the return of the child was not realistic or feasible since the father's plan did not include any measures to establish a relationship with his child for her entire life.

In formulating a proper plan, the parent must demonstrate to the court good faith effort and minimal adequacy as a planning parent.[13] The plan must be feasible and realistic.[14]

In *Matter of Santosky*,[15] the Family Court of Ulster County held that in determining whether the parents of allegedly neglected children have failed to plan for the future of the children, the parents' plan is not to be judged by the same standards applicable to an affluent social elite; nor is the plan to be judged in light of the class mores of the poor, black and uneducated, and that some middle ground should be set.[16]

It can be seen from this brief review of the case law interpreting the statute that there is no general rule as to what constitutes a failure to plan under FCA § 614(d). If that is so, then question arises as to what type of quantum evidence is needed to establish a failure to plan or, on the other hand, is insufficient to do so.

Matter of Orlando[17] is exemplary. In *Orlando,* the Court of Appeals held that a failure to plan was proved when the child's mother: failed to take affirmative steps to insure the child would have the benefit of an adequate home if returned; missed appointments with the child welfare authorities; failed to satisfy promises to secure her own apartment; and failed to obtain employment as a result of non-attendance at a rehabilitation center.

Again, in *Matter of Candie Lee W.,*[18] a failure to plan was found where the mother was unable to establish a stable residence and failed to regularly attend weekly group counseling sessions.[19]

Conclusion

Although there is not yet a rule that can be specifically formulated as to what constitutes a failure to plan for the future of the child under FCA § 614(d) leading to a termination of the natural parents' rights over the biological child, it is evident amid the myriad of case law interpreting the statute that it is really a question of fact and involves an assessment of the good faith efforts on the parents to plan; real efforts to plan in the sense of solving any emotional or personal problem that may be said to interfere with the ability of the parents to eventually care for child; and realistically planning in light of the natural parents' situation and circumstances. In short, it is the facts that will govern both objectively, in the sense that the plan must be real and actual and, subjectively, in light of the parents' problems and their ability to provide in light of whatever personal or practical problems that may exist or impact.

Notes

1. Artificial Insemination and Paternity

1. 190 Misc. 786, 78 N.Y.S.2d 390 (Sup. Ct., New York Co. 1948).
2. 39 Misc. 2d 1083, 242 N.Y.S.2d 406 (Sup. Ct., Kings Co. 1963) .
3. 41 Misc. 2d 886, 246 N.Y.S.2d 835 (Sup. Ct., Suffolk Co. 1964).
4. 74 Misc. 2d 99, 345 N.Y.S.2d 430 (Surr. Ct., Kings Co. 1973).
5. 131 Misc. 2d 823, 501 N.Y.S.2d 969 (Surr. Ct., Bronx Co. 1986).
6. L.1974, c. 303 § 1.
7. See also *People ex rei Abijan v. Dennett,* 15 Misc. 2d 260, 184 N.Y.S.2d 178 (Sup. Ct., New York Co. 1958); *People v. Sorensen,* 68 Cal. 2d 680, 437 P. 2d 495, 25 ALR 3rd 1093.

2. Artificial Insemination and Paternity: Part Two

1. See *Strnad v. Strnad,* 190 Misc. 786, 78 NY.S. 2d 390 (S. Ct. New York County, 1948); *Gursky v. Gursky,* 39 Misc. 2d 1083, 242 NY.S. 2d 406 2d 99, 345 NY.S. 2d 430 (Surrogates Court, Kings County, 1963); *Estate of Bernard H. Gordon,* 131 Misc. 2d 823, 501 NY.S. 2d 969 (Surrogates Court, Bronx County 1986).

4. The Permanently Neglected Child: Certain Criteria

1. See *Matter of Melanie Ruth JJ,* 76 A.D.2d 1008, 429 N.Y.S.2d 773 (3d Dept. 1980); *Matter of Ikem B.,* 73 A.D.2d 359, 427 N.Y.S.2d 3 (1st Dept. 1980).
2. 72 A.D.2d 851, 421 N.Y.S.2d 849 (3d Dept. 1979).
3. 50 A.D.2d 791, 377 N.Y.S.2d 502 (1st Dept. 1975).
4. See also *Matter of Orzo,* 84 Misc.2d 482, 374 N.Y.S.2d 554 (Fam. Ct., N.Y. Co. 1975) (Held: Mother's consistent visitation with her children met statutory requirements of maintaining contact); *Matter of Barbara P.,* 71 Misc. 2d 965, 337 N.Y.S.2d 203 (Fam. Ct. N.Y. Co. 1972) (Held: Where the child was visited only three times over four and one-half years, a finding of permanent neglect sustained parental rights termination despite the contention that the parent's failure to maintain contact with the children should have been weighed in light of class mores of poor, black and unschooled persons); *Matter of Melanie Ruth JJ, supra* (Held: Permanent neglect finding sustained where the father left the state for a period of 17 months and only spoke to child, during that period, once or twice over the phone); *Guardianship of Sonia Vanessa R.,* 97 Misc. 2d 694, 412 N.Y.S.2d 257 (Fam. Ct., N.Y. Co. 1978) (Held: One visit by father and failure to keep appointment with agency coupled with failure to write or telephone sustained finding of

permanent neglect); *Matter of Marilyn H.*, 106 Misc.2d 972, 436 N.Y.S.2d 14 (Fam. Ct., N.Y. Co. 1981) (Held: Failure to maintain contact for two years by natural mother sustained finding of permanent neglect); *In re Wood*, 78 Misc. 2d 344, 355 N.Y.S.2d 885 (Fam. Ct., Laurence Co. 1974) (Held: Finding of permanent neglect sustained where mother saw child no more than three times in three years).

5. See *Matter of Ikem, supra.*

6. See *Matter of Kimberly, supra.*

7. See *In re P., supra.*

8. See *Matter of Sonia, supra.*

9. See *Matter of Orlando F.*, 40 N.Y.2d 103, 386 N.Y.S.2d 64, 351 N.E.2d 712 (1976); *Matter of Melanie Ruth JJ*, 76 A.D.2d 1008, 429 N.Y.S.2d 773 (3d Dept. 1980); *Matter of Roxann Joyce M.*, 75 A.D.2d 872, 428 N.Y.S.2d 264 (2d Dept. 1980); *Matter of Judy V.*, 60 A.D.2d 719, 400 N.Y.S.2d 916 (3d Dept. 1977); *Matter of Amos HH*, 59 A.D.2d 795, 398 N.Y.S.2d 771 (3d Dept. 1977); *Matter of Lee Ann N.*, 110 A.D.2d 479, 487 N.Y.S.2d 891 (3d Dept. 1980); *Matter of Ray AM*, 37 N.Y.2d 61, 370 N.Y.S.2d 431, 339 N.E.2d 135 (1975); *Matter of Ikem B.*, 73 A.D.2d 359, 429 N.Y.S.2d 3 (1st Dept. 1980).

10. See *Matter of Melanie Ruth JJ, supra*; *Matter of Sydel D.*, 58 A.D.2d 800, 396 N.Y.S.2d 263 (2d Dept. 1977).

11. 48 N.Y.2d 117, 397 N.E.2d 374, 421 N.Y.S.2d 863 (1979).

12. *Id.*

13. See *In re Joyce Ann R.*, 82 Misc. 2d 730, 371 N.Y.S.2d 607 (Fam Ct., Kings County 1975).

14. *In re B.*, 6 Misc.2d 662, 303 N.Y.S.2d 438 (Fam. Ct., N.Y. Co. 1964).

15. 89 Misc.2d 730, 393 N.Y.S.2d 486 (Fam. Ct., Ulster Co. 1970).

16. See also *In re Jones*, 59 Misc. 2d 69, 297 N.Y.S.2d 675 (Fam. Ct., N.Y. Co. 1969).

17. *Id.*

18. *Matter of Candie W.*, 91 A.D.2d 1106, 458 N.Y.S.2d 347 (3d Dept. 1983).

19. On this, see also *Matter of Terry D.* 153 A.D.2d 957, 385 N.Y.S.2d 844 (3d Dept. 1976) (Held: Conduct of children's mother including her use of narcotics and involvement in a bizarre sexual crime failed to support the mother's contention of serious planning); *Matter of Ames S.*, 98 Misc.2d 650, 414 N.Y.S.2d 477 (Fam. Ct., Monroe Co. 1979); *Matter of Orzo*, 84 Misc. 2d 482, 374 N.Y.S.2d 554 (Fam. Ct., N.Y. Co. 1975); *In re P*, 71 Misc.2d 965, 337 N.Y.S.2d 203 (Fam. Ct., N.Y. Co. 1972); *Matter of Alfredo HH*, A.D.2d 480, 486 N.Y.S.2d 689 (3d Dept. 1985); *Matter of Guardianship and Custody of Kareem B.*, 135 Misc.2d 324, 515 N.Y.S.2d 179 (Fam. Ct., N.Y. Co. 1987); *Matter of Lee Ann N.*, 16 A.D.2d 979, 487 N.Y.S.2d 891 (3d Dept. 1985).

Introduction to Labor and Employment Law Reprinted Articles

These articles primarily analyze and examine issues involving the interpretation and construction of the Discrimination Statutes in the United States Code, including Title VII, the statute barring discrimination in the workplace based on gender, religion, national origin, and race, as well as the statutes barring Age discrimination and discrimination based on Disability. One of the articles specifically analyzes and comments on the issue of Supervisory liability in Title VII Age and Disability Discrimination cases. A second article, following that, considers the requirement of a showing of Adverse Action in a Prima Facie Employment Discrimination case. Two of the articles have as their subject whether sexual orientation should be protected under Title VII, and whether it will be. The law in this respect is in a state of evolution. Finally, one of the articles examines the significant policy issue whether clauses in employment contracts mandating arbitration and barring and preventing a worker from enforcing his rights in the Federal Court System are right and, indeed, constitutionally permissible.

Chapter 5
Labor and Employment Law
Reprinted Articles

1. *Termination at Will as an Evolving Concept*

The doctrine of termination at will of the non-tenured, non-governmental employee and an employee's option to resign at will have for some time been acknowledged and promoted as the proper vehicle and desideratum for the continued growth and vitality of our free enterprise system.

Each day, however, we read in the business section of our daily newspaper or the front page itself that the highest company executive has, in euphemistic terms, resigned; that 100 middle managers have been slated for early retirement; or a vast army of clerical workers have been laid off due to a purported slowdown in the economy or terminated, perhaps, in a drive for efficiency in the company's operation under new management. Thus, the doctrine of termination at will and its effects, both economic and human, permeate our system from the smallest business to the giant corporate conglomerate. The only workers apparently immune from the doctrine are the tenured academic, whose permanent employment is based on the theory of academic freedom; the government civil service employee, whose employment is originally based on merit and must continue to be so absent gross misconduct; and the union member, whose termination, if attempted, must deal with the collective bargaining unit.

The effects of termination at will in human terms are profound since an employee may be served for any reason whatsoever, except for palpable prejudice based on age, sex or color. Hence the employee may lose his position by reason of the shape of his nose, his inability to smile in sufficient quality and quantity, or, as is most often the case, the fact that a manager simply has conceived an emotional aversion to a particular personality. Until quite recently, however, neither the courts nor the legislature of this state has addressed themselves to the question of whether the doctrine, in this age of social legislation and humane concerns, should continue to exist.

Recent decisions apparently are beginning to call into question this doctrine. The leading case is *Murphy v. American Home Products Corp.*, 58 N.Y.2d 293, 461 N.Y.S.2d 232 (1983). In *Murphy*, a discharged middle management employee brought a lawsuit alleging abusive discharge and breach of contract. The plaintiff claimed that he was fired because he revealed certain accounting improprieties to the management of the company. The court rejected the plaintiff's claim for abusive discharge stating that where employment is for an indefinite term, it may be freely terminated by either party for any reason or no reason at all and that there can be no cause of action for abusive discharge. The court concluded that "tort liability for abusive discharge should await legislative action."

The court also rejected the plaintiff's argument that a breach of contract cause of action existed on the ground that, although the contract was indefinite, the law implied an obligation on the part of the corporation of fair dealing and good faith. The court reasoned that where no definite contract term was agreed upon initially, there could be no implied contractual obligations.

Thus, the Court of Appeals in *Murphy*, though sympathetic to the plaintiff's plight, rejected the tort action as the proper mechanism to redress such an injury and forced the discharged employee to await legislative action. See also *Potrawich v. Chemical Bank,* 98 A.D.2d 318, 470 N.Y.S.2d 599 (1st Dept. 1984); *Gould v. Community Health Plan of Suffolk,* 99 A.D.2d 479, 470 N.Y.S.2d 415 (2nd Dept. 1984); *O'Donnell v. Westchester Community Service Council, Inc.,* 96 A.D.2d 885, 466 N.Y.S.2d 41 (2nd Dept. 1983).

There are, however, two exceptions to the doctrine of termination at will. The first is found in *Wiener v. McGraw Hill, Inc.,* 57 N.Y.2d 458, 457 N.Y.S.2d 193 (1982). The plaintiff accepted employment with the defendant with the assurance of job security and signed an application of employment which stated that his position would be subject to the rules and regulations of the defendant's personnel handbook, which stated that any dismissal of an employee must be for a just cause and only after appropriate steps were taken. The plaintiff was discharged for alleged lack of application and sued for wrongful termination. The Court of Appeals held that the plaintiff had stated a cause of action for breach of contract since he left his previous employment with the assurance that defendant would not discharge him without cause and this assurance was incorporated into the employment application. The court noted that plaintiff rejected other offers of employment in reliance on this assurance and on the assurance that any discharge of an employee would be for cause and in accord with the strict procedures stated in the defendant's personnel handbook. (See also *Citera v. Chemical New York Corporation,* NYLJ, 1/12/84, p. 11, col. 4; *O'Donnell v.*

Westchester Community Service Council, Inc., supra.; *Wernham v. Moore*, 77 A.D.2d 262, 432 N.Y.S.2d 711 (1st Dept. 1980).

The second exception to the *Murphy* rule is when there is a violation of public policy. In *Waldman v. Englishtown Sportswear, Ltd.*, 92 A.D.2d 833, 460 N.Y.S.2d 552 (1st Dept. 1983), the Appellate Division held that, "No case lies for willful or abusive discharge absent a showing by plaintiffs that the discharge was in violation of public policy. . . ." *See* also *Sherman v. St. Barnabas Hospital*, 535 F. Supp. 564 (S.D.N.Y. 1982) and *Brink's, Inc. v. City of New York*, 523 F. Supp. 1123 (S.D.N.Y. 1982).

In the view of this writer, the time is soon upon us when our courts and/or legislature will establish a system of employee tenure, even where the employment is at the will of either party. For if our capitalist system does not bow to the greater good and voluntarily accept the system of tenure, then just as social security, the labor union and other social reforms were written into law, free enterprise will bow again to the force of law.

This article previously appeared in an edition of The Nassau Lawyer, a publication of the Nassau County Bar Association, and is being reprinted here with the permission of The Nassau County Bar Association.

2. Should Title VII of The United States Code Prohibiting Sex Discrimination Be Based on Sexual Orientation: An Argument

42 D.S.C. Sec. 2000e-2 prohibits employer discrimination against an employee (1) by failing or refusing to hire or to discharge an individual or otherwise to discriminate against any individual with respect to his compensation, terms, conditions, or privileges of employment, because of such individual's race, color, religion, sex or national origin, or (2) by limiting, segregating, or classifying employees or applicants for employment in any way which would deprive or tend to deprive any individual of employment opportunities or otherwise adversely affect his status as an employee, because of such individual's race, color, religion, sex, or national origin.[1]

In its large and apparent import the statute is clear in its prohibition of discrimination in the workplace based on sex, race, religion, or national origin. The issue this article proposes to consider and argue is whether the term sex may be said to encompass, under the 2000e statutory language, sexual orientation as well. In short, is "homosexuality" inclusive within this statutory direction against sex discrimination in the workplace.

Up to now, the federal courts have uniformly denied Title VII protection to individuals alleging employment discrimination based on sexual orientation. *DeSantis v. Pacific Telephone and Telegraph Co.*[2] is illustrative of this point. In *DeSantis*, male and female homosexuals brought three separate Federal District Court Actions charging their employers or former employers discriminated against them in employment decisions because of their homosexuality and sexual orientation.

The plaintiffs argued that such discrimination violated Title VII, arguing that Congress in prohibiting discrimination on the basis of sex meant also to include discrimination on the basis of sexual orientation.

The United States Court of Appeals for the Ninth Circuit rejected their claim holding that

> giving the statute its plain meaning, this Court concludes that Congress had only the traditional notions of 'sex' in mind. Later legislative history makes this narrow definition even more evident. Several bills have been introduced to amend the Civil Rights Act to prohibit discrimination against 'sexual preference'. None have [sic] been enacted into law.
>
> Congress has not shown any intent other than to restrict the term 'sex' to its traditional meaning. Therefore, this court will not expand Title VII's application in the absence of Congressional mandate. The manifest purpose of Title VII's prohibition against sex discrimination in employment is to ensure that men and women are treated equally, absent a bona fide relationship between the qualifications for the job and the person's sex. *Id.* At 663. (quoting *Holloway v. Arthur Anderson & Co,* 566 F.2d 659 [9th Cir. 1977]).[3]

Similarly in *Williamson v. A.G. Edwards and Sons, Inc.,*[4] the United States Court of Appeals for the Eighth Circuit stated, citing *DeSantis,* that Title VII did not prohibit discrimination against homosexuals.

By the same token, the Title VII prohibition against sex discrimination in employment has been held not to encompass discrimination based on transsexualism.[5]

This writer would argue that the time has come for the courts of this country to recognize that one's sexual preference is part and parcel of sex and gender and that Title VII should be extended, or rather understood in its meaning, to afford to homosexuals and lesbians the same statutory prohibition against employment discrimination as that given women or men who may be subject to sex discrimination.

The issue at hand for discussion and argument in this article is whether a homosexual or lesbian preference is within the protected class within the meaning of Title VII or, to repeat the issue, whether homosexuality is to be understood, under Title VII, as an aspect of sex or sexuality.[6]

The objective of the law of Title VII to prohibit employment discrimination on the basis of sex was to place women on the same footing as men in the workplace. Women were and are discriminated against because of the unfair and incorrect perception they are weak, inferior, and generally unequal to men. Likewise homosexuals but, more to the point homosexual males are discriminated against for basically the same reason as women: namely that they are seen as weak, inferior, and unequal within the traditional male dominated society. Furthermore, in this day and age, with the onset of the AIDS epidemic there is an unwarranted fear of homosexuals as deadly disease carriers, another factor in a possible laundry list of bogus reasons for the unequal and inferior treatment of this group in the workplace.

Without a doubt, sexual orientation is an aspect of sex and thus should be counted within the rubric of Title VII protection. Law is dynamic, not static. Courts have refused to remain with their hands tied behind their back in the past when the law needed to be modified to fit the times. It is time to recognize that an individual's sexual orientation is part of their sex, whether that individual is a male or female or whether that person is heterosexual or homosexual.

The Supreme Court of the United States once said blacks were "chattel" and then later stated the principal, "separate but equal." Those rules were rightly changed and so should this too.

The analysis of a claim for sex discrimination may be analogized to that of sexual harassment resulting in unwanted sexual advances. Harassment is harassment regardless of whether it is caused by a member of the same or opposite sex.[7] It has even been ruled that sex discrimination is sex discrimination regardless of whether it is inflicted upon a heterosexual or homosexual person.[8]

In fact the United States Court of Appeals for the Fourth Circuit[9] has left open the question of whether, where the acts involved in a Title VII case of sex discrimination are the same sex, homosexuality may make the claim nevertheless cognizable as one of discrimination because of the victim's sex.

Law is ongoing and must adjust to continued societal development. The time has come to recognize that discrimination is not limited to outdated traditional definitions and roles, time to recognize that any and all forms of discrimination linked or connected with sexuality, whether gender or affectional preference, should be banned and barred as abhorrent to the purpose of Title VII which was passed by the Congress to ensure equal treatment for all whether homosexual, transsexual, male or female, in the employment arena.

3. *Trial by Jury—Is There a Doubt?*

In the past ten years, in a trio of decisions of great significance and effect, the United State Supreme Court has, in the view of this writer, cast into doubt the continued future of the constitutional right to Trial by Jury in the Federal Courts of this country. The significance and impact of those decisions have not been fully explained and discussed. In this article, it is to be hoped that a careful analysis of these three decisions and opinions will reveal their full impact and meaning.[1]

I) Gilmer v. Interstate/Johnson Lane Corporation

The first of these far reaching societally impacting decisions was *Gilmer v. Interstate/Johnson Lane Corporation*.[2] In *Gilmer*, the Respondent, Interstate/ Johnson Lane Corporation hired Mr. Gilmer as a manager of Financial Services and, as required by his employment, registered as a securities representative with several stock exchanges, including the New York Stock Exchange. Mr. Gilmer's registration application provided that Mr. Gilmer agreed to arbitrate any dispute, claim or controversy between him and Interstate, under the rule of the organizations under which Mr. Gilmer would register. NYSE rule 34 provided for arbitration of any controversy between a registered representative and any member or member organization arising out of the employment or termination of employment of such registered representative. Interstate terminated Mr. Gilmer's employment at age 62, and Mr. Gilmer, after filing an age discrimination charge with EEOC, subsequently brought suit in the United States District Court for the Western District of North Carolina, alleging Interstate discharged him because of his age in violation of the ADEA. Interstate filed in the District Court a motion to compel Arbitration of the ADEA claim, relying on the arbitration agreement in Mr. Gilmer's arbitration application as well as the Federal Arbitration Act (FAA) 9 U.S.C Sec. 1. The Federal District Court denied Interstate's motion based on *Alexander v. Gardner Denver Co.*[3] because it concluded that Congress intended to protect ADEA claimants from the waiver of a judicial forum. The Fourth Circuit reversed holding there was nothing underlying the purpose of the ADEA indicating a congressional intent to preclude enforcement of arbitration agreements.[4]

Initially, the United States Supreme Court stated, upon analysis of the FAA, that statutory claims may be subject of an arbitration agreement pursuant to the FAA. The Court went on to state that Mr. Gilmer conceded that nothing in the text of the ADEA or its legislative history expressly precluded arbitration, but Mr. Gilmer argued that compulsory arbitration of ADEA claims pursuant to an arbitration agreement would be inconsistent with the statutory framework and purpose of the ADEA The court stated that both arbitration and judicial resolution of the same claim focus on the specific dispute and that the arbitral forum is an equally valid mode for enforcement of the statutory cause of action.

The court rejected the argument that arbitration would undermine the role of the EEOC since an individual ADEA claimant would still be free to file a charge with the EEOC, although the claimant would not be able to institute a private judicial action.

In response to the argument of *Gilmer* that compulsory arbitration was improper because it deprived claimants of the judicial forum provided by the ADEA, the court stated that Congress did not explicitly preclude arbitration or non-judicial resolution of claims and, in any event, there was intention deductible for the statute that the protection afforded by the ADEA included protection against a waiver of the right to a judicial forum.

The court then rejected Mr. Gilmer's contentions that the arbitration would be biased; that the discovery allowed in arbitration is more limited than the federal court which would make it more difficult to prove age discrimination; that the arbitrators would not issue a written opinion, resulting in a lack of public knowledge of the employer's discriminatory policies, an inability to obtain appellate review, and a stifling of the development of law; and that arbitration procedures cannot further the purpose of the ADEA because they do not provide for broad equitable relief and class action relief.

The court also rejected Mr. Gilmer's claim that there would be unequal bargaining power between employers and employees.

Finally, the court rejected the argument that *Alexander v. Gardner-Denver*[5] and *Barrentine v. Arkansas-Best Freight System Inc.*[6] and *McDonald v. West Branchix*[7] precluded arbitration of employment discrimination claims. The court rejected this argument, citing these cases did not involve the issue of the enforceability of an agreement to arbitrate a statutory claim, but occurred in the context of a collective bargaining agreement, a process distinct from and not precluding a subsequent statutory claim.

In strongly worded and well-reasoned dissent, Mr. Justice Stevens and Justice Marshall reasoned that the arbitration clause contained in the employment contracts is not within the coverage of the FAA and, for that reason, Interstate/Johnson Lane Corporation cannot, pursuant to the FAA, compel the petitioner to submit his claim arising under the Age Discrimination in Employment Act of 1967.

II) Circuit City Stores v. Adams

In *Circuit City Stores v. Adams*,[8] the employer brought an action under the FAA to enjoin the employee's state case employment discrimination action and to compel arbitration. The United States District Court for the Northern District of California ordered arbitration. The employee appealed. The United States Court of Appeals for the Ninth Circuit reversed, holding all employment contracts were beyond the FAA's reach. Certiorari was granted.

The United States Supreme Court, in a finely worded and detailed opinion interpreting Secs. 1 and 2 of the FAA, confirmed that the exemption of Sec. 1 that excluded from the Act's coverage contracts of employment of seamen, railroad employees, or any other class of workers engaged in foreign or interstate commerce did not exempt all employment contracts from the FAA's reach, except those of transit workers.

III) EEOC v. Waffle House

In *EEOC v. Waffle House*,[9] the EEOC brought an enforcement action against a former employer on behalf of a former employee under the ADA (Americans with Disabilities Act). The United States District Court for the District of South Carolina denied the employer's petition to stay litigation and compel arbitration under the Federal Arbitration Act (FAA) and to dismiss the action. The employer filed an interlocutory appeal The United States Court of Appeals for the Fourth Circuit held that the arbitration agreement did not foreclose the enforcement action, but precluded the EEOC from seeking victim-specific relief in court. Certiorari was granted.

More specifically, the respondent employee was compelled to sign an agreement requiring employment disputes to be settled by binding arbitration. Mr. Baker suffered a seizure and was fired and then filed a timely discrimination charge with the Equal Employment Opportunity Commission alleging that his discharge violated Title I of the Americans with Disabilities Act. The EEOC filed an enforcement action to which Baker was not a party, alleging the respondent's employment practices, including Mr. Baker's discharge because of his disability, violated the ADA and that the violation was intentional and done with malice and reckless indifference. The complaint requested injunctive relief to eradicate the effects of the respondent's past or present wrongful employment practices and, specifically, relief designed to make Mr. Baker whole including back pay, reinstatement, compensatory damages, and punitive damages for malicious and reckless conduct.

More specifically, the United States Court of Appeals for the Fourth Circuit concluded that the arbitration agreement between Baker and the respondent did not foreclose the enforcement action because the EEOC was not a party to the contract, but had independent statutory authority to bring suit in any Federal District Court where venue was proper. Nevertheless, the Circuit felt the EEOC was limited to injunctive relief and precluded from seeking victim-specific relief because the FAA's policy favoring enforcement of private arbitration agreements outweighed the EEOC's right to proceed in the Federal Court when it seeks to primarily vindicate private rather than public interests.

The United States Supreme Court held that an agreement between employer and employee to arbitrate employment-related disputes does not bar the EEOC from pursuing victim-specific judicial relief such as back pay, reinstatement, and damages in an ADA enforcement action. The court reasoned that prior law does not suggest that the existence of an arbitration agreement between private parties materially changes the EEOC's statutory function or the remedies otherwise available. The Court held that the FAA does not mention enforcement by public agencies, but ensures the enforcement of private agreements to arbitrate, and that because the EEOC is not a party to the contract and has not agreed to arbitrate its claims, the FAA's pro-arbitration policy goals do not require the agency to relinquish its statutory authority to pursue victim-specific relief regardless of the forum that the employer and employee have chosen to resolve their disputes.

Analysis and Conclusion

Both *Gilmer* and *Circuit City* are far reaching decisions since they permit the individual to waive his right to judicial resolution of his employment dispute also waiving the rules of evidence, a hearing in a forum open to the public, and the right of appeal and discovery. *Waffle House* took a step back stating the EEOC pursue its private remedies in the face of an arbitrary contract clause, agreeing to submit all employment disputes to arbitration. What then may be said? It is beyond the scope of this article to delve into the fact and law specific reasons of the United States Supreme Court in these cases. That reasoning and those decisions have, to a degree, been summarized in this article. By way of somewhat imprecise and brief analysis, it is clear that the United States Supreme Court, in *Gilmer* and *Circuit City,* held that where an employee possibly or not fully comprehending and understanding the material meaning of the agreement he is lending his signature to, in the rush and desire to obtain employment or keep it, signs an employment contract where he agrees to submit any dispute or claim to arbitration, including material that might be brought under Title VII, the ADA and the ADEA, the agreement will be enforced and considered. The Supreme Court held, in those cases, that the FAA includes within its statutory reach all employment contracts, excluding transportation workers. The court in *Gilmer* rejected the view that the ADEA did not include protection against waiver of the right to a judicial forum and that Congress did not explicitly preclude arbitration or non-judicial resolution of claims.

In sum, the United States Supreme Court, in both *Gilmer* and *Circuit City,* based its decision on the interpretation of the ADEA, its legislative history, and the reach and meaning of the FAA. In the view of this writer, the United States Supreme Court, on a broader, and if you will constitutional, basis, in its reasoning and result is faulty.

The right to trial by jury, the most basic right of access to the courts of this country, is the most seminal of rights, and it is, as has been stated, a constitutional right. It has as its basis the idea or notion that proceedings should be public and that there should be rules of evidence and procedure governing the litigation event and, most importantly, that fact finding and decision shall rest in the common wisdom of our fellow citizens and not in one person, denominated an Arbitrator, mistakenly perceived as one more knowledgeable and expert at this work than his peers in the general public.

Trial by jury has, as its raison d'etre, that power should be dispersed and not concentrated or collectivized. That is, power should rest, as much as possible, not in the hands of one overseer, but should reside in the many.

The right to trial by jury has as its underpinning that the not so common man and our fellow citizens, far from being incapable or stupid or unequal to the task, are, in fact, eminently qualified to make significant factual determinations.

As such, trial by jury cannot, and should not, be subject to waiver in favor of a non-judicial forum such as Arbitration having, as it does, no right to appeal, no rules of evidence, minimal discovery and closure to the public. Arbitration has as its underlying principle that decisions should be made by the knowing and more knowledgeable and that the public is not up to par for this work, a principle contrary to our constitutional and democratic system of government that entrusts the people with the ultimate power to elect their representatives that they chose to govern. In short, in our system, it is the people who are the masters and not a purported panel of experts, appointed, who are thought to know better and fuller and more fully, and thus are more qualified decision makers and rulers.

Trial by jury may be said to rest in the notion that the common man is not at all so common.

Trial by jury must be said to rest in the idea that a wealth of intellect and expertise rests in our fellow citizens.

Gilmer and *Circuit City* attack this deeply rooted concept. They permit a company with overwhelming economic power to offer an employee, as a condition of an employment contract, to sign away his or her right to be heard and tried in a public forum by his peers. *Gilmer* and *Circuit City* attack the understanding of our democratic system that make and entrust the people as the experts.

Gilmer and *Circuit City* substitute secrecy for an open forum, expertise and authority for the dispersal of power; they say that one is better than 12, that the people have no business in this process, that we need no right of appeal since arbitrators make no mistakes, that we need no rules of evidence and discovery since "father knows best." *Gilmer* and *Circuit City* say we need no controls on falsehood or inaccuracy since, after all, "Big Brother," who knows all, presides over all.

Waffle House puts a brake on *Gilmer* and *Circuit City* allowing the EEOC to continue to do its work. *Waffle House* does not, however, at all change the results and far-reaching effects of *Gilmer* or *Circuit City,* which permit a powerless employee, seeking to survive economically, to sign away his access to the Courts and a public trial to be decided by his peers. *Gilmer* and *Circuit City* concentrate power rather than disperse it. They reject the intellect and wisdom of the People for the wisdom of experts. *Gilmer* and *Circuit City* reject the truth of it all that there is more wisdom, knowledge and intellect in our fellow citizens than is dreamt of in our philosophy. Perhaps, it might be said that *Gilmer* and *Circuit City* radically and irrefutably and irrefragably deny the elective process, and that, in truth, the People are our Masters, and all officialdom their servants.

4. Naming as Prerequisite

Title VII of the Civil Rights Act of 1960[1] prohibits unequal or unfair treatment or discrimination in the employment relationship between employers and their employees and applicants; between unions and their members and potential members; and between employment agencies and their clients. The statute prohibits the covered entities from discriminating on the basis of race, color, national origin, sex, or religion. The age discrimination in employment is also prohibited under a separate Act, as is discrimination against disabled or handicapped persons.[2]

Prior to the enactment of these statutes, employees subject to discriminatory treatment in the workplace, whether based on sex, national origin, religion, race, age, or handicap, had no recourse from the unfair or disparate treatment that may have brought about their discharge.

With the enactment of these statutes, however, employees subject to discriminatory tactics at the hands of their employers now may be said to be armed to challenge in the courts the employer who may have unfairly discharged them.

Hence, these statutes have given rise to, and will continue to give rise to, a plethora of lawsuits in the Federal and State courts.

This article, however, will consider one small area of this complex and burgeoning field: more specifically, the basic Federal discrimination statute prohibiting discrimination based on sex, race, national origin, or religion, 42 U.S.C.

Sec. 2000(e) states in part, in Sec. 5(e), that the prerequisite to commencing a Title VII action against a defendant is the filing with the EEOC, or authorized state agency, a complaint naming the defendant.[3] A corollary of this statutory rule is that a party not named in the EEOC charge cannot be named as a defendant in the subsequent federal civil suit brought under 42 D.S.C. Sec. 2000(e).[4]

The purpose of naming a party as a respondent in an EEOC charge prior to bringing it under Title VII, it has been held, is twofold: (1) to notify the charged party of the alleged violation and (2) to afford that party an opportunity to participate in conciliation and to comply with the Title VII.[5]

There are a number of exceptions to this basic overriding rule. One exception is stated in terms of an identity of interests. Thus, in *Romain v. Kurek*,[6] the U.S. Court of Appeals for the Sixth Circuit held that a party not named in an Equal Employment Opportunity Commission charge may not be sued under Title VII, unless there is a clear identity of interests between it and that party named in the EEOC charge.

A more general exception is stated in *Allen v. City of Chicago*.[7] In *Allen*, the Northern District of Illinois stated initially that not naming a party as a respondent in an EEOC charge and subsequently bringing a Title VII action is not a jurisdictional prerequisite and that the requirement is comparable to a Statute of Limitations and subject to equitable modification.

In explanation of this, the Federal District Court went on to state that the courts have consistently recognized an exception to the general rule where the unnamed party or parties had adequate notice of the charge and had an opportunity to participate in conciliation where holding it to the requirement could deprive him or her of redress of any legitimate grievances.

Another general exception to the rule is stated in *Brewster v. Shockley*.[8] In that case, the District Court of West Virginia stated another and second more general exception to the basic rule: that before the defendant can be sued in court in a Title VII action, he must have been named in the EEOC charge, i.e., where the named and unnamed defendants are substantially identical; or in an agency relationship; or where the defendant and unnamed defendant are engaged in a common discriminatory scheme; or where the plaintiff has alleged facts in the EEOC charge from which the EEOC could infer that the unnamed defendant also violated Title VII.

Again in *Bapat v. Conn. Dept. of Health Services*,[9] the Connecticut Federal District Court stated a third and more general rule and exception. The court stated that an employment discrimination action can be brought against parties not named in the complaint with the EEOC if one of four factors is present: (1) the complainant could not ascertain the role of the unnamed party; (2) the interests of the unnamed party are so similar that omitting the named party from the EEOC proceeding would not have impeded conciliation efforts; (3) the unnamed party suffered no actual prejudice; and (4) the unnamed party represented in some way that relationship with the complainant was to be through the named party. In summary, there are three general exceptions that the party not named in the EEOC charge may not be sued in the Title VII action.

First, there is the rule stated in *Allen v. City of Chicago*[10] that the requirement is comparable to the Statute of Limitations and is subject to equitable modification and, most importantly, is not a jurisdictional prerequisite.

Second, there is the rule stated in *Brewster v. Shockley*[11] that the exception is recognized to function where the named and unnamed defendants are substantially identical; or are in essence in an agency relationship; or where the named and unnamed defendants are engaged in a common discriminatory scheme.

Third, there is the rule stated in *Barat v. Conn. Dept. of Health Services*[12] that the exception is favored where one of four factors is present. These factors have been recited.

It should be noted that a subrule is stated in *Sosa v. Hiroaka*[13] where the Ninth Circuit stated that where community college administrators not named as defendants in an Equal Employment Opportunity Charge in the EEOC could be sued in a Title VII suit brought by a community college professor in that the administrators should have anticipated being defendants in a subsequent suit where the professor specifically alleged that all the administrators named participated in acts giving rise to the charge.

Three general, and one more specific, exceptions have been found to the basic naming requirements as a prerequisite to bringing a Title VII action. There is, it would appear, a seminal overriding rule stated in part in *Brewster, Bapat,* and *Johnson*—namely, that where there is an identity of interests, a party not named in an Equal Employment Opportunity charge may be sued in a subsequent Title VII plenary action; or whether, as stated in *Bapat,* the interest of the named and unnamed party are so similar; or, as stated in *Brewster,* where the named and unnamed defendant are substantially identical or are, in essence, in an agency relationship.

One final point should be noted. The basic identity of interest exception is not available to the plaintiff who is represented by counsel when filing the EEOC complaint. Thus, in *Tarr v. Credit Suisse Asset Mgmt. Inc,*[14] the U.S. District Court for the Eastern District of New York held that as a threshold matter, the exception only applies where the plaintiff was not represented by counsel at the time of the EEOC filing.

5. Employment Discrimination and Individual Liability: A Comparison

Employment Discrimination as a field of law, though of relatively recent origin, has burgeoned greatly in the past 15 years. The significant federal statute, Title VII of the Civil Rights Act of 1964,[1] prohibits discrimination based on race, color, sex, religion, or national origin and extends to all terms, conditions or privileges of employment, including such areas of employment practice as the refusal to hire and promote; unequal pay; and, most importantly, discriminatory discharge.

The Americans with Disabilities Act of 1990[2] generally prohibits disability discrimination by an employer, employment agency, labor organization, or joint labor management-management committee against a qualified individual with a disability in hiring, advancement, or discharge.

The Age Discrimination in Employment Act[3] prohibits an employer from failing or refusing to hire or from discharging any individual or otherwise discriminating against any individual with respect to his compensation, terms, conditions, or privileges for employment, because of such person's age.

Although these are the essential and seminal federal worker discrimination statutes controlling workplace discrimination, there are others.[4]

The analogous state statute[5] prohibits discrimination because of age, race, creed, color, national origin, sex, disability, genetic predisposition or marital status of any individual against such individual in hiring, refusing to hire, or employ, or from barring or discharging such individual from employment.

A full and comprehensive analysis and understanding of these statutory provisions, protections, and mechanisms would require essays and treatises far beyond the scope of this article. What this article will focus on and consider will be the possible individual liability, if any, of corporate officers or officials under Title VII 42 U.S.C. 2000(e) and the analogous state statute, Sec. 296 of the New York State Executive Law.

It is the law that individuals cannot be held liable on a plaintiff's Title VII claim, *Tomka v. Seiler Corp.*, 66 F.3d 1295, 1313 (2d Cir. 1995). In *Tomka* the Second Circuit explicitly held that individual defendants, even those with supervisory control over a plaintiff, "may not be held personally liable under Title VII."

The facts in *Tomka* were that a female employee sued her former employer and three male co-employees, claiming various violations of Title VII. In dismissing the charges against the supervisory employees allegedly responsible for the harassment, the court relied on two factors. First, it considered Title VII's definition of "employer," which is "a person engaged in an industry affecting commerce who has fifteen or more employees . . . and any agent of such a person." 42 U.S.C. Sec. 2000e(b). The court concluded that the inclusion of "agent" in the definition did not create individual liability, but was simply an expression of respondent superior liability. *Tomka*, 66 F.3d at 1313.

Second. the Court noted that the damages scheme adopted by Congress in the Civil Rights Act of 1991, 42 U.S.C. Sec. 1981a, which exempted employers with fewer than fifteen employees from liability for compensatory and punitive damages under Title VII, but was silent as to individual liability, confirmed that Title VII did not contemplate individual liability. "[I]f Congress had envisioned individual liability . . . it would have included individuals in this litany of limitations and discontinued the exemptions for small employers." *Id.* 1315.

Based on this unequivocal and controlling holding, individual defendants[6] cannot be held individually liable on a plaintiff's Title VII claim. At least under Title VII it is clear there can be no individual liability for corporate officers.

The rules under Sec. 296 of the New York Executive Law, the basic state discrimination statute, present a different picture.

The leading case is *Patrowich* v. *Chem. Bank.*[7] In *Patrowich*, the plaintiff brought an age and sex discrimination action against a corporation. Construing Sec. 296, the Court of Appeals held that a corporate employee, even if he has a title as an officer and is the manager or supervisor of a corporate division, is not individually subject to suit, with respect to discrimination based on age or sex under the New York Law. The Court of Appeals held the individual must be shown to either have an ownership interest in the company, or he must have the power to do more than carry out personnel decisions made by others.

Under *Patrowich*, unless, under Section 296, ownership interest can be shown or the ability to carry out more than personnel decisions, then an individual corporate officer may not be held liable if sued under this statute.

What may be said to be the ability to carry out more than personnel decisions has been defined twofold.

There is a line of cases that holds an individual may be liable under the New York Executive Law if the defendant actually participated in the conduct giving rise to the claim of discrimination.[8]

There is a second line of authority on this issue. *Hicks* v. *IBM* is exemplary.[9] In *Hicks*, the Federal District Court held that a supervisor could not be liable for race discrimination against an employee who was half native American and half African, under the provision of the New York Human Rights Law allowing individual liability against a person that aids or abets another in committing discriminatory acts. The Court reasoned the supervisor alleged to have committed, and incited other unnamed employees to commit, discriminatory acts was the primary actor and so could not be an aider and abettor under this statute. Citing *Tomka* v. *Seiler Corp.,*[10] *Hicks* went on to state that individual liability may not be had under that part of Section 296 of the New York State Executive Law which states that "it shall be an unlawful discriminatory practice for any person to aid, abet, incite, compel or coerce the doing of any of the acts forbidden under this article."[11]

The rules that may be gleaned on the issue of individual liability, under Section 296 of the Executive Law, are first, if the individual does have a company ownership interest then he may be held liable under Section 296 of the New York State Executive Law. Second, if the ability to carry out more than personnel decisions is shown in the form of active participation, then the individual may be held liable. Third, if the individual can be shown under Section 296 as aiding and abetting the doing of the acts of discrimination then the individual may be held liable.

Finally, as a subrule, one cannot be an aider and abettor of one's own acts.[12]

It is hoped that this basic review of corporate individual liability under 42 U.S.C. Sec. 2000(e)-2 and the analogous state statute, Sec. 296 of the Executive Law, will at least point the way to the rule connecting individual liability under the statute. If there is any final point following the analysis it is that if the employment discrimination plaintiff wishes to sue an individual and is in Federal Court, or contemplating doing so, he would be wise to add a count in his Complaint under Sec. 296, thus preserving the possibility of individual liability, which would not be possible under *Tomka*.

6. Law in the Workplace

At one time or another most of us will be faced with stress or harassment on the job which may lead to termination or outright firing without notice. The loss of a job to someone, just as with divorce or the death of a spouse, must be considered one of life's most traumatic events.

Traditionally and historically it has been through organization that workers have gained protection and security on the job. However, roughly 100 million U.S. workers are not covered under the national labor laws; only about 10% of the U.S. workforce is unionized, the smallest percentage of any industrialized nation in the world.

New York State is an "employee at will" state. That means, by and large, that one has few protections on the job and can be fired or "laid off" for no reason. However, through a series of statutes—federal, state, and city—our legal system allows some recourse and help for some employees in some limited circumstances. I will outline those here, as a first step in arming readers to fight for what limited legal recourse is available that they might not otherwise have been aware of.

If an employee can make a showing either by acts, words, or circumstances, that he or she has been subject to discriminatory treatment based on his or her race, age, disability, national origin, sex or religion, that person can succeed in a case against his employer for the violation. There are three sets of statutes. The federal statute, Title VII of the 1964 Civil Rights Acts, 42 USC Sec. 2000e-2, prohibits discrimination in the form of refusing to hire, promote or pay and also prohibits discriminatory firing. A discriminatory, hostile work environment, where by act, treatment, or words, the worker can show discrimination in his work environment short of firing or demotion is equally prohibited.

The Americans with Disabilities Act (ADA) prohibits discrimination based on a disability. Employers under the Statute are required to accommodate disabled persons and a disabled person, treated unfairly and fired, but able to work, may be successful in a case in the U.S. District Court.

The Age Discrimination in Employment Act (ADEA) prohibits discrimination based on age where the person is age 40 or over.

These are the basic federal statutes. There are others such as the Equal Pay Act which makes it unlawful for employees to discriminate in compensation on the basis of sex; the Older Workers Benefit Protection Act which prohibits a worker over 40 from undue pressure by management to have his rights waived under the Age Act in return for benefits contained in early retirement agreements and programs; the Family and Medical Leave Act which allows employees with a serious health problem or the pressure of child care to take an unpaid leave; and the Pregnancy Discrimination Act which protects against discrimination based on pregnancy.

The State Executive Law, Sec. 296, prohibits all forms of discrimination in the workplace and is the complementary state statute allowing redress in the State Court System.

There is also a New York City statute providing protection against workplace discrimination similar to the federal and state statutory systems.

What is one to do if faced with the signs of harassment that the worker fears will lead to the loss of his job? Keep records! Document every act, word and event. Preserve all memos! Sign no memos which are unduly or unfairly critical! Make no admissions! If meetings are called, delay and say you want to consult with a family member or friend. Do not say you are seeing a lawyer. This will alert management to take quick and final action against you.

If you are suddenly called to a meeting and your boss is present, ask for time. If you are pressured to sign an agreement giving up your right to sue under the law I have just mentioned, sign nothing and ask for time to consider the "package you are being presented with." You have the right to time and the right to consult a lawyer.

By delaying, documenting, and maintaining silence you are paving the way to a successful negotiated settlement whereby you may obtain a money package, or to a lawsuit which may bring you substantial damages or even reinstatement to your job.

Knowing your rights as an employee, as stated here, is a first step to arming you with certain defenses and rights that can help you succeed in today's workplace.

7. A Second View

In a previous Article published in the *Queens Bar Bulletin*,[1] this writer concluded that Title VII of the United States Code,[2] although it prohibited discrimination in the workplace based on the employee's Race, National Origin, Sex, or Religion, did not prohibit discrimination in the workplace based on sexual orientation, whether Homosexual or Transgender.[3]

The law in this regard appears to be set and clear that Title VII, in this sense, is solely a gender or sex discrimination statute, insofar as it prohibits discrimination based on sex.

Recently, however, there has been a spate, or rather developing line, of cases, holding that if a Gay or Lesbian person is discriminated against because he or she is perceived not to conform to stereotypes how men and women are supposed to act and behave, this conduct may constitute sex discrimination under Title VII.

A recent case, pointing to the way, to this new rule is *Higgins v. New Balance Athletic Shoe*.[4] In *Higgins*, a former employee brought an action against a former employer, alleging retaliation and discrimination based on Sex; Sexual Orientation; and Disability, all in violation of Title VII; the Americans with Disabilities Act (ADA); The Maine Whistle Blower's Protection Act (MWPA); and The Maine Human Rights Act (MHRA). The United States District Court for the District of Maine entered Summary Judgment in favor of the former employer and the former employee appealed. The First Circuit Court affirmed part; vacated in part; and remanded.

More specifically, the court held that the District Court did not err in granting Summary Judgment in New Balance's favor on the Hostile Work claim; the Retaliation claim; and also the Disability Claim, on the issue of the employer's failure to accommodate. The Court, however, in its analysis of the Hostile Work Environment claim, held that the statute prohibited harassment by reason of sex and that even though the statute is inclusive of sex discrimination in same sex harassment cases, citing *Oncale v. Sundowner Offshore Services, Inc.*, 523 U.S. 75, 118 S. Ct. 998, 140 L.Ed.2d 201 (1998), the court went on to state that even in same-sex harassment, as well as more normative sex harassment cases, the plaintiff must prove that the conduct at issue in fact, constituted discrimination because of sex.

The court, however, stated, most explicitly, that Title VII does not proscribe harassment because of sex orientation citing *Hopkins v. Baltimore Gas and Electric Co.*, 77 F.3rd 745 (4th Cir. 1996), and *Williamson v. A.G. Edwards & Sons*, 876 F.2d 69, (8th Cir. 1989).

The Circuit Court, however, considered the argument of the Appellant who cited *Price Waterhouse v. Hopkins,* 490 U.S. 228, 109 S. Ct. 1775, 104 L.Ed.2d 268 (1989), where the appellant in that case was mocked by his peers, by their speaking in high pitched voices and mimicking feminine movements. The *Price Waterhouse* Court concluded that this was sexual harassment because the Appellant had failed to meet his coworkers stereotyped standards of masculinity and so was harassed by reason of his sex.

The First Circuit Court, although it rejected this argument as not having been raised at the District Court level, noted in a Footnote that a Plaintiff can ground a Title VII claim on evidence that other men discriminated against him because he did not meet stereotyped expectations of masculinity, albeit upholding Summary Judgment for the employer where, as has been stated, the employee first raised this issue on appeal.

It is clear that the *Higgins* Court opened the door to the validity and viability of Sexual Stereotyping claims as Sex Discrimination within the ambit of Title VII.

Nichols v. Azteca Restaurant Enterprises[5] took further, specified, and amplified the Dicta in *Higgins.* In *Nichols,* a male former employee sued a former employer for sexual harassment and retaliation, alleging he was harassed by male coworkers and a supervisor because he did not meet their view of a male stereotype.

The U.S. District Court for the Western District of Washington entered Judgment for the employer and the former employee appealed.

The Ninth Circuit Court of Appeals considered the Plaintiff's claim of a Hostile Work Environment and harassment based on sex. More specifically, the plaintiff claimed that he was subject to a relentless campaign of insults; name calling; and vulgarities, wherein male coworkers, and a supervisor referred to Sanchez, the plaintiff, in English and Spanish as "her" and "she"; mocked Sanchez for walking like a woman; and taunted him in Spanish and English as a "faggot" and "Fucking female whore" based on the perception that he was effeminate and therefore these events and actions occurred by reason of his sex and constituted discrimination and harassment based on his sex.

In short, the issue before the court was the plaintiff's contention that he was harassed because he failed to conform his behavior to a male stereotype. The court noted that the Plaintiff's Argument was derived from *Price Waterhouse v. Hopkins,* 490 U.S, 228, 109 S. Ct. 1775, 104 L.Ed.2d 268 (1989), in which the Supreme Court held that a woman who was denied partnership in an accounting firm because she did not match a sex stereotype had an automatic claim under Title VII. The facts in *Price Waterhouse* were that the Plaintiff was described by various partners as "macho," "in need of a course in charm school," "a lady using foul language," and someone had labeled her a "tough-talking somewhat masculine hard-nosed manager."

In fact, the Plaintiff was advised that she could improve her partnership chance if she would "walk more femininely," "talk more femininely," "wear makeup," "have her hair styled," and "wear jewelry." The Supreme Court held that an employer who acted on the basis or belief that a woman must not or cannot be aggressive has acted on the basis of gender.

The *Nichols* Court, citing *Price Waterhouse*, held that sex stereotyping applies with equal force to a man who is discriminated against for acting too femininely and that *Price Waterhouse* established a rule that barred discrimination on the basis of sex stereotyping and applied it to preclude the harassment here.

The Court distinguished its decision in *DeSantis v. Pacific Telephone and Telegraph Co., Inc.*, 608 F.2d 327 (9th Cir. 1979), where the Ninth Circuit held that discrimination based on a stereotype that a man should have a virile rather than effeminate appearance did not fall within the purview of Title VII as conflicting with the Supreme Court holding in *Price Waterhouse* and that for this reason *DeSantis* was no longer good law.[6]

The *Nichols* Court, applying *Price Waterhouse*, held that sex stereotyping applied with equal force to a man who is discriminated against for acting too femininely and that *Price Waterhouse* set a rule that barred discrimination on the basis of sex stereotyping.

In sum, the Ninth Circuit concluded that sexual stereotyping which occurs because of and by reason of sex was and can be actionable under Title VII and a Hostile Work Environment claim, should no termination occur.

A later case in 2002, *Heller v. Columbia Edgewater Country Club*, 195 F. Supp.2d 1212 (D. Or 2002),[7] follows suit on this issue.

In *Heller*, a Lesbian employee's allegation that she suffered sex or gender discrimination by reason of the actions of her former supervisor, who allegedly harassed and ultimately discharged her because the employee did not conform to the supervisor's notions of how a woman should behave, was actionable under Title VII and that the protections of Title VII were not confined to heterosexual employees. The Actions and Acts at issue in *Heller* were that the supervisor ridiculed the plaintiff for wearing men's shoes and with comments such as, "I thought you were a man" and "Do you wear Dick in the relationship?" On this evidence the Defense Motion for Summary Judgment was denied and the Title VII Action was allowed to proceed on the basis that sexual stereotyping was considered to be sex discrimination.

Finally, in *Centola v. Potter,*[8] the Massachusetts Federal District Court held that the Plaintiff set forth a Title VII claim where the evidence showed the plaintiff's coworkers taped pictures of Richard Simmons in pink hot pants to the Plaintiff's letter carrier cage; asked if he would be marching in the gay parade; asked if he had gotten AIDS yet; and placed cartoons mocking gay men at his cage. The Court concluded these facts suggested discrimination based on sexual orientation. The Massachusetts Court held that although discrimination based on sexual orientation is not allowed or included in Title VII, sexual stereotyping is, so long as based on sex, and so is actionable under Title VII.

Conclusion

What rule or pattern can be drawn from this brief review and analysis? It is clear that the Federal Courts are clear in interpreting Title VII as a prohibitive Sex Discrimination Statute and applies it only to harassment and actions by reason of sex and is not directed to discrimination by reason of sexual orientation. The Federal Courts, however, are clearly moving to a view or position that where sexual stereotyping is a skewed perception of how men and women should behave, this action is by reason of sex and is within the ambit of Title VII.

A "rose by any other name should smell as sweet." Under Title VII, as understood in its legislative history, this statute was enacted and directed to prohibit, among others, discrimination in the workplace based on sex. It did not originally include or prohibit discrimination by reason of sexual orientation. Society moves on. To stereotype someone by a wrong, right or any perception, incorrect or not, as to their sexuality is to effectively to attack their sexual orientation.

The Federal Courts have corrected and are correcting an injustice and wrong. Sexual discrimination and sexual stereotyping, in truth, skirt the issue when we all know it is gays or lesbians who are being attacked for their Orientation and not their given bodies. Thus, this trend in the Federal Courts solves this problem at least temporarily and moves society forward.

One day soon Title VII will and should be amended to prohibit discrimination based on sexual orientation, or another bill will be passed. A system and society that includes and does not prohibit; that gives more than it takes; that offers opportunities and chances for the most people is the best for us all. The homosexual who discovers a cure for cancer but cannot work or is belittled and driven out of his job makes losers of us all.[9]

8. Tomka: A Comment on Supervisory Liability

This article proposes to set forth an analysis of the seminal and landmark case of *Tomka v. Seiler Corp.*[1] and to offer an evaluation and criticism of its reasoning and holding, and offer, in addition, an alternative.

The facts in *Tomka* were that a female employee brought suit against her former employer and three male co-employees asserting claims of a Hostile Environment, Sexual Harassment, and Retaliatory Discharge, in violation of Title VII and the New York State Human Rights Law (HRL). The plaintiff also asserted an unequal pay claim, under the Equal Pay Act (EPA) and the HRL, as well as common-law Assault and Intentional Infliction of Emotional Distress claims. The United States District Court for the Western District of New York granted the defendants' Motions for Summary Judgment and the plaintiff appealed.

The Court of Appeals for the Second Circuit held that the evidence raised genuine issues of material fact, precluding Summary Judgment on the Sexual Harassment claims, under Title VII and the HRL; and that the evidence raised genuine issues of material fact, precluding Summary Judgment on the claim of Retaliatory Discharge. The Court also ruled that the plaintiff's EPA claim as to four of seven named male employees could not be resolved on Summary Judgment; that the claim of unequal pay for equal work under Title VII and the HRL was properly dismissed on the ground that the plaintiff presented no evidence that the employer acted with discriminatory intent in paying the plaintiff less than male employees; that the individual defendants could be sued in their personal capacities for sexual harassment under the HRL; that the employer could not be held liable under New York Law, on the basis of Respondeat Superior, for alleged sexual assaults committed by male co-employees and the emotional distress stemming from those acts; and that the employer could not be held liable under New York Law for negligence in retaining or supervising male employees alleged to have sexually harassed the plaintiff absent evidence that the employer had notice of prior assaults or sexual misconduct.

Most importantly, the Circuit Court held that the individual defendants with supervisory control over the plaintiff could not be held personally liable under Title VII. Thus, the United States Court of Appeals affirmed in part and reversed in part.

This article will consider discretely and exactly the holding and analysis of the Second Circuit in *Tomka* that the individual defendants with supervisory control over the plaintiff could not be held personally liable under Title VII.

The Court of Appeals opined that the courts in the Second Circuit are divided over whether an employer's agent may be held individually liable. The Court went on to analyze the meaning of Title VII's definition of an employer. The Court stated that some courts have held that the meaning of "agent" in Title VII includes "employers," who may be held individually liable for discriminatory acts. The Court went on to state that at least three Circuits and a number of District Courts have interpreted this section as not creating individual liability but as a simple expression of Respondeat Superior. The Court concluded that the term agent was not a statutory employer under Title VII, analyzing and considering the statutory scheme and Title VII's remedial provisions.[2]

This writer and lawyer finds the holding in *Tomka* disturbing, if not shocking. Judge Parker, in his strongly worded dissent in *Tomka*, stated that, "the express language of the statute permits individual liability under Title VII and . . . sound jurisprudence counsels giving that statutory language that full effect."[3] Furthermore, Judge Parker saw no basis, "in the statute, or elsewhere for reading the agent clause to impose only Respondeat Superior liability, to the exclusion of joint and several liability, between an employer and his or her agent . . . under Title VII."[4]

In addition, the meaning of "agent" in the Title VII definition of employer, as the *Tomka* Court pointed out, has engendered a significant split of views and opinions among the federal courts. Some courts have held that the plain meaning of the statute means supervisory personnel and others that are agents of the employer are statutory "employers" who may be held individually liable for their discriminatory acts.[5]

This writer believes that the dissent of Judge Parker, and the views of other federal courts on this issue, point to a better rule than that articulated in *Tomka*. *Tomka* shields malefactors from their maledictions and malefactions. There would have been no Nuremberg Trials if Hitler were the only defendant and his agents were excused as nonemployers. Workers are at the mercy, on the basis of the at-will employment doctrine, of their employers. To shield individuals who wreak harm and vengeance on helpless employees on the basis of their not being employers, serves little or no purpose but to protect wrongdoers from paying for their wrongdoing, at least out of their pockets.

Clearly these supervisors are not mere puppets, but are doing the will and carrying out the dictates of the behemoth corporate Goliath employer, which crushes individuals that stand in its way, like checkers on a checkerboard.

There are other policy considerations that can be articulated and argued here. The United States District Court for the District of Rhode Island, in *Iacampo v. Hasbro, Inc.*,[6] set forth a different view of this matter, opposing the *Tomka* holding entirely. In *Iacampo*, an employee brought state and federal claims against her employer and others for gender and disability discrimination. The defendants moved to dismiss or, alternately, for a more definite statement of the claims. The United States District Court held that plaintiff's immediate supervisor and her supervisor's supervisor could be held individually liable under the Americans with Disabilities Act (ADA) and Title VII. The Court further held that plaintiff stated prima facie claims for violations of the Rhode Island Fair Employment Practices Act; the ADA; and Title VII; and for simple assault, battery, and second-degree sexual assault. The Court also held that common-law discrimination claims against defendant, as a third-party beneficiary of contracts between defendant and state government, could not be decided on a motion to dismiss in light of factual disputes over whether the employer signed agreements of which the plaintiff was the intended beneficiary. Finally, the District Court held that the plaintiff failed to state a claim of the Negligent Infliction of Emotional Distress and that the Rhode Island Workers' Compensation Act shielded the employer from the Intentional Infliction of Emotional Distress claim.

More specifically, the Rhode Island District Court engaged in extensive analysis of the question of supervisory /individual liability under the Americans with Disabilities Act and Title VII. The Court noted that there had been a division of authority among the circuits and districts on the issue of individual liability and supervisory employees under Title VII, citing a number of cases for this particular proposition.[7]

The Court then went on to state, over the impassioned dissent of Judge Parker, that in *Tomka*, the majority held that supervisor employees are not individually liable under Title VII. The Court then noted that they were persuaded as to the reasoning of Judge Parker's dissent and found that supervisory employees could be individually liable under Title VII and the ADA. The Court reasoned that

> the imposition of individual liability on supervisory employees under Title VII and the ADA promotes judicial restraint while providing greater redress for victims of discrimination. Courts ignore their constitutional role when they peer beyond the clear language of the statute in search of ascribed congressional purpose, thus to rewrite the law. As Judge Parker notes, Title VII is unambiguous, and a literal reading of the agent clause does not do such violence to the statutory scheme as to justify inquiry into legislative intent. To ignore the plain language of the Title VII (and the ADA) is set forth on uncertain, unmarked, and forbidden judicial waters. . . . Moreover, threatening supervisory employees with individual liability under Title VII and the ADA deters those who would use their positions and power to discriminate, and guarantees that victims of discrimination will receive redress not only from amorphous corporate entitles, but from their very present oppressors.

Clearly, Booth, as Iacampo's immediate supervisor, and Godfrin, Booth's supervisor, are Hasbro's agents. Thus, the Court opines that Booth and Godfrin may be found individually liable under Title VII and the ADA.[8]

Kramer v. Windsor Park Nursing Home[9] also sheds a great deal of light in its reasoning as to why the *Tomka* holding is inappropriate, if not incorrect. In *Kramer*, an employee who was formerly employed by a nursing home brought an employment discrimination action against the nursing home and the co-owner of the home. The nursing home and co-owner moved for Summary Judgment. The United States District Court for the Southern District of Ohio, Western Division, held, in pertinent part, that the nursing home which was named in the Equal Employment Opportunity Commission Complaint and the co-owner shared an identity of interest sufficient to excuse the employee's failure to name the co-owner in the caption of her EEOC Complaint. The Court further held that the co-owner could be held individually liable for violations of Title VII, the Rehabilitation Act, and the Americans With Disabilities Act (ADA), and that material issues of fact precluded Summary Judgment for the employer in the employee's ADA and Rehabilitation Act claims. The *Kramer* Court proceeded, more specifically, to analyze the question of individual liability under federal discrimination statutes. The Court initially noted that Ms. Kramer had sued Mr. Byars in his individual capacity as owner/administrator of Windsor Park. Mr. Byars argued that he could not be held individually liable under Title VII. The Court went on to state that although it recognized that the majority of circuits disagreed with it, the Court stated that it continued to adhere to the view that Title VII does provide for individual supervisory liability, citing *Johnson v. University Surgical Group Associates of Cincinnati.*[10] The Court stated that in *Johnson* it identified three reasons why Title VII provides for individual supervisors' liability.

First, the Court stated the prior holdings of the Sixth Circuit gave at least tacit approval of co-employee supervisor liability.[11] The Court went on to state, as a second reason, that individual liability promotes the purposes of Title VII, referencing the Civil Rights Act of 1991, PL 102-66, Section 3(1). Third, the Court stated that agency principles are followed throughout Title VII and that these principles support shared liability on the part of both the employer and the agent, referencing Restatement (2d) of Agency, Section 359 C(1) (1957). The Court concluded that it would continue to adhere to the conclusion that Title VII does provide for individual liability until the Sixth Circuit or the Supreme Court decided otherwise.

In short, both *Kramer* and *Iacampo* point in a different direction on the issue of individual supervisory liability, and it is urged that their view is the right and correct view.

Conclusion

This brief critical analysis of the *Tomka* holding offers the following view. Clearly the holding of *Tomka*, in effect, is to shield management from liability in Title VII actions. Title VII gives the definition of employer as a person engaged in an industry effecting commerce that has 15 or more employees . . . and any agent of such a person.[12] The issue is, What is an agent? The fact of the matter is that it is stretching the point to say that corporate management is not in an agency relationship with the corporate entity. *Tomka* says they are not within the Title VII definition of an employer. The reality of the *Tomka* holding is that corporate officials are shielded from their wickedness, indifference, callousness, and the pain they cause others. They act badly and are excused and shielded. They fire the worker, at will, who must support his wife and children, and in light of this, *Tomka* says that they are immune from suit. On the plain meaning of agent in the Title VII definition of employer, it surely cannot be said that a corporate supervisor is not an agent. He is doing the will of his fictional boss and should not be allowed to escape. It is no excuse that United States soldiers killed and tortured civilians in Iraq on the ground that they were following orders. If those more humble citizens should be subject to the rule of law, how much more so should well-heeled, prosperous corporate officials be brought to task for their violations and malicious actions? *Tomka* is wrong in the view of this writer, legally and morally, and should be changed. *Tomka*, in the view of this writer, is a step back rather than a step forward. A democratic society places worth on each and every individual irrespective of race, sex, sexual orientation, class, height, or weight. The prosperous should no more be excused than the powerless and weak should be prosecuted.

Reprinted with permission from the <u>Labor and Employment Newsletter</u>, Fall/Winter 2007, Vol. 32. No. 3, published by the New York State Bar Association, One Elk Street, Albany, New York 12207.

9. Adverse Action: An Analysis

Title VII of the Civil Rights Act of 1964, 42 U.S.C. §. 2000(e-2), entitled "Unlawful Employment Practice," states in pertinent part that

> It shall be an unlawful employment practice for an employer-
>
> (1) to fail or refuse to hire or to discharge any individual, or otherwise to discriminate against any individual with respect to his compensation, terms, conditions, or privileges of employment, because of such individual's race, color, religion, sex, or national origin; or
>
> (2) to limit, segregate, or classify his employees or applicants for employment in any way which would deprive or tend to deprive any individual of employment opportunities or otherwise adversely affect his status as an employee, because of such individual's race, color, religion, sex, or national origin.

The basic thrust of the statute is to prohibit discriminatory practice in the workplace based on sex, religion, national origin, and race. It is beyond the scope of this article to provide a full analysis of this most complex and important statute. This article will attempt to analyze one element of proof of what may constitute a prima facie case of national origin, race, color, or religious discrimination, under this statute.

In order to prove national origin, race, color, gender, disability discrimination and age discrimination under Title VII; the Americans with Disabilities Act; and the Age Discrimination Act, a complainant must satisfy the burdens of proof initially established in *McDonnell Douglas v. Green*[1] and *Texas Department of Community Affairs v. Burdine*,[2] as recently affirmed in *St. Mary's Honor Center v. Hicks*.[3] A complainant's initial burden is to establish a prima facie case of discrimination by presenting admissible evidence of "actions taken by the employer," from which one can infer, if such actions remain unexplained, that it is more likely than not that such actions were "based on a discriminatory criterion illegal under the Act." *Furnco Constr. Corp. v. Waters*[4] (citing *International Bd. of Teamsters v. United States*[5]); see also *Hicks*;[6] *Burdine*;[7] and *McDonnell Douglas*.[8]

More specifically, in order to establish a prima facie case of national origin, race, color, or religious discrimination, disability, or age discrimination, the complainant must demonstrate that (1) he belonged to a protected class, (2) his job performance was satisfactory, and (3) he was discharged under circumstances which give rise to an inference of discrimination. See *McDonnell Douglas Corp. v. Green*;[9] *Vaughn v. Mobil Oil Corp.*;[10] *Scott v. Federal Reserve Bank*;[11] *Fahie v. Thornburgh*;[12] and *Fisher v. Vassar College*.[13]

This article proposes to analyze and consider one separate and discrete element of what may be said to constitute a prima facie case of employment discrimination. That element is that the terminated employee, allegedly subjected to some form of discrimination, was the subject or object of an adverse employment decision.

The leading case on that element of an employment discrimination prima facie case is *Galabya v. New York City Board of Education*.[14] The facts in *Galabya* were that a teacher brought an action against the Board of Education alleging his transfer from one school to another violated the Age Discrimination in Employment Act. The United States District Court for the Eastern District of New York entered Summary Judgment in favor of the Board. The teacher appealed. In *Galabya*, the specific facts were that the appellant was "excessed," meaning that that appellant was not fired, but reassigned to another position in the school system. Specifically, the appellant was reassigned to teach keyboarding at Van Ardsdale High School. To that point, in the appellant's 14-year teaching career, his work had been in Special Education. The transfer did not affect the appellant's salary, and there was no evidence that the ultimate reassignment resulted in a loss of benefits, prestige, or opportunities for advancement. However, it was undisputed that the facilities at Van Ardsdale were inferior to the facilities at P.S. 4, where the appellant had taught, to the extent that the teachers at Van Ardsdale did not have their own classrooms, desks, or closets. After a series of disputes at Van Ardsdale, the appellant took a leave of absence. The Second Circuit considered the issue of what was to be considered an adverse employment action here. They apprehended the appellant's argument to be that he was denied assignment to the PS. 4 computer lab, not assigned for the start of the 1994 school year, mis-assigned to Sara Hale, and then ultimately assigned to Van Ardsdale, where he was forced to teach outside his area of expertise, Special Education, and at a school with inferior facilities to PS. 4. The Court then proceeded to analyze what constituted an adverse employment action as a matter of law. The Court stated that a plaintiff sustains an adverse employment action if he or she endures a "material adverse change" in the terms and conditions of employment. The Court went on to state that to be "materially adverse" a change in working conditions must be "more disruptive than a mere inconvenience or alteration of job responsibilities." The Court then stated that "a materially adverse change might be indicated by a termination of employment, a demotion evidenced by a decrease in wage or salary, a less distinguished title, a material loss of benefits, significantly diminished material responsibilities, or other indices . . . unique to a particular situation."

The United States Court of Appeals concluded that there was no evidence that the delay in reassignment, followed by the mis-assignment to Sara Hale, was an adverse employment action. The Court noted the appellant did not allege that the appellee denied him an available transfer, that the appellee failed to pay his salary during the interim period, or that the delay in any way harmed his career. The Court went on to state that the inconvenience that the appellant endured, because of the relatively minor administrative miscues that occurred during the reassignment process, was not cognizable as an adverse employment action. The Court further noted that the allegedly inferior facilities the appellant faced at Van Ardsdale did not render the assignment an adverse employment action. The Court went on to state further that the disparity in working conditions—which was reduced to the fact that teachers in Van Ardsdale rotated through classrooms, whereas the teachers at P.S. 4 had their own classrooms—could be characterized as minor. The Court also concluded that the transfer of the appellant out of Special Education classes also did not constitute an adverse employment action, noting that the plaintiff offered no evidence the transfer was some sort of demotion that would constitute a serious professional setback and stigma to his career. The Court opined that a transfer is an adverse employment action if it results in a change in responsibilities so significant as to constitute a setback to the plaintiff's career. Weighing all these factors, the Second Circuit concluded that what occurred here was not an adverse employment action.

A second authoritative decision on what may be said to constitute an adverse employment action is in *Wanamaker v. Columbian Rope Co.*[15] In *Wanamaker*, the plaintiff brought an age discrimination claim with respect to his termination. Again, the United States Court of Appeals for the Second Circuit initially set forth in *Wanamaker* what may be said to be a prima facie case of retaliation. The Court held that a prima facie case of retaliation under the ADEA requires proof that: (1) the plaintiff was engaged in an activity protected under the ADEA; (2) the employer was aware of the plaintiff's participation in the protected activity; (3) the plaintiff was subject to an adverse employment action; and (4) there is a nexus between the protected activity and the adverse action taken.

The *Wanamaker* Court stated that in retaliation cases brought under Title VII the ADEA does not define an adverse employment action solely in terms of job termination or reduced wages and benefits, and that less flagrant reprisals by employers may be adverse. The Court took note of the decision of the Seventh Circuit in *Collins v. State of Illinois*,[16] where that court stated that in a Title VII case, an employer can make a job undesirable not affecting money or benefits. On the other hand, the Second Circuit, citing *Welsh v. Derwinski*,[17] noted that not every unpleasant incident creates a claim for retaliatory discharge. The Court noted that because there are no bright-line rules, the Courts must pore over each case to determine whether the challenged employment action reaches the level of "adverse."

Finally there is a further consideration, in *Richardson v. New York State Department of Correctional Services*,[18] of what may be said to constitute an adverse employment action. The *Richardson* Court noted the two performance reviews that stated that the plaintiff's job performance was "average" rather than "excellent" did not constitute an adverse employment action, and that the transfer and reassignment, which involved different job responsibilities, and a move to a position involving contact with the prisoner population, constituted an adverse employment decision.

In short, the law appears to be in stated, as set forth in *Galabya*, *Wanamaker*; and *Richardson*. For the action of an employer to constitute a adverse action, the change in employment must be substantive and not a mere annoyance, inconvenience, or alteration. This could be evidenced by a termination of employment, a demotion evidenced by a decrease in wage or salary, or something similarly substantial. On the other hand, in *Wanamaker*, that Court noted that less flagrant actions can be an adverse employment action, even when the action does not affect money or benefits. Similarly in *Richardson*, the Court noted that a move to a position in the correctional system involving contact with the prisoner population constituted an adverse employment action.

There are other cases that analyze this issue more specifically. For example, in *Grube v. Lau Industries, Inc.*,[19] the United States Court of Appeals for the Seventh Circuit stated that the employer's decision to change a female employee's working hours by transferring her from a first-shift manager position to a second-shift manager position did not rise to the level of an adverse employment action as required for the employee's prima facie case of gender discrimination. The Court of Appeals held that the employee's paying job title remained the same and she suffered no significantly diminished job responsibilities.

Similarly, in *Stockette v. Muncie Indiana Transit System*,[20] the United States Court of Appeals for the Seventh Circuit held that requiring an employee to submit to a drug test is not an "adverse employment action," and thus is not actionable under Title VII, where the employee requested that the employee take the test only after it had received the report that he was using drugs and after a trained observer determined that he exhibited signs of being under the influence of a controlled substance.[21]

Lumhoo v. Home Depot USA, Inc.[22] is an interesting case. In that case, the United States District Court for the Eastern District of New York held that the termination of an African-American employee from his position in a home improvement retail chain store followed by a subsequent reinstatement to part-time position at a different location did not constitute adverse employment action required to establish a discriminatory discharge in violation of Title VII and Section 1981. The United States District Court for the Eastern District of New York held that the store investigated the incident leading to termination and reinstated the employee with full back pay, the same salary and benefits, and the same seniority status, and removed all record of his termination from store records.[23]

Conclusion

This analysis of what may be said to constitute an "adverse employment action" in the context of a prima facie case brought under Title VII, the ADA, or the ADEA, shows a basic pattern that the action much be substantive. There must be a significant effect on the employee's employment situation, whether loss of salary, loss of benefits, or some negative change in the employee's working situation. There is authority, however, as stated in *Wanamaker*, that something less than that can be said to constitute an "adverse employment action" and there is no set rule on the issue and that each case must be considered on its own facts.

Reprinted with permission from the Labor and Employment Newsletter, *Summer 2007, Vol. 32. No. 2, published by the New York State Bar Association, One Elk Street, Albany, New York 12207.*

Notes

2. Should Title VII of The United States Code Prohibiting Sex Discrimination Be Based on Sexual Orientation: An Argument

1. 42 United States Code 2000(e)-2.

2. 608 F.2d 327 (9th Cir. 1979).

3. In fact, Congress rejected a Proposal to add a provision to Title VII prohibiting sexual orientation discrimination. Employment Non-Discrimination Act 1994 (ENDA), S.2238, 103d Cong Sess. (1994). Congress' refusal to pass such legislation buttresses the federal courts' holdings that Congress did not intend to include sexual orientation discrimination within the proscriptions of Title VII.

4. 876 F.2d 69 (8th Cir. 1989); on this See also *Blum v. Gulf Oil Corp.*, 597 F.2d 936 (5th Cir. 1979), where the Fifth Circuit held that discharge for homosexuality is not prohibited by Title VII or the prohibition 1981; See also *Polly v. Houston Lighting and Power Co.*, 835 F. Sup. 135 (S.D. Texas 1993); *Kelley v. Vaughn,* 760 F. Supp. 161 (W.D. MO 1991). The EEOC, it should be noted, has also concluded that purported sexual orientation discrimination is not unlawful under Title VII; See EEOC Dec. 77-28 FEP Cas. (BNA) 1789, 1790 (1977). Held: Discharge of the charging party because she is a lesbian is not unlawful under Title VII.

5. On this See also *Sommers v. Budget Marketing Inc.*, 667 F.2d 748 (8th Cir. 1982); *Holloway v. Arthur Andersen and Co.*, 566 F.2d 659 (9th Cir. 1977); *Dobre v. National R.R. Passenger Corp.*, 850 F.Supp 284 (E.D. Pa. 1993); *Voyles v. Ralph K. Davies Medical Center,* 403 F. Supp. 456 (D.C. Cal. 1975).

6. *Rosen v. Thornburg,* 928 F.2d 528, 532 (2d Cir. 1991); *O'Mailley v. AIDS Institute, MNYRO et al.,* No. 95 Civ. 5561 (PKL) 1996 U.S. Dist. LEXIS 11319 (S.D.N.Y. 1996).

7. *Saulpaugh v. Monroe Community Hospital,* 4 F.3rd 134, 148 (2d Cir. 1993) (Van Graafeiland, J. concurring).

8. See *Sullivan v. National Railroad Passenger Corp.,* No. 95-0037 1996 U.S. Dist. LEXIS 20699 (S.D. Pla. 1996).

9. *McWilliams v. Fairfax County BD of Supervisors,* 72 F.3rd (1191) (4th Cir. 1996).

3. Trial by Jury—Is There a Doubt?

1. *Gilmer* v. *Interstate/Johnson Lane Corporation,* 500 U.S. 20, 114 L.Ed. 2d 26, 111 50 1647 (1991); *Circuit City Stores v. Adams,* 532 U.S. 105, 121 S.Ct. 1302, 149 L.Ed 2d 234 (2001); *EEOC v. Waffle House, Inc.* 122 S.Ct. 754 (2002).

2. 500 U.S. 20, 114 L.Ed. 2d 26 111 S.Ct. 1647 (1991).

3. *Id.*

4. 415 U.S. 36, 94 S. Ct. 1001, 39 L. Ed. 2d 147 (1974).

5. 895 F.2d at 97.

6. *Id.*

7. 450 U.S. 728, 101 S. Ct. 1437, 67 L.Ed 2d 64 (1981).
8. 466 U.S. 284, 104 S.Ct. 1799, 80 L. Ed. 2d 302.
9. *Id.*

4. Naming as Prerequisite

1. 342 U.S.C. Sec. 200(e).
2. 29 U.S.C. Secs. 621-634; 42 U.S.C. Sec. 12101-12113.
3. 42 U.S.C. Sec. 200(e)(5).
4. *Johnson v. Palma,* 931 F.2d 203 (2d Cir. 1490 1991); *Eggleston v. Chicago Journeymen Plumbers; Local Union No. 130,* 657 F.2d 890 (7th Cir. 1981); *Drummer v. DCI Contracting Corp.* 772 F.Supp. 828 (S.D.N.Y. 1991); *Williams v. Mass General Hospital,* 449 F Supp. 55 (D.C. Mass. 1978); *Seacrist v. Burns Intern. Sec. Services,* 926 F.Supp 823 (E.D. Wis. 1960); *Lane v. David P. Jacobson and Co. Ltd.,* 880 F.Supp 1091 (Ed. Va. 1995); *Ciker v. Marrion Group Inc.,* 455 F.Supp. 398 (D.C. S.C. 1978); *Allen v. Colgate Palmolive Co.,* 539 F.Supp. 57 (S.D.N.Y. 1981).
5. *Schnellbrecher v. Baskin Clothing Store Co.,* 887 F.2d 124 (7th Cir. 1989); *Stephenson v. CNA Fin. Corp.,* 775 F. Supp. 238 (N.D. Ill. 1991).
6. 772 F.2d 281 (6th Cir. 1985).
7. 828 F.Supp 543 (N.D. Ill. 1993). See also *Feng v. Sandrick,* 636 F. Supp. 77 (N.D. Ill. 1988); *Williams v. Southern Bell,* 464 F.Supp. 367 (D.C. Fla. 1979); (Held: rule not absolute, but is subject to federal policy-crated exceptions.)
8. 554 F.Supp 365 (U.S. Dist. Court W.D. Va. 1983).
9. 815 F. Supp. 525 (D. Conn. 1992).
10. *Id.*
11. *Id.*
12. *Id.*
13. 920 F.2d 1451 (9th Cir. 1990).
14. 958 F.Supp 785 (E.D.N.Y. 1970). See also on this *Harrigan v. Hudson Sheraton Corp.,* 2 F.Supp. 2d 475 (S.D.N.Y. 1998); *Alfano v. Costello,* 940 F. Supp. 4598 465 (N.D.N.Y. 1996); *Sharkey v. Lasmo (Aul. Ltd.),* 906 F.Supp. 949 (S.D.N.Y. 1996). For further case law· in general on these exceptions to the general rule see *Paulsen v. City of North Tonawanda,* 811 F.Supp 884 (W.D.N.Y. 1993); *Matthew v. Houston Ind. School District,* 595 F.Supp. 445 (D.C. Tex. 1984); *Kramer v. Windsor Park Nursing Home Inc.,* 944 F.Supp. 844 (S.D. Ohio 1996); *Stefanovic v. University of Tenn.,* 935 F.Supp 950 (E.D. Tenn. 1996); *Goldstein v. Bombardier Capital Inc.,* 889 F.Supp 760 (D. Vt. 1995); *Jackson v. University of Pittsburgh,* 405 F. Supp 607 (D.C. Pa. 1975).

5. Employment Discrimination and Individual Liability: A Comparison

1. 42 U.S.C. Sec. 2000(e)(2).
2. 42 U.S.C. Sec. 12112(a).
3. 29 U.S.C. 623FF.
4. Equal Pay Act (EPA) which makes it unlawful for employers to discriminate in compensation on the basis of gender: 29 U.S.C. Sec. 206(D)(l); The Older Worker benefits Protection Act (OWBPA) 29 U.S. Sec. 626 prohibits workers of 40 years of age or over from undue pressure by management to waive rights under the ADEA in return for benefits contained in early retirement agreements and programs; The Family and Medical Leave Act (FMLA) allows employees who have a serious health problem or the pressure of child care to take an unpaid leave and protects their right to return in good form to

their employment: 29 U.S.C. Secs 2601-2654. Finally, the Pregnancy Discrimination Act (PDA) protects against discrimination based on pregnancy: 42 U.S.C. Sec. 2000 (e)-(k).

    5. New York State Executive Law Section 296.

    6. 66 F.3rd 1295 (2d Cir. 1995). See also *Cook* v. *Arrowsmith Shelburne Inc.*, 69 F.3rd 1235 (2d Cir. 1995) (dismissing Title VII claims against supervisory personnel in light of the decision in *Tomka*); *Torres v. New York University*, 1996 U.S. Dist. Lexis 356 (S.D.N.Y. Jan 15, 1996); *Persuad* v. *S. Axelrod Company*, 1996 U.S. Dist. Lexis 160 (S.D.N.Y. Jan. 4, 1996).

    7. 63 N.Y.2d 541, 483 N.Y.S.2d 659 (1984).

    8. *Perks* v. *Town of Huntington*, 96 F Supp 222 (E.D.N.Y. 2000); *Shephard v. Frontier Communications Service Inc.*, 92 F. Supp. 279 (S.D.N.Y. 2000); *McCoy v. City of New York*, 131 F Supp 363 (E.D.N.Y. 2001); *Turner v. Olympic Regional Development Authority*, 89 F Supp.2d 241 (N.D.N.Y. 2000); *Schallop v. New York State Department of Law*, 20 F Supp.2d 384 (N.D.N.Y. 1998); *Bush* v. *Raymond Corp. Inc.*, 954 F. Supp. 490 (N.D.N.Y.1997).

    9. 94 F Supp.2d 593 (1 S.D.N.Y. 1999).

    10. 66 F.2d 1295 (2d Cir. 1995).

    11. See also *Sometime v. DAOR, Inc.*, 43 F Supp.2d 477 (S.D.N.Y. 1999); *Graef* v. *North University Hospital*, IF Supp.2d 318 (S.D.N.Y. 1998); *Chamblee v. Harris and Harris, Inc.*, 154 F. Supp.2d 670 (S.D.N.Y. 2001); *Beattie v. Farnsworth Middle School*, 143 F. Supp.2d 220 (N.D.N.Y. 1998).

    12. *Hicks v. IBM, id.*; *Graff v. North Shore University Hospital, id.*

7. A Second View

    1. *Queens Bar Bulletin*, Vol. 63, No. 8, May 2000.

    2. 42 U.S.C. Sec. 2000(e).

    3. See also *Bibby v. Philadelphia CocaCola Bottling Co.*, 260 F.3rd 257 (3rd Cir. 2001) (Held: Harassment based on sexual orientation is not actionable under Title VII; *Simonton v. Runyon*, 232 F.3rd 33 (2d Cir. 2000); *Hammer v. St. Vincent Hospital and Health Care Center, Inc.*, 224 F.3rd 701 (7th Cir. 2000); (Held: Harassment based solely upon a person's sexual preference or orientation [and not one's sex] is not an unlawful employment practice under Title VII, *Higgins v. New Balance Athletic Shoe, Inc.*, 194 F.3rd 252 [1st Cir. 1999].)

    4. 194 F.3rd 252 (1st Cir. 1999).

    5. 256 F.3rd 864 (9th Cir. 2001).

    6. See also *Schwenk v. Hartford*, 204 F.3rd 1187 (9th Cir. 2000) (Held: Employer who acts on the basis or belief that a woman must not and cannot be aggressive has acted on the basis of gender and so a Title VII action lies.)

    7. 195 F. Supp.2d 1212 (D. Or. 2002).

    8. 183 F. Supp.2d 403 (D. Mass, 2002).

    9. For an interesting and informative and relevant decision on this issue see *Weaver v. Nebo School District*, 29 F Supp.2d 1279, 1291 n. 10, (Held: Defendant violated lesbian teacher's rights to equal protection under 142 U.S.C. Sec. 1983 by prohibiting her from discussing her sexual orientation while permitting other teachers to discuss their heterosexual orientation.)

8. Tomka: A Comment on Supervisory Liability

1. 66 F.3d 1295 (2d Cir. 1995).
2. See *Tomka v. Seiler Corp.*, *supra* at 1313-1317.
3. *Id.*, 1318.
4. *Id.*, 1320.
5. See, e.g., *Jones v. Continental Corp.*, 789 F.2d 1225 (6th Cir. 1986) (individuals may be held liable as "agents" of an employer under Title VII); *Paroline v. Unisys Corp.*, 879 F.2d 100, 104 (4th Cir. 1989), rev'd in part, aff'd in relevant part, 900 F.2d 27 (4th Cir. 1990) (en banc) (individual liability under Title VII for supervisory positions); *Bridges v. Eastman Kodak Co.*, 800 F. Supp. 1172, 1179-80 (S.D.N.Y. 1992) ("agents" includes supervisors and other individuals who participate in discriminatory decision-making process); *Cheng v. Tams Consultants, Inc.*, 1991 U.S. Dist. LEXIS 6095, at *4-7 (S.D.N.Y. May 2, 1991) (supervisory employees are agents of the actual employer for purposes of Title VII liability); *Goodstein v. Bombardier Capital, Inc.*, 889 F. Supp. 760, 763-65 (D.Vt. 1995) (agents may be personally liable under Title VII).
6. 929 F. Supp. 562, 572 (D.R.L 1996).
7. *See Paroline v. Unisys Corp.*, 879 F.2d 100, 104 (4th Cir. 1989), rev'd in part, aff'd in relevant part, 900 F.2d 27 (4th Cir. 1990) (supervisory individuals may be liable under Title VII) with *Miller v. Maxwell's Intern. Inc.*, 991 F.2d 583, 587-588 (9th Cir. 1993), cert. denied, 510 U.S. 1109, 114 S. Ct. 1049, 127 L.Ed. 2d 372 (1994) (no individual liability), and *Grant v. Lone Star Co.*, 21 F.3d 649, 651-653 (5th Cir. 1994), cert. denied. See also *Caldwell v. Federal Express Corp.*, 908 F. Supp. 29, 36 (D.Me. 1995); *Ruffino v. State Street Bank and Trust Co.*, 908 F. Supp. 1019, 1047-48 (D.Mass. 1995); and *Miller v. CBC Companies, Inc.*, 908 F. Supp. 1054, 1064-1065 (D.N.H. 1995). See *Iacampo v. Hasbro, Inc.*, *supra* at 571-572.
8. *Iacampo*, *supra* at 572.
9. 943 F. Supp. 844 (S.D. Ohio 1996).
10. 871 F. Supp. 979, 986 (S.D. Ohio 1994).
11. The Court cited in support of this proposition *Jones v. Continental Corp.*, 789 F.2d 1225, 1231 (6th Cir. 1986); *Romain v. Kurek*, 772 F.2d 281 (6th Cir. 1985).
12. 42 U.S.C § 2000e(b).

9. Adverse Action: An Analysis

1. 411 U.S. 792 (1973).
2. 450 48 (1981).
3. 509 U.S. 502 (1993).
4. 438 U.S. 567 (1987).
5. 431 U.S. 432, 358 (1977).
6. 509 U.S. at 506-07.
7. 450 U.S. at 1253-54.
8. 411 U.S. at 802.
9. *Id.*
10. 707 F. Supp. 595 (S.D.N.Y. 1989).
11. 704 F. Supp. 441 (S.D.N.Y. 1989).
12. 746 F. Supp. 310 (S.D.N.Y. 1990).
13. 114 F.3d 1332 (2d 1994). See also *Parika v. United Artist Theater Circuit, Inc.*, 934 F. Supp. 760 (S.D. Miss. 1996); *Plair v. E.J. Brach & Sons, Inc.*, 931 F. Supp. 555 (N.D. Ill. 1995); *Dean v. Pepsi-Cola Beverages Corp.*, 894 F. Supp. 600 (N.D.N.Y.

1995); *Mulero Rodriguez v. Ponte, Inc.*, 891 F. Supp. 680 (D. Puerto Rico 1995); *James v. Ranch Mart Hardware, Inc.*, 881 F. Supp. 478 (D. Can. 1995); *Mills v. Gibson Greetings, Inc.*, 872 F. Supp. 366 (E.D. Ky. 1994); *Thomsic v. State Farm Aut. Ins. Co.*, 870 F. Supp. 318 (D. Utah 1994); *Lopez v. Schwan's Sales Enterprises, Inc.*, 845 F. Supp. 1440 (D. Kan. 1994); *Edwards v. Interboro Institute*, 840 F. Supp. 222 (E.D.N.Y. 1994); *Alie v. NYNEX Corp.*, 158 F.R.D. 239 (E.D.N.Y. 1994); *Evans v. Ford Motor Co.*, 768 F. Supp. 618 (D. Minn. 1991).

14. 202 F.3d 636 (2d Cir. 2000).

15. 108 F.3d 462 (2d Cir. 1997).

16. 830 F.2d 692 (7th Cir. 1987).

17. 14 F.3d 85 (1st Cir. 1994).

18. 180 F.3d 426 (2d Cir. 1999).

19. 257 F.3d 723 (7th Cir. 2001).

20. 221 F.3d 997 (7th Cir. 2000).

21. See also *Primes v. Reno*, 190 F.3d 765 (6th Cir. 1999); *Bragg v. Navistar Intern. Trans. Corp.*, 164 F.3d 373 (7th Cir. 1998) (No adverse employment action under Title VII when alleged performance demonstration, during which the employee was allegedly evaluated without her knowledge to determine whether she deserved a promotion and after which she was not promoted, was not an adverse employment action). See also *Ledergerber v. Stangler*, 122 F.3d 1142 (8th Cir. 1997); *Zhou v. Pittsburg State University*, WL 1564249 (D. Kan. 2003) (Held: Oral and written reprimands that a State University employee received did not constitute adverse employment actions as would support a prima facie case of national origin discrimination under Title VII absent showing that the employee suffered negative consequences as a result of the reprimands).

22. 229 F. Supp.2d 121 (E.D.N.Y. 2002).

23. See also *Martin v. Bowing-Oak Ridge Co.*, WL 31994282 (E.D. Tenn. 2002). In that case the United States District Court for the Eastern District of Tennessee held that the employer's assignment of an African-American employee who had complained of racial harassment by co-workers from the first shift to the second shift was not an adverse employment action as required for employee's prima facie case of retaliation under Title VII and Section 1981 and the Tennessee Human Rights Act (THRA). That Court held that the assignment was a lateral transfer within the employee's same job classification with the same job title, seniority, and pay.

Introduction to Civil Rights Reprinted Articles

These articles have as their subject issues under the Civil Rights Statute, 42 U.S.C. Sec. 1983. This statute is one of the most frequent denizens in the Federal Court system and many cases are brought under its rubric, particularly cases involving improper and excessive use of force by police officers and similar abuse by corrections officers.

Chapter 6
Civil Rights Reprinted Articles

1. A Point of Pleading in 1983 Civil Rights Actions

One of the most common actions today, found both in the federal and state courts, is the action brought to redress the alleged deprivation of a citizen's civil rights by one acting under color of law of a statute or custom of a state or territory.[1]

The action is brought under Title 42, Section 1983 of the United States Code, and though as brought under Section 1983 it is an action to redress the purported violation of a citizen's civil rights, it is often, in its root and essence, little more than a tort claim for false arrest, false imprisonment, assault and/or battery.

Thus for example, when a citizen has allegedly been falsely arrested and thereafter assaulted with excessive force and imprisoned by the police officer or officers of a municipality, whether employed or acting on behalf of a Town, Village, City or County, and the complaint or charges brought against our offended citizen by the District Attorney are withdrawn or dismissed, this citizen will often bring his damage suit in the form of a civil rights action in federal court under 42 U.S.C. Section 1983, rather than a simple tort action in state court. It should be noted that, under the doctrine of pendent jurisdiction set forth by the United States Supreme Court in *United Mine Workers of America v. Gibbs,* 383 U.S. 715, 86 S. Ct. 1130, 16 L. Ed. 2d 218 (1966), the plaintiff in a Civil Rights Action under Section 1983 may include the related or pendent tort claim of false arrest, assault, battery and the intentional infliction of mental distress, provided that it is shown to the District Court that both the Federal Civil Rights claim and the pendent state tort claims arose from a common nucleus of operative fact.

Our Civil Rights plaintiff moreover, in his pleading, if sufficiently inclusive and properly framed, will sue not only the individual police officer or officers who supposedly falsely arrested, attacked and imprisoned him, but also the Police Department and Municipality that employed these officers.

In short the civil rights action under Section 1983, in this day and age of the assertion of the individual right, has become a frequent, if not omnipresent denizen of our courts. The action however, presents certain problems and particulars of pleading which the practitioner must be ever wary of in framing the complaint on behalf of this injured plaintiff.

This brief article proposes to specify and analyze, one particular nicety of properly pleading a Civil Rights action under Section 1983.

The Problem

As has been stated, the civil rights action may be and indeed often is brought not only against the offending police officers, but also against the municipality and police department that employed them.

The uninitiated member of the bar who is confronted with pleading and pursuing a Section 1983 action on behalf of an aggrieved citizen who has been falsely arrested and violated will, to be sure, sue the individual police officers and the police department and municipality that employed them, if he fails to examine with care the case law interpreting and construing this statute. His suit, however, against the municipality may very well be based solely on the theory of respondeat superior; that is to say, on the notion that the municipality and the police department may be sued in this Civil Rights Action, and ultimately recovered from, on the single and simple ground that they employed the police officers that allegedly deprived our citizen plaintiff of his civil rights, for which he now seeks redress.

If a civil rights action brought against a municipality is pleaded solely on the ground of respondeat superior, the action as a matter of law must be dismissed, as against the municipality, on the face of the pleadings alone.

The case establishing this rule, not only of law, but more specifically of pleading is *Monell v. Department of Social Services of the City of New York*, 436 U.S. 658, 98 S. Ct. 2018, 56 L. Ed. 611 (1978).

In *Monell*, female employees of the Department of Social Services and Board of Education of the City of New York brought an action challenging the policy of these agencies which required pregnant employees to take unpaid leaves of absences before these leaves were required for medical reasons. In the course of its decision the Supreme Court of the United States held that although a municipality may be sued as a person under Section 1983 there must be an allegation in the complaint that the official policy of the municipality or custom is responsible for the deprivation of the plaintiff's civil rights. *Monell v. Department of Social Services, supra*, at 2036, 2037.[2]

The cases following *Monell* in the Second Circuit and the Federal District Courts as well have adhered to the rule in *Monell*, explained it fully and uniformly concluded that there must be an allegation in the complaint of a Civil Rights Action brought under 42 U.S.C. Section 1983 that the municipality is somehow involved in the deprivation of the plaintiff's civil rights through its official policy or its execution due to long-standing custom and practice.[3]

   Leonhard v. United States, 633 F.2d 599 (2d Cir. 1980), is apropos. In *Leonhard*, an action was brought by a father on behalf of his three children against the United States various Federal Agencies, New York State Agencies and the City of Buffalo, seeking damages for the separation and concealment of his children. It was alleged that police officer Giambione participated in the removal and concealment of the children under and by full authority of the City of Buffalo. The court held that dismissal of the action against the City was appropriate because the complaint did not allege that Giambione acted pursuant to the official policy, regulation, or custom of the City of Buffalo. *Leonhard v. United States, supra* at 622.

   In *Singleton v. City of New York*, 632 F.2d 185 (2d Cir. 1980), the Second Circuit again had occasion to consider the effect of *Monell* with respect to what constitutes a proper allegation in a civil rights complaint against a municipality. The United States District Court for the Southern District of New York dismissed the plaintiff's complaint. The Second Circuit affirmed and stated that with respect to the plaintiff's claim against the City of New York,

> a municipality may be sued for damages under § 1983 only where the constitutional violations have been committed pursuant to an official policy or custom. . . . No such policy or custom is alleged here. Moreover, in *Turpin v. Mailet*, 619 F.2d 196 (2d Circuit 1980), we noted that an "official policy" cannot ordinarily be inferred from a single incident of illegality, such as a first false arrest, or excessive use of force, absent some additional circumstances. *Singleton v. City of New York, supra*, at 195.[3]

   It is not within the scope of this Article, nor is it its purpose, to consider what may, under the case law, constitute that official policy or custom that must be alleged and pleaded as responsible for the deprivation of a plaintiff's civil rights if a municipality is sued under 42 D.S.C. Section 1983. This much however is clear: unless there is, in a Section 1983 complaint brought against a municipality, a specific allegation that some official policy or custom is involved in and responsible for the deprivation of the Civil Rights of the plaintiff, that Section 1983 action must fail and the complaint must be dismissed.[4]

Conclusion

   In sum, if defeat is not at first blush to be snatched from the prospective possibility of victory by the Attorney for the Section 1983 plaintiff, the Section 1983 complaint must include the allegation that the custom or policy of the municipality is intertwined and involved in the deprivation of the plaintiff's civil rights, lest all be lost, through the loss of a few key words, the keys as it were to the kingdom.[5]

2. *"Official Policy" Under 42 U.S.C. Section 1983*

Where a municipality, be it a city, town, village, or school district, is sued under
42 D.S.C. Section 1983 by an aggrieved citizen for the purported violation of his
civil rights, it is the law that there must be an allegation in the complaint that the
supposed unconstitutional action of the municipality resulted from the implementation or execution of an official statute, ordinance, regulation, or decision
adopted or promulgated by that municipality's body, and that this official policy
is responsible for the alleged deprivation of the plaintiff's rights, or that the constitutional deprivation visited or occurred pursuant to some informal custom of
the municipality. In a word, there must be an allegation in the Section 1983 civil
rights complaint that official policy or informal custom caused the constitutional
tort or deprivation.

A municipality cannot, however, as a matter of law, be held liable for the
deprivation of a citizen's civil rights on the sole ground of *respondeat superior,*
or on the ground that the culpable municipal entity simply employed the tortfeasor. There must be a specific allegation, in the Section 1983 civil rights complaint that the municipality is somehow causally inextricably involved or intertwined in the deprivation of the plaintiff's civil rights, due to execution of
official policy or due to long-standing custom or practice.[1]

The question arises, then, as to what, under the case law, constitutes the
requisite official policy or settled informal custom or practice that will pass muster under Section 1983 and the cases construing and interpreting the statute and
allow a federal civil rights litigant not only his day in court, since the absence of
an allegation in a 1983 civil rights complaint that official policy or informal custom caused the unconstitutional deprivation of the plaintiff's civil rights will result in dismissal of the action, but will bring ultimate victory on the merits of the
case.

This article proposes to present, in summary and schematic form, a short
overview of the relevant case law on what may constitute the needful official
policy or settled informal custom to permit suit against a municipality under 42
U.S.C. Section 1983.

Specific Regulation Policy or Decision

Under *Monell* and the cases following it, where the action of the municipality resulting in the deprivation of the plaintiff's civil rights is taken pursuant to
an unconstitutional ordinance or regulation, or where a local government formally adopts a policy or makes a decision which when executed by the municipal body itself or its employees gives rise to an unconstitutional civil rights vio-

lation, then the local government may be held liable under 42 U.S.C. Section 1983. *Kingsville Ind. School District v. Cooper,* 611 F.2d 1109 (5th Cir. 1980) (School District Personnel decision by Board of Trustees is official decision or policy of the school district municipality since a school district legally acts through its Board of Trustees); *Huemmer v. Mayor City Council of Ocean City,* 632 F.2d 371 (4th Cir. 1980) (unconstitutional towing ordinance); *Owen v. City of Independence Missouri,* 445 U.S. 622 (100 S.Ct. 1398, 63 L.Ed.2d 673 (1980) (where police chief was fired by the city manager and sued the municipality for stigmatizing actions in connection with his discharge, resolution of city council directing city manager to take action against persons involved in unlawful activities, and dissemination of an investigative report, constituted official acts of city for Section 1983 purposes). See also *Gordon v. City of Warren,* .579 F.2d 386 (6th Cir. 1978); *Sterling v. Village of Maywood,* 579 F.2d 1350 (7th Cir. 1978); *Katris v. City of Waukeegan,* 498 F.Supp. 48 (N.D. Ill. 1980).

In the absence of a specific and discernable unconstitutional official ordinance, regulation, decision, or policy, the causal connection between the unconstitutional deprivation brought about by a local official or employee, and the official policy or custom of the municipality, becomes elusive and difficult to discern.

Acts of High Ranking Officials

Policies, practices or decisions ordered by high level municipal officials or officers represent official policy under the *Monell* standard. Thus, where an action is taken pursuant to an illegal or unconstitutional directive of the mayor, police chief, or other municipal department or agency head, the municipality may be held liable if the implementation of the directive leads to an unconstitutional deprivation. *Quinn v. Syracuse Model Neighborhood Corp.,* 613 F.2d 483 (2nd Cir. 1980) (claim for municipal liability under Section 1983 made on showing that mayor directed campaign to stigmatize the plaintiff); *Black v. Stephens,* 662 F.2d 181 (3rd Cir. 1981) (Regulation of police chief and policy of chief of police encouraging use of excessive force held sufficient link with unconstitutional actions of officer); *Tinker v. Des Moines Community School,* 393 U.S. 503, 89 S.Ct. 733 (1969) (Policy of principals of Des Moines Schools, mandating removal of black armband by student wearing it, and his suspension if he failed to remove it held policy of municipality under Section 1983).

Custom

Even in the absence of specific legislative rule or an expressed policy set forth by a municipality's high ranking officials, liability, under *Monell,* can be premised on the existence of a general custom or practice on the part of the municipality, or its high ranking officials, which caused the constitutional deprivation. Under *Monell* the custom or practice involved must be "persistent" or "well settled." (*Monell, supra* at 691).

Under the relevant case law, custom is unwritten de facto policy with no direct formal evidence of its existence. *Adickes v. S.H. Kress & Co.,* 398 U.S. 144, 90 S.Ct. 1598, 26 L.Ed. 2d 142 (1970) (settled actual practices of state officials showing existence of state enforced custom of

3. False Arrest and Sec. 1983: A Short Analysis

42 USC Sec. 1983 is one of the most important of the Reconstruction Civil Rights Acts. The litigation brought under this statute constitutes one of the most numerous categories of cases in the Federal Docket. The statute, originally passed as Section 1 of the Ku Klux Klan Act of 1871[1] creates a claim for equitable and legal relief against every person who, acting under the color of state legislation, custom, or usage, subjects or causes another to be subject to the deprivation of rights secured by the federal constitution and laws.[2]

Many kinds and varieties of cases are and may be brought under this statute. One of the major types of claim brought under this statute are those brought by persons who have been arrested and purportedly assaulted by state, city, or county police officers, alleging the use of excessive force. In *Graham v. Connor*[3], the United States Supreme Court held that the Fourth Amendment of the United States Constitution was the exclusive source of constitutional protection against the use of excessive force in the course of the arrest process. The high court adopted an objective reasonableness test for the Fourth Amendment excessive force claim. On the other hand, the U.S. Supreme Court held in *Whiteley v. Albers*[4] that the Eighth Amendment ban against cruel and unusual punishment protects convicted persons against the use of excessive force.

False arrest claims may also be brought under Sec. 1983 alleging a warrantless arrest or an arrest without probable cause. Although the analysis here must be under the Fourth Amendment of the U.S. Constitution, i.e., that the arrest was made without the prior issuance of a warrant or without probable cause, it may be said that the elements of a 1983 false arrest claim are substantially the same as the elements of the false arrest claim under New York Law.[5]

The Problem

Let us posit that a plaintiff in a Sec. 1983 cause brings his claim under the rubric of false arrest. This plaintiff, however, let us hypothesize, has pled guilty to criminal charge in the State Court, to either assault, or resisting arrest. The question arises whether this Sec. 1983 false arrest claim is precluded by reason of the conviction.

The leading case, is *Cameron v. Fogarty*.[6] In *Cameron*, the Second Circuit held that the prior court conviction for the possession of stolen property did not, by res judicata or collateral estoppel, preclude the 1983 claim, since the constitutionality of the false arrest was not included in the criminal proceeding. The court held, however, the 1983 claim was nevertheless barred by the common law principle and rule that the conviction gave the police officers a complete defense to the false arrest claim. The Court, in *Cameron*, also held that policy considerations favored this reasoning and result. *Cameron* is most certainly the law, at least in the Second Circuit, although other federal circuit and district courts have reached differing rules and results.[7]

Thus, in *Malady v. Crunk*,[8] the Eighth Circuit adopted the rule that the common law defense of conviction defeated the Sec. 1983 claim. On the other hand, in *Howlett v. Rose*[9] the U.S. Supreme Court parted ways with *Cameron*, holding that the elements and defenses of a federal cause of action are defined by federal law and that, with respect to persons that Congress subjected to liability, individual states may not exempt such persons from federal liability by relying on their own common law heritage.

The *Cameron* rule and analysis is still the law in the Second Circuit. For example, in *Roundtree v. City of New York*,[10] the U.S. District Court for the Eastern District of New York followed *Cameron* even to the extent of holding that a conviction pursuant to a plea of guilty to a reduced charge still voids the Sec. 1983 action and that, the albeit reduced plea, is still relevant.

Indeed, it has even been held by the U.S. Supreme Court in *Heck v. Humphrey*[11] that to recover damages for an alleged unconstitutional conviction or imprisonment or for other harm caused by actions whose unlawfulness could render a conviction or sentence invalid, a Sec. 1983 plaintiff must prove that the conviction has been reversed on direct appeal; expunged by executive order; declared invalid by a state tribunal authorized to make such determination; or called into question by the federal court's issuance of a writ of habeas corpus.

It has even been held, again by the Eastern Division of New York that a false arrest 1983 claim is barred, even if the plaintiff pled guilty to a reduced charge but then asserts the plea was not knowing or voluntary.[12]

Conclusion

The rule articulated in *Cameron* makes good sense, at least on the surface. As we all know as lawyers and judges, however, most criminal convictions result from a plea of guilty, unless there has been a suppression hearing on the legality or validity of the arrest and whether there was probable cause or a legally sufficient warrant issued. When these issues were never considered, and, in particular, whether probable cause existed was never scrutinized by the criminal court, when a plaintiff brings a Sec. 1983 claim under false arrest, his claim should not be precluded. Civil is not criminal. The burdens are different. Sec. 1983 is a federal statute with its own standards and laws and rules. *Cameron*, in the view of this writer, is mistaken in that it ignores the plain fact that pleas do not address the validity of the arrest and, at times, nor do suppression hearings, or even trials. If a plaintiff has been injured and wishes to bring a Sec 1983 action, he should be allowed to also do so whatever his decision as to a plea. He should be allowed to civilly litigate and have considered the issue of his arrest that was never considered. The issue of probable cause should not be barred by a criminal conviction and the 1983 plaintiff should be permittted to have his day in court and obtain the redress he deserves.

4. The State Danger Doctrine

Actions brought pursuant to 42 U.S.C § 1983, the Reconstruction Civil Rights Statute are frequently encountered on the federal court docket. These cases involve deprivations of constitutional rights based upon the acts of state officers who act unlawfully under color of law. The cases are varied and may involve police actions with the use of excessive force, inflicting injury, or cases otherwise denominated false arrest cases. Where a state is sued, state officials not be held personally liable merely because they were in a position of authority. There must be a showing of proof that the state officials were somehow personally responsible and involved in the violation of the plaintiff's Constitutional rights.[1]

Thus, some degree of personal involvement must be shown or alleged to sustain a § 1983 action for the violation of civil rights where state officials are named defendants. The rule is stated fully in *Colon v. Coughlin.*[2] In that case, the United States Court of Appeals for the Second Circuit held that the personal involvement of a supervisory defendant can be shown by evidence that (1) the defendant participated directly in the alleged constitutional violation; (2) the defendant, after being informed of the violation through a report or memorandum failed to remedy the wrong; (3) the defendant created a policy or custom under which unconstitutional practices occurred or allowed the continuance of such policy or custom; (4) the defendant was grossly negligent in supervising subordinates who committed the wrongful acts; or (5) the defendant exhibited deliberate indifference to the rights of victims by failing to act on information indicating that unconstitutional acts were occurring.

Under the criteria set forth in *Colon*, it is difficult to impose personal liability on state officials.

The federal courts, however, and the United States Supreme Court have devised a doctrine whereby, under certain conditions, if it can be shown that a great danger was created that would not otherwise have existed, and those state actions foreseeably lead to an individual's deprivation of his life, liberty, or property, a constitutional infringement may be found. The doctrine was originally articulated by the United States Supreme Court in *DeShaney v. Winnebago Cty. D.S.S.*[3] *DeShaney* held that the Constitution can be interpreted to protect its citizens from harm where the state acts in a manner that places a person in extraordinary danger. More specifically, the United States Supreme Court in *De-*

Shaney considered whether the due process clause of the 14th Amendment imposed upon the state an affirmative duty to protect an individual against private violence where a special relationship exists between the state and the individual. The Court found that the special relationship which would impose such an affirmative duty existed only in certain limited circumstances, such as when the state takes a person into its custody and holds him there against his will.

In *DeShaney*, however, the Supreme Court of the United States stated that a constitutional violation might occur despite the absence of a special relationship when the state plays some part in the creation of the dangers and renders the plaintiff more vulnerable to them.

Indeed, two United States Court of Appeals decisions predating *DeShaney*, recognize the state-created danger theory as a basis for establishing a Constitutional claim under § 1983.[4]

This doctrine was further and specifically developed and articulated in *Dwares v. City of New York.*[5] In *Dwares*, a rally was held on July 4, 1989, in Washington Square Park in New York City. At the rally there was a demonstration that included the burning of an American flag. Mr. Dwares did not physically participate in that event, but attended the demonstration and voiced his support for those who did. Also present in the park at the time of the rally was a group of· individuals known as "skinheads" including a Mr. Kreitman, who were all known by the city police department in general, and to the defendant officers in particular, to have a history of racism and engaging in violent attacks on individuals engaged in lawfully protected First Amendment activity.

At 6 p.m. on July 4, Mr. Dwares, who was demonstrating in support of the flag burning, was physically attacked by Mr. Kreitman and other skinheads who repeatedly hit him on the head with a bottle. Finally, after being hit and chased for some 10 minutes Mr. Dwares escaped with head and face bloodied and took refuge in a nearby EMS vehicle. The attack occurred in the presence of the defendant police officers, but the officers made no attempt to intervene or protect Mr. Dwares or arrest the assaulting "skinheads."

The Second Circuit reviewed the Supreme Court's decision in *DeShaney*, where the Supreme Court had held that the State had no duty to protect a child under the Due Process Clause against beatings by his father, even though the State had received reports that the father physically abused the child. Again, analyzing *DeShaney*, the Court noted that while the State may have been aware .of the dangers the child faced, it played no part in their creation, nor did it do anything to render the child more vulnerable to them.

Applying this rationale to the facts in *Dwares*, the Second Circuit ruled that, even though the plaintiff in *Dwares* alleged that the police officers had failed to act upon reports of past violence, and that this would not create a constitutional difficulty, if true, there was also an allegation that the officers had in some way assisted in creating or increasing the danger to the victim and that this implicated and compromised the victim's constitutional rights.

More specifically, the *Dwares* Court concluded that the officers aided and abetted the deprivation of Mr. Dwares' civil rights by allowing him to be subject to the prolonged assault in their presence without interfering in the attack. It is significant that in *Dwares* the alleged failure of the officers to prevent harm despite their knowledge of what was occurring was the basis of the constitutional violation, and not any action of the officers in affirmatively causing harm.

Rodriguez Cirilo v. Garcia, 908 F. Supp; $5 (D. Puerto Rico, 1995) is useful on this issue. There the Puerto Rico District Court held that the state may be liable if the state actors have done anything to make an individual more vulnerable to the harms of a private actor.[6]

Armijo v. Wagon Mound Public Schools[7] is also highly relevant. In that case, after being suspended and driven home without parental notification, a special education student at a public school committed suicide. His parents brought an action against the school district and various school officials. The Court held that state officials can be liable for the acts of third parties where those officials created the danger that caused the harm. The Court, citing *Uhlrig v. Harder,*[8] noted that, in that case, the danger creation theory must be predicated on reckless or intentional injury-causing state action which shocks the conscience. Further noting that the 10th Circuit in *Uhlrig* established a five part test, the Court specifically stated that the plaintiff must also show that the charged state entity and the charged individual defendant actors increased the plaintiff's vulnerability to the danger in some way. The 10th Circuit concluded in *Armijo* that the five part test in *Uhlrig* was satisfied and, in particular, that two of the individual defendants, Schutz and Herrera, increased the· risk of harm to *Armijo*.

Monfils v. Taylor[9] is also helpful. In that case the 7th Circuit Court of Appeals held that the evidence was sufficient for the jury to conclude that the Deputy Police Chief placed the anonymous. informant in a position of danger greater than he otherwise would have faced in violation of the informant's substantive due process rights, by not preventing release of the tape recording of the informant's tip. The Court held that the Deputy Chief knew of the increased danger and assured the Assistant District Attorney that he would make sure the tape was not released, but did not follow through.[10]

Conclusion

This short analysis of the State Danger Doctrine reveals two strands or threads. First, the Federal Courts in applying this doctrine do not limit its applicability to affirmative acts placing a plaintiff in serious danger. They also apply it where the State is indifferent, negligent, or reckless in allowing danger to happen. In short, the doctrine does not apply only when the State assists in creating or increasing the danger, but also where the State demonstrates indifference and fails to act. This doctrine allows the plaintiff who would otherwise be without recourse to successfully bring the State to task where it creates danger, assists in danger occurring, or allows danger to happen through private actors through indifference and carelessness. Without this doctrine, State officials could successfully escape their inaction, negligence, recklessness and, of course, affirmative actions.

In sum, this doctrine is a saving doctrine for plaintiffs whose constitutional rights, though violated, would have no recourse or hope against State officials who failed to act.

This article previously appeared in an edition of The Nassau Lawyer, a publication of the Nassau County Bar Association, and is being reprinted here with the permission of The Nassau County Bar Association.

Notes

1. A Point of Pleading in 1983 Civil Rights Actions

1. Every person who, under color of any statute, ordinance, regulation, custom or usage, of any State or Territory, subjects or causes to be subjected, any citizen of the United States or other person within the jurisdiction thereof to the deprivation of any rights, privileges or immunities secured by the Constitution and Laws, shall be liable to the party injured in an action at law, suit in equity, or other proper proceeding for redress.

2. . . . local governing bodies, therefore can be sued directly under § 1983 for monetary, declaratory or injunctive relief where, as here, the action that is alleged to be unconstitutional implements or executes a policy statement, ordinance, regulation or decision officially adopted and promulgated by that body's officers. Moreover, although the touchstone of the § 1983 action against government body is an allegation that official policy is responsible for a deprivation of rights protected by the Constitution, local governments, like every other § 1983 'person', by the very terms of the statute, may be sued for constitutional deprivations visited pursuant to governmental 'custom' even though such a custom has not received formal approval through the body's official decision making channels. . . . Congress did not intend municipalities to be held liable unless action pursuant to official municipal policy of some nature caused a constitutional tort. . . . We conclude that a municipality cannot be held liable solely because it employs a tortfeasor. . . . [The statute] plainly imposes liability on a government that, under color of some official policy 'causes' an employee to violate another's constitutional rights. . . . We conclude, therefore that a local government may not be sued under § 1983 for an injury inflicted solely by its employees or agents. Instead it is when execution of government's policy or custom, whether made by its lawmakers, or by those whose edicts or acts may fairly be said to represent official policy, inflicts the injury that the government as an entity is responsible under § 1983. . . . *Monell v. Dept. of Social Services, supra,* 2035 at 2036, 2037 and 2038.

Cf. *Quem v. Jordan,* 440 U.S. 332, 99 S.Ct. 1139, 39 L.Ed.2d 358 (1979), where the Supreme Court held that States could not be sued under Sec. 1983, but could be sued if the State consents and *Knight v. Carlson,* 478 F. Supp. 55 (B.D. Cal. 1979) where it was held that counties could be sued under Sec. 1983.

3. For other Federal District Courts and circuits following *Monell*, see *Holland v. Rubin*, 460 F. Supp. 1051 (E.D.N.Y. 1978); *Smith v. Ambrogio*, 456 F. Supp. 1130 (D. Conn. 1978); *Reimer v. Short* (5th Cir. 1978).

4. It is true that, on application of the plaintiff or the court sua sponte in the face of a motion to dismiss under Rule 12b(6) of the Federal Rules of Civil Procedure, the Section 1983 complaint might be amended to properly plead the involvement of the custom or policy of the municipality in the deprivation of the plaintiff's civil rights. There is no assurance however that the application will be made by the court or if made by the plaintiff that it will be granted. Indeed this writer has had the experience of seeing on his application, a Section 1983 complaint dismissed by a Federal District against a municipality on the basis of the *Monell* holding and the dismissal affirmed by the U.S. Court of Appeals for the Second Circuit, all in the absence of an application by the plaintiff to amend this complaint, or a motion by the court to that end.

5. It should be noted that, under *Bivens v. Six Unknown Named Agents of the Federal Bureau of Narcotics*, 403 U.S. 388, 91 S.Ct. 1999, 29 L.Ed.2d 619 (1971), a direct action for the violation of constitutional rights might be brought by an aggrieved plaintiff against a municipality and its officials. If a direct constitutional action under *Bivens* is brought against a municipality, the same rules of pleading apply as applied in a Section 1983 action, that the custom or policy of the municipality is included in the deprivation of the plaintiff's civil rights, making the municipality an active wrongdoer. See, *Turpin Mallets*, 579 F.2d 152 (2d Cir. 1978); *Ekland v. Hardiman*, 526 F. Supp. 941 (N.D. Ill. 1981).

The seriousness of the dismissal of a Section 1983 action or a *Bivens* action, under the Rule of *Monell*, is highlighted by the fact that any pendent tort claims attached, as it were, to the Section 1983 or *Bivens* complaint will also fall if the Section 1983 or *Bivens* claim is dismissed. See *United Mine Workers v. Gibbs, supra*, at 715; *Federman v. Empire Fire and Marine Inc. Co.*, 597 F.2d 798, 809 (2d Cir. 1979).

2. *"Official Policy" Under 42 U.S.C. Section 1983*

1. *Monell v. Dept. of Social Services of the City of New York*, 436 U.S. 658, 98 S.Ct. 2018, 56 L.Ed. 611 (1978); *Leonhard v. United States*, 633 F.2d 599 (2nd Cir. 1980); *Singleton v. City of New York*, 632 F.2d 185 (2nd Cir. 1980); Andrew J. Schatkin, "A Point of Pleading in 1983 Civil Rights Actions," *Brooklyn Barrister*, Vol. 35, No. 4, p. 131.

3. *False Arrest and Sec. 1983: A Short Analysis*

1. Ch. 22, Sec. 1, 17 Stat. 13 (1871).
2. 42 USC Sec. 1983.
3. 490 U.S. 386 (1989). See also *Tennessee v. Garner*, 471 U.S. 1 (1985).
4. 475 U.S. 312 (1986).
5. *Hygh v. Jacobs*, 961 F.2d 359, 368 (2d Cir. 1992).
6. 806 F. 2d 380 (2d Cir. 1987) cert. den. 481 U.S. 106, 107, S. Ct. 1984 (1987).
7. See also Schwartz; Sec. 1983 Claims and Defenses. 3rd Ed. Vol. 1A pp. 348·357.
8. 902 F. 2d 10 (8th Cir. 1990). See Schwartz; Sec. 1983 Claims and Defenses. 3rd Ed. Vol. I A p. 351.
9. 496 U.S. 356 (1992).
10. 778 F. Supp. 614 (E.D.N.Y. 1991). See also *Allison v. Farrell*, 2002 U.S. Dist. (Lexis 975).

11. 512 U.S. 477, 114 S. Ct. 2364 (1994). See also *Spies v. Brown*, 2002 U.S. Dist Lexis 4093 (E.D.N.Y. 2002); *Berman v. Turecki*, 885 F. Supp 528 (S.D.N.Y. 1995); *Morris v. Reynolds*, 264 F. 3rd 38 (2d Cir. 2001).

12. *Sealey v. Fishkin*, 1998 U.S. Dist. Lexis 20142 (E.D. N.Y. 1998).

4. The State Danger Doctrine

1. *Colon v. Coughlin*, 58 F. 3d 865 (2d Cir. 1995); *Wright v. Smith*, 21 F. 3d 496 (2d Cir. 1994); *Wright v. Smith*, 781 F. 2d 319 (2d Cir. 1986); *Estate of Phillips v. District of Columbia* (DDC 2003).

2. *Id.*

3. *DeShaney v. Winnebago County Dept. of Soc. Serv.*, 489 U.S. 189, 109 S. Ct. 998, 103 L. Ed. 2d 249 (1989).

4. See *Kneipp v. Tedder*, 95 F. 3d 1199, 1205 (3d Cir. 1996) citing *Cornelius v. Town of Highland Lake*, 880 F. 2d 348 (11th Cir. 1989), cert. denied, 494 U.S. 1066, 110 S. Ct. 1784, 108 1. Ed. 2d 785 (1990); *Wood v. Ostrander*, 879 F. 2d 583 (9th Cir. 1989), cert. denied 498 U.S. 938, 111 S. Ct. 341, 112 L. Ed. 2d 305 (1990); *Brown v. Grabowski*, 922 F. 2d 1097 (3d Cir. 1990), cert. denied 501 U.S. 1218, 111 S. Ct. 2827, 115 L. Ed. 2d 997 (1991).

5. *Dwares v. City of New York*, 985 F. 2d 94 (2d. cir. 1993).

6. *Rodriguez Cirilo v. Garcia*, 908 F. Supp. 8589 (D.P.R. 1995); See also *Frances-Colon v. Ramirez*, 107 F. 3d 62 (1st Cir. 1997); *Berman v. Turecki*, 885 F. Supp. 528 (S.D.N.Y 1995).

7. *Armijo v. Wagon Mound Public Schools*, 159 F. 3d 1253 (10th Cir. 1998).

8. *Uhlrig v. Harder*, 64 F. 3d 567 (10th Cir. 1995).

9. *Monfils v. Taylor*, 165 F. 3d 511 (7th Cir. 1998).

10. See also *Kallstrom v. City of Columbus*, 136 F. 3d 1055 (6th Cir. 1998) (Held: City's actions placed officers and their family members in special danger by substantially increasing the likelihood that a private actor would deprive them of their liberty interest in personal security. In affirmatively releasing private information from the officers' personnel files to defense counsel in the Russell case, the city's actions placed the personal safety of the officers and their family members in serious jeopardy. The Court held that the city either knew or clearly should have known that releasing the officers' addresses, phone numbers, and driver's licenses to defense counsel in the Russell case substantially increased the officers' and their families' vulnerability to private acts of vengeance. The Court held that the city's policy of freely releasing this information from the undercover officers' personnel files under these circumstances created a Constitutionally cognizable "special danger" giving rise to liability under §1983); See also *Morse v. Lower Merrion School District*, 132 F. 3d 902 (3d Cir. 1997) (Held: State danger doctrine applicable where Diana Morse, who worked at a daycare center, was permitted access to by a mentally deranged and homicidal third party. See also *Kneipp v. Tedder, supra*, where the United States Court of Appeals for the Third Circuit engaged in an intensive analysis of the special danger theory as the basis for establishing a Constitutional violation under 42 U.S.C §1983.

Introduction to Tort Law Reprinted Articles

These articles reprinted here cover fairly specific issues of Tort Law. One of them, on baseball liability, examines the liability of the baseball park or the team for foul balls that may injure a spectator during the course of a baseball game. Another article, "Loss of Consortium and Wrongful Death," examines the play and interaction between a Loss of Consortium Claim and a Wrongful Death Action. A third article examines the ever-present tort of the Intentional Infliction of Mental Distress.

Chapter 7
Tort Law Reprinted Articles

1. *Baseball Liability: Recent Developments*

A recent spate of appellate and trial court decisions have considered the question, with varying conclusions, of the duty, if any, owed to the spectator at a baseball game by the proprietor of the ball park and the professional sports team, and the precise scope of that duty.

It is the purpose of this article to trace the history of the legal duty, if any, owed by the proprietor of a ball park and/or the owner of the team fielded in that park to a spectator of a game at that park, indicate the most recent developments in this field of law, and offer an opinion with respect to future trends in the area.

The Past Law

It had long been the law of the State of New York that a spectator at a sporting event, such as a baseball game, assumed the risks necessarily incident to such game and could not recover in a negligence action for an injury suffered by reason of the assumption of this risk. The Court of Appeals gave its imprimatur to this general principle, to cite one example, in *Robert v. Deposit Cent. School District,* 13 N.Y.2d 809 241 N.Y.S.2d 843 (1963). In *Robert*, a high school student's father brought an action against a school district for injuries sustained by a student when she was struck by a baseball while watching a baseball game played on school grounds. The Trial Court denied the motion of the school district for summary judgment dismissing the complaint on the ground that the student had assumed the risk of her injuries as a matter of law. The school district appealed. The Appellate Division, Third Department, reversed the order of the Trial Court and granted summary judgment to the defendant school district, holding that the student-plaintiff had assumed the risk of being struck and injured by a wildly thrown ball. The Court of Appeals affirmed without comment the order of the Appellate Division, Third Department.

Baker v. Topping, 15 A.D.2d 193, 222 N.Y.S.2d 658 (3rd Dept. 1961) is also relevant. In *Baker,* the plaintiff, a spectator, was struck by a ball hit by one of the players in a baseball game and brought a negligence action against the owners and operators of the Yankee Baseball Club and of Yankee Stadium and against the corporation supplying ushers to the stadium. The plaintiff had been to the Yankee Stadium six times before the day in which he was struck by a baseball as he was being conducted by an usher through an aisle leading to his reserved seat in the unscreened section of the stadium, on the first base line. When he purchased his ticket, he merely asked for a good seat, not requesting one behind the protective screen. The Trial Court granted the defendant's motion for summary judgment dismissing the complaint, and the plaintiff appealed. The Appellate Division, Third Department, affirmed the Trial Court's dismissal of the plaintiff's complaint, holding that the plaintiff, as a spectator in a baseball game, assumed the risk of being struck by a foul or wildly thrown ball when sitting elsewhere than behind the screen in back of home plate and so was precluded from recovering in a negligence action, as a matter of law, under the doctrine of the assumption of the risk.

The law was clear then in both *Robert* and *Baker* that a spectator who, while attending a baseball game, professional or otherwise, was struck by a wildly thrown or batted ball, whether he was seated or was in the process of being conducted by an usher to his seat, unless he was seated in the screened area behind home plate, assumed the risk of being struck by such a ball and was barred, as a matter of law, from pursuing a negligence action against the owners or operators of the stadium or field, by reason of such injury sustained by him, under the doctrine of the assumption of risk. See also *Blackhall v. Albany Baseball and Amusement Co., Inc.,* 157 Misc. 801, 285 N.Y.S. 695 (Albany County Court 1936); *O'Bryan v. O'Connor,* 59 A.D.2d 219, 399 N.Y.S.2d 272 (3rd Dept. 1977); *Adonnino v. Village of Mount Morris,* 171 Misc. 383, 12 N.Y.S.2d 658 (Sup. Ct., Livingston County, 1939); *Zeitz v. Cooperstown Baseball Centennial, Inc.,* 29 N.Y.S.2d 56 (Sup. Court, Westchester County, 1941); *Bennet v. Board of Education of the City of New York,* 16 A.D.2d 651, 226 N.Y.S.2d 593 (2nd Dept. 1962), aff'd 13 N.Y.2d 1104, 246 N.Y.S.2d 634 (1963); *Hornstein v. State of New York,* 30 A.D.2d 1012, 294 N.Y.S.2d 320 (3rd Dept. 1968); *Kozera v. Town of Hamburg,* 40 A.D.2d 934, 337 N.Y.S.2d 761 (4th Dept. 1972); *Cadieux v. Board of Ed. of City School Dist. of City of Schenectady,* 25 A.D.2d 579, 266 N.Y.S.2d 895 (3rd Dept. 1966); Warren, Negligence in the New York Courts, Volume 3, Persons Injured, § 3.02[2]; Warren, Negligence in the New York Courts, Volume 4A, Places, § 1.02-1.03.

There is no doubt that formerly, under the overwhelming weight of case law authority of this state, there could be no recovery by a spectator injured in an unscreened area in the stands at a baseball game by a wildly thrown or batted ball unless the spectator was in the screened area behind home plate, established for his protection, since this spectator was barred from recovery in a negligence action under the doctrine that he had assumed the risk of this type of accident and injury.

The Current Law

With the passage, however, of C.P.L.R. § 1411, entitled "damages recoverable when contributory negligence of assumption of risk is established," the defenses of contributory negligence and assumption of the risk can no longer serve to completely bar the recovery of a potential plaintiff in an action seeking redress for personal injuries.

As a result of this statute, the Court of Appeals was compelled to define, or rather redefine, the legal duty owed by the proprietor of a baseball stadium to the spectators attending its games, since the doctrine of assumption of the risk no longer served to bar a spectator in the stands, but not seated in the screened area behind home plate, from obtaining a recovery for his injuries, but only could reduce his potential recovery, under the doctrine of comparative negligence.

It was in *Akins v. Glens Falls City School District,* 53 N.Y.2d 352, 441 N.Y.S.2d 644 (1981) that the Court of Appeals considered and defined the duty owed by the proprietor of a baseball park to the spectators therein in light of C.P.L.R. § 1411, which had eliminated the assumption of risk as a complete bar to recovery under this section. In *Akins,* the plaintiff attended a high school baseball game that was being played on a field owned and maintained by defendant, the Glens Falls City School District. The field was equipped with a backstop 24 feet high and 50 feet wide, located 60 feet behind home plate and positioned in front of bleachers that could seat 120 adults, and had additional standing room. Two chain link fences three feet in height ran from each end of the backstop along the base lines to a distance approximately 60 feet behind first and third base.

The plaintiff arrived at the game 10 minutes after its commencement and chose to view the game from a position behind the 3-foot-high fence along the third base line, 10 to 15 feet from the end of the backstop and 60 feet from home plate. The plaintiff, in the absence of seating facilities in this area, had to stand, along with a number of other spectators. There is no proof that the screened bleachers behind home plate were filled or that the plaintiff was prevented from watching the game behind the backstop. In the course of the game, the plaintiff was struck in the eye by a foul ball, causing her alleged serious and permanent injury. The plaintiff then initiated an action against the defendant School District, sounding in negligence, alleging that the defendant School District failed to provide safe and proper screening devices along the base lines of its field. After trial, the jury returned a verdict in the plaintiff's favor of $100,000.00, apportioning 65% of the fault to the defendant School District and 35% to the plaintiff. The Appellate Division affirmed. *Akins v. Glens Falls City School District,* 75 A.D.2d 239, 429 N.Y.S.2d 467 (3rd Dept. 1980). The majority in the Appellate Division held there was no error of law holding that the defendant, having screened the area behind home plate, had fulfilled its legal duty to the plaintiff and could not be held liable in negligence when the plaintiff herself had selected a position outside of the screened area.

These were the facts and the history of *Akins* prior to its consideration by the Court of Appeals. The court initially noted that the doctrine of the assumption of the risk had had, previous to the case before it, wide application in a number of cases involving spectators struck my misguided baseballs, but that these cases arose before the adoption of the comparative negligence rule, C.P.L.R. § 1411, and that the doctrine of the assumption of the risk formerly served a complete bar to a plaintiff's cause of action, without regard to the degree of care that must be exercised by the owner of a baseball park. The court further stated that, aside from some few lower court decisions, there was no case law per se which defined the duty of care owed by the proprietor of a baseball field to its spectators. The Court of Appeals then, in this case, proceeded to precisely and exactly define the duty owed by the proprietor of a baseball stadium to a spectator therein, with respect to wildly thrown or batted balls which may, in the course of a game, strike and possibly injure him.

The court stated that the owner of a baseball field, like the owner or occupier of land, is under a duty to exercise reasonable care under all the circumstances, but that the scope of due care required by the owner of a baseball field does not demand that the entire playing field be screened and that, in fact, many spectators may prefer to sit in an area unobstructed by fences or protective netting, and that the proprietor of a baseball park has a legitimate interest in catering to these desires. The court, then, narrowed and defined the critical question of the duty owed by the proprietor of a baseball park to a spectator, with respect to wildly thrown or batted balls which may happen to strike and injure that spectator, to be

> what amount of screen must be provided by an owner of a baseball field before it will be found to have discharged its duty of care to its spectators. *Akins v. Glens Falls City School District, supra,* at 646.

The court proceeded to review the standards of other jurisdictions defining the duty of ball park proprietor to protect its spectators from stray balls. It concluded that it would adopt the rule that the owner or proprietor of a baseball stadium must screen the most dangerous section of the field, the area behind home plate, and the screening must be sufficient for those spectators who may reasonably be expected to seek and sit in such protected seating on an ordinary occasion. The court held thus that the scope of an owner's duty to provide protective screening for the patrons of a baseball game held at its field is to screen the most dangerous section of the field, the area behind home plate, and that this screening must be sufficient for those spectators who may be reasonably anticipated to desire protective seats on an ordinary occasion, concluding that

> we hold that, in the exercise of reasonable care, the proprietor of a ballpark need only provide screening for the area of the field behind home plate where

the danger of being struck by a ball is the greatest. Moreover, such screening must be of sufficient extent to provide adequate protection for as many spectators as may reasonably be expected to desire such seating in the course of an ordinary game. In so holding, we merely recognize the practical realities of this sporting event. As mentioned earlier, many spectators attending such exhibitions desire to watch the contest taking place on the field without having their view obstructed or obscured by a fence or protective net. Administering to those desires, while at the same time providing adequate protection in the most dangerous area of the field for those spectators who wish to avail themselves of it, a proprietor fulfills its duty of reasonable care under such circumstances. . . . We do not attempt to prescribe precisely what, as a matter of law, are the required dimensions of a baseball fields backstop. Nor do we suggest that where the adequacy of the screening in terms of protecting the area behind home plate properly is put in issue, the case should not be submitted to the jury. We merely hold that where a proprietor of a ballpark furnishes screening for the area of the field behind home plate where the danger of being struck by a ball is greatest and that screening is of sufficient extent to provide adequate protection for as many spectators as may reasonably be expected to desire such seating in the course of an ordinary game, the proprietor fulfills the duty of care imposed by law and, therefore, cannot be liable in negligence. *Akins v. Glens Falls City School District, supra*, at 647.

The court, as a further basis for the statement of the broad rule of law in this case, noted that the plaintiff in *Akins* presented no evidence that the backstop was inadequate in terms of providing protection for the area behind home plate where there was a likelihood that a spectator might be struck by a misguided baseball, or that there was an insufficient number of screened seats for those who might reasonably be expected to desire such protection. Under these facts, the court went on to state that, inasmuch as the defendant provided adequate protection for the spectators, whether seated or standing, in the area behind home plate, liability could not be imposed on the School District for failing to provide additional screening along the base lines of the field where the risk of being struck by a wildly batted or thrown ball was less.

In a final word, the Court of Appeals stated that on the facts of the case before it, as a matter of law, the defendant School District fulfilled its duty of reasonable care to the plaintiff, and therefore there was no question of negligence for the jury's consideration. *Akins v. Glens Falls City School District, supra*, at 647, 648.

The holding of *Akins* is clear and not subject to interpretation. It is, quite simply, that the proprietor of a baseball park, in pursuit of fulfilling its duty of care owed to spectators therein who may be struck by a wildly batted or thrown ball in the course of a baseball game, need only provide a protective screening in the area behind home plate, where the danger of being struck by a ball is greatest, and that the screening must be of sufficient extent to provide protection for those spectators who may reasonably be expected to desire such seating in the course of an ordinary game. This, according to the Court of Appeals, defines the duty of care, imposed by law, upon the proprietor of a baseball park to its spectators. To the extent such protective screening exists in the area of home plate, as prescribed by the Court of Appeals in *Akins,* an owner or proprietor of a baseball park cannot be held liable in negligence for spectators struck and injured by a wildly batted or thrown ball, and liability

> may not be imposed on the school district for failing to provide additional screening along the base lines of its field where the risk of being struck by a stray ball was considerably less. (Accord *Cates v. Cincinnati Exhibition Co.,* 215 N.C. 64, 1 S.E. 2d 131; *Curtis v. Portland Baseball Club,* 130 Or. 93, 279 P. 277; see also, *Leek v. Tacoma Baseball Club,* 38 Wash. 2d 262, 229 P. 2d 329, *supra.*). *Akins v. Glens Falls City School District, supra,* at 647.

The rule in holding of *Akins,* under any interpretation, is clear: simply that the sole duty of care owed by the proprietor of a baseball park to a spectator in that park is to provide such protective screening in the area behind home plate of sufficient extent for the spectators who may reasonably be expected to desire such seating in the course of a game. No screening is required, under the *Akins* rule, along the base lines where the bulk of the spectators will be seated, and so, by inevitable implication, no duty is owed to those spectators at all. *Akins* would seem to be clear in its holding and, to coin a phrase, if it does not hold the field on this question, it would appear to, at least, clear it.

Recent trial and appellate court decisions, however, have cast confusion and doubt, at least to this writer, on the lucid rule of law set forth in *Akins.* The first case was *Davidoff v. The Metropolitan Baseball Club, Inc. and The City of New York,* N.Y.L.J. 7/13/82, p. 6, col. 1. *Davidoff* was a personal injury action in which the plaintiff, Jennifer Davidoff, alleged in her complaint that on May 25, 1979, while attending a baseball game in Shea Stadium in Queens, and while seated in the stands behind the first base line, she was struck in the face by a baseball hit in the course of the game and was seriously injured. She further alleged that her injury was solely due to the negligence of the defendants, the Mets and the City of New York, in failing to provide adequate safeguards to spectators and in failing to warn spectators of the dangers of batted balls.

Examinations before trial[1] were had of the Metropolitan Baseball Club, Inc., by Mr. John McCarthy, the press manager of Shea Stadium and its manager on May 25, 1979, the date of the accident, and the plaintiffs, Richard Davidoff and his daughter, the infant plaintiff, Jennifer Davidoff. Mr. McCarthy stated, in his examination, that on May 25, 1979, he became aware of the fact that a young person was struck by a baseball in the course of a night game at Shea Stadium and that the plaintiff, Jennifer Davidoff, was the person struck by the batted ball and had been sitting behind the first base line. Mr. McCarthy also testified that, behind home plate, there was a protective netting and that behind the first base line, where the plaintiff was seated at the time of the accident, was fence made of galvanized steel 3 feet wide by 3 ½ feet high.

At the plaintiff Jennifer Davidoff's examination before trial, she testified that on May 25, 1979, she was struck by a baseball at a night game at Shea Stadium while seated in a box seat behind first base line. Mr. Richard Davidoff, the father of the plaintiff, testified in his examination that he too had gone to professional baseball games at Shea Stadium and that his daughter, the plaintiff, Jennifer Davidoff, had attended the baseball game on May 25, 1979, at Shea Stadium with his knowledge and permission.

On March 11, 1982, the defendant, the Metropolitan Baseball Club, Inc., moved, pursuant to C.P.L.R. 3212, for summary judgment against the plaintiffs, a motion which was joined in by the defendant, City of New York.

In supporting affidavits by Mr. Jeffrey Silberfeld, the attorney for the defendant, Metropolitan Baseball Club, Inc., and Mr. McCarthy, the manager of Shea Stadium at the time of the incident, it was argued by defendant Mets that, based upon the undisputed fact that Shea Stadium had, at the time of the accident on May 25, 1979, and continues to have a screened area behind home plate 50 feet to 130 feet wide and 10 feet high, and that the screened area was known to the plaintiff, who had previously attended games at Shea Stadium and other stadiums, and that the plaintiff, Jennifer Davidoff, had sat in a box seat guarded by a 3 foot high by 3 foot wide fence and that, based on the decision of the Court of Appeals in *Akins,* the plaintiff had failed to state a cause of action.

In particular, Mr. McCarthy, in his affidavit in support of the motion of the defendant Mets for summary judgment, testified that the seating behind the home plate area contained 408 seats, that the amount of seating was more than adequate to provide for the number of spectators who would be reasonably expected to desire such seats in the course of a game, and, while he was present at almost every Mets game, he personally saw empty seats in the screened area behind home plate. He further stated that he had reviewed the records of season ticket holders and found that the area behind home plate was not totally occupied on the day in question, that tickets were available to the general public, and that this was true on May 25, 1979.

In an order and decision dated July 8, 1982, the Honorable Manuel A. Gomez, Judge of the Supreme Court, New York County, denied the motion of the defendants for summary judgment. Mr. Justice Gomez initially reviewed the facts of the case noting that the 14 year-old plaintiff, on May 25, 1979, attended a game at Shea Stadium with her brother and two friends with the knowledge and permission of her father, that she sat in the first base row in a box seat along the first base line, that a 3½ foot fence separated her from the playing field, that the tickets were a gift from her uncle, that she had previously attended 5 professional baseball games, that she was a baseball fan who watched baseball games on television, and that she suffered a permanent loss of vision in her left eye as a result of this accident. Judge Gomez also noted, in his review of the facts of this case, that the defendant, New York Mets, fielded the New York Mets baseball team, leased Shea Stadium from the stadium's owner, the City of New York, and that both defendants operated, maintained, and controlled the facility.

After this review of the facts, Judge Gomez went on to summarize the applicable law with respect to the duty of a proprietor of a baseball field to its spectators, as stated in the *Akins v. Glens Falls City School District* case, *supra.* Judge Gomez stated that the owner or operator of a baseball field, under the

Akins holding, is not an insurer of the safety of its spectators, but is only under a duty to exercise reasonable care under the circumstances. The owner of a baseball field, he stated, is not under a duty of care to screen the entire playing field but, in the exercise of reasonable care, need only provide screening for the part of the field behind home plate where danger of being struck by a ball is greatest. This screening, under *Akins,* he stated, must be of such extent as to provide adequate protection for as many spectators as may reasonably be expected to desire such seating in the course of a baseball game.

After this review of the facts of the *Davidoff* case and the law as set forth in *Akins,* Judge Gomez held that the question of the sufficiency of the screening could not be determined from the papers submitted, but was within the province of the jury. Judge Gomez also stated that it was a question of fact for the jury whether the defendants should have provided additional screening along the base lines of the field where the risk of being struck by a stray ball is great, since the manager of Shea Stadium stated in his examination before trial an affidavit in support of the defendant Mets' motion for summary judgment that the area behind home plate was protected by a wire netting, that seats in the protected area were available to the public on May 25, 1979, and that there was no question but that adequate protection existed on that date for the spectators seated in the area behind home plate. Hence, the trial court concluded that there was a question of fact whether the defendant Mets should have provided additional screening along the base lines of the field where the risk of being struck by a batted ball was greatest.

Finally, Mr. Justice Gomez noted that a spectator at a sporting event such as a baseball game, accepts the obvious danger incidental to the game so long as the risk is not unduly enhanced by the owner of the ball park and that there was a question whether the defendant enhanced that risk by inviting the plaintiff to sit in an area which should allegedly be screened, and that this was also a question of fact for the jury that precluded the granting of the defendant's motion.

Judge Gomez, thus, in his decision, claimed as the basis and ground for denying the motion of the defendant for summary judgment, that three issues of fact existed in the case: (1) whether the protective screen behind home plate was sufficient; (2) whether the defendant should have provided additional screening along the base lines of the field; and (3) whether the defendant enhanced the risk of harm to the plaintiff by inviting her to sit in an area that allegedly should have been screened.

It is the view of this writer that the bases on which Judge Gomez grounded his decision denying the defendants' motion for summary judgment not only totally misconstrued the clear holding of the Court of Appeals in *Akins,* but failed utterly to take account of it at all. The clear and unassailable law in *Akins* is that the duty of care of the proprietor of the baseball park to the spectators attending games is to screen the area behind home plate of sufficient extent to provide adequate protection for as many spectators as may reasonably be expected to desire such seating in the course of a game. When this sort of screening exists, the legal duty of care owed by the proprietor of a ball park to the spectators attending games therein is fulfilled. Nothing more than this need be done by the proprietor of a baseball park under the *Akins* rationale. Judge Gomez, in his decision, found facts that compel the case to go to the jury. Yet, the salient and uncontroverted facts in this case are that the plaintiff was sitting in a box seat along the first base line and not in the screened area behind home plate. Indeed, Judge Gomez so noted this fact in his decision and went on to state that

> the manager of Shea Stadium stated in an examination before trial that the area behind home plate is protected by a pie-shaped galvanized wire netting. Furthermore, in an affidavit submitted in support of the motion he additionally states that seats in the protected area were available to the general public for the May 25, 1979 game.

Judge Gomez in fact concluded that adequate protection was provided for the spectators seated in the area behind home plate.

In short, Judge Gomez admits in his decision, first, that the plaintiff, at the time of the accident and injury, was seated along the first base line and, second, that the area behind home plate was sufficiently protected by a wire netting. Hence, under these facts as admitted by Judge Gomez in his decision, the questions of fact he raises are not questions of fact.

Two more recent trial court decisions, apparently, more clearly adhere to the *Akins* rule, calling into question and, indeed reversing, the rationale, wisdom, and truth of the trial court's decision in *Davidoff*.

Clapman v. City of New York, N.Y.L.J., p. 13, Col 4, 11/24/82, like *Davidoff*, was a motion for summary judgment brought by the defendants City of New York, the owner of Yankee Stadium, its lessee the New York Yankees, and the architect of the Stadium against the plaintiff, a baseball fan injured while viewing a game at Yankee Stadium on July 21, 1977.

The facts of the case, as set forth in the decision of Mr. J. Cotton, were that the plaintiff, David Chapman, on the evening of July 21, 1977, was a spectator at a baseball game at Yankee Stadium. He came as a guest of the European American Bank and was seated in one of their box seats in the second row of field seats, near first base and the Yankee Dugout. The plaintiff was struck in the left eye in the course of the second game of a doubleheader and, as a result of this accident, lost the sight of his left eye. He and his wife thereafter commenced a personal injury action against the defendants City of New York, The New York Yankees, and the architect of the Stadium, Maligan-Praeger, Inc. The plaintiffs complained that the defendants negligently constructed and designed the stadium by failing to provide protective screening, not only in the area of the backstop, but also in the area of the Yankee Dugout near first base. The defendants denied any negligence as a matter of law, under the *Akins* rule, and moved to dismiss the plaintiffs' complaint under that decision.

Mr. J. Cotton initially held that the uncontested documentary evidence revealed that the spectator seats around the home plate area were protected by a metallic screen and that the plaintiff was seated 3 and ½ sections away from the screened area in an unprotected area.

The Court went on to observe that if the plaintiffs' accident had occurred prior to September 1, 1975, the doctrine of the assumption of the risk would have served to totally bar the plaintiffs' cause of action whatever the degree of care exercised by the owner of the ball park, and that since the instant case arose after the adoption of the comparative negligence rule under C.P.L.R. Section 1411, the rule of assumption of the risk could not serve to bar the plaintiffs' recovery.

The Court then went on to review and apply the Court of Appeals decision in *Akins v. Glens Fall City School District, supra,* holding that, inasmuch as the area behind home plate was in fact screened and the plaintiff was seated elsewhere, the defendants had fulfilled, as a matter of law, their duties of care to the plaintiff, and so, the plaintiffs' complaint must be dismissed under *Akins.*

By way of an addendum to this decision, Mr. J. Cotton rejected the plaintiffs' argument that liability could be imposed on the defendants because there were no available seats in the protected area adjacent to which he was seated, since the plaintiff never requested an usher to change his seat, did not attempt to sit elsewhere, and, in any event, the defendants were not required to provide protected seats for all who might apply for them, but only seats in a protected area for as many patrons as might be expected to request them on ordinary occasions.[2]

The *Clapman* decision, in the opinion of this writer, correctly interprets the holding in *Akins,* namely that when a spectator is not seated behind the protective screen at home plate, no legal duty is owed him, and so no liability can attach to the proprietor of a baseball park, its lessee, or even its architect.

The trial Court in *Uzdavines v. Metropolitan Baseball Club, Inc.,* 454 N.Y.S.2d 238 (Civil Court of the City of New York, Queens County, 1982), also considered the issue of the duty owed by the proprietor of a baseball park to its spectators. In *Uzdavines,* the plaintiff alleged that on July 5, 1978, while seated in a Box Section 40 feet behind home plate, some 3 or 4 rows back from the playing field fence, adjacent to her husband, son and daughter-in-law, she was struck in the face by a foul ball, which, she stated, ripped through a hole in the protective netting behind home plate, causing her injury. The plaintiff predicated her complaint on the theories of common law negligence and on the doctrine of res ipsa loquitur. The trial was bifurcated and the court held, after hearing all the testimony, that there was no triable issue of fact as to the plaintiffs' contributory negligence, pleaded by the defendant under New York's comparative negligence law, and directed a verdict in favor of the plaintiff in that respect.

The court also granted the third-party defendant City of New York's motion to dismiss the third-party complaint of the Metropolitan Baseball Club, Inc., against it on the ground that the indemnification and insurance sections of the case between the City of New York and the Metropolitan Baseball Club, Inc., rendered null and void any lawsuit by the Mets against the City of New York.

At the conclusion of the trial and the Court's charge on the plaintiff's two theories of the lawsuit, the jury, by a vote of 5 to 1, did not find the Mets negligent under the theory of common law negligence but did find the defendant negligent, by a unanimous vote, under the theory of res ipsa loquitur. The plaintiff moved to set aside the finding of the jury that the defendant was not negligent on a common law theory, as against the weight of the evidence, and moved for a directed verdict in favor of the plaintiff under the common law theory of negligence, while the defendant moved to set aside the verdict of the jury, fixing the defendant's liability under res ipsa loquitur, as against the weight of the facts and law.

The Court denied both the plaintiff's and the defendant's motions. What is of great import in this decision, however, are not the precise issues it considered, but the fact that the Court, albeit in dicta, held the duty owed by the defendant Baseball Club to the plaintiff-spectator, struck and injured by a batted foul ball, was fully defined and set forth by the Court of Appeals in *Akins*, which, as has been so often stated in this article, held that the sole and delimited duty owed by the proprietor of a baseball club to a spectator is to screen the most dangerous section for the spectators who might be expected to desire such protective seating on an ordinary occasion, *Uzdavines v. Metropolitan Baseball Club, supra*, at 244, 245.

The Court, however, in *Uzdavines*, even extended *Akins*, stating that the duty, however limited, of reasonable care owed by the proprietor of a baseball park to a spectator includes a duty to see that the protective netting around home plate is safe for its intended use and free of defects. The Court, however, in *Uzdavines* failed, it should be noted, to state or even imply, as the *Davidoff* trial Court did, that the proprietor's duty of care to a spectator included a duty to warn or a duty to provide protective netting beyond the home plate area.

Epilogue

If there was any doubt on the issue of the duty of care owed by the proprietor of a baseball park to its spectators and the correct interpretation of *Akins*, the Appellate Division, First Department, laid to rest all doubts and fears in *Davidoff v. Metropolitan Baseball Club, Inc.*, 92 A.D.2d 461, 459, N.Y.S.2d (1st Dept. 1983).

This case was an appeal from the order of Mr. J. Gomez, dated July 9, 1982, which denied defendant's motions for summary judgment based on the *Akins* holding.

The Appellate Division reversed, holding that since the plaintiff was sitting elsewhere than behind the screened home plate area, under *Akins*, no duty was owed to the injured party concluding that

> the plaintiffs' attempt to distinguish the situation in *Akins* from the one included here is unpersuasive. The issue is not whether the game is played at a high school field or professional stadium, but the standard of care imposed

upon the owner or proprietor of the playing field. Thus, Special Term should have granted summary judgment to defendant on the authority of *Akins v. Glens Falls City School Dist. (supra).*"

In short, the Court of Appeals in *Akins*, as interpreted and construed by the First Department in *Davidoff*, has blown the last trumpet in the history of the duty owed by a proprietor of a baseball club to the spectator. We can only wait upon the other Appellate Departments of this state to differ.

Copyright 1984 by the Brooklyn Bar Association and the <u>Brooklyn Barrister</u>. Reprinted with permission.

2. Loss of Consortium and Wrongful Death

Under the early English common law, there was no right to recover damages for wrongful death and so, there could be no compensation for loss of consortium due to the negligently caused death of one's spouse.

Thus, in *Higgins v. Butcher*, 80 Eng. Rep. 61 (K.B. 1606), the plaintiff brought an action alleging that the defendant had assaulted and beat his wife. The plaintiff's wife died some months later as a result of the beating. The court held that no civil action could be brought for wrongful death since, under the felony merger doctrine, both negligent and intentional homicide were considered felonious. Hence, there could be no civil suit for wrongful death since the civil action was merged into or succeeded by the prosecution of the felony.

More to the point, in *Baker v. Bolton*, 170 Eng. Rep. 1033 (K.B. 1808), the plaintiff's wife died as a result of injuries received when the defendant's coach overturned. The plaintiff sought recovery for the loss of the society and services of his wife. The court did note that the plaintiff's wife had been a great help in conducting her husband's business, but concluded that

> in a Civil Court, the death of a human being could not be complained of as an injury; and in this case the damages as to the plaintiff's wife, must stop with the period of her existence. *Baker v. Bolton, supra.*

It is the rule in England, then, that no common law action for wrongful death may lie, nor may damages be recovered for, loss of consortium due to wrongful death.

The courts of this State have also held, relying on this English rule, that there can be no common law action for loss of consortium in the context of wrongful death. The landmark case is *Green v. Hudson Riv. R.R. Co.*, 28 Barb. 9 (Sup. Ct. 1858), aff'd. 2 Abb. Ct. of App. 277 (1866). The widower-husband had alleged in his complaint that his spouse was killed while a passenger on a train on the defendant railroad. He claimed that he had lost the comfort, benefit and assistance of his wife. The action then was for the loss of the wife's consortium. The court initially defined the question to be whether, at common law, a husband may maintain an action for the death of his wife. It is true that, in 1847, the State of New York created a statutory action for wrongful death[1] and *Green* was decided some time later, in 1858. That statute, however, did not provide that a husband was one of the persons for whose benefit the personal representative of the estate could institute an action.[2] Hence, the court correctly defined the issue to be one whether the fact that the action was outside of the statutory scheme could a common law action lie. The court proceeded to review the English and American authorities on the issue, including *Higgins v. Butcher, supra,* and *Baker v. Bolton, supra,* and, although it disposed of the felony-merger doctrine as a basis for the rule, since that doctrine no longer existed in Great Britain and the United States, and speculated that origin of this law was either to be found in the maxim that the right of action was personal to and died with the deceased, or that the value of life was so great as to be incapable of estimation by money, and concluded that the rule had long existed in England, as evidenced by the passage of Lord Campbell's Act, the statutory death act.

The court also reviewed the relevant American case law and found that all but one of the cases[3] supported the proposition that, in the absence of a statute, no action for loss of consortium due to death will lie.

The court, in its final words, reaffirmed the 'common law' rule excluding recovery for loss of consortium in the context of a wrongful death action, stating

> I am constrained by these considerations, to reject the authority of this case, and abide by the common law rule, that an action by a husband for the loss of his wife by the careless and negligent act of a third party can only be sustained where some period intervenes between the time of the injury and the time of dissolution, during which he could be said to have suffered the loss of her service and society and to have incurred expense and underwent anxiety and distress on her account. Where death is the concomitant of the collision and life departs at the instant the shock is received, no action for loss of service can be sustained, because there is no time during her life when it can be said that the husband has lost the service and society of his wife in consequence of the injury complained of. This may be thought a narrow ground on which to place any right of recovery, but there is no other on which the common law rule can be overcome, which declares that the mere death of a human being cannot be complained of as a civil injury, to be compensated in damages. *Green v. Hudson Riv. R.R. Co., supra,* at 21, 22.

The Court of Appeals affirmed *Green* in 1866, merely stating, after a similar review of the English and American authorities, that the case required no further discussion than that previously offered by the lower court and that the court had added little to it. 2 Abb. Ct. App., *supra,* at 282. *Green v. The Hudson River R.R.* has been consistently followed in this State. Thus, the most recent case reaffirming this rule, which does not permit a common law wrongful death action or a common law action for loss of consortium due to the wrongful death of the other spouse, is *Grant v. Guidotti,* 66 A.D. 2d 545, 414 N.Y.S. 2d 171 (2d Dept. 1979).

Here the action was one for wrongful death, but there was also a separate claim for damages for loss of consortium. The lower court entered judgment for the defendants on the ground that the wrongful death action was not commenced within 2 years, as mandated by the wrongful death statute.

The Appellate Division surveyed the history of the wrongful death action under the common law, traced the content and development of the British and New York wrongful death statutes, noted certain current developments in the case law in this field, and held that, under the current law, no common law action for wrongful death or for loss of consortium due to wrongful death, existed apart from the wrongful death statute. Since the statute contained within itself a two-year statute of limitations, that statute of limitations barred the plaintiff's cause of action. The Appellate Division affirmed the order of the Supreme Court dismissing the plaintiffs' complaint on this basis.[4]

To date, under the New York law, no common law, non-statutory action for wrongful death or loss of consortium resulting there from will lie in this state.[5]

The Current Law

In 1846, in Great Britain, with the passage of Lord Campbell's Act,[6] a wrongful death action was created by statute. In the following year, 1847, the State of New York created a similar statutory action for wrongful death. The New York statute differed in three respects from the English statute. First, the damages were limited to the pecuniary injury resulting from such death. Second, the action was only for the benefit of the wife and next of kin, while the English statute included the surviving husband.[7] Third, the American statute had a two year statute of limitations, while the English statute had a one year statute.

The right of action, then, for wrongful death in the State of New York is solely a creature of statute. Hence, the elements and conditions of this statutory tort are delimited and defined by the specific statutory language following the language in the original New York wrongful death statute.[8] E.P.T.L. § 5-4.3, Amount of Recovery, limits the damages awarded to the plaintiff to

> such sum as the jury or where issues of fact are tried without a jury, the court or referee deems to be fair and just compensation for the pecuniary injuries resulting from the decedent's death to the persons for whose benefit the action is brought.

The limiting language "pecuniary injuries," the standard by which damages in wrongful death are to be measured, has been strictly construed by the courts of this State to mean that a person seeking to recover must have a reasonable expectation of pecuniary or financial loss based on his right to anticipate pecuniary benefits from the continued existence of decedent.[9] The pecuniary loss or injury is not limited to the deprivation of financial support theretofore provided by the decedent but may be extended to other elements of damage capable of monetary measurement.[10]

It has long been the law of this State that the loss of consortium is not a compensable item of damage under E.P.T.L. § 5-4.3, since it cannot be considered a pecuniary or financial loss.[11] In *Horton v. State of New York, supra*, at 1021, the Court of Claims, citing an authoritative line of case law, effectually summarized the New York position on this issue. The court held that

> the Decedent Estate Law (§§ 130-132) provides that damages may be such sum as is deemed to be a fair and just compensation for the pecuniary injuries, resulting from the decedent's death, to the person or persons for whose benefit the action is brought.

The amount of the damages depends upon the value of the reasonable expectation of pecuniary benefits from the continuance in life by the decedent to the husband and next of kin. (*Dimitroff v. State of New York*, 171 Misc. 635; *Gaccione v. State of New York*, 173 Misc. 367.)

It has been indicated that the word 'pecuniary' is not used in the statute to . the immediate loss of money or property (sic). If that were so there is scarcely a case where any amount of damages could be recovered. It looks to prospective advantages of a pecuniary nature which have been cut off by a premature death of the person from whom they would have proceeded. (*Tilley v. Hudson Riv. R.R. Co.*, 24 N.Y. 471.)

Courts have held that there is no mathematical formula upon which an award of damages for wrongful death may be based, specifically rejecting:

1. Sentiment, grief, loss of society and suffering of survivors. (*Arnold v. State of New York*, 163 App. Div. 253; *Costello v. Buffalo Gen. Elec. Co.*, 183 App. Div. 48; *Dimitroff v. State of New York*, 171 Misc. 635; *Grasso v. State of New York*, 177 Misc. 690, aff'd. 264 App. Div. 745, aff'd. 289 N.Y. 552; *Lewis v. State of New York*, 234 N.Y. 587; *Sternfels v. Metropolitan St. Ry. Co.*, 73 App. Div. 494, aff'd. 174 N.Y. 512)

Thus, the courts of this state have held, and continue to hold, with some few exceptions to be considered at a later point in this article, that there can be no recovery for loss of society under E.P.T.L. § 5-4.3, in the absence of amendment of the statute or its reinterpretation by the Court of Appeals. *Archambeault v. Draper*, 101 F.Supp. 1004 (E.D.N.Y. 1951); *Campbell v. Westmorland Farm, Inc.*, 270 F.Supp. 188 (E.D.N.Y. 1967); *Amerman v. Lizza & Sons, Inc.*, 45 A.D.2d 996, 358 N.Y.S.2d 220 (2nd Dept. 1974); *Bell v. Cox*, 54 A.D.2d 920, 338 N.Y.S.2d 118 (2nd Dept. 1976); *Fornaro v. Jill Bros., Inc.*, 42 Misc.2d 1031, 1036, 249 N.Y.S.2d 833 (Sup. Ct., Kings Co. 1964), rev'd. on other grounds 22 A.D.2d 695, 253 N.Y.S.2d 771 (2nd Dept. 1964), aff'd. 15 N.Y.3d 819, 257 N.Y.S.2d 938 (1965); *O'Neil v. State of New York*, 66 Misc.2d 936, 323 N.Y.S.2d 56 (Ct. of Claims 1971); *Osborn v. Kelley*, 61 A.D.2d 367, 402 N.Y.S.2d 463 (3rd Dept. 1978);[12] *Grant v. Guidotti, supra*; *Rowe v. Home*, 72 A.D.2d 578, 421 N.Y.S.2d 21 (2d Dept. 1979); *Liff v. Schildkraut*, 67 A.D.2d 299, 413 N.Y.S.2d 625 (2d Dept. 1979); *Tucker v. City of New York*, 54 A.D.2d 930, 388 N.Y.S.2d 133 (2d Dept. 1976); *Walkes v. Walkes*, 465 F.Supp. 638, 642-643 (S.D.N.Y. 1979); *Hentze v. Curry Chevrolet Sales and Services, Inc.*,

46 A.D.2d 800, 362 N.Y.S.2d 1016 (2d Dept. 1964). There can be no doubt but that the statutory requirement of a "pecuniary injury" has long been and continues to be construed by the appellate courts of this state to exclude the loss of consortium as a compensable item of damage in a wrongful death action.

Recent Trends in the State of New York

Two appellate courts, *Martins v. Ford*, 53 A.D.2d 887, 385 N.Y.S.2d 620 (2d Dept. 1976), and *Ventura v. Consolidated Edison*, 65 A.D.2d 352, 411 N.Y.S.2d 277 (1st Dept. 1978), have held that the loss of consortium was a "pecuniary injury" and so recoverable in a wrongful death action by the widow of the decedent suing individually and as administratrix of the estate of the deceased husband in *Martins* and the administrator of the estate in *Ventura*. These cases, however, in the opinion of this writer, constitute virtual aberrations and eccentricities in the law of the consortium action, lack logical and probative force and cite case law in support of their position that is inapposite and irrelevant.

In *Martins v. Ford, supra*, the defendant appealed from a lower court order which denied her motion to dismiss the negligence action for loss of consortium. The Second Department reversed the trial court and granted the motion stating that

> the plaintiff, suing individually and as administatrix of the estate of her deceased husband, has a valid claim for loss of consortium.

Martins would appear to allow recovery for loss of consortium under E.P.T.L. § 5-4.3. Subsequent, however, to the decision in *Martins*, the Second Department clearly held that the loss of consortium was not compensable under the New York wrongful death statute as a pecuniary injury. *Martins v. Ford, supra*, was decided on July 12, 1976. On November 8, 1976, some four months later, the Second Department decided *Bell v. Cox, supra*. In *Bell*, the appellate court explicitly rejected the notion that loss of consortium may be compensable as a "pecuniary injury" under E.P.T.L. § 5-4.3. The court cited *Amerman v. Lizza & Sons, supra*, as the controlling precedent, and, in response to the plaintiff's argument that the law should be changed to allow recovery for loss of society under the New York wrongful death statute, the court concluded that (at p. 920)

> if the law in this regard is to be changed it must be by an amendment of the statute or by its reinterpretation by the Court of Appeals.

It is clear that *Bell* v. *Cox*, decided after *Martins*, implicitly overrules that case.[13] If there can be any doubt on this question, the Second Department made its position on this issue clear in *Rowe v. Home, supra*. In that case, the court tersely stated that loss of consortium is not a pecuniary injury recoverable in a wrongful death action . . . . If the law in this regard is to be changed it is a matter for the Legislature.

In *Ventura v. Consolidated Edison, Inc.*, *supra*, the Supreme Court denied a motion by the administrator of the decedent's estate to include a separate action on behalf of the decedent's widow for loss of consortium. The First Department held that loss of consortium was a pecuniary injury and so compensable in a wrongful death action. The court admitted that a wrongful death action was purely statutory and that there could be no common law action for wrongful death. The court, however, cited dicta in *Millington v. Southeastern Elevator Co.*, 22 N.Y.2d 498, 504-505, 293 N.Y.S.2d 305, 309-310, 239 N.E.2d 897, 900-901, that loss of society is pecuniarily measurable, referred to *Tilley v. Hudson Riv. R.R. Co.*, 24 N.Y. 471 (1862), 29 N.Y. 252 (2d Appeal) (1864), which permitted damages to children deprived of a parent's services due to his or her wrongful death, noted that a Florida case, *Florida Cent. & P.R. Co. v. Foxworth*, 41 Fla. 1, 25 So. 338, permitted loss of society under the Florida wrongful death statute, and further cited *Sea-Land Services, Inc. v. Gaudet*, 414 U.S. 573, 94 S. Ct. 806, 39 L. Ed. 2d 9 (1974), which allowed recovery for loss of consortium in the context of a wrongful death action brought under the General Maritime Law and *Martins v. Ford*, *supra*. These cases are, however, inappropriate and irrelevant to the issue of whether there may be recovery for loss of consortium in a death action where the damages are limited, in this State, to "pecuniary injuries" alone. *Martins v. Ford*, *supra*, is a case no longer binding in light of *Bell*. *Ventura's* citation of *Millington* is also misplaced. In *Millington*, the husband of plaintiff became paralyzed from the waist down as a result of an elevator accident. His wife brought an action for loss of consortium on the ground that her husband would spend the rest of his life as an invalid. *Millington* was, therefore, in the nature of a common law tort action for personal injuries, i.e., loss of consortium of a living husband, and has no applicability to the instant case, a statutory death action. Moreover, the seminal issue facing the court in *Millington* was not whether, as in the case at bar, the loss of consortium is a compensable loss under exclusive statutory language, or even whether said right of action may exist, but whether, given a husband's historical right to sue for the loss of his wife's society, a wife may be prevented from maintaining an action for the loss of consortium, where society moves daily apace towards full equality between the sexes. *Millington v. Southeastern Elevator Co.*, *supra*, at 501.

Ventura also cited *Tilley*, *supra*, for the argument that the loss of consortium was pecuniarily measurable, since, in *Tilley*, the Court of Appeals

had long before discounted the argument that sentiment was impossible to measure, when it allowed damages to children who had been deprived of parental services due to wrongful death, because they were owed a duty of nurture.

The Court in *Ventura* conceded that there was a difference between the "duty of nurture" owed by the parent to the child, and consortium between spouses, but concluded that the importance of *Tilley* was that the Court compensated an injury not explicitly provided for in the wrongful death statute. *Ventura* not only wrongfully cites *Tilley*, but its reasoning and interpretation thereon is inconsistent and weak. The decision in *Tilley* cannot be cited for the notion that the allowance of damages to children deprived of parental services due to wrongful death constitutes a discounting of the argument that sentiment was impossible to measure. In fact, the *Tilley* Court closely analyzed the employment of the word "pecuniary" in the statute, stating that it excluded the loss of society of relatives and the grief and mental suffering attendant on their death, since both are incapable of monetary evaluation. The *Tilley* Court, however, explicitly held that the duty of nurture owed by parents to children is measurable in financial terms, analogizing it to a loss of instruction received from teachers employed for pecuniary compensation, and concluded that

> the injury in these cases is not pecuniary in a very strict sense of the word, but it belongs to that class of wrongs as distinguished from injuries to the feelings and sentiments; and in my view, therefore, it falls within the term as used in the statute. *Tilley v. Hudson River Railroad Co., supra*, at 476.

In addition, the importance of *Tilley* does not lie in the fact that it compensates an injury not specifically provided for in the Wrongful Death Act, since the wrongful death statute does not list explicit categories of compensable injuries, but, rather, defines any injury to be remedied under the Act only to the degree that it must have financial value. Thus, *Tilley* closely analyzed and applied the language of the statute to the facts presented therein and concluded that "the duty of nurture" owed by parents to children was a compensable item of loss under the wrongful death statute.

Ventura's citation of a Florida case, *Florida Cent. & P.R. Co. v. Foxworth*, 41 Fla. 1, 24 So. 338, permitting loss of society under its wrongful death statute, and *Sea-Land Services, Inc. v. Gaudet*, 414 U.S. 573, 94 S. Ct. 806, 39 L. Ed.2d 9, are equally unfitting since the Florida statute did not limit recovery to pecuniary damages alone, but simply reads that the jury may award such damages as are just[14] and in *Sea-Land Services*, the plaintiff lived for some time after his accident. In addition, *Sea-Land Services* was a case decided under the General Maritime Law, a body of law apart from the common law. Thus, in *Alvez v. American Export Lines*, 46 N.Y. 634 2d (1979), the Court of Appeals permitted recovery by the wife of an injured harbor worker, in a personal injury action, for loss of consortium due to her husband's injury and, in dicta, noted the existence of such a right in wrongful death actions under the General Maritime Law, citing *Sea-Land Services*. *Alvez v. American Export Lines, supra*, at 638. The Court observed, however, that under the Death on the High Seas Act (46 U.S.C. §§ 761, 762), recovery for wrongful death is limited to pecuniary loss and so there is no remedy for a wife's loss of consortium (*Alvez, supra*, at 641), and, that under the Jones Act (46 U.S.C § 688), the wife of an injured seaman has no action for loss of consortium (*Alvez, supra*, at 637). It is clear that where the statutory language is specific, it must be held to fully govern the scope of an action for loss of consortium as opposed to the more flexible decisional law.

In addition to the appellate decisions in *Martins* and *Ventura*, holding that the loss of consortium is compensable as a pecuniary injury under the New York Wrongful Death Statute, a number of trial courts have also held that the loss of consortium is a pecuniary injury under E.P.T.L. § 5-4.3. *Lehman v. Columbia Pres. Med. Ctr.*, 93 Misc.2d 539, 402 N.Y.S.2d 951 (Sup. Ct., N.Y. Co. 1978); *Ciaccio v. Hausman*, 97 Misc.2d 741, 412 N.Y.S.2d 557 (Sup. Ct., Queens Co. 1979); *McGale v. Metropolitan Transportation Authority, et al.*, 97 Misc. 20d 20, 410 N.Y.S.2d 751 (Sup. Ct., N.Y. Co. 1978); *Sullivan v. Southside Hospital*, Sup. Ct., Kings County, 4/18/79, N.Y.L.J., p. 13, col. 6 ; *Como v. Ilene Properties*, Sup. Ct., Kings County, 5/29179, N.Y.L.J., p. 12, col. 1. These cases add little to the elucidation of this issue since they fail to truly consider the clear statutory language, pecuniary injury, and, for the most part, support their arguments by citing *Sea-Land Services, supra*; *Tilley, supra*; *Millington, supra*; *Martins, supra*; and *Ventura, supra*, ending with a peroration that compensation for loss of consortium in a wrongful death action is, as it were, an idea whose time has come.

In any event, both the appellate and trial court decisions recognize the loss of consortium as a valid "pecuniary injury" under E.P.T.L. § 5-4.3 blithely ignore the language of the statute and the overwhelming weight of authority in this State whereby damages for wrongful death have been limited to injuries capable of monetary measurement, so specifically excluding the loss of consortium.

Conclusion

The Courts of this State have been most wary of what may be encompassed within the term "pecuniary loss," including the loss of support, services, and inheritance, but excluding grief, mental suffering and loss of society.[15] To extend the clear meaning of E.P.T.L. § 5-4.3, which has received uncontroverted and consistent interpretation by the courts of the State of New York, to include the loss of companionship as a pecuniary loss is, as a matter of logic, to stretch the English language beyond its very linguistic limits and, as a matter of law, to attempt to make whole what are in essence broken, emotional bonds, and to assuage the loss of society and consequent loneliness that every man must suffer at one time in this life. For the Courts to remedy a right such as this is to seek to bind the bonds of a broken spirit and not compensate a concrete temporal loss.

It is for the Legislature to amend this statute, not for the Courts to impose a gloss on its obvious meaning.[16] The question, however, will inevitably be resolved by the Court of Appeals since both *Ventura v. Consolidated Edison, Inc., supra*, and *Grant v. Guidotti, supra*, are presently on appeal and pending before that Court.[17]

3. The Intentional Infliction of Mental Distress: An Analysis

This article proposes to analyze what may be said to constitute the elements of the tort, and to look at a recent trend in the law in the area. Under New York law, in order to establish a claim for the tort of the intentional infliction of mental distress the plaintiff must demonstrate four elements: 1) that the defendant engaged in extreme and outrageous conduct; 2) that the defendant intended to cause severe emotional distress; 3) that the plaintiff suffered severe emotional distress; 4) that the defendant's conduct caused plaintiff severe emotional distress.

Bender v. New York[1] sets a high threshold for an emotional distress claim, holding that the conduct must be sufficiently outrageous to constitute the tort of the Intentional Infliction of Mental Distress.[2] It has been held that to state the claim the conduct must be so outrageous in character and so extreme as to be beyond all possible bounds of decency and must be regarded as atrocious and utterly intolerable in a civilized society.[3]

It has been further held that the tort is stated where severe mental anguish is inflicted through a deliberate and malicious campaign of harassment.[4] The Supreme Court of the State of New York in *Gurkin v. Siegel*[5] states the rules well. In that case the trial court stated that to allege the claim for the Intentional Infliction of Mental Distress, the complaint must allege that

1. The defendant's conduct is or was so outrageous and shocking as to exceed all bounds of decency as measured by what the average member of the community would tolerate;
2. That the defendant's conduct caused serious mental distress to the plaintiff; and
3. That the defendant acted with the desire to cause such distress or acted recklessly and under circumstances that made it certain that the defendant knew that mental distress would result.

The standard of "outrageousness" is rigorous, and it has been held that the plaintiff must show that the defendant's conduct was so outrageous and so extreme in degree to go beyond all bounds of decency and is to be regarded as atrocious and utterly intolerable in a civilized society.[6] The tort is particularly frequent in the employment discrimination context where harassment and resulting termination have occurred, although the tort may and can be found in virtually every kind of case. In *Sanchez v. Orozco,*[7] the Appellate Division, First Department, held that the lower court erred in dismissing the action for emotional distress based on the allegation that a psychiatrist persuaded his psychiatric patient to have a sexual relationship with him, especially in view of the fact that the psychiatrist placed numerous harassing telephone calls to the patient after she had terminated their sexual relationship.

Similarly, in *Atherton v. 21 East 92nd Corp.*,[8] in an action for breach of the implied warranty of habitability where the complaint alleged water seepage, collapse of ceilings, damage to walls, and malfunction of the heating system which caused soot and carbon monoxide to be emitted, the court held the tenant should have been permitted to amend the complaint to add a cause of action for mental anguish based on her fear of the dangerous conditions present in the apartment.

In *O'Reilly v. Executone of Arby*,[9] the Appellate Division, Third Department, held that a complaint alleging sexual harassment on the job by superiors and coworkers and the employer's refusal to take corrective or remedial action forcing the plaintiff to resign and take other employment stated a cause of action for the intentional infliction of mental distress. The New York standard for this tort is strict and rigorous and should a claim for the Intentional Infliction of Mental Distress not be deemed sufficiently outrageous, dismissal or summary judgment on the claim may often result.

Kovich v. Manhattan Life Insurance Company[10] is an example of the tort found not lying in the context of an employment discrimination case. In *Kovich*, the plaintiff alleged that she was terminated while less qualified employees were retained, that her employer falsified her time records to portray her as habitually late, and that her employer threatened her with blacklisting and told her that she would never work in the insurance industry again.

The Federal District Court in *Kovich* held that even if the plaintiff's claim of mistreatment were true, the allegation failed to meet the strict New York standard.[11]

Similarly in *Hirscheimer v. Associated Metals and Minerals*,[12] the United States District Court for the Southern District held that no Intentional Infliction of Emotional Distress claim lay despite plaintiff's exclusion from two meetings; the promotion of a younger subordinate to a position equal to the plaintiff's which resulted in diminished role for the plaintiff; health-related comments directed at the plaintiff; the absence of the plaintiff's name from an essential employee list; employer's refusal to address plaintiff's objections to the promotion of her subordinate and to the former subordinate's conducting business without consulting the plaintiff; the employer's reprimand of the plaintiff for his wife's refusal to greet the former subordinate at a business dinner; the employer's deception in leading plaintiff to believe his job was not in jeopardy; and the employer's public termination of the plaintiff without notice.[13]

In sum, it may be said under the present state of the law, that unless the tort is pled as somewhat beyond the pale, the claim may fail at some point in the course of litigation.

There has been a recent trend in this area of law to permit the tort to be pled with allegations of conduct that are less than outrageous. Thus in *Flatley v. Hartman*,[14] the Appellate Division, Second, Department, held that the plaintiff stated a cause of action for the Intentional Infliction of Mental Distress by alleging that the defendant made repeated phone calls to the plaintiff's house only to hang up as someone answered.

In similar fashion in *Halio v. Lurie*,[15] it was held that a taunting letter from a former boyfriend boasting of his marriage was held sufficient to state a cause action for mental distress. In *Flamm v. Van Nierop*,[16] the trial court held that the cause of action for the Intentional Infliction of Mental Distress was made by allegations of harassing the plaintiff by driving too closely and making threatening looks. These cases show that even if the tort does not meet the traditional standard of "outrageous" under the old and still binding New York standard, the tort may survive to and through trial where less than outrageousness is pled and proven, under this recent case law trend.

Notes

1. Baseball Liability: Recent Developments

1. This writer wrote the brief to the Appellate Division, Second Department, in this case and is familiar with the Record on Appeal, which includes the Examination before Trial and motions at the trial level.

2. Mr. J. Cotton also disposed of the contention of the plaintiffs that the vendors, employed by the defendant-Canteen Corp., obstructed the plaintiff's vision of the game by constantly moving around in front of the area where he was seated and by placing their wares on top of the dugout, and that the defendants City of New York and New York Yankees were negligent in their supervision of the defendant Canton Corp.'s employees, with the observation that spectators at a sporting event, such as a baseball game, will occasionally have their vision blocked, whether by spectators or vendors, and that a seated spectator solves this slight dilemma by leaning in his seat and that "solution" removes any claim of liability to offending vendors or spectators.

2. Loss of Consortium and Wrongful Death

1. L. 1847, ch. 450.

2. In 1870, the New York wrongful death statute was amended to include the husband as one for whose benefit the action could be maintained, L. 1870, ch. 78.

3. *Ford v. Monroe*, 20 Wend. 210 (1838). There the plaintiff was allowed to recover damages for the death and the loss of his services of his son, who was killed by a servant of the defendant. The court stated the case was an anomaly sustained by no precedent, and in conflict with all previous authority. The court observed that the discussion of damages is limited to 4 lines, solely to the effect that they are special damages, specially laid. The court stated that

> a case thus presented, and thus disposed of, can hardly be accepted as an authority which shall overthrow a principle of the common law, so long settled and acquiesced in as to have become quite elementary. *Green v. Hudson Riv. R.R. Co., supra*, at 20-21.

4. See also *Ratka v. St. Francis Hospital,* 44 N.Y. 2d 604, 407 N.Y.S. 2d 458 (1978). In *Ratka,* 3 years passed after the death of the decedent before letters of administration were granted and the action commenced. Plaintiff urged the court to recognize a common law action for wrongful death and so not bar the action by the two year statute of limitations provided by the New York wrongful death statute. The court per Cooke, J. held that the court must

> reject the request to establish a common-law cause of action for wrongful death. The decisions of other jurisdictions are, in our view, based on considerations not present here, and, to the extent that they may suggest a contrary result, we respectfully decline to follow in their steps. . . . [I]t is neither necessary nor appropriate to change established law as a means of saving this cause of action for wrongful death from the bar of the Statute of Limitations.

5. For excellent discussions and analyses of the case law relevant to this question, see Gutman, A SEPARATE CAUSE OF ACTION FOR LOSS OF CONSORTIUM IN DEATH CASES: EXORCISING GHOSTS OF THE PAST, 43 ALBANY LAW REVIEW 1, (1978); *Grant v. Guidotti, supra.*

6. Lord Campbell's Act 9 & 10 Vict., Ch. 93 [1846].

7. In 1870, the statute was amended to include the husband (L. 1870, ch. 78).

8. See 67 N.Y. Jur., Wrongful Death; *Ratka v. St. Francis Hospital, supra.*

9. See *Horton v. State of New York,* 50 Misc. 2d 1017, 1021 (Ct. of Claims, 1966); *Loetsch v. New York City Omnibus Corp.,* 291 N.Y. 308 (1943); *Didocha v. State of New York,* 54 A.D. 2d 786 (3rd Dept. 1976); 67 N.Y. Jur., Wrongful Death, §§ 157, 163-170.

10. 67 N.Y. Jur., Wrongful Death, §§ 157, 163, 167, 169.

11. For overview of recent trends in the case law in this area, see Joseph Kelner and Robert S. Kelner, LOSS OF CONSORTIUM IN WRONGFUL-DEATH CASES, N.Y.L.J. 1/9/80, p. 1, col. 1.

12. *Osborn v. Kelley, supra,* must be distinguished from the other cases listed here since *Osborn* was not decided on the ground that the loss of consortium is not a "pecuniary injury" under E.P.T.L. 5-4.3. In *Osborn,* plaintiff sought recovery in her individual capacity, and not her representative capacity as the administratrix of the decedent's estate, for the loss of the decedent's services, society, companionship, consortium, and support. The court held that a cause of action was stated for the loss of consortium for the period prior to the decedent's death. The court also stated that the individual action for loss of consortium is a derivative one and (at p. 370) concluded that

> the wrongful death statute created a new cause of action based not upon damage to the estate of the deceased because of death, but rather for the pecuniary injury to the surviving spouse and next of kin of the decedent (*Greco v. Kresge Co.,* 277 N.Y. 26, 32, 12 N.E.2d 557, 560). Since a decedent has no cause of action to recover damages for his death (E.P. T.L. 11-3.3), plaintiff has no derivative cause of action to recover for loss of consortium due to decedent's death. Recovery for funeral expenses paid by distributee of the decedent's estate is specifically provided for in E.P.T.L. 5-4.3. In our opinion, the sole remedy available is an action pursuant to the wrongful death statute (EPTL 5-4.1 et seq.) which must be brought by the personal representative of the deceased (EPTL 5-4.1). Therefore, plaintiffs' "Eighth" cause of action was properly dismissed except insofar as it states a cause of action by the individual plaintiff for loss of consortium prior to decedent's death.

13. See *Grant v. Guidotti, supra*, where the Court in footnote 10, explained its decision in *Martins*:

> While the language in our memorandum decision [*Martins v. Ford, supra*] was not as clear as it might have been, we reach no such conclusion [that plaintiff-widow had a valid claim for loss of consortium in a death action]. Our phraseology was used in the context of a record which left an inference that the decedent might have survived for some period of time after the accident. In a subsequent case, *Bell v. Cox*, 54 A.D.2d 920, 388 N.Y.S.2d 118, we made our views clear.

See also *Hromin v. Port Authority of New York and New Jersey* (Sup. Ct., N.Y. Co.), N.Y.L.J., 2/11/79, p. 6, col. 5, where plaintiff moved to amend his complaint to include damages for loss of consortium in a wrongful death action. The court noted that the Second Department case of *Martins* appeared to be no longer viable in light of *Bell v. Cox, supra*.

14. See *Hromin v. Port Authority of New York and New Jersey, supra*.
15. 67 N.Y. Jur., Wrongful Death, §§ 163, 165.
16. See *Bell v. Cox, supra*; *Rowe v. Home, supra*.
17. See N.Y.L.J. 5/3/79, p. 13, col. 3; also, *see Hromin v. Port Authority of New York and New Jersey, supra*; *Bell v. Cox, supra*; and *Rowe v. Home, supra*

3. The Intentional Infliction of Mental Distress: An Analysis

1. 78 F.3rd 787, 790 (2d Cir. 1991).
2. See *Howell v. New York Post Company*, 81 N.Y.2d 115, 596 N.Y.S.2d 350, 612 N.E.2d 699, 701 (1993).
3. *Murphy v. American Home Products*, 58 N.Y.2d 293, 461 N.Y.S.2d 232, 448 N.E.2d 86 (1983).
4. See *Belanoff v. Grayson*, 471 N.Y.2d 91, 98 A.D.2d 353 (1st Dept. 1989); *Brinks Inc. v. City of New York*, 533 F. Supp. 1123, 1125 (S.D.N.Y. 1982).
5. 122 Misc. 2d 302 (S. Ct. New York County 1983).
6. *Howell v. New York Post Company, id.* at 353. See also on this *Fischer v. Maloney*, 43 N.Y.2d 553, 402 N.Y.S.2d 991 (1978), citing Restatement (Second) of Torts Sec. 46 Subd. (1) comment.
7. 178 A.D.2d 391, 578 N.Y.S.2d 145 (1st Dept. 1991).
8. 149 A.D.2d 354, 539 N.Y.S.2d 993 (1st Dept. 1989). See also on this *Tighe v. Ginsberg*, 146 A.D.2d 268, 540 N.Y.S.2d 99 (4th Dept. 1989).
9. 121 A.D.2d 772, 503 N.Y.S.2d 185 (3rd Dept. 1986); See also on this *Collins v. Wilcox, Inc.* 158 Misc.2d 154, 600 N.Y.S.2d 884 (S. Ct. New York Co. 1992); *Neufeld v. Neufeld* 910 F. Supp, 977 (S.D.N.Y. 1996); *Kirwin v. New York State Office of Mental Health*, 665 F. Supp. 1034, 1040 (E.D.N.Y. 1987) (Held: Intentional Mental Distress claim dismissed when the plaintiff employee alleged she was given unjustifiably poor evaluations; that she was ostracized and isolated from the staff; that the employee engaged in a campaign of harassment against her; that she was falsely accused of time abuse; and that she was improperly denied personal and leave time); *Bradley v. Consolidated Edison*, 657 F. Supp 197 (S.D.N.Y. 1987) (Held: alleged negative job evaluation and job assignments),
10. 690 F. Supp. 134 (S.D.N.Y. 1986).
11. *Kovich v. Manhattan Life Insurance Company, id.*

12. No. 94 Civ. 6155, 1997 WL 528057 (S.D.N.Y. Aug. 27, 1997),

13. See also *Dirschel v. Speck.* No. 940502, 1994 WL 330262 (S.D.N.Y. July 8, 1994) (Held: Allegations in Title VI unlawful discharge case that the plaintiff was excluded from meetings; unable to meet with the CEO; and was not consulted on relevant matters; generally subjected to disrespect, and then terminated without notice did not constitute claim for the intentional infliction of mental distress.)

See also *Burger v. Health Insurance Plan of Greater New York,* 684 F.Supp. 46 (S.D.N.Y. 1998) (employee failed to state claim where he alleged physical assault and verbal harassment by co-employees); *Sigmon v. Parker Chapin Flattau & Kimpl,* 901 F. Supp. 667 (S.D.N.Y. 1995) (employer's alleged discriminatory conduct insufficient to state intentional infliction of emotional distress claim); *Cucchi v. New York City OTB,* 818 F.Supp. 647 (S.D.N.Y. 1993) (harassment claim insufficient to state claim); *Persuad v. Axelrod,* 1996 U.S. Dist. Lexis 160 (S.D.N.Y. Jan. 4, 1996) (allegations of sexual harassment including instances of physical touching do not rise to level of outrageousness required); *Marlor v. Manufacturers' Hanover Trust Company,* 1993 W.L. 15481 (S.D.N.Y. Jan. 8, 1993) (claim for emotional distress dismissed where plaintiff alleged racial harassment); *Vardi v. Mutual Life Insurance Company of New York,* 136 A.D.2d 453, 523 N.Y.S.2d 95 (lst Dept. 1988) (employee failed to state a claim where he alleged that his employer falsely accused him of forgery and of defrauding his employer); *Liebowitz v. Bank Leumi Trust Co. of New York,* 152 A.D.2d 169, 548 N.Y.S.2d 513 (2d Dept. 1989) (alleged frequent use of derogatory terms regarding employee's religion did not state claim).

14. 138 A.D.2d 345, 525 N.Y.S.2d 637 (2d Dept. 1988).

15. 15 A.D.2d 62, 67, 222 N.Y.S.2d 759, 754 (2d Dept. 1961).

16. 56 Misc.2d 1059, 1061, 291 N.Y.S.2d 189, 191 (West Cty. Sup. Ct. 1968).

Introduction to Federal Procedure Reprinted Articles

These five articles include a consideration of an exception to the Finality Requirement for Perfecting a Federal Appeal; another article analyzes Rules 15 and 16 of the Federal Rules of Civil Procedure; a third article examines the enforceability of Oral Settlements in the Federal Court System. Finally, the last two articles in this section include a survey of the law surrounding Federal Pre-Trial Orders, and the last and final article considers a recent seminal United States Supreme Court case on Eminent Domain.

Chapter 8
Federal Procedure Reprinted Articles

1. Essay: An Exception to the Finality Requirement

In federal appellate practice the general and set rule is that an appeal may only be made or taken from a final order which ends the litigation on the merits and leaves nothing for the court to do but execute judgment.[1] For example, a District Court's denial of a 12(b)(6) motion to dismiss, which leaves controversy pending, is not a "final decision or order" and so is not appealable.[2] Stated differently, within limited parameters and exceptions to be discussed in this essay, interlocutory appeals are effectively barred.[3] However, federal courts have carved out one exception to this set rule of finality. As set forth in *Cohen v. Beneficial Indus. Loan Corp.*,[4] interlocutory appeals may be taken from "collateral orders."

In *Cohen*, stockholders sued the defendant corporation and certain of its managers and directors, alleging that they engaged in a continuous and successful conspiracy to enrich themselves at the expense of the corporation from the year 1929 and on. The suit alleged mismanagement and fraud. The corporate defendant moved pursuant to New Jersey law to post security for the defendant's costs including attorney's fees and appealed from the denial of that motion.

The United States Supreme Court held that the order denying the motion was appealable, finding that the decision fell within that small class of decisions which finally determines a claim of rights separable from and collateral to rights asserted in the action, rights which are too important to be denied review and too independent of the case itself to require that appellate consideration be deferred until the case gets adjudicated.

The Supreme Court concluded that the order appealed from was in some sense a final disposition of claimed right, not as part of the original cause of action and not requiring consideration with it.[5]

More specifically, the definition of the Collateral Order Doctrine has been said to be a narrow exception to the Final Judgment Rule limited to those trial court orders affecting rights that would be irretrievably lost in the absence of an immediate appeal. For a collateral order to be subject to interlocutory appeal, three requirements must be met. The order must: (1) conclusively determine the disputed question or questions, (2) solve an important issue completely separate from the merits of the action and, (3) be effectively unreviewable on appeal from the final judgment.[6] Thus, it has been held that an order decertifying a class action cannot be the subject of an interlocutory appeal or an order disqualifying counsel.[7] This essay considers a separate discrete issue: Is the denial of a claim, in a case of qualified or absolute immunity, appealable when dismissal of the pending claim has been denied?

In general, the rule is that an interlocutory appeal is permitted from an order denying immunity, either absolute or qualified. The reasoning is that the immunity is permanently lost if the case is permitted to go to trial, as subsequent review would be ineffective. This rule is succinctly and well stated in *Mitchell v. Forsyth*.[8] In *Mitchell*, the petitioner, the Attorney General, authorized a warrantless wiretap for the purpose of gathering intelligence regarding the activities of a radical group that had made tentative plans to take actions threatening the nation's security. Relying on *United States v. United States District Court*,[9] the United States Supreme Court held that the Fourth Amendment did not permit warrantless wiretaps in cases involving domestic threats to national security. The respondent then filed a damages action in the federal District Court against the Attorney General, alleging that the surveillance to which he had been subject violated the Fourth Amendment of the U.S. Constitution and Title III of the Omnibus Crime Control and Safe Streets Act. The District Court granted the respondent's motion for summary judgment on the issue of liability and held that the petitioner was not entitled to either absolute or qualified immunity. The Court of Appeals agreed with the denial of absolute immunity, but held, with respect to the denial of qualified immunity, that the District Court order was not appealable under the Collateral Order Doctrine.

The United States Supreme Court reversed, stating the District Court's denial of qualified immunity was the denial of an entitlement not to stand trial under certain circumstances, and such entitlement constituted immunity from suit rather than a mere defense to liability and, like absolute immunity, is effectively lost if the case is erroneously permitted to go to trial. Thus, the United States Supreme Court held the claim of qualified immunity is appealable under the "Collateral Order Doctrine" since it conclusively determines the disputed question and makes a claim for rights separable from and collateral to rights asserted in the main action.

Similarly, in *Puerto Rico Aqueduct and Sewer Authority v. Metcalf & Eddy, Inc.*,[10] an engineering firm, which had entered into a contract with a Puerto Rican Agency to provide services regarding the subject matter of an environmental consent decree, brought an action seeking a declaration of rights with respect to the agreement alleging damages for alleged breach of contract. The Agency moved to dismiss based on the Eleventh Amendment immunity and the Agency appealed. The Court of Appeals dismissed the appeal. The United States Supreme Court held that the same reasoning that allowed and permitted an order denying individuals' and officials' claims of absolute and qualified immunity to be appealed applied here and that this case fell within the Collateral Order Doctrine of *Cohen*. Once the State and its entities are held to be immune from suit under the Eleventh Amendment, the elements of the Collateral Order Doctrine are satisfied.

Moreover, the Court reasoned that a motion to dismiss on Eleventh Amendment grounds involves a claim to fundamental Constitutional protection, whose resolution will have no bearing on the merits of the underlying action. Finally, the Court held that the value to the states of their Eleventh Amendment immunity gets lost as the litigation proceeds. Thus, the U.S. Supreme Court held that the Order here fulfilled the *Cohen* criteria: (1) conclusively determining the disputed question, (2) resolving an important issue separate from the merits of the main case, and (3) effectively being unreviewable from the final judgment.

Conclusion

This examination of final and interlocutory appeals, in addition to examining the appealability of the denial of absolute and qualified immunity claims, reveals the existence of a collateral order exception comprised of three parts: (1) conclusive determination of a disputed question; (2) resolution of an important issue separate from the merits of the action; and (3) unreviewability from an appeal of the final judgment

As to the denial of absolute or qualified immunity, this much is clear: Should the case proceed to trial, immunity is irretrievably and absolutely lost. Unless an interlocutory appeal is permitted, there can be no review that can undo the damage, change the result, or alter the facts. Thus, when immunity is denied and the case proceeds to trial, immunity is effectively lost. Despite the ability to appeal at the conclusion of the case, the damage is done and the loss of immunity, though reviewed in and through the final judgment, is effectively gone. The reason for the rule is obvious: Appeal would be ineffectual at the end of the trial. Instead, parties should be allowed to make interlocutory appeals of such orders.

Reprinted with permission from: N.Y.Litigator. Spring 2006, Vol.11, No, published by the New York State Bar Association, One Elk Street, Albany, New York 12207.

2. Rule 15 and 16 of the Federal Rules of Civil Procedure: A Comparison

Rule 15 of the Federal Rules of Civil Procedure, entitled "Amended and Supplemental Pleadings" in subsection A., defines the conditions under which a party may amend his or her pleadings.[1] In essence, that section provides that a party may amend his pleadings as a matter of course, in general, and that otherwise a party may amend his pleadings only by leave of Court or by written consent of the adverse party. Rule 16 of the Federal Rules of Civil Procedure entitled "Pretrial Conferences; Scheduling; Management" in subsection (b) states that when the judge or magistrate enters a Scheduling Order the schedule may not be modified except by leave of the judge or magistrate when authorized by district court rule upon a showing of good cause.[2]

It is the purpose of this article to compare the provision for amendment under Rule 15(a) of the Federal Rules of Civil Procedure with Rule 16(b), which includes a "good cause" requirement governing the amendment of pleadings after a Scheduling Order has been entered.

Rule 15(a) in its text provides that leave to amend "shall be freely given when justice so requires".[3] The law interpreting Rule 15(a) generally provides for liberality in permitting amendments to pleadings and favors a liberal construction so that cases are decided on the merits rather than on bare bone pleadings.[4] It has been held that the purpose of Rule 15(a) is to provide for a full and fair hearing on the merits and the burden of further discovery and motions resulting from the granting of a motion to amend a complaint is not a satisfactory basis to deny such motion.[5]

As a further point, complementing the rule that leave to amend is generally freely given, is the rule that the decision to grant or deny the motion to amend the pleadings is within the sound discretion of the trial court. Thus, in *Lewis v. Curtis*[6] the Pennsylvania Court of Appeals held that the decision whether to grant or deny leave is within the discretion of the District Court and the Court's decision to deny leave to amend is subject to reversal only for abuse of that discretion.[7]

It has been held that, ordinarily, the courts exercise their discretion liberally in permitting amendments so as not to deprive a litigant of a chance to bring his case to trial.[8]

To review and sum up, it is the law that leave to amend is generally freely given absent prejudice, but is always within the wide discretion of the District Court Judge. Surprise, futility, and undue delay can also be considered in denial of the leave to amend.

What will now be considered are the specific discrete factors determining the granting or denial of the amendment. In general, the facts of each case are taken as controlling.[9] More specifically, it has been held that amendment will be denied where a claim is not stated. Thus, in *Jafree v. Barber*[10] the Illinois Circuit Court held that the denial for leave to amend a discrimination claim was not an abuse of discretion where the plaintiff in the first amended complaint failed to suggest actual predicate to support the claim that the Federal Bureau of Investigation actions in failing to investigate charges were prompted by racial animus and where at the time of the request for leave to file a second amended complaint the plaintiff did not explain how he would cure defective allegations.[11]

Another rule the courts have promulgated in determining whether to grant or deny a motion to amend is where the motion is made in bad faith. Thus, in *Posadas de Mexico, SA de C.V. v. Dukes*,[12] the Southern District of New York held that leave to amend is to be freely given when justice requires, but leave to amend must be denied where the parties' motion to amend is compelled by bad faith or dilatory motive; the parties adversary can demonstrate actual prejudice if the motion to amend is granted; or the proposed amendment would constitute no more than a futile exercise.[13]

Another reason for granting this motion in where there has been a change in the law. Thus, in *Gregory v. Harris Teeter Supermarkets, Inc.*,[14] the District Court held that a Civil Rights plaintiff's motion to emend the complaint and his second motion to amend the complaint would be granted where each motion was filed immediately after an apparent change in the law occurring after the plaintiff had filed his complaint.[15]

It has been held that a motion to amend a complaint cannot be used as a basis to avoid summary judgment.[16]

It has been further held that a court is not required to deny a motion to amend simply because of a failure to comply with a Local Rule.[17]

It should be further noted that delay alone is an insufficient basis to deny leave to amend a pleading, but the party[18] seeking leave to amend has an obligation to exercise due diligence, and unwarranted and unseemly delay combined with other factors may warrant denial of the amendment.

Another point on this issue is where the delay goes beyond excusable neglect. Hence, the law is that an unexcused delay in seeking to amend pleadings coupled with the probability that the addition of new claims would lead to a new wave of discovery is an adequate basis for denying leave to amend.[19]

It is significant that there is some law that the retention of a new attorney coupled with other factors can be a basis for granting a motion to amend. Thus, in *Davis v. Yellow Cab Co.*,[20] the Pennsylvania District Court held that the delay in amending the complaint was not unreasonable where the injuries were sustained on January 23, 1961, the action was brought on August 30, 1961, and the petition to amend was filed or October 31, 1963, after the plaintiff! had retained new counsel.[21]

It is interesting to note that although a very lengthy delay is not alone sufficient to support a denial of this motion it can be a basis, coupled with other factors.[22]

Another important factor that the law has held to be a basis for denying the amendment to a complaint is a showing of prejudice to the nonmovant, coupled with other factors. Thus, in *Quaker State Oil Refining Corp. v. Garrity Oil Co., Inc.*,[23] the Massachusetts Court of Appeals held that the defendant was not entitled to leave to amend a counter-claim for the fifth time. The court held, that defendant's tardiness in filing the amendment was extreme; the facts upon which the proposed counterclaim rested were known to the defendant all along; and a great deal of discovery had taken place without reference to the new theory, thus prejudicing the plaintiff.[24]

There is law to the effect that this motion will be denied even where a new claim or cause of action is sought to be added even where the delay is great. Thus, in *Manhattan Life Ins. Co. v. J Stratton Syndicate*,[25] the New York United States District Court held that a reinsurers' motion to amend the complaint to add a fraud claim against an insurer for including multiple employer trust insurance under "losses occurring" policy for reinsurance had to be denied because of an extensive delay in seeking amendment.[26]

In the same way, it has been held that a party may be allowed to amend his/her complaint to add a new theory or theories of recovery.[27]

The Federal Courts have held that it is not proper that plaintiff be given leave to append frivolous or repetitious allegations to the complaint at any stage of the proceedings.[28]

There is a general rule worth noting that amendments to pleadings are allowed in the general interest of justice. Thus, in *J.O. v. Alton Community Unit School Dist. #11*,[29] the Court of Appeals of Illinois held that justice would be served by returning the case to the District Court to allow parents to amend pleadings in an attempt to state a claim against Illinois school authorities under Sec. 1983 for failure to prevent the alleged sexual abuse of school children by a teacher.[30]

The courts have noted on this particular issue that doing justice means paying attention and rendering justice to both parties.[31]

Other factors figuring in denial of a leave to amend are where subject matter jurisdiction never existed; where the proposed amendment fails to allege facts which would support a valid theory of liability; or where the party moving to amend has not shown that the proposed amendment has substantial merit. Thus, in *N.A.A.C.P.-Special Contribution Fund v. Jones*,[32] the Northern District of Ohio held that the district court had no authority to allow the plaintiff to amend the complaint to substitute another party as a plaintiff where there was never complete diversity so that subject matter jurisdiction never existed. Similarly, on the matter of meritless claims, the Court of Appeals of Wisconsin held in *Verhein v. South Bend Lathe, Inc.* [33] that a motion for leave to amend the pleading may be denied where the proposed amendment fails to allege fact, which would support a valid theory of liability or where the party moving to amend has not shown that the proposed amendment has substantial merit.[34]

In the same vein as adding new claims and new theories, it has been held that this motion will be granted where newly discovered facts are alleged. Thus, in *Thomas v. Medesco, Inc. vs. Division of Harvard Industries, Inc.*,[35] the Pennsylvania District Court held that the amendment of the complaint to add a claim for punitive damages based on newly discovered implications from facts revealed in discovery would be granted.[36]

An added factor in granting this motion is when the parties have actual notice of an unpleaded issue and have been given an adequate opportunity to cure any surprise resulting in the change in the pleadings.[37]

As an added note to this review of the factors that are determinative of granting or not granting a motion to amend, the Federal Courts have uniformly held that cases should be determined on their merits as far as possible. Thus, in *Cooper v. American Emp. Ins. Co.*,[38] the Court of Appeals of Ohio held that cases should be decided on their merits as much as possible and not on technicalities, where no prejudice or disadvantage is suffered by the opposing side.

It has been held, in addition on this rule, that although there is a favoring of decision on the merits of litigation before the Federal Courts, the courts always have discretion on this issue, in particular where successive amendments are sought.[39]

Finally, unfair surprise can be a basis for denying this motion, often coupled with other factors.[40]

In conclusion, the following pattern emerges on the factors and bases whereby a complaint may be permitted to be amended under Rule 15(a) of the Federal Rules of Civil Procedure.

First, leave to amend is generally liberally and freely granted, absent prejudice, and is within the wide discretion of the District Court Judge. However, leave to amend will not be granted where claim is not stated; is made in bad faith; is made with dilatory motive; or where actual prejudice can be shown. A motion to amend a complaint, it has been held, cannot be used as a basis to avoid summary judgment, but a court is not required to deny a motion to amend simply for failure to comply with a Local Rule. A reason for granting a motion is where there has been a change in the law, but it has been held, that delay alone is an insufficient basis to deny leave to amend a pleading. On the other hand, the party seeking leave to amend has an obligation to exercise due diligence, and unwarranted and unseemly delay combined with other factors may warrant denial of the amendment.

It has been held that an unexcused delay in seeking to amend pleadings coupled with the probability that new claims would be added that would lead to a new wave of discovery is an adequate basis for denying leave to amend.

There is some law that the retention of an attorney with other factors can be a basis for granting a motion to amend. It is also true that a motion to amend can be denied where prejudice can be shown to the nonmovant, coupled with other factors. Although the Federal Courts have held that it is not proper that the plaintiff be given leave to amend to add frivolous or repetitious allegations to the complaint, it has been held that a party may be allowed to amend his/her complaint to add a new theory of recovery.

There is a general rule that amendments to pleadings are allowed in the general interest of justice.

The Federal Courts have held that leave may be denied where subject matter jurisdiction never existed; where the proposed amendment fails to allege facts which would support a valid theory of liability; or where the moving party has not shown substantial merit. The motion may be granted when newly discovered facts are alleged, but will be denied where the proposed amendment fails to allege facts which would support a valid theory of liability.

An added factor in granting the motion is where the parties have actual notice of an unpleaded issue and have been given an adequate opportunity to cure any surprise in the change of the pleadings.

There is a general rule that cases should be determined on their merits as far as possible, but unfair surprise can be a basis for denying the motion, coupled with other factors, as is also true where successive amendments are sought.

Rule 16 presents a totally different rule governing amendment of the pleadings or, rather, amendment of the complaint where a Scheduling Order has been entered. Under Rule 16 the law is that a schedule should not be modified except upon a showing of good cause. The question is what constitutes "good cause"?

The leading case on the interpretation of the good cause provision of Rule 16 is *Parker v. Colombia Picture Industries*.[41] In *Parker*, a former employee sued his employer and sister corporation claiming a discriminatory discharge under the Americans with Disabilities Act (ADA) and the New York State Human Rights Law. The defendants moved for summary judgment and the employee cross-moved for breach of contract. The United States District Court for the Southern District of New York granted the defendants' motion for summary judgment on plaintiff's discriminatory discharge claims, but otherwise denied the motion. Following partial settlement and entry of a final judgment, the employee appealed and the sister corporation cross-appealed. The United States Court of Appeals for the Second Circuit held, among other things, that the employee's statement in an application for Social Security and long-term disability benefits that he was "completely incapacitated" and "unable to work" would not preclude the jury in the ADA action from finding that the employee had the ability to work with reasonable accommodation. The Second Circuit also held that such statements did not subject the employee to judicial estoppel; that there were genuine factual disputes precluding summary judgment as to whether the employee was capable of performing the job with reasonable accommodation when he was terminated, and as to whether the employer had terminated the employee "because of" his disability. The Court also held that the mixed-motive analysis available in the Title VI context applied equally to cases brought under the ADA. The Court further held that there was a genuine issue of material fact regarding whether the sister corporation had acted as the plaintiff's employer.

Most importantly, the Second Circuit held that the District Court did not abuse its discretion in denying the employee's motion to amend the complaint on the ground that the motion was brought after the court-ordered deadline for amending the pleadings. The court entered into an extensive analysis of Parker's motion for leave to amend the complaint to add a breach of contract claim. The court noted that the District Court denied Parker's motion on the ground that it was untimely and futile, finding that Parker had not alleged facts to support a breach of contract claim, and that, in any event, the motion did not comply with the schedule that the court had set for the proceedings in its Order. The Second

Circuit held, however, that the request was not futile to add a breach of contract claim. The court rejected the District Court's contention and analysis that Parker could not allege a claim for breach of contract because he was an at-will employee, finding Parker's argument valid that the company's short term benefits policy constituted such a contract or a promise. The court held that under the benefits plan, Parker's salary and length of service entitled him to six months leave which would take the form of salary continuation benefits and that Parker's at-will status would not alter that entitlement. The court, however, went on to rule that the district court did not abuse its discretion in denying Parker's motion on the ground that the motion was brought after the court-ordered deadline for amending the pleadings. The Court held that the Rule 16(b) "good cause" standard rather than the more liberal standard of Rule 15(a) governed a motion to amend filed after the deadline district court had set for amending the pleadings. The Circuit Court held, citing a number of circuit decisions, that despite the lenient standard of Rule 15(a), a district court does abuse its discretion in denying leave to amend the pleadings after the deadline set in the scheduling order where the moving party has failed to establish good cause. The court noted that a finding of "good cause" depends on the diligence of the moving party. The Court reasoned that the District Court was correct in finding that Parker had not demonstrated good cause for his failure to comply with the Court's deadline. The court considered Parker's claim that he did not discover his contractual entitlement to six months paid leave until receiving SPE's motion for summary judgment, in which SPE referred to Parker's "entitlement" to benefits. The Circuit court held that this argument lacked merit since Parker received a copy of SPE's leave policy, on which he based his contract claim, when he began work at the company in 1993 and further, upon terminating him in September of 1995, SPE specifically informed Parker that his leave had begun on March 17, 1995, and that he had exhausted his maximum period of leave benefits. The court went on to state that Parker was aware both of his rights under the policy prior to and throughout the course of this litigation but also of SPE's allegedly wrongful conduct in beginning his leave on March 17. The court concluded that when he commenced this action, Parker had all the information necessary to support a breach of contract claim.

Parker is the leading and authoritative decision on the interpretation of the "good cause" provision of Rule 16(b) of the Federal Rules of Civil Procedure. *Parker* makes clear that Rule 16 sets a higher and more thorough standard whereby a pleading may be amended after the Scheduling Order has expired. For that purpose there must be a finding of good cause, which can be founded on an untimeliness basis where the moving party had some knowledge or grounds for knowing of the claim or change in the pleadings prior to the expiration of the Scheduling Order time frame .

The interpretation of the "good cause" standard under Rule 16(b) does not reward tardiness and lack of diligence.[42]

In *City of Chanute, Kansas v. Williams Natural Gas Co.*,[43] the District Court of Kansas shed further light on what could be considered good cause under Rule 16 of the Federal Rules of Civil Procedure. In *City of Chanute,* the court ruled that good cause was shown for modification of a scheduling order to allow anti-trust defendants to file a summary judgment motion, which would have been untimely under the original order. The court suggested in its reasoning on this issue that filing a summary judgment motion, which tested the propriety of all claims and employment of such procedure, would render the whole case appealable at the same time.[44]

Conclusion

This brief review and comparison of Rules 15(a) and 16(b) reveals a rule of liberality taking into consideration a multitude of factors leading to and allowing amendment of pleadings or complaint under Rule 15(a) of the Federal Rules of Civil Procedure. Rule 16(b) sets a standard of good cause where the time established by a scheduling order has expired, interpreting good cause to mean a reasoned and actual basis for untimeliness that could not have been avoided. In short, under Rule 16(b) laches, unwarranted and inexplicable delay will not be rewarded or permitted.

3. *Enforceability of an Oral Settlement: A Consideration and Analysis*

Settlement as a resolution of a civil dispute is to be preferred. Trial and litigation are costly and time-consuming. Moreover, trial is always a risk for all.

Hence, the desirability of settlement as the preferred mode of dispute resolution. Each party, in a settlement, walks away somewhat satisfied, and somewhat dissatisfied. Both have given up something. The plaintiff acquires income, fixed and guaranteed. The defendant is relieved of the further cost of litigation and the prospect of losing at trial and being subject to a large verdict.

In general, and it is the sounder practice, the settlement should be reduced to a detailed and formalized writing, covering every facet of the agreement, and signed by each party and their attorneys, thus guaranteeing that each party had the time to reflect on the details of the agreement, understand it, and fully agree to it. What, however, of the event or circumstance when a party may orally agree to a settlement and then changes his mind, all prior to his having taken the time to consider a detailed and a operative written instrument. Under this set of facts and scenario, is the agreement enforceable, or, to put it more clearly, must a settlement, to be enforced, invariably and always be in writing?

The leading cases are *Ciaramella v. Reader's Digest Association*[1] and *R. G. Group Inc. v. Horn and Hardart Co.*[2] In *Ciaramella,* the employee sued his former employer for discrimination under Federal and State laws, i.e., the A.D.A. and Art. 15 of the New York State Executive Law, alleging a failure to give a reasonable accommodation for his disability of chronic depression. The facts in *Ciaramella* were that, after the commencement of the action, the parties negotiated a settlement, which Ciaramella later refused to sign. The Readers Digest Association moved for an order to enforce the settlement Agreement. The Southern District of New York granted the Motion and dismissed the plaintiff's complaint.

Initially, the Second Circuit held that, under New York Law, the parties are free to bind themselves orally and the fact that they contemplate later memorializing their agreement in the executed document will not prevent them from being bound by an oral agreement. The court went on to state, however, that if the parties intend not to be bound until the agreement is set forth in writing and signed, they will not be bound until then. The Second Circuit further noted that the intent of the parties in this respect is a question of fact to be determined by the totality of the circumstances.

The Circuit Court of Appeals went on to hold that there are four factors to guide the enquiry whether the parties intend to be bound by a settlement agreement in the absence of a document executed by both sides, *Ciaramella v. Readers Digest Association*[3] quoting *Winston v. Mediafore Entertainment Corp.*[4] The four factors stated in *Ciaramella* are: (1) whether there has been an express reservation of the right not to be bound in the absence of a signed writing, (2) whether there has been partial performance of the contract, (3) whether all of the terms of the alleged contract have been agreed upon so that all that remains to be done is to sign what has already been fully agreed to, and (4) whether the agreement at issue is the type of contract that is usually committed to in writing.

The *Ciaramella* court, applying four factors to the case before it, held that the District Court erred in concluding that the parties intended that that unexecuted draft settlement constituted a binding agreement.

First, the Second Circuit found numerous indications in the proposed settlement agreement that the parties did not intend to bind themselves until the settlement had to be signed. Second, the court found no evidence of any partial performance. Third, the court found the parties had not yet agreed on all material terms. Fourth, the court found this type of settlement is one generally reduced to writing or, at a minimum, made on the record in open court. The court also made note that the complexity of the underlying agreement is an indication whether the parties reasonably could have been expected to bind themselves orally. The court thus concluded that the totality of the circumstances indicated that Mr. Ciaramella never entered into a binding settlement agreement with his former employer.

R.G. Group Inc. v. Horn and Hanlart Co.[5] is also relevant. In *R.G. Group*, franchisees brought an action alleging prospective breach of an agreement to grant the Franchisees, and Promissory Estoppel. The Southern District of New York granted Summary Judgment. The agreement was never signed. Again, the Second Circuit held that, under New York law, if the parties do not intend to be bound by an agreement until it is in writing and signed, then there is no contract until that event occurs. The court went on to state that this rule holds even if the parties have orally agreed upon all the terms of the contract. The court further held that, where there is no understanding that an agreement shall not be binding until reduced to writing and finally executed, and where all the substantial terms of a contract have been agreed on and there is nothing left to future negotiation and settlement, then an informal agreement can be binding even though the parties contemplated memorializing their contract in a formal document.

The *RG* court noted that what matters here is the parties' expressed intentions by their word or deeds. Again, the Second Circuit in *RG* set forth and listed four factors upon which to decide whether the parties' words or deed, in a given bargaining context, show an intent to be bound only by a written agreement, including: (1) whether there is present an express reservation of the right not to be bound in the absence of a signed writing, (2) whether there has been partial performance of the contract and whether that performance has been accepted by the party disclaiming the contract, (3) whether all, at the time the alleged contract was negotiated, was agreed to, so that all that remained to be done was to sign what had been agreed to and, (4) whether the agreement is of the type and so complex that it is the norm that the contract be in writing .

Again, as in *Ciaramella*, *RG* applied the same four factors and the Second Circuit held that the District Court acted properly in granting Summary Judgment to the defense, finding that the parties intended to be bound by the written agreement, and since the agreement was not signed, there was no contract under New York law. The court further stated that, even if an oral agreement was reached, that agreement was void under the Statute of Frauds. The court also held that the claim of promissory estoppel was properly rejected for lack of a clear promise and for lack of reliance. Reading *Ciaramella* and *R.G. Group* together, we find a rule that parties may bind themselves orally to a contract or settlement, but if the parties intend not to be bound until the agreement is set forth in writing and signed, they will not be bound. The Second Circuit bids us to apply four factors to the parties' intentions considering the totality of the circumstances and cites a preference that an oral settlement to be enforced should be made in open court.

Conway v. Brooklyn Union Gas Co.[6] adds a gloss to this four-factor totality of circumstances rule. In *Conway*, the United States District Court for the Eastern District of New York initially applied the four factors to an oral settlement agreement in an employment discrimination case based on race and gender brought pursuant to 42 U.S.C. Sec. 2000(e) but also considered the issue that although the decision to settle must rest with the client, the courts will presume that an attorney who enters into a settlement agreement has the authority to do so, and that a party challenging an attorney's authority to settle a case on his or her client's behalf bears the burden of showing the attorney lacked the requisite authority to settle the case.

Clearly, the properly delegated authority to settle the case is a significant factor impacting on the enforceability of the settlement.

It is important to note that, although the court in *Conway* did enforce the oral agreement, the *Conway* court was initially and then completely involved in every cause and facet of the negotiation of the settlement from the initial settlement conference in court, where everything was agreed to but the monetary amount, to the subsequent series of phone conferences with the attorney concerning the issues. Thus, the decision in *Conway* to enforce the oral settlement in the view of the court was largely based on the open court nature of the settlement entered into. *Conway* clearly adopts and follows the dicta in *Ciaramella* approving open court settlements. If there can be any doubt that there is strong authority that, for an oral settlement to be enforced, it must be made in open court, the Southern District of New York, in *Wilgerodt on behalf of Maj. Peoples v. Hohri*,[7] laid all fears to rest. In *Wilgerodt*, the Southern District specifically held in a most detailed analysis, citing *Dolgin v. Dolgin*[8] and *Monaghan v. SZS 33 Associates L.P.* and CPLR 2104,[9] that an oral settlement is only binding if it is made in "open court" and that the "open court" requirement is to ensure that there are formalities, if only in the clerk's minutes, to memorialize the critical litigation events. The court noted that in the issue before it, a complete transcript of the proceedings documented the oral settlement agreement between MPF and Hohri and so the requirements of CPLR Sec. 2104 were met.[10]

Conclusion

This brief analysis of the enforceability of oral settlements reveals two, or rather three, strands. First, there are four factors that must be applied to determine whether an oral settlement will be enforced. Second, upon applying the factors, the court will also look at the totality of the circumstances to determine the intentions of the parties to be bound by an oral agreement. Third, the court will look at the complexity of the agreement as a factor.

Finally, even applying these factors and considerations, it would appear that to enforce oral settlement, it must have, in some sense, been made and recorded or transcribed in open court.

4. The Perils and Pitfalls of Pre-Trial Orders

Before a federal lawsuit proceeds to trial, in general, a Joint Pretrial Order must be submitted by the attorneys on behalf of the parties in the case. In the rush to comply with the discrete time frame set forth in the Scheduling Order and mandated by the Federal Magistrate or District Court Judge, items may inadvertently be omitted from the Joint Pretrial Order by either or both of the attorneys representing the plaintiff and defendant. When this happens and, for example, a witness is omitted or an item of evidence is left out, what recourse does the attorney have, especially if he or she has left out a significant item in the Joint Pretrial Order? This is of particular significance because the Pretrial Order sets forth the parameters of how the case will proceed and what will occur at trial. For example, in a disability case, the inadvertent omission of a treating doctor or expert can significantly prejudice the plaintiff's ability to present his or her evidence of the disability.

This dilemma has its solution in the provisions of Rule 16 of the Federal Rules of Civil Procedure and the case law that has interpreted Rule 16. Entitled "Pretrial Conferences; Scheduling; Management," the relevant sections are subsections (a) through (f).[1]

Subsection (e), entitled "Pretrial Orders,"[2] provides in pertinent part that a Pretrial Order can only be modified to prevent "manifest injustice." The issue, therefore, is what constitutes "manifest injustice" under Rule 16(e) of the Federal Rules of Civil Procedure.

Some general rules

The purpose of a Pretrial Order, as a procedural tool, is to insure economical and efficient trial of every case on its merits without chance or surprise.[3] One purpose of a Pretrial Order is to simplify the litigation process by avoiding unnecessary expense and delay and to eliminate surprise by sharpening and simplifying the issues that must be tried.[4] Pretrial Orders are to be liberally construed to cover any of the legal or factual theories that may be embraced by their language.[5] A Pretrial Order is definitive and represents a complete statement of all contentions of the parties and measures the dimensions of the lawsuit both in the trial court and on appeal. Plaintiff is obligated to reveal the theory of his case, to state the issues for trial with sufficient certainty and clarity, and to apprize the trial court and opposing defendants of what they must expect in the course of trial.[6]

Discretion of court

The District Court Judge has discretion as to whether to allow modification of a Pretrial Order, and that discretion is broad.[7]

Some general considerations of manifest injustice

The District Court should generally allow amendments of the Pretrial Order when no substantial injury to the opposing party would result, when the refusal to allow the amendment might result in injustice to the movant, and when the inconvenience to the Court is slight.[8] A Pretrial Order should not be lightly set aside, is not an inexorable decree, and may, under certain circumstances, be modified.[9] Allowing modification of a Pretrial Order balances the need for doing justice on the merits against the need for maintaining orderly and efficient procedural arrangements.[10] In addition, the modification of Pretrial Orders during trial takes into consideration the possible hardship to the parties and doing justice to the merits of the claim.[11]

Prejudice

The general rule is that where prejudice by the opposing party can be shown, a modification of a Pretrial Order will not be permitted. Thus, in *McFadden v. Sanchez*[12] the Second Circuit Court of Appeals held that a District Court may permit modifications of a Pretrial Order to prevent manifest injustice, though modification should not be allowed that would seriously prejudice one of the parties.[13]

Party as attorney

When a party is an attorney, a Pretrial Order will not be reopened.[14]

Time of amendment

Where the amendment is at the last hour of the case and perceived as untimely, it may be denied, although this is not always the case. Thus, in *Petree v. Victor Fluid Power, Inc.*,[15] the United States Court of Appeals for the Third Circuit held that the District Court did not abuse its discretion in refusing to grant an eleventh-hour motion to amend Pretrial Order where no compelling reason was given why the proposed continuing duty to warn of defects theory of liability was not disclosed at Pretrial Conference. In *McFadden v. Sanchez*,[16] however, the United States Court of Appeals for the Second Circuit held that late amendment of a Pretrial Order entered in a Civil Rights action to include a claim for punitive damages was not so prejudicial that the plaintiff should have been caused to lose her opportunity to retry that claim, since there was an error independent of the amendment precluding the punitive damages award as made.[17]

Stipulations

In general, the rule is parties are bound by stipulated facts and admissions in the Pretrial Order, but these too may be set aside to prevent manifest injustice.[18]

Witnesses

The trial judge is granted positive discretion and broad discretion in allowing modification to admit witnesses to prevent manifest injustice.[19]

Issues

The general rule is that the issues defined by the Pretrial Order ought to be adhered to in the absence of some good and sufficient reason and it is within the discretion of the trial Judge to amend the order.[20]

Consolidation of actions

A Pretrial Order, providing that a State Death Action and Admiralty Cause of Action be consolidated for trial and that separate verdicts and judgments be entered in respect to each claim, was not binding on the trial judge, but rather was a decision to be made by the trial judge.[21]

Counterclaims

Seneca Nursing Home v. Secretary of Social and Rehabilitations Services of Kansas[22] held that the trial court did not abuse its discretion or cause manifest injustice when it interpreted its Pretrial Order in such a way as to preclude consideration of certain asserted offsets and counterclaims. The Kansas Federal Circuit Court rejected the attempt of the Kansas Secretary of Social and Rehabilitation Services to assert offsets and counterclaims in response to the nursing home's suit to recover for services provided to welfare patients. The court rationalized that the proposed offsets and counterclaims would further delay resolution of an already stale matter that had been before the court of appeals twice.

Damages

The damage amount may be altered or modified by way of amendment of the Pretrial Order under certain circumstances. Thus, in *Brooks v. Wootton*,[23] the United States Court of Appeals for the Second Circuit held that permitting plaintiff in an automobile accident case to offer proof on issue of punitive damages, which was not included in the Pretrial Order, was permitted. The court held that the defendant had been given protection from unfair surprise since the Pretrial Order conceded that defendant had been convicted of driving while intoxicated. As a result, the court reasoned that plaintiff had every right to expect he would be able to show all the circumstances of the accident and rejected the defendant's attempt to preclude evidence of the intoxication by conceding liability.[24]

Defenses

In general, a Pretrial Order may not be modified or amended to add defenses not previously stated.[25]

Evidence

The Pretrial Order generally controls the admission of evidence at trial unless modified to prevent manifest injustice.[26] More specifically, unless particular evidence or theories are not at least implicitly included in the Pretrial Order, they are barred, unless manifest injustice can he shown.[27]

Records

A Pretrial Order may be amended to permit the introduction of certain records. Thus, in *Central Distributors, Inc. v . M.E.T., Inc.,*[28] the lessee was entitled to amend a stipulation incorporated into Pretrial Order to permit the introduction of records and to prove damages resulting from the lessor's failure to cooperate, as required by the License Agreement, in taking inventory upon the lessee's termination of the agreement. The Circuit Court of Florida held that the District Court's failure to permit such amendment was reversible error.[29]

Conclusion

The standards and criteria concerning modification and amendment of a Joint Pretrial Order under Rule 16 of the Federal Rules of Civil Procedure are governed by the standard of manifest injustice. In general, the law is that a Pretrial Order is binding in the absence of violation of the manifest injustice standard, but the discretion of the District Court Judge in this area is wide. The general rule that parties are bound by stipulated facts and admissions in the Pretrial Order may be set aside to prevent manifest injustice. Discretion of the District Court Judge is wide in this area and "manifest injustice" will be decided on an issue by issue, case by case basis.

This article previously appeared in an edition of The Nassau Lawyer, a publication of the Nassau County Bar Association, and is being reprinted here with the permission of The Nassau County Bar Association.

5. Eminent Domain: A Novel Approach

A few months ago, while reading *The New York Times* of January 25, 2006, I ran across an article which caught my attention that day. The article was about a church in San Springs, Oklahoma, the Centennial Baptist Church in an industrial hub west of Tulsa, Oklahoma, which was about to fall into the hands of the wrecker because the town of Sand Springs was moving ahead with a redevelopment plan to clear the church and other occupants from an allegedly run down district to make way for a group of super stores, including Home Depot. The City was moving to do this on the basis of a Supreme Court ruling in the summer of 2005 that approved the condemnation of private property by the City of

New London, Connecticut, for resale to other private profit interests for what the Court referred to as a "public purpose." The article went on to state that bills to block such a seizure as was occurring here were on the docket in Oklahoma and many other states, including Texas. The article stated that in Sand Springs, a city of 7,600 people on the Arkansas River, the redevelopment plan at issue dated from 2003. This article caught my attention because it involved a church that was being razed to be replaced by business interests in the name of Eminent Domain for a purported "public purpose."

The New York Times article led me to do a bit of research on Eminent Domain and look at the United States Supreme Court case in question. It is beyond the parameters of this article to detail, analyze, or examine the law of Eminent Domain, except in a general fashion as a prelude to the examination of the controversial United States Supreme Court case referred to in *The New York Times* article, *Kelo v. City of New London, Conn.*[1]

In general, Eminent Domain may be defined as the power vested in the State, as sovereign, to take private property for public use without the consent of the owner, whenever necessity demands, upon making just compensation.[2] In general, it may be said that the prohibitions and parameters of the State Constitution govern the exercise of the power of Eminent Domain, and these restrictions and conditions require that a taking be for a public use and require the payment of just compensation.[3] In New York, for example, the New York State Constitution declares that no person shall be deprived of property without due process of law and that private property may not be taken for public use without just compensation.[4] These provisions do not confirm or deny the power of Eminent Domain, but merely state the conditions under which it shall be exercised, namely that the taking be for a public use, that just compensation be given or provided for, and that due process of law be observed.[5]

The Federal Constitution by way of the Fifth Amendment similarly provides that private property shall not be taken for public use without just compensation, and although this amendment does not, by its own force, apply to or restrict the power of the States with regard to Eminent Domain, the command of that amendment has effect on the states by virtue of the 14th Amendment, which prohibits the States from depriving any person of his/her property without due process of law. Thus, with the adoption of the 14th Amendment there is a possibility of a Federal question in every taking by Eminent Domain under State authority, even where there has been full compliance with the requirements of a State Constitution.[6]

There are two prongs to every Eminent Domain case and seizure. First, there is the "taking" issue. As has been noted, the 5th Amendment provides that private property may not be "taken" by the Federal government without just compensation. The basic issue in Eminent Domain cases is whether the government's action on a person's private property amounts to a "taking."[7]

The second element of an Eminent Domain case, in addition that there be allowed a "taking," is that even when the government wants to take a person's property and is even willing to compensate him for it, that individual may be unwilling to part with his property and under the Fifth and Fourteenth Amendment to the United States Constitution, even upon payment for the property, the property must be taken for a "public use." The early interpretations of the public use test were interpreted as property taken for the public good, public necessity, or the public utility. In the latter half of the 19th Century, however, that broad interpretation of "public use" limitation was abandoned and what was substituted was a "use by the public test." That is to say, that the public had a right to use or enjoy the property taken. At the beginning of the 20th Century the United States Supreme Court gave up the "use by the public test" and returned to the broader "public benefit" test in determining when a use was public. The leading case defining what constitutes a public use is the 1954 United States Supreme Court decision in *Berman v. Parker*.[8] That case involved the constitutionality of the 1945 District of Columbia Redevelopment Act. The Act created the District of Columbia Redevelopment Land Agency and granted that Agency the power to assemble real property for the redevelopment of blighted areas of the City through the exercise of Eminent Domain. After assembling the necessary real-estate, Congress authorized the Agency to lease or sell portions of the land to private parties upon an agreement that the purchasers would carry out the redevelopment plan.

The appellants in *Berman* argue their property could not be taken, first because their property was commercial and not residential or slum housing, and second because by condemning the property for sale by a private agency for redevelopment the land was being redeveloped for a private and not a public use. The Supreme Court upheld the use of the Eminent Domain power in *Berman* holding that the Congress was exercising the "police power." Berman gave the public use limitation of the 5th and 14th Amendments an expansive view. The Court approved the concept of redevelopment

Similarly, the Supreme Court followed this broad public benefit test in *Berman* in upholding the Hawaii Land Reform Act of 1967. In that case, *Hawaii Housing Authority v. Midkiff*,[9] where the state legislature in Hawaii through this Act created a system for taking residential real property from lessors and transferring title to the lessees of the property in order to reduce the concentration of land ownership in the State, the Court found that this exercise of the Eminent Domain power was rationally related to the public purpose of correcting deficiencies in the real-estate market and social problems attributable to concentrated land ownership. The United States Supreme Court held that the fact that the property was transferred to private individuals did not invalidate the "taking," finding that the public use requirement was in line with the scope of the State's police powers.[10]

This short review of the law of Eminent Domain and its elements constitutes a preface to a full analysis and consideration of the groundbreaking, if not disturbing, decision of the United States Supreme Court in *Kelo v. City of New London, Conn.*[11] *Kelo v. City of New London, Conn.* bears careful analysis and consideration, since it presents a somewhat radical development in the law of Eminent Domain and, more specifically, in its interpretation of what constitutes a public use. The facts in *Kelo* were that the City of New London was targeted by State and Local officials for economic revitalization and to this end the New London Development Corporation, a private nonprofit corporation established some years earlier to assist the city in planning economic development, was reactivated. Bond issues were issued to create a Fort Trumbull State Park, and the pharmaceutical company Pfizer announced that it would build a 300 million dollar research facility on a site immediately adjacent to Fort Trumbull. Local planners hoped that Pfizer would draw new business to the area. Finally, the New London Development Corporation finalized a development plan focused on 90 acres of the Fort Trumbull area. That area formally consisted of 115 privately owned properties, as well as 32 acres of land formerly occupied by the naval facility. The development plan encompassed several parcels for various hotels, restaurants, shopping, marinas, a pedestrian river walk, 80 new residences, a U.S. Coast Guard museum, 90,000 square feet of research and development office space, parking and retail services for visitors to the adjacent State park or the nearby marina, a renovated marina, an office and retail space, and parking. The City Council approved the plan.

More specifically, the facts of the case were that the petitioner, Susette Kelo, had lived in the Fort Trumbull area since 1997 and had made extensive improvements to her house, which she prized for her water view. Petitioner Wilhelmina Dery was born in her Fort Tumbull house in 1918 and had lived there her entire life with her husband, Charles, also a petitioner. In all, nine petitioners owned 15 properties in Fort Trumbull. Ten were occupied by an owner or family member, and the other five were held as investment properties. There was no allegation that any of these properties were blighted or otherwise in poor condition, but in fact they were condemned only because they happened to be located in the development area. The petitioners brought action in the New London Superior Court claiming that the takings of their properties would violate the "public use" in the 5th Amendment in the United States Constitution and after a 7 day trial, the Superior Court granted a permanent restraining order prohibiting the taking of the properties located in parcel 4, but denied the petitioners relief as to the properties located in parcel 3.

Both sides appealed to the Supreme Court of Connecticut and that court held that all of the City's proposed takings were valid. The Court reasoned that the takings were authorized by a specific statute, Conn. Gen. Stat. Sec. 8-136, that the Court held expressed a legislative view that the taking of the land, even as part of an economic development project, is a "public use" and in the "public interest" relying on *Hawaii Housing Authority v. Midkiff*[12] and *Berman v. Parker.*[13] The Supreme Court granted certiorari to determine whether the City's decision to take property for the purpose of economic development satisfied the "public use" requirement of the 5th Amendment. The Court proceeded to reason that it was the long accepted rule that the State may not take the property of a private party for the sole purpose of transferring it to another private party, even though one party is paid just compensation. On the other hand, the Court stated that it is also equally clear that the state may transfer property from one party to another if future "use by the public" is the purpose of the taking. An example of future use, the Court said, would be condemnation of land for a railroad. The Court went on to reason that the City here would be forbidden from taking the petitioners' land for the purpose of conferring a private benefit on a particular private party. Nor, the Court said, would the City be allowed to take property under the pretext of a public purpose when its actual purpose was to bestow a private benefit. The Court noted, however, that the takings here would be executed pursuant to a carefully considered development plan, and the City's development plan was not adopted to benefit a particular class or identifiable individuals, again citing *Midkiff*. The Court went on to note that this was not a case in which the City was planning to open the condemned land to use by the general public. The Court then stated that the concept of use by the general public or use by the public was no longer the law and that that view of "public use," a narrow one, had steadily eroded over time. The Court then went on to analyze this area, noting that at the close of the 19th Century the concept and bright line in this area was changed to a "public purpose."

The Court then stated that the disposition of this case turned on whether the City's development plan served a "public purpose." The Court stated that that concept has been interpreted broadly and referenced *Berman v. Parker*[14] and *Hawaii Housing Authority v. Midkiff*[15] and also made note of *Ruckelshaus v. Monsanto*.[16] The Court then opined that a strong theme of Federalism was the "great respect" the Court owed to State legislatures and State courts in discerning local public needs. The Court then went on to analyze the development plan in question, and judged that the area, although not blighted, was sufficiently distressed to justify a program of economic rejuvenation and that that decision of the City was entitled to great deference. The Court stated that the city had formulated an economic development plan that it believed would provide substantial benefits to the community, including new jobs and increased revenue, and that the City was endeavoring to coordinate a variety of commercial, residential, and recreational use of land.

The Court rejected the petitioners' argument that economic development does not qualify as a "public use," noting that promoting economic development is a traditional, long accepted function of government. Again citing *Berman v. Parker*,[17] *Midkiff*,[18] and *Monsanto*,[19] the Court further noted that economic development could not be distinguished from other public purposes that the Court has recognized.

The Court rejected the petitioners' argument that using Eminent Domain for economic development impermissibly blurs the boundary between public and private takings. The Court noted, citing *Midkiff* and *Berman,* that the government's pursuit of a public purpose would often benefit private individual parties. The Court rejected the petitioners' argument that nothing would stop a City from transferring a citizen's property to another citizen for the sole reason that the benefited citizen would put the property to more productive use and pay more taxes. The Court stated that such a one-to-one transfer of property executed outside the confines of an integrated development plan is not presented in this case.

The Court also rejected the petitioners' argument that for takings of this kind we should require a "reasonable certainty" that the expected public benefits will actually accrue. The Court stated that such a rule, however, would represent an even greater departure from its precedent, citing *Midkiff.*[20]

The Court declined to second guess the City and the City's determination as to what lands it needed to acquire in order to effectuate the project. In short, the Court affirmed the City's authority here to take the petitioners' property, albeit not minimizing the hardship that these condemnations may entail, notwithstanding the payment of just compensation. The Court emphasized that nothing in this opinion precluded any state from placing further restrictions on its exercise of the takings power. In sum, the Court ruled that the Court's authority only extended to determining whether the City's proposed condemnations are for a "public use" within the meaning of the 5th Amendment to Federal Constitution and, in light of the case law, the Court said that this question must be answered in the affirmative.

Analysis and Conclusion

The *Kelo* decision is a groundbreaking and potentially societally impacting decision. *Kelo* posits the rule that the State, through its Eminent Domain power, can take private property with just compensation and seize it for economic development. It is admitted by the Court, in *Kelo*, that the people whose property was involved here were not economically disadvantaged, nor did the property present a blight to society. Their property was not an eyesore, yet the *Kelo* Court permitted property to be taken for private business and profit. It is not as if the property were seized to build a road, to make way for a railroad, or to serve some other truly public use. What the *Kelo* Court permitted here was property to be taken for economic development, which in reality was taken for business and corporate purposes and profit. The petitioners in *Kelo* were there for many years and valued and treasured their homes. What the property in *Kelo* was taken for was, in effect, to establish some kind of mall, a combined recreation and business area. The *Kelo* Court offers several reasons and justifications for this radical decision. The Court in *Kelo* says that deference is owed and due to the state legislature and what it determines is a good use to be put to land it may seek to seize and take for the general public. The Court also says that the criterion of "public use" has been modified and extended in its meaning and reach to "public purpose." Third, the *Kelo* Court cites two cases *Berman v. Parker*[21] and *Hawaii Housing Authority v. Midkiff.*[22] Both of those cases are distinguishable in the import and meaning they give to the Eminent Domain power. *Berman v. Parker* involved the assemblage of real property in the District of Columbia for redevelopment of blighted areas of the city. *Hawaii Housing Authority v. Midkiff* involved state legislation providing for the taking of residential real property from lessors and transferring titles to the lessees of the property in order to reduce the concentration of land ownership in the city. *Kelo*, on the other hand, admittedly did not involve solving the social problem of concentrated land ownership or eradicating slum housing, as was true in *Midkiff*, respectively, and *Berman*. The petitioners in *Kelo* were not the owners of blighted or slum housing. There was no allegation that any of the properties in *Kelo* were shanties or buildings in otherwise poor condition. Thus, the *Kelo* Court citations of *Berman* and *Midkiff* are irrelevant and serve to extend the meaning of *Midkiff* and *Berman* beyond their original intent and understanding in their interpretation of the Eminent Domain power. Moreover, the *Kelo* Court's argument that it is the term "public purpose" that governs and not "public use" also misses the mark and extends the Eminent Domain power far beyond its original meaning and thrust. Obviously, a "public purpose" can be interpreted broadly to mean any purpose that serves the well being of the general public, including an upscale mall complete with restaurants, parking, office space, and park land, as was contemplated by the City of New London in *Kelo*.

In short, "public purpose" can mean anything that happens to be seen and envisioned as good for the public. Glitz and upscale stores might be seen as good for the public, but is that the true meaning and conclusion to be attached and drawn out of the Eminent Domain power? As for deference to be given to state legislation, if such legislation is unconstitutional and wrong, it is appropriate to examine it and weigh what should be done, rather than simply to stamp it with some sort of Good Housekeeping Seal of Approval.

The interpretation that *Kelo* affords to the term "public use" and the manner in which it interprets that term extend the term to a meaning beyond its original import. Public use must mean and be interpreted as a common use, not a use connected to corporate profits. If the *Kelo* decision is allowed to stand then we are all, however modest our means and however lacking in funds, victimized by the forces of greed, business, and money. The *Kelo* decision is a disturbing precedent since it allows money to rule over persons and their homes. *Kelo* is capitalism and greed gone rampant, allowing the humble and the powerless, who have saved to establish a homestead and place for their children and grandchildren, to have their homes razed and taken for the sake of a better look. *Kelo*, in some sense, wants to make the world a world of Starbucks and Ruby Tuesdays. *Kelo* is a decision that enshrines profits and money and makes them the desiderata for all of us. Finally, *Kelo* opens the door to razing anybody's home if it stands in the way of modernity and what is perceived as upscale and raising the class level. It puts all of us in danger of destruction for the bulldozer of business interests. It is hoped that the Congress will pass legislation, and the state legislatures should pass such legislation, to provide for persons to be secure in their homes and personal possessions from the corporate power mongering that *Kelo* permits and gives operation to.

This article is reprinted from the November 2006 issue of the Queens Bar Bulletin, Vol. 70, No. 2 with the permission of the Queens County Bar Association.

Notes

1. Essay: An Exception to the Finality Requirement

1. See *Catlin v. United States,* 324 U.S. 229 (1945); *see also Lauro Lines SRL v. Chasser,* 490 U.S 495 (1978).

2. *EEOC v. Am. Exp. Co.* 588 F.2d. 102 (2d Cir. 1977); *CES Publ'g Corp. v. St. Regis Publ'n, Inc.,* 531 F.2d 11 (2d Cir. 1975).

3. 28 U.S.C. §1291 (1994). *See Firestone Tire and Rubber Co. v. Risgord,* 449 U.S. 368 (1981) (explaining that the finality requirement preserves rule and independence of the district court judge, eliminates successive appeals, and promotes effective judicial administration); *see also Di Bella v. United States,* 369 U.S. 121 (1962); *Allis-Chalmers Corp. v. Philadelphia Elec. Co.,* 521 F.2d 360 (3rd Cir. 1975).

4. 337 U.S. 541 (1949).

5. See also *United States v. Alcon Labs,* 636 F.2d 876 (1st Cir. 1981).

6. *See Richardson-Merrell, Inc. v. Koller,* 472 U.S. 424 (1985); *Flanagen v. United States,* 465 U.S. 259 (1984); *Coopers and Lybrand v. Livesay,* 437 U.S. 463 (1978) (orders decertifying class action not subject to Collateral Order Doctrine and therefore not appealable).

7. *See Coopers and Lybrand,* 437 U.S. 463 (1978).

8. 422 U.S. 511 (1981).

9. 407 U.S. 297 (1972).

10. 506 U.S. 139 (1993). *See* generally *Nixon v. Fitzgerald,* 457 U.S. 731 (1982); *Armendariz v. Penman,* 75 F.3d 1311 (9th Cir. 1996); *Taylor v. Bowers,* 966 F.2d 417 (8th Cir. 1992) (to the extent the district court's denial of claim of qualified immunity turns on issues of law, denial is appealable final decision, despite absence of final judgment); *Robinson v. Volkswagenwerk AG,* 940 F.2d 1369 (10th Cir. 1991); *Crymes v. DeKalb County,* 923 F.2d 1482 (11th Cir. 1991) (absolute immunity: county commissioners); *Auriemma v. Montgomery,* 860 F.2d 273 (7th Cir. 1988) (governmental officers); *Marx v. Gumbinner,* 855 F.2d 783 (11th Cir. 1988) (holding that absolute immunity did not adhere where defendants announced to the media the discontinuation of the prosecution; no immunity adhered to a press release); *Agromayor v. Colberg,* 738 F.2d 55 (1st Cir. 1984) (holding that the press officer position question was sufficiently essential to the legislative process to confer immunity).

2. Rule 15 and 16 of the Federal Rules of Civil Procedure: A Comparison

1. (a) Amendments. A party may amend the party's pleading once as a matter of course at any time before a responsive pleading is served or, if the pleading is one to which no responsive pleading is permitted and the action has not been placed upon the trial calendar, the party may so amend it at any time within 20 days after it is served. Otherwise a party may amend the party's pleading only by leave of court or by written consent of the adverse party; and leave shall be freely given when justice so requires. A party shall plead in response to an amended pleading within the time remaining for response to the original pleading or within 10 days after service of the amended pleading, whichever period may be the longer, unless the court otherwise orders.

2 (b) Scheduling and Planning. Except in categories of actions exempted by district court rule as inappropriate, the judge, or a magistrate when authorized by district court rule, shall, after consulting with the attorneys for the parties and any unrepresented parties, by a scheduling conference, telephone, mail, or other suitable means, enter a scheduling order that limits the time (1) to join other parties and to amend the pleadings; (2) to file and hear motions; and (3) to complete discovery. The scheduling order also may include: (4) the date or dates for conferences before trial, a final pretrial conference, and trial; and (5) an other matters appropriate in the circumstances of the case. The order shall issue as soon as practicable but in no event more than 120 days after filling of the complaint. A schedule shall not be modified except by leave of the judge or a magistrate when authorized by district court rule upon a showing of good cause.

3. *Id.*

4. See *Davenport v. Ralph N. Peters & Co.*, 386 F.2d 199 (C.A. N.C. 1967); *Manhattan Fuel Co., Inc. v. New England Petroleum Corp.*, 422 F. Supp. 797 (D.C.N.Y. 1976), *aff'd.* 578 F.2d 1368; *Walder v. Paramount Publix Corp.*, 135 F. Supp. 228 (D.C. N.Y. 1955); *McHenry v. Ford Motor Co.*, 269 F.2d 18 (C.A. Mich. 1959); *Fuhrer v. Fuhrer*, 292 F.2d 140 (C.A. Ind. 1961).

5. *Middle Atlantic Utilities Co. v. SMW Development Corp.*, 392 F.2d 380 (2nd Cir. 1968); again in *Brown v. Dunbar and Sullivan Dredging Co.*, 189 F.2d 871 (2nd Cir. 1951), the United States Court of Appeals for the Second Circuit held that the Federal Rules were intended to facilitate the application of substantive law and not to fight it and they contemplate free amending privileges; similarly in *Reeves v. Sielaff*, 382 F. Supp. 472 (D.C. Pa. 1974), the Pennsylvania District Court held that the purpose of allowing amendment of the pleadings is to permit a final decision on the merits and not on technicalities. *See also David v. Crompton and Knowles Corp.*, 58 FRD 444 (D.C. Pa. 1973), where the Pennsylvania District Court held that the purpose of a permissive or liberal attitude towards amendments of pleadings is to encourage decision of the case on the merits by allowing the parties to present the real issues of the case. *See also Dussouy v. Gulf Coast, Inv. Corp.*, 660 F.2d 594 (C.A. La. 1981); cf. however, *Scott v. Crescent Tool Co., Inc.*, 306 F. Supp, 884 (D.C. Ga. 1969), where the Georgia District Court noted that amendments should be freely granted unless the rights of the adverse party are prejudiced and that even if some prejudice is found, such prejudice must be balanced against hardship to the moving party if leave to amend is denied.

6. 671 F.2d 779 (C.A. Pa. 1982).

7. On this *see* also *Barrett v. Independent Order of Foresters*, 625 F.2d 73 (C.A. Ga. 1980); *Freeman v. Continental Gin Co.*, 381 F.2d 459 (C.A. Miss. 1967); *Cassell v. Michaux*, 240 F.2d 406 (D.C. Cir. 1956).

8. *Wilson v. Lamberton*, 102 F.2d 506 (C.A. Pa. 1939); on the District Court's wide discretion to grant or deny motions for amend *See also Taylor v. National Group of Companies, Inc.*, 765 F. Supp. 411 (N.D. Ohio 1990); *See also Spampinato v. M. Breger & Co.*, 176 F.Supp. 149 (D.C.N.Y. 1958); and *Poloron Products, Inc. v. Lybrand Ross Bros. & Montgomery*, 72 F.R.D. 556 (D.C.N.Y. 1976), where the New York District Court noted that the District Court's discretion could not be an unbridled discretion. For further cases on liberality in granting of the amendment see *Toth v. USX Corp.*, 883 F.2d 1297, (C.A. 7 1989) (Held: Amendments freely granted so long as amendments do not unfairly surprise or prejudice the defendant.) Thus, *Layfield v. Bill Heard Chevrolet, Co.*, 607 F.2d 1097 (C.A. Ga. 1979), as a further refinement of this rule, held that leave to

amend a complaint is by no means automatic. *See also U.S. for Benefits and Use of Ehmcke Sheet Metal Works v. Wausau Ins. Companies,* 755 F. Supp. 906 (E.D. Cal. 1991), where the California District Court held that the amendments to pleadings are liberally allowed, but they may be denied as a result of undue delay, bad faith, undue prejudice to the opposing party, or futility of a proposed amendment. On this *see also, Foremost-McKesson Inc. v. Islamic Republic of Iran,* 759 F. Supp. 855 (D.D.C. 1991), where the District Court held that leave to amend a complaint should be freely given absent undue delay, undue prejudice, or futility of the amendment.

9. *Standard Title Ins. Co. v. Roberts,* 349 F.2d 613 (C.A. Mo. 1965) and *Caddy-Imler Creations, Inc. v. Caddy,* 299 F.2d 79 (C.A. Cal. 1962).

10. 689 F. 2d 640 (C.A. Ill. 1982).

11. See also *S.S. Silberblatt, Inc. v. East Harlem Pilot Block-Bldg. 1 Housing Development Fund Co., Inc.,* 608 F.2d 28 (C.A. N.Y. 1979) and *Rohler v. TRW, Inc.,* 576 F.2d 1260 (C.A. Ind. 1978).

12. 757 F.Supp. 297 (S.D.N.Y. 1991) 41.

13. *See also* on "bad faith" *GSS Properties, Inc. v. Kendale Shopping Center, Inc.,* 119 F.R.D. 379 (M.D.N.C. 1988) and *Moll v. Southern Charters. Inc.,* 81 F.R.D. 77 (D.C.N.Y. 1979).

14. 728 F. Supp. 1259 (W.D.N.C. 1990).

15. See also *Schempp v. School Dist. of Abington Twp., Pa.,* 195 F. Supp. 518 (D.C. Pa. 1961); *Hood v. P. Valentine & Sons,* 38 FRD 502 (D.C.N.Y. 1965).

16. See *Artman v. Int'l Harvester Co.,* 355 F.Supp. 476 (D.C. Pa. 1972) and *Glesenkamp v. Nationwide Mutual Ins. Co.,* 71 FRD 1 (D.C. Cal. 1976).

17. *Bernstein v. National Liberty Int'l Corp.,* 407 F. Supp. 709 (D.C. Pa. 1976); *Cf. Krzske v. CIR,* 548 F.Supp. 101 (D. C. Mich. 1982) (Held: Noncompliance with Federal Rules and Statutes resulted in denial of leave to amend complaint.)

18. *See United States For and on behalf of Maritime Admin. v. Continental Illinois Nat'l Bank & Trust Co. of Chicago,* 889 F. 2d 1248 (C.A. 2 N.Y. 1989); *Quaker State Oil Refining Corp. v. Garrity Oil Co., Inc.,* 884 F.2d 1510 (CA. 1 Mass. 1989); *Nevels v. Ford Motor Co.,* 439 F.2d 251 (C.A. Ga. 1971). See also *Boyle v. Texas Gulf Aviation, Inc.,* 696 F.Supp. 951 (S.D.N.Y. 1988); *Sanders v. Thrall Car Mfg., Co.,* 582 F. Supp. 945 (D.C.N.Y. 1983); *Hare v. Family Publications Service, Inc.,* 342 F.Supp. 678 (D.C. Md. 1972).

19. *Richardson Greenshields Securities, Inc. v. Muihin Lau,* 113 FRD 608 (S.D.N.Y. 1986); *Daves v. Payless Cashways, Inc.,* 661 F.2d 1022 (C.A. Tex. 1981).

20. 35 FRD 159 (D.C. Pa. 1964).

21. See *Rhodes v. Amarillo Hospital Dist.,* 654 F.2d 1148 (C.A. Tex. 1981) and *Kleiner v. First Nat'l Bank of Atlanta,* 526 F.Supp. 1019 (D.C. Ga. 1981).

22. *Villa v. City of Chicago,* 924 F.2d 629 (C.A.7 Ill. 1991); *Morongo Band of Mission Indians v. Rose,* 893 F.2d 1074 (C.A. 9 Cal. 1991); *Middle Atlantic Utilities Co. v. S.M.W. Development Corp.,* 392 F.2d 380 (C.A.N.Y. 1968). See also *Robinson v. Cuyler,* 511 F.Supp. 161 (D.C. Pa. 1981) (3 year delay coupled with other factors including futility and prejudice); *Rogers v. Valentine,* 306 F.Supp. 34 (D.C.N.Y. 1969) (5 year delay, though not conclusive, was a salient consideration); *Vibrant Sales, Inc. v. New Body Boutique, Inc.,* 105 FRD 553 (D.C.N .Y. 1985).

23. *Id.*

24. *Dole v. Arco Chemical Co.,* 921 F.2d 484 (C.A. 3 1990) and *Deasy v. Hill,* 833 F.2d 38 (C.A. 4 Va. 1987).

25. 132 F.R.D. 39 (D.C.N.Y. 1990).

26. Compare, however, *Jenn-Air, Products Co. v. Venn Ventilator, Inc.*, 283 F.Supp. 591 (D.C. Pa. 1968) (plaintiff permitted to amend despite unexplained delay where trial was several months away, the patents in a patent infringement action were related, and if the motion were denied the plaintiff could institute a separate action.) See also *Computer Associates, Inter., Inc. v. Computer Automation, Inc.*, 678 F.Supp. 424 (S.D.N.Y. 1987) (New claim permitted where no undue delay and no bad faith were shown.)

27. On this see *Mir. V. Fosburg*, 646 F.2d 342 (CA. Cal. 1980); *Mateza v. Walker*, 469 F.Supp. 1276 (D.C. Mass. 1979); *Continental Bank, N.A. v. Caton*, 136 FRD 691 (D. Kan. 1991).

28. See on this rule *Coleman v. Ramada Hotel Operating Co.*, 933 F.2d 470 (C.A.7 Ill. 1991); *Slavin v. Benson*, 493 F.Supp. 32 (D.C.N.Y. 1980); *Glover v. City of New York*, 446 F.Supp. 110 (D.C.N.Y. 1978); and *Johnson v. Helicopter & Airplane Services Corp.*, 389 F.Supp. 509 (D.C. Md. 1974).

29. 909 F.2d 267 (C.A.7 Ill. 1990).

30. *See also Huse v. Consolidated Freightways*, 227 F.2d 425 (C.A. Wis. 1955); *Canister Co. v. Leahy*, 182 F.2d 510 (C.A. Del. 1950).

31. *Byrne v. Buffalo Creek R. Co.*, 536 F.Supp. 1301 (D.C.N.Y. 1982); *Pollux Marine Agencies, Inc., M.V. Captain Demosthenes v. Louis Dreyfus Corp.*, 455 F. Supp. 211 (D.C.N.Y. 1960); and *Hirshhorn v. Mine Safety Appliances Co.*, 101 F.Supp. 549 (D.C. Pa. 1951).

32. 732 F.Supp. 791 (N.D. Ohio 1990).

33. 598 F.2d 1061 (C.A. Wis. 1979).

34. On meritless claims see *Ross v. Zavarella*, 732 F.Supp. 1306 (M.D. Pa 1990); *Truehart v. Blandon*, 684 F.Supp. 1368 (E.D. La. 1988); and *Sentner v. Amtrak*, 540 F.Supp. 57 (D.C.N.J. 1982).

35. 67 FRD 129 (D.C. Pa. 1974).

36. See also *Kas v. Financial General Bankshares. Inc.*, 105 FRD 453 (D.C.D.C. 1984).

37. See *Nielson v. Armstrong Rubber Co.*, 570 F.2d 272 (C.A.N.D. 1978); *Hageman v. Signal L.P. Gas, Inc.*, 486 F.2d 479 (C.A. Ohio 1973); *Hanson v. Hunt Oil Co.*, 398 F.2d 578 (C.A.N.D. 1968).

38. 296 F.2d 303 (C.A. Ohio 1961).

39. *Kartell v. Blue Shield of Massachusetts, Inc.*, 687 F.2d 543 (C.A. Mass. 1982); *Dostert v. Crowley*, 394 F.2d 178 (C.A. Md. 1968); and *Williams v. Lewis*, 342 F.2d 727 (C.A. Va. 1965).

40. *Esquire Radio & Electronics, Inc. v. Montgomery Ward & Co., Inc.* 804 F.2d 787 (C.A. 2 N.Y. 1986); *Hanson v. Hunt Oil Co.*, 398 F.2d 578 (C.A.N.D 1968); *Hicks v. Resolution Trust Corp.*, 738 F.Supp. 279 (N.D. Ill. 1990).

41. 204 F.3d 326 (2d Cir. 2000).

42. See also on this *Colorado Capital v. Owens*, 227 FRD 181 (E.D.N.Y. 2005), where the court held that, while under Rule 15 leave to amend should be freely granted, it is important to distinguish where rule 16 and a scheduling order is involved. In *Colorado Capital* the court noted that because the request was made after the deadline imposed by the Magistrate's Scheduling Order, the different standard of review, the good cause standard under Rule 16, governed. The court went on to state, citing *Parker and Rent-A-Center, Inc. v. 47 Mamaroneck Avenue Corp.*, 215 F.R.D. 100, 101 (S.D.N.Y. 2003), that good cause has been defined to mean that a party must show that despite their diligence the court timetable could not have reasonably been met. The court concluded that the August 30 motion to amend was filed over five months past the deadline for amended pleadings and that the movant did not specifically state his reasons for amending the

complaint in his letter motion to amend, or in any other supporting document. Hence, the court ruled that the movant had failed to establish good cause for missing the Scheduling Order deadline.

43. 743 F.Supp. 1437 (D. Kan. 1990).

44. Cf. on this *Amcast Indus. Corp. v. Detrex Corp.* Cercla 132 F.R.D. 213 (N.D. Ind. 1990) where the district court of the Northern District of Indiana held that in a circla action brought by a corporation and its wholly owned subsidiary against the subsidiary's former shareholders, neither the plaintiff's explanation nor the assertive absence of prejudice to defendants was a sufficient showing of "good cause" to warrant modification of the scheduling deadline for filing amendments to the pleadings. The court noted that the plaintiffs failed to explain why they did not allege that the former shareholders were "operators" of the facility at which ground water pollution was discovered as well as "owners" of the facility before the deadline expired, but instead waited to make amendment until the former shareholders moved for Summary Judgment on the ground that they were not "owners."

See also on "good cause" *Gestetner v. Case Equipment Co.*, 168 FRD 138 (D.C. Me. 1985); *Forstmann v. Culp*, 114 FRD 83 (M.D. N.C. 1987) (Held: Even though good cause shown, motion denied where defendants would be substantially prejudiced as discovery had been closed.); *cf. Spiller v. Ella Smithers Geriatric Center*, 919 F.2d 339 (5th Cir. 1990) (Held: Trial court granted motion to amend Scheduling Order to allow additional time to file motions by allowing defendant to move for Summary Judgment after original cut off date, notwithstanding the plaintiff's objections.)

3. Enforceability of an Oral Settlement: A Consideration and Analysis

1. 131 F. 3rd 320 (2d Cir. 1997).
2. 751 F. 2d 69 (2d Cir. 1984).
3. *Id.*
4. 777 F. 2d (2d Cir. 1985).
5. *Id.*
6. 236 F. Supp. 2d 241 (E.D.N.Y. 2002).
7. 953 F. Supp. 557 (S.D.N.Y. 1997).
8. 31 N.Y.2d 833, 334 N.Y.S.2d 228 (1972).
9. 73 F.3rd 1276 (2d Cir. 1990).
10. Cf. however, *Sunrise v. Consolidated Rail Corp.*, 992 F. Supp 146 (N.D.N.Y 1998), where the District Court noted, citing *Hartford Fire Insurance v. SS 'AN CUHN,'* No. 96 Civ 7738 (O.L.C), 1997 WL 790578 (S.D.N.Y. Dec. 29, 1997), that commitment to writing or placement on the record are not absolute requirements for the enforcement of settlement agreements.

4. Perils and Pitfalls of Pretrial Orders

1. (a) Pretrial Conferences; Objectives
   (b) Scheduling and Planning
   (c) Subjects to be discussed at Pretrial Conferences
   (d) Final Pretrial Conference
   (e) Pretrial Orders
   (f.) Sanctions

2. After any conference held pursuant to this rule, an order shall be entered reciting the action taken. This order shall control the subsequent course of the

action unless modified by a subsequent order. The order following a final pretrial conference shall be modified only to prevent manifest injustice.

3. *Smith v. Ford Motor Co.*, 626 F.2d 784 (10th Cir. 1980).

4. See *Seneca Nursing Home v. Secretary of Social and Rehabilitation Services of Kansas*, 604 F.2d 1309 (10th Cir. 1979); *Walker v. West Coast Fast Freight, Inc.*, 233 F.2d 939 (9th Cir. 1956). *See also U.S. v. First Nat. Bank of Circle*, 652 F.2d 882 (9th Cir. 1981) (Unless Pretrial Orders are honored and enforced the object of the Pretrial Conference to simplify issues and avoid unnecessary proof will be jeopardized if not nullified.).

5. *Rodrigues v. Ripley Industries, Inc.*, 507 F.2d 782 (1st Cir. 1974).

6. *Trujillo v. Uniroyal Corp.*, 608 F.2d 815 (10th Cir. 1979); *American Home Assur. Co. v. Cessna Aircraft Co.*, 551 F.2d 804 (10th Cir. 1977); *Johnson v. Geffen*, 294 F.2d 197 (D.C. 1960).

7. See *Sadowski v. Bombardier Ltd.*, 539 F.2d 615 (7th Cir. 1976); *De Laval Turbine, Inc. v. West India Industries, Inc.*, 502 F.2d 259 (3d Cir. 1974); *Bettes v. Stonewall Ins. Co.*, 480 F.2d 92 (5th Cir. 1973); *Wallin v. Fuller*, 476 F.2d 1204 (5th Cir. 1973); *Ely v. Reading Co.*, 424 F.2d 758 (3d Cir. 1970); *Washington Hospital Center v. Cheeks*, 394 F.2d 964, 129 U.S. App. D.C. 339 (1968); *U.S. v. State of Tex.*, 523 F.Supp. 703 (E.D. Tex. 1981); *Matter of Beefeaters, Inc.*, 27 B.R. 848 (Bankr. Mich. 1983).

8. *Campbell Industries v. M/V Gemini*, 619 F.2d 24 (9th Cir. 1980).

9. See *Bettes v. Stonewall Ins. Co.*, supra.; *Jeffries v. U.S.*, 477 F.2d 52 (9th Cir. 1973).

10. *Laguna v. American Export Isbrandtsen Lines, Inc.* 439 F.2d 97 (2nd Cir. 1971).

11. *Washington Hospital Center v. Cheeks*, supra. See also *Cruz v. U.S. Lines Co.*, 386 F.2d 803 (2nd Cir. 1967) ("Interest of Justice"); *Case v. Abrams*, 352 F. 2d 193 (10th Cir. 1965) (Balance between preserving essential integrity of order and adaptability to meet changed or newly discovered conditions or to respond to special demands of Justice); *Sill Corp. v. U.S.*, 343 F.2d 411 (10th Cir. 1965) (Pretrial Orders are blueprints for trial and should not be relaxed in absence of good cause, but may always be modified in interest of administration of justice.).

12. *McFadden v. Sanchez*, 710 F.2d. 907 (2nd Cir. 1983).

13. *See also* on prejudice *Angle v. Sky Chef*, 535 F.2d 492 (9th Cir. 1976); *Manbeck v. Ostrowski*, 384 F.2d 970, 128 U.S. App. D.C. 1 (1967); *Hale v. Firestone Tire and Rubber Co.*, 756 F.2d 1322 (8th Cir. 1985).

14. *Associated Beverages Co. v. P. Vallantine & Sons*, 287 F.2d 261 (5th Cir. 1961).

15. *Fischer & Porter Co., Inc. v. U.S Intern. Trade Com'n*, 831 F.2d 1191 (3d Cir. 1987).

16. *Id.*

17. *See also, Colvin v. U. S. for Use and Benefit of Magini Leasing and Contracting*, 549 F.2d 1338 (9th Cir. 1977); *Stahlin v. Hilton Hotels Corp.*, 484 F.2d 580 (7th Cir. 1973); *Payne v. S.S. Nabob*, 302 F.2d 803 (3d Cir. 1962); *Dozier v. J.A. Jones Const. Co., Inc.*, 587 F.Supp. 289 (E.D. La. 1984); *Vanlandingham v. Ford Motor Co.*, 99 F.R.D. 1 (N.D. Ga. 1983); *Marble v. Batten & Co.*, 36 F.R.D. 693 (D.D.C. 1964).

18. See *Islamic Republic of Iran v. Boeing Co.*, 771 F. 2d 1279 (9th Cir. 1985); *United States v. Tampa Bay Garden Apartments, Inc.*, 294 F.2d 598 (5th Cir. 1961); *Coastal States Marketing, Inc. v. Hun*, 694 F.2d 1358 (5th Cir. 1983); *E.H. Boly & Son Inc. v. Schneider*, 525 F.2d 20 (9th Cir. 1975); *Mull v. Ford Motor Co.*, 368 F.2d 713 (2d Cir. 1966); *Associated Press v. Cook*, 513 F.2d 1300 (10th Cir. 1975); *Central Distributors, Inc. v. M.E.T., Inc.*, 403 F.2d 943, 5th Cir. 1968); *Chatzicharalambus v. Petit*, 430

F.Supp. 1087 (E.D. La. 1977); *Peter Pan Seafoods, Inc. v. U.S.*, 272 F. Supp. 888 (W.D. Wash. 1967).

19. *United States v. International Business Machine Corp.*, 87 F.R.D. 411 (S.D.N.Y. 1980); *Lirette v. Popich Bros. Water Transport Inc.*, 660 F.2d 142 (5th Cir. 1981).

20. *Trujillo v. Uniroyal Corp., supra.; United States v. Joyce*, 511 F.2d 1127 (9th Cir. 1975); *Commercial Ins. Co. of Newark, N.J. v. Smith*, 417 F.2d 1330 (10th Cir. 1969); *Manbeck v. Ostrowski*, 384 F.2d 970, 128 U.S. App. D.C. 1 (1967); *Case v. Abrams*, 352 F.2d 193 (10th Cir. 1965); *Becker v. Marketing and Research Consultants, Inc.*, 526 F.Supp. 166 (D. Gol. 1981); *United States v. An Article of Drug, Acnotabs*, 207 F. Supp. 758 (D.N.J. 1962); *Olson v. Shinnihon Kisen K.K.*, 25 F.R.D. 7 (E.D. Penn. 1960); *Flanders v. U.S.*, 172 F. Supp. 935 (N.D. Cal. 1959); *Neuspickle v. City of Knoxville, Tenn.*, 48 F.R.D. 441 (E.D. Tenn. 1969); *Washington v. General Motors Acceptance Corp.*, 19 F.R.D. 370 (S.D. Fla. 1956); *Yale Transport Corp. v. Yellow Truck & Coach Mfg. Co.*, 3 F.R.D. 440 (S.D.N.Y. 1944).

21. *First Nat. Bank in Greenwich v. National Airlines, Inc.*, 288 F.2d 621 (2nd Cir. 1961).

22. *Seneca Nursing Home*, 604 F.2d 1309 (10th . Cir. 1979).

23. *Brooks v. Wootton*, 355 F.2d 177 (2nd Cir. 1966).

24. *See also Draft Systems, Inc. v. Rimar Mfg., Inc.*, 524 F.Supp. 1049 (E.D. Penn. 1981). *Cf. Associated Press v. Cook*, 513 F.2d 1300 (10th Cir. 1975) (Record in breach of contract action failed to disclose any manifest injustice such as would entitle the defendant to amend the Pretrial Order in which the parties conceded that the amounts claimed by the plaintiff were the proper measure of damages, unless the defendant had the right to terminate the agreement.); *See also Clemones v. Alabama Power Co.*, 250 F.Supp. 433 (N.D. Ga. 1966) (Where no exception was filed to Pretrial Order wherein parties stipulated as to the measure of damages, it controlled the case thereafter.).

25. *G & R Corp. v. American Sec. and Trust Co.*, 523 F.2d 1164, 173 U.S. App. D.C. 215 (1975) *See also Canal Ins. Co. v. First General Ins. Co.*, 889 F.2d 604 (5th Cir. 1989).

26. *Colvin v. U.S. for Use and Benefit Magini Leasing and Contracting*, 549 F.2d 1338 (9th Cir. 1977).

27. *United States v. First Nat. Bank of Circle*, 652 F.2d 882 (9th Cir. 1981).

28. *Central Distributors, Inc. v. M.E.T. Inc.*, 403 F.2d 943 (5th Cir. 1968).

29. *Cf Lucra v. Snyder*, 599 F.Supp. 1459 (D. Col. 1984) where the Colorado District Court held that the trial court did not err in allowing the defendants to introduce a videotape of the incident giving rise to litigation where such videotape was included in a Pretrial Order. It did not err in prohibiting plaintiffs from introducing other videotapes that were not included in the Pretrial Order.

5. Eminent Domain: A Novel Approach

1. 545 U.S. 469, 125 S. Ct. 2655, 162 L.Ed. 439 (2005).

2. Vol. 51, N.Y.Jur.2d, Eminent Domain, p. 24, Sec. 1, Thomson West, 2005. *See also People v. Adirondack Ry. Co.*, 160 N.Y.225, 54 N.E.689 (1899); *West 41st Realty, LLC v. New York State Urban Development Corp.*, 298 A.D.2d 1, 744 N.Y.S. 121 (1st Dept. 2002).

3. Vol. 51, N.Y.Jur.2d, Eminent Domain, pp. 30-31, Sec. 5, Thomson West, 2005. *See also Cannata v. City of New York*, 24 Misc.2d 694, 204 N.Y.S. 982 (S. Ct. Kings County 1960); *Kahlen v. State*, 223 N.Y.383, 119 N.E.883 (1918); *Gilman v. Tucker*, 128

N.Y.190, 28 N.E.1040 (1891); *In Re Brooklyn Battery Tunnel Plaza*, 186 Misc. 603, 62 N.Y.S. 303, (S. Ct. Kings County 1946).

    4. N.Y.Const. Art.#1, Secs. 6, 7(a).

    5. Vol. 51, N.Y.Jur.2d, Eminent Domain, p. 31, Sec. 5, Thomson West, 2005.

    6. Vol. 51, N.Y.Jur.2d, Eminent Domain, p.32, Sec. 6, Thomson West, 2005 and U.S. Constitution Amendments V and XIV.

    7. For an analysis on "taking" see CONSTITUTIONAL LAW, 7th Ed., JOHN E. NOWAK & RONALD D. ROTUNDA, Sec. 11.12, pp. 509-542, Thomson West, 2000.

    8. 348 U.S. 26, 75 S Ct. 98, 99 L.Ed. 27 (1954).

    9. 467 U.S. 229, 104 S. Ct. 2321, 81 L.Ed.2d 186 (1984).

    10. CONSTITUTIONAL LAW, 7th Ed., JOHN. E. NOWAK AND RONALD D. ROTUNDA, Sec. 11.13, pp. 542-544, Thomson West, 2000.

    11. *Id.*

    12. *Id.*

    13. *Id.*

    14. *Id.*

    15. *Id.*

    16. 467 U.S. 986, 104 S. Ct. 2862, 81 L.Ed.2d 815 (1984).

    17. *Id.*

    18. *Id.*

    19. *Id.*

    20. 0467 U.S. 242, 104 S. Ct. 2321 (1984). Here the Supreme Court held that when the legislature's purpose is legitimate and its means are not irrational, the cases are clear that empirical debates over the wisdom of takings—no less than debates over the wisdom of other kinds of socioeconomic legislation—are not to be carried out in the Federal Courts.

    21. *Id.*

    22. *Id.*

Table of Cases

Gonzalez v. Medina, 69 A.D.2d 14, 470, N.Y.S.2d 953 (1st Dept. 1979)
Goodstein v. Bombardier Capital, Inc., 889 F. Supp. 760, 763-65 (D.Vt. 1995)
Gordon v. City of New York, 401 F. Supp. 632 (E.D.N.Y. 1975)
Gordon v. City of Warren, .579 F.2d 386 (6th Cir. 1978)
Gordon v. Eastern Airlines, Inc., 391 F. Supp. 31 (S.D.N.Y. 1975)
Gould v. Community Health Plan of Suffolk, 99 A.D.2d 479, 470 N.Y.S.2d 415 (2nd Dept. 1984)
Graef v. North University Hospital, IF Supp.2d 318 (S.D.N.Y. 1998)
Graham v. Connor, 490 U.S. 386 (1989)
Grancaris v. J.I. Hass Co., 79 A.D. 2d 551, 434 N.Y.S.2d 19 (1st Dept. 1980)
Graney Development Corp. v. Taksen, [66 A.D.2d 1008, 411 N.Y.S.2d 757 (4th Dept. 1978)
Grant v. City of Rochester, 68 Misc.2d 358, 326 N.Y.S.2d 691 (Sup. Ct., Monroe Co. 1971)
Grant v. Guidotti, 66 A.D. 2d 545, 414 N.Y.S.2d 171 (2d Dept. 1979)
Grant v. Lone Star Co., 21 F.3d 649, 651-653 (5th Cir. 1994), *cert. denied.*
Grasso v. State of New York, 177 Misc. 690, *aff'd.* 264 App. Div. 745, *aff'd.* 289 N.Y. 552
Greco v. Kresge Co., 277 N.Y. 26, 32, 12 N.E.2d 557, 560
Green v. Hudson Riv. R.R. Co., 28 Barb. 9 (Sup. Ct. 1858), *aff'd.* 2 Abb. Ct. of App. 277 (1866)
Greenberg v. City of Yonkers, 45 A.D.2d 314, 358 N.Y.S.2d 453 (2d Dept. 1974)
Gregory v. Harris Teeter Supermarkets, Inc., 728 F. Supp. 1259 (W.D.N.C. 1990)
Grigorian v. Poluszek, 22 A.D.2d 704, 253 N.Y.S.2d 804 (2d Dept. 1964)
Grube v. Lau Industries, Inc., 257 F.3d 723 (7th Cir. 2001)
GSS Properties, Inc. v. Kendale Shopping Center, Inc., 119 F.R.D. 379 (M.D.N.C. 1988)
Guardianship of Sonia Vanessa R., 97 Misc. 2d 694, 412 N.Y.S.2d 257 (Fam. Ct., N.Y. Co. 1978)
Gurkin v. Siege, 122 Misc. 2d 302 (S. Ct. New York County 1983)
Gursky v. Gursky, 39 Misc. 2d 1083, 242 N.Y.S.2d 406 (Sup. Ct., Kings Co. 1963)

Habenicht v. R. K. O. Theaters, Inc., 23 A.D.2d 378, 260 N.Y.S.2d 890 (1st Dept. 1965)
Habersham v. Grimaldi, 18 A.D.2d 615, 234 N.Y.S.2d 599 (1st Dept. 1962)
Haehl v. Village of Portchester, 463 F. Supp. 845 (S.D.N.Y. 1978)
Hageman v. Signal L.P. Gas, Inc., 486 F.2d 479 (C.A. Ohio 1973)
Hager v. Hutchins, 91 Misc. 2d 402, 398 N.Y.S.2d 316 (Sup. Ct., Orange Co. 1977)
Hairston v. Broadwater, 73 Misc.2d 523, 342 N.Y.S.2d 787 (Supreme Court, Nassau County 1973)
Hale v. Firestone Tire and Rubber Co., 756 F.2d 1322 (8th Cir. 1985)
Halio v. Lurie, 15 A.D.2d 62, 67, 222 N.Y.S.2d 759, 754 (2d Dept. 1961)
Hall & Co. of N. Y. v. Orient Overseas Assoc., 65 A.D.2d 424 (1st Dept. 1978), *affd,* 48 N.Y.2d 958 (1979)
Hammer v. St. Vincent Hospital and Health Care Center, Inc., 224 F.3rd 701 (7th Cir. 2000)
Hancock v. Ingersoll-Rand Co., 21 A.D.2d 703, 249 N.Y.S.2d 43 (3d Dept. 1964)
Hanson v. Hunt Oil Co., 398 F.2d 578 (C.A.N.D 1968)
Harbor Associates, Inc. v. Asheroff, 35 A.D.2d 667 (2d Dept. 1970)
Hare v. Family Publications Service, Inc., 342 F.Supp. 678 (D.C. Md. 1972)
Harrigan v. Hudson Sheraton Corp., 2 F.Supp. 2d 475 (S.D.N.Y. 1998)
Harris v. New York, 401 U.S. 222 (1971)

Appendix – Original Sources

Chapter 1
Criminal Law Reprinted Articles

1. "The Right to a Speedy Trial: C.P.L. Sec. 30.20: An Overview." *The Mouthpiece, Newsletter of the New York State Association of Criminal Defense Lawyers,* May/June 1993.
2. "Suppressing the Beeper in the Drug Sale." *The Suffolk Lawyer,* April 1993.
3. "Due Diligence under C.P.L. Sec. 30.30(4)(c): A Recent Development." *The Queens Bar Bulletin,* April 1993.
4. "C.P.L. Sec. 30.30: A Sequel." *The Queens Bar Bulletin,* May 1993.
5. "A Note on Burglary in the Second Degree." *The Suffolk Lawyer,* October 1993.
6. "*Brady*: Part One." *The Suffolk Lawyer,* November 1993.
7. "Conspiracy: The Necessity of an Overt Act." *Atticus, the Newsletter of the New York State Association of Defense Lawyers,* Vol. 20, March/April 2007.
8. "*Brady*, Part Two." *The Suffolk Lawyer,* December 1993.
9. "The Accidental Showup." *The Suffolk Lawyer,* January 1994.
10. "Psychiatric Examination of the Complainant in Criminal Law: Some Case Law." *The Mouthpiece, Newsletter of the New York State Association of Criminal Defense Lawyers,* January/February 1994.
11. "A Question of Value." *The Suffolk Lawyer,* March 1993.
12. "Express Consent and the Two Hour Rule." *Queens Bar Bulletin,* February 1993.
13. "Notice and the Confirmatory Identification." *Queens Bar Bulletin,* March 1993.
14. "Juror Note Taking." *The Suffolk Lawyer,* December 1992.
15. "Recent *Batson* Developments." *The Suffolk Lawyer,* December 1992.
16. "Border Searches: An Overview." *The Mouthpiece, Newsletter of the New York State Association of Criminal Defense Lawyers,* September/October 1992.
17. "AIDS Dismissal and the Clayton Motion." *The Mouthpiece, Newsletter of the New York State Association of Criminal Defense Lawyers,* June/July 1992.
18. "Dismissal of an Indictment under 190.50 of the C.P.L. (Part Two)." *Kings County Criminal Bar Association Journal,* January 1993.
19. "*Sandoval* and Severance." *The Suffolk Lawyer,* June 1992.

20. "Production of the Complainant in a Wade Hearing: Some Recent Law." *The Suffolk Lawyer,* April 1992.
21. "Undercover Closure." *Queens Bar Bulletin,* March 1992.
22. "The Confirmatory Identification: Wade Hearing or No." *Queens Bar Bulletin,* April 1992.
23. "The Confirmatory Identification." *Queens Bar Bulletin,* October 1992.
24. "Violation of Probation in Criminal Law: One Small Point." *The Suffolk Lawyer,* October 1992.
25. "Defendant's Presence at Trial: Recent Developments." *The Suffolk Lawyer,* February 1992.
26. "Recent *Payton* Decisions." *Queens Bar Bulletin,* October 1991.
27. "Standing Under *Wesley.*" *Nassau Lawyer,* September 1991.
28. "Advocacy Over Etiquette: Preserving the Prosecutor's Misconduct in Summation as Reversible Error." *Nassau Lawyer,* June 1991.
29. "Possession as 'Dominion and Control'." *Nassau Lawyer,* May 1991.
30. "Dismissal of a Misdemeanor Complaint: Victory Before Trial." *Nassau Lawyer,* December 1990
31. "Suppressing Cash in a Drug Sale Case." *Nassau Lawyer,* November 1990.
32. "The Requirements of a Physical Injury in Assault Cases." *Nassau Lawyer,* April 1990.
33. "Unconstitutional DWI Checkpoints: A Basis for Suppressing the Chemical Test." *Nassau Lawyer,* December 1989.
34. "Dismissal of Interfamily Disputes." *Queens Bar Bulletin,* November 1989.
35. "Residue of Cocaine." *Queens Bar Bulletin,* October 1989.
36. "The Presentence Report in New York Law." *Queens Bar Bulletin,* April 1991.
37. "Bolstering: Part One: Notes Toward Definition." *The Suffolk Lawyer,* 1994.
38. "Bolstering: Part Two: A Recent Case." *The Suffolk Lawyer,* March 1994.
39. "A Note on Chargeable Time." *Queens Bar Bulletin,* April 1994.
40. "The Undefined Bulge and Probable Cause." *The Suffolk Lawyer,* May 1994.
41. "Three Pretrial Hearings." *Queens Bar Bulletin,* May 1994.
42. "*Sandoval* and the Grand Jury: A Recent Case." *The Mouthpiece Newsletter of the New York State Association of Criminal Defense Lawyers,* November 1994.
43. "A Question of Weight." *The Mouthpiece, Newsletter of the New York State of Criminal Defense Lawyers,* September 1994.
44. "A Note on Misdemeanor, Criminal Trespass." *The Suffolk Lawyer,* December 1994.
45. "A Recent *Rosario* Decision." *The Queens Bar Bulletin,* December 1994.
46. "A Recent Development in New York State Criminal Motion Practice." *The Suffolk Lawyer,* January 1995.
47. "*Batson* II." *The Suffolk Lawyer,* November 1994.
48. "The Confirmatory Identification: A Way to a Hearing." *The Mouthpiece Newsletter of the New York State Association of Criminal Defense Lawyers.*
49. "A Note on Sentencing." *The Queens Bar Bulletin,* March 1995.
50. "Why I Am Opposed to the Death Penalty." *The Summation,* March 1995.
51. "Some Cases on Alias." *The Suffolk Lawyer,* March 1995.
52. "Mental Competency and the Grand Jury." *New York State Bar Journal,* December 1994.
53. "The Forty-Five Day Rule." *The Queens Bar Bulletin,* April 1995.
54. "Three Recent *Ryan* Cases." *The Queens Bar Bulletin,* October 1994.
55. "Three More Pretrial Hearings." *The Queens Bar Bulletin,* November 1994.

56. "A Recent Case on Presence." *The Mouthpiece Newsletter of the New York State Association of Criminal Defense Lawyers,* March 1995.
57. "Failure to Pay A Fine: Incarceration or Not." *The Queens Bar Bulletin,* February 1994.
58. "*Rosario* Material: A New Category." *The Mouthpiece, Newsletter of the New York State Association of Criminal Defense Lawyers,* November/December 1995.
59. "A Novel Motion in Limine." *The Mouthpiece, The Newsletter of the New York State Association of Criminal Defense Lawyers,* July/August 1995.
60. "The Voluntariness Hearing in Criminal Law." *The Suffolk Lawyer,* December 1995.
61. "The Station House Identification." *New York Criminal Law News,* November 1995.
62. "The Rape Shield Law: A Recent Case." *The Suffolk Lawyer,* May 1995.
63. "The Motion for A Mistrial in a Criminal Case." *New York Criminal News,* April 1995.
64. "Possession with Intent to Sell: A Matter of Sufficiency." *Queens Bar Bulletin,* May 1995.
65. "A Note on the Scope of Criminal Discovery in New York." *Queens Bar Bulletin,* October 1978.
66. "Three Final Pretrial Hearings." *Queens Bar Bulletin,* November 1995.
67. "Constructive Possession: An Overview." *The Nassau Lawyer,* May 1990.
68. "Dismissal of an Indictment under Sec. 190.50 of the Criminal Procedure Law (Part II)." *Brooklyn Barrister,* May 1991.
69. "The Speedy Trial Consequences of an Unavailable Prosecution Witness." *New York Criminal Law News,* May 1997.
70. "Defendant's Presence at Trial: Recent Developments." *Suffolk Lawyer,* 1995.
71. "DNA Admissibility in New York State Criminal Cases." *New York Criminal Law News,* March/April 1998.
72. "Readiness and Relation Back." *New York Criminal Law News,* June/July 1996.
73. "CPL 30.30: A Kind of Delay." *The Mouthpiece, The Newsletter of the New York State Association of Criminal Defense Lawyers,* May/June 1997.
74. "A Case of Interplay." *The Mouthpiece, The Newsletter of the New York State Association of Criminal Defense Lawyers,* March/April 1996.
75. "The Batson Hearing." *The Mouthpiece, The Newsletter of the New York State Association of Criminal Defense Lawyer,* July/August 1997.
76. "Withdrawal of the Guilty Plea under the Federal Rules of Criminal Procedure: An Analysis." *Criminal Justice Journal,* Vol. 7, Winter 1999.
77. "Probable Cause and Pretrial Hearings." *The Mouthpiece, The Newsletter of the New York State Association of Criminal Defense Lawyers,* September/October 1999.
78. "Extending the Time for Taking an Appeal in a Criminal Case." *New York Criminal Law News,* March/May 2000.
79. "The Criminal Defense Interview." *Queens Bar Bulletin,* December 2000.
80. Is It a Dwelling or Building? A Significant Factor in Determining the Type of Criminal Conduct." *New York Criminal Law News,* November/December 1996.
81. "Good Cause under C.P.L. Sec 180.80: Analysis." *Queens Bar Bulletin,* March 1996.
82. "The Motion for Severance in New York Criminal Law." *Queens Bar Bulletin,* December 1995.
83. "Stay of Judgment and Bail Pending Appeal." With Spiros Tsimbinos. *New York Criminal Law News,* January/February 1996.
84. "Withdrawing the Guilty Plea." *New York Criminal Law News,* July/Aug. 1998.
85. "Duplicative Counts: An Analysis." *Suffolk Lawyer,* May 2003.

86. "Section 450.50 Appeal by the People from an Order of Suppression: An Overview." *New York Criminal Law Newsletter,* Spring 2005.
87. "The Pen Register: A Constitutional Excursus."*Atticus, The Newsletter of the New York State Association of Criminal Defense Lawyers,* Vol. 18, No. 5, September/October 2005.
88. "Waiver of the Right to Appeal." *New York Criminal Law Newsletter,* Vol. 4, No. 2, Spring 2006.
89. "The Motion to Set Aside a Sentence: The Criteria and Bases." *Nassau Lawyer,* Vol. 55, No. 10 June 2006.
90. "Peremptory Challenges Under Attack." *Queens Bar Bulletin,* Vol. 68, No. 6, March 2005.
91. "Motion to Dismiss an Indictment under C.P.L. 190.50. Time-barred? Maybe Not." *Nassau Lawyer.* Vol. 42, No. 4, April 1994.
92. "A Note on Criminal Appellate Practice." *Queens Bar Bulletin,* February 2003.

Chapter 2
Evidence Reprinted Articles

1. "Polygraph Evidence: Admissibility in Civil and Criminal Cases." *The Queens Bar Bulletin,* Vol. 57, October 1993.
2. "Admissibility of Polygraph Evidence in the State of New York." *Nassau Lawyer,* April 1978. Reprinted in February 1979 Advance sheet of the *New York Supplement.*
3. "DNA Test: The Mechanism." *The Queens Bar Bulletin,* February 1995.
4. "The Polygraph Confession." *The Mouthpiece, The Newsletter of the New York State Association of Criminal Defense Lawyers,* September/October 1995.
5. "A Note on Circumstantial on Evidence." *The Mouthpiece, The Newsletter of the New York State Association of Criminal Defense Lawyers,* March/April 2000.
6. "Three Cases on Laboratory and Ballistics Reports." *Mouthpiece, Newsletter of the New York State Association of Criminal Defense Lawyers,* Vol. 10, September/October 1997.

Chapter 3
Civil Procedure Reprinted Articles

1. "A Note on the Notice of Claim." *Queens Bar Bulletin,* May 1992.
2. "Some Points on the Writing of an Appellate Brief." *Queens Bar Bulletin,* November 1991.
3. "Appealing the Mistrial Order." *Queens Bar Bulletin,* Fall 1984
4. "Conforming the Pleadings to the Proof." *Bronx Journal,* Winter 1985.
5. "Rule for *Lex Loci* has Received New Impetus in Conflicts Cases." *Nassau Lawyer,* March 1984.
6. "A Note on the Note of Issue." *Queens Bar Bulletin,* Winter 1983.
7. "Non Sui Juris: An Overview of the New York Law." *Brooklyn Barrister,* January 1983.
8. "The Law of Conflicts: A Recent Trend." *Nassau Lawyer,* November 1982.
9. "Settlements Under Section 15-108 of the General Obligations Law: Two Means to the End." *Nassau Lawyer,* June 1982.
10. "Section 50-e: The Importance of Filing a Notice of Claim." *Brooklyn Barrister,* March 1982.

11. "Amendment of the Pleadings and the Notice of Claim." Advance Sheet, *New York Supplement*, July 1981.
12. "Bifurcation and Trifurcation." *Nassau Lawyer*, June 1991.
13. "The Art of Cross Examination." *The Suffolk Lawyer*, April 1994
14. "A Note on the Compromise Verdict." *Queens Bar Bulletin*, February 1996.
15. "C.P.L.R. 325(d) and the *Ad Damnum.*" *Suffolk Lawyer*, December 2003.
16. "Filing a Late Notice of Claim: One Basis and Analysis.", *Queens Bar Bulletin*, Vol. 64, No. 5, February 2001.
17. "A Note on the Workers' Compensation Law." *Torts, Insurance & Compensation Law Section Journal, NYSBA*, Vo. 34, No. 1, Summer 2005.
18. "Trial By Jury Revisited." *Queens Bar Bulletin*, Vol. 69, No. 3, December 2005.

Chapter 4
Family Law Reprinted Articles

1. "Artificial Insemination and Paternity." *Family Law Review, Family Law Section of the New York State Bar Association*, December 1994, reprinted from the Article appearing in the *Queens Bar Bulletin,* November 1992.
2. "Artificial Insemination and Paternity: Part Two." *Family Law Review, Family Law Section of the New York State Bar Association*, March 1994, reprinted from the Article appearing in the *Queens Bar Bulletin*, December 1992.
3. "Child Abuse and Neglect: A Limit." *Brooklyn Barrister*, November 1985.
4. "The Permanently Neglected Child: Certain Criteria." *Family Law Review, Family Section of the New York State Bar Association*, September 1996.

Chapter 5
Labor and Employment Law Reprinted Articles

1. "Termination at Will as an Evolving Concept." *Nassau Lawyer*, February 1985.
2. "Should Title VII of The United State Code Prohibiting Sex Discrimination Be Based On Sexual Orientation: An Argument." *Queens Bar Bulletin*, May 2000.
3. "Trial by Jury—Is There a Doubt?" *Queens Bar Bulletin*, March 2004.
4. "Naming as Prerequisite." *Queens Bar Bulletin*, December 2003.
5. "Employment Discrimination and Individual Liability: A Comparison." *Queens Bar Bulletin*, April 2003.
6. "Law in the Workplace." *The Gavel*, Summer 2003.
7. "A Second View." *Queens Bar Bulletin*, Vol. 69, No. 6, March 2006.
8. "*Tomka:* A Comment on Supervisory Liability." *Labor and Employment Newsletter*, Vol. 32, No. 3, Fall/Winter 2007.
9. "Adverse Action: An Analysis." *Labor and Employment Newsletter*, Vol. 32, No. 2, Summer 2007.

Chapter 6
Civil Rights Reprinted Articles

1. "A Point of Pleading in 1983 Civil Rights Actions." *Brooklyn Barrister*, May 1984.
2. "Official Policy under 42 U.S.C. Section 1983." *Queens Bar Bulletin*, 1986.
3. "False Arrest and Sec. 1983: A Short Analysis." *Queens Bar Bulletin*, November 2003.
4. "The State Danger Doctrine." *Nassau Lawyer*, Volume 55 No. 6 February 2006.

Chapter 7
Tort Law Reprinted Articles

1. "Baseball Liability: Recent Developments." *Brooklyn Barrister,* January 1984.
2. "Loss of Consortium and Wrongful Death." *Brooklyn Barrister,* May 1980; Reprinted in the July 1981 Advance Sheet of the *New York Supplement* and in January by the Division of Claims, American Insurance Association.
3. "The Intentional Infliction of Mental Distress: An Analysis." *Queens Bar Bulletin,* October 2000.

Chapter 8
Federal Procedure Reprinted Articles

1. "Essay: An Exception to the Finality Requirement." *NY Litigator,* Vol. 11, No. 1, Spring 2006.
2. "Rule 15 and 16 of the Federal Rules of Civil Procedure: A Comparison." *Brooklyn Barrister,* Vol. 57, No. 9, June 2006.
3. "Enforceability of an Oral settlement: A Consideration and Analysis." *Queens Bar Bulletin,* April 2004.
4. "The Perils and Pitfalls of Pre-Trial Orders." *Nassau Lawyer,* November 2006.
5. "Eminent Domain: A Novel Approach." *Queens Bar Bulletin,* November 2006.

Subject Index

Index of Cases